وَإِذَا قِيلَ لَهُمُ اتَّبِعُوا مَا أَنزَلَ اللَّهُ قَالُوا بَلْ نَتَّبِعُ مَا أَلْفَيْنَا عَلَيْهِ آبَاءَنَا أَوَلَوْ كَانَ آبَاؤُهُمْ لَا يَعْقِلُونَ شَيْئًا وَلَا يَهْتَدُونَ

And when they were asked to follow what Allah has revealed, they answered that instead we follow what we have found our forefathers doing. But even if their forefather did not understand anything or were misguided

The Mushaf: Chapter 2, Verse 170

Muslims' Greatest Challenge

Muslims' Greatest Challenge

Choosing between Tradition and Islam

Omar M. Ramahi

Books
Black Palm Books

Copyright © Omar M. Ramahi 2019

All rights reserved.
No part of this book may be reproduced in any form without written permission from the publisher.

Printed and bound in the United States of America

ISBN: 978-1-9991630-0-6 (paperback)
ISBN: 978-1-9991630-1-3 (hard cover)

2 3 4 5 6 7 8 9 10

Published by Black Palm Books

To my father who provided me space to think;
◇
to all who value the truth more than their parents, family, health, profession, and religion;
◇
to all who do not aspire for superiority, authority, power or grandeur;
◇
to that person who I met somewhere in the world and encouraged me to write this book;
◇
and to that little giant who initiated my journey, I humbly dedicate this work.

◊ Contents ◊

Author's Note x

Conventions xiv

The Cause for the Beginning 1

Science of Marginalization 18

War on Reason 54

Manufactured Extremism 110

Guidance or Magic? 159

The Mushaf 184

Naskh: Fraud in the Name of God 236

New Doctrines: Sunnah and Hadith 261

Legislation beyond the Revelation 336

Towards a Muslim Renaissance 393

Bibliography 401

Index 408

Author's Note

This book is an attempt to find why Muslims are in conflict with themselves, why Muslims have been living in an intellectual isolation and intellectual vacuum. This book is an attempt to find why Islam, as embodied in the Mushaf, calls for sharply different norms than those adopted by the majority of Muslims. To search for the answers, the book uses, as much as possible, two sources: the first is critical reasoning, and the second is the Mushaf. The order of use of these two sources is important. In sharp contrast to the vast majority of books on Islam, this book does not base the validity of any argument on the stature of past or present personalities and scholars, irrespective of their high status and reverence amongst the majority of Muslims. Therefore, the reference for validity is different from what is used in those books.

The book takes a methodical approach to analyzing the techniques that evolved throughout the ages to marginalize the Muslims mind and to project reason as the archenemy of Islam. The book analyzes alleged prophetic narratives (Hadith) and interpretations of the Mushaf (*tafsir*) by prominent jurists to confirm that rationalism and reason were both, and largely, disconnected from Muslims intellectual discourse, at least in the overwhelmingly dominant religious material that has reached us.

This book analyzes fundamental contradictions in the way the vast majority of Muslims perceive Islam, and how the conceived and practiced Muslim or "Islamic" doctrines lack foundation in the Mushaf. The book goes behind the scene, so to speak, to understand the reasons behind such a vast disconnect. The book provides a context to the severe intellectual underdevelopment amongst most Muslims vis-à-vis their understanding of their religion. It looks at canonized practices and doctrines that emerged throughout the ages through dubious scholarship to maintain a docile, hopeless, aimless, and subservient Muslim *umma*. It brings to the forefront stark contradictions between the canonized Muslim doctrines and the Mushaf, contradictions that many Muslims choose to ignore.

The book challenges the use of Hadith as a source of Islamic legislation. It takes an unconventional perspective of the Mushaf's exegeses and reaches conclusions that are based on reason and the Mushaf's direct text, yet contradictory to the conventional Muslims' doctrines.

The book looks at the culture of violence championed by the historically triumphant Muslim scholars, jurisprudents and clergy, whose "scholarship" triumphed and morphed that of the other scholars who put the Mushaf first and everything else as secondary. It questions whether such culture inspired past and contemporary violent movements. The book revisits fundamental doctrines and canonized laws and looks carefully at their evolution and their connection to the Mushaf. Two chapters in the book address the two most important sources of Islamic Law: Hadith and the Mushaf. The analyses in these two chapters leads to unconventional conclusions, thus establishing a new perspective that stems purely from the Mushaf and critical reasoning. The conclusions in these two chapters put Hadith in a perspective and context completely non-convergent with prevailing Muslims doctrines. The conclusions will also have direct implications on what is typically perceived as Islamic law and the controversial doctrine of Sharia.

The book is not an attempt to reform Islam. The claim to reform Islam is highly offensive to most Muslims simply because reform means change, and typically carries the temporal connotation in the sense of "change to suit the times". The book is not an attempt to "modernize" Islam. This is because Islam as embodied in the Mushaf is immutable for all times, otherwise, we would witness new revelations and Prophets to provide new revelations to suit the "modern" times. The book advocates the thesis that Islam, as embodied by the Mushaf, the divine revelation, is immutable and absolute. Rather than questioning the suitability of Islam for "the times", the book advocates an understanding of the Mushaf through a persistent and gradual process that lead to absolute understanding of at least parts of it.

The book is neither an attack on Islam nor an appeasement of Muslims. It is a serious and methodical attempt to create a genuine discussion and reflection on the so-called Islamic doctrines that were developed many years after the death of the Prophet Muhammad, doctrines that have thin connection, if not detrimental, to Islam. For the reasons outlined in the book, it is expected that some Muslims, or possibly many, will perceive the material of the book as highly provocative and controversial.

Many books on Islam can be grouped into four major categories. The first category includes books that have strong anti-Islam bias. These include two sub-categories: those with explicit bias and those with implicit bias disguised as pseudo-scholarship. Second, books written by Muslims or non-Muslims who try to justify that everything within Muslims' religious doctrines is perfect but misunderstood. This category of books attempt to reinterpret these doctrines to achieve convenient goals (perhaps these books can be considered as an attempt to "modernize" Islam and make it "compatible with the times", i.e., an *asri* understanding of Islam). Third, books by Muslims (mostly) that show discomfort with "Islamic" doctrines and attempt to present a "modern" understanding of these doctrines rather than challenging the doctrines themselves. Such a "modern" understanding is perceived by some as an attempt to reform Islam. The fourth category includes books by non-Muslims who are genuinely interested in Islam but are deeply confused by the seas of contradictory doctrines. The authors of the last category are careful not to offend Muslims, but find themselves struggling with complex and deeply contradictory doctrines that were considered by most Muslim scholars and jurisprudents as integral to Islam. The vast majority of these books (from the four categories) base their arguments on the Mushaf's traditional exegeses and what is believed to be authentic Hadith. This book challenges the fundamental "Islamic" doctrines.

Finally, the key feature of this book is that it does not take the commentaries and opinions of famed Muslim scholars (including the most celebrated Muslim jurisprudents) as an integral part of Islam. Some of the ideas and discussion presented in this book will appear controversial to many Muslims and even traditional scholars of Islam. However, in support of my ideas, I used the same two sources mentioned above: God's greatest gift to humankind and the Mushaf.

There were numerous people who helped me shape my thoughts. To all, I am deeply indebted, especially to those long conversations with many of my brilliant engineering graduate students, whose clarity of thought and unwavering and scrutinizing intellect helped me refine my ideas. It is enthralling how the ideas of this book and the intellectual stimulus that it generated had a profound impact on my research group's scientific philosophy. This is a strong testimony that for a religion to be meaningful, it has to be based on reality, i.e., the physical world.

Several Mushaf and Hadith databases have been used heavily throughout this work. An indispensable database for any Mushaf researcher is available online at http://www.readverse.com/home/. The Tafsir al-Quran (https://sensortower.com/ios/us/pakistan-data-management-services/app/quran-tafsir-tfsyr-lqran/442158525/overview) is available as an App on the iPhone platform only. The www.quran.com and www.sunnah.com are two helpful databases for anyone interested in Islam and especially in the way the vast majority of Muslims view and interpret their religion.

I am very grateful to my daughter Zainab for her review of the first draft and for her superb editing and valuable feedback that helped improve the presentation significantly. I acknowledge most highly Professor Andreas Christmann for reviewing the first draft of the book and his valuable feedback and encouragement. I like to thank Ms. Kelly Comeau for her superb copyediting. Finally, thanks to my son Yousuf for his help in editing the final manuscript.

The most important and overwhelming gratitude I have is for the enormous privilege of having the time and space to think and write. I see so many people in the Muslim world who do not have a minute to sit and think about anything let alone their religion, simply because they are busy making ends meet by working more than 12 hours a day just to get by. Perhaps my modest effort, through this book, may contribute to improving their condition somehow. This silent majority of the Muslim world, identified easily by their deeply sad and silent faces, need to have their say someday.

Omar M. Ramahi
oramahi@gmail.com
Waterloo, Ontario
2019

CONVENTIONS

Since this is a book about Islam, reference to the Mushaf (conventionally, but incorrectly referred to as the Qur'aan) on which the entire religion is based is essential. The Mushaf, the divine revelation, contains 114 chapters and a total of 6,236 verses. In practically all printed Mushafs, a verse is a text that is separated from other verses within a chapter by two circles. Throughout this book, when a Mushaf verse is stated in Arabic, it is followed by an English translation, which is partially an interpretation since converting one language into another is essentially an interpretation. My approach is to keep the translation/interpretation to a minimum. When I am not convinced of the proper translation/interpretation of a certain Arabic word, it is left untranslated (i.e., transliterated).

Mushaf verses are referenced as Mx:y, where x is the Chapter number and y is the verse number. All Arabic words are italicized. Dates of death for prominent authors, jurisprudents, clergy, scholars, etc., (if available) are presented as x/y where x and y refer to the Hijri and Gregorian calendars, respectively. Only the Gregorian calendar is used for publication dates.

Hadith refers to the collections of narratives attributed to Prophet Muhammad. A single narrative will be referred to as hadith. The Plural would be hadiths. The traditional books of Hadith have been organized into chapters or divisions (*kutub*) and then into sub-chapters (*abwaab*). Online compilation of some Hadith books have tried to preserve the original organization of the Hadith chapters but the task has proven to be difficult. The numbering system of the online database www.sunnah.com will be adopted. For example, the first hadith in Sahih al-Bukhari, Kitaab al-Hajj (Pilgrimage), will be referenced as Sahih al-Bukhari, Kitaab al-Hajj, no. 1513. The sub-chapter designation will be omitted.

Muslims history involves people who contributed to the doctrines that have become accepted by most Muslims as Islam. Some of these people were scholars, some were clergy, some were historians, etc. Some even had overlapping roles. I claim that these roles are distinct and therefore, I will use the label that I see most fit and relevant.

1

The Cause for the Beginning

يَا أَيُّهَا الَّذِينَ آمَنُوا كُونُوا قَوَّامِينَ بِالْقِسْطِ شُهَدَاءَ لِلَّهِ وَلَوْ عَلَىٰ أَنفُسِكُمْ أَوِ الْوَالِدَيْنِ وَالْأَقْرَبِينَ

O those who believed, adhere to equity, and witnesses for Allah, even if it be against yourselves or parents and nearest kin.

M4:135

This book chronicles the story of my journey in search of answers to questions that I consider fundamental and essential to my existence as a human being. This book came about as a need to realize meaningful and satisfying answers to so many questions I have encountered in my journey. This work is not entrenched in abstract religion and spirituality but rather in the simple realities that surround me: societal realities; economic realities; and the realities of power, politics, and life in general. The story in this book is my religion, Islam, which embodies the sources that have formed my perspective on life and all things around me, from the tangible to the intangible and from the physical to what we perceive as the non-physical, and even the meta-physical.

Expressing one's life experiences can be cathartic and may connote a sense of completeness and satisfaction. However, my intention here is not to write about my life experience and all its boring and exciting turns and twists. My intention is to bear witness to what I understand to be important and to share it far and wide. This book is part of the human urge to share what we believe to be the truth, not necessarily what we believe to be right. While it might be obvious to many, for emphasis, truth and right are not synonyms. Truth is reality and right is a perspective. Without sharing what we believe to be the truth, whether in the fields of chemistry, biology, physics, history, or even archeology, there will be no advancement in human civilization. A static society is indeed the anathema of progress. Movement, dynamism or renewal are fundamentals of the creation in at least its material manifestation. Nothing stays the same. Those mysterious electric charges that make all living and non-living things, after all, are not idle, they are in constant motion, or to use the Mushaf term, they are in constant *tasbeeh*. No one yet knows what would have happened if electrons were frozen in motion. Perhaps we can consider this eternal dynamism (i.e., motion) as the primary axiom of life sciences.

Why should I write another book about religion and in particular about Islam? To many non-Muslims, the topic of Islam is already controversial with perceptions largely conceived and crafted by politically motivated think-tanks and propagated by media venues with multiple political agendas. For the most part, non-Muslims, sadly, have a negative perception of Islam and consequently of Muslims. Such negative feelings towards Islam and Muslims at times are manifested in the most aggressive, repugnant and inflammatory ways, and are at times wrapped with academic gloss and diplomatic façade. Many Muslims, on the other hand, are of the opinion that what they do and say is always right but simply misunderstood and maligned due to media coverage that, according to their common belief, serves all types of mischievous agendas. These Muslims believe that Islam is misunderstood and if only non-Muslims would stay away from mainstream media and independently delve into the religion then they would be able to understand the true greatness of Islam and consequently "see the light". Despite all this, however, the religion of more than one and a half billion people cannot be meaningfully discussed independently of prevailing perceptions. Whether politically motivated or not, perceptions are not to be dismissed.

Prior to the 1979 revolution in Iran, which was spearheaded by individuals who identified Islam as the overriding force and ideology behind the revolution, the Western media had little interest in Islam. Even during the peak of the Middle East oil crises of 1973, which had significant effects on the economies of Western countries, Islam was not considered a center-stage player by either the media or academic establishments despite religiously-loaded rhetoric from King Faisl of

Saudi Arabia, whose country spearheaded the embargo. The Iranian Islamic revolution of 1979 changed that back seat coverage dramatically. Since then, it seems that any conflict within the Middle East and its geo-political extensions in North Africa and central Asia has been contextualized and framed within something Islamic. All of a sudden, the West discovered all things Islamic, and Muslims found themselves at the center of global attention with conflicting forces pulling them towards all Islamic persuasions as well as revived and newly minted doctrines. A cottage industry of Islamic experts subsequently emerged. For a variety of reasons, money was poured endlessly to study everything that is Islamic. Universities and think tanks hired Islamic experts to decipher and interpret all Islamic and Islamic-inspired phenomena sweeping the Muslim World.

When Islam was a collection of rituals, a simple faith or an exotic spirituality, the global interest in it was minimal. When Islam became relevant to the geo-political game, it became amusing, interesting or dangerous. There is little evidence to suggest that the dramatic explosion in the interest to study Islam occurred for purely noble ends or for genuine understanding of the faith, unlike general fascination with Eastern religions such as Buddhism, Hinduism or exotic spiritual cults. There was too much at stake to delegate the interest in Islam to purely noble ends. At stake were things much more important than the correctness or validity of a religion. At stake was political influence, dominance, money, oil, more oil, and a lot of oil.

To the West, since the late 19th Century, the Middle East has two things of grand importance: oil and Israel. The two are strongly, if indirectly, connected. After all, Israel is considered part of the West that happens to be physically located in the Middle East, and oil was referred to in the annals of American colonial political discourse as "our oil."[1] So by coincidence, Israel and oil happened to be in that area called the Middle East. The East and its Islam had to be rediscovered since the West thought it belonged to it (but happened to be in the Middle East) and all of a sudden had come under threat. Islamic experts had to be minted, and fast. Muslim and non-Muslim experts on Islam mushroomed from everywhere, having proven their efficacy in earlier conquests of the Middle East and North Africa.[2] Journalists who interviewed some Muslims, academics who studied a group of Muslims, and expatriates who stayed for a short period of time in a Muslim country all became highly touted Islamic experts. Think tanks employed academics as mercenaries to interpret Islam in service, mostly, of carefully-orchestrated political agendas.

In hindsight, and after all the bombs had fallen on Iraq, Syria, Libya, Afghanistan, Pakistan, Somalia and Yemen, Islamic experts proved to be more effective than bombs in decimating Muslim societies and planting the seeds for future perpetual mayhem. University academic programs were regrouped and energized by government funding and grants to complement the agendas of conquest.[3] In summary, the West approached the East and its Islam with a colonial lens, all in the context of its vital interests, no matter how widely and broadly defined.

Muslims too became equally interested in the religion they call their very own. Ancient rivalries between antiquated Muslim groups were revived along with the emergence of new rivalries. The Arabic term *khawaarij* (denoting a rebellious group) was revived from the first Muslim century and brought back with full vigor for the same purpose to which it was introduced to marginalize and excommunicate with absolute ease from Islam the "enemies of the state". Muslims who started to question doctrines that are generally accepted as Islamic and especially those who started to think about the "Islamic" tradition were labeled as Mu'tazalites, another derogatory ancient label.[4] Centuries old Arabic terms were dusted off and reintroduced to cast a religious gloss on activities and movements that had nothing "Islamic" about them. All of a sudden, a successful revolution in the Middle East posed a fundamental challenge to the post-WWI political dominance of French-British-American imperialism, the dismantling of the Ottoman domain, and ensuring that shipping lanes remained under Western control to guarantee the flow of cheap energy resources to the West and its network of beneficiaries.

Regardless of whether one refers to the 1979 revolution in Iran as Islamic or not, one can safely say that Islam was the primary ideological force behind it. The prominent leaders and ideologues of the revolution were Muslim scholars, sociologists, intellectuals and jurisprudents. Islam was the core of the message for struggle against the Iranian monarchy and against the West's exploitation of Iranian resources. The fact that the Iranians were predominantly adherents of the Shia school of jurisprudence (a sizable minority amongst Muslims) made things more exciting, and even exotic to the West. The West and those who were comfortable with the pre-1979 geopolitical order in the Middle East realized that the challenge to the rise of what was then termed political Islam had to be formidable, effective and swift. Direct military intervention by Western countries could not be used as the only option to put the brakes on the revolution in Iran. Instead, the canonized doctrines that evolved throughout many centuries and that were largely considered as part of Islam had to be used to present the most effective challenge to the expansion of the revolutionary fervor that swept the Middle East in those early years of the 1980s. The West and its allies in the Middle East watched with dread the powerful new Islam that had emerged and noted that it was loaded with political and economic overtones that jeopardized their two most precious "possessions" in the Middle East. This "new" Islam was not the one that existed elsewhere and for the most part did not challenge the status quo. The older "Islam" was sustaining the status quo that was favorable to the West and in fact, it was a tool that reshaped the Middle East to favor the West's interests.[5] To address the new phenomenon that created an unprecedented awakening in the Middle East with effects felt from Morocco all the way to the remote Islands of Indonesia, the West fell back on the proven tactic of turning Muslims against each other.

It can be argued that many Muslims had minimal interest in understanding Islam prior to 1979, aside from understanding how to perform the rituals and understanding what will give the faithful worshipper more rewards in the paradise of the hereafter. People's tendency to direct attention to whatever is powerful and impressive is perhaps innate. When a politician utters something exceptionally imbecilic, a serious debate in the public sphere starts to analyze the merits of his or her comment. If someone without the same fame made the same comment, then it is generally considered unworthy of attention. After the 1979 revolution in Iran, Muslims became interested in Islam for various reasons, including to understand the ideological drive behind the revolution. Some became interested when they recognized the potential of Islam as a means through which the status quo can be changed, and some for realizing that Islam might help to deconstruct the post-WWI geopolitical order imposed by the victors of WWI, the British Empire and France.[6] Some renewed their interest in Islam simply because it was exciting to be at the center stage after a long absence since the grandeur of the Umayyad, Abbasid, or the Ottoman times. Many felt nostalgic for the "Islamic" glories of the past, glories and grandeur that had nothing fundamentally

Islamic about them except the politically-motivated appellation. But there were also those Muslims who saw the potential of Islam to bring social justice and legitimate equity and distribution of wealth to a Middle East that was reeling under dictators of kingly and presidential flavors ruling with absolute power not seen since the ancient pharaohs.

Millions of Muslims wanted to turn towards the faith; but which faith to turn to? Here started the competition for the minds and souls of Muslims. Money was poured into the mix by Western countries and Muslim states to persuade the Muslim populace to believe in a particular sect, school of thought, a distinct school of jurisprudence, or an "Islamic" philosophy. Several "Islams" emerged: the radical, the extremist, the conservative, the liberal, the Sufi, and the *wasati* (of a middle ground) to name a few. In the past few years, the number of websites related to Islam has exploded for reasons that had to do with the natural and unprecedented revolution in information sharing fueled by the Internet, but also for reasons related to the equally unprecedented interest in Islam from foes and supporters alike, and to win adherents to the new emerging Islams. The number of TV and radio channels advocating the philosophy of Islamic groups has reached hundreds. Again, so much was at stake indeed, from interests championed by the West to those championed by many Muslim groups and governments. Authors were commissioned to churn books discrediting one sect of Islam for purely political gains. The vast majority of these books were published with heavy patronage from the government of Saudi Arabia, who appeared to agree with the West that the rise of political Islam in Iran was a destabilizing threat to their monarchy and to the geopolitical balance in the Middle East that favors the Saudis and the interests of all their supporters. Evidence cannot be found to substantiate claims that the rise of Shia Islam in Iran, Lebanon or the Persian Gulf was a threat to Islam as understood by non-Shia sects. The Persian Shias of Iran could possibly have had plans to conquer the Middle East and beyond, but there was no evidence to support such claims. The major contribution of the Iranian revolution, whether intended or not, was the sensitization of the people of the Middle East to the fragility of their political systems that were products of Western machinations, secret treaties and connivance.

A word of caution on the use of the term "Muslim sect". For the sake of clarity, it is used in this book to denote a group of Muslims who believe in the primary source of the religion of Islam, namely the

The Cause for the Beginning

Mushaf, which represents the entire revelation to the Prophet Muhammad. According to this definition, different interpretations of the Mushaf would not imply exclusion from Islam, and by extension its sects. Consequently, this definition would imply that any group or any philosophy that claims the Mushaf as a non-godly revelation and does not accept the Mushaf is not considered a Muslim sect or belonging to Islam. Aside from these qualifications, it is not only a fruitless exercise to categorize Muslims, but sheer arrogance even if this takes place within the realm of what is typically considered religious studies and most abstract forms of Islamic theology.

Following the Iranian revolution and the overwhelming global curiosity about Islam, many Muslims also became interested in Islam. However, most of those Muslims were living in Muslims-majority countries having social and political environments that were heavily controlled by the state and with very little, if any, freedom of expression. There were competitions for who should truly represent Islam, with confusing and varying interpretations of the religious text (primarily the Mushaf). Those competitions were not natural, but rather driven by political agendas. This is primarily because they occurred under the watchful eyes of highly oppressive dictatorships. From the most politically passive forms of Sufism to the most militant and conservative forms of Wahhabism, there was so much to choose from in this expansive marketplace of "Islamic" ideologies and persuasions.[7] Most of these sects were vague and contained conflicting religious directives and numerous contradictions. A good friend once told me that Islam can be used to justify anything one wishes to do. He was right only if he was referring to the man-made "Islam", not Allah's revelation. Many choices are available within one Islamic doctrine or the other. Here, Muslims are confronted with a dilemma: either accept the multiple choices as being part of Islam, accept only one persuasion, or better yet, follow the *à la carte* approach selecting what one finds most convenient for various situations.

I am not rehashing and giving credence to the plethora of fabricated and alleged prophetic sayings and illusive traditions that intend to prove the superiority of one sect over all others. Again, I do not intend to judge who amongst Muslims is more pious and more rightful than others, which is an exercise of sheer arrogance and elitism. What I am after is to understand how a single faith can lead to dramatically conflicting ideas and principles of governance (an example is the belief by some sects that mercy should be granted to prisoners of war while other sects believe they all prisoners should be executed).

Sciences present models to understand the material world and to help make predictions. A scientific theory is considered meaningful if it can lead to correct predictions, but much more importantly, if it does not lead to contradictions. If Newtonian mechanics predict that a specific bridge will fail when twenty trucks drive on it at one time but will not fail if the same number of trucks drive on it an hour later (assuming that the weather has not changed), then Newtonian mechanics cannot be adopted as a system of beliefs for civil or bridge engineers. So either a theory has to be revisited and scrutinized to make sure that it is sound, or must instead be rejected altogether. If Islam embodied by the Mushaf was meant to be a way of life or, as the Mushaf describes itself as a book of guidance (see M2:2 and M2:185), if it leads to contradictions and confusion, then either Islam is not only irrelevant, but possibly ineffective as a doctrine for guidance and community governance.

One of my co-religionists might question what makes me believe that my interpretation of the Mushaf is the right one and that of everyone else's is wrong. This book will show that the problem here does not lie in the Mushaf, or even in its interpretation, but in the body of the parallel doctrines that have been thrust upon the faithful in the name of religion. These doctrines largely formed the interpretation of the Mushaf and effectively became dominant over the Mushaf and, thus in effect, became the primary source of the religion. These new "Islamic" doctrines include incredible compendia of deeply confusing and contradictory material, making the Mushaf pale in comparison in terms of complexity, scope, depth, perceived intrusiveness, and inclusiveness.

The strength of faith is commendable, but if it blinds a person from seeing, understanding and dealing with reality (and I will refrain from saying what is right as that can be a subjective concept with sordid philosophical implications), then faith has the potential to solidify into dogma and an instrument of oppression, control, subjugation, a method of hierarchical classification and justification for superiority. This is the "faith" that many religious antagonists most likely had in mind when they turned against all religions and became agnostics. Or perhaps this is the faith-religion that Karl Marx described as the "opium of the people". If religion is incompatible with the physical laws of nature, then it will not attract intellectuals, thinkers and physical scientists, but only those who are least educated and who try to seek refuge from responsibility with superstitions disguised as articles of faith. Charles Darwin turned against the incompatibility between the divinity studies he learned at Cambridge and what he discovered during his voyage around the globe. He could not reconcile the two and he opted for the truth or reality.

There is a difference between faith (as in believing) and truth (as in reality). This difference can be understood by turning to science, where faith plays a central and pivotal role. Faith is typically considered part of religion; something to be frowned upon from a purely scientific perspective. Scientific assumptions are essentially articles of faith as they cannot be proven or unproven. Once certain articles of faith (of the scientific variety) are accepted as assumptions, science is supposed to help us cope with and understand reality, and better yet, adapt and survive socially and physically. Science could not have started with assumptions, but they were instituted later on and essentially became part of the faith of science. These fundamental assumptions cannot in any way contradict the science they lead to or vice-versa.

Therefore, science is firmly based on assumptions. Similarly, in religion, faith and truth should not be jumbled. A religion that is a faith should be differentiated from a religion that is based on faith. In the faith-based religion, the faith is not an end by itself but a foundation on which to build a system for a way of life (in the broader context). If the faith-based religion does not lead to practical consequences to make our collective lives, the lives of not only the faithful but of all of humanity better, then I would argue such a religion has limited utility or effect in one's life. Faith that is a means of individual comfort may be different from a faith that leads to justice and equality. Some religions and faiths give a feeling of satisfaction and contentment, while others agitate its adherents to work for the common good; in other words, to achieve tangible goals based on the core articles of faith.

This book can be thought of as my personal story in discovering my religion while resisting untold intimidation by my co-religionists; a discovery and a journey that would have been made exponentially more difficult and likely impossible had I been living within one of the "Islamic" countries and amongst Muslims who have largely become intolerant to any discussion of Islam that questions historical dogma and canonized doctrines. In fact, a fraction of what is presented in this book might warrant labels of apostasy, heresy or even outright *kufr* (denial of

Islam). My "story" as narrated in different forms in this book contains parallels to the story of others who discovered that their religion had been thrust to the center stage, and who realized that they were hypnotized into accepting an Islam different from that of the Mushaf. With the magnitude of respect and attention most Muslims, including myself, give to their religion, and to the centrality Islam commands in one's own life, I spent serious efforts to understand and hopefully dispel any contradictions in the religion that I adhere to and that I call Islam. Guided by my understanding of reality, I felt that a self-consistent understanding of Islam was needed to make sense of it all. The need is even more acute considering the potential Islam has to affect all humanity and Planet Earth, for the better, of course.

To understand anything, most specifically religion, one has to live in an environment where there is no intellectual intimidation or intellectual bullying. To understand anything requires intellectual abilities. If the intellectual processes are inhibited, intellectual freedom does not exist and independent understanding is impaired. Fear and love, for better or worse, are two powerful attributes that can indeed blind one from realizing reality. If intellectual intimidation is a barrier to understanding and learning, then one expects it would stifle creativity and progress. The intellect of the Muslims is practically in solitary confinement in a vast prison. The prison warden is communal with many contributors. The giant potential within Muslims is tamed by overwhelming intimidation and fear. The potential of Islam is suppressed by its very own people. Imagine the following simple thought experiment. Bring an iconic figure with incredible achievements, such as Albert Einstein or Leonardo Da Vinci, then lock him up in a cell. What would be expected to come out such geniuses who have been isolated and imprisoned? Most likely nothing at all. The potential of Islam resembles the contributions of these two iconic figures when let out of imprisonment. Muslims live largely within an atmosphere of severe oppressive intellectual intimidation and fear amounting to intellectual imprisonment. In fact, for many Muslim sects and Muslim governments, the threshold for committing apostasy and *kufr* has been made horrifyingly low to deter any Muslim from exercising uninhibited thinking. Once a person is declared an apostate (a definition equivalent to that of an "infidel" coined by the Church in Medieval Europe.[8]) then shedding the blood of that "apostate" will not be frowned upon, if not outright condoned by a wide range of Muslims. Many chilling examples are available. Once on a TV talk show, in the heat of a debate of two Muslims who represented different sects, one of the two guests used his left hand to drink from a glass of water. The opposing guest, who represented the second sect, immediately pointed that one of the signs of *zandaqa* (a horrific-sounding word used throughout Muslim history to refer to people who commit transgression against Islam) was to hold a glass of water in the left hand.

Historical records do not suggest that Muslims have been in this state of intimidation and bullying throughout their history. Major Muslim scholars contributed significantly to philosophy and science, even proposing evolutionary theories many centuries before Darwin. Nevertheless, many Muslim luminaries and scholars were accused of *kufr, zandaqa* and apostasy simply because they proposed ideas that were not conventional to the four dominant Sunni sects. The parallel between the attitude of Muslims of the past towards their scholars and thinkers and the attitude of the Church in medieval times towards Galileo and Darwin are amazingly striking. What the world of Christianity experienced before the Renaissance has strong similarity to what Muslims are experiencing today. It is not unreasonable to expect parallel consequences.

My personal story has numerous examples of intellectual intimidation and outright bullying disguised under a variety of instruments and concocted "Islamic" principles, such as "enjoining good and preventing of evil", or scare tactics such as "you will be misleading many people if your reasoning turns out to be wrong". Surprisingly, these tactics that are presumably intended to protect Islam from evils, wrongs, and heresy were not applied to the likes of ibn Kathir (d. 774/1373) the most prominent Mushaf exegete (amongst Sunni Muslims) when he claimed that the Prophet transmitted Satanic verses.[9] In the Canadian town in which I have lived for many years, the elites of the Muslim establishment accused me of *fitna*, an Arabic term that can be translated as mischief, although the religious and historical connotations of the term imply more profound imagery than mere children's play. My sin deserving of the *fitna* accusation was to inquire about the financial transactions of a local masjid and to support an online petition exposing the possible financial mischief that was taking place in that masjid. On a recent trip to a Middle Eastern country, I committed the "sin" of discussing the "creation" in the Mushaf and made the implication that both transformation and evolution can be a direct implication of the Mushaf text. In a matter of seconds, my interpretation was declared by a close relative of mine to be *kufr*. *Kufr*, a term that I will revisit later in this book, appears repeatedly in the Mushaf. It refers to a deeply serious transgression against God that involves denial of truth. Of course, once a person is labeled as *kafir* (the actor of *kufr*), then perhaps shedding his blood would be a matter of time and opportunity. Perhaps the person who take it upon himself to get rid of a *kafir* would be considered a hero and a savior and purifier of the faith.

To make this system of intimidation far-reaching and most effective, it has to be in the name of religion or it has to be structured and embedded within the faith itself. After all, faith is extremely powerful as it needs no proof at all. The faithful cannot prove what he has faith in and the disbeliever has no proof to counteract the faithful. What can be more powerful than something one believes in without any rational proof? It has to be that in itself!

The seeds of a grand conspiracy to create grand intimidation of Muslims were implanted early in the history of Muslims by Muslims who realized the amazing power of faith. Indeed, it is a conspiracy of Eastern origins without infidels. This conspiracy most likely evolved during or immediately after the death of Prophet Muhammad and climaxed and perfected during the Umayyad and Abbasid dynasties (41/661-656/1258), a conspiracy that was hatched or largely patronized by the power elites to ensure their monopoly on power. The conspiracy succeeded to a certain extent as exemplified by the grand wars that took place in the first Muslim Century (wars that were led by the companions of the Prophet) but needed steady infusion of "Islamic" religious doctrines to keep the multitudes in line and in servitude to the state. The copious body of doctrines produced in the course of this long running scheme has been one of the most formidable challenges to understanding Islam, by Muslims and non-Muslims alike, but more importantly and practically, it has been a force that impeded progress in the Muslim communities and for Muslims at large.

European colonialism of most Muslim countries over the past 300 years contributed significantly to their systemic economic weakness and broad social injustice.[10] Despite its long-term horrific consequences, colonialism contributed only partially to the overall retardation of Muslim societies. It is extremely hard to gauge the effect of colonialism on the prevailing religious doctrines within Muslim nations. Indeed colonial powers undoubtedly exercised influence on local governments and religious clergy under their rule, but there is no evidence showing that these colonial powers created religious doctrines to serve their needs.

The present practiced "Islam", which is a religion sanctioned by practically all states with Muslim majority, and especially by states that define themselves as Islamic, in my opinion, is the cause behind the backwardness and misery that inflicts the Muslim world. This state-sanctioned religion stifles every noble principle Islam came to uphold, most important of which is freedom. It sabotaged the true Islam and diverted it into a doctrine of submissiveness and fatalism. The liberating and energizing concept of agency of humans along with free will, both overly stressed in the book of Islam, the Mushaf, were completely circumvented and replaced with predestination, for no purpose but to turn Muslims into a flock succumbing to the will of the political ruler rather than the will of Allah.

When a person dies under the hands of a careless surgeon, the tendency among Muslims is to accept the tragedy and human loss as a predestined event, an event that was decreed before Allah created the universe or was decided upon when that person was born, or simply an "act of God". In fact, Muslims typically frown at those who do not accept and exercise patience towards these "acts of God" for their presumed lack of faith, and accepting the untimely death as predestined and unavoidable. Fatalism, to name only one disease, became a de-facto pillar of Muslims religion.

The Arabic language and grammar were retooled to serve a grand plan of turning Islam, whose core principle is upholding truth, into a tranquilizer. The Muslims lost the will to live and to participate in this world, with a restructured ideology that made them oscillate between a fictitious past utopia and the pleasures of the hereafter. Muslims came to resemble an old sick man who lost hope in life.

Laying the blame where it belongs is important, but colonialism is only part of the factors that led to the retardation of the Muslim world. The colonialists are no longer amongst Muslims occupying their lands, however, Muslims with predominant doctrinal thinking inherited from the Umayyad, Abbasid and possibly successive Muslim empires are amongst us. Colonialism of the direct and military type is long gone, but religious doctrines that have no foundation in the Mushaf have remained amongst Muslims and have penetrated their innermost psyche. Those religious doctrines (the Sunnah, Hadith, Usool al-Fiqh, Ijtihad, etc.) were so meticulously interwoven within the fabric of the state-sanctioned Islam that one can only counter and negate them, not by mere rejection of these doctrines, but only through serious efforts to understand and engage with the primary source of Islam, the Mushaf.

Many Muslims refuse to believe that there is anything wrong with their understanding of Islam. This happens for a variety of reasons, including institutionalized marginalization and sometimes for fear of a backlash. While decrying non-Muslims lack of patience to understand Islam, any serious discussion of the faith is harshly condemned under a systematic and methodical procedure of intimidation that intends to silence any dissent from classical modes of religious interpretation and thinking.

I am not advocating an Islamic reformation, nor am I advocating a modern (whatever the often-used term "modern" typically invokes) interpretation of the Mushaf. Advocates for modernizing or reforming Islam are mostly non-Muslims who I will not necessarily characterize as Islam antagonists but typically have an impression and a perspective of Islam that was shaped by traditional Muslim doctrines, the types that evolved throughout the ages. Of course, there are some who have hatred and hostility towards Islam and Muslims for a variety of reasons, but these, I hope, would have gained a more positive impression of Islam had Muslims left aside the inherited dogmas and the "Islamic" tradition.

Am I advocating for an age of Muslim enlightenment or a Muslim renaissance? These are partial possibilities. Yes, Muslims need enlightenment and renaissance of their own. Muslims should not fear or be alarmed by a Muslim, or better yet, Islamic Renaissance or Islamic Enlightenment. If the European historical model is any lesson, Europe went through a transformation where rationality, causality and common sense prevailed over actions that were explained only by invoking the divine and the wisdom of the Church. Europe started to deal with reality first, then the unseen, not the other way around. Yet, through and after the Age of Enlightenment, Europeans did not cease to be religious. There was no purge of the Christians nor of religion from Europe.

What I am after is a serious and rigorous approach to understanding Islam as a religion. I may not be able to provide a fully satisfactory definition for seriousness, but I find it easier to attempt seriousness with potential shortcomings than attempting correctness. Seriousness might

The Cause for the Beginning

not be easily defined, but specifying or preaching a correct approach implies elitism and a sense of superiority.

This book is not about the good or bad intentions of non-Muslims. It is not about answering misconceptions held by non-Muslims. It is not about proving that Muslims are right and everyone else is wrong. It is not about interfaith dialogue, yet it hopes to contribute towards that effort. This book is an attempt to answer a question that haunted me for years, about identifying and taking a closer look at the cause behind deeply entrenched stagnation in Muslims' engagement with their religion. This book questions dogma and traditional thinking amongst Muslims that has gone unquestioned for hundreds of years, or perhaps had gone questioned but has been repeatedly silenced whenever and wherever such dissent has surfaced. A cursory look into the history of Muslim thinkers, scholars and scientists reveals accusations of apostasy, *zandaqa, kufr,* etc. leveled against many scientists and thinkers such as ibn Hayyan, ibn Arabi and ibn Sina by Salafi sects.[11] I expect the attack against Muslim intellectuals and thinkers will continue, however, the monopoly over religion is waning dramatically.

To Muslim readers, a warning is in order: if you believe that everything that needs to be known about Islam is known, then this book is certainly not for you. If you are a Muslim and believe that no one can introduce material to help Muslims and non-Muslims understand Islam better than the multitudes of "Islamic scholars" who have produced thousands of volumes and commentaries on the Mushaf and traditions of prophet Muhammad, then this book is definitely not for you. If you are a Muslim and believe that everything that can be understood about the Mushaf has been explained fully by numerous highly respected exegetes and nothing more can be added, then this book is certainly not for you. If you are a Muslim and believe that it is wrong to challenge famous "scholars of Islam" simply because they are "People of Knowledge", then this book will offend you in many ways. For those Muslims who are happy and satisfied with all that is going on around them, reading this book can be a wasteful exercise. This book is also not for Muslims who are comfortable with the status quo and do not see any reason to be uncomfortable at the unimaginable loss of lives, destruction and helplessness sweeping the "Islamic World" or wherever injustice is taking place. If you are a Muslim and have deep scorn and disrespect for the intellectual ability of humans, this book will aggravate you immensely. Finally, for those who believe intellectual inquiry is dangerous, this book is equally dangerous!

To non-Muslim readers, I have no warnings at all. The book will show you that Muslim-made doctrines are largely concoctions that evolved without much scrutiny, that Islam is embodied in one book, the Mushaf, and no one is divinely ordained to be its official interpreter. The non-Muslim reader will even be surprised to learn that even the Prophet of Islam did not provide an interpretation of the Book or an appendix to the Mushaf detailing his commentary. The non-Muslim reader might find comfort in seeing the parallels between how Islam was diverted to become an instrument of control and war and how similar diversions occurred in other religions, including Judaism, Christianity, Hinduism and Buddhism. Most critically, this book will show that the message of the Mushaf is universal and extends beyond those who embrace Islam. This book will empower non-Muslims to understand the Mushaf without Muslim or non-Muslim intermediaries, an understanding that is essential to know Islam and to dispel man-made mysteries that have become synonymous with Islam.

Finally, this book is not an attempt to modernize Islam, but rather to understand Islam from its original and only source.

---

1. Chomsky, Noam. *On Power and Ideology.* South End Press, 1990.
2. Said, Edward. *Orientalism.* Vintage, 1979.
3. Kurzman, Charles and Ernst, Carl. "Islamic Studies in U.S. Universities". *Review of Middle East Studies,* vol. 46, Middle East Studies Association of North America (MESA), 2012.
4. In general, the Mu'tazalites in Muslim history refers to rationalists who believed that the mind has a central role in understanding Islam. Their opponents, the advocates of strict adherence to the Prophetic traditions, succeeded in projecting the Mu'tazalites as heretics or as a fringe group not worthy of respect or even inclusion in the body of the Muslim *umma*. It is important to note that the label Mu'tazalites

was given to them by their enemy since it connotes isolation or desertion. As the Mu'tazalites evolved, they referred to themselves as Ahl al-Adl wa al-Tawheed.

5. Lacey, Robert. *The Kingdom: Arabia and the House of Saud.* Harcourt Brace Jovanovich, 1981. Lacey gives an excellent expose of the rise of the Saudi dynasty and how the British supported the Wahhabi Muslims of Arabia to rally the Arab tribes in support of ibn Saud conquests.
6. The Sykes-Picot treaty was a 1916 secret treaty between the UK and France to divide and colonize the Middle East.
7. Wahhabism refers to a religious sect based on the writings of Muhammad ibn Abdulwahhab (d. 1206/1792), and borrows heavily from ibn Taymiyyah (d. 728/1328) and Ahmed ibn Hanbal (d. 241/855).
8. According to the Catholic Encyclopedia, infidel refers to non-Christians or those who were not baptised.
9. Ibn Kathir, abu al-Fida Imaduddin Ismail. *Tafseer al-Qur'aan al-Azeem (Tafsir ibn Kathir).* Dar al-Salaam, 2012.
10. Williamson, Jeffrey G. and Clingingsmith, David. India's Deindustrialization in the 18th and 19th Centuries (PDF). Harvard University, 2005. Accessed 18 May 2017. An example is the decline of India's economic power during the British colonization. Under the British rule, India's share of the world economy declined from 24.4% in 1700 to 4.2% in 1950,[12] and its share of global industrial output declined from 25% in 1750 to 2% in 1900.
11. Al-Fahid, Nasir ibn Hamad. *Haqiqat al-Hadharah al-Islamiyya.* Manbar al-Tawheed wa al-Jihad, 2006.

2

SCIENCE OF MARGINALIZATION

يَا أَيُّهَا الَّذِينَ آمَنُوا لَا يَسْخَرْ قَوْمٌ مِّن قَوْمٍ عَسَىٰ أَن يَكُونُوا خَيْرًا مِّنْهُمْ وَلَا نِسَاءٌ مِّن نِّسَاءٍ عَسَىٰ أَن يَكُنَّ خَيْرًا مِّنْهُنَّ ۖ وَلَا تَلْمِزُوا أَنفُسَكُمْ وَلَا تَنَابَزُوا بِالْأَلْقَابِ ۖ بِئْسَ الِاسْمُ الْفُسُوقُ بَعْدَ الْإِيمَانِ ۚ وَمَن لَّمْ يَتُبْ فَأُولَٰئِكَ هُمُ الظَّالِمُونَ

O you who have believed, let not a people ridicule another people lest they may be better than them; nor let women ridicule other women; perhaps they may be better than them. And do not insult one another and do not call each other by offensive nicknames. Wretched is the name of disobedience after belief. And whoever does not repent - then it is those who are the oppressors.

M49:11

WHO QUALIFIES TO SPEAK ABOUT ISLAM

Who are you to speak about Islam? What qualifications do you have to discuss the Mushaf, let alone write a book about Islam? Are you a *sheikh* (religious figure)? Are you a *mufti* (religious edict issuer)? Are you a *hujjat* (high-ranking jurisprudence scholar)? Are you an *alim* (religious scholar)? Have you studied at al-Azhar, Medina, Najaf, or Qum? Do you have an *ijaza* (certificate) from a *sheikh*? How many Prophetic narratives have you memorized after all? Did you memorize the Mushaf? But what if your claims were wrong, are you not afraid of committing a sin and ending up in hellfire? Are you more knowledgeable than all those *ulama* (Muslim scholars) to challenge their consensus or their commentaries on religion and their respected knowledge and *ilm* (science)? Are you claiming that everyone else is wrong in his or her understanding of Islam and you are the only one who is right? Are you an expert in the Arabic language to comment on the Mushaf? These are a few examples of the types of interrogatory and intimidating questions that I have encountered whenever I have presented what I believe to be logical, if unconventional, interpretations of the Mushaf, or whenever I questioned prevailing doctrines considered by many as an integral part of Islam. These questions are valuable material for a university philosophy course on common fallacies, therefore, I will leave their analysis from the logical perspective for that venue. These questions are mentioned here only to suggest the type of Muslim culture they reflect: a culture that has largely succumbed to intimidation and bullying; the antithesis of Islam's core philosophy of infinite intellectualism, infinite eternal curiosity and unlimited progress.

Marginalization and intimidation, brewed to perfection since the dawn of the Umayyad and Abbasid dynasties, are two overriding features that color Muslims' religious culture.[1] While I wholeheartedly assume the non-malicious intent of those who ask any of the questions listed above, these questions represent the first line of defense (or denial) one encounters when attempting to provide a logic-based and reality-based interpretation to the Mushaf. These are the same questions one encounters when questioning conventional orthodox doctrines and Islamic jurisprudence principles that were created, as evidence suggests, from whims and opinions. These questions which I have encountered too often are products of a static and intellectually-petrified culture, frozen in time and space, negating intellectualism and fiercely resistant and opposed to intellectual progress. The broad intellectual stagnation amongst Muslims may be rooted in what has evolved as a religious culture deeply embedded in their thinking irrespective of the commitment to religious rituals.

Who is entitled to speak about Islam and what constitutes Islam? What constitute things and practices that are "Islamic"? An analogy to a subject different from religion, such as perhaps mathematics, will help answer these questions. Who is entitled to speak about mathematics? If we circulate this question amongst mathematicians all over the world, what answer would we expect? Should only Harvard mathematicians be entitled to speak about math or only those who were mentored by Professor X, the recipient of the grandest prize in mathematics and who is known to be the most brilliant mathematician alive today? In the same vein, one may ask who is entitled to present a paper in the most reputable conference on quantum physics. When a person submits a paper to the conference in question, the material of the paper is scrutinized for accuracy, logic, and validity through a stringent review process (as is the custom in reputable scientific venues, where the higher the reputation of the scientific journal, the higher the scrutiny of the submitted manuscripts). In fact, many conferences and journals submit the contribution to a blind review, which means that what matters most is not the lineage, prestige, fame or stature of the contributor but the soundness and correctness of the contribution. For mathematics, anyone can speak about mathematics as long as that person provides mathematics that makes sense and is correct. It may be safe to assume that mathematicians would be interested to hear from anyone who can solve some of the most puzzling problems in their field, regardless of the attributes and accolades of that person. Similarly, anyone can contribute to biomedical technology, as long as the contribution is validated either by reasoning or by experiment. The mind behind all wireless technology, motor technology, hydropower technology, all navigation technology, and most biomedical devices was a man with very little formal education. When Michael Faraday discovered and formalized the laws of electromagnetic induction, he was not ridiculed for having no formal education. No one has a monopoly over correctness. Correct knowledge is assumed to mean that the knowledge was derived based on reasoning or empirical finding, subject to what scientists refer to as the scientific method. Reason is not only essential to correctness but is the epitome of human existence. (Amongst the Salafis and Ahl al-Sunnah wa al-Jamma'ah, reason was considered inseparable from philosophy which was considered a pillar of atheism).[2]

An assertion makes sense when it is based on axioms (and in some fields, assumptions) of the field under study and when it builds upon validated knowledge without contradicting that knowledge. The ability of someone to contribute to mathematics is different from the credibility one has to teach mathematics, for the latter needs credentials and certificates testifying to the knowledge of the applicant and the ability to teach a well-defined subject in an institution that has accepted that knowledge. Contributing to a subject can be helped by having specific credentials but they are not a necessity. Meaningful knowledge contribution needs substantiation and rationality. The one who teaches a subject does not need to be the one who contributes to it. The first reproduces knowledge while the second produces knowledge.

Mushaf uses a spectrum of different terms to distinguish between knowledge, information and inspiration generated by people. For instance, two important verbs in the Mushaf are *qaala* and *talaa*. The first is typically translated as "said" and the second one as "narrated" or "recited". *Qaala* can imply "have said", but not always. *Qaala* can mean "produced", "formed", or "fashioned new information or knowledge". (An understanding of the meaning of *qaala* does not only help to understand issues relating to the production of knowledge, but has significant implications on the relationship between Muslims and non-Muslims, as will be explained in Chapter 4.)

The correctness of an argument, as it stands by itself and backed by evidence, had been the only way science was able to express or uncover truths. Modern understandings of what constitutes science are varied. Also, not all methodologies used to discover science are accepted by all scholars and scientists as scientific methodologies. Nevertheless, what defines science is the methodologies.[3] Science is a system by which truths are found. Scientists do not create truths, they simply discover them. Scientists also exert effort to understand truths. The Mushaf gives prominence to *haqq* (truth) in more than 263 verses. The opposite of *haqq* is *batil* (falsehood). A statement or a piece of information that represents facts is true whereas a statement that conceals facts is untrue, false or *batil*. To speak about mathematics, one must provide substantiation with mathematical proofs rather than invoking lineage, pedigree, prestige, or any type of authority.

Islam's goal, if not its ultimate one, is to reach truths. This means that anyone can speak about Islam as long as that person follows a process of rational reasoning that validates the arguments presented. Even a person who does not believe in Islam can talk about Islam. Contribution to the truth can come from anyone irrespective of believing in Allah, Muhammad, both or neither. The person can be of any color, gender, age, creed or nationality. Contrary to popular understanding amongst most Muslims, anyone can comment on the Mushaf. Whether the commentary is worthy of any respect amongst Muslims or non-Muslims depends on whether or not it makes any sense and does not contradict reality. The preconditions widely imposed by Muslims on who is entitled to comment on the Mushaf, such as having memorized the Mushaf, having perfected the Arabic language, having studied the traditions of Prophet Muhammad, being aware of the "secrets" of Mushaf, being aware of which parts of the Mushaf are abrogated (i.e., nullified) are all methods of intimidation and marginalization, all evolved within the Muslim culture or influenced by political rulers.

These intimidation techniques, whether by design or accident, resulted in separating Muslims into classes. If the Mushaf is based on truths, then it can accept commentary from anyone who is interested in the truth and who uses instruments of rationality and reason rather than falsehood in his or her commentary. Even the commentaries on the Mushaf by contemporaries of the Prophet cannot be accepted without substantive and validated arguments. The fact that a certain companion narrated something is not sufficient to establish the truth of the substance of the narrative, no matter how important that companion was.

Of course, any commentary, irrespective of its source, should be subjected to analysis and scrutiny. Commentaries either make sense or not. Philosophy, which has traditionally served to develop a process of reasoning to arrive at truths, had been turned into an archenemy of most Muslim sects. In effect, the majority of Salafi scholars equate philosophy with *zandaqa*, thereby forging a divide between Islam and rationality.[4]

Another important question concerns what constitutes Islam, Islamic knowledge, Islamic studies or anything deserving of the adjective "Islamic". Many Muslim scholars would argue that the field of Islamic studies refers to evolving Muslim legal doctrines that evolved throughout the ages. At many North American universities, Islamic Studies might also include "Islamic" architecture, art, philosophy, economics, sociology, and mysticism. Some even attempted to "Islamize" knowledge itself.[5] Ironically, missing from the rush to Islamize things are "Islamic" mathematics, "Islamic" Chemistry, "Islamic" Biology and "Islamic" Physics; after all, these disciplines have connection to the Mushaf in one way or another. Even the body of knowledge that encompasses the jurisprudential output of major Muslim sects (such as Hanbali, Shafi'i, Hanafi, Maliki, Ja'fari, Imami, Zaidi, Abadhi, etc.) was produced after the end of Muhammad's Prophethood, and thus have nothing "Islamic" about it. The skeptics need to look no further than M5:3

Science of Marginalization

اَلْيَوْمَ أَكْمَلْتُ لَكُمْ دِينَكُمْ وَأَتْمَمْتُ عَلَيْكُمْ نِعْمَتِي وَرَضِيتُ لَكُمُ الْإِسْلَامَ دِينًا

[On this day, I have completed your religion for you and finalized my providence on you and contently have chosen Islam as your religion.] Thus, any knowledge produced after the completion of religion is outside of the "Islamic" realm. Not surprisingly, the adjective Islamic never appears in the entire Mushaf.

Scholars, Muslims or non-Muslims, never provided a rationale for qualifying a specific discipline, science, art, or profession as "Islamic". Once something is declared Islamic, there are others that must be non-Islamic or un-Islamic. There are numerous references in the Mushaf to astronomical phenomena, but the astronomy or cosmology mentioned in the Mushaf has nothing Islamic about it. The Mushaf prohibits usury () and one may indeed create a link between injunctions regarding the specific act of usury in the Mushaf and an economic system. But is such a link sufficient to qualify that particular economic system as Islamic?[6] It is also possible to make a link between certain injunctions in the Mushaf specifying social manners of entering a house and culturally-dependent social etiquettes. Can we then start carving a social behavior that we might label as Islamic etiquette?

What about Islamic architecture? One of the oldest masjids in existence is Uqba ibn Nafi'i in the city of Qairawan, Tunisia. The domes of that masjid look Byzantine. What would characterize particular architecture as Islamic? The adjective "Islamic" qualifies a noun to be connected or related to Islam, the religion, with an implication of the existence of the "un-Islamic". Of course, spending time to analyze the precise use of the adjective "Islamic" might be a waste of time. If we all understand the definition, then we all should bu'qe content. However, the problem, and arguably the danger is that whatever is referred to as "Islamic" can be conveniently grouped under the religion of Islam (and consequently be included in a curriculum on Islamic studies) where in reality, the religion Islam is a different thing altogether.[7]

According to M5:3, the religion was completed by the end of Muhammad's Prophethood. It only makes sense to consider Islam, in its purest form, the religion that was completed then. As can be inferred directly from the Mushaf, Islam could not have been waiting for someone who would be born centuries after Muhammad's death to complete or put the final touches on the religion. A belief in such a possibility contradicts Islam's divine revelation. Also, had that been the case, the companions of Muhammad would have experienced an incomplete religion. It must be emphasized here that completeness of the religion is different from understanding all that needs to be understood in this universe, including full understanding of the Mushaf itself. Any work that would be produced after the end of the Prophethood to help understand the religion would indeed be welcomed and needed, but not new rules and doctrines, or a new religion packaged under different guises. Therefore, it is reasonable to study Islam from its unadulterated source if one is interested in the religion itself.

Muslims undoubtedly enriched the sciences, but their contributions were a result of many factors, including the patronage of rich empires whose foundations and practice were not necessarily based on the principles of Islam. The magnificent contributions of the great Muslim scientists and philosophers were part of a human chain of visionaries and brilliant individuals, some of whom we know and some we may never know. In fact, the label "Islamic" can be a double-edged sword. If the adjective Islamic refers to an action performed by Muslims, then distasteful and wrong actions committed by Muslims will be justifiably referred to as Islamic. One can argue that particular interpretations of the Mushaf inspired a generation of backwardness and servitude. Neither science and progress nor backwardness can justifiably be labeled "Islamic". If a country that calls itself Islamic commits blunders, Muslims should not be surprised that non-Muslims would perceive that Islamic country or government in a negative light. In fact, if a Muslim commits terrorism, we should not be surprised either if the act is labeled as Islamic terrorism.

INFATUATION WITH PERSONALITIES

Many Muslims have become absorbed by dogma, mysticism, irrationality and infatuation with personalities and scholarly figures of past centuries. Many Muslims have also elevated the status of the companions of the Prophet to extraordinary levels along with near-divine attributes. It is not clear who can be considered to be the "companions of the Prophet", or more precisely those who are referred to as *sahaaba*. In fact, no consensus is available as to who the *sahaaba* were. Some defined the *sahaaba* broadly and include anyone who lived during the time of the Prophet. Others defined *sahaaba* as anyone who had any interaction with the Prophet, no matter how brief the interaction was. According to al-Bukhari (the compiler of the Sahih al-Bukhari Hadith compendium), the *sahaaba* are people who accompanied the Prophet or have seen the Prophet with their own eyes.[8] Others restricted the definition to those who accompanied the Prophet for extended periods.[9] Al-Nawawi (d. 676/1277) had a very expansive definition that considered as part of *sahaaba* anyone who saw the Messenger of Allah even if for a moment.[10] Most interestingly, according to al-Nawawi's definition, the hypocrites who came and met with the Prophet (see M63:1) are also classified as *sahaaba*.

These different categorizations are hardly important unless one realizes the significance attributed to the *sahaaba* and the enormous implications that follow and impact the way Muslims practice their religion. Interestingly, despite these varying definitions, ibn Salah, (d. 643/1245), the author of one of the major books on the Sciences of Hadith, after giving different definitions for who qualifies to be a *sahaabi* (singular of *sahaaba*), dismisses the different definitions altogether and highlights the unique attributes of the *sahaaba*, particularly their *adaalat* (ability to execute absolute justice).[11] Ibn Salah's reasoning is equally interesting. He claimed that their *adaalat* is sanctioned by the Qur'aan, the Sunnah and the Ijma (collective agreement on religious matters) of who is worthy of making Ijma from the *umma* (the collective Muslim body).[12] He supports his assertion by invoking M3:110 and makes the profound claim that the exegetes (presumably all) have agreed that the verse was related to the companions of the Prophet. (He even cites M2:143 and M48:29 to buttress his claim).

The Shia sects, on the other hand, did not give any special status to the *sahaaba* but elevated the status of certain descendants of Prophet Muhammad, later to be called imams, to levels not only higher than all people that proceeded Muhammad but also to a status not even attained by prophets.[13] Notice the parallelism to Christianity, where the apostles of Jesus were elevated to a near-Prophet or near-divine status. Naturally, one wonders if there were motives behind the prevalent practice of developing a hierarchical structure of importance amongst people and even prophets. In hindsight, one can assume that establishing the importance of a specific person or group of individuals is a prelude to establishing high importance to what is attributed to that person or group. The outcome of the manufactured hierarchy of significance and closeness to Allah resulted in accepting what was said and done by the *sahaaba* and imams as doctrines integral to Islam. Such elevation of the *sahaaba* and imams indeed had very detrimental effect on understanding Islam, possibly similar to the detrimental effects the writings of the Apostles had on understanding Christianity.

If a Muslim is confronted with an implausible and illogical conclusion about a certain explanation of some religious subject, about a certain physical phenomenon or something else, one should not be surprised if the answer comes in the form: "Allah is capable of anything". Granted that the religion, any faith, or even modern sciences begin with some assumptions, but it appears that all of Islam has been turned into assumptions, and a mixture of irrationalism, unseen, and inexplicable phenomena, all in the name of the same mantra "Allah is capable of anything". From articles of faith counted by the fingers of one hand, the Muslims transformed Islam into numerous articles of faith. In the end, the religion was turned into a faith. These numerous additions, together with larger-than-life religious figures, both contemporary and ancient, are never to be questioned. The opinions, judgments and interpretations of these figures became the truth, not because of logic or reason but mostly because of whom they were and the alarmingly inflated reverence they have acquired throughout the ages. Even if these personalities make disastrous errors, they are still viewed with utmost reverence. Even if they make catastrophic blunders, they are still heroes and champions in the eyes of millions of Muslims (see the discussion on the concept of Ijtihad in Chapter 9).

The attribution of authority to celebrated individuals has had a profound effect on how Muslims think, live, on the evolution of Muslim schools of jurisprudence, and most critically, on how they understand Islam. Infatuation with personality served to mentally shackle Muslims and discouraged independent inquiry based on reason, reality and the Mushaf. It will take a considerable effort and time to liberate Muslims from the dominance of a culture that discourages inquiry and inhibits free thinking and elevates personalities to divine status. It is not surprising to see two, three, or four lines, if not more, of the most flowery accolades bestowed upon Muslim historical figures that even Prophet Muhammad's accolades pale in comparison. As an example, in one book ibn Taymiyyah (d. 728/1328) is introduced by five lines of honors never bestowed upon the Prophet:[14]

قال شيخنا وسيدنا الإمام العلامة القدوة الزاهد العابد الورع الكامل شيخ الإسلام مفتي الفرق ناصر السنة قامع البدعة سيد الفقهاء والحفاظ تقي الدين أبو العباس أحمد بن شيخنا الإمام العلامة مفتي المسلمين شهاب الدين أبي المحاسن عبد الحليم بن الإمام العلامة شيخ الإسلام مجد الدين أبي البركات عبد السلام بن عبد الله بن أبي القاسم بن محمد بن تيمية الحراني جزاه الله عن نصر دينه ونصر سنة نبيه عليه السلام خيرا

[Our Sheikh, the master imam, the erudite example, the austere, the worshipper, the pious, the complete, the sheikh of Islam, the edict-giver, the Sunnah supporter, the eliminator of innovations, the master of jurisprudents and memorizers, Taqi al-Deen abu al-Abbas Ahmed, the son of our Sheikh the erudite Imam, the edict-giver of Muslims, Shahab al-Deen Abi almahasin Abdulhalim, the son of Sheikh al-Islam Majd al-din abi albarakat Abdussalam, the son of Abdullah, the son of abi al-Qasim son of Muhammad, the son of Taymiyyah al-Harrany, may Allah reward him for supporting His religion and supporting the tradition of his prophet...] In more recent times, an entire conference was dedicated to interpreting a single edict given by ibn Taymiyyah.[15] It is truly amazing that never a single saying or tradition of the Prophet had been given such dedication and importance, let alone a single verse from the Mushaf.

Even the Prophet did not escape such irrational and misplaced reverence. Many Muslims have attached divine attributes to the Prophet, such as "the lord of the two universes and the lord of jinn and humans", and have attributed *ismat* (infallibility) to the Prophet, implying that he did not commit any errors in anything he did or in any of the judgments or decisions he made in spite of repeated references in the Mushaf that he is incapable of performing acts beyond man's physical capacity and attributes. This unsubstantiated elevation of the status of the Prophet suggests that the Muslims were competing with Christians in showing off the supernaturalism of their Prophet, and hence, the subnarrative would imply, his alleged superiority over that of the Christians' Prophet.

The supernatural attributes bestowed upon Prophet Muhammad are contrary to his message and distract from and diminish the strength and effectiveness of the message. One can see similarities here with many Christian sects, in a conception of Muhammad based on a model adopted by those sects where Jesus was considered not only a prophet but also the son of God, and hence was infallible with divine attributes. Despite emphatic denial by many Muslims, there is a striking similarity between the perception of Jesus amongst the majority of Christians and of Muhammad amongst the majority of Muslims. Throughout history, when intellectualism diminishes, personality worship increases. The history of Muslims is not an exception.

Attaching divine attributes to Muhammad deviated the focus from the Message that Muhammad delivered, which is the essence of Islam. The Mushaf emphasizes the physical limitation of Muhammad due primarily to him being a *bashar* (the physiological form of the human being) in numerous verses (see M3:144, 7:188, 11:31 amongst others). The Mushaf never even came close to giving divine attributes to Muhammad, but stressed the contrary. The underlying assumption by many Muslims is that the higher the status a believer bestows upon the Prophet, the stronger the faith of the believer becomes. According to the prevailing attitudes amongst not only many Muslims but also their scholars is that if one questions the Prophet's divine attributes, then one's faith is in peril!

This Mushaf-contradictory status of Muhammad, manufactured from narratives and legends, whether by design or by excessive zeal, facilitated a grand diversion of Muslims from the pure religion to an infinitely mercurial new religion that can be shaped to fit one's objectives as and when needed. In fact, the diversion of Muhammad status from that described in the Mushaf to a divine status has paved the way to legitimizing a huge body of manufactured and falsified religious material wrongly and intentionally attributed to the Prophet. The inflated, incorrect, and Mushaf-incompatible image of the Prophet has led some of the major scholars of Islam to invoke or reference narratives and traditions of the Prophet with low probability of authenticity, on the assumption that even if the authenticity of the tradition was weak (i.e., highly improbable), some benefits might be achieved without even giving any slight reason of how the benefit might come about.[16]

Ask the People of *Thikr*

Another common practice to silence whoever attempts an independent and reasoned approach to understanding Islam is by invoking a phrase from M16:43

Science of Marginalization

$$\text{فَاسْأَلُوا أَهْلَ الذِّكْرِ إِن كُنتُمْ لَا تَعْلَمُونَ}$$

[Ask the people of *thikr* if you do not comprehend/understand.] This phrase is used to distance Muslims from direct engagement with the Mushaf by deferring its interpretation to an exclusive group of people, those of *thikr*. Despite not providing an interpretation of *thikr*, by invocation of this verse, the implication is that Muslims are incapable of understanding on their own, and therefore must ask those who are knowledgeable, meaning the "scholars of Islam", for help in interpreting and understanding the Mushaf, and by extension, anything related to the religion. Many from the Shia sect, on the other hand, believe that the people of *thikr* are the infallible imams who are the only ones who effectively have monopoly on understanding the religion or the imams and the Prophet (those Shias do not provide any validation for either interpretation).[17] Tabatabaa'i (d. 1401/1981), a leading Shia scholar of the 20th Century and a highly respected scholar amongst Shias, deviated from the classical Shia thinking by providing a logical argument rather than reliance on earlier hadiths and believes that the people of *thikr* could be the people of Torah (specifically rather than the Jews).[18]

The problem with the typical usage of the above phrase in M16:43 becomes clear when realizing that the phrase is only a part of a verse. In fact, it is not only a part of a verse but the verse is also a part of a sentence. If the complete sentence, which extends to two verses is considered, we arrive at a different meaning. Here is M16:43, 44

$$\text{وَمَا أَرْسَلْنَا مِن قَبْلِكَ إِلَّا رِجَالًا نُوحِي إِلَيْهِمْ ۚ فَاسْأَلُوا أَهْلَ الذِّكْرِ إِن كُنتُمْ لَا تَعْلَمُونَ}$$
$$\text{بِالْبَيِّنَاتِ وَالزُّبُرِ ۗ وَأَنزَلْنَا إِلَيْكَ الذِّكْرَ لِتُبَيِّنَ لِلنَّاسِ مَا نُزِّلَ إِلَيْهِمْ وَلَعَلَّهُمْ يَتَفَكَّرُونَ}$$

[And we have sent before you but men that we revealed unto them. Thus, ask the people of *thikr* if you did not understand of the clear sign and *zubur*, and we have revealed to you the *thikr* so you may clarify to people what had been revealed to them and list they contemplate.] The full sentence indicates that the people of *thikr* are those who have knowledge of the previous books, not those "who know". There is simply no rationale or reference in the Mushaf or a Prophetic narrative to stretch the meaning of the people of *thikr* to self-appointed, socially-appointed, or politically-appointed scholars, or as specialists, scientists or scholars in general. It is comforting that the majority of exegesis adopted this contextual and logical understanding of who the people of *thikr* are; yet part of the verse is used widely in contradiction to this understanding and repeatedly and almost universally amongst Muslims as a tool of intimidation and marginalization.

The most intimidating and offensive tactic of suppressing intellectual and religious inquiry is the invocation of the "people of *thikr*" or its modern variant, "consult the specialists". The underlying assumption is that not anyone can discuss or understand Islam independently; that one needs to consult those who are specialists in Islam. The proponents of the "specialists" tactic often refer to medical specialization that one consults when in need of medical attention rather than seeking the help of anyone else[19].

There are numerous problems with these arguments. In fact, not all medical doctors are licensed for consultation or practice. For this, exams, certifications and licensing are all needed and only then can a medical doctor be allowed by the governing authority to practice medicine. There is an important distinction between controlled practice and knowledge. After all, medical doctors obtain significant amounts of their knowledge from scientists who are not allowed to practice medicine. Similarly, a PhD in electrical engineering, while having an amazing amount of knowledge about electronics, may or may not be allowed to do the wiring of a one-room cottage simply because he may not be licensed for such practice. In fact, the electrician who is licensed to do the wiring may or may not know electrical engineering or the physics of wiring altogether.

The confusion arises when religion is considered as a vocation or a practice.[20] The definition and context of the "specialist", nevertheless, is typically lost in the heat of these very feisty and convoluted debates. Many Muslim scholars consider themselves as specialists on Islam. But how did this come about? Or a better question yet is what constitutes an Islam specialist? Most Muslim religious scholars would consider having a Bachelor of Arts degree in Sharia, Fiqh, or Qur'anic studies from a recognized Muslim university be sufficient to qualify as a specialist. Indeed, this person will be a specialist in what the respective university considers as an approved subject. But the problem here lies in that the subjects that Muslim or "Islamic" universities teach have no connection to science and no matter how vast and complex the subject might be, it remains a collection of information most of which is contradictory (as will be discussed in Chapters 6-9).

There could be a benefit to study such vast amounts of information, but that makes the student a specialist in this information, but not a specialist in religion. For example, a historian studies history and historical records and perhaps adds analysis that sheds light on historical events. However, the historian is not a scientist of history. Analyzing the Sahih al-Bukhari Hadith compendium for various objectives does not make the person a religious scholar. Similarly, having impressive knowledge of the amazingly complex classification of Hadith (exceeding twenty-seven types according to several prominent Muslim scholars) does not make a person a religious scholar, but simply a specialist in the historical classification of Hadith.[21] Being not aware of or studying all these Hadith types does not disenfranchise a Muslim from the ability to understand Islam. In the same vein, to understand Islam and be a learned Muslim scholar or "Islamic" scholar, one does not need to study fourteen volumes of al-Asqalani's (d. 852/1449) commentary and interpretation of Sahih al-Bukhari, where each volume exceeds 700 pages. Islam is not a concoction of a body of knowledge made by humans.

Of course, it is an open question whether such studies deserve to be labeled as "Islamic" or even to be housed under Religious studies departments or faculties. Even having a PhD degree that is related to Muslim jurisprudence and Fiqh would certainly make the person an imminent scholar in the subject but not a religious scholar. Consider for instance a much celebrated Salafi scholar, Muhammad al-Arifi. He is highly celebrated as a religious scholar but his PhD thesis was on collecting and studying ibn Taymiyyah's opinions of Sufism. Undoubtedly there is some value in this thesis, however, this effort by al-Arifi would make him a specialist in ibn Taymiyyah (or even partially) but not a religious scholar worthy of belonging to "the people of *thikr*." Despite the fact that al-Arifi's PhD studies took place in the Faculty of Usool al-Deen (theology), he cannot be considered a religious scholar or even a religious edict issuer (*mufti*). In contrast, the University of Chicago, one of the most highly reputed universities for studies related to Islam, minted numerous scholars specializing in different topics that are conventionally classified as "Islamic", but these scholars are never considered by Muslims as religious scholars despite being highly learned in "Islamic" law, Sharia and Fiqh. It is worth noting that the University of Chicago houses its Islam studies program under the Department of Near Eastern Languages and Civilizations. If the same studies were to be conducted in an "Islamic" university, they would be housed under Fiqh, Sharia, Qur'anic studies, or theology departments or faculties. If the graduate of these "Islamic" universities meets the approval of the religious establishments, then and only then will he be labeled as a religious scholar.

THE GREAT MUSHAF-MUSLIM DIVIDE

Many Muslim individuals and Muslim organizations are ready and quick to hand out copies of the Mushaf to spread the message of Islam. This would give the indication that Muslims want everyone to read the Mushaf independently and learn Islam from its primary (if not only) source. However, the reality is completely different. Once any individual starts contemplating and inquiring about certain verses, the more learned and seasoned Muslims would direct that individual to the "scholars of Islam" who, the scholars believe, interpreted everything that needs to be interpreted for the "rest of us". So one wanders why there is this unusual enthusiasm to hand out the Mushaf if one needs to go through specific channels or certified clergy to understand it. At one time, the Catholic Church did not allow commoners to possess a copy of the Bible. The argument of the Church then was that the interpretation of the Bible had to be made by the Church's sanctioned clergy. The parallel between the Church then and the Muslim clergy now is striking.

The prevailing pattern of behavior amongst many Muslims vis-à-vis inquiry amounts to self-censorship, and worse, self-appointed policing of intellectual inquiry. This pattern of behavior not only violates the Mushaf injunctions, but is detrimental to the intellectual health of Muslim societies. In fact, the Mushaf characterizes different types of offenses that vary in degree of *haram* (eternally forbidden by Allah). Such caution when analyzing the Mushaf verses should not be confused with honest attempts to understand those verses based on one's best ability. Whether the misrepresentation of the Mushaf text is intentional or unintentional, the behavioral pattern that emerges, nevertheless, enforces an atmosphere of servitude and subjugation that encourages blind following and disempowerment. The Mushaf does not invoke obedience to anyone but Allah, and in a different verse, simultaneous obedience to the Messenger Muhammad and those who are in command of the affairs of the Muslims. Moreover, obedience to Allah is unlike obedience of a servant towards his master; it is not servitude. (For more on the concept of obedience, see Chapter 8 and in particular, the difference between the Messenger and the Prophet.)

A Mushaf verse that is also used repeatedly to dissuade anyone from developing confidence to understand and learn the Mushaf is M17:36

وَلَا تَقْفُ مَا لَيْسَ لَكَ بِهِ عِلْمٌ ۚ إِنَّ السَّمْعَ وَالْبَصَرَ وَالْفُؤَادَ كُلُّ أُولَٰئِكَ كَانَ عَنْهُ مَسْئُولًا

[Do not pursue that you have no *ilm* of. You will be questioned on the mechanism of hearing, mechanism of vision, and mechanism of comprehension]. The verse is part of a series of commandments from M17 that delineates a blueprint for a just and peaceful life based on broad principles, including not committing murder and adultery. The first part of the above verse instructs the reader not to follow that in which one is not well versed or one does not understand. A closer and more precise translation necessitates translating the word *ilm* to the English word "understanding" or "comprehension" instead of "knowledge". The distinction between knowledge and *ilm* appears repeatedly in the Mushaf, possibly to stress the unique importance of science in the life of the Muslim or human in general. Here, science refers to understanding and confidence that the knowledge begotten is based on truth (See Chapter 9 for further discussion of *ilm*.)

In the context of M17:36, Allah stresses the importance of verification of information before accepting it as facts. In fact, the verse is an indictment for anyone who repeats what he or she hears or sees without full understanding of the subject matter rather than an indictment of someone who attempts to understand the Mushaf on his own. Here, Allah stresses in an emphatic expression invoking all the faculties that the human needs for comprehension (mechanisms of hearing, seeing and understanding) to verify facts and not to repeat what cannot be verified. It is a tall order indeed and a very serious one. Therefore, repeating the commentaries of a certain exegete, no matter how esteemed and trustworthy he happened to be, without verification, falls under the warning of M17:36.

Allah clearly states in the Mushaf that it is a book of guidance (see M2:2). The caste system that separated people into saints and clergy, "people of authority and knowledge", "common people" (*al-awaam*) and "special people" (*al-khawaas*) and was institutionalized years after the completion of the message of Muhammad is in violation of the most basic dictates of the Mushaf, which classifies people based on metrics beyond human abilities. Since Muslims believe that the Mushaf is a direct revelation from Allah, one can always turn to the Mushaf itself to address point of confusion that might arise rather than referring to any particular designated authority.

Using the Mushaf to silence inquiry is not effective if those who are silenced put some energy into researching the Mushaf with confidence, realizing that the Mushaf is a guidance for all, including the most erudite and also the "commoners". Understanding the Mushaf, however, is not a trivial exercise; it needs patience, persistence, knowledge of the meaning of words and understanding the context of the verses. If one needs guidance in any area, one needs to spend sufficient effort to achieve that guidance. If one wants to protect one's village from flooding, good education and training in civil engineering is essential. This training is certainly not trivial and would take dedication, time and effort. There is a price for guidance. The price for the alternative, however, is even more costly. The fact that Allah stated at the very beginning of M2 that the Mushaf has guidance for the pious does not eliminate the effort that this group of people has to exert to achieve this guidance.

It is all Downhill from Here

An equally effective intimidation mechanism to silence inquiry and to marginalize is to invoke Hadith. Take, for example, a certain hadith that is repeated too often during Friday sermons, especially in South Asian Muslim communities. The hadith claims that the best of people are those that accompanied the Prophet, then the next best are those who succeeded them and the next best are those who succeeded the immediate successors (the first "next best"). This hadith has several variants, one of which is available in Sahih al-Bukhari[22]

> The Prophet said, "The best people are those living in my generation, and then those who will follow them, and then those who will follow the latter."

This hadith has many problems. First is how could the Prophet have known the future despite crystal clear Mushaf injunctions indicating such impossibility? Being capable of knowing the future is different from having the ability (or gift) of interpreting dreams, as was the case with prophet Yousuf. In the case of the Prophet, according to the Mushaf, any prediction of the future was exclusive only to Allah (see M3:44, 6:50, and 7:188). Second, the hadith implies classification of people based on piety and knowledge, which is contrary to the Mushaf injunctions. However, even if these contradictions are dismissed, the average person (Muslim or non-Muslim) wonders why the contemporaries of the Prophet were better than those who were not fortunate to have accompanied him?

Why should the second generation be better than the third? These are simple questions that seem to have no relevance or possibility for consideration because of the overbearing weight of "the Prophet said so". What can be sensed from the hadith above is a theme of arbitrariness that is manifested in many other hadiths (as will be shown throughout this book), characterizing the behavior of not only the Prophet but also Allah. The hadith above invokes many important questions. Why should someone who accompanied the Prophet and was deceitful be better than a pious and good person who, of no fault of his own, was born centuries later? What about people like us who succeeded the Prophet after many generations? Are we doomed to a much lower status than that of all those who preceded us? Why is there a focus on the companionship and contemporariness of the Prophet and on temporal proximity to the Prophet instead of on the message (i.e., the Mushaf) that the Messenger delivered?

Where does *taqwa* (piety and fear of Allah), which matters the most to Allah, and performing righteous deeds fit into these classifications? Why should the decisions and opinions of any of the contemporaries of the Prophet, including those of the four Righteous Caliphs who governed Medina and the government that the Prophet established, be considered as the right decisions for all space and time and the consequential implication that these decisions should be binding on all future generations of Muslims?

The battles of Saffin and Jamal pitted many companions against many other companions. The historical facts accepted by the very proponents of the above hadith showed that many *sahaaba* killed other *sahaaba*. Who was right and who was wrong? The above hadith thrusts the naïve believers into a labyrinth of contradictions especially when combined with other hadiths that stress if a Muslim goes to war with another Muslim, then both Muslims are in hellfire. If these hadiths were to be believed, then many important *sahaaba* are doomed to hellfire. Nevertheless, aside from the confusion and contradictions such hadiths create, could there have been a deliberate effort by the political and religious establishments, working hand-in-glove, to compel the faithful to accept a specific religious doctrine without any scrutiny or any analysis? As we show in Chapters 8 and 9, there may have been a massive effort to derail the focus of Muslims from the Mushaf to new doctrines that appear to be "Islamic" in flavor but devoid of compatibility with the Mushaf. Most likely, these new doctrines were politically motivated.

The Mushaf is replete with incidents involving the Prophet and the people whom he was dealing with on a daily basis. Those included people of all types of characters: pious, believers, supporters, hypocrites, opportunists, good, bad, troublemakers, and even people who never accepted Islam. Even the people who accompanied the Prophet on the Muslims' first battle with Quraish, the battle of Badr, were not all pure and pious-perfect. In their zeal to elevate the companions of the Prophet to angelic status and to the deflect any shortcomings from the companions, or Muslims in general, the majority if not all of Mushaf exegetes associated any reference to wrongdoing or negative attributes to the Jews and Christians. The Jews and Christians, in broadest terms, became the punching bag for all Muslims, while the concept of *sahaaba* with its subsequent corollaries, such as the *salaf* (the generation that proceeded the *sahaaba*) and the *khalaf* (the generation that proceeded the *salaf*), was spun most likely to achieve nefarious political objectives.

Despite the fundamental problems the above hadith has, the average Muslim has a tendency to seek the opinions and perspectives of the *sahaaba*, the *khalaf* and the *salaf* all the way down to even obscure scholars whose only credentials are the lavish accolades bestowed upon them by yet other obscure scholars. The fact that a specific person in Muslim history did a specific scholarly work, such as commenting on Hadith or the Mushaf, does not warrant seeking the opinion of that scholar on matters that took place centuries later.[23] The above "downhill" hadith is repeated so often on Friday sermons; but why? What would the average Muslim feel hearing this hadith over and over? No doubt that this average and hapless Muslim will look backwards in time for salvation, for advice and for guidance, and will waste a lifetime digging into an avalanche of historical records hailed by the self-appointed guardians of the faith as the religious material that constitutes the Islamic *ilm*. The framers of this hadith and others of similar spirit paved the way for a methodology of backwardness under which the Muslims continue to reel.

In their zeal to glorify the too distant past, numerous Muslim scholars have gone beyond elevating the status of the Prophet's companions to elevating all people of Arab descent, contradicting the universality of the message of Islam and its basic dictum that only faith and good deeds are the ultimate indicator of one's value. Al-Bukhari dedicated part of his famous book *al-Taareekh al-Kabir* (The Grand History) to present the Arabs of Quraish as the best of people.[24] (The same Arabs that ibn Hanbal described as the most noble of people were described by ibn Khaldun as violent, uncivil, and brutal, with a tradition of violence, anarchy and incapability of governance.[25]) In justifying the importance of the Arab contemporaries of the Prophet, and by extension Arabs in general, al-Zarqani describes the companions of the Prophet as "pure Arabs, enjoying all attributes of Arabism and qualities such as strong memory, brilliance, taste for clarity, ability to discern purpose of forms, etc., so they were able to absorb and understand the sciences of the Mushaf and its inimitability through their nature and the clarity of their instinct; an achievement and ability that we cannot come close to despite the copious sciences and arts available to us today."[26] Al-Zarqani, who taught at al-Azhar University, is exalting the same Arabs who took pride in raiding and looting their neighboring tribes and the same Arabs who buried their female newborns for fear of bringing shame to their families.

Such a description of the companions of the Prophet in a textbook on the "sciences" of the Mushaf and strong emphasis on their Arabness should not be taken lightly, especially when considering that al-Zarqani was a professor and taught the same material at al-Azhar, the most prominent institution for the study of religion amongst Sunni Muslims. From the prominent scholars of the 2nd Century such as ibn Hanbal (d. 241/855) and al-Bukhari, all the way to 20th Century scholars such as al-Zarqani, all have stopped just short of suggesting that the companions of the Prophet were infallible.

For Muslims, the Arabic word for a companion, *sahaabi*, has come to denote reverence and veneration while simultaneously implying that future generations, despite their advances in sciences and knowledge, will forever pale in comparison in their attempts to understand the Mushaf. More on this subject will be covered in other chapters of this book, however, here it suffices to state that an image has been created in the minds of Muslims that the companions of the Prophet understood the Mushaf better than anyone who succeeded them, and consequently their actions must have been in full compliance with the Mushaf directives. Some Muslims would even state that the *sahaaba* were pure Muslims. The available historical records, however, do not give any indication that the *sahaaba* understood the Mushaf better than later generations.

The Mushaf is precise about rejection of blind following, or blind imitation of forefathers (along with teachers and caretakers). One questions the purpose of the above Sahih al-Bukhari hadith that contradicts logic, common sense or even the Mushaf itself. The end outcome of this and other hadiths was to marginalize Muslims and to make them feel sufficiently insignificant to succumb to whatever was done, written, decreed or speculated by earlier people. This outcome was precisely one of the tenants of the Salafi sects: complete acquiescence to whatever the *salaf* said or did and the creation of a temporal religious hierarchy in Muslim societies. In broader perspective, the results have had a disastrous effect on Muslims, stratifying their society into religious castes and petrifying any intellectual activities coupled with blind allegiance to people who we do not know much about, and furthermore, a de-facto allegiance to people who lived in different times under circumstances completely different from ours. But most important, those hadiths institutionalize allegiance to people, and servitude and obedience to a class of so-called scholars, noblemen, and companions of the Prophet, and by extension to the caste of "religious men" who command undeserving reverence simply because of being repeaters for what was said by yet people of underserving reverence.

The system of subjugation and servitude contextualized within religion is similar to one adopted by military trainers where the young recruits are subjected to rigorous psychological self-effacement to evaporate their personalities and originality and then build them up as per the dictates of the military program to turn the recruits into obedient robots. Turning the Muslim into a robot that practically seeks the guidance and imitation of hundreds, if not thousands, of people is very different from the respectful position of *khalifa* (vicegerent) that Allah bestowed upon humans.

Since nothing comes from nowhere, including hundreds of thousands of hadiths churned during the first and second Muslim centuries, we must assume that if the probability of the validity of a certain hadith is low, then the probability that the hadith was fabricated to serve a specific objective is high. The blind acceptance of the "downhill" hadith and many others continues to prevent Muslims from asking why Allah would predestine some people to be better and more trustworthy and knowledgeable than others. Why do the companions of the Prophet have an automatic privilege whereas other people who were born fourteen centuries later, like you and me, should be doomed to a much lesser status? While the Sahih al-Bukhari hadith defies the Mushaf and the Prophet's behavior as archived in the Mushaf, it is used to send a message to every Muslim not to doubt or question the sayings and edicts of the companions and their successors. The fact that a genre of hadiths serves to condemn inquiry to the point of associating inquiry with sin suggests influence from political rulers or religious authority, either of whom were strongly interested in preserving authority and its privileges and silencing the Muslim masses.

The system of intimidation, disenfranchisement and disempowerment that had been developed based on the doctrine of Hadith that contradicts the Mushaf appears to be effective. Many Muslims have come to accept, without challenge, exegeses of early scholars. One can find numerous weak hadiths cited in these exegeses (for a particularly compelling example, see ibn Kathir's interpretation of M4:138). These hadiths are included in these highly respected compendia despite their dubious and mysterious origins.

Muslim religious literature exaggerate the piety of the companions, their successors and the successors of the successors. At times the hyperbole borders on the absurd and impossible.[27] The objective, once again, is to provide validation for the uniqueness of the *salaf* and their supernatural qualities that put them apart from all humankind. It is common when Muslim intellectuals present new ideas or new interpretations of the Mushaf to be confronted with the question "do you have the *taqwa* that those scholars possessed?"

Interpreting the Mushaf, however, does not need the *taqwa* prerequisite, as mentioned earlier. One example is the manufactured image of al-Shafi'i (d. 204/820) intended to make him a holy man, and consequently, severely discourage questioning his religious contributions. The reported story of al-Shafi'i's (d. 204/820) practice of reciting the entire Mushaf twice daily during Ramadan is a representative example. Simple math shows that it is humanly impossible to recite the entirety of the Mushaf twice daily. This is because reciting the Mushaf non-stop would require an average of fifteen hours for the average reciter without *tajweed* (the art of slow and melodic recitation of the Mushaf). So to recite the Mushaf twice daily requires more than thirty hours. This leaves no time for sleeping and attending to bodily functions and other duties such as the obligatory prayers. Perhaps it is physically possible if you speedread, but then what would be the benefit of speedreading the Mushaf. Based on common sense, human capacity and the fact that the day has only twenty-four hours, it is impossible to recite the Mushaf as al-Shafi'i is alleged to have done.

Of course, there are Muslims who invoke the *karamaat* (special privileges believed to be given only to extremely pious and good people) argument to imply that al-Shafi'i had special unique attributes given only to those whom Allah favors.[28] This explanation for al-Shafi'i's superhumanism cannot be proven or disproven. What stands against the plausibility of the *karamaat* argument is the physical impossibility or the triviality of the act itself, in this case, speedreading the Mushaf. But then there is the possibility that such stories had another purpose: to preoccupy the faithful with non-stop recitation under the lure of high rewards in the hereafter. Ahmed ibn Hanbal is reported to have had categorically pronounced that no one can be part of Ahl al-Sunnah (the family and proponents of the Sunnah, the body of knowledge that relates to the Prophet's life and sayings) unless he leaves argumentation and submits and believes in the traditions.[29] Ibn Hanbal discourages further discussion and interpretation of a specific verse in the Mushaf by asserting these interpretations are the privilege and ability of scholars of religion because of the "special" knowledge that they have.[30]

Scholars are essential to help us understand various subjects from soil mechanics to the Mushaf, but their explanations must be substantiated and conveyed to the non-scholar in a logical and meaningful way instead of invoking special privileges that intend to prevent questioning those scholars. The concept of the expert has been overlooked in the rush to glorify Muslim scholars as possessing the "sacred knowledge", as many Muslims would claim. The opinion of an expert is highly respected, but the expert must substantiate the opinion based on facts and information.

Science of Marginalization

The stories of the supernaturalism of so many *sahaabas* and the *salaf* and the *khalaf* convey a sense of helplessness, despair and belittlement. They convey the message that one needs to attain an incredible level of piety (as for instance the ability to recite the Mushaf twice daily for thirty days in a row) before one achieves a status that would allow interpreting the Mushaf, participate in the development of Islamic-inspired jurisprudence, or for one's opinion on religion ever to be respected. *Taqwa*, on the other hand, cannot be a prerequisite to understand Islam for the simple reason that the Mushaf is a book that provides guidance. If *taqwa* was a precondition, then a non-Muslim will never be able to understand Islam in the first place. If *taqwa* was a precondition to understand the Mushaf, then Muslims should never distribute the Mushaf to any non-Muslims as is commonly done on many US and Canadian university campuses. Understanding the meaning of a verse does not need *taqwa*, it needs exercising one's intellect in the absence of any type of intimidation. Lest we forget that the Mushaf is for those who have *taqwa* and for those who do not. The Mushaf is also for Muslims and non-Muslims.

MEMORIZATION AND *TAJWEED*

Memorization is a tradition that remained in Arab society and has affected Muslims in so many ways. Memorization has become synonymous with knowledge. I once attended a social function where a local Imam was invited to address the gathering. He went on to recite a very long poem to the ecstasy of the audience that included women (most disenfranchised of Muslims), in particular, presumably thrilled by the Imam's perceived command of the religion. It was my closest experience to seeing hypnotization in action.

Amongst many Muslims, memorization is a tradition where the strength of one's memory, not intellect, can help advance one's social and religious standings or even one's career. In the years following the Prophet's death, written media was not widely available. Memorization was important to help transfer knowledge from one generation to the next. It served an important function then, and memorizers were held in high esteem and had an important social status, if not a respected profession. This can be discerned from the respect and reverence given to the *huffadh* (memorizers) in a variety of scholarly works on Islam.

Amongst the Arabs, or possibly non-Arabs, listening to the narration of hadiths from memory creates an illusion that the narrator is a scholar.

Legends have been woven around memorization and memorizers of Hadith and the Mushaf. There are abundant reports of Muslim scholars who memorized hundreds of thousands of hadiths. In fact, al-Bukhari was reported to have memorized several hundred thousand hadiths (the reports vary between three hundred thousand and one million). If one were to question if such ability was humanly possible, one would be silenced with the classical retort that "Allah can make anything possible" and that Allah chose to give those people the incredible power (conveniently referred to as *karamaat*) to memorize these many hadiths. Of course, the perpetrators of either argument never provided any proof. Nevertheless, a question arises as to why the Prophet asked his companions during his lifetime to write the Mushaf instead of relying on the memory of super-humans for its preservation. Why did the alleged super-humans arrive in later years instead of being available early on to prevent all the tragedies that emerged from the presence of the hundreds of thousands of hadiths that were deemed invalid (i.e., fabricated)? What about the concept of *karamaat*, which Muslims did not seem to put to scrutiny. In fact, the *karamaat* concept is simply a concept. The *karamaat* designation cannot be proven or disproven; it is simply one additional escape mechanism wrapped in an "Islamic" garb to avoid explaining the unexplainable and to rationalize the irrational. If the claims of al-Shafi'i and many of his disciples and followers are true that there were two types of *wahi* (divine revelation), one being the Mushaf and the other Sunnah, then why was the first *wahi* documented immediately but the other had to wait 200 years? Instead of dispelling any possibility of super-humans, many Muslims invoke Allah's ability to do whatever He wishes to justify the presence of something that cannot be justified by rationality, common sense, human knowledge and history, experience, Allah's laws and above all, the Mushaf.

Muslims typically have higher respect for someone who has memorized the Mushaf. Memorizing the Mushaf is desired by most committed Muslims; it is, nevertheless, a formidable task. It takes native Arabic speakers years to memorize the Mushaf. For non-Arabic speakers, memorizing the Mushaf is possible but exceptionally difficult and might take a lifetime to accomplish. A barrier that excludes non-Arabic speakers from full participation in Islam diminishes the universality of the religion. Memorization and understanding are two separate matters. As

Muslims' literature suggests, Muslims had never paused to reflect on why Allah would favor those who memorize the Mushaf over others. What magical power would memorization of the Mushaf bring about to enable a person to have good understanding of the Mushaf, let alone become the ubiquitous better, to be entrusted with important and high profile responsibilities within the Muslim community, which has nothing to do with memorization, such as presiding over the Friday sermon? Memorizing the Mushaf can be useful for someone who leads the daily prayers, for purely technical reasons, but should it be assumed that the person who memorizes the Mushaf also understands it? It can be argued that memorization of the Mushaf can potentially be distracting from its understanding since the process of memorization requires significant concentration and time that can better be spent on understanding the Mushaf or improving the conditions of one's community.

One should keep in mind that memorization of the Mushaf requires constant "maintenance". It is a continuous and highly demanding process rather than a one-time deal. The Mushaf does not have any verse that exalts the believers to commit it to memory. There may have been times when memorization of the Mushaf was of importance because mass printing was not available; today, the Mushaf is widely available in printed and electronic media. In fact, with the proliferation of Mushaf databases, it takes only a few seconds to list all the Mushaf verses that address a specific topic. Such technology can be significantly more important and useful than reciting a complete chapter of the Mushaf from memory. Believing that mere utterance of the Mushaf words bring heavenly rewards, as many Muslims believe, again cannot be substantiated (see Chapter 5).

Was the Mushaf revealed as a physical, metaphysical, magical protector or shield from physical adversities for those who memorize it? Or was it revealed as a book of guidance, as stated in its very beginning? If you want to excel in college Physics 101 and you were given a book of guidance for Physics 101, then what benefit would be gained from memorization of the book rather than understanding it? What purpose would reciting the physics book twice a day serve if the concepts of the book were not understood? Many Muslims claim or believe that the mere recitation of the Mushaf is a form of worship. This claim can never be found anywhere in the Mushaf.[31]

The first person or group who emphasize the importance of committing the Mushaf to memory could have been influenced by either incorrect interpretation of the Mushaf, reliance on a host of alleged hadiths, or had other motives. The end result, however, was to distract the believer from understanding the Mushaf and to impose on the Muslim community classifications of piety and goodness for the purpose of marginalization and disempowerment that further enriches a caste system.

Let us assume that a Muslim passes the test of Mushaf memorization. Still a bigger task would be expected from the memorizer in order to reach a position worthy of having sufficient credibility to be taken seriously on matters related to the religion. This brings us to the next hurdle of *tajweed*, an Arabic word that stems from the past tense of the verb *jawwad*, which means to enhance something. *Tajweed* embodies the meaning of perfection or completeness. *Tajweed* of the Mushaf, however, connotes a specific way of reading or reciting the Mushaf where all the annotations are precisely pronounced to eventually render a semi-melodic rhythm. Achieving the ability for proper *tajweed* is a formidable task for the native Arab speaker. For the non-Arab, it is simply an incredibly difficult task that requires many years of continuous training. According to *tajweed* experts, there are multiple methods by which the Mushaf can be recited. (Interestingly, some of these recitations are contradictory (see Chapter 6)). If a believer cannot perform *tajweed,* or if she recites a verse of the Mushaf improperly, then she would not be considered qualified enough to interpret the Mushaf text. This would exclude a majority of the people of earth even if all were to convert to Islam.

The message of the Mushaf emphasizes the diversity of creation, comprising nations and tribes having different tongues not to be amalgamated into one nation speaking one tongue (see M49:13). The universality of Islam transcends temporal and physical boundaries; Islam is not a religion for a distinct region, tribe or specific period of time. Just like any book or document that is intended to serve as guidance, understanding the Mushaf is much more important than the ability to recite it. The verb *iqra* and its derivatives imply comprehension or understanding. *Tala*, on the other hand, means to recite. The confusion of or lack of interest amongst so many Muslims in understanding the difference between these two verbs, *iqra* and *tala,* has serious effect on their understanding of the Mushaf and their religion in general. This lack of interest, primarily and most surprisingly amongst Muslim Arabs, to understand the meaning of the words of the Mushaf could be due to many reasons, such as disinterest in the Mushaf, not taking the Mushaf with the seriousness it deserves as Allah's revelation, or not to challenge traditional interpretation of the Mushaf, or possibly believing that the Mushaf is fully interpreted and there is no need for any additional work. Nevertheless, unsubstantiated emphasis on *tajweed* led to the emergence of an elite group dominated largely by Arabs who seduced non-Arabs with their melodic recitation of the Mushaf. The consequences of such confusion did not stop here but led high-profile Muslim scholars to believe that Arabs, inherently, have superior status, as al-Zarqani claimed.[32]

From a simplistic perspective, it is highly problematic if not puzzling why many Muslims have placed high priority on *tajweed* while giving much less priority to understanding the Mushaf. A Muslim is encouraged to exercise *ihsaan* (performing to one's best abilities) in every aspect of his/her life. Reading or reciting the Mushaf to the best of one's ability is not an exception. However, what has become known as *tajweed* has become a distraction to busy the faithful with something "Islamic" but devoid of both practical utility and meaning. Grand international competitions are held yearly under the patronage of Muslim establishments and governments for the best *tajweed*. To fortify the efforts to busy or engage Muslims with the excessive *tajweed* activities, hadiths were advocated highlighting the *ajr* (the reward one achieves in the hereafter) that the believer receives from memorizing the Mushaf and performing *tajweed*. (More on *tajweed* will be discussed in Chapter 5).

KNOWLEDGE OF HADITH

Another method of disenfranchisement of Muslims is to question one's knowledge of hadiths and especially if one commits many hadiths to memory. (See Chapter 8 for an extensive discussion of Hadith.) Hadith is loosely defined as reports summarizing what the Prophet or his companions said, did, commented on, and includes descriptions of the Prophet's behavior. The prevailing Muslim culture necessitates memorization of a good number of hadiths before one's credibility to interpret the Mushaf is established. In the pursuit of establishing credibility to participate in dialogues or discussions on Islam, the next test would be to question one's understanding of Hadith. One *khateeb* (the title given to the lecturer of the Friday religious sermon) in a nearby town to Toronto once reminded the audience of the difficulty to understand Hadith and how a certain ancient scholar wrote several thick volumes deciphering the meaning of only forty hadiths. The poor and helpless listener might then imagine that if several volumes of books were necessary to understand only a few hadiths, then a lifetime might be needed to understand the remaining thousands of hadiths.

With all that time needed to understand Hadith, one wonders how much time is left to pay attention to or even understand a tiny part of the book that Allah intended as guidance for humankind. The message from all of these exaggerated legends and stories about the expanse of the Hadith corpus and its expansive commentary and the importance of its study is that before attempting to comment on the Mushaf, or have a sufficiently respected credibility on subjects related to Islam, one needs to immerse oneself in the study of these copious compendia of tens of volumes, written in archaic styles, and to achieve yet a better understanding, one needs to study the commentaries on the commentaries. (Notice for example how Sahih al-Bukhari was interpreted by al-Asqalani, who lived six centuries after al-Bukhari, and al-Asqalani in turn had to be interpreted by a host of scholars.)

These copious volumes of Hadith commentaries might be of interest to many scholars of history but they should be considered purely as historical records. The value of these records, as we show in Chapter 8, to understanding Islam is very low. I would even argue that these records are detrimental to understanding Islam. From the scholarly perspective, these compendia would not pass minimal modern academic and publishing standards, especially since they are replete with arguments substantiated by ghost figures, and heavy reliance on the perceived credibility, integrity and honesty of figures who spanned hundreds of years. Even considering the standards of the times during which these commentaries were published, one questions whether these Hadith and commentaries books were written with academic integrity or clear methodologies.

Acceptance of or rather respect for, these commentaries is most likely attributed to the reverence and respect Muslims have developed for Muslim scholars. When non-Arab Muslims are faced with such commentaries, the discouragement and feeling of hopelessness and despair reaches unimaginable heights! To accept all these volumes as expressing facts means that one should have faith in the authenticity of every hadith and faith in the goodness, honesty, erudition and correctness of the commentators of Hadith (see Chapter 8). An entire religion that is based on few articles of faith (that cannot be either proven or disproven) becomes a religion of millions of articles of faith, or simply the entire religion is turned into a faith. Accepting, understanding, and to a lesser degree memorizing the body of Hadith and studying all commentaries were all turned into prerequisites for establishing credibility to comment on the Mushaf or the Sunnah, or on Islam in general.

CLASSICAL AD HOMINEM

Ad hominem is a classical logic fallacy that is essentially a personal attack with the objective to discredit the argument or thesis by discrediting the person who asserted the argument. Ad hominem is a direct attack on the person's character rather than a rational and logical negation of an argument. Questions such as "who do you think you are to comment on religion?" or "what credentials you have that qualify you to comment on Mushaf?", amongst other similar variants, are all ad hominem attacks. In addition to its illogical and fallacious construction, this line of personal attack reflects a lack of humility that Islam is supposed to instill in the Muslim in the first place. In light of the teachings of the Mushaf, ad hominem is essentially an accusation, which is universally considered by Muslims and non-Muslims as a negative behavior that attempts to distract from the substance of the argument.

If the direct character assassination fails, a typical line of attack is to question one's religious education. Having a bachelor degree from any religious institution, or even a higher degree, only implies that the awardee of the degree has mastered subjects sanctioned by the particular institution that offered the degree. Islam, however, cannot be a monopoly of any religious or non-religious institutions. Some religious institutions may adopt specific subjects that fall under what is commonly referred to as Islamic sciences. If one were to disagree with the entire premise that such subjects are sciences at all, or if one does not accept the methodologies that lead to such subjects, then one cannot beholden to conformity with such "sciences".

Many Muslims exercise double standards when considering the religious education credentials of Muslim scholars. Going centuries back, the scholastic or religious credentials of many ancient scholars had never been put under scrutiny. Examples in modern times include highly reputable and famous Muslim figures such as al-Albani (d. 1420/1999) and Sayyid Qutb (d. 1386/1966). Al-Albani was self-taught and became at one point the modern face of the Salafi sect, receiving high respect from a significant sector of Sunni Muslims. In fact, many Muslims gave al-Albani extraordinary reverence to the point that they accepted his reclassification of certain hadiths in Sahih al-Bukhari from *sahih* (authentic) to *thaeef* (weak). Sayyid Qutb, the author of one of the respected Mushaf exegeses, never had any formal or informal religious education or training. In fact, Qutb's formal education concluded with a Bachelor of Arts in Education, a subject that was looked upon by religion scholars of Egypt as secular. Despite his lack of any religion-based education or attending officially sanctioned religious schools or universities in Egypt, not many, if any, appear to have questioned his "Islamic" credentials or any credibility he might have had to be sufficiently fit to comment on the Mushaf, let alone have his own exegesis. Behind the acceptance of both al-Albani and Qutb, however, lies political ideologies rather than religious scholarship. The Salafis championed al-Albani because he championed the theology of Ahmed ibn Hanbal and ibn Taymiyyah. In the case of Qutb, the Society of Muslims Brotherhood with its millions of followers were his champions because he was one of their members. From these contemporary examples, one can extrapolate backwards in time to realize how considerations for scholarly eminence and high religious erudition were largely politically and partisan tainted.[33]

If all fails, one's own attire and facial features from the length of the beard and trimming of the moustache to the particular clothes one wears, all would play a role in establishing the "religious" credibility of the person. Many Muslims have come to accept superficial features and dress code as signs of piety and of closeness to Allah, and by extension, importance. This applies equally to men and women. Muslim women often intimidate each other for merely revealing a few strands of hair. All this acquiescence, once again, came from no source but an abundance of hadiths that cannot be accepted as part of Islam for reasons that will discussed extensively in Chapter 8.

Science of Marginalization

Concluding Thoughts

There are fundamental reasons for the stagnation of Muslims in practically all aspects of life. Evidence indicates that the elemental mechanisms for advancement of religious understanding have been resisted with vigor by the majority of Muslims. Muslim societies' approach to religion reflects a state of schizophrenia. Muslims have high respect for the classical methods by which knowledge is advanced, e.g., research based on consistent, proven and established methodologies; peer reviewed journals and publications; books; etc. However, they refuse to consider compatibility between the divine revelation and reason, as if the two are irreconcilable or incompatible.

The culture of Muslims is predominantly a culture of monologues: a never-ending one-way "lecture" rather than a discussion or a genuine dialogue. Whether in the family, the school, or the masjid, one is always on the receiving end of a lecture. In the culture of the masjid, the imam is held in unnecessarily high reverence and his sermons are delivered as if they were Godly revelations, to be received by the captive Muslim audience without the slightest inquiry or challenge. Practically, silencing of the faithful has turned into a religious prerogative. A whisper during the Friday sermon (*khutba*) is considered a religious violation (if not a sin); by extension, questioning the imam would then be a sin. A two dimensional space-time hierarchy developed in the Muslim's culture over time that relegated the Muslim populace to an abyss of marginalization. In turn, the marginalization and disenfranchisement, irrespective of its origin and evolution, created a Muslim culture with little respect for the individual's potential and significance while elevating select Muslim scholars and personalities to gods that monopolize knowledge, virtue and infallibility. Those Muslim scholars have strong resemblance to medieval priests in Christendom. Of course, it is a vicious and self-feeding cycle. These Muslim priests would not have been given enormous power, prestige and reverence if it had not been for subservient Muslims whose confidence eroded with time under the dilapidating weight of numerous fabricated hadiths and privilege-serving interpretations of the Mushaf.

The bottom line is that many Muslims have been made to believe that there are "those who know" and "those who do not know". This belief has become almost sacred and has prohibited many Muslims from exercising their Allah-given right, as specified explicitly in the

Mushaf, to question, think, contemplate, analyze, synthesize and contribute to the understanding of their own religion. The Muslim clergy, fortified by doctrines that have nothing to do with Islam, waged an all-out war against reason. In Chapter 3, I will elaborate further on this war on reason in both traditional and modern Muslim societies. Chapter 9 will discuss the importance of differentiating knowledge from science; a prelude to do away with the entitlement of scholarship monopoly.

Different forms of intimidation, marginalization and bullying have all become part of the Muslim culture. Some forms are practiced by the elite religious class towards "the commoners", while others are institutionalized within the Muslim psyche, perhaps better described as self-intimidation or self-marginalization. All these forms have found firm roots in Muslim societies to the point that many Muslim women believe and fiercely argue that they are inherently inferior to men and go to the extent of approving men's physical violence towards their wives as justified and sanctioned by Islam. This belief, even if found amongst a small group of Muslim women, is, nevertheless, a triumphant climax of decades-old self-colonization of the Muslim mind with its fruits of eroding the self-esteem of not only women but the entire Muslim *umma*.

Breathing is a very simple exercise that any healthy person does effortlessly and as an uncontrolled reflex. However, if a heavy weight is pushing against the chest, the simple exercise of breathing becomes hard, if not impossible. If Muslims are relieved of the incredible weight of religious intimidation and bullying, then the empowerment of *every* single Muslim, child, woman and man, becomes a possibility. Only then can Muslim societies truly advance to take a position of relevance in the world.

1. The Umayyad (41/661-132/750) and Abbasid (132/750-656/1258) dynasties were the earliest dynasties to embrace Islam as an official religion and to govern in the name of Islam.
2. Salafis and Ahl al-Sunnah wa al-Jamma'ah, are broad designations for Muslim sects that largely follow the teachings of Ahmed ibn Hanbal and ibn Taymiyyah.
3. Di Francia, G. Toraldo. *The Investigation of the Physical World.* Cambridge University Press, 1981.
4. Sabiq, Sayyid. *Fiqh al-Sunnah.* Vol. 2, Dar al-Kitaab al-Arabi, 1973, p. 461. Muslim scholars provided different definitions for *zandaqa* ranging from deception all the way to *kufr.*
5. *Islamization of Knowledge: General Principles and Work Plan.* The International Institute of Islamic Thought, Islamization of Knowledge, Series no. 1, 1989. Also see Chapter 9.
6. Muhammad Baqir al-Sadr aptly named two of his books as *Our Philosophy* and *Our Economics* opting out of the "Islamic" designation.
7. The rationale to name things Islamic is not clear even in major scholarly works such as Bosworth's *The Islamic Dynasties,* Coulson's *A History of Islamic Law,* Ullmann's *Islamic Medicine,* Watt's *Islamic Political Thought,* Ahmad's *History of Islamic Sicily,* etc.
8. Ibn al-Salah, abu Amr. *Uloom al-Hadith.* Sa'adah Press, 1908, p. 294. Sahih al-Bukhari is the most respected Hadith compendium amongst the Sunni Muslim sect. It was compiled by abu Abd-Allah Muhammad al-Bukhari (d. 256/870).
9. Ibn al-Salah. *Uloom.*
10. Al-Kannouji, abi al-Tayyeb. *Al-Hittah fi Thikr al-Sihah al-Sittah.* Dar al-Jeel, [n.d.], p 160.
11. Ibn al-Salaah. *Uloom,* p. 294.
12. See Chapter 9 for an extensive discussion on Ijma.
13. Khomeini, Roohallah. *Islam and Revolution: Writings and Declarations of Imam Khomeini.* Translated and annotated by Hamid Algar, Mizan Press, 1981, p. 63. Muslims do not believe and in fact ridicule the concept of sainthood in Catholicism, yet the practice of blind following of certain personalities is an implicit assumption of infallibility that elevates those personalities above sainthood.
14. Ibn Taymiyyah, Taqi al-Deen Ahmad. *Al-Sarim al-Maslool ala Shatim al-Rasool.* Al-Ramadi, 1997, p 5.
15. International Conference on ibn Taymiyyah's Mardin's Fatwa, March 30-31, 2010, Mardin, Turkey, Islam Today, https://muslim-

matters.org/2010/06/29/the-mardin-conference-%E2%80%93-a-detailed-account/. Accessed 2 June 2019.
16. Al-Jewziyyah, ibn Qayyem. *Kitaab al-Rooh*. Dar al-Turath, 2003, p. 267.
17. Al-Razi, abu Jafar. *Al-Kafi*. 3rd ed., vol. 1, Dar al-Hadith, 1972, p. 522.
18. Tabatabaa'i, Muhammad Husayn. *Al-Mizan*. Vol. 12, al-Aa'la, 1997, p. 254.
19. These intimidating tactics are often accompanied by a deceptive humility emphasizing that the religious scholar (invoking the argument) is not the right person to be consulted for medical issues. Considering that the Hadith prescribed remedies for all ailments even for scorpion bites, one may avoid expensive healthcare by consulting these religious scholars even for medical issues.
20. The idea that Islam or religion has been turned into a practice is not far-fetched. In numerous Muslim countries, the mufti (a religious edict issuer) and the speakers for Friday sermons are regulated by the government.
21. Ibn al-Salah. *Uloom al-Hadith*.
22. Sahih al-Bukhari, Kitaab al-Manaqib.
23. Sayyid Qutb was a prominent 20th Century Mushaf exegete. Despite his scholarly work on the Mushaf and other Islam related topics, he is considered by many Muslims as a controversial figure whose writings led to an extremist ideology. From the religious authority point of view, Qutb was never trained in traditional Muslim religious schools. One can learn from this example to emphasize the point that scholarship is different from religious authority.
24. Al-Athari, abu al-Zahra'a. *Ia'that al-Nathar fi Tahqiq Qawl al-Bukhari Fihi Nathar*. [.n.d.], p. 29.
25. Ibn Khaldun. *Al-Muqaddimah*. Vol. 1, Dar al-Awdah, 1981, p. 118.
26. Al-Zarqani, Muhammad. *Manahil al-Irfan fi Uloom al-Qur'aan*. Dar al-Kitaab al-Aarabi, 1995. Muhammad al-Zarqani was a Professor of Qur'aan and Hadith Sciences in the Faculty of Usool al-Deen, al-Azhar University. Al-Azhar university is the foremost center of Sunni religious learning and the most prominent university to teach the doctrines of the Sunni sects.
27. Al'aika, Sultan and al-Ssahib, Muhammad. *Asbab Tafawuk al-Sahaaba fi Thabt al-Hadith*. Dar ibn Aljaoozi, 2010, p. 49.
28. Al-Athari. *Ia'that*, p. 29.
29. Ibn Hanbal, Ahmed. *Usool Ahl al-Sunnah*. [n.d.], p. 25.
30. Ibn Hanbal, Ahmed. *Al-Rudd ala al-Jahamiyyah wa al-Zanadiqah*. Dar al-Thabaat, 2003, p. 60.

31. Hadiths abound on the power of memorization of the Mushaf and the protection it provides to the believer from the torture of the grave or even hellfire. Indeed, this brings into question the authenticity of such hadiths, a subject that will be addressed in greater details in Chapter 8.
32. Al-Zarqani. *Manahil.*
33. There are too many examples that one can draw from Hadith books where credibility and scholarship are directly tied to one's religious sect. This strong partisanship and sectarianism emerged in the first Muslim century after the major split between the Muslim camps that gave rise to the Sunni and Shia sects.

3

WAR ON REASON

أَفَلَمْ يَسِيرُوا فِي الْأَرْضِ فَتَكُونَ لَهُمْ قُلُوبٌ يَعْقِلُونَ بِهَا أَوْ آذَانٌ يَسْمَعُونَ بِهَا ۖ فَإِنَّهَا لَا تَعْمَى الْأَبْصَارُ وَلَٰكِن تَعْمَى الْقُلُوبُ الَّتِي فِي الصُّدُورِ

So have they not traveled through the earth so they may have *quloob* by which to reason or ears by which to hear? For indeed, it is not the means by which seeing takes place that become blinded, but blinded are the *quloob* which are within the *sudoor*.

M 22:46

Faith and Religion

I fondly remember during my high school years when we had a new Religious Studies teacher who did not object to us leaving our prayer carpets open after completing our midday ritual prayers. Our former teacher insisted that such a practice was not sanctioned in Islam because, according to the teacher, if one were to leave the prayer carpet open, there would be a serious consequence: Satan will pray on it. When we informed our new teacher of the concern of the former one, the new teacher was surprisingly delighted. In a sigh of relief, the teacher exclaimed: "Satan will pray and repent after all!" The teacher and all of us would have never been happier.

This simple true story reflects a strain of irrationality that has traditionally colored Muslims' collective thinking. It is a type of irrationality that most likely is not exclusive to Muslims and might very well be common amongst many groups, not only religious but also social, scientific, or academic. It is a type of irrationality that can be described by a schizophrenic behavior that affects fully rational humans who make fully rational decisions and choices, but who become irrational when the matter relates to certain practices or subjects of faith or religion. There seems to be certain reason-inhibiting mechanisms that kick in when religion, broadly defined, is the subject, as if religion and reason should not necessarily be compatible, or, more specifically, as if reason has no room in religion. The possible explanation for this schizophrenia is connecting the faith or religion with excessive fear or excessive love, or possibly depriving rationality and reason from being part of religion.

Reason, rationality, or rationalism, all describe a process of deduction whereby one starts with certain assumptions or axioms and then reaches specific conclusions that depend on those very assumptions one started with. Islam is based on a number of beliefs. In science, beliefs are typically referred to, rather surreptitiously, as assumptions or axioms. I use the word "surreptitiously" because scientists like to have an explanation for everything or a link between cause and effect. In fact, scientists like to have a proof for everything, but assumptions or axioms do not have a proof. A belief or faith, by definition, does not come with an explanation, proof or validation.

Clearly, there is a simplistic distinction between seeing a boy holding an apple and believing that he is holding the apple. Assumptions and axioms are articles that are assumed to be too simple or possibly too complex to require a proof. Axioms can be considered as pieces of information that are self-evident. (We must remember, however, that even what is believed to be self-evident is a subjective perspective). An example of an axiom is that two halves of one apple make a whole apple. Assumptions, on the other hand, may not be self-evident, but are intended to lead to fundamental practical consequences that cannot be mutually contradictory or self-contradictory. Assumptions cannot be proven or disproven, but they make a connection to something or a phenomenon that can be proven, based on the assumptions. One can think of an assumption as the essential initial point. For instance, in physics, two primary assumptions are the conservation of energy and causality. (The first implies that energy cannot be created or consumed, and the second implies that an effect requires a cause that precedes it in time.) Using the language of religion, these two assumptions can be considered as articles of faith in the field of physics. Therefore, an uncomfortable conclusion for physicists and scientists in general is that physics, just like Islam, has articles of faith. However, beyond these two articles of faith, within physics, no physical principles can be taken at face value. In other words, everything else aside from these articles of faith needs to be proven or deduced without violating these two fundamental articles.

Similar to science, Islam, as a complete (or closed) religion (*deen*), has a few articles of faith, namely believing in Allah, believing in the Angels, believing in the Prophets, believing in the scriptures that were revealed to earlier prophets, and believing in the Day of Accountability (typically, but incorrectly, translated as the Day of Judgment.) (Whether in physics or Islam, articles of faith cannot be proven or disproven. In Islam, for instance, the Latter Day, or the hereafter has yet to come, so it cannot be either proven or disproven. The Mushaf states that there is nothing like Allah. Proving or disproving something relies on understanding its nature, thus the impossibility of disproving or proving the existence or the nature of Allah.) Different Muslim schools of jurisprudence add to these articles, but here, for simplicity and without loss of generality, I will consider the above five articles as the common denominators among those schools. Again, these articles of faith cannot be proven or disproven; therefore, the one who believes and the one who does not believe stand on equal footing as far as the strength of their belief or disbelief is concerned. No one has a logic capable of proving or disproving these articles, since logic has no relevance to faith.

Therefore, initially, logic and belief must be non-convergent. A person either believes or rejects the articles of faith of a specific religion. Such a decision is purely binary. If a person believes in these articles, then everything else within the religion depends on and, more importantly, cannot contradict these articles. Just like a physicist whose faith in the principles of conservation of energy allows him to establish proofs and validity for a variety of phenomena, the Muslim needs articles of faith so that she or he can move forward to establish a system that is practical, logical, compatible with reality, and most critically, meaningful and relevant to life. The Muslim needs faith in addition to other things to establish a framework where everything fits in well and makes sense, primarily of his or her present reality, before making sense of either the past or the future. In Islam, faith is a beginning, not an end in itself. Islam as a religion includes few articles of faith, but much more; therefore, Islam cannot be called a faith or a tradition, but a *deen*. The articles of faith in Islam should not contradict reality. Faith as an end in itself, as simply based on unproven axioms, cannot be the primary tool for navigating the challenges of the intricately complex existence, and especially for knowing more about humans past and future.

There is a difference between faith, belief in something, and bearing witness.[1] If someone saw a murderer committing a crime, he is a potential witness in a court of law. However, if he has a strong belief about who committed the crime without having seen the murderer do it, this "believer" cannot be asked to bear witness in a court of law. By default, a Muslim is a believer in the five articles of faith of Islam (Allah, the Angels, the Prophets, earlier revelations or scriptures, and the Day of Accountability), but the Mushaf is explicit about who bears witness to the oneness of Allah as stated in M3:18

شَهِدَ اللَّهُ أَنَّهُ لَا إِلَهَ إِلَّا هُوَ وَالْمَلَائِكَةُ وَأُولُو الْعِلْمِ قَائِمًا بِالْقِسْطِ

[Allah bore witness that there is no deity except Him and the Angels and those who were given or possess *ilm*, ever upholding fair distribution.] Contrary to all English translations of this verse, *ilm* cannot be translated as knowledge (see Chapter 9). The most suitable translation of *ilm* would be understanding or science, which is the translation adopted here. The interest of this verse in the discussion here is not to understand how the Angels can bear witness to the oneness of the deity, but to realize the importance of the process of understanding in enabling the act of witnessing, rather than believing in the oneness of deity/Allah.

The singular importance of M3:18 becomes more transparent when we find that Allah stresses in M42:11 that there is nothing like Him. Nothing like Him implies that it is impossible to see, hear, touch, smell, measure, detect, observe or imagine Him having a form and shape. Nevertheless, even assuming that experiencing Allah using any of the human senses is possible, as stipulated by alleged highly controversial narratives attributed to the Prophet (see Chapter 5 and 8), the oneness of Allah does not necessarily follow; there could be a plurality of gods! Notice that the Mushaf speaks of those who were in possession of understanding as those who bore witness to the deity's oneness, not bore witness to Allah or to a specific god! Again, the emphasis is on the oneness. (It is interesting to note that the precision of the wording in M3:18 is as remarkable as the imprecision used to interpret it in the books of Mushaf exegeses.)

According to the Mushaf, witnessing the oneness of the Deity can only be achieved through the mind, which is the faculty that facilitates understanding and/or comprehension. The people who were given or are in possession of the understanding in the above verse are not the so-called scholars of Islam (see Chapter 9). Knowledge of something is different from understanding something. Bearing witness to the oneness of Allah resembles being a witness to the reasoning that reveals the oneness of the solution to a mathematical problem. The parallel to mathematics, which can be described as a highly symbolic form of reasoning, is too stark to be overlooked. It is to be emphasized, however, that establishing the oneness of the solution (existence and uniqueness in the jargon of mathematics) is totally different from finding the solution itself.

Interestingly, M3:18 does not invoke belief, Islam, or the nature of Allah; all these are distinct concepts and are not to be confused or conflated with the idea of bearing witness. The Mushaf unequivocally stresses that achieving the highest level of awareness of the oneness of Allah can only be possible through understanding. To understand something (law, nature, behavior, etc.) would need what is commonly referred to as science. Therefore, science, irrespective of its exact definition, is a process through which humans achieve understanding. A scientist produces knowledge whereas a knowledgeable person reproduces already available knowledge. Science implies a process of understanding phenomena and the relationship between cause and effect. Indeed M3:18 presents the Mushaf's most significant emphasis on the importance of science and reason. M3:18 is an indication that science is the key to understand the universe and its creator, and to realize the oneness of the Deity. The Mushaf is not a book of science and cannot create scientists, but certainly encourages humanity to embrace science.

Disparaging the Intellect

The Mushaf invokes the *aql* (mind) in forty-nine verses, *al-albab* (brains or minds) in twenty-six verses and *faqaha* (comprehended) in twenty.

The Mushaf repeatedly encourages the believer and humanity in general to use the mind to understand the universe, the creation, and the signs attesting to both. The Mushaf, however, never mixes the process of understanding with faith. It is through the mind, not primordial instincts, that humans can evolve intellectually, politically, economically and socially within a civil framework. Through Muslim history, a process has evolved to mystify and question reasoning and to isolate intellectuals from a leading role to understand and interpret the Mushaf. After all, the Arabic term *aklani,* which literally means a person who advocates rationalism, has been used derisively by early and contemporary Salafis to describe intellectually-engaged Muslims.[2]

In a variety of Muslim literature, *aklani* is used as a derogatory term to refer to Muslims who propounded a rational approach to understanding the Mushaf text.[3] The work *aklanyyoon* (plural of *aklani*) was used in Muslim history to refer to heretics or to people who rejected Islam. Accusingا Muslim of heresy amounts to accusing him of rejecting the revelation and consequently abandoning the religion altogether. In fact, rejection of the Mushaf revelation automatically implies that the person is no longer a Muslim.

Not different from Christian history, throughout Muslim history rivalries ensued between different groups of Muslims with each group claiming the highest moral and religious grounds while discrediting the others with caustic labels. Particularly, the turn against rationalism, or aklanism, could have started, most likely when the Arabs of the Arabian Peninsula started interacting with the surrounding Roman and Persian cultures and civilizations, many of which embraced the new religion but approached it with curiosity and intellectualism rather than with the spirit of tribal allegiance, or inherent privilege. Review of early Muslim literature, especially debates between two major rival groups, the Ash'aris and Mu'tazalites, reveals that this war against reason had oscillating intensity depending on the persuasion of the ruling elites and the political climate.[4]

Nevertheless, despite a lack of clarity on the timeline for the inception of hostility towards rationality, reason and *akl* were made de facto enemies of Islam by Muslim groups that fiercely promoted the Sunnah as the second revelation (second to the Mushaf). The new doctrine, packaged as "the Sunnah", was extremely difficult to rationalize and sell to Muslims, so rationality had to be ridiculed and degraded to a point that it became associated with transgression against Islam. The opponents of rationalism fanatically championed their embrace of the Sunnah and even labeled themselves Ahl al-Sunnah wa al-Jamma'ah (the family of the Sunnah and the collective). These groups put forth a methodology for the interpretation of the Mushaf to fiercely oppose rationalism. While Ahl al-Sunnah wa al-Jamma'ah claimed to defend and champion the Mushaf and considered it the supreme source of the religion and particularly the primary fountain of legislation, in practice, however, their primary and only source for understanding and practicing Islam was the loosely defined Sunnah doctrine.[5]

The ideologues of Ash'aris and Ahl al-Sunnah wa al-Jamma'ah were triumphant over the rationalists as evidenced by the fact that the vast majority of Sunni Muslims today are followers of the Sunnah doctrine. The Sunnah advocates had to retool the Arabic language to explain the Mushaf in light of their strong hostility towards rationalism. The interpretation of the Mushaf by leading Sunnah advocates, such as ibn Kathir and many others pursued an ideologically motivated approach that focused least on consistency, logic, compliance with the text of the Mushaf, and compatibility with the Mushaf itself. Under the guise of opposition to Aklanis, Mu'tazalites, Mantiqees, Jahamiyya, and other Muslim philosophical and theological schools that advocated critical thinking, reason became a sworn enemy by the mainstream Sunni sects.[6]

It is not an exaggeration to say that the Sunnah (not Sunni) camps, largely declared full war against reason. A striking example is how the word *qalb* in the Mushaf became synonymous with the heart rather than the brain. This was a convenient interpretation, or possibly a diversion since it would automatically connect any reference to all *qalb* derivatives in the Mushaf to emotions rather than to an intellectual process, hence creating a divide between rationalism and Islam. This interpretation would immediately render a total of 49 occurrences of the *aql* derivatives in the Mushaf, many of which were used to emphatically emphasize the importance of the signs of Allah, to the domain of emotions. Take for instance M22:46

أَفَلَمْ يَسِيرُوا فِي الْأَرْضِ فَتَكُونَ لَهُمْ قُلُوبٌ يَعْقِلُونَ بِهَا أَوْ آذَانٌ يَسْمَعُونَ بِهَا فَإِنَّهَا لَا تَعْمَى الْأَبْصَارُ وَلَكِن تَعْمَى الْقُلُوبُ الَّتِي فِي الصُّدُورِ

[So have they not traveled through the earth so they may have *quloob* by which to synthesize (create understanding) or ears by which to hear? For indeed, it is not the means by which seeing takes place that become blinded, but blinded are the *quloob* which are within the *sudoor*.] This Mushaf verse was interpreted by almost all Mushaf exegetes as if the Arabic word *quloob* meant hearts rather than brains. Since the heart is not an instrument for intellectual activity, analysis, synthesis, comprehension, or thinking, the importance of reasoning had been removed from the Mushaf altogether.[7] The fact that the Arabic word *qalb* in modern Arabic denotes the heart is not a proof that its meaning in the Mushaf is identical. This particular legacy interpretation of *qalb* is only but one example of how deconstruction and reconstruction of language were used effectively and without much curiosity by the majority of Muslim clergy to create a convenient interpretation of the Mushaf, as will be shown repeatedly throughout this book.

The linguistic challenges and apparent paradoxes arise when the Mushaf is interpreted in light of the Arabic language commonly used nowadays. There is no proof to suggest that the Mushaf available today is different from the one the Prophet asked the Muslims to write during his lifetime. If the Mushaf has not changed, then there is no reason to substantiate that the Arabic of today is precisely that of the Arabic of the Mushaf. The grammatical structure of the language of the Mushaf is different from the modern Arabic grammar. For example, *sudoor* in M22:46 has different meanings in Arabic, one of which is a cavity or an empty space.[8] In a different context, *sudoor* refers to the central part of the house. A man or a woman has organs within the chest's cavity but also has other cavities, most prominent of which is the cavity within the head. Insistence on translating the word *qalb* in the Mushaf as the heart instead of the brain appears to suggest that comprehension is a mysterious process of non-physical or even metaphysical nature. The heart has a primary function of pumping and circulating blood throughout the human body. Since no thinking or reasoning can take place within the heart, one would conclude, if *qalb* indeed refers to the heart, then all that matters is faith. Reason had to submit to faith, which is the prevailing conclusion of most available English translations (that were based on conventional and major exegeses of the Mushaf).

The brain and anything related to it, such as the act of using the brain, invoking the brain, contemplating with the brain (or the mind) and products of the mind and the brain (i.e., sciences), all had been given heightened importance in the Mushaf. The mind is invoked to encourage the believer to contemplate the existence of everything from the nearest to the farthest. The Mushaf does not limit discussing, thinking, or contemplating the essence of anything, and it even invokes the believers to challenge the Qur'aan itself as in M4:82

أَفَلَا يَتَدَبَّرُونَ الْقُرْآنَ وَلَوْ كَانَ مِنْ عِنْدِ غَيْرِ اللَّهِ لَوَجَدُوا فِيهِ اخْتِلَافًا كَثِيرًا

[Will they not contemplate the Qur'aan and if it were from other than Allah, they would have found in it numerous contradictions/differences.] Most profoundly, the Mushaf even encourages contemplating the nature of Allah.[9] M3:18 declares that bearing witness to the oneness of Allah is the capability of the people who understand or the people of science. Notice that the prophets and believers were not necessarily included amongst those who are capable of bearing witness to the oneness of Allah.

The stress on rationalism, comprehension and science in the Mushaf is overwhelming. It can be argued that the Mushaf is the ultimate instrument of demystification in order to empower humanity to achieve closeness to Allah. Since Allah is not described by space or volume, proximity to Him implies getting close to his attributes that he listed in the Mushaf. Being close to Allah, in the context of M4:82, is achieving higher or better understanding of the world, the universe and the laws that govern them. Allah placed so much significance on science that should be the highest goal of every Muslim.

The insistence of the Mushaf's on using mental faculties to understand all that is there to understand sharply contradicts numerous Muslims' writings that canonized intellectual docility and deprivation. A dramatic reversal took place from a religion that does not place any limit on inquiries, including contemplating the nature of Allah to a religion that implicitly forbids inquiry and launches caustic virulent attacks against individuals whose ideas do not comply with the politically-motivated interpretations of the sanctioned Muslim clergy. The Arabic term *bid'ah* (innovation in religion or heresy) has been made synonymous with deviation from Islam, a deviation that can lead to going astray from the path of the religion. Most often, the accusation of *bid'ah* is used as a veiled accusation of *kufr* (which, according to the Mushaf, is one of the highest forms of transgression against Allah). Since *bid'ah* has a direct path to hellfire (in the doctrine of Ahl al-Sunnah wa al-Jamma'ah), the fear of the *bid'ah* label likely discouraged Muslims for many centuries from daring to produce any new interpretation of the Mushaf despite the irrelevance of most of the existing interpretation.[10]

The intellectual output of early Muslim societies was a natural evolutionary response to a divine revelation that constantly enticed and invited the mind to reflect on the nearest and the farthest, and the smallest and grandest. The divine revelation challenged scientists, historians, sociologists, economists and others to excel in every aspect of life. When one looks back at earlier Muslim societies, one finds that the nature of then competing influences are typical of any society with scientific, religious and political elites. Political patronage had a strong role to play in the emergence of the so-called fundamentalists, traditionalists, or Salafis. Ample evidence from narratives attributed to the Prophet and a specific class of companions and their followers reveals that the philosophical and religious persuasions of most of the historically dominant Muslim sects were aligned with the ruling elites, whose patronage was a natural consequence. (Take, for example, the genre of hadiths that command the believer to obey the ruler even if he was a tyrant and unjust, as long as he allows Muslims to freely perform the daily prayers).[11]

When Islam reached non-Arabs, different perspectives on life emerged, perspectives sharply different from those of the Arab tribes who lived simple lives where governance was patriarchal with unwritten rules administered by the tribe's elders. For many Arabs, the spread of Islam to non-Arabs who were familiar with other philosophies and civilizations constituted a possible threat to the way of thinking prevalent amongst simple tribal societies. Tribalism was and remains the antithesis of organized civil society. Instead of perceiving the influx of non-Arab cultures into the domain of Islam as a positive development, evidence indicates the opposite happened, especially amongst Arabs with strong nationalistic zeal.[12] Many Arabs could have felt that the inclusion of non-Arabs in the nascent Muslim empire was a threat instead of a positive manifestation of the globalization of the Islamic domain with the cultural and civilizational riches that it brings with it. The newcomers to Islam were part of rich and old civilizations and found in the Mushaf a book that unleashed, in the most revolutionary way, their intellectual capacities.[13]

The approach of the non-Arabs to the Mushaf was different from that of the Arabs. The non-Arab newcomers accepted Islam and, more importantly, adopted an Islam-inspired outlook in different aspects of their civilizations, including the arts, sciences, and philosophy. The "original" Arab Muslims, from a mostly tribal background, found their influence and prestige dwindling. Arab nationalism and jingoism have old roots, and despite the skillful governance of the Prophet in Medina where different Arab tribes were reconciled to a unity government, feuds surfaced immediately after the Prophet's death, contesting the rightful heir to Muhammad. The strong nationalism amongst Arabs and their feelings of superiority affected their interpretation of the Mushaf.[14] Ample evidence from the historical records suggest that the Arabs wanted to mold the language of the Mushaf to fit their customary use of the language and, furthermore, to use it as an instrument of control and subjugation of the vast number of non-Arabs who became part of the new Arab empires.

Language is the most sensual form of the Mushaf.[15] It is a form that can be read or listened to in order to convey either information, understanding or both. Allah insisted that the Mushaf was presented in a clear Arabic language, a language that was most likely fully comprehensible to the Arab tribes at the time of the Prophet.[16] Nevertheless, despite their strong command of Arabic, especially their renowned poetic prowess, the early Arab Muslims may have attempted to interpret the Mushaf in light of familiar poetic styles. We find reference to the Arabs' attitude towards the language of the Mushaf in M69:41

وَمَا هُوَ بِقَوْلِ شَاعِرٍ قَلِيلًا مَّا تُؤْمِنُونَ

[And it is not the saying of a poet; little do you (plural) believe.] Here, Allah stresses that the Mushaf was not the product or outcome of a poet, and thus Muhammad was never a poet. The Mushaf insisted that the revelation was not to be treated as a book of stylistic poetry with its customary imprecision and where synonyms are conveniently interchanged to create rhymes. Rather, the Mushaf conveyed precise and logical information. Imprecision in the use of words and exaggeration were two prominent features that made Arabic poetry distinct from the Mushaf. (This verse is typically invoked by Muslims as if Allah was challenging the Arabs to produce a similar document to the Mushaf.)

Early and contemporary Muslim writings hint that non-Arabs were perceived by the Arabs as cultural invaders. The Arabs felt a threat from cultures and civilizations that were far more sophisticated and advanced than their own simple mostly nomadic and tribal culture. The attitude of the incoming non-Arabs towards Islam and the Mushaf in particular could have been significantly different from that of Arabs accustomed to the seduction of their language and poetry. Based on the rich experience of the civilizations that embraced Islam, perhaps non-Arabs were more sensitive to the precision of the Mushaf than Arabs. Naturally, if one were versed, say in philosophy, mathematics or manufacturing, one would take note of the context and precise usage of words more than one with a much less sophisticated life. The Mushaf is expected to resonate more with a sophisticated and learned society than a simple one, just as a sophisticated painter would view a painting with more cognizance of its composition, medium and techniques than an ordinary person who never took any lessons in painting. Just like a good painting, which is for the most sophisticated of painters and the art-illiterate person who sees something soothing in it but cannot explain why, the Mushaf is certainly also for the least and most sophisticated and for the least and most learned. However, expectedly, the level of one's engagement with the Mushaf differs. For the least sophisticated and least learned Arabs, the sophistication, complexity and universality of the Mushaf had to be tamed in favor of a petrified image of the "ideal Muslim society"; the image that was convenient and familiar to the Arabs. Since the new Arab empires used Islam to establish their legitimacy, Arabic, the presumed language of Islam, was a strategic tool to maintain their dominance.

Conformist Language

Conflicts between different schools of Arabic grammar during the early years of the Abbasid dynasty suggest the possibility of diverging jurisprudential opinions based on different understandings of Arabic.[17] This could have affected the schools of jurisprudence in significant ways, and more critically, the interpretation of the Mushaf.

M16:103 states that the Qur'aan was revealed (and transformed) into a clear Arabic tongue, but is it the same tongue the Arabs are using fourteen hundred years after the death of the Prophet? Take for instance the word *dharaba* that appears in several places in the Mushaf. The root of the word *dharaba* appears fifty-eight times in the Mushaf. Based on the context, not a single occurrence of *dharaba* in fifty-seven verses would logically imply physical beating or striking. How could it be then that the word *adhriboohun* in M4:34 had come to be translated by ibn Kathir, al-Qurtubi, al-Tabari, al-Manar, amongst other prominent exegeses of the Mushaf, as physical beating and striking of women? Let us consider M4:34

الرِّجَالُ قَوَّامُونَ عَلَى النِّسَاءِ بِمَا فَضَّلَ اللَّهُ بَعْضَهُمْ عَلَى بَعْضٍ وَبِمَا أَنْفَقُوا مِنْ أَمْوَالِهِمْ فَالصَّالِحَاتُ قَانِتَاتٌ حَافِظَاتٌ لِلْغَيْبِ بِمَا حَفِظَ اللَّهُ وَاللَّاتِي تَخَافُونَ نُشُوزَهُنَّ فَعِظُوهُنَّ وَاهْجُرُوهُنَّ فِي الْمَضَاجِعِ وَاضْرِبُوهُنَّ فَإِنْ أَطَعْنَكُمْ فَلَا تَبْغُوا عَلَيْهِنَّ سَبِيلًا إِنَّ اللَّهَ كَانَ عَلِيًّا كَبِيرًا

[*Rijal* are *qawwamoon* on *nisa* by what Allah has given some (masculine and feminine) over the other (masculine and feminine) and what they spend from their money. So those who are suitable (feminine) are devout, protecting the unseen by what Allah has protected. And those from whom you fear their *nushooz* advise them and forsake them in bed and *adhriboohun*. But if they obey you, seek no means against them. Indeed, Allah is exalted-Grand.] It is instructive to contrast this translation with the one provided by Sahih International (SI): [Men are in charge of women by [right of] what Allah has given one over the other and what they spend [for maintenance] from their wealth. So righteous women are devoutly obedient, guarding in [the husband's] absence what Allah would have them guard. But those [wives] from whom you fear arrogance - [first] advise them; [then if they persist], forsake them in bed; and [finally], strike them. But if they obey you [once more], seek no means against them. Indeed, Allah is ever Exalted and Grand.][18] Notice the stark difference between the two translations. The first one was mine and I only translated each Arabic word using its English counterpart without any additions of conjunctions or insertion of any extraneous words reflecting any particular preconceived interpretation.

The probability of inaccuracy in my translation is due to choosing the wrong English counterparts for Arabic words. In fact, a matter that has not yet been settled amongst Arabic linguists is the meaning of *nushooz* and thus I intentionally left it untranslated. The SI translation, on the other hand, is essentially a translation of a specific interpretation. Surprisingly, neither the SI authors nor other reputable exegetes considered where else and how else *adhriboohun* was used in the Mushaf. They could have avoided this in the first place and likely opted for a translation that found resonance with societies favoring power hierarchy and acceptable violence towards the most vulnerable and least powerful members of the society.[19] The question of context is paramount to understanding the meaning of a word in Arabic, if not in all languages. Arabic words, in particular, have multiple meanings and the only way to buttress the intended meaning of the word is to understand the entire context. The context cannot provide an absolute meaning of a word but certainly serves to narrow the range of meanings considerably. In this process of understanding the context there lies yet another call for additional invocation of the mind.

The word *dharaba* is used here as an example to help understand whether the intentional misuse and abuse of language was a factor in creating schism between different competing camps and means to justify self-serving interpretations of the Mushaf. Literalism, fundamentalism, and traditionalism are typically attributed to one of the early camps that have come to be known as the Salafi School. The connotation arising from the words fundamentalism and traditionalism can be either positive or negative depending on which side the person rests. Literalism, on the other hand, deserves careful attention. Literalism implies adhering to the literal meaning of the word. In the case of the *dharaba* example, literalists cannot be exonerated for not consulting the Mushaf itself for the most likely meaning of the word that is based both on a possible meaning of the word and its context.

Another example is the interpretation of *wazna* in M18:105

أُولَٰئِكَ الَّذِينَ كَفَرُوا بِآيَاتِ رَبِّهِمْ وَلِقَائِهِ فَحَبِطَتْ أَعْمَالُهُمْ فَلَا نُقِيمُ لَهُمْ يَوْمَ الْقِيَامَةِ وَزْنًا

[Those are the ones who rejected the signs of their Lord and in meeting Him, so their deeds have become worthless; and We will not assign to them on the Day of Resurrection any *wazna*.] The word *wazna* is kept untranslated. Interpretation of *wazna* by al-Bukhari can be both entertaining and instructive. Al-Bukhari archives a hadith attributed to the

Prophet that states: "the fat man will come on the day of judgement and not having the weight of the wing of a mosquito" and then he (the Prophet) recited the underlined part of the verse above. *Wazna* could mean the weight associated with the gravitational force, but it could also mean status, value, prestige, or dignity. The hadith does not explain the relevance between the weight due to gravity and the worth or value of the person.[20] Thus, al-Bukhari is implying that the correct interpretation of *wazna* in M18:105 is gravity-induced weight. Al-Bukhari sacrificed the context of the verse in order to advocate a truly bizarre interpretation.

Debating the correct meaning of a word that requires some intellectual effort might sound worrisome to most Muslims and particularly Arab Muslims who believe that Allah has promised to preserver the Arabic language according to M15:9

إِنَّا نَحْنُ نَزَّلْنَا الذِّكْرَ وَإِنَّا لَهُ لَحَافِظُونَ

[We have revealed the *thikr* and we shall preserve/protect it.] The most common understanding of this verse, amongst Muslims, is that Allah gave an assurance that the Arabic language will be preserved from alternation or extinction.[21] However, before reaching the conclusion that Allah will preserve the spoken and written Arabic and thus Arabic becomes immutable, an understanding of the meaning of *thikr* is in order. *Thikr* cannot be translated into English without first understanding what it means in Arabic. The translations available today translate *thikr* into "remembrance", "reminder", "message", or "Qur'aan". The casual reader of the Mushaf may accept all of these translations as synonymous; however, this is not the case as M36:69 explains:

وَمَا عَلَّمْنَاهُ الشِّعْرَ وَمَا يَنبَغِي لَهُ إِنْ هُوَ إِلَّا ذِكْرٌ وَقُرْآنٌ مُبِينٌ

[And We did not teach him poetry and it was not befitting/allowed for him; indeed it (هو) was nothing but *thikr* and clear/apparent Qur'aan.] The conjunction "and" at the end of the phrase clearly indicates the difference Qur'aan and *thikr*.

It might come as a surprise to many Muslims and Arabs in particular that the written and spoken Arabic of today is not sufficient to help us understand the Mushaf since there is more than one school of Arabic grammar.[22] In fact, there are sufficient indications that applying contemporary grammatical structures might make the Mushaf more difficult, if not impossible, to understand.

From early on, logical and reasonable interpretations of the words of the Mushaf were frowned upon. In the name of religion, logic and reason were effectively circumvented with the aid of alleged Prophetic narratives or hadiths (see Chapter 8 for an extensive discussion of Hadith). Definitions for Arabic words were produced independently of context and etymology. As a rule, most, if not all, exegetes did not value the meaning of Arabic words or the context that might illuminate their meaning.[23] In fact, a distinct methodology was developed to bypass the original meaning of the Arabic words by inventing a new system of definitions with religious context that fits what the interpreter wished to justify. The typical approach to decipher and eventually understand a certain word in the Mushaf became as follows: first, the word is explained using traditional Arabic usage (as in pre-Islam poetry or, in modern times, reference is made to *Lisan al-Arab*.[24]) Then, inexplicably, a different definition is produced and is qualified as *fi al-Sharia* (in the context of Sharia) or *fi al-istilah* (in the context of methodology).[25] The new definition is based on perceptions that arose from particular interpretations of the text of the Mushaf or Hadith; interpretations that were based on opinions.

The concept of *fi al-Sahria* and *fi al-istilah* amounts to pure subversion of the religion to achieve all types of objectives.[26] The framers of this concept used religion as if it were their own scholarly fiefdom, thus endowing themselves with the power to redefine Allah's words as they saw suitable to engrain specific self-serving interpretations.[27] This concept with its significant and wide reaching implications silently made its way into the Muslim scholars' common consciousness without any appreciable (if any) scrutiny or challenge by either the scholarly or non-scholarly Muslim community. (Non-Muslim scholars are historically too intimidated to delve into the apparent complexities of the definitions of Arabic words so they mostly opted to be sidelined or stay as mere observers, perhaps by the fear of being ridiculed as incapable to understand the "secrets" of the Arabic language.) The outcome of the new opinion-based system of definitions is that the meaning of the Arabic words of the Mushaf can be adjusted (or perhaps manipulated would be a more apt description) to fit a specific ideology or persuasion. An example is the concept of *ismah* (infallibility).[28] The derivative of *ismah* appeared in the Mushaf in several verses. Muslim scholars fully agree on its meaning as "protection", yet, the so-called *fi al-istilah* concept provides a completely different meaning.[29]

The irony is the Qur'aan (not the Mushaf) emphasizes that it was revealed using a clear Arabic language, not an ambiguous Arabic language with words having definitions outside of the language boundary.[30] This process can be made infinitely more mercurial when one brings to the mix the compendia of alleged prophetic narratives that are inconsistent with other narratives and even contradictory to the Mushaf itself. The outcome of these definitions suggests that the meaning of the words of the Mushaf are very fluid. This fluidity severely diminishes the respect Muslims and non-Muslims have towards the Mushaf as practically exemplified by treating the Mushaf as a collection of words that can be recited for worship rather than a substance of guidance.

The system of definitions of Arabic words that Muslim scholars refer to as the *fi al-istilah* resulted in a rift between the meaning of words in Arabic and the meaning for which certain exegetes wanted to advocate. Let us consider M12:2

إِنَّا أَنزَلْنَاهُ قُرْآنًا عَرَبِيًّا لَعَلَّكُمْ تَعْقِلُونَ

[We have revealed it an Arabic Qur'aan in order that you may *ta'qiloon*]. For the purpose of understanding this verse, and without losing generality, *ta'qiloon* here will be translated as "to comprehend".[31] The verse emphasizes the Arabic nature of the Qur'aan (rather than the entire Mushaf) that enables comprehension. Whether this verse implies that the language of the Qur'aan is Arabic or the nature of the Qur'aan is Arabic is not clear to this author.[32] Regardless, the words of the Mushaf have to be understood from and within the Arabic language. (See also other verses in the Mushaf that the emphasized the Arabness of the revelation or at least part of it such as M12:2, 13:37, 16:103, 20:113, 26:195, 39:28, 41:3, 42:7, 43:3, and 46:12).[33]

CAUSALITY

Sababiyyah (causality) is another casualty of the dominant Muslims sects including their far right, such as the Salafis and Ahl al-Sunnah wa al-

Jamma'ah, and their far left, such as the Hanafis. Since the first Muslim century, different political camps (with partial intellectual leanings) debated the connection between cause and effect. Those who denied any connection between the two employed Islam to help advocate their opinion, not by using complete argument from within the Mushaf but rather by simply using specific Mushaf words or phrases to bestow derogatory labels on their opponents. Frightening mouthful Arabic and non-Arabic labels borrowed from the Muslims religious lexicon, such as *bid'ah, kufr,* and *zandaqa,* amongst other effective verbal weapons, were bestowed lavishly on the causality opponents.

The opponents of causality viewed religion and Islam in particular, as a mixture of mysteries and miracles. This is not surprising since anything, be it Islam or science, if not understood, can be perceived as a confusing mixture of mysteries and miracles. Both require no effort to believe or have faith in, but to understand Islam or to understand science requires hard work, deep contemplation, deep intellectual engagement, or all the above. To a large extent, the founders of the major Muslim schools of jurisprudence considered the belief in causality to be equivalent to a denial of Allah's capabilities, His will, or even denial of— or even *kufr*—in the revelation. The Mushaf, however, proves them wrong. The initial Muslim opposition to causality reflected a strong tendency not to disconnect from the pre-Islam habits and thinking of the Arabs; habits that were repackaged, after embracing Islam, with an Islamic vocabulary but devoid of Islam's spirit.

Causality means that every effect has a cause, thus establishing a connecting path between two sequential events. If the cause is inexplicable, then it cannot be a cause but an illusion or a myth. Equally, if no reasonable connection is established between two sequential events, then causality cannot describe the relationship between them. The analysis that establishes the connection between cause and effect requires concerted effort that might require hard work including the types of work that customarily are referred to as scholarship and science. An alternative to accepting causality is demonstrated by the oft-repeated mantra, "Allah is capable of doing whatever He wishes". This phrase is used too often by the anti-causality camp to dismiss any connection between cause and effect by invoking a God with an arbitrary behavior who is modeled after the arbitrariness of a temperamental ruler or a dictator. If one tries to use causality to reason through any subject, from life, theories of evolution, modern medicine, to death, the vast majority of Muslims and their scholars reply with the Mushaf phrase *kun fayakoon*, which typically translates as "be and it becomes" or "be and it is". Muslims who invoke the *kun fayakoon* phrase imply an outright dismissal of the application of the concept of causality in understanding the universe and creation with their physical and social laws. Causality is in essence the most profound manifestation of nature whereby a natural process leads from the cause to its consequential effects. This natural process embodies the fundamentals and laws of creation; however, the predominant Muslim sects associated the processes of nature with disbelief in Allah and rejection of all his powers. The invocation of nature and its processes is typically associated with materialism despite the fact that the signs of Allah (*aayaat*), those that He asks humans to contemplate on, are all part of nature, i.e., pure material signs.

Before we go into any analysis of the relevance of the cause-effect relationship in our attempt to understand our complex existence and reality, we need to consider the context of the misused phrase *kun fayakoon*, which appeared in M2:117, 3:47, 3:59, 6:73, 16:40, 19:35, 36:82, and 40:68. As an example, we consider M2:117

بَدِيعُ السَّمَاوَاتِ وَالْأَرْضِ ۖ وَإِذَا قَضَىٰ أَمْرًا فَإِنَّمَا يَقُولُ لَهُ كُن فَيَكُونُ

[The originator of the heavens and earth (or earths) and if He decreed an order, then He *yaqool* (pronounces) to *kun fayakoon*]. Notice first that the *kun fayakoon* in this verse is connected with a divine decree (*qadha*). Clearly, there is no connection between the creation and Allah's decree culminating in *fayakoon* (being). In fact, this can also be concluded from all other verses listed above that contain *kun fayakoon*. Specifically, Allah's creation and design precedes his decree, whereas the *kun fayakoon* follows Allah's pronouncement (*qawl*). Thus, the generalization of the conventional interpretation of *kun fayakoon* as commanding something to emerge from nothingness cannot be substantiated from this or any verse in the Mushaf. Thus, there is no connection between *kun fayakoon* and *khalq* (creation). In fact, the Mushaf affirms causality in numerous verses, and in particular, stresses that Allah's will and causality are not divergent concepts (or processes). Take for instance M9:26

War on Reason

ثُمَّ أَنزَلَ اللَّهُ سَكِينَتَهُ عَلَىٰ رَسُولِهِ وَعَلَى الْمُؤْمِنِينَ وَأَنزَلَ جُنُودًا لَّمْ تَرَوْهَا وَعَذَّبَ الَّذِينَ كَفَرُوا ۚ وَذَٰلِكَ جَزَاءُ الْكَافِرِينَ

[Then Allah sent/provided His tranquility upon His Messenger and upon the believers <u>and sent/provided soldiers that you did not see</u> and punished those who rejected, and that was the recompense of the *kafiroon*] and M9:40

إِلَّا تَنصُرُوهُ فَقَدْ نَصَرَهُ اللَّهُ إِذْ أَخْرَجَهُ الَّذِينَ كَفَرُوا ثَانِيَ اثْنَيْنِ إِذْ هُمَا فِي الْغَارِ إِذْ يَقُولُ لِصَاحِبِهِ لَا تَحْزَنْ إِنَّ اللَّهَ مَعَنَا ۖ فَأَنزَلَ اللَّهُ سَكِينَتَهُ عَلَيْهِ وَأَيَّدَهُ بِجُنُودٍ لَّمْ تَرَوْهَا وَجَعَلَ كَلِمَةَ الَّذِينَ كَفَرُوا السُّفْلَىٰ ۗ وَكَلِمَةُ اللَّهِ هِيَ الْعُلْيَا ۗ وَاللَّهُ عَزِيزٌ حَكِيمٌ

[If you do not aid and support the Prophet, Allah has already aided and supported him when those who disbelieved had driven him out as the second of two, when they were in the cave as he said to his companion, do not grieve; indeed, Allah is with us. Thereafter, Allah sent down his tranquillity upon him and supported him with angels you did not see and made the word of those who rejected, the lowest, while the word of Allah the highest. And Allah is *Aziz-Hakim*.] The interest in these verses here is only to point out that the outcome of the events in the above two verses, the victory of the believers (in M9:26) and the safe passage of the Prophet and his companion (in M9:40), were made possible by the presence of soldiers, unseen to humans, sent directly by Allah. For humans, those events could be classified as "miraculous" or "supernatural", but they were indeed causal; a clear case of cause and effect rather than the perceived "miracle" of *kun fayakoon*.

The Mushaf presents the creation emphatically within a cause-effect context. In M23:14

ثُمَّ خَلَقْنَا النُّطْفَةَ عَلَقَةً فَخَلَقْنَا الْعَلَقَةَ مُضْغَةً فَخَلَقْنَا الْمُضْغَةَ عِظَامًا فَكَسَوْنَا الْعِظَامَ لَحْمًا ثُمَّ أَنشَأْنَاهُ خَلْقًا آخَرَ

[Then We created the zygote into a clinging clot, then We created the clot into a lump of flesh, then We created from the lump, bones, and then We covered the bones with flesh; then We developed/initiated him into another creation.] In most of the popular Mushaf translations, *khalaqa* was translated as "made" instead of "created". The Arabic word for "made" is *sana'a*. Only in two translations was *khalaqa* translated as "created" and as "fashioned".[34] Whatever the correct English counterpart for *khalaqa* is, it denotes a progressive process of growth (rather than transformation). A Muslim who lived fourteen hundred years ago would believe in M23:14 without fully realizing the expansive scope of *khalq* (creation) but could not understand its full meaning and implication. To a modern biologist, however, the very process of *khalq* is understood in its entirety with its minutest details. So according to the Mushaf, creation includes the development process that takes the zygote into a much different form. Creation here does not imply that a human being appears out of nothingness. However, abu Hanifa, the grandfather of the Hanafi Sunni sect, theorizes that Allah creates things from nothingness, without providing any validation for his theory.[35] In fact, the theory that creation comes from nothingness, touted by a majority of Muslims, is not only unsubstantiated by any Mushaf evidence, but is in sharp contradiction to what M23:14 most explicitly indicates. Other prominent Muslim jurists had fundamentally similar attitudes towards creationism, albeit with modulated hostility towards those who differed from their opinions.

PREDESTINATION, DESTINY AND ALLAH'S KNOWLEDGE

Predestination refers to the concept of believing that all events, including life and death, have been decided or willed by God thousands of years before the events took place. While the concept may find roots in other religions, the Mushaf does not provide any validation for predestination but rather disproves it altogether. In fact Islam negates predestination whether attributed to Allah as the One who willed or to any other agent. Here I will try to discuss how the concept came to be intertwined with other Islamic concepts such as *qadar* and *qadha*. These two Mushaf terms, which will be discussed here, are typically invoked by Muslims to imply predestination. Since no validity of predestination can be found in the Mushaf, its roots in Muslim history can be traced to narratives attributed to the Prophet and narratives attributed directly to Allah through Qudsi Hadith, which are a type of hadiths that most Muslims believe to be revealed to the Prophet but attributed to Allah directly while not being part of the Mushaf.[36] Most Muslims consider Qudsi hadiths as a direct revelation. Perhaps no other concept has deeply affected the Muslim culture than predestination. Perhaps no other concept has devastated the Muslim culture than predestination, with colossal consequences. It can be argued that the singular reason for the retardation of the Muslim countries is the embodiment of predestination as the primary pillar of their faith.

It is difficult to ascertain the origin of the predestination theory amongst Muslims, but it is easy to speculate about the motives behind its inceptors. The sensitivity of the concept of destiny and its implication on the political climate, especially the desire of rulers not to have their reign challenged, did not escape the rulers and their patrons. Jurists that are patronized by the ruling elites may have been tempted to manipulate the Mushaf through fabricated hadiths, thereby creating an atmosphere of despair coupled with fear and coercion.

The alleged Prophetic narratives commenting directly or indirectly on *qadar* erase the role of the human will and agency, again in sharp contradiction to the pronouncements of the Mushaf. The Mushaf does not hint that one's actions were decided before birth nor does it imply that one's net earnings were predetermined in advance. It seems unjust that the Lord of the universe, the Lord of infinite justice, decided in advance to commit a 20th Century Somali man to misery and poverty but a Swedish woman to a life full of riches and comfort. In light of the general understanding amongst Muslims that life and its vicissitudes are tests, one wonders why would the misery of the Somali man be justified or reconciled as a test? Why would Allah test one with misery but test the other with riches? Why would Allah with His infinite justice give to a Nordic man a life expectancy of eighty-five years but only forty-five to that of a Somali nomad?

The implications of predestination suggest that Allah favors some people over others, including the ultimate favor of who will be sent to hellfire and who will be sent to paradise. The predestination theory implies that Allah practices favoritism or arbitrariness. The construct "act of God", whether in the form of a person dying under the hands of a surgeon or a tree falling and crushing a person in a house, had been fashioned to dilute any sense of responsibility from either a potentially careless surgeon or from a builder who built a house next to a tree that can be brought down by a storm. The concept of preordained deeds and fortunes can lead to reclusion and a lifestyle of hopelessness and carelessness. Many Muslims typically and casually justify variance in income as a divine test. The Mushaf, however, does not provide any validity to the "test" theory. Having a test in what one has and achieves in life is one thing, but being tested with divinely preordained largess or poverty is a different matter altogether.

Predestination is one of the most confusing concepts in Muslim history with far reaching consequences. The concept is shrouded in mystery in all Abrahamic faiths. For Muslims, however, the roots of the mystery can be traced back to specific verses in the Mushaf, especially those involving the Arabic words *kitaab, kataba, qadha and qadar*. The roots of the predominant theories of predestination can also be traced to certain hadiths. These claim that all things were planned in advance, with some narratives alleging that all that relate to a human were planned fifty thousand years before his birth, while others claiming that all deeds and future earnings were prescribed by Angels when the fetus is developing inside the mother's womb.[37] All such hadiths are accepted as part of the most common understanding of predestination, yet despite being deeply contradictory to the Mushaf.

Amongst Muslims, the concept of predestination originated from the translation of the Arabic word *qadar* as "destiny". Additional complications were added when the word *qadha* was also connected to the predestination discourse despite lack of any relevance between *qadar* and *qadha*. The peculiar, selective and inconsistent interpretations of the words *kitaab, kataba, qadha and qadar* appear to be the primary cause for the prevalent theories about predestination. Conflating all these words into a single concept of predestination, in addition to adding Allah's knowledge to the confusing mix, as typically found in the intellectual and religious discourse of most Muslims, is another reason for making the predestination theory highly intractable and seemingly distant from any approach by the average Muslim.

To begin unraveling the predestination puzzle, we need to realize that these Arabic words are different, implying that they have different meanings and implications. *Kitaab* and *kataba* are two hugely important terms that are key to understanding predestination, however, for now, they will be left untranslated but will be discussed later. The propounded theories of predestination conjectured by many Muslim jurists suffer from self-inconsistency, self-contradiction, and incompatibility with the Mushaf. The development of these theories can be traced back to the first century of Islam when power struggles between competing camps fueled mass scale fabrication of hadiths to justify a variety of practices, from denying women their rights and keeping many in abject servitude to sanctioning the ill-gotten wealth of despotic rulers and their conquests, all in the name of Islam and Allah, and all in the name of a predestined outcome that the pious Muslim must accept with calm, patience and as part of Allah's grand scheme of things. The Mushaf challenged rulers and elite groups who realized that the new religion championed equality, fairness and justice, and especially scrutiny of war bounty.

Therefore, the power centers advocated an interpretation of the Mushaf that directed the Muslim multitudes to succumb to the "will of Allah", which was a brilliant cover for the will of the ruler. The courtiers of the kings of the new "Islamic" empires brilliantly interpreted the *khilafa* (vice-regency) of the human being strictly as that of the ruler who was readily lavished with the religiously-connoted title of *khaleefa* (vicegerent). In Islam, the term *khaleefa* originated in M2:30 with reference to Adam (irrespective of being a single person or humans) representing humanity, who Allah has made as a representative on earth.[38] This connection strongly suggests the origin of framing political governance within an Islamic context. The framing simply hinged on bestowing the label of *khilafa* on governance.[39] The acceptance by the majority of Muslims followed without much challenge. The catastrophic consequence is that the *khilafa* (the alleged Islamic government) and the *khaleefa* (the Islamic governor) both became the will of Allah. Obedience to the representative of the *khilafa*, the *khaleefa*, had to follow. The most dangerous consequence is the *khaleefa's* will to eliminate his opponents. Executions of the *khaleefa's* opponents became "Islamic".

Predestination is an extremely powerful concept since it provides an "Islamic" instrument for those in power to entice Muslims to accept misery and embrace hopelessness, all in the name of Allah. Muslim rulers with self-bestowed "Islamic" titles of *amir* and *khaleefa* and their courtiers of theologians and jurisprudents installed the tools of oppression within Muslims' system of beliefs, turning the Muslim into an instrument of self-oppression and, by extension, collective oppression. The state, which was equally lavished with the new religiously-connoted title *khilafa*, had only to reinvigorate, when needed, the religious dogma that kept the Muslim masses in "religious" servitude, or more aptly "Islamic" servitude. The state, emboldened and blessed by the institution of the *khilafa*, needed to expend less effort to keep its subjects under control and the vast financial interests of the ruler and his courtiers intact. After all, the Muslims, according to numerous Muslim theologians and jurisprudents, were religiously mandated to pledge their allegiance to the *khilafa*. Connecting *khilafa* to political control, and essentially tyranny and despotism, and, of course, the will of Allah, was truly the work of genius.

The Mushaf articles of faith were the foundation on which the entire system of Islam had to be structured. Believing in the Day of Accountability is one of those articles of faith. (Accountability, which is *hisaab*, is different from resurrection, which is *ba'th*). Accountability is meaningless if every human action has been planned in advance. The primary source or foundation on which the advocates of predestination rely on is the Hadith corpus, and as a secondary source, the Mushaf. A representative example are the following two hadiths from Sahih Muslim, which are stated here in English directly instead of the original Arabic since the vast majority of hadiths were transmitted by meaning rather than verbatim, and therefore providing the original Arabic version will be of little value:[40]

> Abdullah (ibn Mas'ud) reported that Allah's Messenger said: The constituents of one of you are collected for forty days in his mother's womb in the form of blood, after which it becomes a clot of blood in another period of forty days. Then it becomes a lump of flesh and forty days later Allah sends His Angel to it with instructions concerning four things, so the angel writes down his livelihood, his death, his deeds, his fortune and misfortune. By Him, besides Whom there is no God, that one amongst you acts like the people deserving Paradise until between him and Paradise there remains but the distance of a cubit, when suddenly the writing of destiny overcomes him and he begins to act like the denizens of Hell and thus enters Hell, and another one acts in the way of the denizens of Hell, until there remains between him and Hell a distance of a cubit that the writing of destiny overcomes him and then he begins to act like the people of Paradise and enters Paradise.

> Hudhaifa ibn Usaid reported that Allah's Messenger said: When the drop (zygote) remains in the womb for forty or fifty (days) or forty nights, the Angel comes and says: My Lord, will he be good or evil? And both these things would be written. Then the Angel says: My Lord, would he be male or female?

And both these things are written. And his deeds and actions, his death, his livelihood; these are also recorded. Then his document of destiny is rolled and there is no addition to and subtraction from it.

These two hadiths indicate that all the deeds of the newborn were planned, decreed, ordained, or fixed in advance. They also suggest that Allah decisions are arbitrary in making the new born a male or a female. Clearly if that were the case, the Day of Accountability would be a theatrical play. In fact, the two hadiths contradict the Mushaf in so many ways. In particular, let us focus on M91:7-10

وَنَفْسٍ وَمَا سَوَّاهَا
فَأَلْهَمَهَا فُجُورَهَا وَتَقْوَاهَا
قَدْ أَفْلَحَ مَن زَكَّاهَا
وَقَدْ خَابَ مَن دَسَّاهَا

[And a soul that He leveled, then He inspired within it its tendency towards treachery and its tendency towards piety. Successful is he who purifies it and unsuccessful he who suppresses it.] Even if the precise meaning of the words in these four verses were not established, the message in the four verses is simple and clear: good and evil are direct consequences of one's own deeds. The predetermination of the gender of the newborn finds no support in the Mushaf, but rather one finds emphasis that the creation involves females and males. The contradiction between Sahih al-Bukhari's hadiths and the Mushaf is too stark. If contradictions are not to be accepted, the Muslim must believe in either the Mushaf or Sahih al-Bukhari; the two cannot exist in a single self-consistent religion. (See Chapters 7 and 8 for a discussion of the claim by many Muslim clergy that the Hadith serves to explain the Mushaf and thus the Hadith overrides the apparent meaning of the Mushaf.)

There are many other hadiths that have a similar flavor to the above, with some implying a random god who creates and disposes of people as he pleases. Some hadiths claim that Allah sends droves of people to heaven while others to hellfire, again, only because "He pleases". Significantly, in such hadiths, "pleases" is inseparable from "wills". Ahmed ibn Hanbal, one of the five grand Muslim jurists, reported in the Book of al-Sunan, that when Allah created Adam, Allah struck Adam's left shoulder and from it came out a nation of dark people, then He struck Adam's right shoulder and from it came out a nation of white people, then Allah commanded those to Adam's right to proceed to heaven and those to his left to proceed to hellfire while saying: "I care the least".[41] It is inconceivable that any learned Muslim jurist would believe in such bizarre stories, let alone endorse the racist overtones connecting a dark skin color with evil (perhaps to justify or buttress the practice of enslaving dark-skinned people). This narrative gives an image of a god who is random and temperamental, a sharp contrast to the precision of God of the Mushaf.

These are but a few of many other hadiths attributed to the Prophet that are highly suspicious and are not only deeply contradictory to the Mushaf but give an alarming image of a god whose attributes not only include arbitrariness and temperament, but also despotism. Since these hadiths are contradictory in principle to the Mushaf, they need to be rejected outright rather than attempting to reconcile their contradictions with thin sophistry attributed to men of equal or higher credibility to that of ibn Hanbal. One should not be surprised that such hadiths appeared in Sahih Muslim, as the same Sahih compendium is replete with other incredulous hadiths of greater implausibility (see Chapter 8 and 9).

Instead of refusing to recognize the validity of suspicious and bizarre hadiths since the first century of Islam, methodologies have been developed to reconcile volumes of suspect hadiths with each other and with the Mushaf. In fact, the practice of reconciling contradictory or suspect narratives with each other has not abated, as it is still part of the Hadith Sciences curricula in some of the leading religion schools in Muslim countries (this "science" is conventionally designated as Ilm Mukhtalaf al-Hadith). Despite the huge efforts to the degree that these endeavours were turned into "scientific" curricula, the contradictions within the Hadith corpus and between Hadith and the Mushaf remain irreconcilable.[42]

The interpretation of Allah's will in the hadiths mentioned above and many others (including depictions mentioned in numerous stories by ibn Kathir) was modeled after the will of a tyrant who decrees as he wishes and orders the torture or reward of people as he pleases.[43] The god that these narratives and stories glorify has strong resemblance to a despotic king in one of Dr. Suess' brilliant depictions. To buttress this "randomness" will theory, phrases from the Mushaf were interpreted, not only out of context, but also out of meaning, such as the following Mushaf phrase expunged from M2:284

$$\text{فَيَغْفِرُ لِمَن يَشَاءُ وَيُعَذِّبُ مَن يَشَاءُ ۗ وَاللَّهُ عَلَىٰ كُلِّ شَيْءٍ قَدِيرٌ}$$

[Then He forgives whomever He wishes and tortures whomever He wishes]. This phrase is part of a verse that is part of a context that includes the preceding verse where the addressees are those who conceal the testimony. Here is M2:284 in its entirety

$$\text{لِّلَّهِ مَا فِي السَّمَاوَاتِ وَمَا فِي الْأَرْضِ ۗ وَإِن تُبْدُوا مَا فِي أَنفُسِكُمْ أَوْ تُخْفُوهُ يُحَاسِبْكُم بِهِ اللَّهُ ۖ فَيَغْفِرُ لِمَن يَشَاءُ وَيُعَذِّبُ مَن يَشَاءُ ۗ وَاللَّهُ عَلَىٰ كُلِّ شَيْءٍ قَدِيرٌ}$$

[To Allah belongs whatever is in the heavens and whatever is in the earth (or earths). And whether you reveal what is within your *anfusikum* or conceal it, Allah will bring you to account for it. Then He will forgive whom He wills and punish whom He wills, and Allah is over all things competent.][44] Notice that the entirety of the verse indicates that Allah's will (*mashi'ah*) to forgive or punish is related to an offense. Yet the broader context can be even more revealing. M2:283 (not reproduced here for brevity) indicates that Allah's forgiveness or punishment is related to concealing testimonies. Thus, the broader context narrowed down the relevance of Allah's choice between forgiveness and punishment to a specific human behavior with sufficient severity to warrant punishment; yet, Allah leaves open the option of forgiveness. The broader context changes the interpretation of one phrase in M2:284 from a god that is temperamental to God who is willing to forgive a serious offense.

Absent a methodology to understand the Mushaf, random interpretations of phrases and verses, as explained above, remain the rule rather than the exception. Such random approaches to the Mushaf led many Muslims to fashion the will of Allah in the image of the will of a king, infused with randomness and arbitrariness, devoid of cause-effect connection except the absolute inexplicable "will".

KATABA

The Arabic word *kataba* has enormous significance for understanding whether or not predestination has roots in the Mushaf. This highly important word, which is used to buttress the claim of predestination by its proponents, is the same one that holds the key to dismantling the entire theory.[45] The derivatives of *kataba* appear 319 times in the Mushaf with different meanings dependent on the context. For instance, *kutiba alai'kum* had been generally translated and understood to imply "it had been decreed upon you (plural)," whereas *kataba la'kum* is generally accepted by most Muslim exegetes to mean "it had been decreed or decided for you (plural)." Understanding the Mushaf verses that contain *kataba* and its derivatives is an exercise that warrants extra diligence since the traditional interpretation of *kataba* is "he wrote" or "he scribed", connoting the process of scribing information on a medium. This interpretation, as we show below, leads to confusion with major implications for the concept of predestination as widely perceived by Muslims.

By now the reader sees that manipulation of language can indeed be a source of misunderstanding. Above, we showed that the context is critical and essential to developing an understanding of Arabic words, especially in the Mushaf. Language is a collection of words positioned in a context. The context is typically the first casualty when Muslims and non-Muslims use the Mushaf to justify a peculiar interpretation. But the context is only one component that helps to determine the meaning of a word. Different possible meanings for a single word is the second component (as was the case when the word *qalb* was considered earlier in this chapter). Arabic grammar, no matter how important it is claimed to be, can be of little use to understand the precise meaning of a word when present in a particular context. In fact, one can argue that Arabic grammar can potentially provide multiple meanings to a word when considered in a specific context (example is al-Tabari's interpretation of M54:49.[46]) In the context of the Mushaf, the personification of Allah, prevalent in the works of Muslim clergy, played a major part in diverting the meaning of words. The interpretation of verbs associated with Allah in the Mushaf were based on personifying Allah to have human-like physical qualities and attributes. Most likely, early Muslims' lack of abstraction ability coupled with bizarre hadiths contributed to the prevalent personification in early Muslims' writings. An example of such hadiths is one in Sahih al-Bukhari where Allah is portrayed as having a leg with which He stuffs evil doers deep into hellfire on the Day of Resurrection.[47] (Another hadith in al-Darimi (d. 255/869) claims that the Prophet will see Allah and even talk at him on the Day of Resurrection.[48])

The interpretation of the Arabic verb *kataba* was molded in the image of a person who inscribes or records information on a medium such as stone or paper, whereas in the Mushaf context, *kataba* is indicative of establishing an entity whose constituents are all interconnected in the sense of affecting each other. (Such entity can be considered a self-consistent and integrated system). Therefore, *kataba* is closer in meaning to "authored" or "composed" rather than wrote. In fact, the Arabic language distinguishes between *kitaab* (book) and *makhtoot* (something which is written or inscribed). A book denotes a collection of interconnected information grouped together to constitute a meaningful system, a standalone body of knowledge or a standalone theme. A mere collection of notes or information, on the other hand, does not necessarily constitute a book.[49]

The verse with the most familiarity amongst Muslims that is commonly used to support the prevailing understanding of predestination is M9:51

قُل لَّن يُصِيبَنَا إِلَّا مَا كَتَبَ اللَّهُ لَنَا هُوَ مَوْلَانَا وَعَلَى اللَّهِ فَلْيَتَوَكَّلِ الْمُؤْمِنُونَ

[Pronounce/promulgate that nothing will befall us except whatever Allah has *kataba* for us; He is our *mawla* (with whom we are entrusted) and on Allah shall the believers rely].[50] The word *kataba* appears a total of eight times in the Mushaf. If the word *kataba* in M9:51 were to be interpreted to mean "it was ordained" or "it was recorded", then it could lead to the understanding that whatever befalls humans has been planned and designed fully ahead of time. So if you live in misery, your misery with all its unpleasant consequences and associated hardships has been decreed by Allah in advance! In frank language, such understanding would imply that a person cannot change his misery since Allah planned it for him many years before he was born. And if the same person was able to undo his misery, then, using identical logic, Allah must have planned the same. Giving this philosophy more specificity, a woman who is gang raped should not blame anyone but Allah for what had befallen her (to comfort such woman with the cliché that her ordeal was a test from Allah can be difficult to stomach as the woman wonders why Allah singled her out for such a "strenuous" test while other women were "tested" with life's luxuries and material goods and comfort). But before such conclusions can be made, let us consider the word *kutiba* (derived from *kataba*) which appears thirteen times in the Mushaf. The first sentence of M2:178 is

يَا أَيُّهَا الَّذِينَ آمَنُوا كُتِبَ عَلَيْكُمُ الْقِصَاصُ فِي الْقَتْلَى الْحُرُّ بِالْحُرِّ وَالْعَبْدُ بِالْعَبْدِ وَالْأُنْثَى بِالْأُنْثَى

[O you who believed, legal retribution was *kutiba* on you for those who were killed, the free person for the free person and the slave for the slave and the female for the female.] This verse gives guidelines for punishing murderers. If the prosecution and punishments were predetermined or predestined, the understanding of *kutiba* to imply preordained becomes meaningless since the punishment for the killers is yet to be administered through the will of the believers (followers of Muhammad). If enacting the punishment was preordained or predestined, the instructional Mushaf verse would be superfluous. Had the verse been a truism (i.e., a factual statement), it would find contradictions in reality and from Muslims' own history.

Another appearance of *kutiba* is in M4:77

أَلَمْ تَرَ إِلَى الَّذِينَ قِيلَ لَهُمْ كُفُّوا أَيْدِيَكُمْ وَأَقِيمُوا الصَّلَاةَ وَآتُوا الزَّكَاةَ فَلَمَّا كُتِبَ عَلَيْهِمُ الْقِتَالُ إِذَا فَرِيقٌ مِنْهُمْ يَخْشَوْنَ النَّاسَ كَخَشْيَةِ اللَّهِ أَوْ أَشَدَّ خَشْيَةً

[Have you not looked at those who were told keep your hands off and perform prayers and give charity/*zakat*? After that, when fighting was *kutiba* on them (after they were told), a group of them become fearful of people as being fearful of Allah or even higher.] The *kutiba* decree in this verse has a temporal context, as it was preceded by the Arabic conjunction *falamma*, which implies temporal succession. Clearly *kutiba* in this verse refers to a divine decree that was established after a specific event.

Another example is M2:183

$$\text{يَا أَيُّهَا الَّذِينَ آمَنُوا كُتِبَ عَلَيْكُمُ الصِّيَامُ كَمَا كُتِبَ عَلَى الَّذِينَ مِن قَبْلِكُمْ لَعَلَّكُمْ تَتَّقُونَ}$$

[O you who believed, *kutiba* on you fasting as was *kutiba* on those who preceded you so you may practice piety (*tattaqoon*).] If *kutiba* were to be interpreted to imply that the act of fasting was willed by Allah, or the act of fasting was planned in advance, then everyone (instinctively) must fast, but that is not the case, at least as far as the understanding of fasting is concerned. The same argument would apply to M2:180

$$\text{كُتِبَ عَلَيْكُمْ إِذَا حَضَرَ أَحَدَكُمُ الْمَوْتُ إِن تَرَكَ خَيْرًا الْوَصِيَّةُ لِلْوَالِدَيْنِ وَالْأَقْرَبِينَ بِالْمَعْرُوفِ حَقًّا عَلَى الْمُتَّقِينَ}$$

[*kutiba* on you when death approaches one of you (plural) if he leaves wealth a bequest for the parents and near relatives according to what is acceptable; a duty upon the righteous.] Clearly not all of the people or the followers of the Prophet Muhammad write a will during their lifetime. Even if one were to consider the word *kutiba* in this verse as a command (which is not), then a command can be either fulfilled or rejected. In either case, *kutiba* does not imply an event that was planned in advance, thousands if not millions of years before the event took place, and that was planned to happen at a particular instant in time.

Therefore, the critical part of M9:51 (see above) can be understood in light of the logical interpretation of M2:178 and M4:77 and other verses where *kataba* refers to something or an event that might or might not happen, yet the event, when and if it occurred, cannot be outside a set of possibilities. Accordingly, in M9:51, *kataba* refers to the set of occurrences, calamities, challenges or other events that might take place without specifying or ensuring that any specific one will take place. *Kataba*, essentially, defines the realm of possibilities rather than a certainty. M9:51 strictly recognizes that Allahs' laws are in charge and no one else's.

Lastly, we consider M35:11

وَاللَّهُ خَلَقَكُم مِّن تُرَابٍ ثُمَّ مِن نُّطْفَةٍ ثُمَّ جَعَلَكُمْ أَزْوَاجًا وَمَا تَحْمِلُ مِنْ أُنثَىٰ وَلَا تَضَعُ إِلَّا بِعِلْمِهِ وَمَا يُعَمَّرُ مِن مُّعَمَّرٍ وَلَا يُنقَصُ مِنْ عُمُرِهِ إِلَّا فِي كِتَابٍ إِنَّ ذَٰلِكَ عَلَى اللَّهِ يَسِيرٌ

[And Allah has created you from dirt then from a zygote then made you pairs, and that a female conceive or gives birth except with His *ilm* (understanding), and in no way can anyone be given a long age, nor is anyone diminished in his age, except that it is in a *kitaab*, that is easy for Allah.] Our focus here is on the underlined part of the verse which explains that there is a possibility that someone's age might be increased or decreased, and that the allowance or permissibility for this variance in age is part of a system or *kitaab*. This would also imply that one's age is not fixed, contrary to what most Muslims believe. The traditional Mushaf exegeses, however, bypassed the direct meaning of the verse and choose to enforce an interpretation that is based on the belief that one's age is fixed before birth. The exegetes of the Mushaf differed on the precise interpretation of M35:11. Some chose to completely ignore the implication of extending the age or decreasing it altogether as Sayyid Qutb did in his *Fi Thilal al-Qur'aan,* or going to extreme and unusual (if not bizarre) lengths to interpret the use of pronouns contrary to the Arabic of the Mushaf or any other Arabic only to enforce the preconception that one's age is fixed at or before birth, as did ibn Kathir.[51] Tabatabaa'i in his al-Mizan had a different understanding of Arabic grammar than ibn Kathir and admitted that the age of a person can be increased or decreased, yet he claims that it is written in the book (a metaphor for "it had been decided") that one's age will be extended or decreased for specific reasons. Tabatabaa'i appears to have admitted that there is a possibility for an increase or a decrease in one's age yet he claims that these different possibilities have been decided in advance.

QADAR

The first century of Islam witnessed the emergence of Muslim individuals and groups who did not believe that the human behavior and fate were planned in advance. Those groups, referred to in the annals of Muslim history as Qadaris, were discredited and their ideas attacked fiercely, most notably by ibn Hanbal and his followers to the point that torturing and even killing Qadaris was advocated.[52] The majority of

Muslims interpret *qadar* as one's destiny, fate, or Allah's divine will, with the understanding that both were decreed in advance. This interpretation originates from M54:49

$$\text{إِنَّا كُلَّ شَيْءٍ خَلَقْنَاهُ بِقَدَرٍ}$$

[We, everything, have created in measures/proportions]. Of the most widely used translations of the Mushaf (such as Yusuf Ali, Muhsin Khan, Sahih International (SI), Ghali, Pickthall and Shakir,) only SI translates *qadar* as predestination. The word *qadar*, however, does not mean predestination but rather a proportion or measure, even by the admission of the prominent exegetes themselves. Yet the same exegetes interpreted it to imply predestination. The SI translation is directly based on earlier exegeses that do not provide any credible argument or even a hint of how *qadar* is related to predestination. The extrapolation amongst the prominent exegetes is indeed extravagant. An example is ibn Kathir who begins his interpretation of M54:49 by stating "We have created everything with a measure/proportion that we proportioned and decreed". Notice ibn Kathir's addition of "that we proportioned and decreed."[53] It is not apparent why this most popular of exegetes made an insertion in his interpretation to essentially add information that carries significant implications unless ibn Kathir was either biased by a preconceived notion or inspired by other "religious" material that, in his assessment, carries higher weight than that of the Mushaf.[54] Through his insertion, ibn Kathir encapsulates an understanding of *qadar* that is almost universal amongst Muslims.

No one can find in the Mushaf a rationale for connecting the word *qadar* to destiny or predestination; therefore, the proponents of predestination resort to Hadith. A famous hadith that is often taught in Islamic curricula is one from Sahih Muslim, typically referred to as Jibril hadith:[55]

> While we were one day sitting with the Messenger of Allah there appeared before us a man dressed in extremely white clothes and with very black hair. No traces of journeying were visible on him, and none of us knew him. He sat down close by the Prophet rested his knees against the knees of the Prophet and placed his palms over his thighs, and said: "O Muhammad! Inform me about Islam." The Messenger of Allah replied: "Islam is that you should testify that there is no deity

worthy of worship except Allah and that Muhammad is His Messenger, that you should perform salah (ritual prayer), pay the *zakat*, fast during Ramadan, and perform Hajj (pilgrimage) to the House (the Ka'bah at Makkah), if you can find a way to it (or find the means for making the journey to it)." He said: "You have spoken the truth." We were astonished at his thus questioning him and then telling him that he was right, but he went on to say, "Inform me about *imaan*." He (the Prophet) answered, "It is that you believe in Allah and His Angels and His Books and His Messengers and in the Latter Day, and in *qadar*, both in its good and in its evil aspects." He said, "You have spoken the truth." Then he (the man) said, "Inform me about *ihsaan*." He (the Prophet) answered, "It is that you should serve Allah as though you could see Him, for though you cannot see Him yet He sees you." He said, "Inform me about the Hour." He (the Prophet) said, "About that the one questioned knows no more than the questioner." So he said, "Well, inform me about its signs." He said, "They are that the slave-girl will give birth to her mistress and that you will see the barefooted ones, the naked, the destitute, the herdsmen of the sheep (competing with each other) in raising lofty buildings." Thereupon the man went off. I waited a while, and then he (the Prophet) said, "O Umar, do you know who that questioner was?" I replied, "Allah and His Messenger know better." He said, "That was Jibril. He came to teach you your religion."

Muslims universally interpret the word *qadar* **in this hadith as fate or predestination. The most noticeable aspect of this hadith is its elevation of the belief in predestination to a level equivalent to belief in Allah. Therefore, the direct implication would dictate that not believing in** *qadar* **amounts to rejecting Islam. Another variant of this hadith is found in the same Sahih Muslim collection:**[56]

One day the Messenger of Allah appeared before the public that a man came to him and said: Prophet of Allah, (tell me) what is *imaan*. Upon this he (the Prophet) replied: "That you affirm your *imaan* in Allah, His Angels, His Books, meeting Him, His Messengers and that you affirm your faith in the Resurrection hereafter." He (again) said: Messenger of Allah, (tell me) what is Islam. He (the Prophet) replied: "Islam is that you worship Allah and do not associate anything with Him and you establish the ordained prayer and you pay the obligatory *zakat* and you fast Ramadan."

Notice that the second hadith did not designate *qadar* as part of *imaan* nor Hajj as part of Islam. Surprisingly, according to Sahih Muslim, both hadiths are authentic; however, there is no mention by Muslim or later commentators on his Sahih that the two hadiths define Islam and imaan differently. Sahih al-Bukhari, on the other hand, provides a different version of Jibril hadith:[57]

> One day while the Prophet was sitting in the company of some people, Jibril came and asked, "What is *imaan*?" Allah's Messenger replied, *imaan* is to believe in Allah, His Angels, the meeting with Him, His Messengers, and to believe in Resurrection." Then he further asked, "What is Islam?" Allah's Messenger replied, "To worship Allah alone and not to associate anyone with Him, to offer prayers and to pay the obligatory *zakat* and to fast Ramadan." Then he further asked, "What is *ihsaan*?" Allah's Messenger replied, "To worship Allah as if you see Him, and if you cannot achieve this state of devotion then you must consider that He is looking at you." Then he further asked, "When will the Hour be established?" Allah's Messenger replied, "The answerer has no better knowledge than the questioner. But I will inform you about its portents. 1. When a slave (lady) gives birth to her master. 2. When the shepherds of black camels start boasting and competing with others in the construction of higher buildings. And the Hour is one of five things that nobody knows except Allah." The Prophet then recited: "Verily, with Allah (Alone) is the knowledge of the Hour." (M31.34) Then that man (Jibril) left and the Prophet asked his companions to call him back, but they could not see him. Then the Prophet said, "That was Jibril who came to teach the people their religion." Abu Abdullah said: He (the Prophet) considered all that as a part of *imaan*.[58]

Despite the fact that Sahih al-Bukhari takes precedence over Sahih Muslim amongst almost all Sunni Muslims, its version of Jibril hadith is not given preference over that of Sahih Muslim when the topic of *qadar* is debated. Of course one can argue that Sahih al-Bukhari's version of Jibril hadith had omissions due to memory lapses of Hadith transmitters, but irrespective of its authenticity, the Sahih Muslim version appears to introduce a concept entirely absent from the Mushaf and to position this innovative concept amongst the most highly held Muslims' beliefs (in addition to including Hajj as one of the pillars of Islam). Finally, it is important to realize that Muslim included two hadiths in his compendium that attest, according to some *sahaaba,* to the possibility that Jibril hadith is either incomplete or contained additions.[59]

QADHA

The third pillar of the predestination theory is the Arabic word *qadha*. This is a word that is typically invoked to designate that which Allah has already planned, ordained, decreed, etched on stones or had in store for all humans tens of thousands of years before their birth. Clarity and precision were the victims whenever *qadha* has been debated amongst Muslims. Let us consider M17:23

وَقَضَىٰ رَبُّكَ أَلَّا تَعْبُدُوا إِلَّا إِيَّاهُ وَبِالْوَالِدَيْنِ إِحْسَانًا

[And your lord has made *qadha* that you worship no one but Him and provide parents with goodness and kindness.] For the vast majority of Muslims, the word *qadha* means that events, phenomena, or one's actions have all been decreed or decided in advance. This understanding carries the implication that the decree would have an effect on one's life irrespective of whatever one does; meaning that nothing that can affect or change Allah's act of *qadha*. In light of this conventional understanding of the word *qadha*, M17:23 presents a real quandary. Since not everyone worships the Lord and not all people are kind to their parents, the act of *qadha* in M17:23 cannot indicate the certainty of what *qadha* refers to, as in worshipping the Lord or being kind to parents.

Whenever predestination is debated, most Muslims immediately invoke Allah's knowledge of the unseen (*ghaib*), as if rejecting predestination carries with it a negation of Allah's knowledge of the future. The lack of connection between the common understanding of predestination on the one hand, and *qadha*, *qadr*, and *kitaab* on the other, does not have any implication on Allah's capability to be knowledgeable or not of the unseen, or knowledgeable or not of the past or the future, or having an understanding of all universal laws that makes perfect prediction of future events. Believing that our actions, rather than the outcome of the actions, are based on our free choice and free will in no way implies that Allah cannot predict (rather than knows) what will happen in the future. Past and future are relative terms and need not be confused with predestination. (Chapter 9 focuses on the importance of differentiating between *ilm* (science or understanding) and *ma'rifa* (knowledge), and the strong implications such a distinction has on Allah's relationship with the future.)

Naturally, one wonders if all has been planned, why hellfire must be the consequence for a helpless person burdened with Allah's plan for him to commit a sin. If all has been planned in advance, then what would be the purpose of the Day of Accountability? If all has been preordained, the Day of Accountability becomes a divine injustice. Indeed, there would be no incentive for anyone to embrace a religion that will place a person in hellfire for no wrongdoing of his own. This would put into question one of the major articles of faith in Islam: belief in the Day of Accountability. The overbearing of the culture of Hadith and the overbearing dominance of the clergy (see Chapters 8 and 9) hypnotized the Muslims to not even contemplate the absurdity of such divine injustice.

At the personal level, accepting predestination absolves a person from taking responsibility for the consequences of his own actions. In practice, predestination can turn the population from humans with free will to pre-programmed robots in human flesh. Such an invented concept had been used very effectively to mask reason from understanding the causal connection between events and actions, and taking full responsibility for these actions. Muslims often find sufficient comfort in blaming anything that goes wrong on Allah. At the societal and state levels, disconnecting one's actions from one's will in the name of predestination can again serve the ruling elites by resigning the masses to senseless and hopeless existences.[60] This senselessness led a prominent Muslim leader who was thrown in jail to be fully content with what had befallen him and to further claim that Allah was behind his incarceration rather than the brutality of his oppressor.[61] The incompatibility of the predestination understanding led so many women to accept the abuse of their husbands as Allah's will. The narrative of oppression would go even further to exalt women who patiently tolerate such abuse as being close to Allah and deserving of His rewards in the hereafter.

Rejecting predestination and taking responsibility of one's action can lead to a dramatic change in the Muslims' collective life, from Muslim's approach to healthcare and physicians' malpractice to community practices that affect the environment. Rejecting predestination will force Muslims to stop blaming all problems on the "will of Allah" and take responsibility, and above all, take the most precious gift God gave to humans very seriously.

Muhammad's Literacy

Muslims' gravitation towards the extraordinary affected their interpretation of the Mushaf in so many ways. A prominent example is the belief by most Muslims that the Prophet was illiterate. The literacy or illiteracy of Prophet Muhammad is possibly of interest to historians and sociologists who are interested in understanding the relationship between the qualities and educational pedigree of a leader and his effect on his society or history at large, or his overall impact. Muslims, largely, used the claim that Muhammad was illiterate as an additional proof that the source of the Mushaf was Allah since Muhammad did not know how to write or read and he could not have authored a book as complex as the Mushaf. Contrary to the atmosphere shaped by many Muslim clergy and scholars, defending the alleged illiteracy of the Prophet should not be construed as defending Islam. Non-Muslim scholars of history and religion were divided on whether Muhammad was illiterate or not. Believing in his literacy does not necessarily weaken one's belief that the Mushaf was a divine revelation. Despite the lack of scientific or historical evidence to support the theory that the Prophet was illiterate, the majority of Muslims, however, believe that he was illiterate. Nevertheless, believing that Muhammed was illiterate or literate is not related to Islam. Believing that Muhammed was literate does not make one an enemy of Islam, a supporter of the enemies of Islam, or part of the Western "crusade" to weaken Islam.[62]

The source for the confusion surrounding the literacy or illiteracy of the Prophet is related to the Mushaf reference to Muhammad in M7:158 as the *ummy* Prophet, where *ummy* is typically translated as "illiterate". Many Muslim scholars argue that the authenticity and the divine source of the Mushaf are validated by invoking the illiteracy claim that an illiterate man is incapable of authoring such an expansive and complexly composed book. Such line of reasoning is weak because under the assumption that Muhammad was indeed illiterate, he could have instructed any literate person to write the revelations that he received from Allah. The Mushaf specifically defines *ummy* in M2:78

وَمِنْهُمْ أُمِّيُّونَ لَا يَعْلَمُونَ الْكِتَابَ إِلَّا أَمَانِيَّ وَإِنْ هُمْ إِلَّا يَظُنُّونَ

[And among them are *ummyyoon* not knowing the scripture/book except in wishful thinking and indeed they are only assuming] *Ummyyoon*, the plural of *ummy*, is explained in the verse as those who do not understand the Book. One can be illiterate and still have knowledge of the Book through instruction that does not involve reading or writing. In M62:2

هُوَ الَّذِي بَعَثَ فِي الْأُمِّيِّينَ رَسُولًا مِنْهُمْ يَتْلُو عَلَيْهِمْ آيَاتِهِ وَيُزَكِّيهِمْ وَيُعَلِّمُهُمُ الْكِتَابَ وَالْحِكْمَةَ وَإِنْ كَانُوا مِنْ قَبْلُ لَفِي ضَلَالٍ مُبِينٍ

[He who has sent among the *ummyyoon* a Messenger from themselves reciting to them His verses and purifying them and teaching them the Book and laws/rules despite their previous state of apparent confusion]. The Mushaf speaks of a Messenger that was sent to the *ummyyoon*. The Arab tribes were well-versed in literature and were renowned for displaying their works of poetry on the walls of the Ka'bah. The Arab tribes were also known for their celebrated literary works and poetry duels that were held during the annual trade meetings in Mecca's environs. In the pre-Prophethood years, Kadijah, Muhammad's first wife, hired Muhammad prior to their marriage to manage her trade caravan to the North. Despite Muhammad's pre-Prophethood reputation for exemplary honesty, it would have been highly improbable that Khadijah entrusted her vast trade and riches to an illiterate person no matter how honest.

Based on the Mushaf, an understanding of the meaning of *ummy* emerges. *Ummy* refers to someone who was not versed in the religious scriptures that were revealed to prophets preceding Muhammad. However, thousands of hadiths (whether authentic or unauthentic) related to the Prophet's life do not indicate that he was illiterate. On the contrary, the Mushaf hints that Muhammad was versed in writing and reading. Consider M29:48

وَمَا كُنتَ تَتْلُو مِن قَبْلِهِ مِن كِتَابٍ وَلَا تَخُطُّهُ بِيَمِينِكَ إِذًا لَّارْتَابَ الْمُبْطِلُونَ

[And you did not recite before it any scripture/book, nor did you inscribe/write one with your hand otherwise the falsifiers would have had cause for doubt.] If the Prophet was indeed illiterate, the Mushaf would not have referred to Muhammad's ability to read and write.

Muhammad's literacy or illiteracy does not have any bearing on the validity of the divine revelation. It is the Muslims' infatuation with the extraordinary and miracles in all forms that led to the evolution of the illiteracy theory. The illiteracy or literacy of Mohammed could not have been a precondition for receiving revelation from Allah. Even under the assumption that Muhammad was illiterate, this "miracle" would have temporal effect (on his contemporaries only) rather than on all humankind for the simple reason that authenticating the alleged illiteracy claim cannot be included in the faith since it was outside the Mushaf text or even outside the body of Hadith.

THE COMFORT OF MIRACLES

Pre-Islam society in Arabia was overwhelmed with superstitions and myths. The tribe of Quraish worshipped idols made of stones and food in the hope of being provided with a better life and wealth. The idols were thought to bring people not only prosperity but also closer to Allah. The Mushaf's primary message is the rejection of the *batil* (falsehood or illusion) that is the opposite of *haqq* (truth), and is intended to direct humans to a life of reason and rationality in order to progress, advance, and survive. Perhaps the most stressed theme in the entire Mushaf is the *haqq-batil* duality, which is distinct from the right-wrong duality.[63] Realizing or understanding the truth has more far reaching implications than simply realizing the presence or absence of something. The laws of nature are part of the truth. The cause-effect relationship is a part of the truth. The mechanism by which bacteria spreads is part of the *haqq*, whereas believing that reading Chapter 2 of the Mushaf four times a day cures depression is part of the *batil*. Realizing the truth of soil mechanics would extend the survivability of a fishing village that is located very close to seawater tides. Worshiping a structure made of a stone in the belief that it will bring prosperity is part of the *batil* as much as believing that putting a Mushaf in the compartment of a car will protect the car from accidents.

The Mushaf provides a historical snapshot of the consternation of many contemporaries and some companions of the Prophet by the message of Islam. One would expect that after the death of the Prophet, some of those who were challenged by the principles of Islam, and especially the rise of the Muslims power, two factors that cost them prestige, status and power, to have repackaged their old ways, habits and conceptions into an "Islamic" format. Waning the early Muslim community from being mesmerized by *batil* could not have come about easily and suddenly. That which is commonly accepted today as the slow death of old habits could have most likely applied then. Before the advent of the Prophet, the concept of the supernatural was entrenched in Arab societies. Also, because miracles were integral components of Christianity and Judaism, their influence facilitated the broader acceptance of the possibility of supernatural events. Adherents of religions consider miracles to be supernatural phenomena, occurrences or events that are not subject to the laws of nature. The Arabic word for miracles, *mo'jiza*, does not appear in the Mushaf at all. That which appears as a supernatural event to a person might be a well-explained causal event or explicable phenomenon to another.

The Mushaf alludes to occurrences during the lives of earlier prophets that could be perceived as miracles; however, the Mushaf refers to those events as *aayaat* (signs or clues) rather than miracles. A prominent example is the staff of Moses which, according to M7:117, became a serpent upon Allah's command. In the story of Prophet Ibrahim, Allah assured him that He would order the fire to be cold and peaceful (see M21:69). In the case of the Propht, the Mushaf does not speak of any miracles. The supernatural events ("miracles") associated with Ibrahim, Moses and Jesus were reported explicitly in the Mushaf, but none were attributed or linked to the Prophet Muhammed.

One would expect that if there were miracles associated with Muhammed, the Mushaf would be the first to document them. But there were none! On the contrary, the Mushaf states categorically in M17:90-93 that there are no supernatural events or miracles associated with Muhammad.[64] Still many Muslims believe that Muhammad experienced some miracles, but such belief is based on stories that were not substantiated by historians. Even from the perspective of Hadith, most if not all narratives that reference such miracle claims have weak authentication.

In fact, historical records do not show the Prophet to have had any association with miracles, aside from unauthenticated reports of a cloud believed to have had hovered above him during one of his pre-Islam trade journeys to the North, and the Splitting of the Moon event.[65]

Some hadiths report the miracle of water springing from within the Prophet's hands.[66] Such hadiths generate more questions than answers. If the Prophet indeed managed to spring water from his hands, why was that miracle was revealed to his close companions only and not shared with Quraish, which demanded precisely such a miracle from Mohammad as the Mushaf carefully documents. After all, his companions had believed in him so there was no need for a miracle for them only. These hadiths seems to be the most brazen in the entire Hadith fabrication history because the Mushaf specifically, directly and emphatically stated the impossibility of such a miracle in M17:90-93

وَقَالُوا لَن نُّؤْمِنَ لَكَ حَتَّىٰ تَفْجُرَ لَنَا مِنَ الْأَرْضِ يَنبُوعًا
أَوْ تَكُونَ لَكَ جَنَّةٌ مِّن نَّخِيلٍ وَعِنَبٍ فَتُفَجِّرَ الْأَنْهَارَ خِلَالَهَا تَفْجِيرًا
أَوْ تُسْقِطَ السَّمَاءَ كَمَا زَعَمْتَ عَلَيْنَا كِسَفًا أَوْ تَأْتِيَ بِاللَّهِ وَالْمَلَائِكَةِ قَبِيلًا
أَوْ يَكُونَ لَكَ بَيْتٌ مِّن زُخْرُفٍ أَوْ تَرْقَىٰ فِي السَّمَاءِ وَلَن نُّؤْمِنَ لِرُقِيِّكَ حَتَّىٰ
تُنَزِّلَ عَلَيْنَا كِتَابًا نَّقْرَؤُهُ قُلْ سُبْحَانَ رَبِّي هَلْ كُنتُ إِلَّا بَشَرًا رَّسُولًا

[and they promulgated/declared we will not establish peace with you until you spring from earth a fountain or you possess an orchard of palm trees and grapes so that you make rivers gush through it *taf'geerah*, or you make the heaven fall upon us in fragments as you have claimed or you bring Allah and the Angels before us, or you have a home of wonderful decoration, or you ascend into the heaven, and we will not believe your ascent till you keep sending down on us a book that we can understand, promulgate/declare that *subahaana* my Lord have I been anything except a *bashar* (the physiological form of the human being) Messenger.] The manufacturers of the water spring hadith that contradict these verses showed complete contempt for the Mushaf or even mockery.[67]

From a logical point of view, one can ask what is the lasting objective of a "miracle" that was intended to convince a contemporary of the Prophet of the validity of the Prophethood or the divine source of the

Message. Would the same miracle be of any value to anyone who did not witness the miracle, or even to anyone who lived many years after the occurrence of the miracle? By then the miracle would have been long gone and becomes nothing but a belief, hence it is no longer a miracle for those who did not witness it. If it is not considered a belief, then it will be perceived as a legend or a myth. Regardless, its effect would be long gone.[68]

On the assumption that miracles did occur, a critical question is why would Allah favor someone or a group of individuals with a proof of the authenticity of Muhammad as a Prophet or as a Messenger while excluding others? The possible temporal and national relevance of pre-Islam messages in comparison to the non-temporal and universal message of Islam could give indications to the absence of miracles in Islam. If Islam is intended to be a religion for all people, not a specific nation or tribe, and for all times, then the miracles of Islam need to be eternal, equally accessible to all or none at all. The hallmark of the message of Muhammad has to be embodied within the Mushaf instead of supernatural events with limited temporal and special impressions or effects. The validity that Jesus was a prophet or connected with or part of God in some capacity, as believed by different Christian denominations, could have been provided by miracles then. The validity that the Mushaf was a revelation from Allah is then expected to be embedded within the Mushaf itself rather than an incident related to Muhammad. The *aayaat* of the Mushaf are indeed what Allah refers to as validation of the Message. But all of the *aayaat* are related to physical or natural phenomena or events; not one is related to a supernatural event. Not one!

Even the *aayaat* that were intended for the Prophet himself were usurped and churned into hundreds of miracles. The so-called night of Isra and Miraj is the finest example of Muslim mythology that supersedes Greek and Jewish mythology. Out of only one verse in the Mushaf, Muslim clergy spun hadiths that filled tens of pages followed by many more pages of narratives interpreting these hadiths. The verse in question is M17:1

سُبْحَانَ الَّذِي أَسْرَىٰ بِعَبْدِهِ لَيْلًا مِّنَ الْمَسْجِدِ الْحَرَامِ إِلَى الْمَسْجِدِ الْأَقْصَى الَّذِي بَارَكْنَا حَوْلَهُ لِنُرِيَهُ مِنْ آيَاتِنَا إِنَّهُ هُوَ السَّمِيعُ الْبَصِيرُ

[Subhana who made his *abd* (servant) set forth at night from the sacred masjid to the distant masjid that which we *barakna* its surroundings (or possibly its year) <u>so we show him from our signs</u>. Indeed He is the all hearing all seeing.] Notice that the underlined words indicate that whatever happened to the Prophet during this special night was to show him the signs of Allah. Irrespective of what the Prophet (presumably the *abd* in the verse) saw, it was not for anyone but the Prophet. On the assumption that the Prophet alone saw those miracles, then they would be miracles only for him but to no one else. Hearing about a miracle is not the same as witnessing it.[69]

The infatuation with miracles crept into the "Islamic" ethos. Many Muslims resort to the belief in the supernatural to seek comfort or to avoid responsibility and effort. An example is the belief that reading (not understanding or studying) a specific combination of certain Mushaf chapters every Friday will help in one's salvation, or believing that uttering a certain phrase seventy times every night before going to sleep (presumably the precise number is important, so sixty nine will not be effective) will facilitate comfortable and deep sleep devoid of nightmares and possibly cleanse some of the sins committed that day. These supernatural "comfort *duaa*" not only lack any foundation in the Mushaf, but lead to the creation of a hypnotized culture that has minimal connection to the substance of the revelation.[70] By extension, one may argue that many Muslims seek comfort in the extraordinary or unreasonable. The intent here is not to research the subject of miracles from the perspective of Islam, but only to highlight how illusion (*batil*) became intransigent in Muslim culture. The comfort sought by many Muslims in miracles and, thus the extension, the belief that miracles can happen at any time and the "miraculous" effect of uttering certain "Islamic" phrases, all became a substitute for assuming responsibility and agency. The reliance on illusions had a very profound consequence: it prevented Muslims from exerting serious efforts to understand cause-effect relationships.

A prominent theme in Muslims' collective thinking is the infatuation with the extraordinary rather than the ordinary. Hostility towards reason is prevalent, as if reason and reality negate the will and power of Allah. Disbelief in miracles, however, does not necessarily connote disbelief in the power of Allah to effect supernatural events.

Concluding Thoughts

Islam's pinnacle lies in its emphasis on reason, which represents one of the essential elements to reach and understand the truth. There lies the logic of Islam's finality. Falsehood and irrationality can sedate the person from action and from searching for the cause behind natural phenomena. If the sedation continues, progress in its broadest definition will be halted. The objective of Islam is not to make a person spiritually "high" but to enable humanity to engage with reality through reason. The belief in falsehood, mystery, myth and miracles decreases one's ability to affect one's future or destiny. The more one knows through the mechanism of reason and science, the more one can affect one's destiny. Having full determinism, on the other hand, is impossible since we live within a complex environment with complex interactions involving multiple players with a variety of physical and non-physical phenomena. Believing in the supernatural absolves the person from exercising control and responsibility. Additionally, it makes the Qur'aanic concept of agency irrelevant. Control by others, be it authority, enemy, supervisor, friend, spouse or whomever, becomes easier the more one believes in myth and mystery, the true antitheses of Islam.

Using critical thinking and common sense, and without any intellectual intimidation or superfluous conjectures disguised as the Qur'anic interpretation of the "people of *thikr*, knowledge, or science", one would expect to find the Mushaf as a book that was intended to help humanity conform to the laws and order of a universe that was in existence long before the Prophet was born. Allah's laws that created all things known or unknown to humans were in effect for millions of years as science and discoveries have revealed, and as the Mushaf stressed by numerous references to the signs of Allah. The message of the Mushaf is to redirect humanity towards a harmonious organic existence with nature in its most complex physical and non-physical manifestations. The message of the Mushaf is replete with references to what is commonly referred to as the "material world", which is all that exists and can be touched, seen, heard, smelled or measured. The religion of Islam does not nullify nor negate the importance of the material world, but on the contrary uses it as means to comprehend what cannot be touched, seen, heard, smelled or measured. The material world, or nature in general, should not have a negative connotation, but on the contrary, a very positive one. Understanding the laws that govern the material world is the right approach to strengthen one's understanding of religion. The tools of science are essential in this effort. Uncertainty cannot be eliminated by using uncertain information. Not surprisingly, the validation for Muhammad's prophecy were material signs or signs of nature, not theories and ideas.

If Muslims believe that the Mushaf is complete and certain, it cannot be explained through material that is incomplete, imperfect and has varying degrees of certainty. Islam is based on a number of beliefs, not the other way around. Any intact body of knowledge must be self-consistent. For example, Newton's classical mechanics theory describes the forces between macroscopic objects; for it to be a complete theory, it has to be self-consistent to be acceptable by humans. Newtonian mechanics cannot explain the forces between sub-atomic particles, but we expect the theory to be consistent when explaining how a bridge deforms during a hurricane. Realizing contradiction is a primordial pre-programmed attribute that humans have, rather than an instrument of reasoning invented by the Greeks or earlier peoples. If the Mushaf is to be believed as a divine revelation, it has to be self-consistent and it has to be compatible with reality, otherwise, it lacks validation. Therefore, the verses of the Mushaf can be neither contradictory to each other nor leading to contradictions with anything that is true (*haqq*). The alternative would place the Mushaf in doubt. The Mushaf needs to be convincing, implying that its validity must be within reach to all people, even considering their wide spectrum of learning. The Mushaf emphasizes the problem of contradictions in M4:82

أَفَلَا يَتَدَبَّرُونَ الْقُرْآنَ وَلَوْ كَانَ مِنْ عِندِ غَيْرِ اللَّهِ لَوَجَدُوا فِيهِ اخْتِلَافًا كَثِيرًا

[Then do they not reflect upon Qur'aan? And if it had been from other than Allah, they would have found within it much contradictions.] The implication here is that contradictions arise from anything that does not come directly from Allah. Also implied by the verse is that anything that comes from Allah cannot embody contradictions. Therefore, self-consistency is not a pure mathematical fantasy but is grounded in reality. In physics (the essence of reality), laws do not change. These laws are the foundation of self-consistent theories that we depend on for our safety when we fly in an airplane or stand next to a high-voltage transmission wire. Apparent contradictions in the Mushaf arise, however, when attempts are made to understand phrases within verses without recognizing the importance of considering not only the entire verse but also the broader context that might spill over to several verses or even an entire chapter. This can lead to compounded confusion when Hadith is brought into the mix.

The Mushaf does not have red lines for inquiry. The Mushaf encourages contemplating the beginning of the universe or its finality, the creation, heaven and hellfire, even the nature of Allah. Prophet Ibrahim was intrigued by Allah's ability to bring the dead to life. He asked Allah directly to explain the process to him.[71] Not only did Ibrahim ask Allah such a daring question, but also Allah chose to archive Ibrahim's question along with the answer in the Mushaf. There was no reprimand to Ibrahim for his apparently audacious attitude. The red lines were created and imposed upon the Muslims by people who were enemies of reason, afraid of inquiry, or both.

Intellectual freedom was one of the most prominent casualties when Muslims viewed reason with enmity. A stark correlation between intellectual freedom amongst Muslims and their political and scientific prominence is noticeable. Despite the "un-Islamicness" of the Umayyad and Abbasid dynasties, and despite their monopoly on power, intellectual freedom had some space during the first two centuries of Islam. The emergence of Muslim sects with strong enmity against reason could have been the beginning of a major intellectual decline that Muslims have been reeling from until today with consequences that curtailed not only intellectual freedom but other freedoms. Any notion of true freedom without intellectual liberation is simply meaningless.

1. It had been typical in physics to de-emphasize the difference between the physics articles of faith (assumptions) and bearing witness (experimentation, measurements or empirical findings).
2. Al-Affani, Sayed ibn Hussein. *Riyadh al-Jannah fi al-Rudd ala al-Madrasa al-Akliyya wa Munkiri al-Sunnah*. Dar al-Aaffani, 2006.
3. Al-Akl, Nasir ibn Abdul Karim. *Al-Itijahat al-Aklanyya al-Haditha*. Dar al-Fadhylah, 2001. (Based on a university thesis).
4. The Ash'aris were adherents of a school of thought or sect founded by abu al-Hasan al-Ash'ari (d. 376/936). The school is considered one of the orthodox schools of theology amongst Sunni Muslims. The Mu'tazilites is an umbrella label for early Muslim sects who advocated reason and rationality.
5. There is a likelihood that a tendency against rationalism is inherent in the makeup of humans. The Mushaf gives credence to this possibility through numerous verses that strongly encouraged those who lived around the Prophet, whether adversaries, hypocrites, polytheists, or believers, and humans to use their mind in questioning, comprehending and contemplating (see M2:44,73,76,164,171,242, 3:118, 5:103, 6:32,151, 7:169, 10:16,42, 12:2, 13:4, 16:12,67, 21:10,67, 22:46, 23:80, 24:61, 25:44, 26:28, 28:60, 30:24,28, 36:62,68 and many others.) If this tendency is not inherent to humans, then it is likely that societal factors, including the power structure in societies, exert pressure to mitigate disposition towards rationalism.
6. The Aklanis, Mu'tazilites, Mantiqees, and Jahamyya, were designations for intellectual or theological Muslim schools that largely stressed the importance of rationalism in understanding Islam and the Mushaf in particular.
7. Shahrour, Muhammad. *Al-Kitaab wa al-Qur'aan: Ro'ya Jadeedah*. Dar al-Saqi, 2011, pp. 298-307. It is very unusual that the understanding of the word *qalb* has gone unnoticed for so many years. One can have a heart transplant operation and remain who he is in terms of values, religion, understanding, behavior, manners, feelings and knowledge; but would a brain transplant, on the assumption that it is possible, put one person in the body of the other?
8. Shahrour. *Al-Kitaab*, pp. 298-307.
9. See M42:11
10. Keller, Nuh Ha Mim. *The Concept of Bid'ah in the Islamic Shari'a*. The Muslim Academic Trust, 1999.
11. Ibn Hanbal, Ahmed. *Usool Ahl al-Sunna*, p. 38.

12. Al-Zarqani, Muhammad Abdul-Adhim. *Manahil al-Irfan fi Uloom al-Qur'aan.* Dar al-Kitaab al-Arabi, 1995, p.138.
13. An example is ibn Sahl (d. 390/1000), who is credited with being the first scientist to explain the phenomenon of optical reflection and refraction.
14. Al-Zarqani. *Manahil,* p. 138.
15. Part of the Mushaf, the Qur'aan, was transformed into a language for comprehension according to M43:3. Notice that other parts of the Mushaf, such as the first verse of M2, is not an Arabic word.
16. See M39:28, 41:3, 42:7, 43:3, and 46:12.
17. Dhaif, Shawky. *Al-Madaris al-Nahawiyya.* 7th ed., Dar al-Ma'arif, 1968. The book exposes the proliferation of Arabic grammar schools in Muslims' history and how there was no uniformity between the different schools.
18. Sahih International is a translation of the Mushaf by three Muslim women who converted to Islam. The women remain anonymous, however the translation is widely championed by many Sunni and particularly Salafi sects. Interestingly, it is the only exegesis that is named as "Sahih", following the tradition of the Hadith books that are canonized by the majority of the Sunni Muslims.
19. It is instructive to note that the context of M4:34 does not imply a marital relationship between a husband and a wife. Additionally, since the verse is generally addressing men and women (broadly), not all women end up as wives. Since interpretation of the entire Mushaf has not been achieved yet, one would expect that English translations of the Mushaf convey that fact by leaving many words transliterated unless the translator is convinced of their meanings, or at least despite its difficulty, the translators need to maintain utmost minimalism in their approach by translating the words but not the conventional meanings or interpretations. It might be a worthwhile project for Muslims to develop methodologies for translating the Mushaf into English and other languages without inserting any sectarian influence.
20. Ibn Hanbal. *Usool,* p. 30
21. Notice that in this verse, the pronoun "we" is used, which indicates that other agents participated with Allah in preserving the *thikr.*
22. Dhaif. *Al-Madaris.*

23. The classic and modern Mushaf exegeses are largely based on the opinions of early Muslims including the companions of the Prophet and their successors. These opinions are commonly stated without any support or proof; their validity is implicitly assumed to be the status or reverence of those who made them.
24. Ibn Manzur, Muhammad ibn Mukarram. *Lisan al-Arab.* 3rd ed., Dar Sader, 2000. This dictionary is considered by most Arabs to be the most authoritative dictionary of the Arabic Language. It was compiled by ibn Manzur (d. 712/1312). It is very important to keep in mind when consulting this dictionary that many Arabic words were defined according to their interpretation by Muslim clergy. In fact, these interpretations were not expunged from the Mushaf but rather from purely partisan or sectarian foundations. An example is the word *nasakha* (see Chapter 7.)
25. As an example, see Al-Zarqani's *Manahil*, p.138, where *naskh* is framed within the *fi al-istilah* definition.
26. The concept of *fi al-istilah* is adopted by both Sunnis and Shias.
27. It is common in scholarly works to define certain words or terms in order to facilitate a better understanding. However, such definitions remain peculiar to that particular discipline, or even to a specific work but cannot be given absolute generalization.
28. More on *ismah* will be discussed in Chapter 8.
29. Murtadha, Muhammad Mahmoud. *Falsafat al-Ismah ind al-Shia.* Dar al-Wila'a, 2015, p. 146. Murtadha uses several verses from the Mushaf to conclude that the linguistic meaning of *ismah* is protection, then he switches to the *fi al-istilah* definition and starts by stating that the *fi al-istilah* meaning does not differ much from the linguistic meaning while producing a *fi al-istilah* meaning that is thinly connected to the linguistic meaning.
30. The use of the word Arabic in the Mushaf, particularly in M26:195, could be a reference to the specific language spoken by the Arabs then or to a feature of that language, particularly it being generative and youthful, as some scholars have theorized.
31. When invoking the reader to use the mind, the Mushaf uses two words, namely *ta'qiloon* and *tafakkaroon*. These two words are translated often as "to comprehend". However, there is an important difference between them. The first is derived from the past tense *a'qala*, which means to connect things together whereas the second is derived from *fakkara*, meaning to dismantle (and repeatedly). Thus, it is most likely that the closest English translation of *ta'qiloon* would be "to synthesize" whereas for *tafakkaroon*, it would be "to analyze". The difference would imply that *tafakkaroon* precedes *ta'qiloon* in

terms of intellectual ability or hierarchy.
32. Shahrour. *Al-Kitaab,* p. 53-64.
33. It is interesting that the Mushaf specifies that the Qur'aan was revealed in Arabic. In light of the difference between Kitaab, Furqaan and Qur'aan that Muhammad Shahrour introduced in *al-Kitaab wa al-Qur'aan*, it is worthwhile to reconsider whether the word "Arabic" was used as an adjective or reference to the Arabic language.
34. See Ghali and Pickthall translations.
35. Al-Khamis, Muhammad ibn Abdulrahman. *Etiqaad al-A'imma al-Arb'ah abi Hanifa wa Malik wa al-Shafi'i wa Ahmed.* Dar al-Ismah, 1992, p. 16.
36. Qudsi Hadith is a class of hadiths revealed to the Prophet where, according to the Qudsi Hadith theory, Allah speaks directly in the first person. These hadiths are studied, in as far as their level of authenticity is concerned, using the methodologies of classical Hadith Science, which means they have similar classifications to the non-Qudsi hadiths (see Chapter 8).
37. Sahih al-Bukhari, Kitaab al-Qadar, nos. 1 and 2. Sahih Muslim, Kitaab al-Qadar, nos. 1-6, 27.
38. The anglicized term Caliph, implying an Islamic ruler, originated from the Mushaf term *khalifa*.
39. "Islamization" of different behaviors and different systems, whether in economics, politics, or even social life, has been attempted by many Muslims by using a medieval Arabic label (see Chapter 9).
40. Sahih Muslim, Kitaab al-Qadar.
41. Ibn Hanbal, Ahmed. *Kitaab al-Sunnah.* Al-Matba'ah al-Salafiyyah, 1930, pp. 147-148.
42. The practice of excluding rationality from religion studies is not exclusive to Muslims, as it is common amongst people of other religions and beliefs. It seems a natural phenomenon amongst all people to justify and validate tradition rather than question it, with no better example than the tradition of religion. In the case of religion, political motivations for this exclusion are abundant. In the case of the Muslim tradition, nevertheless, one cannot rule out the effect of years of intellectual depravity and intimidation that created multiple gods whose commentaries and narratives, in practice, became of equal or higher value than divine revelation.
43. Ibn Kathir. *Stories of the Prophets.* Dar-us-Salam Publications, 2016. Ibn Kathir's Mushaf exegesis is amongst the most respected in the Sunni Muslim world.
44. Contrast this verse with M3:29 where revealing and concealing are

related to the mind rather the *nafs*.

45. Shahrour. *Al-Kitaab*, p. 53-64. Shahrour is arguably the first person in history to provide an analysis of the meaning of *kataba*. According to this author, Shahrour's analysis could have the most significant impact on Muslims' modus operandi and entire outlook on life.
46. Al-Tabari, Muhammad ibn Jarir. *Jami al-Bayaan ann Taweel al-Qur'aan (Tafsir al-Tabari)*. Dar al-Kutub al-Ilmiyyah, 2009. Al-Tabari (d. 310/923) is considered one of the major exegetes of the Mushaf and possibly the first.
47. Sahih al-Bukhari, Kitaab al-Tawheed.
48. Al-Darmi, AbdAllah ibn Abd al-Rahman. *Sunan al-Darmi (aka Musnad al-Darmi)*. Dar al-Mughni, 2000, p. 199.
49. Shahrour. *Al-Kitaab*, pp. 53-64.
50. It is instructive to compare this translation with the one by Sahih International: [Say, "Never will we be struck except by what Allah has decreed for us; He is our protector." And upon Allah let the believers rely.] Notice that the SI translated *qul* as say.
51. Qutb, Sayyid. *Fi Thilal al-Qur'aan*. Dar al-Shurooq, 2008.
52. An excellent summary of the attacks on the Qadaris and other groups of similar theological leanings can be found in hadiths included in ibn Kathir's exegesis of M54:49. Despite most of the cited hadiths being classified as technically *thaeef* (weak) or *ghareeb* (strange), their presence in a large number of these *tafsir* works may give the unassuming reader a feeling that even if the hadiths are not fully *sahih* (authentic), their spirit somehow validates the conventional interpretation of predestination. The practice of overwhelming the reader with all types of hadiths, irrespective of their authenticity, is common amongst numerous Muslim clergy.
53. It is worth highlighting that the Mushaf states "We, everything, have created it..." rather than "We have created everything...". This may suggest that the creation preceded the act of proportioning.
54. It is very common in most Mushaf exegeses to find commentaries that appear as if attempting to read Allah's mind in the sense that the commentary intends to explain what Allah intended to express. This type of commentary is not rooted in the Mushaf text but inspired by a peculiar understanding the exegete had and that was influenced, most likely, by Hadith, which was widely considered as an explainer of the Mushaf (see Chapter 8).
55. Sahih Muslim, Kitaab al-Imaan.
56. Sahih Muslim, Kitaab al-Imaan.
57. Sahih al-Bukhari, Kitaab al-Imaan.

58. Notice that towards the end of the hadith, *imaan* and Islam, both are lumped as *imaan*.
59. Sahih Muslim, Kitaab al-Imaan.
60. The incorrect understanding of *qadha*, implying an a priori decision by Allah with a specific action to follow or, in general, predestination, affected Muslims' understanding of other verses in the Mushaf that contained the same word, most notably M17:4, which had been interpreted to predict and guarantee the demise of the state of Israel. In the case of the state of Israel, Jews on the one hand justified the colonization of Palestinian land using the religious pretext of God's decision to grant the land to them, while Muslims are waiting the fulfillment of Allah's decision to liberate the land and return it to its rightful owners. Both groups relied on a self-serving and convenient interpretation that led to either extreme violence or to servitude and docility.
61. Raed Salah, the leader of the Islamic Movement in Israel, declared that it was Allah's will to be jailed rather than the will of the Prime Minister of Israel, see http://www.alquds.co.uk/?p=530573. Accessed 9 May 2016.
62. Mutahari, Murtadha. *Al-Nabi al-Ummi*. MSA of US & Canada (PSG), [n.d.]. Mutahari's book is a defense of the Prophet's illiteracy. The book was inspired by an article written in 1964 by Syed Abdul Latif who was the president of the Academy of Islamic Studies, Hyderabad. The article (also presented at the Fourth All India Islamic Studies Conference, The Osmania University, Hyderabad, 1964) claimed that the Prophet was literate and that the Mushaf has verses clearly proving the Prophet had mastery of both reading and writing. A worthy note is that Mutahari refers to Abdul Latif (p. 40) as "this Indian scholar". Since Abdul Latif was a Muslim with lofty credentials, there was no relevance to his Indian nationality. One would surmise that Mutahari wanted to diminish Abdul Latif's credibility. Mutahari, however, should have realized that his implicit argument backfires since he was a Persian. This marginalization pattern could be observed in Muslim history where the Arabs glorified themselves as the most noble (see Chapter 2 and particularly al-Zaraqani's *Manahil*) whereas the modern Persians, perhaps, saw themselves as the guardians of Shiaism and then the rest would follow in importance and hence credibility. Interestingly, this hierarchy was reversed in North American non-Arab Muslim cultures where a white American or white European Muslim clergy would garner the highest respect.

63. The predominant Muslims attitude towards the Mushaf is that it focuses on the right-wrong duality. One may argue that this attitude exists amongst not only Muslims but Christians and Jews, vis-à-vis their divine scriptures. This attitude led to a sense of supremacy amongst members of the three Abrahamic groups. For each of them, rather than focusing on and preaching what leads to the creed, the focus is typically on the rightfulness of their respective faiths. In fact, the Mushaf concept of *shahadah* is directly related to truth. The Mushaf does not speak of what is correct and what is wrong.

64. The purpose of a miracle is to convince humans of the validity of a divine message. If earlier prophets produced (through Allah) miracles, then their messages were local in space and time. Thus those messages were intended for a specific group of people who lived during a specific time. Most Christians, for example, believe in the miracles of Jesus because they were told the miracles happened, not because they witnessed the miracles themselves. If Muhammad did not produce any miracles, then his message is not confined by either space or time and thus is intended for all humans and for all times. In fact, the Mushaf addresses all humans in M2:185.

65. Sahih al-Bukhari, Kitaab al-Manaqib. Al-Bukhari lists four hadiths claiming that the moon was split. None of these hadiths, however, explicitly state that the Prophet himself said that the moon was split.

66. Sahih al-Bukhari, Kitaab al-Wu'du. Al-Darmi, *Sunan*, p. 177.

67. The belief in miracles is also prevalent amongst Shias who believe that spectacular miracles occurred during the conception of Fatima, the daughter of the Prophet from his first wife Khadija, where Angels with golden utensils were part of both the conception and delivery of Fatimah.

68. Muhammad Metwali al-Sha'raawi (d. 1419/1998) was a former Egyptian Minister of Endowments, Muslim scholar and professor, and argued that Muhammad's miracles were the Qur'aan, a non-physical miracle, and physical occurrences, such as the splitting of the moon. The Qur'aan, al-Sha'raawi claims, is a miracle for all people but the physical miracles were for the people who were around the Prophet only. The major problem with this argument is that it would still favor the people around the Prophet more than later generations since the sensual is easier to accept than the non-sensual. The second problem is that al-Sha'raawi's extrapolation has no validation in either the Mushaf or Hadith.

69. The Isra and Miraj mythology spanning tens if not hundreds of pages and occupying Muslim clergy's scholarship distracted the Muslims

from a very simple message embedded within the M17:1. When Muhammad received the revelation, he could have questioned what had befallen him. In this verse, Allah took him on a journey, the details of which should not be of interest to Muslims since the journey was intended only for Muhammad to most likely assure him and to validate to him that the revelation was from Allah. Aside from the elaborate mythology in the Hadith, the stories of Isra and Miraj detail bizarre negotiations that took place between the Prophet and Allah to reduce the number of the obligatory daily prayers from fifty to five.

70. An example is a hadith related to Fatimah, the daughter of the Prophet, where she is believed to have said: "My father, the Messenger of Allah, entered when I had gone to bed to sleep and said: 'O Fatimah! Do not go to sleep before doing four things: reciting the whole of the Qur'aan, making the Prophets your mediators (with Allah), making the believers satisfied with you and performing the pilgrimage and visit (hajj and 'umrah to Makkah)'. Then he started praying! So I stayed in bed until he finished the prayer and said: 'O Messenger of Allah! You ordered me to do four things that I could not do in this hour!' The Messenger of Allah smiled and said: 'If you recite the Tawheed chapter (al-Ikhlas Chapter) three times it is as if you have recited the whole of the Qur'aan; and if you recite prayers to me and the prophets before me then we shall be your mediators in the Day of Judgment; and if you pray that Allah forgives the believers (say istighfar) they shall be satisfied with you; and if you say: Subhan Allah (praise be to Allah) and al-Hamdu Lillah (gratitude to Allah) and La Ilaha Illa Allah (there is no God but Allah) and Allahu Akbar (Allah is greatest) it is as if you have performed the pilgrimage and visit.' From: *Awaalim al-Zahra*, p. 580. *Musnad Fatimah al-Zahra*, Dar al-Safwah, [n.d.], pp. 218-9.

71. See M2:260.

4

MANUFACTURED EXTREMISM

لَا إِكْرَاهَ فِي الدِّينِ ۖ قَد تَبَيَّنَ الرُّشْدُ مِنَ الْغَيِّ ۚ فَمَن يَكْفُرْ بِالطَّاغُوتِ وَيُؤْمِن بِاللَّهِ فَقَدِ اسْتَمْسَكَ بِالْعُرْوَةِ الْوُثْقَىٰ لَا انفِصَامَ لَهَا ۗ وَاللَّهُ سَمِيعٌ عَلِيمٌ

There is no compulsion/enforcement in the religion right-mindedness has already been evidently (distinct) from misguidance, so whoever disassociates through *taghut* and believes in Allah, then he has already upheld fast the most binding grip, it can never be disconnected and Allah is hearing *aleem*.

M 2:256

A BRIEF HISTORY

Toward the end of the 20th Century AD, the image of Muslims around the globe had been largely manipulated to project extremism, violence and intolerance. This partially manufactured image has been in the making since the early 1980s and reached epic proportions following the terrorist attacks of 9/11. The negative propaganda that Muslims found themselves subjected to — and the subjects of — was done with the objective of justifying war against two predominantly Muslim countries, namely Afghanistan and Iraq, as the days following 9/11 have proven. If we accept that the negative depiction of Muslims was for reasons related to Islam itself, it would be difficult to make sense of the selective media coverage of the violence perpetrated by several Middle Eastern states against both non-Muslims and Muslims. Western media and Western governments shielded the brutality of "Islamic" political regimes. Terrorism by governments that rule in the name of Islam and whose flags bear "Islamic" phrases was not considered a problem, but terrorism by Muslim groups was sufficient to designate Islam as a global menace. Expectedly, many Muslims in the West and the East found themselves defending against an unjust campaign that associated Islam with violence and savagery. Mysterious groups alleged to be part of a global Islamic movement striving to revive the Caliphate emerged with no clear path to establishing their objective but beheading Westerners and Easterners and distributing their gruesome actions on social media for the entire world to watch in horror.

While it cannot be ascertained who is the mastermind behind the illusive, ghostly and mercurial global al-Qaida movement, it is highly likely that the movement has or had roots in the Saudi and US intelligence establishments.[1] Notably, "Islamic" extremism was perceived favorably by the Western media during the fight against the Soviet invasion of Afghanistan (1399/1979-1409/1989) and during the Chechen wars of independence (1414/1994-1417/1996). Nevertheless, evidence points to a concerted campaign initiated and financed by western governments, western think tanks and media organizations to portray Muslims as extremists and terrorists. This campaign helped to justify the invasions and occupation of Iraq and Afghanistan and, by extension, helped to further legitimize Israel's anti-Palestinian policies (Palestinians are predominantly Muslim) and occupation of Palestinian territories.[2] The overtones of the campaign to demonize Islam were political.

Western interests found in al-Qaida and its self-replicating derivatives, such as the Islamic State of Iraq and al-Sham (ISIS), organizations that can be used to further geopolitical interests. But one wonders what made the West cultivate and harbor a group with a controversial and extremist religious doctrine that views the world through a binary lens of absolute right vs. absolute wrong, halal (religiously allowed) vs. haram (religiously prohibited), Sharia (rule through religious codes) vs. *kufr* (rule through non-religious doctrine), *Dar al-Islam* (the geographic and political domain of Islam) vs. *Dar al-Harb* (the geographic and political domain of the enemies of Islam). While solid evidence is not yet available to prove the link between al-Qaida and Western and Arab intelligence organizations, a preponderance of evidence shows that al-Qaida morphed out of direct Saudi government patronage.[3] The conflict in Syria that started in 2011 is a case in point. While any identified alleged al-Qaida operative is targeted worldwide and most likely unable to cross international borders, a large migration of al-Qaida operatives from the Horn of Africa and the Arabian Peninsula into Syria through neighboring Turkey took place after 2011. For such an influx of terrorists could have taken place without the knowledge of the surrounding countries with strong ties to the West is highly unlikely.

The West, in the pursuit of global dominance, found in the religious doctrine to which al-Qaida and ISIS operatives adhere a selectively extremist and exclusionist outlook susceptible to manipulation due to its fundamental unspoken doctrine of imitation of and submission to the *amir* (leader). Al-Qaida's ideology evolved from Wahhabism, which is attributed to Muhammad ibn Abdulwahhab (d. 1206/1792).[4] The foundation of Wahhabism is Salafism, which is derived from the word *salaf* (forefathers). Salafism, in summary, refers to the doctrine of imitating the companions of the Prophet in practically everything known about them. For Western governments with deep interests in the Middle East, those who commit violence in the name of Islam contribute to a positive feedback loop. The higher the level of violence by the "Islamic" extremists, the higher the justification for intervention, the more easily geopolitical objectives are achieved, the higher the responding violence, and so on; it is an unending vortex until the objectives of the West change and the religious leaders are instructed to change the focus to a new *jihad*.

The Wahhabi brand of violence may have been known to the British from the time of their occupation of Egypt. Muhammad Ali (1183/1769-1265/1849), the Ottoman governor of Egypt, was the first to confront the zeal of the Wahhabis and the first Saudi Kingdom (1157/1744-1233/1818). Ali suppressed the revolt of Muhammad ibn Saud against the Ottomans and destroyed Der'eya, the seat of the government of the first Saud dynasty in 1233/1818. By looking at the history of the Arabian Peninsula over the past century, one finds the al-Qaida and the seemingly modern jihadi movements to be a reconstitution of older ones. The founder of the Kingdom of Saudi Arabia effectively used the same Wahhabi doctrine to subdue and unify most of the Arabian Peninsula under his command. However, his conquest could have never been possible without the financial and intelligence support of the British, to which Orientalists' understanding of the Salafi doctrine was critical in their full manipulation to fulfill the grand designs of the British Empire.[5] Since the British were the primary financiers of the then exiled and fragmented clan of ibn Saud, they exerted strong influence over his political and territorial ambitions. In the diehard Wahhabis, known then as the Ikhwan, ibn Saud found a zeal and fervor that could conquer mountains in the name of Islam, or perhaps in the name of the rewards promised if one achieves "martyrdom" during "God sanctioned campaigns."

Ibn Saud brilliantly struck a strategic alliance with the Aal al-Sheikh clan, who were direct descendants of ibn Abdulwahhab (Aal al-Sheikh means "the family of a religious leader or chieftain"), to practically divide the influence and booty from his grand campaign to reclaim the Arabian Peninsula and unify most of it under his control. The Aal al-Sheikh clan became the de facto guardians and reincarnation of the Wahhabi doctrine. In return for their invaluable favors to ibn Saud, they and their Wahhabism were given unprecedented powers to enforce their extreme views and to project Wahhabism as the true unadulterated Islam. Whether it was ibn Saud or the British behind this brilliant scheme is a matter for speculation. However, it seems likely that the British were aware of the fervor of the Wahhabis and both ibn Saud and the British used them with efficiency and devastating effectiveness.[6]

The British grand plans were at work and Abdulaziz ibn Saud was given financial rewards and rule over vast tracts of land and sand. The Hijaz, which is mostly the western part of the Arabian peninsula, was of no strategic interest to the British, and moreover had the potential to become a liability if they had to occupy it (raising the wrath of millions of already agitated Muslim subjects under their colonial reach), so it was strategically used to reward ibn Saud, bringing along enormous consequent financial benefits. Ibn Saud with his extremist fanatical fighters could have wiped clean all of the scattered Arab fishing villages dotting the western side of the Persian Gulf coast. In fact, he could have sent a small crowd, not even a battalion, to spread the domain of his nascent kingdom, but the British had to draw a line in the sand, figuratively and literally. The British Empire global scheming was indeed brilliant and strategic. The tiny remote fishing villages, in the British grand geo-political scheme, had to be reinvented as little kingdoms and sheikdoms (the latest reinvention was the Kingdom of Bahrain with 305 square miles in area). The First and Second Gulf Wars of 1411/1991 and 1424/2003 were direct consequences of the British Empire's machinations in those early days.

From an obscure extremist sect that held on to selective parts of Ahmed ibn Hanbal's doctrine, the Wahhabis were thrust into global prominence as they became the spiritual and ideological backbone of one of the richest dynasties in the world; a dynasty that forged strong ties with the USA, the most powerful country in the world. The discovery of oil in the Arabian Peninsula and the official role of the Aal al-Sheikh clan as the guardians of Islam was a major turning point in establishing Wahhabism as a force to reckon with. The extremist and most violent doctrines that were claimed as part of Islam, by their adherents, of course, were no longer confined to a desolate faraway desert. These doctrines are now easily reachable and their spread is facilitated with ease whenever the political needs arise.

A book about religion is typically not about history. I take cues from the Mushaf, which presents specific content in a historical context. After all, history is the story of people and their lives. The brief history mentioned above is strikingly relevant to Muslims today. The same strain of doctrines attributed unjustly to Islam that helped the British, and later the Americans take control of the vast energy resources of the Middle East are back in full motion to help the US and the West this time strengthen their claim over what could potentially slip away from their control. Rationality dictates that if a plan was successful before, one should pursue the same plan again since it was tested and proven workable. The players here are all rational; hence, the revival of Wahhabism and its extreme views and actions is a repeat of a very successful precedence.

CONFRONTING THE PAST

M2:256, stated and translated/interpreted on the first page of this chapter, unambiguously emphasizes that there can be no *ikraah* in religion. *Ikraah* is an Arabic word denoting forcing a person to do or believe what that person hates, does not like, does not believe in, or does not want to do. In summary, *ikraah* means coercion. The verse neither includes a command that is limited in its application to a specific group nor does it necessarily denote applicability to all people in general. M2:256 presents a truism rather than an injunction. The following conclusion would then unfold: it is not possible to force anyone to believe in anything or to do any commandments decreed directly from Allah.

In plain English, one cannot shove faith, ideology or religion down anyone's throat.

This would also include anything within the faith, ideology or religion. Religion is neither governance nor bondage. Governments have the tools and authority to establish enforcement, but religion does not. Unfortunately, the simplicity of this verse is lost in the labyrinth of contradictory narratives attributed to Prophet Muhammad where compulsion became the rule, even if it leads to bloodshed. Lost in the transmission of Hadith is whether Muhammad was acting as a messenger or a governor (of Madinah) whenever he gave a specific command. Instead of developing a sound methodology to understand the Mushaf, Salafism, the broader domain from which the Wahhabis derived their ideology, and Wahhabism were determined to reconcile contradictory narratives, not only vis-à-vis the Mushaf but among the narratives themselves.

An important question is how the Wahhabi-Salafi extremist philosophy evolved over centuries to become a genuine threat to Muslims and non-Muslims alike. Radicalism or fundamentalism are not necessarily synonymous with extremism. Wahhabism-Salafism is a philosophy based on specific mercurial and contradictory interpretations of the Mushaf and on the belief that a class of clergy have the exclusive privilege of interpreting the religion and of declaring what is permissive and forbidden for all Muslims. Wahhabism, however, is not as rigid as it appears. In fact, a cursory look at what Wahhabis consider as haram and halal had been shifting with time. One example is their view of still photography. Prior to the 1980s, Wahhabi scholars forbade the depiction of the human or animal figure without a white line drawn across the neck. This requirement has long been dropped without any explanation. The concept of jihad is continuously modified by religious authorities to meet the political objectives of the *amir* by invoking a major loophole in their doctrine that is used very skillfully to practically justify whatever the *amir* calls for. *Amir*, in itself, through the prism of Wahhabism, has an expansive definition that stretches to include the ruler, governor, king or anyone, legitimate or not, who has control of the political destiny of the country; yet, the definition shrinks to confine the *amir* to what the guardians of the Wahhabi sect see fit. Overall, the underlying religious doctrine of Wahhabism-Salafism is not a new phenomenon but rather a repackaging of a mixture of the ancient Ahl al-

Sunnah wa al-Jamm'ah doctrines that were developed in the early centuries of Islam to give legitimacy to the Umayyad and Abbasid empires, and to marginalize trends amongst Muslims that advocated rationality and more inclusive systems of governance.

The Wahhabi-Salafi doctrines have gained significant ground over the past thirty years, with an alarming expansion rate in practically all Arab countries and strong influence in some non-Arab countries such as Pakistan, Afghanistan, Mauritania, Malaysia and parts of India and Africa. The roots of the doctrines can be traced back hundreds of years to the writings of ibn Taymiyyah and his disciple ibn Qayyem al-Jawziyyah (d. 751/1350). Both ibn Taymiyyah and al-Jawziyyah borrowed heavily from Ahmed ibn Hanbal, one of the primary jurists in early Muslim history. The followers of ibn Hanbal claim that their school is the purest of all schools of Islamic jurisprudence. The undeclared, underlying principles of the Salafis dictate never to question the authenticity of the Prophetic narratives and the interpretations of the Mushaf by a specific group of Muslim jurisprudents and clergy. Ibn Hanbal, his followers and the school of jurisprudence that emerged implicitly advocated following the tradition (the Sunnah) of the Prophet and used the Mushaf largely for philosophical duals to disenfranchise other groups and exclude them from the domain of Islam.

While the Wahhabism-Salafism doctrines appear extreme, interestingly, the roots of these doctrines are the same as those of other jurisprudence schools, including the more liberal ones. The difference between the Salafi and other major schools of jurisprudence is the emphasis on particular Prophetic narratives and their interpretation rather than on the principles of jurisprudence (see Chapter 9). It is safe to say that the vast majority of Muslims who describe themselves as Sunni Muslims derive their understanding of the Mushaf and their understanding of the religious doctrine and laws from the works of the leading Muslim jurist Muhammad ibn Idris al-Shafi'i (d. 204/820). In his most famous work, *al-Risala*, al-Shafi'i developed a system of expunging legislation that he intended to be the foundation of Islamic jurisprudence.[7]

Historians argue as to whether al-Shafi'i was the very first to originate a system of Islamic law or whether he only collected and elaborated on previous works. Irrespective of who was first, *al-Risala* constituted a milestone in canonizing new rules for jurisprudence derived using the tools of classical philosophy that is much decried by Salafis. These rules, whether attributed to al-Shafi'i himself, his contemporaries or predecessors, have entered the history of Muslims with little scrutiny. Al-Shafi'i and other jurists, such as ibn Hanbal, Malik ibn Anas (d. 179/795), and abu Hanifa (d. 150/767), eventually created what later became the major schools of Sunni jurisprudence. From the Shia side, Ja'far al-Sadiq (d. 148/765), a descendant of Ali ibn Abi Talib (the 4th Righteous Caliph), established the Ja'fari jurisprudence school, which is respected if not followed by most contemporary Shia Muslims.

A culture of exclusivity and elitism was already present among several groups of Muslims during the rise of Islam. The period that followed the death of the Prophet was incredibly tumultuous in Muslims history. After the Prophet's death, many tribes attempted to break away from the new Muslims' domain, resulting in what has become known as the Riddah Wars (Wars of Rebellion). Three of the immediate successors of the Prophet for the governorship of the nascent Muslim State were assassinated and a major schism emerged, splitting the Muslims into several camps that engaged in destructive wars, and leading to consequences that continue to affect Muslims very significantly even after so many centuries have passed by. Major conflicts emerged that even pitted Ayesha, the youngest of the wives of the Prophet against his cousin Ali. Not only the Muslims were divided in wars, the very house of the Prophet was also split.

Most Muslims have a tendency to portray the years of the *sahaaba* and Salaf (the companions and the immediate successors of the Prophet) as the rosiest of Muslims history. The facts, regrettably, do not support this depiction. Only fifty years after his death, Madinah, the city that provided refuge to Prophet Muhammad and hosted the first government established by the Prophet, was sacked. Many of the Prophet's companions and Mushaf memorizers of Madinah were bludgeoned to death. Soon thereafter, the savagery did not spare Mecca and the House of Allah. Mecca was brutalized and the Ka'ba was partially destroyed. Medina and Mecca, the cities of the Prophet and the most respected cities amongst Muslims, were not sacked by Persians, Romans, or "infidels", but by fellow Muslims!

Perhaps many Muslims are discomforted by these historical events and like to forget them or dismiss them altogether for fear it might project Islam as a religion of violence and extremism. Most Muslims or non-Muslims who want to probe and study the root causes that led to destructive violence and tension between early Muslims are often labeled as enemies of Islam or accused of fostering *fitna* (religiously-rooted mischief) between Muslims. The prevailing attitude, at least amongst most Sunni clergy, is that it is better to leave that unfortunate history alone. Of course one can learn from historical events no matter how pleasant or bloody they were.

It is more important that the study of history for history sake is to understand the root cause of extremism and intolerance that Muslims are experiencing today and most likely will experience in the future as long as they continue to show disinterest in these root causes. The interest in studying the early Muslim years should not be for the purpose of enhancing the abject sectarianism amongst Muslims or for proving that one sect was righteous and the rest were astray. The highest value in studying the tumultuous early history of Muslims lies in preventing further bloodshed between Muslims and sheer violence in the name of Islam.

Muslims should not be alarmed as to why such violence and destruction followed the death of the Prophet. Practicing Islam helps towards achieving justice and peace, but not necessarily utopia. Since an ideal society was never a stated objective of the Mushaf, then Muslims can be at ease confronting the tragic twists of their past history, irrespective of the key players in these tragedies. The historical facts, including those archived in the Mushaf, never even projected the society that the Prophet established as ideal. That was not the mission of Muhammad the Messenger. In fact, careful reading of the Mushaf reveals numerous challenges that Muhammad and the nascent Muslim community faced. Questioning the violence in early Muslims history and finding answers should make Muslims reflect deeper into whether or not the early Muslim community was ideal in any sense. This is indeed a difficult and provocative request for many Muslims. The answer to these questions can lead to major unexpected revisions of the prevailing religious dogmas, but more critically and importantly, a window into understanding alien doctrines that crept into Muslim culture and with time became accepted as part of Islam. Muslims largely contextualized the study of their early history as an attempt to bridge the difference between their sects instead of understanding how multiple doctrines, instead of the Mushaf, became the de facto core of Islam.

The catastrophic events and schisms that affected the nascent Muslim community could have helped in the emergence of utmost intolerance and the willingness to go to extremes to justify conquest, destruction, killing, plundering, usurpation and rape, all in the name of Islam and in the name of the purity and idealism of the Salaf. In the years that followed the death of the Prophet, many Muslims and non-Muslims went to extraordinary measures to fabricate hadiths, allegedly attributed to the Prophet and to his contemporaries and immediate successors. The fabrication of hadiths was a reaction to competing influences and conflicting political objectives. Of course the "enemies of Islam" could have contributed to fake hadiths, but their role has to be justly calibrated with respect to other, more substantial, factors.

The elevation of Ayesha, one of the Prophet's wives, to a status never bestowed upon any other woman, and the elevation of Ali, the Prophet's cousin and son-in-law, along with Ali's progeny, to a status not held by previous prophets, all took place during those years and for political and monetary objectives.[8] The fabrication of prophetic narratives during the first Hijri century was a flourishing and profitable cottage industry to such a point that when al-Bukhari started his grand mission of collecting authentic narratives attributed to the Prophet and his companions, it is reported that he had to sift through hundreds of thousands of hadiths. Some have even claimed that the likes of al-Bukhari and al-Shafi'i memorized three hundred thousand to one million hadiths. If al-Bukhari eventually believed that a small fraction (approximately 2600) of these hadiths had been authentic, the vast scale of the Hadith fabrication industry is put into stark relief. The fabricated hadiths, accordingly, would amount to approximately 400 times more than the authentic ones. To put it in a different perspective, for every hadith that al-Bukhari believed to have been a true reflection of what the Prophet intended to convey or said, there were 400 other fabricated hadiths. This alarming number of fake hadiths is an indication that many Muslims advanced personal interest, personal philosophy, marginalization of non-Muslims, abuse of women, taking young girls as wives, dictatorship, violence, denying relatives any inheritance, promoting produce or merchandise and many other objectives by simply commissioning someone with Arabic skills to draft a suitable hadith.

Of course, the enemies of Islam cashed in on the fabrication orgy by inserting material from earlier religious traditions, particularly Judaism (such hadiths are largely referred to as Israeeliyyat). The collections of the Israeelyyat were widely believed to be the works of individuals who converted from Judaism to Islam. In his popular book *Stories of the Prophets*, ibn Kathir reported numerous stories that were almost identical to those found in Jewish scriptures.[9] The stories of ibn Kathir were most likely fabricated by either Muslims with knowledge of the Old Testament, Jews who converted or claimed conversion to Islam, or Jews. Many of ibn Kathir's stories are controversial and even problematic on two counts: first, they have no foundation in the Mushaf, and second, they could not have been narrated by the Prophet, whom the Mushaf characterized as someone who had no knowledge of the unseen nor any knowledge of the earlier divine Scriptures. The problem in essence lies in making the body of knowledge in such stories part of Islam. One can doubt or support the authenticity of such hadiths, but the link to the Mushaf cannot be found. Their value, perhaps, lies in being historical documents only.

The roots of the mythologized early history of the Muslims could have most likely emerged in those tumultuous years following the Prophet's death. Attempts to fabricate hadiths during the life of the Prophet cannot be ruled out, but the task would have been difficult since the Prophet was alive and he and his companions could have challenged any forgeries with ease. After the first Hijri century, the hadiths that were already available were carefully scrutinized, and complex rules were established (later to be canonized as "science") making it much harder, but certainly not impossible, for hadith fabrication to continue. The scrutiny and the "science" of Hadith that was established during the second and third Hijri centuries did not guarantee the authenticity of what was accepted by the likes of al-Bukhari, Muslim, al-Tirmidhi and others as authentic hadiths (the subject of Hadith and its collection will be discussed in Chapter 8). Still today, many hadiths with variable degrees of authenticity (there are many scales of authenticity that do not have uniform definition amongst Hadith collectors) find their way into Muslim culture to justify bloodshed and conquest in the name of Islam and in the name of the Prophet of Islam. Take for instance the collection of hadiths on the importance of Sham (modern day Syria and the territories surrounding it). These hadiths, which exalt the status of the people and region of Sham, were most likely fabricated to favor Muawiyah, the first ruler of the Umayyad dynasty, over Ali, the cousin of the Prophet, during the grand *fitna* (mischief) that divided the nascent Muslim community only 25 years after the death of the Prophet.

If a preponderance of evidence points to massive fabrication of hadiths, we might expect fabrication related to other important contemporaries of the Prophet, such as the prominent Muslim figures and leaders who succeeded the Prophet in governance, including the Righteous Caliphs abu Bakr, Umar, Othman, and Ali, and prominent companions such as ibn Abbas, Malik ibn Anas, and many others. In fact, fabricating narratives attributed to the companions would be much easier since reverence to those individuals would not have been the same as that bestowed on the Prophet.

Opponents of Islam and Muslims, on the other hand, find in the early *fitna* wars a cause of celebration and sufficient reasons to discredit the religion and attribute the dispute to fundamental flaws within Islam itself.[10] Muslims who want to understand their religion correctly and non-Muslims (opponents, enemies or others) who oppose the religion because of un-Islamic doctrines that have inundated Muslim culture, both need to study and reflect on those early years following the Prophet's death in an effort to separate Islam from other doctrines that were attached to it.

The disputes amongst Muslims who could legitimately be considered as contemporaries of the Prophet contributed to the wholesale production of fake hadiths. Of course, financial and material interests could have been additional contributing factors in the same way that such interests play a role today in advocating specific "religious" persuasions or entire doctrines. A hadith that has been used excessively to justify an abhorrent exclusivity practiced by some Muslims' sects is the one that proclaims Muslims will be divided into seventy-three factions; all but one will be doomed to hellfire.[11] Instead of trying to determine the hadith*'s* compatibility with the Mushaf in the first place, many Muslims were quick to establish a philosophy and a worldview based on this hadith. The overwhelming Muslim practice indicates that the question of whether such a hadith is compatible with the message of Islam or not is of little importance. The example of this and other hadiths*s* shed light on doctrines that attempt to fit a square peg in a round hole.

Violence in the Name of Islam

The hadiths collected by al-Bukhari, numbering approximately 4,000 (with thematic duplication), are generally considered by Sunni

Muslims to be the most authoritative and reliable.¹² Amongst the most contentious is the following hadith: ¹³

عن ابن عمر رضي الله عنهما أن رسول الله صلى الله عليه وسلم قال (أمرت أن أقاتل الناس حتى يشهدوا أن لا إلاه إلا الله وأن محمدا رسول الله ويقيموا الصلاة ويؤتوا الزكاة فإذا فعلوا ذلك عصموا مني دمائهم وأموالهم إلا بحق الإسلام وحسابهم على الله تعالى.

[Ibn Umar, may Allah be pleased with both of them, narrated that the Messenger of Allah (S) said: I was ordered to fight people until they witness that there is no god but Allah and Muhammad is his messenger, and perform prayers and give alms; and whence they do, then they prevented me from going after their blood (reference to killing them) and their moneys except in what demanded by Islam and to Allah they shall be eventually judged.] For brevity, henceforth this hadith will be referred to as the Sword Hadith. The presence of this hadith in Sahih al-Bukhari is sufficient for most Muslims to make it legitimate, if not sacred. This hadith is not only terrifying to Muslims and non-Muslims alike, but is contradictory to the content, spirit and text of the Mushaf, and especially the characterization of the Prophet Muhammad in the Mushaf. This hadith is either completely forged, entirely authentic, or partially authentic in wording or intended message.¹⁴ Of course the nature of the methodologies adopted for Hadith collection implies a probability of authenticity in the first place. A cause for concern that significantly diminishes faith in the authenticity of the Sword hadith is the first and second demands on people to witness that there is no deity but Allah and Muhammad is his messenger. The Mushaf, on the other hand, asks people to be in a state of *imaan* rather than to witness anything. *Imaan* and witnessing are drastically different. Also, *imaan* is not always belief. Belief is related to faith but *imaan* can also be related to security. The Mushaf asks the Muslims to achieve a state of *imaan* through Allah.

The imprecision or laxity in understanding the words of the Mushaf led to not only major confusion over the Muslims' treatment of non-Muslims but also to fundamental contradictions in understanding the core of Islam. (The consequences of using belief, *imaan,* and witness interchangeably in many contexts will be discussed in more details in Chapter 9). The other indication that the Sword hadith lacks authenticity is the third demand that would spare people death and destruction, namely performing the daily prayers and paying *zakat* (alms-giving).

Non-believers are conventionally understood to be non-Muslims; therefore, they are not obliged to either perform prayers or pay *zakat*. Only the followers of Muhammad's message are required to perform these religion-based obligations. The enforcement of such obligations does not fall under the mandate of any government, whether "Islamic" or not. In fact, no government, "Islamic" or not, had ever enforced prayers or *zakat* on Muslims let alone non-Muslims.

In M3:18, Allah, the Angels, and the people of science are the only ones to witness that Allah is the only deity presiding over fairness (see Chapter 3 for an extended discussion of M3:18). Even in M3:18, there is no demand imposed on the people of science to witness the oneness of the deity. Again, one can be asked to believe in something, but witnessing it is a different matter altogether. This demonstrates the incompatibility of the Sword hadith with the Mushaf. Another indication that the hadith is most likely a forgery is its use of the word "people". "People" can imply all people or a specific group of people, so the inclusivity or exclusivity aspect of the addressed is not necessarily problematic or hides the clue behind the true meaning of the hadith (as numerous Muslim clergy believed). The problem, however, is that the "fighting" in the Sword hadith is directed against people in general, not even the *mushrikeen* (typically interpreted as idol worshippers or those who associate other gods with Allah) or *kuffar*. This in itself is a major contradiction of the Mushaf. The incredulity of the hadith (or at least its conventional interpretation) can be further highlighted by realizing that the Mushaf did not decree any penal code for not performing prayers or for not giving *zakat*. If under Islam the government cannot punish Muslims who do not perform the Islamic rituals, why would the prophet of Islam demand that non-Muslims, who do not accept his message in the first place, adhere to Islamic commands?

The challenge with any hadith, irrespective of its authenticity, is the absence of context. Surprisingly, based on Hadith commentary books, Muslim scholars' interest in the context seems absent at best (whether interpreting the Mushaf or Hadith). In contrast, the vast majority of Muslim scholars believe that the verses of the Mushaf, the divine revelation of Allah, has a context or a reason for its revelation typically referred to as *Asbaab al-Nuzool* (the reason for the revelation).[15] These challenges led many, from both the Shia and Sunni sects, to develop mechanisms for validation of the contradictory hadiths. These include belief in the correctness of the interpretations of the *Salaf*, the *ismat* (inherent infallibility) of the Ahl al-Bait and the concept of abrogation (which is the subject of Chapter 7).

Whoever forged the Sword hadith was most likely inspired by or attempted to create a parallel to M9:5:

فَإِذَا انسَلَخَ الْأَشْهُرُ الْحُرُمُ فَاقْتُلُوا الْمُشْرِكِينَ حَيْثُ وَجَدتُّمُوهُمْ وَخُذُوهُمْ وَاحْصُرُوهُمْ وَاقْعُدُوا لَهُمْ كُلَّ مَرْصَدٍ فَإِن تَابُوا وَأَقَامُوا الصَّلَاةَ وَآتَوُا الزَّكَاةَ فَخَلُّوا سَبِيلَهُمْ إِنَّ اللَّهَ غَفُورٌ رَّحِيمٌ

[And when the sacred months have passed, then engage (in fighting) the *mushrikeen* wherever you find them and capture them and besiege them and sit in wait for them at every place of ambush. And if then they repent and establish prayer and give *zakat,* then set them free. Indeed, Allah is forgiving-merciful.] This verse has been referred to by Muslim and non-Muslim scholars as the Verse of the Sword. Notice the apparent parallelism between the Sword hadith and Verse of the Sword. However, there are structural differences. The Sword hadith refers to people in general while the verse refers to the *mushrikeen,* which is commonly translated as polytheists. *Mushrikeen* and polytheists, however, are not necessarily synonyms. Polytheists implies association of others with Allah in his attributes. *Mushrikeen* could also imply worshipping Allah but adding one or more deities.

In light of the verse that immediately precedes this verse, namely M9:4, the Verse of the Sword is clearly addressing only a subset of *mushrikeen,* those that are in active conflict with the Muslim community led by the Prophet. Of course generalization of M9:5 to a standalone principle that governs the relationship between Muslims and *mushrikeen* (irrespective of the meaning of the word) cannot be substantiated by either the full context or other verses from the Mushaf. However, *shirk,* from which *mushrikeen* is derived, literally means a state of association. Therefore, wherever *mushrikeen* appears, it needs to be qualified by the context. Could *mushrikeen* in M9:5 be referring to Muslims who have committed mutiny (i.e., those who accepted the message of Muhammad but revolted against the government of Muhammad) and gave allegiance to other groups. This interpretation has plausibility based on the requirements for cessation of fighting stipulated explicitly in the verse. Notice that one of the demands in the verse is *tawba* (repentance), which is going back to one's earlier state. If the *mushrikeen* were to be fought to enter Islam, the presence of the word *tawba* would be irrelevant.

A Muslim can be a *mushrik*, a *kafir*, both, or neither, just like People of the Book can be *mushrikeen* or *kuffar*. In fact, some hadiths do not dismiss this possibility, such as the reference to pretentiousness as a small *shirk*. Certainly, some might find this interpretation unconventional, but a careful look at the Mushaf reveals that practically every major prophet and messenger was challenged by his own people, from Noah to Jesus. Would Prophet Muhammad be an exception? One wonders why the conventional interpretation of the Mushaf eliminates such possibility. The fact that hunger for power amongst some of the companions of the Prophet was demonstrated immediately upon his death lends credence to the possibility that hunger for power was also prevalent amongst some companions during his lifetime.

Numerous verses were a direct rebuke and questioned the sincerity of people who were living amongst the Prophet. For example, consider M49:14

يَا أَيُّهَا الَّذِينَ آمَنُوا لَا يَسْخَرْ قَوْمٌ مِّن قَوْمٍ عَسَىٰ أَن يَكُونُوا خَيْرًا مِّنْهُمْ وَلَا نِسَاءٌ مِّن نِّسَاءٍ عَسَىٰ أَن يَكُنَّ خَيْرًا مِّنْهُنَّ وَلَا تَلْمِزُوا أَنفُسَكُمْ وَلَا تَنَابَزُوا بِالْأَلْقَابِ بِئْسَ الِاسْمُ الْفُسُوقُ بَعْدَ الْإِيمَانِ وَمَن لَّمْ يَتُبْ فَأُولَٰئِكَ هُمُ الظَّالِمُونَ

[O you who have believed, let not any people scoff at another people who may be better than they; neither let women scoff other women who may be better than they and do not defame yourselves or revile one another by nicknames, miserable is the name, evident immorality, after belief, and whoever does not repent, then those are they who are the transgressors.] Notice the verse explicitly addresses the believers in the Prophet and his message. In M3:123, Allah asks the Muslims who fought in the battle of Badr to exercise caution and *taqwa* (piety):

وَلَقَدْ نَصَرَكُمُ اللَّهُ بِبَدْرٍ وَأَنتُمْ أَذِلَّةٌ فَاتَّقُوا اللَّهَ لَعَلَّكُمْ تَشْكُرُونَ

[Indeed Allah granted you victory at Badr while you were outnumbered; so have *taqwa* in Allah so that you may thank Him.] If all those who fought in in Badr were full of *taqwa*, the reminder or subtle reprimand to this elite group of Muslims would not have been necessary.

The endless sanitization by many Muslim clergy of the excesses and outright crimes by some companions and their successors has created a false image of the early Muslim society, including the society of which the Prophet was part. In a twist with dangerous consequences, the interpretation of the Mushaf succumbed to an imaginary society that many Muslim clergy claimed to have been the best or most just of all times. The danger lies in this perception contributed to a petrification of the concept of idealism. Idealism, in the annals of Muslim history, became exemplified by the behavior, dress code, hygiene practice, political expression and general conduct of the Prophet's companions. This, in turn, stunted the universality of Islam through a confinement of its virtues to space, time, and people. Not surprisingly, in the eyes of many self-appointed Muslim clergy, the credibility of a Muslim is shattered once he is clean shaven or she is without a headscarf.

A second verse that is the hallmark of the principle on which violent Muslims justify their brutality is M9:29

قَاتِلُوا الَّذِينَ لَا يُؤْمِنُونَ بِاللَّهِ وَلَا بِالْيَوْمِ الْآخِرِ وَلَا يُحَرِّمُونَ مَا حَرَّمَ اللَّهُ وَرَسُولُهُ وَلَا يَدِينُونَ دِينَ الْحَقِّ مِنَ الَّذِينَ أُوتُوا الْكِتَابَ حَتَّىٰ يُعْطُوا الْجِزْيَةَ عَن يَدٍ وَهُمْ صَاغِرُونَ

[Fight or engage in war those who do not believe in Allah or in the Last Day and who do not consider unlawful what Allah and His Messenger have made unlawful and who do not adopt the religion of truth from those who were given the book until *you'too* the *jizyah* willingly while they are humbled (or humiliated).] We note that the command in the verse is to fight certain groups from within those who were given the book until they *you'too* the *jizyah*. This verse is different from M9:5 in many ways. Here, the command is to fight a group of people representing a subset of those who were given the book. (Notice that the Mushaf differentiates between those who were given the book and the People of the Book.) First, we realize that the *mushrikeen* are not mentioned in this verse. Second, the verse does not incite hostility towards the broader group who were given the book, believe in Allah and the Day of Accountability, and forbid what Allah and his messenger have made forbidden. Clearly, these two aspects do not reveal the full meaning of the verse. Additionally, if those who were given the book here implies the Christians and the Jews, what about others, including Hindus, Sikhs, Buddhists, animists, atheists, Zoroastrians, devil worshippers, etc. If one were to argue that none of those groups (aside from Christians and Jews) were present at the time of Muhammad, then the verse cannot have universal implication and would only be relevant to temporal circumstances. Again, laxity and imprecision in interpretation where verses, or even parts of verses, were plucked out of their context encouraged a culture of extremism that considered violence and murder (under the pretext of jihad) as the pinnacle of the Islam.[16]

The extremist outlook amongst strains of Muslim sects is further fueled by the following hadith in Sahih al-Bukhari and typically referred to as ibn Masoud's hadith:[17]

عن ابن مسعود عن النبي صلى الله عليه وسلم قال (لا يحل دم امرىء مسلم يشهد أن لا إله إلا الله وأني رسول الله إلا بإحدى ثلاث الثيب الزاني والنفس بالنفس والتارك لدينه المفارق للجماعة)

[Ibn Masoud narrated that the Prophet said: The blood of a Muslim who bears witness that there is no god but Allah and I am the messenger of Allah except under one of three conditions cannot be shed (i.e., killed) unless he commits one of three offenses: Committing adultery while being married; taking the soul of someone else; and leaving his religion and parting from the group.] This hadith implies that Muslims who do not give *zakat* or do not perform the obligatory prayer should not be killed. This would be in contradiction with the Sword hadith, which advocates killing a non-Muslim who does not give *zakat* or performs the obligatory prayers. The contradiction between the above hadith and the Mushaf extends even further. The punishment of adultery in Islam is lashes, not execution, as will be shown below. In addition, the Mushaf never sanctioned killing of someone who disagrees or parts with the majority, either in opinion or in person. Overall, this hadith, which is most likely a forgery, lowers the threshold for taking a life to yet another lower level.[18]

Many self- and government-appointed Muslim clergy have gone to extremes to validate and explain the controversial hadith of ibn Masoud by extending the concept of the general versus the specific as applied to the Mushaf, to prophetic narratives.[19] The problem with this concept lies in that its applicability is typically based on conjecture rather than any substantive proofs. An additional problem with the hadith is the broad reach and vague interpretation. For instance, "leaving the religion" in the ibn Masoud's hadith had been interpreted to encompass *kufr*, *shirk*, sorcery, ridiculing Allah, ridiculing the Prophet, abandonment of prayers, proclaiming knowledge of the unseen and other offenses and infractions certain Muslim scholars believed will lead to *kufr*. These interpretations have even left the door wide open to sanctioning execution for any act that the religious authority defines as *kufr*.

The act of "parting from the group" can be interpreted in many ways. It is not clear which group should not be parted from. Throughout history and now, Muslims have been divided into many groups, with many claiming to be the righteous one worthy of salvation and paradise. These broad, unfounded and unsubstantiated interpretations of alleged hadiths indeed planted the seeds of many conflicts and wars. The problem lies in definitions and precisely lack a methodology to understand Arabic words.

The majority of Muslims accepted *kufr* as the state of becoming an infidel. The word infidel has roots in Christendom to describe anyone who is outside the faith. Such binary classification of all humankind most likely originated in Jewish scriptures where all people were classified as either Jews or gentiles. The Mushaf has no equivalent to infidels or gentiles. In fact, one cannot find in the entire Mushaf a single word or phrase that connotes the meaning of non-believers. A Muslim indeed can be a *kafir* if he covers or conceals the truth willingly. Similarly, a Christian or a Jew can be either a *kafir* or not a *kafir*.

The precision by which the Mushaf uses definitions and terms had been lost in the Arabs' intoxication with seductive Arabic metaphors and poetry. Even the word Muslim has a context and is not absolute, and that is why the Mushaf does not classify all people into either a Muslim or non-Muslim. There is no basis in the Mushaf to consider *kufr* as the opposite of *imaan*. Consider M5:73

لَقَدْ كَفَرَ الَّذِينَ قَالُوا إِنَّ اللَّهَ ثَالِثُ ثَلَاثَةٍ وَمَا مِنْ إِلَهٍ إِلَّا إِلَهٌ وَاحِدٌ وَإِن لَّمْ يَنتَهُوا عَمَّا يَقُولُونَ لَيَمَسَّنَّ الَّذِينَ كَفَرُوا مِنْهُمْ عَذَابٌ أَلِيمٌ

[They have committed *kufr* those who *qala* that Allah is the third of three, and there is no deity except one, and if they do not desist from what they are doing (the act of *qala*), then there will surely afflict those who have committed *kufr* among them a painful punishment.] *Qala* is typically, if not always, translated as "said". In fact, Mushaf translators place within quotes whatever comes after *qala*. In today's Arabic, *qala* implies the meaning of the word "said", but it has broader scope. When Allah refers to Himself as doing the *qala* act, He cannot be spelling out letters from a mouth. The act of *qala* is synonymous with promulgating or conveying a meaning or a concept. (A prominent example is M112:1 where Allah is promulgating or declaring his oneness rather than asking the Prophet, or others, to repeat after Him.) In M5:73, the Mushaf makes a clear distinction between a person who believes in the Christian doctrine of the Trinity and a person who created the concept or promulgated it without a proof. Notice that one who believes in a certain idea is not necessarily the one who originated or created the idea. The precision in the Mushaf in making such distinction should not be taken lightly. The Mushaf, however, uses different words than *qala* to express utterance and pronunciation. Consider M69:44

وَلَوْ تَقَوَّلَ عَلَيْنَا بَعْضَ الْأَقَاوِيلِ

[And if he *taqawwala* on us some *aqaweel*.] Here, *taqawwala*, which is a derivative from *qala* implies fabrication or making up false claims. Clearly "*taqawwala* on us" cannot imply that he uttered or pronounced to us.

Beheading with Ease

Abdullah, the son of Ahmed ibn Hanbal, wrote in *Kitaab al-Sunnah*: "My father mentioned to me, I heard Abdulrahman ibn Mahdi saying who claimed that Allah did not talk to Musa [Prophet Moses] must first be asked to repent, and if not, his neck should be severed".[20] Also, from the same book: "Ghayyath ibn Jafar has mentioned to me, I heard Sufyyan ibn Aynyya say: Mushaf is the *kalam* (narration or words) of Allah. Whoever says it was created, then he is a *kafir*. Also, whoever doubts that this person is a *kafir*, then he too is a *kafir*".[21] Here we find another example of where administering the most severe of punishments, death, for someone whose only sin might be his unconventional interpretation of the word *kall'ama* in the Mushaf. It is to be emphasized that such violence was sanctioned by ibn Hanbal rather than by an alleged attribution (i.e., hadith) to the Messenger or Allah. Even if these punishments are not practiced, their spirit encourages a culture of extreme violence in the name of Islam.

These opinions by ibn Hanbal discourage Muslims from even attempting to think of interpreting the words of the Mushaf beyond what was canonized by the approved (or certified) clergy of Islam for fear of falling into sin or worse, being executed. Of course, one should not rule out the possibility that the book of Abdullah, the son of ibn Hanbal, was a forgery in itself. Nevertheless, whether it was a forgery or not, ibn Hanbal is not the main concern in this discussion but rather these historical documents (i.e., *Kitaab al-Sunnah* by ibn Hanbal and others) that became part of Muslim religious doctrines.

Jurisprudents could not have handed down death punishments without the direct or tacit approval of the political authorities. Ibn Hanbal, for example, studied and worked as a *mufti* (edict giver) under Abbasid rulers. The intermixing of religion and jurisprudence (see Chapter 9) suggests that lavishing the death penalty on different groups was politically motivated then as much it is today. Manipulating Islam for political ends was the hallmark of the Umayyad and Abbasid dynasties. Nevertheless, the incredible latitude by which jurisprudents, the likes of ibn Hanbal, lavished the death penalty with ease gave rise to a culture that encouraged further extremism and violence sanctioned under a religious veneer. Excessive zeal towards the personality of the Prophet culminated in yet a higher level of violence towards anyone who vilifies the Prophet. Ibn Hanbal's opinion on who vilifies the Prophet is summarized by his son Abdullah, who said: I heard my father saying that whoever vilifies the Prophet, his head must be severed".[22]

Ibn Taymiyyah, a prominent figure in Muslims' history, was a major exponent behind narratives advocating extremism and violence and most likely the ideologue, but not the originator, of the violent culture propagated by the Salafi zealots and their followers. Ibn Taymiyyah wrote a two-volume book on the subject of vilifying and verbally insulting the Prophet. Insulting the Prophet is considered a most abhorring and egregious of acts amongst Muslims. A person who insults the Prophet might be punished proportionately under codes for language that can be inflammatory or might incite violence, or language that can be construed as deeply offensive to a religious group or a population minority.

The Salafis advocated direct obedience of the Salaf's opinion and direct imitation of their actions and behavior. The imitation part is typically accompanied by disdain for those who advocate the use of intellect in understanding Islam and its injunctions. The Salaf use deductive and inductive syllogism to deduce opinions and different punishments for a variety of offenses. For instance, ibn Taymiyyah invokes analogy to justify a death sentence for vilifying the Prophet despite the absence of such punishment in the Mushaf (ibn Taymiyyahs's book *al-Sarim al-Maslool ala Shatim al-Rasool* is a manifesto for sheer terrorism and violence in the name of Islam.)[23] By making the vilification of the Prophet equivalent to marrying one of his wives, which was forbidden by the Mushaf, the punishment for vilification, according to ibn Taymiyyah, would be death. Marrying any of the Prophet's wives was an injunction relevant only to the contemporaries of the Prophet (see M33:53). The analogy invoked by ibn Taymiyyah was as follows: since vilifying the Prophet is an offence of higher magnitude than marrying his wives, the death sentence would be justified. The problem with ibn Taymiyyah's logic is two-fold. First is the liberty he takes in assuming that the offense of vilifying the Prophet is worse than marrying one of his wives (it could or could not be). Second, despite the gravity of marrying any of the Prophet's wives, the death punishment was never prescribed in that case either. Notice that ibn Taymiyyah's argument is based on classical logic, something his adherents despise.

In a different narration, ibn Taymiyyah projects the Prophet as unjust, brutal and who champions extreme violence. In one story, the Prophet learns of someone who was accused of committing adultery with one of his wives.[24] According to ibn Taymiyyah, the Prophet commissioned his cousin Ali to simply go and sever the head of the accused. Ali did not chop the poor man's head because Ali claimed that he did not find him to be a man (i.e., having male genitals). The message that one takes from this bizarre story, taken for granted by a highly respected figure as ibn Taymiyyah and reported in numerous Hadith books, is that the Prophet made no attempt to verify the facts and ask the accused to appear before him or in a court of law. For ibn Taymiyyah, who is considered the arch-philosopher of the Salafi sect, advocating violence, even if based on suspect stories, was an expression and manifestation of faithfulness and closeness to Allah. Ibn Taymiyyah advocated for even harsher forms of violence, including torching to death not only a woman who was believed to have married the Prophet and remarried after his death, but also her alleged new husband.[25]

The ideological debates between numerous philosophical schools during the second Hijri century became extreme and resulted in further extremism to the point that the declaration or the verdict of *kufr* was dispensed generously upon those who dared to interpret the Mushaf using a methodology not sanctioned by ibn Hanbal. Such edicts and opinions are available in books highly respected by millions of Muslims. My objective here is not to analyze the bizarreness of such narratives or their authenticity but rather the language used in such highly regarded books legitimizing the beheading penalty for a variety of acts that cannot be elevated to the level of offences mentioned in the Mushaf. Rejecting these Mushaf-contradictory dubious stories (packaged in the form of hadiths) cannot be a cause for distancing one from Islam but the contrary.

The ease by which the verdict of *kufr* is administered was not exclusive to ibn Hanbal's jurisprudence. According to abu Hanifa, "Whoever says I do not know if my lord is in the heavens or in earth, then he has become a *kafir*, and same applies to whoever said He is on the throne and I do not know if the throne is in the heavens or in earth."[26] (Notice that the original text states "in earth" rather than "on earth".) Malik ibn Anas, one of the four grand jurisprudents of Sunnis, expressed equal readiness to execute a person for merely having a different interpretation of the Arabic language than his.[27] Al-Shafi'i, who is widely considered a moderate jurisprudent, did not find any problem in issuing a death penalty for a Muslim who does not perform the ritual daily prayers.[28]

The opinions of highly respected jurisprudents such as ibn Hanbal, ibn Anas, abu Hanifa and al-Shafi'i, as they relate to different interpretations of the Mushaf and to those who do not observe Islamic rituals are deeply troubling because of their potential consequences. Those opinions were based on a particular interpretation of a language that changed with time. In fact, the conclusions and subsequent conclusions of *kufr* were based on specific interpretations of specific Arabic words whose usage and connotation have shifted and whose context was deemed irrelevant. Moreover, a consistent definition of *kufr* was never given in these most respected of religious compendia.

The contradictions between the Mushaf and the philosophies of ibn Hanbal, ibn Anas and abu Hanifa should be a cause of serious concern for any Muslim. It is highly relevant to realize that the penal code of the Mushaf is confined to offences that have an impact on society, such as murder or taking innocent lives, committing sexual acts in public, and theft. Eating pork, not performing prayers, not giving *zakat*, drinking alcohol or not fasting in Ramadan, are all offenses that have no declared, explicit or implicit punishment in the Mushaf. In effect, the jurists have created a new Sharia that is not only alien to the Mushaf but transgresses the limits that the Mushaf imposes. This is itself a serious offense in Islam.

These are but a few examples of unsubstantiated directives that demonstrate the violence inherent in the doctrines that evolved following the death of a man who was declared by the Mushaf to be a mercy and kindness to humanity. Of course, one can dismiss these extreme opinions as inflammatory, un-Islamic, misguided, or completely wrong. However, a near-infallibility status that had been bestowed upon ibn Hanbal, abu Hanifa, ibn Malik, al-Shafi'i, ibn Taymiyyah, ibn Abbas, Abdullah ibn Umar, the Four Righteous Caliphs and many others that makes challenging their opinions extremely difficult aside from getting the challenger extreme ridicule for attempting to question the opinions of men who are held with such extreme esteem by most Muslims.

Similar to ibn Hanbal's advocacy of the death sentence for those who interpret parts of the Mushaf in a way different from his own interpretation, ibn Taymiyyah follows a similar course of reasoning buttressed by a plethora of additional horror stories. One story that ibn Taymiyyah cites needs special attention for its potentially serious implications. The story describes two men who went to the Prophet to seek his judgment on a specific dispute between them.[29] After learning the Prophet's opinion on the dispute, the one whom the Prophet judged against was not satisfied and sought to consult abu Bakr (the first Righteous Caliph). Abu Bakr ruled identically to the Prophet. Still not satisfied, the two men went to seek the opinion of Umar (the second Righteous Caliph). Umar, learning of the outcome of the two men's experience with the Prophet and his ruling, went inside his house, picked up his sword and immediately chopped off the head of the person who disagreed with the Prophet's ruling. The incredulity of the story does not end here as it continues by claiming that M4:65

$$\text{فَلَا وَرَبِّكَ لَا يُؤْمِنُونَ حَتَّىٰ يُحَكِّمُوكَ فِيمَا شَجَرَ بَيْنَهُمْ ثُمَّ لَا يَجِدُوا فِي أَنْفُسِهِمْ حَرَجًا مِمَّا قَضَيْتَ وَيُسَلِّمُوا تَسْلِيمًا}$$

[By your Lord, they will not become *mu'minoon* (having *imaan*) in you until they make you a judge in what they controvert amongst themselves then they would not find in themselves any hesitation or restriction in what you have decreed and would submit *tasleema*,] was revealed immediately in response to this incident and especially to exonerate Umar.[30] Another variant of this blood soaked story is that after the severing of the head of one of the two men, Umar narrated M4:65 as a justification for what he did. Notice the contradiction between the two stories, where one assumes M4:65 had already been revealed, whereas the other claimed that the incident triggered the revelation.

One can dismiss the jurisprudence and works of ibn Taymiyyah as an aberration or as not representative of the religion of the majority of Muslims. Such a dismissal can be shortsighted because of the implications of ibn Taymiyyah's edicts and opinions. Ibn Taymiyyah is revered amongst a large segment, if not the majority of Sunni Muslims. His writings are deeply respected, as exemplified by his commonly used title: Sheikh al-Islam (Sheikh implies a highly respected religious figure). To give a glimpse at the level of reverence ibn Taymiyyah holds amongst Muslims, in 2010 an entire conference was organized for the sole purpose of deciphering what has become known as the Mardin Fatwa (Mardin's Edict), which was issued by ibn Taymiyyah in the 14th Century AD. The *fatwa* was named after the city of Mardin in modern-day Turkey.[31] It is hard to recall a single conference ever held to decipher a single verse of the Mushaf, let alone a single chapter.

It is important to take note that ibn Hanbal, ibn Taymiyyah, and abu Hanifa, amongst many others, based their death penalty deductions not only on the body of Hadith but also on stories from the time of the Prophet. The accuracy of these stories was never substantiated by either jurisprudents or historians and can best be described as a concoction of legends, partial truths, and extreme exaggerations. Nevertheless, largely respected books of Hadith, such as those of Muslim and al-Bukhari, have their fair share of violence-laden hadiths. Take for instance this Sahih al-Bukhari hadith:[32]

> Narrated Anas: Some people from the tribe of Ukl came to the Prophet and embraced Islam. The climate of Medina did not suit them, so the Prophet ordered them to go to the (herd of Milch) camels of charity and to drink their milk and urine (as a medicine). They did so, and after they had recovered from their ailment (became healthy) they turned renegades (reverted from Islam) and killed the shepherd of the camels and took the camels away. The Prophet sent (some people) in their pursuit and so they were (caught and) brought, and the Prophets ordered that their hands and legs should be cut off and that their eyes should be branded with heated pieces of iron, and that their cut hands and legs should not be cauterized, till they die.

While this story is intriguing in its evasiveness and cruelty, it evokes many questions. Why would "some people" migrate to Medina and leave their tribe? If those people truly migrated to Medina, then they would have settled in Medina. Why would the Prophet prescribe medication for their strange ailment while he never practiced medicine? The Prophet was not known, either before or after the Prophethood, to have practiced medicine and there is no proof that he received medically related revelations or any medical training. Did the "some people" recover so quickly or did it take days or months for their full recovery? Why would the Prophet prescribe such cruel and unusual punishment for an offense that is not found in the Mushaf? If he did, he would have transgressed against the limits that were precisely prescribed in the Mushaf (*hudood*). If the Prophet exceeded the prescribed limits, he would have violated the message that he was supposed to deliver, which in itself would have been a serious transgression. Was this hadith a fabrication together with a long list of others, to sanction severe violence by political rulers?

The problem of using stories, whether authentic or not, to deduce what is haram and to deduce an Islamic penal code has led to a culture that encourages and implicitly sanctioned arbitrariness in leveling the death punishment for a variety of offenses never alluded to directly nor remotely in the Mushaf. The guidelines that ibn Taymiyyah expunged using deduction, analogy, or sheer speculation were not only broad but also elastic. The problems do not lie in ibn Hanbal, ibn Taymiyyah, or the jurisprudence they invented, but in a culture of lax and irrational adoption of a broad range of Prophetic and non-Prophetic narratives, whose authenticity is not only in doubt but belief in it is not binding on Muslims.

JIZYAH

Jizyah is historically understood to refer to a type of tax levied against non-Muslims living under Muslims' rule (i.e., an "Islamic" state). Muslim clergy differed widely on who should be taxed. Some considered the *jizyah* applicable to Christians and Jews while some clergy added Zoroastrians and religious groups.[33] Numerous clergy provided what they believed to be a rationale behind *jizyah,* such as taxation for protection or taxation in lieu of the *zakat* that Muslims pay, which is not required on non-Muslims.[34] Muslim clergy, almost universally, base the concept of *jizyah* on M9:29 (repeated here for clarity. See above for translation)

قَاتِلُوا الَّذِينَ لَا يُؤْمِنُونَ بِاللَّهِ وَلَا بِالْيَوْمِ الْآخِرِ وَلَا يُحَرِّمُونَ مَا حَرَّمَ اللَّهُ وَرَسُولُهُ وَلَا يَدِينُونَ دِينَ الْحَقِّ مِنَ الَّذِينَ أُوتُوا الْكِتَابَ حَتَّىٰ يُعْطُوا الْجِزْيَةَ عَن يَدٍ وَهُمْ صَاغِرُونَ

The Arabic word *jizya* is derived from *ja'za,* which implies either retribution or reward. This becomes apparent when considering all other verses in the Mushaf that used the word and its derivatives. For example, in M2:191, 3:87, 4:93, 5:29, 5:38 the relevance was to punishments and in M3:136, 3:145, 9:121 the relevance was to a reward. Missing from the numerous scholarly works on *jizyah*, however, is the meaning of a key word in M9:29, namely *you'too* (يُعْطُوا), which is underlined above. *You'too* is universally translated as "to give". Accordingly, *you'too al-jizyah* (يُعْطُوا الْجِزْيَةَ) would then be interpreted as "to give the *jizyah*". The problem with this interpretation and translation becomes apparent when considering another verse in the same chapter where M9:29 appears, namely M9:58

وَمِنْهُم مَّن يَلْمِزُكَ فِي الصَّدَقَاتِ فَإِنْ أُعْطُوا مِنْهَا رَضُوا وَإِن لَّمْ يُعْطَوْا مِنْهَا إِذَا هُمْ يَسْخَطُونَ

[And of them is he who defames you concerning donations, then if they are *ou'too* (أُعْطُوا) some of it, they become satisfied; and if they are not *you'too* (يُعْطَوْا) from it, then are they wrathful.] Here, *ou'too* is the past tense of *you'too* in M9:29. (In all these transliterations, the letter t is the substitute of the Arabic letter ط).³⁵ However, *ou'too* in M9:58 is universally translated and interpreted by Muslim scholars as "they were given" while its past tense in M9:29 is translated and interpreted as "to give". Both words have the same *dhamma* accent on the first and the third letter.³⁶

Why in M9:29 was the meaning of يُعْطَوْا flipped to imply its opposite? The context of M9:58 clearly indicates that *ou'too* implies "to give", otherwise the entire verse becomes meaningless in the sense that those demanding the proceeds of *sadaqat* (charity) need to give it. In the same vein, *jizya,* in M9:29, becomes a punishment to be administered once the conflict ceases rather than a lifetime system of extortion.

Throughout Muslims history, including the first century, there could have been numerous laws, some of which levied tax on certain people for all reasons. Whether these laws were justified, fair, brutal, or coercive is a testimony about the rulers and governors who enacted them rather than a reflection on the spirit of Islam or the religion itself. All those rules were not part of Islam. Furthermore, there is no justification to lump them all under the instrument of *jizya*. In fact, according to historical records, certain Muslim rulers were not happy that mass conversion to Islam was taking place for fear of reducing their *jizya* proceeds.³⁷ The *jizyah* system practiced by many dynasties including, for example, the Ottomans when they ruled over the Balkans, cannot be canonized as Islamic. The economic systems practiced by the Righteous Caliphs, including taxation, irrespective of the authenticity of the historical records that have reached us and that described such systems, cannot be considered as Islamically mandated.

Jizyah is a form of coercion since it encumbers heavy burden on non-Muslims, forcing them to accept Islam or to be subjected to onerous financial conditions. The argument advocated by numerous Muslim scholars and clergy that *jizyah* parallels the *zakat* (financial obligation towards a group of needy people) and *sadaqat* (charity) that Muslims pay has flaws. *Zakat* and *sadaqat* are demanded by Allah and hence they do not fall under the obligations of the state. No Muslim country (ruled by Muslims or by having a Muslim majority) enforces the collection of *zakat* or *sadaqat*. In fact, Muslim scholars and clergy have never had any consensus on the modalities of the *zakat* such as its recipients and its amount and on which capital or possessions it applies to.

The concept of *jizyah* as understood amongst Muslims, their Shias and Sunnis, is not validated by the Mushaf and it contradicts the fundamental spirit of Allah's divine revelation, which stresses the freedom of anyone to choose his or her own belief system and religion or not to believe in anything at all (see M18:29). The freedom to choose cannot exist side-by-side with a discriminatory system based on extortion and coercion.[38]

ADULTERY

Adultery in Arabic is an act that falls under the broad *fahisha* designation. The Arabic word *fahisha* has roots related to something that exceeds a prescribed limit. *Zina*, the Arabic word typically translated as adultery, is a form of *fahisha*. The Mushaf does not distinguish between *zina* when the perpetrators are either married or unmarried. According to M24:2, the punishment for adultery is one hundred lashes provided when there is an availability of four witnesses:

الزَّانِيَةُ وَالزَّانِي فَاجْلِدُوا كُلَّ وَاحِدٍ مِّنْهُمَا مِائَةَ جَلْدَةٍ وَلَا تَأْخُذْكُم بِهِمَا رَأْفَةٌ فِي دِينِ اللَّهِ إِن كُنتُمْ تُؤْمِنُونَ بِاللَّهِ وَالْيَوْمِ الْآخِرِ وَلْيَشْهَدْ عَذَابَهُمَا طَائِفَةٌ مِّنَ الْمُؤْمِنِينَ

[The *zaaniyah* and *zaany* then lash each one of them a hundred lashes, and let not compassion for them take you in the religion of Allah in case you believe in Allah and the Last Day; and let a section of the believers witness their torment.] Practically, all Muslim jurisprudence schools make a distinction between *zina* committed by married or unmarried people. For an unmarried person, the punishment is one hundred lashes, precisely what the Mushaf stipulates, but for the married one, the punishment is *rajm* (death by stoning).

Zina is typically translated as fornication or engaging in intercourse with the opposite sex outside marriage. However, the Mushaf differentiates between *zina* and *fahisha*. According to Mohammad Shahrour, *zina* is an overt *fahisha* that is subject to punishment. Covert *faahish*, as for example fornication in privacy, does not qualify to be *zina* and thus does not warrant any punishment administered by the state.[39] The

Mushaf explicitly enacted *hudood* (boundaries) for all punishments. The punishment for *zina* is the prescribed lashes, but not *rajm*. In fact, the punishment of *rajm* is never mentioned in the Mushaf. Careful scrutiny of the background that led to the adoption or belief in *rajm* or the death-by-stoning punishment for the married adulterer can reveal insight into the dilemma and contradictions facing Muslims who refer to the Mushaf and Islam in general for legal opinions on a variety of offenses.

The proponents of the *rajm* refer to alleged stories about the Prophet, including the following hadith in Sahih al-Bukhari:[40]

> Narrated ibn Umar: A Jew and a Jewess were brought to Allah's Messenger on a charge of committing an illegal sexual intercourse. The Prophet asked them. "What is the legal punishment (for this sin) in your Book (Torah)?" They replied, "Our priests have innovated the punishment of blackening the faces with charcoal and Tajbiya." Abdullah ibn Salam said, "O Allah's Messenger, tell them to bring the Torah." The Torah was brought, and then one of the Jews put his hand over the Divine Verse of the *rajm* (stoning to death) and started reading what preceded and what followed it. On that, ibn Salam said to the Jew, "Lift up your hand." Behold! The Divine Verse of the *rajm* was under his hand. So Allah's Messenger ordered that the two (sinners) be stoned to death, and so they were stoned. Ibn Umar added: So both of them were stoned at the Balat and I saw the Jew sheltering the Jewess."

This hadith brings critical questions to the fore. Was the Prophet then the governor of Medina? If the Jewish subjects were under his jurisdiction, it would be assumed that he would have exacted uniform punishments on all his subjects, especially when considering that the Mushaf does not make a distinction between Muslims or non-Muslims who commit *zina*, or for that matter any other offense.[41]

If the hadith were true, it would have implied that the Prophet believed in multiple penal codes for different people of different religions living under his government. This would then contradict the universality of the Mushaf's message. So if the Prophet made a judgement based on the Torah and not the Mushaf, as the above hadith stipulates, it would have implied that the Prophet believed that the Torah that was brought to him was the true and unaltered Torah. Finally, was it customary for the Jewish tribes within and around

Medina to use the Prophet as the arbitrator in their disputes? Regardless, stoning is prescribed for several punishments in Jewish scriptures but never mentioned in the Mushaf.

It is even difficult to ascertain whether or not stoning was indeed prescribed in the Torah (considered as the divine revelation to Moses), or was it Rabbinical interpretation or addition as part of the Talmud. Nevertheless, Muhammad was commanded by the Mushaf to make judgements based on what was revealed to him (see M5:48). Therefore, if the original revelations were different, then Medina or any other society to be governed by the Mushaf would have had contradictory rulings: stoning for Jews, flogging for Muslims, and different punishments for people of other faiths as prescribed in their scriptures, holy books or traditions. Realizing that *zina* requires four witnesses, it is an overt offense that affects society rather than a private matter related to those who commit the act. The plausibility of having different punishments for subjects living under a singular governance nullifies the principle of justice and fairness in the first place.

Another hadith typically used to sanction *rajm* for *zina* is the following:[42]

> Narrated abu Huraira and Zaid ibn Khalid al-Jjuhani: A bedouin came to Allah's Messenger and said, "O Allah's Messenger! I ask you by Allah to judge My case according to Allah's Laws." His opponent, who was more learned than he, said, "Yes, judge between us according to Allah's Laws, and allow me to speak." Allah's Messenger said, "Speak." He (i.e., the bedouin or the other man) said, "My son was working as a laborer for this (man) and he committed illegal sexual intercourse with his wife. The people told me that it was obligatory that my son should be stoned to death, so in lieu of that I ransomed my son by paying one hundred sheep and a slave girl. Then I asked the religious scholars about it, and they informed me that my son must be lashed one hundred lashes, and be exiled for one year, and the wife of this (man) must be stoned to death." Allah's Messenger said, "By Him in Whose Hands my soul is, I will judge between you according to Allah's Laws. The slave-girl and the sheep are to be returned to you, your son is to receive a hundred lashes and be exiled for one year. You, Unais, go to the wife of this (man) and if she confesses her guilt, stone her to death." Unais went to that woman next

morning and she confessed. Allah's Messenger ordered that she be stoned to death.

According to this hadith, the Prophet used Allah's laws to make a judgment. But the problem with this hadith is that the law in question does not exist in the Mushaf, which is the only place where Allah's laws would have been documented for Mohammad.

As if the proponents of stoning were not fully content with the hadiths mentioned above, the theory of textual abrogation was brought to bear to add additional justification for stoning. Hadith books such as Sahih al-Bukhari and others claimed that the second Righteous Caliph Umar was a proponent for stoning to the point that he believed a specific Mushaf verse was revealed for the purpose of explicitly proclaiming the stoning punishment.[43] Debating the multifarious discourse of the textual abrogation in general and vis-à-vis stoning in particular is problematic (if not extremely comical) from practically every aspect as will be discussed in more details in Chapter 7.

To add further legitimacy to *rajm*, a very bizarre hadith was added to Sahih al-Bukhari.[44] The hadith in question claims that a certain Amru ibn Maymoon, a person that we do not know much about except he was an honest man according to the framers of Hadith. The bizarre narrative claims that ibn Maymoon observed the stoning of a she monkey by a group of monkeys because she committed *zina*.[45] There are numerous discussions of this hadith and its other more expansive variants in so many books (the other variants, not reported in Sahih al-Bukhari, read like a pornographic novel). This hadith can be easily dismissed as a joke; however, the interest here is not to demonstrate that Muslim clergy have a unique sense of humor or to determine whether this hadith is authentic or not. One can find elaborate discussions by Muslim clergy attesting to the sincerity and honesty of ibn Maymoon; but does that imply that any bizarre story coming from any honest and sincere person deserves inclusion in the books of Sahih (i.e., to be made part of the religion?) The interest here is to question its inclusion in Sahih al-Bukhari in the first place. Irrespective of whether ibn Maymoon observed the alleged monkey stoning or not, the major question is what qualified the hadith to have been made part of Islam. It is highly likely that whoever included this hadith in the Sahih al-Bukhari wanted to lend further legitimacy to *rajm* when all other justifications failed.

There are indications that stoning to death was practiced in different Muslim and non-Muslim religious sects such as Yazidis and Jews.[46] The Mushaf considered *zina* a sin and prescribed a punishment that cannot exceed one hundred lashes without specifying whether the perpetrators are married or not. Going beyond this punishment, especially a most cruel and severe punishment of stoning (i.e., severe torture prior to death,) is in fact a transgression against Islam rather than a demonstration of stronger allegiance to it.

APOSTASY

Riddah in Muslim history typically refers to the act of converting from Islam to a different religion, or it refers to a Muslim renouncing his or her religion. Both Shia and Sunni jurisprudence schools consider *riddah,* typically translated as apostasy, to be a major offense punishable by death. None of the Shia or Sunni sects uses the Mushaf directly to justify such extreme punishment but rather refer to the Hadith corpus. From the Sunni perspective, the death penalty for apostasy is deduced from several hadiths in Sahih al-Bukhari. A good example is Ikrama's hadith:[47]

> Narrated Ikrama: Some *zanadiqah* (a word that loosely refers to atheists) were brought to Ali and he burnt them. The news of this event reached ibn Abbas who said, "If I had been in his place, I would not have burnt them, as Allah's Messenger forbade it, saying, 'Do not punish anybody with Allah's punishment (fire). I would have killed them according to the statement of Allah's Messenger 'Whoever changed his religion, then kill him.' "[48]

From the Shia side, Alkafi's collection includes the following hadith:[49]

> I heard (imam) abu Abdullaah (al-Sadiq) saying, "A Muslim from among the Muslims who renounces Islam and rejects the Prophethood of Muhammad and considers him untrue, then verily his blood is lawful for anyone who hears that from him, his wife is to

be separated from him the day he became *murtad*, his wealth will be divided among his heirs, and his wife will observe the *idda* of a widow. The imam is obliged to kill him, and not ask him to seek forgiveness."

Another Shia source is attributed to imam al-Ridha:[50]

I read (a question) in handwriting of a person addressed to (imam) abu al-Hasan al-Ridha: "A person born as a Muslim, then becomes a *kafir* or *mushrik*, and leaves Islam should he be asked to seek forgiveness, or should he be killed and not be asked to seek forgiveness?" The imam wrote: "He should be killed".

Another hadith in Sahih al-Bukhari presents yet another sharp contradiction to the Mushaf. This hadith is widely accepted as direct and unequivocal justification for the punishment of death for apostates. The hadith has variants, but the common thread to all is the phrase attributed to the Prophet stating that "whoever exchanges his religion, then kill him".[51] Despite the stark contradiction to the Mushaf, the proponents of the death penalty for apostasy are adamant that this hadith is fully compliant with the Mushaf.[52] On the other hand, most opponents of the death punishment for apostasy struggle to reconcile Ikrama's hadith, which they claim to be authentic, with M2:256. Notice that Ikrama's hadith did not specify any religion at all, so if we were to take the hadith as authentic, would the punishment for those who convert from Christianity to Judaism be the death penalty too? What about those who convert from Buddhism to Islam?

The Sunnis and Shias considered these three hadiths in addition to a host of other stories as the foundation for justifying killing apostates.[53] The problem with these hadiths is that they contradict the Mushaf. First, the Mushaf states in M2:256 that "There is no compulsion in religion". This verse is typically interpreted as a command to refrain from compulsion, but considering the grammatical structure of the verse, there is no particular group addressed, hence, the verse does not state a command or a directive but rather emphasizes the fact that compulsion in religion is impossible. The Mushaf makes a broad statement on the invalidity or impossibility of coercion in faith. Indeed, a person can be coerced to perform certain acts, but to force belief is simply impossible. Religion (which encompasses faith) implies a conviction that can never be enforced. Clearly M2:256 and the three hadiths above are in contradiction. Therefore, a Muslim who believes in the Mushaf cannot believe in the validity of these hadiths. Therefore, these hadiths were either fabrications or half-truths in the sense that a few words within an otherwise legitimate Prophetic hadith were modified to justify aggression in the name of Islam and in the name of the Prophet.

The Mushaf reserved the death penalty only for two circumstances and these were the intentional or unintentional killing of a person (i.e., murder or manslaughter). In both circumstances the punishment by death takes place only if the family or guardian of the killed person wishes it to take place. This also means that the state cannot enforce the death penalty unless the family wishes so.

The rulings on apostasy are part of a bigger problem of giving higher priority to hadiths that have been altered (intentionally or unintentionally) because their transmitters gave themselves the permission to transmit the hadiths as they understood them rather than verbatim (see Chapter 8). In general, the authenticity of Hadith is probabilistic and its certainty cannot be established beyond any doubt, and to build penal codes including the punishment of execution based on uncertain hadiths puts into question whether divine justice or something else is being applied.

The Mushaf clarified that religion is a personal choice based on a freedom that Allah recognized in the Mushaf. The respect of the human will is demonstrated in M18:29 where Allah acknowledges that the revelation transmitted the truth and it is up to the individual to accept it or not. This accommodating position of the Mushaf is sharply contradictory to the text and spirit of the hadiths that advocate death and violence. These hadiths imply that the Mushaf was revealed as an instrument of coercion and sheer brutality. Coercion and brutality were in fact two hallmarks of the Umayyad dynasty, which most likely commissioned and propagated hadiths that justified brutality and land conquest in the name of Islam.

There are several verses in the Mushaf that have been interpreted by many Muslim scholars as inferring the punishment of death for apostates, such as M2:217, 3:90, 3:91, 5:54, 9:66, and 16:106. As discussed earlier, any verse or a combination of sequential verses cannot be understood without their context. Because of the very serious consequences of ill-found interpretation of these verses, we consider the most prominent two: M3:90 and M2:217.

M3:90

$$\text{إِنَّ الَّذِينَ كَفَرُوا بَعْدَ إِيمَانِهِمْ ثُمَّ ازْدَادُوا كُفْرًا لَّن تُقْبَلَ تَوْبَتُهُمْ وَأُولَٰئِكَ هُمُ الضَّالُّونَ}$$

[Indeed, those who commit *kufr* after *imaan*, then indulge further in *kufr*, never will their repentance be accepted, and they are the ones astray.] Since according to this verse Allah is the One to whom people repent, then *kufr* is dealt with on the Day of Accountability by Allah, not on this earth by people, be they in authority or not. *Imaan* or *kufr* is an expression or act directed towards Allah. He alone has the prerogative either to reward for it or to punish.

M2:217 (only partially given here):

$$\text{وَمَن يَرْتَدِدْ مِنكُمْ عَن دِينِهِ فَيَمُتْ وَهُوَ كَافِرٌ فَأُولَٰئِكَ حَبِطَتْ أَعْمَالُهُمْ فِي الدُّنْيَا وَالْآخِرَةِ ۖ وَأُولَٰئِكَ أَصْحَابُ النَّارِ ۖ هُمْ فِيهَا خَالِدُونَ}$$

[And whomever amongst you *yartadd* (abandons or leaves) on/from his religion and dies on a state of *kufr*, those have lost their deeds in this life and the hereafter, and those are the people of hellfire and they will stay in it for eternity.] Again, there is no mention of killing the one who leaves his religion.

The Mushaf warns the followers of Muhammad in M5:44,45,47 that those who rule by anything but the divine revelation are transgressors, truth deniers and disobedient, respectively. The punishment of death for apostates reflects an act of transgression, disobedience, and *kufr*.

HAND AMPUTATION

Amputation of a hand as a punishment for theft is practiced today in some Muslim countries, including the Kingdom of Saudi Arabia, Yemen and the Islamic Republic of Iran. Practically all Muslim jurisprudence schools claim that the punishment for theft is hand amputation. There are numerous hadiths to justify this type of punishment. The quintessential problems with such hadiths is that they provide a wide range for the threshold of the value of the stolen item that warrants amputation. For instance, some hadiths put the threshold at the fair market value of a chicken egg while others put it much higher. While numerous Muslim clergy are comfortable and at times too liberal with expansive extrapolations based on pure conjectures and opinions to provide the *hikmah* (wisdom) behind certain Islamic injunctions, the severe punishment by severing the thief's hand is never contextualized to explain any *hikmah* behind severing the hand of an egg's thief and doing the same to someone who steals one billion dollars. The same clergy do not provide a justification for serving identical punishment to a bread thief who wanted to feed his starving family and to a banker who defrauds millions of people and turning them into beggars.

Those who justify amputation based on the Mushaf use M5:38

وَالسَّارِقُ وَالسَّارِقَةُ فَاقْطَعُوا أَيْدِيَهُمَا جَزَاءً بِمَا كَسَبَا نَكَالًا مِّنَ اللَّهِ ۗ وَاللَّهُ عَزِيزٌ حَكِيمٌ

[And the male who is engaged in stealing or theft and the female who is engaged in stealing or theft, then *eqta'oo aydeehima* as a consequence for what they have gotten *nakallan* from Allah, and Allah is *Aziz Hakim*.] *Aqta'oo* is the plural imperative tense of the verb *qata'ah*. In modern Arabic, *qata'ah* is used interchangeably with *bata'rah* (to amputate or separate by means of cutting). Another similar verb in the Mushaf is *qatta'ah*, to which I will return shortly. Derivatives of *qata'ah* appeared fifteen times in the Mushaf.[54] In only two verses in M59:5 and M56:33 could the context imply the meaning of cutting off or plucking off something physical (as in dates or fruits). In twelve of the remaining verses, *qata'ah* refers to elimination of a non-physical entity such as any trace of a group of people (see M8:7 and M15:66). In M27:32, the verb *qata'ah* is used to indicate affirmation of a decision:

قَالَتْ يَا أَيُّهَا الْمَلَأُ أَفْتُونِي فِي أَمْرِي مَا كُنتُ قَاطِعَةً أَمْرًا حَتَّىٰ تَشْهَدُونِ

[She said O you chiefs advise me on my affairs as I would not *qate'ah* a matter until you bear witness.] In this verse, the verb *qate'ah* is not related to any physical object. Just like many other languages, the meaning of a verb in Arabic becomes clear when considered within its context, especially when the nature of the object of the verb is recognized. In M5:38, the object is *aydeehuma*, which in modern Arabic is typically translated as "their hands", but *aydee* (hands in modern Arabic) is used in numerous verses in the Mushaf to indicate ability, capability, strengths, and deeds or related meanings. Finally, we come to the word *nika'lan* in M5:38. If the context and the object of the verb were not sufficient to determine its meaning, the consequence of the verb might narrow down the meaning considerably. The consequence to the punishment, as M5:38 stipulates, is *nika'lan* from Allah. In modern Arabic, *nika'lan* connotes torment or torture, thus *nika'lan* is aptly used by the proponents of the amputation theory to further strengthen their claim that M5:38 calls for hand amputation for thieves. Surprisingly, none of the meanings of the root verb *nak'ala* implies torment or torture, but rather distancing, isolation or putting aside. Considering the possible intersection of the different meanings of the three words *aqta'oo*, *aydeehima* and *naka'lan* to produce a meaningful sentence, the punishment for theft would most likely be isolation, exile, or imprisonment rather hand amputation.

The proponents of hand amputation attempt to provide additional validation for their theory using M12:31

فَلَمَّا سَمِعَتْ بِمَكْرِهِنَّ أَرْسَلَتْ إِلَيْهِنَّ وَأَعْتَدَتْ لَهُنَّ مُتَّكَأً وَآتَتْ كُلَّ وَاحِدَةٍ مِنْهُنَّ سِكِّينًا وَقَالَتِ اخْرُجْ عَلَيْهِنَّ فَلَمَّا رَأَيْنَهُ أَكْبَرْنَهُ وَقَطَّعْنَ أَيْدِيَهُنَّ وَقُلْنَ حَاشَ لِلَّهِ مَا هَٰذَا بَشَرًا إِنْ هَٰذَا إِلَّا مَلَكٌ كَرِيمٌ

[and later on when she heard of their scheming, she sent for them and prepared for them a meeting hall and gave each one of them a knife and promulgated or said come out before them and afterwards when they saw him, they greatly admired him and *qatta'na* their hands and said or promulgated, perfect is Allah this is not a man form but a noble angel.] *Qatta'na* is translated by virtually all Mushaf exegetes as "they (feminine form) cut (past tense)" but not "cut off", while without explanation *aqta'oo* in M5:38, which is a different tense of the same verb, is translated as cutting off. Based on the context of M12:31, it seems highly unlikely that the women in this verse have gathered willingly to have their hands amputated after witnessing firsthand the extraordinary beauty of Yousuf. If the verse refers to cutting but not cutting off then the punishment of theft is likely the cutting of the hand as in making cuts that will leave permanent marks on the hand. If that were the case, it would be similar to tribal practices in some African countries where face cutting indicates social attributes.

Another relevant verse is M26:49

قَالَ آمَنتُمْ لَهُ قَبْلَ أَنْ آذَنَ لَكُمْ إِنَّهُ لَكَبِيرُكُمُ الَّذِي عَلَّمَكُمُ السِّحْرَ فَلَسَوْفَ تَعْلَمُونَ
لَأُقَطِّعَنَّ أَيْدِيَكُمْ وَأَرْجُلَكُم مِّنْ خِلَافٍ وَلَأُصَلِّبَنَّكُمْ أَجْمَعِينَ

[He expressed (conveyed or promulgated) you have believed him before I gave you permission. He is your great master who taught you magic (or sorcery) so you will recognize I will *u'qatta'anna* your hands and feet and legs alternately and will crucify you collectively.] The relative close historical proximity between Prophets Moses and Yousuf, and considering that the system of Pharaonic doctrines was common to their respective times suggests, that two verbs *qatta'na* in M12:31 and *uqatta'anna* in M26:49, notwithstanding their different tense, referred to identical acts. Therefore, it is highly plausible that M26:49 does not indicate hand amputation but rather cutting to inflict scars that would identify the person throughout society as an offender or criminal.

In spite of the conclusions reached above, here I argue that a purely linguistic analysis could yet reveal additional support for the imprisonment theory for theft rather than amputation. The verb *qatta'ah,* pronounced similarly to *qata'ah* but with heavy stress on the t, has a similar form to *qata'ah,* as it is composed of the same three Arabic letters but with different diacritical marks. The verb *qatta'ah* and its derivatives appeared in seventeen verses in the Mushaf.[55] Similar to *qata'ah, qatta'ah* might refer to a physical act as in M5:33 or to a non-physical act as in M21:93. Based on a purely Mushaf-based classification, *qatta'ah* implies plurality of objects in the sense that it carries the same meaning as *qata'ah* but is used when multiple physical or non-physical entities are addressed. Here lies a very important clue as to whether M5:38 implies

148

physical cutting. Since the verse starts by addressing the male and female thieves, the combination of which is plural, the object had to be plural. However, *qata'ah* was used, thus indicating that the recipient is singular. If the "cutting" here implied hand amputation, then the recipient should have been plural, and the present form of *qatta'ah* would have been used instead of *qata'ah*. Therefore, the recipient or the object of the verb in M5:38 has to be singular. In light of the meaning of *aydeehuma* discussed above, the subject most likely cannot be a physical entity but rather something else such as, most likely, the offenders' influence, which is singular. This supports the conclusion drawn above that the punishment for thieves is isolation from society such as exile to a remote land or imprisonment. The earlier explanation of the meaning *nika'lan* leads further support to this conclusion.

Cutting off the hand of a thief does not prevent him or her from stealing again. Even if he were to steal twice and even if his two hands were cut off, he could steal a third time by hacking and robbing one's bank account without the use of the hands. But then there will no hands left to cut off. The Mushaf provided the principle or the foundation for the punishment of theft, which is isolation from society. This isolation can be commensurate with the value of the stolen property. The ruling on the punishment for theft is Allah's prerogative (Allah's Sharia); the ruling on how long the isolation should be is the society's prerogative. Allah's ruling is indeed fully compatible with reality.

The above discussion was based on the Mushaf itself. If historical reports indicate that Umar ibn al-Khattaab, the second Righteous Caliph, cut off hands of thieves, or if he suspended Sharia during a famine, his policy, even if the historical records were correct, does not invalidate or replace the Mushaf rulings.

Hirabah

Hirabah, is an umbrella term that covers a variety of ever expansive offenses from drug trafficking, to theft and murder. The term originates from the word *yu'haribon* (those who engage in warfare) in M5:33

إِنَّمَا جَزَاءُ الَّذِينَ يُحَارِبُونَ اللَّهَ وَرَسُولَهُ وَيَسْعَوْنَ فِي الْأَرْضِ فَسَادًا أَن يُقَتَّلُوا أَوْ يُصَلَّبُوا أَوْ تُقَطَّعَ أَيْدِيهِمْ وَأَرْجُلُهُم مِّنْ خِلَافٍ أَوْ يُنفَوْا مِنَ الْأَرْضِ ذَٰلِكَ لَهُمْ خِزْيٌ فِي الدُّنْيَا وَلَهُمْ فِي الْآخِرَةِ عَذَابٌ عَظِيمٌ

[Indeed the punishment for those who wage war against Allah and his Messenger, and strive to create in the land, contamination and mischief, is to be killed or crucified or *tuqatt'a aydeehim* and *arjuluhum* from behind, or be exiled from the land. That will be a disgrace for them in this world and in the hereafter they will have great punishment.] This verse, typically referred to as the *hirabah* (waging war) verse, listed different types of punishments that fall under two offenses: waging war against Allah and his Messenger and simultaneously exerting efforts to create mischief in the land and contamination (which might fall under environmental pollution in today's language).

Hirabah is an expression encompassing a variety of offenses that were arrived at by means of deduction, mere conjecture, or pure political motives. It is not clear how numerous jurisprudents considered the applicability and relevance of M5:33, for instance, to drug trafficking in countries such as the Kingdom of Saudi Arabia and the Islamic Republic of Iran. Also, *hirabah* is used to justify execution of thieves in the Kingdom of Saudi Arabia.[56] Notice that the verse speaks of a war waged against Allah and His Messenger, simultaneously. The question that comes to mind is what does waging war against Allah and his Messenger imply? What does waging war on Allah mean? What does waging war on the Messenger mean? Notice that only one of four types of punishments stipulated in the verse are to be applied to those who meet three criteria: waging war on Allah and His Messenger (simultaneously) and strive to create in the land mischief and/or contamination. A Muslim can believe in the entirety of the Mushaf but choose to traffic drugs. Irrespective of the egregiousness of the offense and its impact on society, the relevance between such an offence and waging war on Allah is not clear if not existent.

Concluding Thoughts

The literature of Muslim religious texts contains an alarming strain of violence and punishment by death lavished with ease at offences such as vilifying the Prophet, having unconventional interpretation of the Mushaf, or even not performing one or more of several Islamic rituals. The ease by which the head severance is sanctioned in the writings of highly respected Muslim scholars sends shivers down the spine of non-Muslims and Muslims alike. The turbulent and most violent period following the death of the Prophet most likely had a major influence on shaping the violent discourse that inundated the opinions of early Muslim scholars. Jockeying for power and naturally in the name of religion must have been the norm rather than the exception. The likes of ibn Hanbal even legitimized dictatorship and absolute tyranny and violence by the rulers. According to ibn Hanbal:[57]

> *Imamat* (leadership/governance) is established through election or inheritance, and both of these methods are valid and there is consensus on their legitimacy. And *imamat* can also be established through coercion and force, and this method, even if not as good as the first, still remains legitimate according to ahl al-Sunnah…full allegiance is given to the leader of the faithful, whether of good character or not from amongst those who have been made leaders through consensus and has taken the reigns of power, and also whoever takes the reigns of power using the sword until he becomes *the leader of the faithful*.

The amazing contrast of these opinions with the Mushaf text and spirit is truly shocking. While the Mushaf abhors violence and calls for a very calibrated violent response only in answer to an initiated violence by an aggressive party, ibn Hanbal approves sheer tyranny even if it was achieved at the cost of mayhem and violence.

The philosophy of extremism invaded the Muslim clergy's ethos to the extent that hardship, severity, pain, agony, difficulty, perseverance, extreme marginalization, and extreme irrationality became the norms contrary to Allah's revelations. Allah archives the extremes of Bani Israeli (not to be confused with Jews in general) not for the purpose of ridiculing them but so that the followers of Muhammad do not behave in the same way. The Muslim clergy, however, built an entire religious philosophy based on extremism not only in violence but also in framing (rather than interpreting) simple Mushaf injunctions. For example, fasting can present hardship to many Muslims. M2:184 specifically gave Muslims the choice to fast or not to fast. The Muslim clergy went to extreme measures to frame a negative as a positive (see Chapter 7, especially the discussion on fasting).

Women received the worst of the extremist ideology. The Hadith equated them with dogs.[58] The Hadith turned women's reproductive system, the source of human beings, into a source of *najas* (impurity). The menstruation blood was turned into *najas* despite the apologetic narratives by so many Muslim clergy and their proponents. Consequently, when women become impure, they were told to abstain from prayers. Worse yet, this severe marginalization of Muslim women was repackaged (using the classically assumed Godly rationale or *hikmah*) as a mercy to women during their period since they would be physiologically and psychologically imbalanced and thus would be in need of comfort and relaxation. Surprisingly, however, Muslim men and women can have severe ailments but Muslim clergy never decreed that such ailments warrant abstaining from prayers. The Mushaf repeatedly stressed the importance of prayers and *zakat*. If women were prohibited from prayers during their menstruation, the Mushaf would have instructed so, but it did not. The Hadith, however, makes the subject much more confusing.[59]

Staunch belief in the authenticity of Sahih al-Bukhari, Sahih Muslim, al-Kafi, the Imams, the Sahaaba, the Prophet's contemporaries and other Hadith compendia (al-Tirmidhi, abu Dawood, etc.), and the fact that these collections were hardly questioned but rather increasingly respected throughout the past twelve centuries, put the Muslims in a serious quandary in reconciling the flagrant contradictions between the Mushaf and the numerous narratives attributed to key figures in Muslim early history. This resulted in two dominant Muslim camps: those who adhered to the letter of the Hadith while completely shunning the Mushaf under the pretext that the Sunnah (i.e., the hadiths and Prophet's practice in this case) provided a context and explanation for the Mushaf. The other camp maintained belief in the hadiths since many of them were found in highly respected collections such as the Sahihs. The second camp, however, advocated a benign interpretation that would lessen the severity of contradictions found between such hadiths and the Mushaf. Both camps, however, refused to realize that the message of Islam is the Mushaf and whatever the Prophet did or said, even if fully authenticated and fully attributed to him, cannot be a replacement for divine powers or divine privilege. The stark contradictions between numerous hadiths and the Mushaf is largely dismissed as an apparent contradiction. It is precisely this incredible body of contradictions that allowed violence and extremism to be sanctified and glorified in the name of Islam. Until Muslims take these contradictions seriously, all aspects of violence against non-Muslims and Muslims will continue to flourish in the name of Islam.

1. Chossudovsky, Michel. *America's War on Terrorism*. 2nd ed., Center for Research on Globalization, 2005.
2. Shaheen, Jack. "Arab and Muslim Stereotyping in American Popular Culture". *Occasional Papers Series*, Center for Muslim-Christian Understanding, Georgetown University, 1997. Shaheen, Jack. *Guilty: Hollywood's Verdict on Arabs After 9/11*. Olive Branch Press, 2007. Luntz, Frank. *The Israel Project's 2009 Global Language Dictionary*. available at: https://www.transcend.org/tms/wp-content/uploads/2014/07/sf-israel-projects-2009-global-language-dictionary.pdf. Accessed 6 February 2019.
3. http://nypost.com/2013/12/15/inside-the-saudi-911-coverup. Accessed 17 March 2019. In a recent interview, the Crown Prince of Saudi Arabia, Muhammad ibn Salman, acknowledged his country's role in the spread of religious extremism around the world, http://www.asianews.it/news-en/Wahhabism,-terrorism-and-the-'confessions'-of-a-Saudi-prince-43465.html. Accessed 6 February 2019.
4. Muhammad ibn Abdulwahhab was a staunch follower of the Hanbali sect and ibn Taymiyyah.
5. Lacey, Robert. *The Kingdom: Arabia and the House of Saud*. Harcourt Brace Jovanovich, 1981.
6. Lacey. *The Kingdom*.
7. Al-Shafi'i, al-Imam Muhammad ibn Idris. *Al-Risala fi Usul al-Fiqh*. Translated by Majid Khadduri. 2nd ed., Islamic Text Society, 1961.
8. From Sahih al-Bukhari: Abu Musa al-Ashari also narrated that the Prophet Muhammad said: "May among men attained perfection but among women none attained perfection except Mary the daughter of Imran, and Asiya the wife of Pharoah, and the superiority of Ayesha to other women is like the superiority of Tharid (an Arabic dish) to other meals." Khomeini, Roohallah, Islam and Revolution: Writings and Declarations of Imam Khomeini, Mizan Press, Berkeley, 1981, p. 63.
9. Ibn Kathir, abu al-Fida Imaduddin Ismail. *Stories of the Prophet*, Darussalam, 2003.
10. The so-called *fitna* wars are the Jamal and Siffin wars that took place 25 and 26 years, respectively, after the death of the Prophet.
11. Sunan ibn Majah, Kitaab al-Fitann: "The Jews split into seventy-one sects, one of which will be in Paradise and seventy in Hell. The Christians split into seventy-two sects, seventy-one of which will be in Hell and one in Paradise. I swear by the One Whose Hand is the soul of

Muhammad, my nation will split into seventy-three sects, one of which will be in Paradise and seventy-two in Hell." It was said: "O Messenger of Allah, who are they?" He said: "The group." A noteworthy variant of this hadith is in Jami al-Tirmidhi, Kitaab al-Imaan: "The Messenger of Allah said: 'The Jews split into seventy-one sects, or seventy-two sects, and the Christians similarly, and my *umma* will split into seventy-three sects.'" In al-Tirmidhi's version, there is no mention of any group heading to Hell or Paradise. These two hadiths, despite their *sanad* (the chain of authorities attesting to the historical authenticity of a particular hadith) going back to the companions of the Prophet, they either escaped al-Bukhari altogether or were amongst the more than six hundred thousand hadiths that he sifted through and found not *sahih* (authentic) or not worthy of inclusion in his Hadith compendium. Interestingly, almost twelve hundred years after al-Bukhari's death, al-Albani elevated the grade of these hadiths to *sahih*.

12. See Chapter 8 for more extensive discussion of Hadith.
13. Sahih al-Bukhari, Kitaab al-Imaan. Sahih Muslim, Kitaab al-Imaan.
14. See Chapter 8 for more discussion on the practice amongst Hadith collectors of transmitting a hadith by its understood meaning rather than verbatim.
15. See Chapter 6.
16. Several hadiths attest that the pinnacle of Islam in jihad. These hadiths, however, are not in the Sahihs.
17. Jami al-Tirmidhi, Kitaab al-Dyyat.
18. Contemporary defenders of such controversial hadiths take a uniquely caustic approach when debating and defending their position. As an example, consider the defense of ibn Masoud's hadith by Khalid ibn Saud al-Belayhid, a member of the Saudi Scientific Organization for Sunnah in http://www.saaid.net/Doat/binbulihed/22.htm despite the contradiction between the hadith and M9:5 and 9:29. Accessed 8 February 2019.
19. The concept of general vs. specific in interpreting the rulings of the Mushaf was championed (and possibly theorized) by al-Shafi'i.
20. Ibn Hanbal, Ahmed. *Kitaab al-Sunnah*. Al-Matb'ah al-Salafiyyah, 1930, p. 10.
21. Ibn Hanbal. *Kitaab*, p. 7.
22. Ibn Hanbal. *Kitaab*, p. 95.
23. Ibn Taymiyyah, Taqi al-Deen Ahmad. *Al-Sarim al-Maslool ala Shatim al-Rasool*. Al-Ramadi, 1997. It is of interest to note that this book was republished by the Saudi National Guard in 1983 during the

height of Saudi intensity in spreading the Wahhabi sect around the world. As of June 2018, the book was viewed more than 20,480 times on waqfeya.com.
24. Ibn Taymiyyah. *Al-Sarim,* p. 46 (Saudi National Guard edition). Ibn Taymiyyah, Taqi al-Deen Ahmad. *Al-Sarim al-Maslool ala Shatim al-Rasool.* Vol. 2, 2nd ed., Dar al-Tawsweeq al-Duwliyya, 2007, p. 121.
25. Ibn Taymiyyah. *Al-Sarim,* p. 123 (Dar al-Tasweeq al-Duwaliyya ed.)
26. Al-Khamis, Muhammad ibn Abdulrahman. *Etiqaad al-A'imma al-Arba'ah, abi Hanifa wa Malik wa al-Shafi'i wa Ahmed.* Dar al-Ismah, 1992, p. 12.
27. Al-Khamis. *Etiqaad,* p. 29.
28. Al-Shafi'i, Muhammad ibn Idris. *Kitaab al-Umm.* Vol. 2, Dar al-Wafa, 2001, p. 564.
29. Ibn Taymiyyah. *al-Sarim,* p. 34, (Saudi National Guard edition).
30. Ibn Taymiyyah. *al-Sarim,* p. 34, (Saudi National Guard edition).
31. Michot, Yahya. "Ibn Taymiyyah's 'New Mardin Fatwa'. Is genetically modified Islam (GMI) carcinogenic? *The Muslim World,* Hartford Seminary, Blackwell Publishing Ltd., 2011.
32. Sahih al-Bukhari, Kitaab al-Hudood.
33. Al-Shafi'i, Muhammad ibn Idrisa. *Kitaab al-Umm.* Vol. 5, Dar al-Wafa, 2001, p. 405.
34. Providing the rationale or the "*hikmah*" (wisdom) behind Islamic rulings is a common practice amongst Muslim clergy. All these rulings are merely extrapolation and guesswork that provide no link to either the Mushaf or Hadith. By these *hikmah* opinions, the clergy in effect play the roles of psychologists, medical doctors, economists, sociologists, etc.
35. The letter ط in يُعْطُو is one of the most difficult to transliterate. See https://en.wikipedia.org/wiki/Teth. Accessed 17 March 2019.
36. Accents in Arabic are critical in understanding the meaning of words. For a brief introduction on the use of these accents, see http://www.arabion.net/lesson4.html. Accessed 2 June 2019.
37. Cahen, Cl., Inalcik, Halil and Hardy, P. "Djizya". *Encyclopaedia of Islam,* edited by P. Bearman, Th. Bianquis, C.E. Bosworth, E. van Donzel, and W.P. Heinrichs. 2nd ed., Accessed 29 August 2016. http://ezproxy-prd.bodleian.ox.ac.uk:2066/10.1163/1573-3912_islam_COM_0192 First published online: 2012 First print edition: ISBN: 9789004161214, 1960-2007.
38. To circumvent the system of *jizya* as historically understood amongst virtually all Muslim schools of jurisprudence and sects, some Muslim

clergy, especially from the Shia sects, devised the concept of *musala'ha* (reconciliation) with non-Muslims. This concept stipulates that during peacetime, the *jizya* is no longer applicable.

39. Shahrour, Muhammed. *Al-Kitaab wa al-Qur'aan: Ro'ya Jadeedah.* Dar al-Saqi, 2011, p. 538.
40. Sahih al-Bukhari, Kitaab al-Hudood, no. 6841.
41. It is noteworthy that the penal code in the Kingdom of Saudi Arabia, a country that upholds the "Islamic" Sharia, does not differentiate between Muslims and non-Muslims when exacting "Islamic" punishments.
42. Sahih al-Bukhari, Kitaab al-Shuroot, no. 2724.
43. Fatoohi, Louay. *Abrogation in the Qur'an and Islamic Law.* Routledge, 2013, pp. 156-160.
44. The word bizarre is used instead of strange since strange (*ghareeb*) is one of the classifications of Hadith. It is difficult to ascertain if all of the hadiths in Sahih al-Bukhari were included in the Sahih by al-Bukhari himself or were added years after his death. Ilal, Rachid. *Sahih al-Bukhari: Nihayat Ustoora.* Dar al-Watan, 2017. This book is arguably the first to question the origin of Sahih al-Bukhari and to highlight the availability of different versions none of which could be traced to al-Bukhari himself.
45. Sahih al-Bukhari, Kitaab Manaqib al-Ansar, no. 3849.
46. The Torah prescribes stoning for a variety of offenses different from sexual offenses. Stoning was practiced by the Yazidi sect in Iraq http://en.wikipedia.org/wiki/Murder_of_Du%27a_Khalil_Aswad. Accessed 17 March 2019.
47. Sahih al-Bukhari, Kitaab Istitaabat al-Murtudeen wa al-Mu'aaneedeen wa Kitaluhum.
48. www.sunnah.com translated the last phrase as 'Whoever changed his Islamic religion, then kill him.'
49. Al-Razi, abu Jafar. *Al-Kafi.* 3rd ed., vol. 7, Dar al-Hadith, 1972, p. 257. Al-Tusi, abu Ja'far Muhammad ibn Hasan. *Tahdhib al-Ahkaam.* Vol. 10, Dar al-Ta'aaruf, [n.d.], p. 136.
50. Al-Tusi. *Tahdhib*, Vol. 10, p.139.
51. Sahih al-Bukhari, Kitaab Istitaabat al-Murtudeen wa al-Mu'aaneedeen wa Kitaluhum.
52. See Saleh al-Fuzan's opinion on the punishment for apostasy, and in particular his interpretation of apostasy hadiths. Al-Fuzan was a member of the Grand Scholars Committee, Kingdom of Saudi Arabia, therefore, his opinion, most likely, reflects the opinions of the religious and political establishments at least at the time the opinion

53. Ibn Taymiyyah, *al-Sarim*.
54. See M2:27, 3:127, 5:38, 6:45, 7:72, 8:7, 9:121, 13:25, 15:66, 22:15, 27:32, 29:29, 56:33, 59:5 and 69:46.
55. See M2:166, 5:33, 6:94, 7:124, 7:160, 7:168, 9:110, 12:31, 12:50, 13:31, 20:71, 21:93, 22:19, 23:53, 26:49, 47:15 and 47:22. M13:31 presents an apparent deviation from the rest in that the object for *qatta'ah* is *ardh* (earth). However, Muslim scholars have differed widely on the plural of earth. Based on M65:12, the plural of *ardh* has to be also *ardh*.
56. http://www.cnn.com/2013/03/13/world/meast/saudi-executions-beheading/index.html. Accessed 17 March 2019.
57. Al-Ahmadi, Abdullah ibn Salman. *Al-Masa'el wa al-Rasa'el*. Vol. 2, Dar Taybeh, 1991, p. 5, 12.
58. Sahih al-Bukhari, Kitaab al-Salah, no. 511.
59. In Kitaab al-Haidh, a chapter completely dedicated to menstruation in Sahih al-Bukhari, one finds some hadiths prohibiting women from prayers during menstruation while others giving them full permission — a case of extreme contradiction.

(Note: item 52 continues at top: was made. https://ar.islamway.net/fatwa/5384/من-بدل-دينه-فاقتلوه. Accessed 17 March 2019.)

5

GUIDANCE OR MAGIC?

إِنَّ اللَّهَ وَمَلَائِكَتَهُ يُصَلُّونَ عَلَى النَّبِيِّ ۚ يَا أَيُّهَا الَّذِينَ آمَنُوا صَلُّوا عَلَيْهِ وَسَلِّمُوا تَسْلِيمًا

Indeed, Allah and His Angels *yusalloona* on the Prophet, O you who have believed *salloo* on him and *sallimoo tasleemah*.

M33:56

THE ILLUSION OF INCANTATIONS

An outstanding feature of the Mushaf is its liberal approach towards thought and its advocacy of extreme critical thinking. The Mushaf does not inhibit or limit the interrogative capability of the mind or absolute curiosity. According to the Mushaf, there are no red lines to inquiry. Allah himself declared in M33:53

[and Allah is not shy from the truth.] Challenging anything is not only not forbidden, but strongly encouraged as the Mushaf repeatedly entices humanity to reflect, travel, think, ponder, inquire, analyze, synthesize, and question all through the use of various functions of the brain. There is no other bodily organ that can be used for all of these functions. Based on the Mushaf and its repeated commands for contemplation, for intellectual analysis and for intellectual synthesis, it is not surprising that reasoning is deeply respected in Islam. The Mushaf recognizes the importance of the intellectual faculty to the degree that it considered those who possess sciences and understanding as witnesses to the oneness of Allah (see M3:18). Yet, the majority of Muslims continue to brush aside one of the primary objectives of the Mushaf, that of guidance, and instead consider it a book of magic and mystery. For example, many Muslims believe that the utterance of a certain verse seventy times daily provides a shield from hellfire or it may net the reciter specific reward in the hereafter or even forgiveness from a week or a year's worth of sins. Another example is the belief that repeating a certain verse a specific number of times before prayer will cleanse all sins encumbered in that day, and there are many other variants on the same theme. All of these claims of rewards or sins-annihilation exercises come from suspect reports attributed to the Prophet. Not surprisingly, none of these reports have any connection to the Mushaf since they contradict its foundational principles: good deeds, justice, fairness and accountability.

Despite the dramatic evolution of human knowledge and scientific achievements, there is insistence by the vast majority of Muslims on using the Mushaf as a form of magic. To illustrate this, take for instance a phrase that is repeated every day by almost all Muslims on Earth, that of the *salawaat*. Whenever the name of Prophet Muhammad is invoked, Muslims immediately utter, preferably loudly, the *salawaat*. The *salawaat* is typically translated as offering praise and blessings to or on the Prophet Muhammad (not clear which proposition to use since the meaning of *salawaat* is not clear in the first place). The utterance of the *salawaat* typically takes the following form: *Allahmua salli wa'sallim ala sayyduna Muhammad* (May Allah *salli* and *sallim* on our Master Muhammad). I had the opportunity to ask many Muslims from around the world, Shias and Sunnis, what the purpose of invoking such praise and blessings is. Some suggested that the intent is the need to offer blessings on the Prophet. Others believed or suggested that by invoking the *salawaat*, the Muslims ask Allah to offer his blessings and peace on the Prophet. Others had no answer at all but to believe or assume that it is simply a good and virtuous thing to do, and, of course, the virtuous things will net the Muslim plenty of *ajr* (rewards). Many Muslims also believe that the *salawaat* grants the believer a reward in the hereafter or

Guidance or Magic

grants him the privilege to qualify for Prophet Muhammad's intercession (*shafaa'at*) on the Day of Accountability. Yet, many others invoke the *salawaat* as an incantation that provides protection from evil eyes. One wonders why there is no common understanding of a phrase that Muslims throughout history invoke endlessly.

To find the connection between *salawaat* on the Prophet and the Mushaf, we turn to M33:56

إِنَّ اللَّهَ وَمَلَائِكَتَهُ يُصَلُّونَ عَلَى النَّبِيِّ يَا أَيُّهَا الَّذِينَ آمَنُوا صَلُّوا عَلَيْهِ وَسَلِّمُوا تَسْلِيمًا

Let us consider three popular English translations. Sahih International gives: [Indeed, Allah confers blessing upon the Prophet, and His Angels (ask Him to do so). O you who have believed, ask (Allah to confer) blessing upon him and ask (Allah to grant him) peace.] Muhsin Khan translates the same verse to: [Allah sends His *salaat* (Graces, Honours, Blessings, Mercy, etc.) on the Prophet (Muhammad SAW) and also His Angels too (ask Allah to bless and forgive him). O you who believe! Send your *salaat* on (ask Allah to bless) him (Muhammad SAW), and (you should) greet (salute) him with the Islamic way of greeting (salutation, i.e., asaalaam u'alaikum).] Pickthall gives: [Lo! Allah and His Angels shower blessings on the Prophet. O ye who believe! Ask blessings on him and salute him with a worthy salutation.] While Ghali gives: [Surely Allah and His Angels shower Serenity (Literally: shower prayers) on the Prophet. O you who have believed, pray for (benediction on) him, and submit in full submission.][1] It should be kept in mind that the Mushaf translations are essentially translations of Mushaf interpretations provided by famous exegetes such as ibn Kathir, al-Qurtubi, al-Tabari, or others. Now, let us use some basic reasoning to decipher the structure of the original verse, but not its full meaning. Particularly, let us carry out a different type of translation where the structure is kept intact, as much as possible, while key (or controversial) words remain transliterated. This gives: [Allah and His Angels perform the act of *salaat* on the Prophet; O you who have become believers perform the act of *salaat* on him and perform *salam tasleemaa*.] According to the first part of the verse, if we accept that Allah and the Angels do *salaat* on the Prophet, then, according to the same verse, Allah commands the believers to perform the *salaat* act on the Prophet. Again, let us keep the verb *salaat* intact for now without any translation. Accordingly, Muslims interpret performing the act of "*salaat* on" as asking Allah to perform *salaat* knowing very well that the verse started by stating that Allah Himself performs *salaat* on the Prophet. If Allah is already doing something, why beg him endlessly to do it? This strange reasoning can be clarified further by using the following analogy. Person A does a certain act and then asks person B to do the same act. Person B then turns around and asks person A to do the same act. This process is clearly fruitless, if not meaningless.

The belief that simple utterance of Mushaf verses or "recommended" phrases can help achieve ultimate salvation in the hereafter reaffirms the predominant view that the Mushaf is a book of supernatural powers rather than a book of guidance. It is hard to imagine any benefit a chemistry student would gain from the utterance of a sentence in a chemistry book without understanding its meaning, let alone uttering the same sentence seventy times.

The belief in the power of the repetition of words finds no place in the Mushaf but in numerous hadiths. There are too many to list but a representative example is one in Sunan abu Dawood:

> Whoever recites ten *aayaat* in *qiyaam* will not be recorded as one of the forgetful. Whoever recites a hundred *aayaat* in *qiyaam* will be recorded as one of the devout, and whoever recites a thousand *aayaat* in *qiyaam* will be recorded as one of the *muqantareen* (those who pile up good deeds).

Most Muslims believe that reciting specific verses of the Mushaf also yields supernatural benefits. According to Sahih al-Bukhari:[2]

> A man was reciting *surah* al-Kahf and his horse was tied with two ropes besides him. A cloud came down and spread over that man, and it kept on coming closer and closer to him till his horse started jumping (as if afraid of something). When it was morning, the man came to the Prophet, and told him of that experience. The Prophet said, "That was *sakina* (tranquility) which descended because of (the recitation of) the Mushaf."

and[3]

> Allah's Messenger said, "Whoever says, subhan Allah wa bihamdihi, one hundred times a day, will be forgiven all his sins even if they were as much as the foam of the sea."

This is only a sample of some of the hadiths that speak about miracles happening not only to the Prophet but to ordinary people who simply recite parts of the Mushaf. In fact, the concept of a miracle was transmuted into other forms of supernatural activity that have the effect of miracles, but to lessen their psychological effect (and possibly not to infringe on Prophetic privileges), it was repackaged under different mechanisms such as *ruqiyah*. *Ruqiyah* is a type of incantation that includes verses from the Mushaf mixed with supplication intended to either protect or cure the person upon whom the *ruqiyah* is administered. No reference to *ruqiyah* can be found in the Mushaf but only in Hadith. A prominent and illustrative example is the following hadith in Sahih al-Bukhari:[4]

> It was narrated that abu Sa'eed said: "A group of the companions of Prophet set out on a journey and traveled until they stopped in (the land of) one of the Arab tribes. They asked them for hospitality but they refused to welcome them. The chief of that tribe was stung by a scorpion and they tried everything but nothing helped them. Some of them said, 'Why don't you go to those people who are camped (near us), maybe you will find something with them.' So they went to them and said, 'O people, our chief has been stung by a scorpion and we have tried everything but nothing helped him. Can any of you do anything?' One of them said, 'Yes, by Allah, I will recite ruqiyah for him, but by Allah we asked you for hospitality and you did not welcome us, so I will not recite ruqiyah for you until you give us something in return.' Then they agreed upon a flock of sheep.' Then he went and spat drily and recited over him Al-hamdu Lillaahi Rabb il-'Aalameen [*surah* al-Fatiha]. (The chief) got up as if he was released from a chain and started walking, and there were no signs of sickness on him. They paid them what they agreed to pay. Some of them then suggested to divide their earnings among themselves, but the one who performed the ruqiyah said, 'Do not divide them until we go to the Prophet and tell him what happened, then wait and see what he tells us to do.' So they went to the Messenger of Allah (peace and blessings of Allah be upon him) and told him what had happened. The Messenger of Allah (peace and blessings of Allah be upon him) asked, 'How did you know that it (al-Faatihah) is a ruqiyah?' Then he added, 'You have done the right thing. Share out (the flock of sheep) and give me a share too.' And the Messenger of Allah smiled.

This hadith has several problems that suggest it is a forgery. First, the hadith projects the Prophet as cunning and greedy whereas the Mushaf speaks of a Muhammad as having high and noble manners. Second, the hadith, if true, would have introduced a cure for snake and scorpion bites. One wonders why hospitals around the world have not established special wards staffed with Muslims available to read the *Fatiha* (first chapter of the Mushaf) on victims of venomous bites, if not universally, at least in Muslim countries, especially for those who consider the utterance of the Prophet Muhammad as a divine revelation.

INFATUATION WITH THE SUPERNATURAL

The Mushaf is a book that encourages the limitless use of intellectual faculties. The Mushaf does not even shy away from contemplating the nature of Allah, specifically in M42:11 which unequivocally states that there is nothing like Him. This verse by itself can lead the believer to an infinite journey of wonders and intellectual pursuits that have no boundaries. The Mushaf does not establish any red lines for inquiry, contemplation, pondering, excelling in science, reflection and searching. At some point in Muslim history, the Mushaf, a book that was intended to be a guidance, was transformed into a book of psychologically comforting incantations. The Mushaf defines itself as a book of guidance not only for the few, the privileged, the elite, but for all humanity, even for those who do not believe in the prophecy of Muhammad (see M2:185 in particular). Considering the enormous social, political and economic relevance of the Mushaf, and particularly its power to affect social transformation, one wonders if there were deliberate and systematic efforts throughout Muslim history to divert Muslims from a doctrine that can empower them.

The Mushaf does not claim to undo the physical and non-physical laws of the universe for the sake of someone who would happen to read one of its chapters, or to create new physical laws to please the believers, irrespective of their virtue. Subversion of the laws of the universe under the guise of Allah's will is essentially a subversion of the core message of the Mushaf. The Mushaf was revealed to help humanity fully realize and adjust to reality and truth rather than to skew the complex laws of nature to humans' fluctuating dispositions. Islam came to synchronize the life of humans with nature.

The core of the message of Islam is to distinguish between illusion or fantasy and reality or truth, which the Mushaf describes as *haqq*. Of course, the Muslims' consideration of the Mushaf as a book of healing for all ailments with metaphysical power is not exclusive to the Mushaf but also to all other doctrines that have evolved to be considered as representing Islam. The Mushaf emphasizes, emphatically and repeatedly, the importance of the dialectic between *batil* (illusion/fantasy/myth) and *haqq* (truth/reality/fact). The dialectic of wrong versus right is not the main concern of the Mushaf. The vast majority of Muslim scholarship has emphasized the latter and negated the former.

The dialectic of *batil* versus *haqq* grounds the Mushaf in reality that does not favor Muslims for simply "believing" while doing the wrong thing or to disfavor a "non-believer" for doing the right thing. The metrics of the Mushaf are firmly rooted in acceptance and understanding the *haqq* versus *batil* dialectic. This requires a firm understanding of the relationship between cause and effect. The belief in chaos or order does not negate the cause-effect relationship that is repeatedly and strongly emphasized in the Mushaf. Even what appears to someone at a specific time in history to be a miracle follows a cause-effect relationship. The Mushaf stories of some of the battles the Prophet participated in describe a direct cause-effect process that tipped the battles' outcome in favor of the Prophet's camp through direct intervention of invisible soldiers, not any magical intervention. Today, invisibility and cloaking are the topics of engineering and science and no longer considered as supernatural.

Instead of focusing on *haqq* and recognizing what *batil* is, the Muslims sought the supernatural or illusion to strengthen their faith. In light of dismissing the laws of the universe, and in particular severe hostility to the material world, a heavy dose of illusion along with the convenient concept of the miracle were needed to buttress the faith. The subliminal competition with Christians whose Prophet had magnificent miracles cannot be overlooked either.

Muslims have been, and continue to be, infatuated with the supernatural, from believing in the splitting of the moon story to mysterious surgeries performed on Prophet Muhammad that, according to some accounts, were performed with surgical instruments made of gold, while other accounts claimed that water sprung from the Prophet's fingers in a brazen contradiction to M17:90-93 that categorically deny such occurrence or possibility.[5] Of course, there is that quick retort if one were to question these alleged miracles: "Allah is capable of doing anything he wishes", which is a common interpretation of the Mushaf phrase *kun fayakoon* (be and it is).

Anything that denies reason and common sense had been institutionalized into the thought process of the average Muslim as if it were a deliberate effort to relegate Muslims to complete irrelevance or mummified societies living in a dimension of irrelevance.

Muslims, rather than the so-called "infidels", are responsible for changing the meaning of the Mushaf's words to fit a peculiar conceived relationship between humans and Allah. As an example, consider M2:186

وَإِذَا سَأَلَكَ عِبَادِي عَنِّي فَإِنِّي قَرِيبٌ أُجِيبُ دَعْوَةَ الدَّاعِ إِذَا دَعَانِ فَلْيَسْتَجِيبُوا لِي وَلْيُؤْمِنُوا بِي لَعَلَّهُمْ يَرْشُدُونَ

[And if my worshipers ask you about Me, I am close by and will fulfill the *duaa* of the one who makes *duaa;* then they should answer towards Me and have *imaan* in Me lest they become righteous.] Muslims invoke this verse widely to stress the benefit of *duaa*. The most common translation of *duaa* is praying to Allah for happiness, prosperity, health, contentment, or whatever the need might be. If this translation of *duaa* is correct, the verse clearly indicates that Allah will answer the prayer of the worshiper no matter the request. After all, Allah is either serious or joking. The understanding that Allah can and should answer the *duaa* neither makes sense nor finds validation in reality. Take the case of two students, Saleh and Taleh. Saleh studied very hard for the chemistry exam while Taleh wasted his time playing videogames. The night of the exam, Taleh called his pious mother to pray for him that he may achieve a good score. Should we expect Allah to answer the prayers of the pious and deeply religious mother? Taleh did not study for the exam and deserved to fail the course. Saleh, irrespective of his piety or that of his mother, studied studiously and deserved to pass. Would Allah interfere unjustly to infuse the knowledge of chemistry into Taleh's brain the night of the exam simply because of the *duaa* of his highly pious mother? If *duaa* means request, then according to the Mushaf, Allah answers all requests. But there is a problem with answering such a request in the example above; it simply violates the principles of justice that Allah upholds everywhere else in the Mushaf.

M2:186 is unconditional and absolute implying that there are no preconditions for accepting *duaa*. The common understanding of the meaning of *duaa* as "request" leads to contradictions. Depending on the context, a large number of verses show that *duaa* could also mean "to call for", "to call upon", or "invite to" (see for example M2:221, 2:26, 3:23, 3:61, 8:24, 10:25, 12:108 and many others). It is more likely that *duaa* in M2:186 is an invitation rather than a request. M2:186 would then imply that if a worshipper were to call Allah into his life, Allah would be willing to oblige. It is an assurance from Allah that he is ready to enter anyone's life if the request is initiated in a sincere way. This interpretation is not only valid linguistically but also avoids violating the Mushaf principles.

Muslim clergy have struggled to understand this verse and typically invoke a host of Prophetic and non-Prophetic hadiths that claim that Allah indeed answers the *duaa*/request, but in ways that humans are not necessarily capable of understanding. Others claim that Allah might answer the *duaa*/request not in this life but in the hereafter. The proponents of the "request" interpretation of the word *duaa* have created a nested labyrinth of narratives too convoluted to discuss here. The underlying message and problem with the conventional and dominant interpretation of M2:186 is to subvert the cause-effect relationship and the laws of the universe. The interpretation provided here, however, does not negate the possibility that Allah may intervene to affect the course of an event. The point to be emphasized here is that Allah's intervention does not deviate from His laws. What triggers an intervention needs to be understood based on the Mushaf text.

Historical narratives indicate that throughout the past fourteen centuries, Muslim scholars who advocated for the study and importance of science and philosophy, and the use of both to understand the Mushaf, were fiercely and violently marginalized. Today, scholars who dare step outside the norms established by the Muslim clergy are ostracized if not accused of outright apostasy. One illustrative example is that of Mustafa Mahmoud (d. 1430/2009). Mahmoud is considered one of the most prominent Arab intellectuals of the 20th Century. In the eye of the established Muslim clergy, Mahmoud's biggest sin and fall from grace was a book he wrote a few years before his death entitled *Shafa'a: an Attempt to Understand the Ancient Disagreement between its Opponents and Proponents*. If a scholar as prolific, popular and highly respected as Mahmoud was dealt with in such a caustic manner, one can imagine the fate of others who dare venture outside the norms established by al-Shafi'i, ibn Hanbal, ibn Malik, abu Hanifa, ibn Taymiyyah, al-Nawawi, ibn Kathir and their disciples and followers.

Many Muslims today appear to subliminally negate the fact that the universe is governed by very strict and precise laws. This attitude has created a defensive approach to philosophical and science-based movements that attempted to explain and understand society, civilizations, the universe and creation. Muslim scholars who eventually prevailed in terms of their opinions and philosophies such as ibn Hanbal, ibn Taymiyyah and later ibn Kathir, were staunch and violent opponents of such movements. These and many other Muslim scholars turned a blind eye to the order and precision of the universe and all its laws as described in the Mushaf.

Numerous Muslim classical scholars and clergy interpreted philosophy and the scientific explanations of society and nature as anti-religion. The material world became synonymous with atheism and transgression against Islam. It is precisely the material world, however, that Allah used for signs and arguments to make people focus on the reality that they see all around them. It is specifically the material world that Allah refers to as his *aayaat* (see Chapter 7). Allah simply used the material world to convince humans of the validity of the Message and Messenger instead of using mysterious non-physical phenomena or even philosophical arguments or ideas. After all, Muslims believe that Allah created the material world, so where is the problem when using it to demonstrate truths? It cannot be a sheer coincidence that the decline of the "Golden Age" of Islam followed the emergence of new doctrines that pushed the Muslims away from reality, and especially the material world.

The overwhelming majority of Muslim scholars dismiss evolution theories as anti-Islamic. In fact, a Muslim can easily be dismissed as *kafir* simply for entertaining the thought that humans evolved through complex processes and over time.[6] Many Muslims seek comfort in finding commonalities with Christian fundamentalists who also reject evolutionary theories despite fundamental disagreement on specific truths that are far more important than whether or not man evolved or popped out of nowhere. The common thread between these two camps, the Christians and Muslims who reject evolution is the severity of their opposition to reason, science and denial of facts or truths. Let us consider some of the Mushaf's verses that mention creation, particularly M23:14, which outlines a process of *khalq* (creation):

ثُمَّ خَلَقْنَا النُّطْفَةَ عَلَقَةً فَخَلَقْنَا الْعَلَقَةَ مُضْغَةً فَخَلَقْنَا الْمُضْغَةَ عِظَامًا فَكَسَوْنَا الْعِظَامَ لَحْمًا ثُمَّ أَنشَأْنَاهُ خَلْقًا آخَرَ فَتَبَارَكَ اللَّهُ أَحْسَنُ الْخَالِقِينَ

[Thereafter We created the zygote into a clot/embryo from which We created the clot into a chewed up morsel, from which We created the chewed up morsel into bones, from which We dressed the bones with flesh; then We brought him into being as another creation, *fatabarak Allah*, The best of creators.] One can start to understand the meaning of *khalq* based on common usage and modern Arabic dictionaries, but such meanings or interpretations can change with time. M23:14 describes a process of development that starts from the zygote and ends with the infant. To the biologist, this process is well understood in its most minute details to the point that it is taught in first-year university biology courses. In the Mushaf, however, this precise biological process is referred to as *khalq*. The Mushaf does not use *khalq* to imply something popping out from nowhere or from nothingness. According to the Mushaf, *khalq* refers to an ongoing process of development rather than a transformation (*ja'ala*). It is unrealistic and wrong to interpret *khalaqa* in M23:14 as if Allah is present in every delivery room, delivering babies from their mothers' wombs. Could it be that the Arab's use of the word *khalaqa* is incorrect, at least as far as modern Arabic is concerned?

While certainly we have the freedom to use any word to describe whatever phenomenon or act we wish, the Mushaf provides what appears to be an absolute reference or a standard that is constant with time. A word as *khalaqa* would then be understood based on its context and the connection of the context to reality. Alternatively, the words of the Mushaf would have mercurial meanings that describe a temporal perception rather than truths (*haqq*). The concept of a "standard" is not a luxury and a preference but essential if one is to make an association with reality.

Derivatives of the verb *khalaqa* appeared 260 times in the Mushaf. The Mushaf uses "*khalaqa* from" in several verses, while using the "beginning of *khalq*" in others. Therefore, most likely, *khalq* designates a process or a development that takes place over time rather than a mysterious act of popping out from nothingness. When such reasoning is shared with many Muslims, they express discomfort as if some powers are taken away from Allah. These Muslims often invoke the *kun fayakoon* phrase that appeared in the Mushaf several times. This phrase is typically translated as "be and it is" and is used to imply that the evolution and development of species sharply contradicts Allah's process of "creation". The Muslims' *kun fayakoon*-based defense, or rather dismissal of all evolution theories is, in many ways, similar to the reaction of the Catholic Church to evolution theories.

The Mushaf neither contradicts nor denies the theories of evolution and other theories that attempt to provide a clue to the origin of humankind. To emphasize, the Mushaf provided neither a theory nor an answer for how humankind evolved; instead, however, it provided an encouragement to spend efforts and specifically, to travel and search to see firsthand how Allah initiated the creation as exemplified by M29:20

قُلْ سِيرُوا فِي الْأَرْضِ فَانظُرُوا كَيْفَ بَدَأَ الْخَلْقَ ثُمَّ اللَّهُ يُنشِئُ النَّشْأَةَ الْآخِرَةَ إِنَّ اللَّهَ عَلَى كُلِّ شَيْءٍ قَدِيرٌ

[Declare/promulgate/proclaim: move in earth and become aware how the *khalq* has started, then Allah brings into being the last *nash'ah* (evolution) and Allah has power over all things.]

The Mushaf verses that mention Adam are typically invoked, especially by Muslims, in discussions related to creation. The Mushaf leaves no doubt that there is a clear distinction between the beginning or "creation" of Adam and the beginning of creation. The problem, or the apparent schism between evolution theorists and creationists lies in not differentiating between the humans of today and those who lived hundreds or possibly millions of years ago. The Mushaf uses two distinct words to shed light on this important subject: *bashar* and *insaan*. The Mushaf uses *bashar* to emphasize the biological form and function of humans. The physiological side of humans is the *bashar* and the psychological side is the *insaan*. This critical distinction could help towards understanding the apparent disconnect between evolution theories and the emergence of Adam as a highly evolved species who underwent a divine "reprogramming", or injecting into the homo heidelbergensis some software that transformed him into "the wise man".[7] The analogy to the computer chip cannot be overlooked. It took hundreds of years to enable the development of the computer chip's hardware, but it was only the software that brought the computer to "life". (The emphasis is on the enabling aspect rather than the development.)

This transformation could explain the missing link in the evolution theories that pertain to humankind.[8] The evolution theories represent a remarkable scholarly achievement, but the so-called missing link was the transformation from a man or a woman having a physiological dimension only to the full human. It may be too difficult to prove this missing link using physical sciences.

Evolution theories were not the brainchild of Darwin or 18th Century England. In fact, Darwin was not the first to propose evolutionary theories. Interestingly, a host of Muslim scholars discussed evolution prior to the publication of Darwin's *On the Origin of Species* in 1859. Here is an excerpt from ibn Khaldun's *al-Muqaddima*:[9]

> The animal world then widens, its species become numerous, and, in a gradual process of creation, it finally leads to man, who is able to think and to reflect. The higher stage of man is reached from the world of the monkeys, in which both sagacity and perception are found, but which has not reached the stage of actual reflection and thinking. At this point we come to the first stage of man after (the world of monkeys). This is as far as our (physical) observation extends.

Ibn Khaldun stretched evolutionary concepts to imply that man evolved from monkeys, which is a significant departure from the essence of modern evolution theories. Al-Jahiz (d. 255/869), al-Farabi (d. 339/950), al-Mas'udi (d. 346/957), al-Khazini (d. 424/1130), ibn Miskawaih (d. 423/1032), ibn Sina (d. 428/1037), al-Biruni (d. 442/1050), Raghib Isfahani (d. 501/1108), ibn Bajah (d. 532/1138), ibn Tufayl (d. 582/1186), ibn Rushd (d. 594/1198), Jalal al-Deen Rumi (d. 671/1273), ibn Khaldun (d. 808/1406) and other notable Muslim scholars all found no cause for alarm in evolution theories.[10] Most likely, evolutionary theories were accepted by leading Muslim scholars and scientists since their science and scholarship enabled them to realize that those theories were important to understand the beginning of the creation and especially that the theories posed no contradictions to the Mushaf. Other Muslim scholars, such as ibn Taymiyyah, were not equipped or even capable of making a connection between specific Mushaf verses and reality. For instance, ibn Taymiyyah, al-Jawziyya and ibn Kathir, just to name few prominent Muslim scholars, hardly had any training or experience in the physical sciences. Based on the fact that those scholars were deficient in scientific training or lacking any interest in science (based on the historical records that have reached us), it appears that they were simply not interested in theories of evolution or theories related to how the creation started despite the clarity of M29:20 (see above). Alternatively, possibly those Muslim scholars were not interested in searching for how the creation began because of the overbearing *kun fayakoon* mantra.

It is not an exaggeration to state that for evolution theorists, the Mushaf is a trove of treasures, from revelations related to the realization by humankind of the benefits of iron (M57:25) to revelations that hint at the first domestication of livestock and humans' early settlements (see M39:6 as an example).

The magnitude of hostility exhibited by early Salafi Muslim scholars and clergy and the broader sects that followed Ahl al-Sunnah wa al-Jama'ah towards philosophers and scientists was extremely intense. The triumphalism of the ibn Taymiyyah camp, however, exaggerated the breadth of the hostility. Different reasons could have contributed to viewing philosophy and reason with suspicion, such as challenge to the authority of jurisprudents and Muslim clergy in general who thought that their expertise was nearly universal, extending to science and practically everything the pious Muslim needs to know from gynecology to cosmology and everything in between. Nevertheless, philosophical and scientific challenges to the *kun fayakoon* theories do not warrant extreme hatred and marginalization unless, possibly, it indirectly infringed on privilege. Absent direct cause-effect data, the claims that are made here are mere conjectures. However, the severe confrontation between scientists and Muslim clergy today and the natural challenge to privilege that it carries are all indications of what could have happened in yesteryears.

Personification of Allah

While most Christians accepted the concept that the Lord can be a person, many Muslims did something similar in essence but without using similar terminology and without any explicit canonized doctrines. If personification means attributing physical qualities to Allah, then key Muslim clergy essentially condoned it. The religious literature compiled by leading early Muslim scholars and clergy makes a compelling case that Allah was personified or objectified. All this led to affecting how Muslims perceived Allah, the creation, the universe and everything in between, including how the Mushaf is interpreted. What scholars of religion, whether Muslims, Christians, or Jews, typically refer to as "theology", and which is mostly kept as the exclusive domain of the "scholars" that relate to the nature of God, is extremely critical to developing the worldview that the religion advocates in the first place. If there is a mix-up, confusion, or even sheer ignorance in comprehending the most fundamental (i.e., "theology") of religion then one would expect catastrophic consequences in terms of understanding and significant confusion later on.

One cannot place a specific period when the personification narratives started appearing in Muslims' history. Nevertheless, the objectification of Allah can be found in the writings of the most respected scholars of Islam. Take for instance a hadith that claims that Allah packs the *kuffar* in hellfire with his foot:[11]

> The Prophet said, "Paradise and Hell (Fire) quarreled in the presence of their Lord. Paradise said, 'O Lord! What is wrong with me that only the poor and humble people enter me?' Hell (Fire) said, 'I have been favored with the arrogant people.' So Allah said to Paradise, 'You are My Mercy, and said to Hell, You are My Punishment which I inflict upon whom I wish, and I shall fill both of you.'" The Prophet added, "As for Paradise, (it will be filled with good people) because Allah does not wrong any of His created things, and He creates for Hell (Fire) whomever He will, and they will be thrown into it, and it will say thrice, 'Is there any more, till Allah (will put) His Foot over it and it will become full and its sides will come close to each other and it will say, 'Qat! Qat! Qat! (Enough! Enough! Enough!)'".

The interpretation of the word *arsh* (throne) in the *Mushaf* as a physical structure would give the Muslim the impression that Allah has physical attributes. Despite fierce denial by Muslim clergy who champion ibn Kathir's exegeses and Sahih al-Bukhari, both of which contain narratives replete with personal attributes of Allah, such vivid imageries inadvertently direct one's thoughts to connecting human or animal attributes to Allah.

M48:10 includes the phrase *yad Allah fawka aydihum,* which carries the conventional interpretation of "the hands of Allah are above their hands." Some contend that this interpretation is essentially a literal translation but it is not. *Aydihum,* as was discussed in Chapter 4, could imply hands but also capability, ability, power, strength or influence. For emphasis, all are literal rather than metaphorical translations of the word *ayadihum,* therefore, it is inaccurate to refer to those who interpret *ayadihum* as hands as literalists (a common similar mistake is to refer to Salafis as literalists).

There are numerous hadiths depicting Allah placing people in his hands and others placing the entire creation on his fingers.[12] Some bizarre narratives claim that on the Day of Accountability eight incredibly mammoth elks will physically carry Allah's throne.[13] To spice up this narrative and to answer any doubters, the size of the elks were made to equal the distance traveled in one hundred years (not specified whether by foot or horse). Interestingly, if one does the math, the size of this god who will be carried by those eight elks would be the equivalent of an insignificant dot compared to the size of the universe as we know it today. Ibn Hanbal goes even further to depict a god who laughs, who can be seen, who leads people in procession, who descends from one heaven to another, a god who occupies a place, a god who created Adam with his hands, planted the *jannah* (Paradise) with his hand and wrote the Torah with his hand.[14] Ibn Kathir's exegesis takes the lead with such imagery with similar stories such as in his interpretation of M20:8, where Allah is claimed to sit on a chair to attend to the matters of His worshippers. The European Renaissance painting of a god positioned within bright clouds and voluptuous children with wings, presumably Angels, hovering around him is not much different in theme than ibn Kathir's depiction. (Michelangelo used his brush whereas ibn Kathir used his pen.) Both are illustrious of personification that has become very creative, if gone wild.

The debate on the interpretation of the attributes associated with Allah, such as *yad* Allah, raged fiercely amongst early Muslims. Because of the epic destruction of grand libraries at the hands of Mongols and others, not all books of early Muslim scholars reached us. Nevertheless, what has reached us strongly suggests that fierce debates occurred during the first two centuries of Islam on the interpretation of Allah's attributes, debates that have led to lasting confusion amongst Muslims and lasting divisions between them. Names of Allah were used interchangeably with his attributes and no distinction was made between the two.[15]

The four early leading grand jurists believed in the physical attributes of Allah, but merely rejected the resemblance to human attributes. This means that they believed in Allah having a physical hand, but one that is different from the human hand. The essence of the personification of Allah is exemplified by the belief that strong believers will see Allah on the Day of Accountability.[16]

Overall, the dominant Muslim scholars and clergy (who were mostly jurisprudents) of the first two Muslim centuries used the sensuous connotation of Arabic words to describe Allah's attributes in order to transform them onto physical attributes. If one uses the sensuous meaning of a word, he or she cannot necessarily be described as a literalist. Both the sensuous and the non-sensuous meanings are legitimate interpretations of an Arabic word and only the context should determine which interpretation is suitable.

The dramatic confinement of the Arabic vocabulary to a narrow set of acceptable definitions even led to an uncanny interpretation of the word *tasbeeh,* which is typically used to refer to the repetitive utterances of short sentences glorifying Allah, to also encompass acoustical vibration of innate objects.[17] If one were to consider the numerous hadiths that depict the hands, feet, legs and other organs of the personified god, it can be concluded with high likelihood that these hadiths did not penetrate Muslim religious literature accidentally or sporadically. It could have been a deliberate effort dating back to the first and second Muslim centuries to incorporate Christian, Jewish and Greek mythology into Islam in shapes and forms that can find apparent linguistic justification in Islamic religious texts, irrespective of whether these texts are authentic or not. Not all interpretations that were based on personification were nefarious in intent. Many Jews and Christians who embraced Islam must have been influenced by the personification of God that was common in their religious scriptures. Expectedly, such influence helped guide their interpretations of the Mushaf.

The personification could have been the outcome of viewing and considering a book authored by Allah in the same way as a book authored by a human. Allah expresses the truth whereas humans model the truth. Nevertheless, it is difficult to ascertain the circumstances behind the inclusion of bizarre hadiths, but their preponderance cannot be the work of careless or incorrect interpretation of Mushaf verses, especially considering numerous verses that can easily shed light on the meaning of others. The works of ibn Hanbal, ibn Taymiyyah and the collections of ibn Kathir, from his highly regarded exegesis to his *Stories of the Prophets* treatise, cannot be brushed aside as an aberration in methodology. It was argued by several Muslim scholars that the scholars of early years used scholarly methods available then and that could potentially be an explanation, or partial explanation, for their interpretations and conclusions. This argument, however, is difficult to accept considering that no methodologies whatsoever were used except for the cardinal rule of forming a particular interpretation by restating the opinions of earlier Muslims, earlier scholars, companions of the Prophet, and highly respected others. Still, there would have been some scholarly merit in stating the opinions of all these people. The problem, however, is that sectarian influence played a major role in which arguments to include and which to exclude. The scholarly merit of most of these earlier works were very little.

The personification of Allah by prominent Muslim scholars and clergy cannot be dismissed as mere fringe opinions. It had a major impact as the preponderance of narratives, stories and hadiths percolated down the Muslims' minds to shape their perception of the processes behind the development of the universe and of creation. Despite the influence of a body of religious literature by leading jurisprudents and scholars, most Muslims remain deeply uncomfortable with any personification of Allah primarily for religious-theoretical reasons. The practical consequences of Allah's personification and/or objectification, however, were never at the forefront of these concerns. Once the personification develops a foothold in the perception of people, irrespective of their religion, the concept of creation would then be narrowed down to a reflection of what a human being might be able to create with his own hands! This narrows the realm of possibilities dramatically, including evolution theories, and creates the schism between the perceived religion and the true religion.

Naturally, scientists who discovered sub-atomic particles, far-away galaxies and incredibly intricate and complex biological processes that take place over long periods of time, all find it difficult to associate a human-like or a physical creature to the cause behind all of their discoveries while at the same time accepting the "from nothingness" idea. Richard Dawkins, a brilliant modern-day scientist and renowned atheist, despite his hostility to religion, cannot be considered as an antagonist of Islam. On the contrary, he advocates the use of validation and evidence as the core of belief. This makes Dawkins an advocate of the truth. The Mushaf text has not been the reason for his alienation or apparent rejection of Islam but rather a host of myths claimed as part of Islam coupled with a hostile attitude many Muslims have towards truth seekers. Not only would Dawkins be surprised that many Muslims believe the Prophet ascended to heavens to meet Allah using a horse with wings but many other Muslims seem very uncomfortable with a such claim in the first place.

Little did Dawkins know that from only one verse in the Mushaf, namely M17:1, the Muslim mythologists (rather than exegetes) churned numerous narratives that have no basis in reality or religion. The parallels between the Isra-Miraj stories and Greek mythology is striking.[18] In Muslims mythology, the Prophet is claimed to have used a horse with wings (named al-Buraaq) to ascend to the seventh heaven. According to the *kun fayakoon* principle, he could have been transferred to the seventh heaven "just like that" instead of traveling on a bird-horse! The Prophet is also believed to have tied al-Buraaq to the wall next to the Aqsa mosque when he stopped in Jerusalem on his way to the seventh heaven. Again, why was the Prophet concerned that al-Buraaq would go astray when it was sent by Allah specifically for this journey?[19]

Generations of Muslims perceived jurisprudents-turned-clergy who were vehemently anti-science as beacons of light and defenders of Islam. These anti-science crusaders were key instruments in the ideological and scientific decline of the Muslims. Centuries of accumulated misplaced reverence installed an aura of perfectness and infallibility on those scholars. Such excessive reverence helped complete the divorce of the Muslim community from rational thinking.

The effective personification and objectification of Allah by many highly revered Muslim jurists and exegetes have led to difficulties in understanding the complexity of the processes that brought the entire universe to where it is now. The processes of objectification and personification imprisoned the Muslim mind in imagery structured around fear. Massive elks holding the throne of Allah, the confinement of Allah to a physical space, the feet of Allah pushing the disbelievers in hellfire, scary Angels waiting for bad people as they enter hellfire, Angels ready in the graveyard to torture every dead person, and a thin straight road on which all people must walk on the Day of Accountability, are only a few of the imageries based on the selective approach to interpret the Mushaf language by leading Muslim exegetes and clergy (and buttressed by Hadith). The objectification penetrated the subconscious of Muslims to the point that the Mushaf narratives of Adams were framed in a sensuous setting with physical players acting as Allah, Iblis, Adam, and the Angels. The verbs in such narratives were interpreted to imply physical performances. The theory of knowledge expressed in the Mushaf was also framed using sensuous acts and objects. (For example, *allama bi al-qalam* in M96:4 was interpreted as "He taught by means of the pen".[20])

Unwilling to accept the complexity of the human creation, the developments and processes that affect species and physical laws and order, fierce hostility to reason and the cause-effect principle, all led to an equally fierce rejection of science-based ideas that contemplate evolution in physical form and in sociological/societal form. The misconstrued understanding of *kun fayakoon* has obfuscated interest in scientific inquiry. Applying this generalization to Muslims of all ages is clearly unjustified, especially to those cultures and societies that produced al-Bayruni, al-Farabi, al-Khawarizmi, ibn Khaldun, ibn Rushd, and other luminaries. Nevertheless, it is a fair characterization of the mummified Muslim societies of this age. It is much more convenient for a lazy believer to dismiss any need to excel in science by simply invoking the magical powers of "the creation" rather than the Godly powers of creation. Once *kun fayakoon* is invoked, all arguments and sciences become meaningless, if irrelevant. Surprisingly, those who stand behind *kun fayakoon* fail to explain why Allah took six days (irrespective of the equivalence between our days and Allah's days), or six time units to create the heavens and the Earth (or earths) instead of creating them in an instant using the *kun fayakoon* mantra.[21]

The language of personification was also instrumental in framing the interpretation of Allah's will (*mashi'ah*). "If God wills, so it will be", so goes the most common Muslims' response to any inquiry that finds the classical explanation of the Salafis and Ahl al-Sunnah wa al-Jama'ah absurd. Yet, no serious attempts were made to understand what is meant by Allah's will. The two fortresses of resistance to inquiry about the creation and the beginning of the universe were the *kun fayakoon* and Allah's will. With these two instruments of faith, a young graduate of a religious school finds himself fit to debate a seasoned scientist. The scientists would be using every instrument emphasized in the Mushaf to find the truth whereas the young religion "expert", "specialist" or "*alim*" would dynamite any potential inquiry with these fortresses of denial.

Objectification of Allah started with attaching the sensuous attributes of words to describe His attributes. The meaning of Arabic words, just like in any other language, depend on the context. Also, just like English and other languages, the meanings of words can shift over time. The context of words, however, is the most essential in understanding what the words convey. After all, the primary objective of words within a sentence is to convey a concept or a message. Focusing only on the sensuous meaning of the word also led to severe logical incompatibilities with cataclysmic implications, such as attempting to understand from within the Mushaf whether humans have free will or not. Again, the confusion stemmed from the lack of a methodical approach to understanding the Mushaf, a topic that will be discussed in Chapter 6.

Concluding Thoughts

Two important themes in the divine revelation are the separation of *batil* from *haqq* and the concept of suitability of one's deeds to society. During the evolution of the Hadith and Sunnah doctrines—an evolution that occurred under the shadow of empires—the power of faith had to be harnessed to achieve benefits for the ruling elites. Under the new doctrines, the easiest road to salvation and having a chance to compete with the Prophet in entering Paradise became the daily utterance of a few words. Mere utterance of words, the meaning of which Muslims disagree upon, became a substitute for participating in society and doing what is suitable (*saleh*) for humankind. These chants and invocations reached absurd levels to the point that Muslims would repeat a supplication in order that Allah may fulfill a promise that He has already promised to fulfill.[22]

For despotic rulers who could not directly confront the power of Islam, diverting the Muslim masses towards anything that did not threaten their wealth and grip on power was a welcome option. To this end, the Muslim clergy reengineered the new religion to construe participation in "politics" as a "worldly affair," in other words, a distraction from *ajr*-based activities promised to take the faithful directly to the gates of Paradise. A Hadith cottage industry ensued to serve this objective. This led Muslims to seek help, comfort, happiness and even Paradise from and through the unreal and the miraculous. Miracles, however, were no longer confined to the Prophets but found their way to every Muslim through *karamat*, piety, supplication, etc.

The infatuation with the miraculous served to distance Muslims from reality; a few verses from the Mushaf became a cure for scorpion stings. Years of retardation left Muslims with hardly anything to compete with against a more advanced reality-based West except for invoking the miraculous. The supernatural would materialize only if one became devotional and close to Allah through the utterance of phrases and words.

Embracing the supernatural, naturally, diminished interest in the natural and material world, both of which became synonymous with atheism and transgression against Islam. The material world specifically, however, is what Allah uses to validate His divine revelation, not the supernatural, metaphysical, or any particular philosophy.

The personification or objectification of Allah by early Muslim clergy framed the messages and words of the divine revelation to reflect actions that a supernatural human might perform. This problem arose from the image of God conceived by those clergy years before the depiction of Angels, God, Moses, hellfire, heaven, etc. of the European Renaissance. Using the pen rather than the brush, Muslim clergy and founders of Muslim sects created vivid imagery of a god having legs, hands, and eyes. The accumulated effect of this imagery, which also became part of the canonized religion through Hadith, affected the perception of God. Anything attributed to God would, at least subliminally, be attributed to a person-like being. This included actions mentioned in the Mushaf such as creation. Since the Hadith created the perception that Allah is an entity, His creation became synonymous with humankind's creation in the sense of using one's own hands to create something. This personification had most severe effect on understanding the concept of creation in the Mushaf, and consequently created a long lasting schism between scientists and Muslims.

The *khalq* (creation) of Allah is unlike the *khalq* of humans. The Mushaf does not separate creation from evolution. The Mushaf explains that evolution is an essential element of creation while creation embodies evolution.

Guidance or Magic

1. From www.quran.com.
2. Sahih al-Bukhari, Kitaab Fadha'el al-Qur'aan, no. 5011.
3. Sahih al-Bukhari, Kitaab al-Da'aawat, no. 6405
4. Sahih al-Bukhari, Kitaab al-Ijaarah, no. 2276.
5. Ibn Kathir, Hafidh Abi al-Fada'ah Ismail. *Book of Evidences: The Miracles of the Prophet.* Translated by Ali Mwinyi Mziwa and ibn R. Ramadhan, Dar al-Ghad, 2001.
6. Thee topic of evolution came up during a casual conversation with one my uncles. I started explaining that the Mushaf does not rule out some evolution theories. His reaction was swift. He immediately declared my statements as *kufr*, which is typically understood as transgression against Allah.
7. Shahrour, Muhammad. *Al-Qasas al-Qur'aani: Qiraa'ah Mu'aasira.* Vol. 1, Dar al-Saqi, 2010, pp. 251-258.
8. Some Muslim scholars have noticed the importance of differentiating between the words *bashar* and *insaan*. Mohammad Shahrour discussed the so-called missing link more extensively in Shahrour. *Al-Qasas*, pp. 251-270. Muhammad Abdo (d. 1323/1905) also realized the difference between the two.
9. Ibn Khaldun. *Al-Muqaddimah: An Introduction to History* Abridged Edition. Translated by Franz Rosenthal. Abridged and edited by N. J. Dawood. Princeton University Press, 2015.
10. Shah, Muhammad Sultan. *Evolution and Creation.* Society for Interaction of Religion-Science and Technology, 2010.
11. Sahih al-Bukhari, Kitaab al-Tawheed, no. 7449.
12. Al-Jewziyya, ibn Qaiyyem. *Shifa al-Aleel fi al-Qada wa al-Qadar.* Almaktaba Altawfeeqyyah, p. 32. Ibn Hanbal, Ahmed. *Kitaab al-Sunnah.* Vol. 1, al-Matba'ah al-Salafiyyah, 1930.
13. Ibn Kathir. *Tafseer al-Qur'aan al-Azeem.* See his interpretation of M69:17.
14. Ibn Hanbal, Ahmed, *Kitaab al-Sunnah.*
15. Today, many Muslims still cannot recognize or are not interested in realizing the difference between the names of Allah and His attributes. In fact, many, if not the majority, believe that Allah has 99 names. The written works that have reached us were most likely sanctioned by the empires that ruled the Muslims in the first Muslim centuries.

16. Al-Khamis, Muhammad ibn Abdulrahman. *Etiqaad al-A'imma al-Arba'ah abi Hanifa wa Malik wa al-Shafi'i wa Ahmed.* Dar al-Ismah, 1992.
17. Al-Jewziyyah, ibn Qayyem. *Kitaab al-Rooh.* Dar al-Turath, 2003.
18. Sahih al-Bukhari, Kitaab Manaqib al-Ansar.
19. See the debate by Richard Dawkins and Hasan Mahdi: https://www.youtube.com/watch?v=9QZcuwWj1CA. Accessed 1 February 2019.

    Dawkins was surprised how anyone would believe in the mythology of the Isra-Miraj story. Mahdi, however, was adamant that such mythology is part of Islam. The deluge of "religious material" essentially demonstrates how Muslims, and especially many of their intellectuals, can be severely hypnotized to believe in myth and to consider it as part of Islam.
20. Shahrour, Muhammed. *Al-Kitaab wa al-Qur'aan: Ro'ya Jadeedah.* Dar al-Saqi, 2011, p. 319.
21. This interesting perspective was made by my good friend Ali Albishi.
22. Sahih al-Bukhari, Kitaab al-Tafsir.

6

THE MUSHAF

يَا أَيُّهَا النَّاسُ قَدْ جَاءَتْكُم مَّوْعِظَةٌ مِّن رَّبِّكُمْ وَشِفَاءٌ لِّمَا فِي الصُّدُورِ وَهُدًى وَرَحْمَةٌ لِّلْمُؤْمِنِينَ

O you humans, warning and advice have come to you from your lord and cure to what is inside your *sudoor*, and guidance and mercy to the believers.

M10:57

ALLAH'S REVELATION

The Muslims believe that the Mushaf is a book produced, created and revealed by Allah, who originated, transformed and created all truths.[1] These truths include the physical laws with their unwavering uniqueness and precision. Muslims also believe that Allah fashioned and designed (*samma'ma*) all living and non-living things with perfection, including the atom and its sub-atomic particles and galaxies and all the laws that govern their motion and interaction.[2] The Muslims also believe that the creator who designed and created the atom and its nuclear forces with mind-boggling precision is the same One who authored the Mushaf. Using the common denominator that all Muslims agreed upon, namely that the Mushaf is Allah's revelation, the Muslims, therefore, would be expected to approach the Mushaf not in the same manner as when approaching any other book authored by a human.

The Mushaf

The Mushaf is different from any other book; it is different in every respect including form, style, grammar, structure and organization.[3] This does not mean that the Mushaf is only for people with advanced scientific training and sensitivity, but rather to emphasize that the Mushaf needs to be approached with a mindset that realizes that the Mushaf has precision similar to the precision of sub-atomic particles.[4] Such an approach would encourage the Muslims to pause and think about every word of the Mushaf, if not every letter. Believing that the Mushaf is the work of Allah makes one ask about the particular organization of the Mushaf in its existing form, its particular "grammar", its particular division into chapters, the naming of the chapters, the division of each chapter into verses, the division of some sentences into verses, the combination of sentences into one verse, and a host of many other questions that relate not only to the meaning of the text but to its structure. Many questions would then accumulate that would demand answers based on reason while being consistent with reality (truths). Similar to demonstrating, say, the principle of conservation of momentum in sub-atomic particles, demonstrating the validity of certain interpretations of the Mushaf needs rationale and truths. The credibility or reverence of a certain exegete should have no value in establishing the validity of his interpretation any more than Einstein's morality has any relevance to the validity of his relativity theory.

THE MUSHAF-MUSLIMS DIVIDE

The general Muslims' attitude towards the Mushaf had been shaped largely by historic Muslim figures and by what is typically considered as the exegeses of the Mushaf. These perceptions resulted in diverting the bulk of the Muslims mental energy towards material of suspicious origin and questionable authenticity, namely the Hadith and *Asbab al-Nuzool* (circumstances for the Mushaf revelations). Despite regular recitation and unmatched respect of the Mushaf, the divide between the average Muslim and the Mushaf widened with time. Consequently, Muslims found themselves at the whims of myths while trying to defend external attacks (from non-Muslims) and answer internal inquiry (from Muslims) with immense difficulty and with sharp contradiction. These shaky foundations made the religion of Mohammad appear as backward and violent to non-Muslims. For Muslims, deep alienation from their own religion took place because the essence of the exegeses presented the Mushaf, practically speaking, as irrelevant, as will be demonstrated throughout this chapter. The alienation within the Muslim community led to divisions and polarization enhanced and sustained by manufactured doctrines that were loaded with contradictions.

In the confusing labyrinth created by exegetes who mostly provided opinions and stories framed as an interpretation of the Mushaf, the central theme of the revelation was lost and the core message embodied by the Mushaf was altered. This is not to say that the works of exegetes have no value; they do, but mostly as historical records. The supreme goals of Islam of achieving justice, peace and seeking the truth were replaced with dominance, power and illusion (*batil*). The concept of salvation was borrowed from Christianity and repackaged under an "Islamic" garb. The *kalima* (pronouncement of the *shahada*: that there is no deity but Allah and Mohammad is his Messenger) became the key to salvation in a complete contravention of Mushaf injunctions. A seven-word phrase became the dividing line between hellfire and paradise. The Mushaf advocated for the truth, not for the superiority of one race, nation, or "religion" over others. The diversion created by the exegetes curtailed the universality of the Mushaf. The Mushaf was contextualized within an image framed around specific people who lived during a specific period.

Criticizing exegetes should not be construed as delegitimizing their efforts. The message here is not to undermine the complexity of the Mushaf but to loosen the clergy's monopoly over its interpretation, especially when the interpretation lacks methodology and confuses more than it clarifies. Numerous Mushaf exegeses were compiled over past centuries. These exegeses (*tafaasir;* singular: *tafsir*) are typically named after their authors. Some of the *tafaasir* that have survived to this day include, from the Sunni school, *Jami al-Bayan ann Ta'weel a'ay al-Qur'aan* by al-Tabari (d. 311/923), Ma'aalim al-Tanzeel by al-Baghawi (d. 516/1122) Tafsir al-Kabir by al-Razi (d. 606/1209), *al-Jami* by al-Qurtubi (d. 673/1274), *Tafsir al-Qur'aan al-Azeem* by ibn Kathir (d. 775/1373), *Tafsir al-Jalalayn* by al-Mahalli (d. 863/1459) and al-Suyuti, (d. 911/1505), *al-Manar* by Rashid Ridha (d. 1354/1935), *Tafsir al-Sa'di* by al-Sa'di (d. 1376/1957), and *fi Thilal al-Qur'aan* by Sayyid Qutb (d. 1386/1966). From the Shia Schools, the prominent exegeses are *Tafsir Imam al-Sadiq* by Jafar al-Sadiq (d. 148/765), *Tafsir al-Qummi* (d.

307/919), *Ma'aajm al-Bayaan fi Tafsir al-Qur'aan* by Tabarsi (d. 548/1153) and Tafsir al-Mizan by Tabatabaa'i (d. 1401/1981).

Some of the *tafaasir* kept the interpretation to the bare minimum while others expanded on it significantly, alluding to subjects that at times deviated considerably from the Mushaf. Most of the *tafaasir* were largely based on the opinions of some highly respected people in Muslim history and the opinions of other people whose identities were never revealed. Additionally, those opinions were stated without providing any background on how they were derived. Each of these *tafaasir* was the effort of a single individual; not a single *tafsir* was a collective effort between groups of individuals. (Even though *Tafsir al-Jalalayn* was authored by two scholars, it was, nevertheless, not an exception since it was initiated by Jalal al-Deen al-Mahalli in 863/1459 and then completed by his student Jalal al-Deen al-Suyuti in 911/1505.) We do not know much about many of the exegetes, under what circumstances they lived, their history, credibility, religious erudition, knowledge of Arabic, knowledge of history or even their knowledge of Arabic grammar and understanding of the Mushaf words. Even what has reached us about these exegetes in terms of their erudition and scholarship has very little relevance to the validity of their exegeses. Some exegetes did not even have a formal religious training in the sense of having graduated from a certified religious school, such as Qutb. Yet, Muslims have come to accept these *tafaasir* as their guide to help them understand the Mushaf. Some *tafaasir* gained wide fame purely based on sectarian influence and patronage of empires.

In practice, Muslims have made the exegetes their conduit to understanding Allah's revelation. In effect, the exegetes became the gatekeepers to Islam. The consequences were catastrophic; the direct link between the Muslim and Allah was severed. Allah's revelation was interpreted based on the opinions of self-appointed clergy; some of these opinions were never supported by any evidence or reason while other opinions were based on a convoluted mix of alleged Prophetic narratives, legends, strange stories, stories attributed to the Torah and a host of confusing deductions.[5] While there are multiple exegeses, the differences between them are insignificant. In fact, even the Shia *tafaasir* borrowed excessively from the Sunni *tafaasir*. All, however, lack an overriding methodology of interpretation as exemplified by confusion when applying the Arabic grammar to the Mushaf and confusion in the applicability of Hadith in general to the interpretation of the Mushaf. Latter exegetes borrowed from earlier ones while favoring certain opinions and omitting others. The exegetes relied largely on narratives (some of which were framed as hadiths) attributed to a very select group from the companions of the Prophet and chosen based on sectarian lines. Despite vehement claims to the contrary, the *tafaasir* did not provide the Prophet's own interpretation of the Mushaf. While this might be a surprise to many Muslims, it should not be since the Prophet never provided any interpretation of the Mushaf; and if he did, none has reached us.[6]

Al-Baqara, which is Chapter 2 of the Mushaf, begins with a strong emphasis that the Book does not contain ambiguities and doubt. The same chapter states that the Book is a guidance for those who are *mutaqeen* (conventionally translated as Allah-conscious.)[7] Allah does not list any academic prerequisites for the *mutaqeen* before deserving guidance. Is it that simple? The answer is an emphatic yes based purely on the Mushaf. I have been asked numerous times, "are you implying that anyone can read the Mushaf and start interpreting it?" The answer is anyone, including non-Muslims. Anyone who is armed with the elements of truth rather than opinions, illusions, feelings, lies, and pre-conceived notions has the ability to understand parts of the Mushaf that Allah refers to as the Book. Some parts of the Mushaf need specialization such as biology or physics or cosmology. We may never be able to understand some parts using our present scientific knowledge. In fact, we may never be able to understand other parts (specifically, some of the *aayaat*) at all until we witness their manifestations (see M3:7). The notion that a complete exegesis of the Mushaf can be produced is a fantasy.

Despite the lack of any consistent methodology to interpret the Mushaf, various scholars and their disciples put forward a list of qualifications they considered as prerequisites for those who wish to attempt interpreting the Mushaf. These qualifications vary according to the scholars' sects and opinions, but typically include knowledge of Arabic grammar, full knowledge of "Hadith sciences", knowledge of history and pre-Islamic history, knowledge of the "secrets of the Qur'aan" such as the *nasikh* and *mansookh* (abrogator and abrogated). A question arises as to why those individuals who excelled in all of these prerequisites still failed to provide a consistent methodical and logical interpre-

The Mushaf

tation of the Mushaf. Why have those supposed experts in Arabic grammar failed to agree on a consistent grammatical interpretation of numerous verses?[8] The fact is that expertise in Arabic grammar, strong knowledge of history, knowledge of Hadith, knowledge of *usool al-deen*, and knowledge of the "Hadith Sciences", none of these helped to produce self-consistent and logical interpretations of the Mushaf. Neither did knowledge of the *nasikh* and *mansookh* help. In fact, the introduction of the concept of *naskh* added significant confusion, creating more doubt in a Book in which Allah stated from its very beginning that there is no doubt within it. (The concept of *naskh*, which introduced the most significant doubt in the Mushaf, will be discussed at length in Chapter 7).

The most perplexing question of all is why those who possessed all "prerequisites" for interpreting the Mushaf gave us so many conflicting interpretations? Muslims need to realize and admit very honestly that there is a genuine Mushaf *tafsir* crisis.

Interpreting the Mushaf without having a consistent methodology for understanding its language is a futile exercise. Without guidelines in interpreting the language of the Mushaf, the "interpretation" itself becomes mere beliefs rather than true understandings. If the Mushaf becomes merely a belief, it then ceases to be a source of guidance. If there is more than one Arabic grammar, then which one is the right one to use in interpreting the Mushaf?[9] Can different Mushaf words have identical meaning? Is there a difference between the Book, the Qur'aan, *al-Furqan* and *al-hikmah*?[10] These are different words derived from different roots. Do these words refer to one thing or different things? How can one differentiate between adjectives and nouns? Does Allah have 99 names or some are names and some are attributes? Is there a difference between names and attributes? Assuming there is a difference, would it matter to understand this difference? Why are certain Mushaf sentences split amongst more than one verse? Is the context important to understand a single verse? Is classical Arabic grammar important for understanding the Mushaf, or does the Mushaf defines its own grammar, or do we need grammar at all to understand the Mushaf? The answers to all these questions and many more lay the framework through which a methodology for interpreting the Mushaf can be established. Are humans today more capable for interpreting more of the Mushaf than Muslims who lived centuries ago? The answer is most likely.

The broad scope of the Mushaf, its complexity, and its breadth of subject matter ranging from science to sociology require a variety of specialities to facilitate a meaningful interpretation. The *ahkam* (general rulings), on the other hand, do not require a scientist of any specialization. The non-*ahkam* part of the Mushaf, which represents its largest portion, can be interpreted and understood through hard work, effort and a variety of sciences in the same way a bridge engineer needs sufficient training in the science and principles of mechanics and civil engineering, or, if phrased using the Mushaf language, one would need guidance in civil engineering to build a bridge that does not fail 98% of the time, and certainly more guidance in civil engineering if the bridge were to not fail 99% of the time.

It is impossible that a single person can provide a meaningful interpretation of the entire Mushaf. Some sections of the Mushaf require an astronomer to understand and explain them to the rest of us, while others require a biologist, a mathematician or a linguist. Other parts require an anthropologist, as for instance when Allah indicates in M29:20 that understanding the beginning of the creation requires excavation and science. More explicitly, to heed the call of M29:20, one needs to be a scientist rather than a tourist. All these specialties are needed to understand different parts of the Mushaf that are related to these specific disciplines. Other parts of the Mushaf do not need specialties to understand them but only sufficient dedication, complete sincerity, energy, and understanding of the meaning of the Arabic language and its structure.

The Mushaf used the Arabic language to express dialogue or interaction between people who spoke all types of languages. The Mushaf contains simple instructions and commands that are easy to understand, provided one knows the Arabic language. Why Arabic? Indeed this is a good question, but before answering this question, we need to realize that irrespective of the type of language used, a language is needed for communication with humans. Mathematics, for instance, is the language of science. It is difficult, if not impossible, to communicate science without the language of mathematics. Is it possible to use other means? Possibly, but will it be as precise and concise? Is there another language other than mathematics that can communicate science? Based on the history of humankind, the answer is most likely not!

The Arabic grammar available to us today is not adequate to aid in interpreting or understanding the Mushaf. Interpreters often invoke a

The Mushaf

host of inexplicable justifications, such as the Mushaf is entitled to "exceptions", "specificities" or "privileges", in order to force specific interpretations that stem from pre-conceived ideas. These interesting "exceptions" are so many that the entire Mushaf became an "exception" rather than the blueprint for what the Arabic language should be. The Arabic language and grammar that is used as a reference for the Mushaf was canonized hundreds of years after the revelation was completed; the Mushaf came first.

INTERPRETING ALLAH'S REVELATION TO FIT PRE-CONCEIVED NORMS

Exegetes base their interpretation on normative understanding or pre-conceived norms rather than rationale, consistency and truths. This method, which is common amongst Muslims in general and exegetes in particular, is illustrated by considering the Mushaf concept of *hidayah* (guidance). The prevailing understanding amongst Muslims regarding *hidayah* is that Allah chooses (presumably in an arbitrary fashion) those upon whom He bestows guidance. This understanding could lead mischievous and violent people to justify their actions and vindicate themselves of any wrongdoing by invoking the prevailing understanding that Allah chose not to guide them, hence their complete exoneration from any accountability, judgement and even punishment. Consider the last sentence of M42:13

اللَّهُ يَجْتَبِي إِلَيْهِ مَن يَشَاءُ
وَيَهْدِي إِلَيْهِ مَن يُنِيبُ

The two phrases of the sentence were placed one above the other so that even those not highly versed in Arabic grammar will notice that the grammatical structures of the two phrases are identical. Let us start with the second verse, the translation of which is [He (Allah) guides towards Him whoever returns (to him)]. The second phrase clearly gives one prerequisite for achieving Allah's guidance, namely returning to Allah. (It does not make sense for Allah to return to Allah). This implies that there is no arbitrariness in who is granted guidance since the "turning back" or "returning to" is a human voluntary act. We can now proceed to understand the first phrase. The translation is [Allah chooses for Him whoever wills]. From the structure of the two phrases, we conclude that the will referred to here is that of the human, not Allah. If we were to interpret the will in the verse as belonging to Allah then the "turning back to Allah" in the second phrase applies to Allah.

If there is no consistency in grammar, then, by definition, it cannot be grammar. (It should be emphasized that inconsistency is different from absence of grammar rules.[11]) Attributing the will to humans is consistent with the Mushaf and with principles of fairness and justice. M42:13 is no simple verse. It is a powerhouse! It unleashes the infinite potential of humanity; it simply states that guidance can be achieved if one wants it. Using the same logic, guidance in bridge construction comes only if one wants it and if one enrolls in a civil engineering program to achieve such guidance.

Another verse conveys a parallel message. The last sentence of M13:27 reads

قُلْ إِنَّ اللَّهَ يُضِلُّ مَن يَشَاءُ
وَيَهْدِي إِلَيْهِ مَنْ أَنَابَ

[Confirm that Allah *yuthillu* whomever wishes and He guides towards Him whomever *anab*.] The parallelism between this sentence and the one in M42:13 is striking and instructive as it sheds further light on who obtains Allah's guidance. Again, starting with the second phrase, the translation can be given as [and He guides towards Him who has returned]. If we accept that it is the human who has returned to Allah, then the first phrase must be translated as "Allah misguides whoever wills". The will is therefore that of the human not Allah.

My own anecdotal experiences with people who claim to be versed in the Mushaf is instructive. Typically, the starting point is acceptance of the parallelism between each of the two phrases in the verses above, but then controversy ensues whenever I propose an explanation based on the grammatical structures of the phrases. There appears to be strong resistance amongst Muslims to the idea that humans control their will and direct themselves either towards guidance or misguidance. The impetus towards either stems from the individual rather than a divine decision that is arbitrary, selective and discriminatory. Muslims attempt

The Mushaf

to fit notions to which they are accustomed, whether now or before Muhammad's Prophethood, into the way they interpret the Mushaf even at the cost of inconsistent grammar or hiding behind the labyrinth of the "specific" and "general" of the Mushaf, which created a loophole for inconsistent and unsubstantiated interpretations.[12]

Muslims view the Mushaf *tafaasir* with high respect in the sense that these works are intended to help Muslims understand and navigate through the complexity of the Mushaf. Muslims, for the most part, are unwilling to express that these *tafaasir* leave the reader, most of the time, with more confusion than guidance and with more doubt than certainty. In fact, one is better off not consulting these *tafaasir* altogether. For example, consider M3:18

شَهِدَ اللَّهُ أَنَّهُ لَا إِلَهَ إِلَّا هُوَ وَالْمَلَائِكَةُ وَأُولُو الْعِلْمِ قَائِمًا بِالْقِسْطِ

This verse was discussed earlier in Chapter 3. Here, we revisit this verse because of its importance and because it illustrates how the *tafaasir* can cipher the Mushaf leaving many Muslims with resignation and disinterest. A literal translation of M3:18 can be given as [Allah bore witness that there is no deity except Him, and the Angels and those who have understanding also bore witness that he is the only deity ensuring fair allowance and fair allocation]. Let us consider one of the most prominent *tafaasir*, that of al-Qurtubi. He divided his commentary into four parts without providing the reader with any hint whether these four parts are different interpretations or complementary. The fact that the four parts give different interpretations is confusing to start with. Al-Qurtubi starts by quoting Said ibn Jubair (who al-Qurtubi does not place in any historical or scholarly context) as saying: "there used to be 360 idols surrounding the Ka'ba, and when this verse was revealed, the 360 idols fell down in prostration." Most interestingly, even on the assumption that if this supernatural event happened, it was neither considered nor documented as one of the supernatural events associated with the life of Muhammad. If such an event truly took place, it would have validated Quraish's practice of associating those idols with Allah, since based on the explanation by ibn Jubair, those idols had incredible and supernatural powers and were obedient to Allah.[13] After all, Quraish did not worship those idols but considered them as conduits to being closer to

Allah (see M39:3). In the second part, al-Qurtubi alludes to the important status of scientists and, quoting a host of different people, he gives the impression that most likely the "scientists" in this verse refers to the prophets, yet he contradicts himself later on. In the third part, he narrates an amusing story that is not related to the verse, then he alludes to a certain hadith by Anas (a companion of the prophet) in which the prophet is alleged to have said "Whomever reads this verse (i.e., M3:18) when going to sleep, Allah will create seventy thousand Angels who will ask Allah to forgive him." These stories are concoctions of irrationalities that were woven at times when Muslims were intellectually obliterated to even ask simple questions as to why would Allah not simply forgive the reciter of the verse directly. One wonders why would Allah go through the hassle of creating these many Angels, seventy thousand in total, in the first place? The fourth part, or rather alternative interpretation, which we skip here, is an exercise in sophistry that leaves the reader profoundly confused.

The *tafsir* of ibn Kathir, which is highly regarded by most Muslims, does not give any interpretation of M3:18. In fact, ibn Kathir introduced few hadiths that sharply contradicted the very verse he was attempting to interpret in the first place. By using some hadiths for validation, ibn Kathir claimed that after the verse was revealed, the Prophet stated that he too bears witness that Allah is the only deity. This clearly contradicts the verse in question and other verses of the Mushaf confining the revelation to the Mushaf only. Clearly, ibn Kathir did not understand the meaning of the word *shahid*, or he considered *shahada* as synonymous with faith. Ibn Abbas, who is considered by many Muslim scholars as the earliest exegete and whose interpretations were excessively referenced in almost all books of Hadith and *tafsir*, included, without any explanation, the Prophets and believers amongst those who bear witness to the oneness of Allah. The extraordinary and expansive arbitrariness in interpreting the Mushaf has become commonplace even amongst modern scholars of Islam.

My objective here is not to provide a comprehensive critique of Mushaf exegeses. However important, this is a task beyond the objective of this book. My aim is to sensitize the reader, and especially the Muslim reader, to the idea that what is referred to as *tafsir* is in fact mostly a blend of opinions, commentaries, legends, stories, sophistry, hyperbole, and information without sources. The *tafsir* also includes commentaries borrowed from Jews and Christians (referred to as "the people of the

The Mushaf

earlier Books"). Without a doubt, al-Qurtubi's interpretation of M3:18 leaves the reader confused. The verse, however, leads to crucial questions: why were the prophets not amongst those who bore witness that Allah is the only deity? Who are those referred to in the verse as "*olu'al-ilm*"? Are *olu al-ilm* people of science, people of learning, or people of knowledge? Is there a distinction between *ilm* (science) and *ma'rifa* (knowledge)? If there is, then Muslims must carefully review their understanding of every single verse in the Mushaf where reference is made to those who possess knowledge and those who possess science (see Chapter 9). Does knowledge and science correspond to awareness of something or knowing something? What does knowing something mean? Who are those humans who bore witness that Allah is the only deity? Why were prophets and messengers excluded from the group of witnesses (except in ibn Abbas's interpretation)? Do not all Muslims bear witness that Allah is the only deity (the declaration of *shahadah*)? What does *shahid* and *shahada* mean?

I encourage the reader to look into al-Qurtubi's explanation of this verse and that of ibn Kathir, as both provide representative samples of two highly venerated *tafaasir*. For a more contemporary example, one can consider *al-Manar* by Rashid Ridha, who starts his *tafsir* of M3:18 by using the consensus of earlier exegetes. Ridha largely repackaged what was done centuries earlier. When he reached the critical part of the verse that refers to the "people of knowledge/science", he presented conflicting opinions. Ridha speculated that the *olu al-Ilm* in M3:18 might refer to those who are capable of providing a rational proof for an event or phenomenon. Nevertheless, this thread in Ridha's commentary provided a new perspective not available in earlier exegeses. The major scientific discoveries and technological advances of Ridha's time could have contributed to his unconventional thinking. Ridha, eventually, however, succumbed to the overbearing influence of earlier exegetes and resigned to interpret *olu al-Ilm* as the companions of the Prophet, or, citing Zamakshari (d. 537/1143), as the Mu'tazilites, or citing al-Razi (d. 313/925), as the scholars of *usool al-deen*. Six hundred years since the death of ibn Kathir, Muslims' ability to interpret the Mushaf seems to have not advanced at all. Ibn Kathir remains one of the highest authorities on Mushaf interpretation.

Another *tafsir*, *al-Mushaf al-Moyassar* (*moyassar* means made easy), is an exegesis that was produced by a group of Muslim scholars under the patronage of the government of the Kingdom of Saudi Arabia. This *tafsir* is minimalist in the sense that it provides interpretation for words that might seem uncommon to modern Arabic speakers. No methodology was provided as to how the translations were arrived at.

EXEGESES METHODOLOGIES: ARE THERE ANY?

Traditional exegetes give the impression that the words of the Mushaf can be interpreted in various ways and lack precision and definite meaning. This mercuriality was justified by yet additional imprecise interpretations of the Mushaf. Conspicuous in the different exegesis is the absence of humility or admission on the part of a scholar in his attempt to interpret the Mushaf when he could not provide a meaningful interpretation, let alone when his explanation did not make sense or was irrelevant or confusing. Also absent is an admission that certain verses could not have been understood or interpreted using the knowledge and science available at the time. As if the fact that Muhammad himself never provided an interpretation for the Mushaf was not sufficient enough to instill humility in any daring interpreter of the Mushaf. Overall, after reading the available exegeses, one is left with confusion, disinterest, and apathy not only towards the Mushaf but also towards Islam as a whole.

There is no particular reason why I choose the verse cited above to compare its treatment by different exegetes. One can choose other verses and observe similar contradictions and approaches that are anything but methodical. The general impression that one achieves from the majority, if not all, available exegeses can be summarized as follows:

1. The interpretations were based largely on legends, undocumented and unsubstantiated stories and hearsay.
2. The interpretations were based largely on hadiths, many of which are not even classified as authentic. In fact, some exegetes knowingly included hadiths with weak authentication.
3. The interpretations mostly gave minimal attention to the meaning of words.
4. The interpreters used inconsistent grammar.
5. The interpretations were not based on logic.
6. The interpreters lacked humility to admit when they were not able to or could not provide a meaningful and logical interpretation.

The Mushaf

7. The interpreters had a habit of mixing what Allah expressed in the body of the revelation and Allah's wisdom or intent behind the revelation. This is typically packaged as the *hikmah* (reasoning or rationale) behind certain Mushaf injunctions such as forbidding intoxicants or pork, or even the benefits of fasting and prayers). What essentially amounts to reading Allah's mind is typically referred to as the "wisdom" behind the revelation. The exegetes provided no clue as to how they deciphered Allah's wisdom and His intentions.
8. The interpreters mostly inserted irrelevant and obscure stories to juxtapose preconceived notions onto the Mushaf text.
9. Some interpretations provide outright contradictory information.
10. Most interpreters used opinions of historical figures who the reader is clueless as to their identity, credibility, scholarship, and above all, their honesty.
11. No information is provided that lists the interpreters' qualifications as far as their possession of all rules that Muslim scholars have made imperative for interpreting the Mushaf.

The laxity, imprecision and carelessness by which the Mushaf was approached and interpreted was neither irrational nor the scheming of conspirators. The principal attitude towards the Mushaf is a manifestation and consequence of the Muslims' approach towards the Hadith and towards the concept of the Sunnah in general. A common understanding amongst the vast majority of Muslims is that the Mushaf, irrespective of its constituents, is not easy to understand; that it must be accompanied by the Sunnah to facilitate its interpretation. The de facto mutiny against the Mushaf as a complete and the only revelation reached epic proportions amongst many Muslim scholars to the point of declaring that the Mushaf is not complete without the Sunnah.[14] This understanding created a chasm between Muslims and the Mushaf that started during the life of the Prophet, as documented by M25:30 in which the Prophet explains his concern that his own people (not the *kuffar* or the *mushrikeen,* but the *mu'meneen*) had migrated away or distanced themselves from the Mushaf.[15]

Most, if not all, available exegeses leave the Muslim with profound confusion. Surprisingly, exegetes did not recognize the potential for this highly inevitable confusion. In fact, exegetes never discussed the fact that many interpretations within any single *tafsir* can be explicitly contradictory, as if the typical ending phrase Allah *a'lam* (which is usually translated incorrectly as "Allah knows best"), stamped at the end of an interpretation of a certain verse, bestows on the exegetes sufficient modesty and humility. The Allah *a'lam* expression, with its façade of humility serves to absolve the exegete from any wrong interpretation and to exonerate him from inconsistent interpretation and flawed logic. The invention of the concept of Ijtihad could most likely have contributed to this overbearing carelessness. (The concept of Ijtihad is discussed extensively in Chapter 9.) A Muslim academic would most likely take a much more serious approach to a doctoral thesis ensuring when the time for the defense of the thesis nears that he/she will be able to defend every single word of the thesis and give a rational justification that stands up to the scrutiny of the examination committee. Would the doctoral thesis defense committee be content with the humility of the PhD candidate by him/her invoking what God knows best about the thesis subject?

The stark uniformity in the exegetes' approach to the Mushaf (even across Muslim sects) distanced and discouraged Muslims from establishing a rational connection to the Divine. If the rational connection is severed, the only one remaining is the irrational one. Thus, the Mushaf was turned into a text that comforts and lends serenity and an atmosphere of "spirituality" to the life of Muslims. In addition, reciting the Mushaf has become more of an instrument of perceived reward for the reader than a manual of guidance. Reading the Mushaf was turned into to an act of worship, rather than means to achieve guidance.[16]

The emphasis in the Mushaf is on the text itself rather than the Messenger or the Sunnah. In fact, the Mushaf declares that the messenger had been instructed by Allah to do nothing but convey (i.e., deliver) the message as M5:92 indicates:

وَأَطِيعُوا اللَّهَ وَأَطِيعُوا الرَّسُولَ وَاحْذَرُوا فَإِن تَوَلَّيْتُمْ فَاعْلَمُوا أَنَّمَا عَلَىٰ رَسُولِنَا الْبَلَاغُ الْمُبِينُ

[and obey Allah and obey the Messenger and be cautious, if you then turn away understand that the only responsibility of Our messenger is clear delivery.] A fact that is hard to accept by many Muslims is that the canonized Sunnah of the Prophet or that of his companions did not explain or provide any interpretation for the Mushaf or the Qur'aan.

The Mushaf

An instructive exercise for those who believe that the Hadith provides an explanation for the Mushaf is to study the most respected and trusted books of Hadith to find, perhaps surprisingly, that they did not have a uniform interpretation of any verse. In fact, and surprisingly for many Muslims, the details of the obligatory *salaat* ritual act, such as the number of prostrations, was not even detailed in any hadith directly related to the Prophet. Yet, the fact that other matters were spelled out explicitly, such as the required ablution for the daily prayers, were not left out of the Mushaf. One would expect that what Allah had left out of the Mushaf should be less important than what He had left in it. The opposite would be extraordinarily problematic.

If the Prophet never interpreted the Mushaf, or at least if he did, none of his interpretation has reached us, then what was the original source on which most exegetes based their interpretation? A figure that is widely cited by exegetes is Abdullah ibn Abbas (d. 69/688), a cousin of the Prophet. Ibn Abbas is credited with interpreting and explaining many, if not most, of the Mushaf. Surprisingly, there is no proof that ibn Abbas received his interpretations directly or indirectly from the Prophet. Had that been the case, the Hadith transmission chain that is related to the Mushaf would have included the Prophet. Ibn Abbas was approximately 14 years of age when the Prophet died, so the postulation that he absorbed knowledge of the Mushaf during the life of the Prophet is doubtful and clearly unrealistic. Furthermore, how could ibn Abbas come to know the interpretation of the Mushaf if the Prophet himself did not provide his own commentary on it?

It is likely that some people during the first century of Islam had a stake in creating an instrument through which their worldview or goals found support in the Mushaf. The hadiths, in general, despite their level of authenticity, have a higher standard of vetting for authenticity. The vetting of non-Prophetic hadiths, however, have lower standards. To buttress credibility in ibn Abbas's interpretations of the Mushaf, a hadith was produced stating that the Prophet prayed to infuse ibn Abbas with knowledge of the Qur'aan. According to several sources, the Prophet is reported to have said "O Allah, make him perceptive and well versed in the religion and teach him the interpretation of the Qur'aan."[17] Whether this hadith is authentic or not still does not serve as a proof that ibn Abbas's interpretation of the Mushaf was accurate. The Prophet could have offered similar prayers for many young children who were brought to his audience. The indisputable credibility of ibn Abbas in his ability to interpret the Mushaf like no one else in the history of humankind hinged solely on a single hadith, which even if fully authentic, proves nothing. Nevertheless, the reverence bestowed upon ibn Abbas led to considering his words as if they were those of the Prophet, if not effectively those of Allah.[18]

Abdullah ibn Masood was another companion credited with his vast knowledge of the Mushaf. Interestingly, the largely accepted credibility of ibn Masood in interpreting the Mushaf is traced to ibn Masood himself. Ibn Masood claimed to have known practically everything about the Qur'aan including the purpose behind each revelation.[19] In the case of ibn Masood, however, there were no hadiths, even of low authenticity, that claim the Prophet prayed to guide ibn Masood in the sciences of the Qur'aan. Where then did ibn Masood receive all of his Mushaf knowledge? No one knows. Did ibn Masood provide any rationale for his interpretation? No. What makes Muslims consider ibn Masood a *tafsir* authority? The answer is most likely his status as a close companion of the Prophet.

Missing from the *tafaasir* compendia that has reached us is the concept of validation. Rules for validation amongst exegetes, if any, appear to have been based purely on the belief that the narratives transmitted by the companions of the Prophet or revered scholars (the likes of ibn Umar, ibn Hanbal, ibn Malik, etc.) were sufficiently credible. In other words, the correctness of the proof relied on who reported the hadith. By inserting information that is contradictory or additive to the Mushaf text, the exegetes have effectively added new information to the Mushaf, thereby becoming partners to Allah in the process of framing the text and its meaning. In fact, the Mushaf provides a very dire warning to anyone who attributes wrong information to Allah as M7:33 explains:

قُلْ إِنَّمَا حَرَّمَ رَبِّيَ الْفَوَاحِشَ مَا ظَهَرَ مِنْهَا وَمَا بَطَنَ وَالْإِثْمَ وَالْبَغْيَ بِغَيْرِ الْحَقِّ وَأَن تُشْرِكُوا بِاللَّهِ مَا لَمْ يُنَزِّلْ بِهِ سُلْطَانًا وَأَن تَقُولُوا عَلَى اللَّهِ مَا لَا تَعْلَمُونَ

[Promulgate/proclaim/declare that my Lord has made haram the *fawahish*, what is apparent of them and what is concealed and the *ithm* and possession without right and to associate with Allah that for which he has not sent down authority and that you attribute to Allah that which you have no understanding of.]

The Mushaf

What would it take for certain exegetes to recognize that there seems to be contradictions between different interpretations in the available exegeses and to conclude that a convincing and logical interpretation is yet to be found? That would certainly require some humility, especially when dealing with what Muslims believe to be the most serious, precise, and important of all books. In fact, the style by which these *tafaasir* had been written is largely alien to the style of writing and research we have come to expect nowadays. This is not a reflection on the intellectual ability of the exegetes of early times. It is possible but not certain that they carried out their scholarly work using their maximum intellectual capacity, but during times that were different in many ways from ours. Perhaps the first exegetes intended to provide the opinions available then and left it for the reader to choose whatever he or she found the most suitable or logical. Perhaps this style in *tafasir* compendia was transformed into the normative form of *tafasir*. Perhaps the exegetes believed that it is possible to provide an interpretation of the full Mushaf and raced to fill their compendia with whatever they believed was relevant.

Humility is an esteemed trait amongst people of all religions including Muslims. Humility manifests itself in Muslim societies by social interaction and behavior. In scholarship, however, many Muslim scholars and clergy, if not the vast majority, disregard or disconnect from humility and assume a behavior that resembles infallibility. Some even become virulently caustic and hostile to any opinion that diverges from theirs, lavishing *kufr* and *zandaqa* labels on their opponents with ease. The essence of scholarship is reaching truths, which necessitates suppression of the ego and consequently necessitates the admission of truth and the avoidance of falsehood and sophistry. Humility requires an unequivocal admission by a true scholar when he cannot explain or understood a certain subject. If a scholar does not know or is not sure of something, he is expected to state that he does not know or does not have sufficient information to make a conclusion or interpretation. According to this understanding, the majority of exegetes lack scholarly humility. Instead of admitting that an interpretation of a verse is not available or cannot be produced in light of present knowledge and science, some exegetes such as ibn Kathir, resorted to admittedly weak hadiths to buttress specific opinion.

Many Muslims come to the defense of exegetes by invoking the concept of Ijtihad. In the context of Islamic scholarship, Ijtihad is understood (or has evolved) to mean that if a person (specifically a Muslim jurisprudent or clergy) makes a serious effort or deduction that leads to a correct conclusion, then he is entitled to two rewards: one for his effort and the other for reaching a correct conclusion. However, if the effort, deduction or interpretation leads to a wrong conclusion, then the person is still entitled to one reward.[20] The concept of Ijtihad, irrespective of its origin, was framed within a context of rewards rather than truths, leading to adventurism, carelessness and laxity in exegeses scholarship, and little accountability for information that is contradictory to the Mushaf and, indeed, to human reason. (The concept of Ijtihad is discussed extensively in Chapter 9.)

Institutions of higher education in Muslim countries largely do not provide critical analyses of well-known exegeses, but stay away from the subject in order not to appease the religious establishment who accepted the venerability and near-infallibility of the high-profile exegetes such as ibn Abbas, ibn Masood, al-Qurtubi, al-Tabari, ibn Kathir, and Tabatabaa'i, amongst others. (This problem is significantly compounded by the absence of institutions that focus on religion but are independent from either governments or religious institutions that are strongly connected to the governments.) Muslims consider exegetes to be amongst the leading scholars of Islam, but their scholarship is questionable. In their defence, it is often argued that they did their best in light of their knowledge and the scientific or research methods available to them. This excuse is problematic on two counts. First, it is effectively an exoneration without trial, and second, it is not substantiated by any proof. These exegetes lived over a span of hundreds of years. Their works were expansive versions of earlier exegeses and a compilation of new material, much of it was irrelevant and distracting. There is no validity to the claim that their works embodied or represented the scholarship of their times.

Honesty and scholarship are two critical elements for authorship of scholarly works. The major fault that appeared in *tafsir* scholarship is de-facto acceptance of infallibility of a host of people, some of which were contemporary to the Prophet and many others were not. Even some of the exegetes themselves became an authority. For example, ibn Kathir believed that it is permissible to use the so-called Israeeliyyat hadiths in Mushaf interpretation. Ibn Kathir's opinion in turn became part of the *tafsir* methodology acceptable to the Salafis and ahl al-Sunnah wa al-Jamma'ah. In theory, Muslim scholars are quick to emphasize that aside from the Prophet, no one is infallible. However, in practice, the acceptance of the works of ibn Abbas and ibn Masood and many others without challenge speaks otherwise.

Many Muslims are compelled by rewards (*ajr*) and intentions. Allah gives rewards as He pleases and He is the only One who would know the intention of humans. The intention of a scholar cannot be used as a factor in judging his or her scholarship. Two verses in the Mushaf dispel major conceptions about intentions. The first is M2:284

$$\text{لِلَّهِ مَا فِي السَّمَاوَاتِ وَمَا فِي الْأَرْضِ ۗ وَإِن تُبْدُوا مَا فِي أَنفُسِكُمْ أَوْ تُخْفُوهُ يُحَاسِبْكُم بِهِ اللَّهُ ۖ فَيَغْفِرُ لِمَن يَشَاءُ وَيُعَذِّبُ مَن يَشَاءُ ۗ وَاللَّهُ عَلَىٰ كُلِّ شَيْءٍ قَدِيرٌ}$$

[to Allah (belongs) whatever is in the heavens and whatever is in the earth (or earths) <u>and whatever you display or disclose of that which is within yourselves or conceal it, Allah will hold you accountable for it</u>, then He forgives whomever He decides, and torments whomever He decides, and Allah is capable of everything.] At first glance, this verse seems to suggest that humans will be accountable for their intentions. It is only through the full context of the verse, which includes M2:283, that we conclude the underlined part in M2:284 is related to concealing evidence. One needs to look also at M33:54

$$\text{إِن تُبْدُوا شَيْئًا أَوْ تُخْفُوهُ فَإِنَّ اللَّهَ كَانَ بِكُلِّ شَيْءٍ عَلِيمًا}$$

[In case you display (or disclose) anything or you conceal it, then surely Allah has full understanding (and awareness) of everything.] Here Allah only specifies that he eventually knows (through His *ilm*) anything that is either concealed or disclosed. M33:54 does not mention accountability and broadens what falls under Allah's *ilm* to encompass everything rather than only what is in one's self. For societies, however, individual rewards and personal intentions cannot be the highest priority. Similar to the bereaved family of a murdered person who cannot be comforted or compensated by knowing the true intention of the killer, Muslims cannot be comforted by debating the intentions of exegetes. The good intentions of exegetes have no bearing on the correctness and logic of

Deciphering Allah's Wisdom

A typical *tafsir* of the Mushaf is narrated as a story, often with details peripheral to the verses in question. Repeatedly, the *tafsir* blurs the line between the meaning of the verse and the wisdom or rationale behind it. What Allah archived is different from the reason or rationale behind what was archived. This important distinction is overlooked in common *tafaasir*. Based on the excessive amount of confusing and contradictory information, the *tafaasir* either cater to the uneducated, the purely faithful or give the impression that it really does not matter what the right interpretation is. A subliminal "who cares" or the American-English colloquial "whatever" appears to be the underlying message the exegetes are advocating. Too often, the exegete interprets what he thinks is Allah's wisdom, thereby deciphering Allah's intentions rather than His revelation. A good example is the very beginning of M5:3

$$حُرِّمَتْ عَلَيْكُمُ الْمَيْتَةُ...$$

[Made haram on you the *almaytah*...] This verse mentions the haram foods including *almaytah*. Ibn Kathir never explained what is meant by *almaytah;* instead, he gave what he believed was the rationale for this exclusion by listing the health problems that arise from eating dead animals. Interestingly, he extrapolated to exclude dead fish. Ibn Kathir assumed *almaytah* referred to a dead animal, but he did not elaborate on the fact that any animal meant for food has to die first. Al-Sa'di explains in his exegesis how the deceased (presumably an animal) would have foul meat because of the blood remaining within the animal. Al-Sa'di excluded fish and grasshoppers without providing any reason for this exclusion. Just like ibn Kathir, al-Sa'di never explained what *almaytah* means.[21]

The *tafaasir* also relied heavily on referencing unknown people or even people whom the reader was never introduced to within the text of the *tafsir* itself. Such people could have been revered by the exegete,

The Mushaf

but what about the rest of us? Are we expected to accept the credibility of those people in the same way the exegetes did? There is a deep infatuation with personalities amongst most Muslims. Respect towards all scholars is commendable, but servitude is counterproductive and contrary to the injunctions of the Mushaf, which goes to the extent of discouraging the blind following of one's own parents and forefathers (see M31:15). In most *tafaasir*, the process of authentication or validation of certain opinions is by evaluating the reverence held for the person who expressed the opinion. The chain of reverence starts from the companions of the prophet (*sahaaba*), then the generation that succeeded the companions (*salaf*), then the generation that came next (*tab'ie*), and sometimes reaching people who lived centuries after the Prophet (such as ibn Taymiyyah and ibn Kathir). For authentication, *tafsir* books also use stories of the life of the Prophet or his companions and their followers. Infatuation with personalities in the Muslims' culture is probably one of the most critical factors that has prevented their understanding of the Mushaf.

The randomness by which exegetes have approached the Mushaf reached epic proportions when resorting to opinions or arguments of not only figures with dubious scholarly credentials, but to unknown people. An example is when using a phrase such as "some of them have said" without specifying who those people were (see for instance al-Baghawi' interpretation of M5:3). In these examples, the exegete is effectively implying that the reader should trust him. What is conspicuously absent from the *tafaasir* is the invocation of logic and rationality. If logic is insufficient for analyzing a certain verse, and if the exegete could not find a *tafsir* by others that makes sense and did not contradict the Mushaf, then based on the principles of honesty and scholarship integrity, the exegete is required to leave the verse untouched. He simply needs to state that a reasonable and logical explanation for the verse is yet to be found. It is apparent that exegetes would rather interpret all verses, even at the cost of filling their *tafaisr* with contradictory, meaningless explanations, legends, and myths.

Aside from the fundamental content of the *tafsir* itself, the style in which it is often presented is highly archaic, thus discouraging many to put in efforts to understand or even to believe that understanding it or parts of it is within the human capabilities. This has left the *tafsir* the domain of an exclusive group of individuals through which the rest of the Muslims must pass to achieve some understanding of their religion.

The Mushaf effectively became interpreted through the lenses of few individuals. Through *tafsir*, a schism has been forged between the Mushaf and the general Muslim populace. This schism is in many ways what Prophet Muhammad had observed during his lifetime and was archived in M25:30

وَقَالَ الرَّسُولُ يَا رَبِّ إِنَّ قَوْمِي اتَّخَذُوا هَذَا الْقُرْآنَ مَهْجُورًا

[And the Messenger expressed/said oh my lord my people/nation have taken this Qur'aan deserted/abandoned.] In the "spiritual" sense, most Muslims are deeply connected to the Mushaf including Muslims that are not too observant of their religious duties. The rational connection, however, remains weak at best.

Mushaf exegeses did not escape the influence of sectarian conflicts. Sectarianism was superimposed onto the Mushaf to arrive at preconceived conclusions that serve political and sectarian interests. An illustrious case can be found in *al-Mizan tafsir* by Tabtaba'i, in his explanation of M28:5

وَنُرِيدُ أَن نَّمُنَّ عَلَى الَّذِينَ اسْتُضْعِفُوا فِي الْأَرْضِ وَنَجْعَلَهُمْ أَئِمَّةً وَنَجْعَلَهُمُ الْوَارِثِينَ

[And we want to confer a favor on those who were oppressed in the land and turn them into *a'immah* and turn them into inheritors.] Tabatabaa'i focused on the underlined word *a'immah*, which is derived from the Arabic root *ammah*, that means to lead or to be the head of a group, nation, philosophy or religion, or possibly from the Arabic noun *umma* (nation). Words derived from *ammah* give a variety of meanings related to leadership status or nations of people, including the word imam. In Shia jurisprudence, *imamat* is a central doctrine that attributes religious leadership, authority and infallibility to specific descendants of the Prophet. An imam designates one of those descendants and *a'immah* is the plural of imam. (According to Shias, imam Ali, the cousin of the Prophet, was the first in the lineage of imams.)

In his interpretation of the word *a'immah*, Tabatabaa'i began by referencing imam Ali's own commentary on this verse where he (Ali) attributed *a'immah* to Prophet Yousuf and his progeny. Then Tabatabaa'i immediately invoked a certain hadith that indicated that the Prophet implied that *a'immah* referred to Ali and his two sons, Alhasan and Alhussein. Not satisfied by Ali's own claim that the *a'immah* refers to prophet Moses and his progeny, Tabatabaa'i declared that numerous Shia sources indicated M28:5 was revealed in direct reference to Ahl al-Bait, the term used by Shias to refer exclusively to the family of the Prophet and his descendants. Finally, Tabatabaa'i invokes *Nahj al-Balagha*, a book authored by Ali that implies M28:5 is related to the suffering and persecution of Ahl al-Bait. Notice that *Nahj al-Balagha*, Ali's own work, sharply contradicted what Tabatabaa'i claimed Ali said.[22] Thus, with Ali being the most senior of all Shia imams, one would expect his interpretation to override those of the latter imams who were, presumably, of lesser status and chronologically farther from the Prophet. Nevertheless, Tabatabaa'i chose to override Ali's own interpretation of M28:5 (by Tabatabaa'i's own admission) to create a connection between M28:5 and Ahl al-Bait. If one were to consider the verses that immediately preceded and proceeded M28:5, one concludes with little doubt that the context of M28:5 is related to Prophet Moses and the Pharaoh of Egypt. In fact, M28:5 is connected grammatically to M28:6, which explicitly mentions the Pharaoh.

Of course, the Sunni sects have their own interpretations of many other verses that juxtapose their claim that the companions of the Prophet are the best of people ever to inhabit the earth. Both the Shia and Sunni sects used the Mushaf to validate their respective assumed superiority and correctness.

THE "SCIENCES" OF QUR'AAN

In the rush to decipher Allah's "wisdom", the grand exegetes did not differentiate between two Arabic words, *ilm* (science) and *ma'rifa* (knowledge). This grand failure led to cataclysmic implications (see Chapter 9). The conflation of the two terms obfuscated a significant difference between the meanings of science, knowledge and practice.[23] Since exegetes paid little attention to the meaning of words, it can be anticipated that different concepts will not be distinguished either. Overall, the confusion led to an elite class of clergy that are quick to designate themselves as *ulama* (scholars or scientists). This class effectively became the gatekeepers for understanding the Mushaf.

It is not known when the expression *uloom al-Qur'aan* (the sciences of the Qur'aan) was first used. According to one of the leading professors of Qur'anic Sciences in al-Azhar, Mohammad al-Zarqani, the earliest treatise on this subject is attributed to al-Hufi (d. 330/942) and entitled *al-Burhan fi Uloom al-Qur'aan*.[24] Other texts followed throughout the centuries. The centrality of the Mushaf to Muslims' life and the vastness of the topics covered in the Mushaf have led numerous scholars to develop ways to understand subjects related to the Mushaf. According to al-Zarqani, the sciences of Qur'aan include the sciences of *tajweed*, the sciences of Othmani inscription, the science of *nasikh* and *mansookh*, the science of reading the Qur'aan, the science of place of revelation, the sciences of the circumstances of revelation (*Asbab al-Nuzool*), the sciences of the strange in Qur'aan, the sciences of the miraculous in the Qur'aan, and the grammar of the Qur'aan. Al-Zarqani, however, did not make clear how these bodies of information became sciences or who developed or discovered these "sciences", or if all or any of these works can be considered as sciences in the first place.

If all that needs to be known about these "sciences" is known, then they cease to be sciences and become a body of knowledge. Take for instance *tajweed*, the practice of reading the Mushaf in a melodic fashion. Art is more suitable to describe *tajweed* rather than science. Inscription of the Mushaf is also an art rather than a science. Furthermore, standard Arabic grammar was conceived and developed many years after the completion of the revelation, therefore it could not be capable of providing a consistent methodology to understand the relationship between the words of the Mushaf, nor could it be sufficient to explain the meaning of these words. The official Arabic grammar today cannot be sufficient to explain the language of the Mushaf. If one were to study the *tafaasir* corpus, one would experience firsthand the vast disagreement between exegetes on the grammatical interpretation of numerous verses. We need to keep in mind that these differences exist despite the exegetes being fully versed in Arabic grammar. Therefore, full knowledge of modern Arabic grammar cannot be a prerequisite to understanding the structure of the Mushaf text and verses. (As discussed

The Mushaf

in Chapter 2, claims to the contrary are designed to disenfranchise people from attempting to understand the Mushaf on their own.)

To understand a scientific paper related to the physics of thermodynamics, one would first need to understand the symbols or notations used to describe the physics of thermodynamics. In this example, the symbols and notations represent the language medium. In the case of the Mushaf, understanding the language is a fundamental prerequisite to understand the message communicated in the Mushaf. This is because humans communicate and convey meanings through words, not signs. The overwhelming exegetes, if not all, have paid little attention to the meaning of Arabic words. Major Arabic dictionaries such as *Lisan al-Arab*, however, do not help much. These dictionaries have a circular approach to interpreting the meaning of Arabic words by using canonized interpretations of the Mushaf.[25]

The concept that some different Arabic words imply or refer to a singular meaning is indicated as *taraaduf*. Scholars of Arabic and Islam argued extensively, especially during the first three Muslim centuries, and fiercely in recent years whether *taraaduf* exists in the Arabic language.[26] The fact that Arabs throughout history and especially famous and grand poets used different words to refer to one thing (tangible or non-tangible) is an indication that *taraaduf* was and remains commonplace in the spoken and written Arabic of many Arabs throughout history. This fact, however, does not imply that *taraaduf* is part of the Mushaf Arabic. For instance, many Arabs marvel at the strength of the Arabic language by claiming that the sword has numerous names in Arabic. This claim, however, is problematic because many of the so-called names are attributes describing features of a sword such as its sharpness, its function in decisive battles, its origin, etc. (Another common example is the lion.) A typical use of a word describing the sword should not be considered as precise but rather choosing an attribute of the sword that makes the entire sentence or phrase sound melodic. If the poet, for instance, is using one of the features of the sword, it should be understood from the context that he is referring to a sword, otherwise, a precise usage would be expected to include the name of the sword alone or the name of the sword followed by one of its attributes when and if needed. If the Mushaf is expected to be infinitely precise in duplicating the precision of the physical creation, then we would expect an attribute to proceed a name rather than appearing singularly in a sentence. Nature does not have *taraaduf* and so neither does the work of Allah, who created both nature and the Mushaf.

Thus, irrespective of whether by accident, ignorance, arrogance or by design, the denotation "science" came to further limit normal people's inquiry into the Mushaf. To attempt to understand a science, one, rightfully, assumes he must be a scientist or a scholar. So rather than "science" referring to a cohesive and consistent set of norms or practices for investigation and discovery, in reference to the Mushaf, it has come to mean a complete set of practices and a body of information. The designation of "scientists" on the other hand has no consistency. Even in chemistry, a bachelors degree graduate is not sufficiently qualified for the scientist designation. His university certificate qualified him to be a chemist (i.e., a practitioner of chemistry). Since chemistry discoveries are on-going, he has yet to produce knowledge to deserve the scientist label. Similarly, a graduate of any religious school is not a scientist or a scholar. Since the religion is complete, there can be no scientists in religion (see Chapter 9).

ASBAB AL-NUZOOL

According to the majority of Muslims, *Asbab al-Nuzool* means the reasons for the revelations. Specifically, *asbab* means reasons and *nuzool* generally means revelation. *Asbab al-Nuzool* is considered one additional "science" that is claimed by most Muslim scholars and clergy to be essential for understanding the Mushaf, and that without this "science", the Mushaf cannot be understood or its message is not complete. This "science" is founded on the assumption that every verse in the Mushaf was revealed in response to a certain event that occurred during the life of the Prophet, or that the revelation took place within a specific context involving humans.[27] Many Muslims, however, struggle to reconcile the idea that the revelations were in direct response to specific incidents while simultaneously believing that the entire Mushaf was revealed during a specific night (the night of Qadar in M97:1) during the lifetime of the Prophet. The advocates of predestination believe that the circumstances that took place during the lifetime of Muhammad were only a trigger to place the revelation in practical context and thus help understand its purpose. In other words, Allah made people do certain things so He could produce the revelation in a real-world context. The Muslims who do not believe in predestination, perhaps a tiny minority, find it difficult to accept that the Mushaf was revealed in response to humans' acts based on free will. If that were the case, the universality of the Mushaf would be questionable since the 23 years during which the Mushaf was revealed did not represent all scenarios that all humans would go through.

When the Muslim clergy discarded the idea that the universe is created with infinite precision and that the Mushaf has equal precision to that of the universe, then confusion abounded. Expectedly, since the clergy are not necessarily versed in the physical sciences, their perspective would be severely limited, especially anything that relates to the meaning of creation. As far as the Mushaf is concerned, the precision in its "creation" should be reflected in its words and the choice of these words. When both are discarded, confusion is inevitable. If all uranium isotopes are considered to be the same, then one will miss the amazing power of nuclear energy. Similarly, if one treats different words (such as al-Furqaan, al-Qur'aan, al-Kitaab) as the same, then one is missing the "nuclear" power that is available in the book of Allah.

One can find diverging opinions on the reasons behind the revelation of numerous verses, while for many others the exegeses provide no reasons at all. An example is M4:65.

فَلَا وَرَبِّكَ لَا يُؤْمِنُونَ حَتَّىٰ يُحَكِّمُوكَ فِيمَا شَجَرَ بَيْنَهُمْ ثُمَّ لَا يَجِدُوا فِي أَنفُسِهِمْ حَرَجًا مِّمَّا قَضَيْتَ وَيُسَلِّمُوا تَسْلِيمًا

[By your Lord, they will not have *imaan* in you until they make you a judge in what they controvert amongst themselves then they would not find in themselves any hesitation or restriction in what you have decreed and would submit *tasleema*.] As was discussed in Chapter 4, ibn Taymiyyah claimed it was revealed to exonerate Umar ibn al-Khattaab for killing a man who did not accept the Prophet's ruling.[28] However, the exegetes ibn Kathir and al-Tabaraani gave two other possible reasons. So thus far, even amongst the Salafi Sunni sect, we find at least three different reasons for the revelation of M4:65.

Even if we were to assume that the revelation came in response to distinct incidents or occasions, there was no agreement amongst exegetes as to what those incidents or circumstances were. This disagreement cannot be dismissed as a minor problem since if the reasons for revelations were relevant to understanding the Mushaf, Muslims would end up with very serious and irreconcilable differences that relate to the very foundation of their religion.

For the reasons mentioned earlier, what is referred to as *Asbab al-Nuzool* is anything but a science. Irrespective of the real meaning of science, it is based on truths, logical deduction and sound reasoning, not guesswork, legends, stories and opinions. Because the fundamental premise behind the *Asbab al-Nuzool* is the belief that the Qur'aan was revealed within or relevant to a specific context, the message delivered by Muhammad would be localized in time, space and social, political and economic context. If that were the case, Islam would be deprived of any universality. The relevance and specificity of some passages of the Mushaf to events that occurred at the time of Muhammad is a strong indication that not everything in the Mushaf addresses all humanity or even all believers of Muhammad or all Muslims. (For instance, injunctions and verses related to the women of the Prophet are not relevant to how Muslims or non-Muslims conduct their lives.) Inclusion of such material in the Mushaf, however, conveys specific messages that have an intended purpose. If the reasons for the revelation, including dates, were essential to the totality of the Mushaf, the Prophet, on the assumption that he was aware of these reasons, could have added an appendix at the end of the Mushaf.

Embedded in *Asbab al-Nuzool* is the concept of the "general" and the "specific". This concept divides many verses of the Mushaf into two groups: one that has narrow or specific applicability and the other with universal applicability (or some of the verses have specific context while others have a much broader context.) Al-Shafi'i's *al-Risala* treatise brought forth, perhaps for the first time in Muslims history, the time-space specificity or relevance of certain verses that relate mostly to rulings and to specific incidents that took place during the Prophet's time.[29] A verse that addresses a specific event that the Prophet experienced clearly was in response to that particular event, otherwise the Mushaf archived theatrical plays. Al-Shafi'i, without a doubt, highlighted the importance of distinguishing between two important categories of verses. Nevertheless, the task of determining which verses are specific and which are general cannot be resigned to guesswork, opinions, hearsay, or unsubstantiated claims. The concept of the general vs. specific

The Mushaf

becomes even more complex and convoluted as al-Shafi'i further claimed that some verses have a general audience or general applicability but, at the same time, are applicable to a specific audience. Al-Shafi'i based the rationale for these broad principles on certain hadiths. The underlying problem in his reasoning is twofold: first, not realizing that the Prophet acted within the limits of the divine revelation (within these limits, there is a continuum of possibilities); and second, not everything reported about the Prophet is accurate (i.e., Hadith).

The absence of any rationale for deciding which verses of the Mushaf are general and which are specific does not negate such possibility. Most, if not all, exegetes do not provide any methodology that helps distinguish between the specific and general verses. The context was never looked upon as an integral part of understanding the Mushaf text. The complex Arabic grammar that was invented almost two hundred years after the death of the Prophet is in fact an impediment to understanding the Mushaf. The context of each verse and the particularity of each Mushaf chapter were sacrificed at the altar of imprecision, the only methodology one can discern from the *tafaasir* books.

The disinterest prevalent in the *tafsir* and *Asbab al-Nuzool* corpus to understand the precise meaning of the Mushaf's words have prevented deciphering the specificity, or lack of, of the Mushaf verses. Without a clear understanding of the grammar of the Mushaf, the prospects for achieving any resolution on this critical subject are severely diminished. Mohammad Shahrour was the first, at least in modern times, to provide a framework for addressing this vexing subject that had effectively created multiple Mushafs. Shahrour categorized the Mushaf revelations as having either a spatial-temporal context or existential one. The evolution in Shahrour's thinking was catalyzed by realizing that a difference exists between the meanings of key Mushaf words including al-*furqaan*, Qur'aan, *thikr*, and *kitaab*.[30] Shahrour's most important contribution is his thesis that the Mushaf contains multiple books (see for instance M98:2) and that the Qur'aan was an archive of truths that includes past events and future prophecies. Other parts of the Mushaf contain archives of the stories of Allah's messengers and prophets including those of Mohammad.[31]

Knowledge of the place where the revelation took place is also referred to in the annals of traditional Qur'aan scholars as a science. The place of revelation is assumed to be either Madinah or Mecca. Revelations that took place in Mecca, or before the Prophet's migration to

Madinah, are referred to as *Meccai* verses while the rest are referred to as *Madani* verses. Nevertheless, the majority of Islam, and particularly Qur'aan scholars believe that knowledge of whether the verse is *Madani* or *Meccai* is an important prerequisite to enable a proper interpretation of the Mushaf. The problem with this assumption is that it once again contextualizes and localizes the revelation to time and space. If the place of revelation was essential to proper interpretation of verses, then the Prophet would have indicated next to each verse its place of revelation; but this was never the case.[32] If such information was vital to the Mushaf, it could not have been left for the scholarship of the Muslim clergy who were born hundreds of years after the conclusion of the revelation. The proponents of the *Meccai/Madani* categorization argue that it is essential since it allows for realizing which verses in the Mushaf were abrogated by temporally succeeding verses. (We show in Chapter 7 that the abrogation theory is fraudulent in its entirety.)

The tendency for excessive contextualization in space and time of Mushaf verses led to a significant divergence in interpretation. This contextualization was incomplete, if not impossible without supplementary historical reports whose proof of authenticity was subjected to much relaxed rules in comparison to those used for Hadith (such reports include the biographies of the Prophet by ibn Hisham and ibn Ishaaq.)

In general, because of the reliance on the Hadith corpus, Muslims could not agree on one reason for the revelation. If *Asbab al-Nuzool* were to be believed as an integral part of Islam, and in particular, of understanding the Mushaf, then one has to believe that there are multiple Mushafs precisely because there are multiple *Asbab al-Nuzool*. The Hadith corpus has played the role of dividing the Muslims and effectively creating multiple Mushafs

The Mushaf contains historical records such as stories of the Prophets who preceded Muhammad. Those stories were not theatrical plays staged by actors prechosen by Allah. All of of those stories, including the stories of Muhammad, were real, took place in specific time and space, and were archived in the Mushaf. But Allah's preservation of history and his archival methods are unlike those of humans. Those historical events took place based on the free will of the participants. Prophet Abraham, according to the Mushaf, was about to immolate his son. Abraham acted out of free will. Allah did not find it important to archive which son it was: Ishaq (Isaac) or Ismail. Clearly, the Mushaf has archived an incident that took place several thousands of years before the revelation. Therefore, the revelation was based on an historical incident. The *asbab* (reasons) behind including the Abrahamic stories in the Mushaf, or the *Asbab al-Nuzool* for these stories are for the Muslims (or the Mushaf reader in general) to ponder. Similarly, the stories that relate to the Prophet have an historic context. However, the messages that Allah chose to archive in the Mushaf need to be considered independently of the details of their historic contexts. In fact, if the reasons for the revelation are known, then by definition, the interpretation of the Mushaf must be correct.

Here we can discern that Allah's way of archiving historical incidents is highly precise and succinct to the point that such historical records appear as historical snippets. Perhaps the message that Allah is sending is that the Muslims need not focus on irrelevant details such as whether Abraham wanted to immolate Ishaq or Ismail, but rather, perhaps, on the transitioning in human history from immolating humans to immolating animals.[33] Similarly, in the case of the Prophet, there are many examples, but a highly illustrative one is M66:1

يَا أَيُّهَا النَّبِيُّ لِمَ تُحَرِّمُ مَا أَحَلَّ اللَّهُ لَكَ تَبْتَغِي مَرْضَاتَ أَزْوَاجِكَ وَاللَّهُ غَفُورٌ رَّحِيمٌ

[O Prophet, why do you eternally prohibit (make haram) what Allah has made eternally lawful for you, thereby seeking the satisfaction of your spouses, and Allah is forgiving-merciful.] Here a broad message emerges that the Prophet has no right to make haram (eternal prohibition) as he wishes; that the prohibition is exclusive only to Allah. However, al-Tabari, ibn Kathir, al-Baghawi and al-Sa'di, just to name few exegetes, did not find the core message of this verse worthy of inclusion or discussion. Instead, they dedicated practically all of their interpretation of M66:1 to a list of numerous opinions by unknown people about what the Prophet made as haram. (The speculation about what the Prophet prohibited varied from sexual intercourse with Maria, one of his wives, to eating honey.) If Allah wanted the Muslims to know what the Prophet made as haram, he could have made that explicit. The Muslim exegetes were more concerned with the details that Allah intentionally left out than a message that is embedded in the text itself and does not need anything further to understand.

All that Allah included in the Mushaf, be it a truism or historical archives, was for a reason. These reasons are embedded within the Mushaf. Deciphering the reason for the revelation is precisely understanding the revelation.

PACIFICATION IN THE NAME OF SPIRITUALITY

Once the rational connection to the Mushaf is curtailed, the only connection that remains is an irrational one. This paved the way for the concept of *ajr* (reward) to play a major role in the relationship between Muslims and the Mushaf. The prevalent understanding amongst Muslims is that the Mushaf is a medium through which one can accrue rewards simply by mere recitation, especially during particular periods such as the month of Ramadan, Hajj or other Islamic occasions.[34] With high emphasis on recitation as a medium for *ajr* generation, the Mushaf was turned into a pacifier. On grand Muslim occasions such as Hajj and Umra, when hundreds of thousands of Muslims congregate, conversations and discussions amongst Muslims of different nations, tribes and colors is considered a distraction and waste of one's precious time during these holy occasions. Instead, the encouragement is on the recitation of the Mushaf, especially when the Muslim clergy introduce all kinds of hadiths claiming the multiplicities of the rewards during these religious occasions.

Transforming the Mushaf into an instrument that generates rewards reached epic proportions. Unique calculus was also introduced to emphasize the *ajr* gained from reading the Mushaf while implicitly trivializing the importance of its understanding. There are numerous hadiths that promise rewards for reading only a very small portion of the Mushaf, even at times just a few verses; rewards that are equivalent to reading the entire Mushaf. An example is a hadith attributed to Fatimah, the daughter of the Prophet[35]:

> Fatimah said: "My father the Messenger of Allah entered when I had gone to bed to sleep, and said: 'O Fatimah! Do not go to sleep before doing four things: reciting the whole of the Qur'aan, making the Prophets your mediators (with Allah), making the believers satisfied with you and performing the pilgrimage and visit (hajj and umrah to

The Mushaf

Makkah).' Then he started praying! So, I stayed in bed until he finished the prayer and said: 'O Messenger of Allah! You ordered me to do four things which I could not do in this hour!' The Messenger of Allah smiled and said: 'If you recite the Tauheed chapter (al-Ikhlas *surah*) three times it is as if you have recited the whole of the Qur'aan; and if you recite prayers to me and the prophets before me then we shall be your mediators in the Day of Judgment; and if you pray that Allah forgives the believers (say istighfar) they shall be satisfied with you; and if you say: Subhan Allah (praise be to Allah) and al-Hamdu Lillah (gratitude to Allah) and La Ilaha Illa Allah (there is no God but Allah) and Allahu Akbar (God is greatest) as if you have performed the pilgrimage and visit.' "

The inclusion of spirituality and *ajr* as defining elements in the Muslim relationship to the Mushaf led to indifference to the meaning of the Mushaf's text and to whether or not it carries any relevance to the life of the individual. The Mushaf is no longer looked upon as a book of guidance. The Mushaf has become the gravy rather than the meat. The meat, of course, is the Hadith. This is encapsulated and exemplified in a footnote by Yousef Meri in his introduction to *Asbab al-Nuzool* by Ali ibn Ahmad al-Wahidi:[36]

> The importance and necessity of the different sciences of the Qur'aan cannot be emphasised enough. However, from the point of view of personal spiritual discipline alone, a Muslim does not need to know all the detailed knowledge that these sciences provide. This is because from this particular point of view, all that matters is how to regain the sense of eternity – which is the aim of any genuine spiritual discipline – and partake in the realm of the 'eternal now' which is the realm of the Qur'aan. All that a Muslim is required to do, in this regard, is to approach the Word of God with awe and utter indigence and make the Qur'aan his point of focus on the Divine.

The "spiritual discipline" and the "eternal now" to which Meri refers are two concepts that have no roots in the Mushaf. The diversion to the "spiritual" could have evolved from certain Sufi persuasions. It is critical to emphasize that the intention here is not to downgrade or belittle any spiritual connection one might have to any divine or non-divine revelation, from a religious text to music to a pure physical phenomenon or manifestation. The point here is to show that the concept of "spirituality" has no connection to the Mushaf.

Non-Arab Muslims, witnessing first-hand the confusion the Arabs have had in exploring a purely Arabic book, created an approach to the Mushaf that is fluid and mercurial. Non-Arab Muslims, mostly Persians, theorized that the Mushaf talks to each person in a different way, and that the Mushaf has secrets and infinite meanings. Under the sheer pressure of the deeply intimidating Qur'anic "sciences", many non-Arab Muslim scholars succumbed to a third-class status by relegating the interpretation of the Mushaf to Arabs without considering themselves equal, if not more qualified, in understanding the Mushaf Arabic than traditional Arab linguists who projected contemporary forms and norms of Arabic onto the Mushaf. The fact that Arabs disagree profusely on the interpretation of even some conjunctions such as the Arabic *itha* (which has no single word equivalence in English) should be a sufficient reasoning to support this claim.

Once the Mushaf was repackaged as a source of "spirituality" and an instrument through which one accumulates divine rewards, or even a source of comfort, it became of minor importance to understand the revelation. The amazing differences between the exegetes and their randomness in approaching the Mushaf and the overwhelming contradictions in their interpretations created additional alienation between the Mushaf and Muslims. It simply did not matter what the Mushaf was talking about as long as one can achieve benefits and "spiritual" comfort from owning a printed copy of it, reading it, or decorating with it, or leaving a copy of it in the car's glove compartment for *baraka* (blessings) and for protection. Once the Mushaf became a source for the illusive and undefined "spirituality", the emphasis in the religion shifted to the Hadith and particularly to the way Muslims believed how the Prophet, his companions and their followers conducted their affairs, from the "Islamic" dress to the so-called Prophetic Medicine. The religion was petrified and molded into a space-time singularity, which led, expectedly, to significantly diminishing appeal amongst the majority of people around the globe.[37]

DIFFERENT MUSHAFS

The idea of different Qur'aans was introduced not many years after the Prophet's death. No one knows precisely when the idea was first intro-

The Mushaf

duced; nevertheless, narratives by Malik ibn Anas indicated that the subject was debated in the first Muslim century.[38] Al-Shafi'i also alludes to different Qur'aan readings in his *al-Risala* treatise.[39] The subject of different *qira'aat* (Qur'anic readings, not recitations) has been downplayed by most Muslims for fear of the obvious, that a conclusion can be drawn that there are different Mushafs.

The meaning of different *qira'aat* is neither clear nor agreed upon by the very scholars of Islam who claimed their existence. It is also not clear whether different *qira'aat* mean different sounds and pronunciations, or different words altogether? Malik ibn Anas reported[40]

> Abd al-Rahman ibn Abd al-Qari narrated: "Umar ibn al-Khattaab said before me: 'I heard Hisham ibn Hakim ibn Hizam reading *surah* al-Furqan in a different way from the one I used to read it, and the Prophet himself had read out this *surah* to me. Consequently, as soon as I heard him, I wanted to get hold of him. However, I gave him respite until he had finished the prayer. Then I got hold of his cloak and dragged him to the Prophet. I said to him: "I have heard this person (Hisham ibn Hakim ibn Hizam) reading *surah* al-Furqan in a different way from the one you had read it out to me." The Prophet said: "Leave him alone [O Umar]." Then he said to Hisham: "Read [it]." [Umar said:] "He read it out in the same way as he had done before me." [At this,] the Prophet said: "It was revealed thus." Then the Prophet asked me to read it out. So I read it out. [At this], he said: "It was revealed thus; this Quran has been revealed in Seven Ahruf. You can read it in any of them you find easy from among them.

This hadith could constitute the first reference to the Seven *Ahruf* theory (*ahruf* is the plural of *harf*, which means a letter in Arabic). This hadith is ambiguous in what exactly was different in the reading of ibn Hizam from the other reading with which ibn al-Khattab was familiar. If the pronunciation of ibn Hizam were incorrect, he would have been corrected immediately as there is no record of variations in pronunciations in the Arabic that the Quraish tribe spoke. If by a different reading ibn al-Khattaab implied that ibn Hizam inserted or deleted letters or words in verses that ibn al-Khattaab heard from the Prophet directly, then ibn Anas's hadith indicates the presence of multiple Mushafs.

Variation in the revelation between different *Ahruf*, according to numerous Muslim clergy and scholars, means precisely variation in the text. Al-Zarqani, a proclaimed authority on the sciences of Qur'aan and who used to teach on the subject in al-Azhar University, gave elaborate examples to convince his audience of the existence of multiple versions of several verses and that each of those multiple readings are legitimate revelations.[41] Al-Zarqani's claim hinges on earlier works by highly respected religious scholars such as al-Razi and al-Asqalani who argued that different *qira'aat* of the Mushaf meant that there could be variations in names, variation in verb tense, variation in grammatical construction, additions or deletions to a verse, variation in placements of words, alternations between specific letters within a word, and finally, variations in the rules of *tajweed*. The reader is strongly encouraged to read al-Zarqani's book to find firsthand how highly respected Muslim religious clergy took the liberty to assume such wide variations in the revelation.

All the alternations, insertions, and deletions that were inflicted on the revealed text most likely were the end product of attempted forgeries. Whether the story of ibn al-Khattaab in the ibn Anas hadith is true or not is a different matter altogether. The hadith could have also been a blatant forgery intended to validate the variations in the revealed text. It is not surprising that the interpretations of Muslim clergy of the above hadith and the entire concept of *qira'aat* are too numerous and too complex even by the admission of the clergy themselves.[42] In fact, whenever key Muslim clergy discuss this subject, they shroud it in mystery and typically remind their audience that even the most prominent of historical Muslim figures could not reach any common understanding of the meaning of *Ahruf* and especially the different *qira'aat*.[43]

Instead of realizing the magnanimity of the claims that there are different Mushafs, the framers of the different *qira'aat* invoked Allah's mercy and infinite wisdom as the essential rationale behind the variations in the *qira'aat*.[44] Particularly, the framers of the *Ahruf* concept claimed that multiple revelations were essential to accommodate various tribes in Arabia that could not pronounce certain Arabic sounds. These theories seem very incredulous since not all people around the world are able to pronounce Arabic words. The Chinese and Japanese peoples have difficulty pronouncing Arabic sounds. It is surprising that none of the *qira'aat* accommodated either people.

Most Muslims like to believe that the Seven *Ahruf* theory implies different pronunciations, or dialects, and therefore the theory of multiple *qira'aat* is really not a contentious issue after all. The traditional scholars of Qur'aan, at least those who believe in the so-called multiple

The Mushaf

qira'aat, however, believed that there are effectively multiple versions of a variety of Mushaf verses, or multiple versions of the Mushaf. These scholars argue that different versions of a verse will lead to a unique meaning. This type of thinking reflects either pure ignorance of the concept of language, let alone Arabic, or an exercise in pure sophistry.[45] To argue the existence of different versions of one verse is to imply imprecision of the language of the Mushaf.

An example of the variations in different *qira'aat* is exemplified in the different versions of M50:19. The version that is available in practically all of the printed Mushafs and that is accepted as the true one is

$$وَجَاءَتْ سَكْرَةُ الْمَوْتِ بِالْحَقِّ ۖ ذَٰلِكَ مَا كُنتَ مِنْهُ تَحِيدُ$$

[And the stupor of death has come attesting to the truth; that is what you were averting.] Al-Zarqani, however, admits the following "alternative reading":

$$وَجَاءَتْ سَكْرَةُ الْحَقِّ بِالْمَوْتِ ۖ ذَٰلِكَ مَا كُنتَ مِنْهُ تَحِيدُ$$

[And the stupor of truth attesting to death; that is what you were averting.] Notice how the سَكْرَة and الْحَقّ were switched in the alternative version. The difference in the meaning between the two versions is stark indeed. The framers of the *Ahruf* theory did not find any problem in this variation despite their claim that Allah promised to preserve the Mushaf, unless the preservation refers to numerous versions.

Following the death of the Prophet, it was likely that attempts were made to introduce variations to the Mushaf verses by minor insertions or deletions. It is of little importance to ascertain who was behind these alterations. The fact is that dubious hadiths were produced to question the uniqueness and precision of the Mushaf, all in the name of multiple *qira'aat*. In effect, these hadiths either questioned the precision and uniqueness of the Mushaf or did not find it important to preserve its precision and in particular the uniqueness of its Arabic. Interestingly, irrespective of its authenticity, al-Bukhari reports a certain hadith that attests to an understanding in those earlier days of Islam that the Arabic of Quraish could have been somewhat different from that of the Mushaf.[46] Later scholars compounded the confusion by sacrificing the precision and uniqueness of the Mushaf for the sake of not questioning or casting doubt on the hadiths that they claimed were authentic (*sahih*). Thus, effectively casted doubt about the Mushaf rather than the Hadith corpus, which is inherently doubtful. Preserving the system of Hadith, or the Hadith doctrine, took precedence over realizing the uniqueness of and the precision of the Mushaf.

TAJWEED AND MEMORIZATION AS A "HOLY" DIVERSION

Many Muslim parents beam with pride when their sons or daughters memorize the Mushaf, even if the children do not understand a single word of what they have memorized. Muslim children are encouraged to first memorize the most complex and difficult parts of the Mushaf, simply because it is easier to memorize in comparison to the lengthy chapters at its beginning. The lengthy chapters, however, are much easier to interpret than the smaller ones. In fact, long chapters have mostly stories that appeal to people of all ages.

The numbering of the chapters was made by the author of the Mushaf, Allah. The chapters of any book are presented in a specific order to achieve an objective. Similarly, the chapters of the Mushaf were ordered to increase the reader's awareness of its content in a gradual manner, starting with the chapter that is simplest and easiest to understand and then moving to the more complex and concluding with the most difficult. This could indicate, perhaps, that the first chapters are important for understanding the latter. Therefore, the logical approach to study the Mushaf is to start from its beginning rather than its end. This should not come as a surprise since all Arabic books start from the right cover. The difficulty in understanding a chapter should not be taken as directly proportional to its length. If Muslim parents like to connect their children with the Mushaf from an early age, then studying the beginning of the Mushaf should take precedence over its latter chapters. Since the focus has shifted from understanding to memorization, starting with the shortest chapters became more appealing.

It is difficult to know the real reason why parents radiate with joy when their kids complete a memorization of the Mushaf. Who is the beneficiary from memorization? Is it the son/daughter or the mother who believes that because of the accomplishment of her son she would be heading straight to paradise? The privileges and benefits one receives from memorization of the Mushaf remain a mystery. Of course, many

The Mushaf

Muslims are quick to produce several hadiths to prove the amazing rewards of memorization, such as protection from torture in the grave, a high status in paradise, etc. But why would memorization be given a much higher priority than understanding? There were times when memorization of the Mushaf was useful and important, however, now print and digital media are omnipresent. Even in those early times, memorization was never a substitute for the written word. At the time of the Prophet's death, the Mushaf was not only memorized but the Prophet made sure it was also written during his lifetime.[47] In fact, the Mushaf never indicates that Allah neither encourages nor asks the believer to memorize the Mushaf but to understand it, to think about its content, to ponder its meanings and to keep reflecting on its injunctions and lessons. The Mushaf never encouraged the Muslims to commit the Mushaf to memory.

The memorization of the Mushaf is part of a culture that believes in the power of utterance irrespective of whether the utterance means anything to its reciter or even if the uttered words are understood by the reciter. It is tempting to speculate as to whether or not the emphasis on memorization was an effort to preoccupy the Muslim masses with a daunting task that requires perpetual and very time-consuming maintenance. If memorization of the Mushaf is very difficult and time-consuming for native Arabs, one could imagine the difficulty experienced by non-Arabs. Considering the respect and undue reverence Muslims give to those who memorize the Mushaf, memorization becomes a discriminating tool to further disenfranchise and marginalize non-Arabs, and to further alienate Muslims.

Muslims understand *tajweed* as the proper recitation of the Mushaf with intonations. The root of *tajweed* is *jawwad*, which means to have done an act or have manufactured or performed something in the best possible way. As applied to the reading of the Mushaf, Muslim scholars have defined *tajweed* as the pronunciation of each letter using stringent rules and further observing rules that apply to each letter in different grammatical contexts. Aside from the melodic recitation, which at times is difficult to differentiate from singing, there are complex rules established by the exclusive scholars of the Mushaf for the sole purpose of proper *tajweed*. Neither the word *jawwad* nor *tajweed* were mentioned in the Mushaf. Most of the *tajweed*-related instructions have made their way to us through the Hadith corpus and even by commentaries made centuries after the death of the Prophet.

According to Sahih al-Bukhari, there are five major benefits to the person who makes *tajweed*:[48]

> The Prophet said: "Verily the one who recites the Mushaf beautifully, smoothly, and precisely, he will be in the company of the noble and obedient Angels. And as for the one who recites with difficulty, stammering or stumbling through its verses, then he will have twice that reward."

In the English translation of this hadith, *qara'ah* was translated into recite to reflect the conventional interpretation. Recite, however, is the translation of *talaa* rather than *qara'ah*. Another benefit for the reciter is stated in another Sahih al-Bukhari hadith: "The best of you are the ones who learn the Mushaf and teach it to others."[49] Again, irrespective of the authenticity of this hadith, it is not related to recitation but rather to understanding the Mushaf and transmitting the understanding to future generations.

According to al-Tirmidhi, the Prophet said "Whoever reads a letter from the Book of Allah, he will have a reward. And that reward will be multiplied by ten. I am not saying that *alif, laam, meem* is a letter, rather I am saying that *alif* is a letter, *laam* is a letter and *meem* is a letter."[50] In the English version of this hadith, *qara'ah* was translated as he read instead of he studied or he understand. According to al-Tabarani (d. 360/971), the Prophet said "The Mushaf is an intercessor, something given permission to intercede, and it is rightfully believed in. Whoever puts it in front of him, it will lead him to Paradise; whoever puts it behind him, it will steer him to the Hellfire."[51] These hadiths, used largely as proof of the importance of muttering Mushaf verses, have three serious problems that significantly diminish their credibility. First, their authenticity is doubtful. Second, their transmission could have emphasized the meaning as understood by the transmitters rather than transmitting what the Prophet said verbatim (a common practice amongst Hadith transmitters; see Chapter 8). Third, these hadiths contradict the principles of the Mushaf.

Thikr, tarteel, and *qira'ah* are three different words that are related in different ways to the revelation and the Mushaf. Despite the fact that most Muslims consider them synonymous, these words are not only

The Mushaf

distinct but provide a methodology for interpreting the Mushaf. *Tajweed*, on the other hand, as understood to imply good and proper recitation of the Mushaf, is a concept alien to Islam that created a significant distraction from the objective of understanding the Mushaf; an objective that is intended for guidance of humankind. By creating an art (far from science) that few people can master, *tajweed* became an instrument that created a class society. The capability or proficiency to perform *tajweed* gives a Muslim the feeling that he is not only doing something worthwhile and getting a divine reward for it, but a feeling of superiority over other people (Muslims and non-Muslims).

If performing *tajweed* is a daunting task for Arabs, one can imagine what would be the case for non-Arabs and specifically people with mother tongues that make it extremely difficult to read Arabic, let alone perform *tajweed*. This leads to disenfranchisement of non-Arabs. *Tajweed* became a science with voluminous treatise. An example is a book by Czerepinski, where, ironically, printed on the front cover of this 260 page *tajweed* manual was a Mushaf verse that appeared four times in M54:17,22,32,40

$$\text{وَلَقَدْ يَسَّرْنَا الْقُرْآنَ لِلذِّكْرِ فَهَلْ مِن مُّدَّكِرٍ}$$

[And We have made the Qur'aan easy for *thikr* (utterance/pronunciation); is there any one capable of *dikr*?][52] *Dikr* is not *thikr*; hence, it was left without translation. I cannot be sure of the precise meaning of *dikr*; nevertheless, the verse gives the message that the Qur'aan was made easy to pronounce. Contrast this statement with the labyrinth of a 260-page treatise by Czerepinski on *tajweed*.

Indeed, for non-Arabs, the mere thought of *tajweed* can be demoralizing. Muslim societies have come to give significant respect to anyone who excels in *tajweed* and memorization of the Mushaf. Sometimes, these accomplishments lead to undeserving leadership positions such as leading group prayers, giving Friday sermons, and presiding over religious or non-religious functions. The ability to be a memorizer and *tajweed* performer would then take higher priority than the moral character of the person and/or his relevant proficiency.

The Mushaf begins with a message of guidance. The first and second chapters emphasize that the Mushaf is meant to be a guide for the *mutaqeen*, those who are cognizant of Allah's presence in every move in their lives, cognizant of their responsibilities towards society, maintain constant touch with Allah, and give to the poor from what Allah has given them. The Mushaf is about guidance, not mystery. It is about guidance, not encrypted messages intended for a "chosen people". The early verses of the Mushaf dispel the notion that it was revealed to an elite and privileged class who will be its guardians, sole interpreters and gate keepers. Humans, not Allah, create linguistic barriers, social barriers, and unsubstantiated interpretations of religious revelations to preserve their privilege and status. Even when a religious text is exceptionally clear and simple, it is interpreted by the protectors of privilege as containing hidden parts that only the gifted (those who possess *karama*) can understand.

Muslims are always eager to show how Islam is a religion of equality and point to how Muslims stand shoulder to shoulder, the rich and the poor, when performing the group prayers. However, when it comes to understanding the Mushaf, suddenly Muslims cease to be equal and a host of complex socio-religious strata emerge. Artificial classifications amongst the Muslim society that have no roots in the Mushaf and no roots in the spirit of the religion start to emerge. Such classifications were canonized with "Islamic" terminology, such as *Awaam* (general public), *Khawaas* (specific public), *Ahl al-Hull wa al-Aqd* (those who are entitled to make decisions), *Ta'beean* (those who lived after the contemporaries of the Prophet), the *sahaaba* (a loosely and expansively defined group of the Prophet's contemporaries), and *Ahl al-Beit* (the household of the Prophet).[53] The prevailing practiced doctrines are far removed from depicting a fair and equal society. These strata within the Muslim society resemble a cast system that effectively kept the average Muslim from experiencing Islam from its primary and only source: the Mushaf, and kept non-Muslims from venturing into Islam and at least trying to understand its Message.

The early verses in the Mushaf are a source of empowerment for the Muslim and non-Muslim alike, an empowerment that was sourced directly from Allah. The Mushaf starts with a declaration of independence from any system no matter how religious. With such an empowering beginning, why then would Muslims become so disempowered? What has gone so wrong that the Book of guidance has turned into a book for justifying exclusion, sheer violence and alarming elitism? Is it a twisted interpretation of the Book that gave rise to a culture of backwardness, exclusion and violence or is it a departure from the Book itself and adhering to different sources of different doctrines that Muslims have given preference to over that of the Mushaf? These are difficult questions that Muslims need to answer.

CONCLUDING THOUGHTS

Had non-Muslims caste doubt on the uniqueness and precision of the Mushaf, they would be immediately accused of anti-Islam scholarship and sinister manipulation of historical records, if not outright hatred and enmity towards Muslims and Islam. However, these "scholarly" manipulations were the works of Muslim scholars and clergy. For Muslims, it takes only the utterance of a few Arabic words to transform a scholar from an Islam hater and enemy into a respected Muslim scholar.

The lack of methodology coupled with inconsistency and sophistry in the *tafsir* corpus was tolerated or perhaps looked upon with an aura of respect by non-Muslim scholars of Islam (mostly Western). These non-Muslim scholars were timid in their critique of *tafsir* for various reasons. Perhaps they were cautious to criticize the contradictions in *tafsir* for fear of being perceived as hostile to Islam. Perhaps they were fearful of being accused of not having sufficient command and understanding of the Mushaf "sciences" or Arabic to critique the *tafsir* in the first place (or not knowing Arabic grammar, the secrets of revelations, the *nasikh* and *mansookh*, *Asbab al-Nuzool*, the Sunnah, etc.) Additional confusion amongst many Arabs arose from a genuine misunderstanding that the Arabic language did not change from the time of the Prophet to now. Muslim scholars and clergy misinterpreted Allah's promise to preserve or protect the *thikr* for preservation of the Arabic language. The language that the Arabs speak has changed; however, the Mushaf has not.

I tried in this chapter to show that science has no connection to what generations of religious scholars have advanced as Qur'anic sciences. Qur'anic "sciences" represent a body of knowledge developed over generations and is based on a specific set of practices and methodologies. One cannot conclude that all of these practices or methods were part of a wicked or sinister conspiracy to harm Islam and Muslims. They could have been. The outcome, rather than the intent, however, is what is important to all Muslims. The outcome led to the creation of a barrier between the Mushaf and Muslims. Not only did this barrier prevent

Muslims and non-Muslims from understanding the Mushaf but contributed to a Muslim culture: that frowns upon precision; that perceives the revelation as fluid, varying and mercurial; that the Mushaf is a pacifier; and that the Mushaf is a collection of words whose mere utterance leads to heavenly rewards. For non-Muslims, the books of exegeses represent a concoction of contradictions and confusion, both of which are discouraging to entice any further interest in Islam.

Tafsir books are mostly the works of one person. It is not possible thus far to find a single *tafsir* that is the work of multiple scholars who discuss and debate the merits of what to include, what to exclude, what does not make sense, which hadith to use in support of certain interpretations and why, which methodology to use, which *Asbab al-Nuzool* to use, and a host of other very important considerations. The Mushaf is Allah's revelation, which is part of his creation. His creation is the truth (reality) and this creation can be understood using tools of science (understanding reality) and logic (use of primordial reasoning mechanism).[54]

If we want to understand the atom, which is a part of the creation, then we start with the realization arising from experimental findings that the atom has complexity. Any mathematical or physical model that we develop and envision for the atom represents a significant reduction of the atom's complexity. The model, however, is a step towards having a better understanding of the atom. In an analogy to the atom and our attempt to understand it, the Mushaf is a divine creation. We may build models to understand it, but we cannot understand it based on the way we do things, and specifically, the way we write language.

While we may write language in a certain way, the way Allah "writes" or expresses language is different from our way. We can easily observe in the Mushaf that there appears to be no connection between successive verses in a single Chapter. For a person versed in the Arabic language and the way it was used for thousands of years, the Mushaf presentation is incoherent and distracting. For example, Prophet Moses is mentioned throughout the Mushaf, not in one Chapter only. The Mushaf themes are scattered. Some sentences are divided amongst two verses while other sentences are completely contained within a single verse. All these styles are not exceptions, or are exceptions to the language the Arabs used and are using today, but not an exception to the way Allah expresses language.[55] We are not necessarily expected to write the way Allah expresses language, but we need to understand His style rather than make our style the reference to understand His.

Shahrour is arguably the first Mushaf exegete (or partial exegete, as he strongly shuns the idea that one person is able to come up with a full *tafsir* of the entire Mushaf) who developed a method to interpret the Mushaf based on *tarteel*, a method that was suggested by the Mushaf itself.[56] Shahrour started a new approach to the Mushaf interpretation. Most Muslim scholars find Shahrour's approach radical and completely unconventional. Those scholars are correct; however, Shahrour's approach is the only logical approach available today that can formulate the seeds of a new beginning for the relationship between humans (Muslims and non-Muslims) and the Mushaf.

1. The word "created" used here does not carry the same connotation that the Mu'tazilites or their intellectual opponents associated with the Mushaf.
2. Perfection is used here to imply consistency, efficiency and clarity of purpose.
3. Shahrour, Muhammed. *Al-Kitaab wa al-Qur'aan: Ro'ya Jadeedah*. Dar al-Saqi, 2011, pp. 212-232.
4. Since Muslims believe that Allah created everything, the Mushaf, in the revealed form (i.e., the summary of certain events, the physical and non-physical laws that govern the interaction between the created things, and future prophesies) is Allah's creation too. This entitles the Mushaf to the same precision as that of other creations. The more humans become aware of the precision in the physical world, the more they would accept the precision of the Mushaf. This idea is completely unrelated to the concept of the creation of the Qur'aan championed by the Mu'tazilites.
5. Ibn Kathir borrowed excessively from the so-called Israeeliyyat, which are narratives attributed to Christian and Jewish sources. He justified his borrowing by using the following hadith from Sahih al-Bukhari, Kitaab al-Anbia: "The Prophet said: 'Narrate about me even if it were a single sentence, and tell others the stories of Bani Israel.'" Even if this hadith was authentic, the Prophet could have implied the stories about Bani Israel that are plentiful in the Mushaf. Nevertheless, ibn Kathir and the Ahl al-Sunnah wa al-Jama'ah believed that it is permissible to include Israeeliyyat as long as they don't contradict the Mushaf and the Sunnah. But one wonders why would ibn Kathir establish the interpretation of the Mushaf, the divine revelation, on these Israeeliyyat in the first place. What guarantees the correctness of a piece of information even if it does not contradict the Mushaf? Especially if such information came from people that ibn Kathir deemed to have gone astray, have acquired Allah's wrath and were doomed to hellfire (see ibn Kathir's interpretation of M1)!
6. Some exegetes claim that the Prophet indeed provided some interpretations such as for M108. The different hadiths that comment on M108, however, do not show any consistent interpretation despite the claim that the Prophet explained the meaning of M108 to his companions.
7. Whenever *taqwa* and its derivatives, including *mutaqeen*, appear in the Mushaf, the context is related to society and social welfare. Therefore, additional study needs to determine the true meaning of *mutaqeen*.

8. Ibn Hanbal, Ahmed. *Al-Rudd ala al-Jihamiyyah wa al-Zanadiqah*. Dar al-Thabaat, The footnote by Sabri Bin-Salama Shaheen on p. 143 provides different interpretations of M6:3 attributed to Muhammad al-Ameen al-Shanqiti. These interpretations allow for different grammatical structures and consequently provide different meanings. Al-Shanqiti implies that different interpretations have equal credibility but one is better than others. This recurring notion amongst the classical exegetes suggest that it is not important to provide a correct interpretation. This notion is buttressed by a widely held conviction amongst Muslims that the Mushaf rewards its readers. The classical narrative would continue to discourage Muslims from uncovering the inconsistencies and exposing the faults of their scholars since it only aids the Jews and the Christians in discrediting Islam.
9. Dhaif, Shawky. *Al-Madaris al-Nahawiyya*. 7th ed., Dar al-Ma'arif, 1968. Ouzon, Zakareya. *Jinayat Seebaaway*. Riyad al-Rayyes Books, 2002.
10. Shahrour. *Al-Kitaab*, pp. 53-67.
11. Modern Arabic grammar and particularly Nahu (the art or science of adding *taskheel* to ending of Arabic words) is inconsistent with the grammar of the Mushaf.
12. The concept of the specific and the general in the Mushaf is traced to al-Shafi'i but it could have been proposed earlier. The concept considers certain verses that appear to have a general scope actually refer to specific people or incidents. Similarly, according to the same concept, some verses that appear to be addressing specific incidents or people are intended to be general. The concept is introduced in al-Shafi'i's *al-Risala* (see page 222) without any validation or even any rationale. The only remote justification for the concept is the specificity or generality of certain hadiths which were assumed by al-Shafi'i and others to have explained certain Mushaf verses. The concept gives the interpreters of the Mushaf extraordinary fluidity, which makes it nearly impossible to arrive at a consistent methodology for Mushaf interpretation.
13. Quraish was the most powerful tribe in Makkah during the Prophet Muhammad's life.
14. Al-Zahrani, Mohammad ibn Matar. *Tadween al-Sunnah al-Nabawiyyah*. Dar al-Hijrah, 1996, pp. 22-23. Brown, Jonathan. *Misquoting Muhammad*. Oneworld, 2014, p. 37.
15. Despite the fact that M25:30 refers to the Prophets' own people, ibn Kathir opted for a different interpretation, claiming that the

Prophet's people refers to the *kuffar*. Ibn Kathir interpretation manifests a methodology amongst exegetes whereby any wrongdoing is attributed to the *kuffar* but none is attributed to the followers of Muhammad.

16. Al-Zarqani, Muhammad Abdul-Adhim. *Manahil al-Irfan fi Uloom al-Qur'aan*. Dar al-Kitaab al-Arabi, 1995, pp. 45, 207. According to al-Suyuti, mere utterance of the Qur'aan is an act of worship.
17. Sahih al-Bukhari, Kitaab al-Wudu, no. 143. Sahih Muslim, Kitaab Fatha'il al-Sahaaba, no. 2477
18. Despite being highly controversial and problematic, this logic appears to be widely accepted as stated explicitly in one of the al-Azhar text books on the Sciences of Qur'aan (see al-Zarqani's *Manahil*).
19. Al-Zarqani, *Manahil*, p. 161.
20. One hadith that is typically cited to support the concept is Ijtihad is found in both Sahih al-Bukhari and Sahih Muslim: "Amr ibn al-Aas reported: The Messenger of Allah, peace and blessings be upon him, said, 'If a judge makes a ruling, striving to apply his reasoning (Ijtihad) and he is correct, then he will have two rewards. If a judge makes a ruling, striving to apply his reasoning and he is mistaken, then he will have one reward.'" Sahih Sahih Muslim, Kitaab al-Aqdhiya, no. 1716.
21. Al-Sa'di, Abdur-Rahman ibn Nasir. *Tayseer al-Kareem al-Rahman fi Tafsir Kalam al-Mannan* (*Tafsir Al-Sa'di*). 2nd ed., Dar al-Salam, 2002.
22. There is more than one version of *Nahj al-Balagha* adding additional confusion to the interpretation of this verse.
23. The concept that some different Arabic words imply or refer to a singular meaning is referred to as *taraaduf*. Scholars of Arabic and Islam argued extensively, especially during the first three Muslim centuries, whether *taraaduf* exists in the Arabic language. The fact that Arabs throughout history, and especially poets, used different words to refer to one thing (tangible or non-tangible) is an indication that *taraaduf* was and remains commonplace in the spoken and written Arabic of many Arabs throughout history. This fact, however, does not imply that *taraaduf* is part of the Mushaf Arabic. For instance, many Arabs claim that the sword has numerous names in Arabic. This claim, however, is not problematic because many of the so-called names are attributes describing features of a sword, such as its sharpness, its function in decisive battles, its origin, etc. A typical use of a word describing the sword should not be considered as precise. If the poet, for instance, is using one of the features of the sword, it should be understood from the context that he is referring to a

sword, otherwise, a precise usage would be expected to include the name of the sword alone or the name of the sword followed by one of its attributes, when and if needed. If the Mushaf is expected to be infinitely precise in duplicating the precision of the physical creation, then we would expect an attribute to proceed a name rather than appearing singularly in a sentence. Nature does not have *taraaduf* nor does the work of Allah who created both nature and the Mushaf.

24. Al-Zarqani. *Manahil*, p. 33.
25. Ibn Manzur, Muhammad ibn Mukarram. *Lisan al-Arab*. 3rd ed., Dar Sader, 2000. This is considered by most Arabs to be the most authoritative dictionary of the Arabic Language. It was compiled by ibn Manzur (d. 712/1312).
26. Shahrour. *Al-Kitaab*, p. 23.
27. The earliest book and possibly most authoritative on *Asbab al-Nuzool* is the work of Ali ibn Ahmad al-Wahidi, (d. 468/1075). A second highly referenced one is *al-Itqaan fi Uloom Al-Qur'aan* by Jalal al-Deen al-Suyuti (the co-author of Tafsir al-Jalalin).
28. Ibn Taymiyyah, Taqi al-Deen Ahmad. *Al-Sarim al-Maslool ala Shatim al-Rasool*. Vol. 2, 2nd ed., Dar al-Tawsweeq al-Duwliyya, 2007, p. 34
29. Al-Shafi'i, Muhammad ibn Idris. *Al-Risala*. Dar al-Kutub al-Ilmiyyah, 1939, p. 64.
30. Shahrour. *Al-Kitaab,* pp. 53-67.
31. Shahrour's contribution regarding the difference between al-Qur'aan and al-Fur'qaan can potentially put to rest the grand dispute that erupted between the Mu'tazalites and Ahl al-Hadith in the second Muslim century. The dispute centered on whether the Qur'aan was created or not. Shahrour's thesis would imply that the Qur'aan was not created but other parts of the Mushaf were.
32. Al-Zarqani. *Manahil*, p. 161.
33. Shahrour, Muhammad. *Al-Qasas al-Qur'aani: Qiraa'ah Mu'aasira*. Vol. 2, Dar al-Saqi, 2010, pp. 109,110.
34. Al-Zarqani. *Manahil*, p. 45.
35. *Musnad Fatimah al-Zahra*. Dar al-Safwah, [n.d.], pp. 218-9.
36. Al-Wahidi, Ali ibn Ahmad. *Asbaab al-Nuzool*. Royal A'al al-Bayt Institute for Islamic Thought, 2008.
37. Out of the world population of 7.2 billion, Muslims constitute approximately 1.6 billion amounting to 22%. Most of the Muslim population growth is through natural birth. Islam did not spread to all corners of the world. Notice that none of the Latin and South American countries has a Muslim majority. The stagnation in Islam's

growth, if measured by the increase of converts to Islam, is very visible.
38. Ibn Anas, Malik. *Al-Muwatta*, 3rd ed., Diwan Press, 2014.
39. Al-Shafi'i. *Al-Risala,* p. 273.
40. Ibn Anas, *al-Muwatta.*
41. Al-Zarqani, *Manahil,* pp. 125,132.
42. Al-Zarqani, *Manahil,* p. 132
43. See https://www.youtube.com/watch?v=81lFOx8DKr8 and https://www.youtube.com/watch?v=sokHQyQDV_c&t=812s Accessed 2 February 2019.
44. Al-Zarqani, *Manahil,* p. 133.
45. Believing that different words, different phrases and different grammatical structures lead to a singular meaning could possibly be the source of the mercurial culture that has colored the scholarship of not only the alleged Qur'anic "sciences" but also that of the collective Muslims behavior towards the Mushaf and life in general.
46. Sahih al-Bukhari, Kitaab Fatha'il al-Qur'aan, no. 4984: Narrated Anas ibn Malik: The Caliph Uthman ordered Zaid ibn Thabit, Said ibn al-As, Abdullah ibn al-Zubair and Abdur-Rahman ibn al-Harith ibn Hisham to write the Qur'aan in the form of a book (Mushaf) and said to them. "In case you disagree with Zaid ibn Thabit (al-Ansari) regarding any dialectic Arabic utterance of the Qur'aan, then write it in the tongue of Quraish, for the Qur'aan was revealed in this dialect." So they did it.
47. Whether the Mushaf was compiled in one book during the life of the Prophet or not is historically debated. However, it is inconceivable that the ordering of the Mushaf chapters was done after the Prophet's death since the order of a book is an integral part of it.
48. Riyadh al-Saliheen, Sahih al-Bukhari, Book 9, no. 94.
49. Sahih al-Bukhari, Kitaab Fatha'il al-Qur'aan, no. 5027.
50. Jami al-Tirmidhi, Kitaab Fatha'il al-Qur'aan, no. 2910.
51. Abu al-Qasim al-Tabarani was one of the most prominent Hadith scholars of the fourth Muslim century.
52. Czerepinski, Kareema. *Tajweed Rules of the Qur'aan.* Sarawar, Part 1, 2003.
53. Ibn al-Salah, abu Amr. *Uloom al-Hadith.* Dar al-Fikr, 2002, p. 294.
54. Logic is claimed to have been invented by the ancient Indians and Greeks. This author believes logic, broadly defined as the tools of rational analysis, was discovered rather than invented. There are interesting parallels to mathematics where certain mathematical principles are claimed to have been invented rather than discovered.

55. This discussion leads to important questions. Was the Arabic language, specifically the Arabic words, created by humans or did it evolve naturally? It is inconceivable that Allah would use a human-made language to express his revelation. This leads to the idea that Arabic words (not grammar) evolved naturally with time.
56. Shahrour. *Al-Kitaab*, p. 49.

7

NASKH: FRAUD IN THE NAME OF GOD

قُلْ إِنَّمَا حَرَّمَ رَبِّيَ الْفَوَاحِشَ مَا ظَهَرَ مِنْهَا وَمَا بَطَنَ وَالْإِثْمَ وَالْبَغْيَ بِغَيْرِ الْحَقِّ وَأَن تُشْرِكُوا بِاللَّهِ مَا لَمْ يُنَزِّلْ بِهِ سُلْطَانًا وَأَن تَقُولُوا عَلَى اللَّهِ مَا لَا تَعْلَمُونَ

State that my lord has only made haram the *fawahish*, those that are apparent and those that are hidden, and the *ithm*, and the *baghi* that is not founded on truth, and to associate with Allah that for which He has not revealed any authority, and that you claim or attribute/ascribe to Allah things that you have no proof or understanding of.

M7:33

THE CONCEPT OF *NASKH*

In Muslim jurisprudence tradition, *Naskh* is the concept that claims some verses of the Mushaf are nullified or modified by other verses. The concept essentially implies that some verses of the Mushaf have no applicability, or they are null and void. Some variations of the concept also imply that some revelation used to be documented in the Mushaf and is no longer there but is still applicable. *Naskh* addresses two types of verses: the first type, the *nasikh* (abrogator), nullifies or voids a second type, the *mansookh* (abrogated). Therefore, the *naskh*, as a concept, rather than the literal meaning of the word, implies nullification. Because of its significant implications on Muslim jurisprudence, resulting in decisions such as to execute or not to execute a human being, the *naskh* concept can be considered as a doctrine, or according to its proponents, it can be considered as a very critical instrument in understanding the full implication of the revelation. Out of all doctrines that were claimed to be part of Islam, none had created confusion and disarray, and none had trivialized the religion and the divine revelation as *naskh* did, and none had belittled the word of Allah and its precision as *naskh* did. The concept of *naskh* not only impeded understanding of the religion of Islam but also infused severe doubt and distrust in numerous verses of the Mushaf, thus creating not only doubt but confusion in the entire revelation and expectedly confusion in the entire religion.

Naskh is typically referred to as a theory or as a science. If it were to be considered as a theory, then it should be subjected to validation. If it were to be considered as a science, then it should be subjected to scientific methods for consistency and methodology. After all, science is not a collection of thoughts and pieces of information but is defined by its methodology. The fact that *naskh* is a complex concept infused with contradictions makes it difficult if not impossible to label it as either a theory or a science. The concept stipulates different types of *naskh* (legal, textual, etc.) The difference between these types is of much less significance to expose here than to discuss the very concept itself.

The vast majority of Muslims may conceal their shock at the extent of the damage *naskh* has caused to their understanding of how their religion should be practiced. This happens, most likely, for fear of being marginalized and labeled as being not knowledgeable of one of the important "sciences" of the Qur'aan. (In their zeal to amplify the importance of the *naskh* concept, its proponents turned it into a science.) This is classically demonstrated when Muslim clergy ridicule and marginalize genuine Muslim and non-Muslim Mushaf scholars by accusing them of lacking the "sacred knowledge" of the *nasikh* and the *mansookh*. While Judaism, Christianity and Buddhism appear to have had doctrines similar to that of Hadith and the Sunnah, not one of those religions had anything that came close to *naskh*.[1] It is highly likely that the doctrine of *naskh* did not have any parallels in any divine, divinely inspired or humanly-constructed religious doctrines; therefore, the concept is unique to Muslims. My objective here is to deconstruct the *naskh* concept, to demonstrate its invalidity, to show how it is shrouded in mystery, contradictions and inconsistencies, and to show how it represents a very powerful example of humans' incredible and unique potential to present myth as a truth.

In this chapter, I will examine the rationale behind the attempt to nullify part of the divine revelation in the name of a highly controversial human-made instrument constructed to serve political, social or economic objectives. My interest here is not to present a theological or a philosophical discussion on the implausibility of *naskh*, or to argue, based on material derived from the Mushaf, Hadith or historical records, why it is not possible for certain verses to have been abrogated. These types of discussions or refutations of *naskh* are available in other works.² Also, I will not attempt to prove that certain verses could not have been abrogated, as this had also been attempted by others. My goal here is to shed light on the concept and demonstrate its invalidity. However, I will present a few examples in order to emphasize the contradictions and hint at the potential motives that prompted the framers of *naskh* to expand the concept in their advocacy for a preconceived perspective on Islam in general.

EXAMPLES OF *NASKH*

Numerous works were written on *naskh* and particularly on which Mushaf verses were abrogated or nullified and which did the abrogation.³ An example of *naskh* is the claim that M9:5

فَإِذَا انسَلَخَ الْأَشْهُرُ الْحُرُمُ فَاقْتُلُوا الْمُشْرِكِينَ حَيْثُ وَجَدتُّمُوهُمْ وَخُذُوهُمْ وَاحْصُرُوهُمْ وَاقْعُدُوا لَهُمْ كُلَّ مَرْصَدٍ ۚ فَإِن تَابُوا وَأَقَامُوا الصَّلَاةَ وَآتَوُا الزَّكَاةَ فَخَلُّوا سَبِيلَهُمْ ۚ إِنَّ اللَّهَ غَفُورٌ رَّحِيمٌ

[And when the prohibiting months are drawn away, then *aktuloo* the *mushrikeen* wherever you find them, and take them, and detain them, and sit for them at every place of observation, and if they repent, and uphold the prayer, and pay the zakat then let them go their way; Allah is forgiving, merciful] abrogated at least three verses that include M53:29

فَأَعْرِضْ عَن مَّن تَوَلَّىٰ عَن ذِكْرِنَا وَلَمْ يُرِدْ إِلَّا الْحَيَاةَ الدُّنْيَا

[So stay away from who turns his back on our revelation and who only seeks the lowly life] and M43:89

$$\text{فَاصْفَحْ عَنْهُمْ وَقُلْ سَلَامٌ ۚ فَسَوْفَ يَعْلَمُونَ}$$

[Then turn away from them (as in not exacting retribution) and pronounce peace then they would understand] and M3:186

$$\text{لَتُبْلَوُنَّ فِي أَمْوَالِكُمْ وَأَنفُسِكُمْ وَلَتَسْمَعُنَّ مِنَ الَّذِينَ أُوتُوا الْكِتَابَ مِن قَبْلِكُمْ وَمِنَ الَّذِينَ أَشْرَكُوا أَذًى كَثِيرًا ۚ وَإِن تَصْبِرُوا وَتَتَّقُوا فَإِنَّ ذَٰلِكَ مِنْ عَزْمِ الْأُمُورِ}$$

[You shall be tested with your money and selves and you will hear from those who were given the book before you and from those who associated great harm, and if you exercise patience and piety that will heed great requests.] Al-Nahhaas (d. 338/949), one of the earliest authors of a dedicated book on *naskh*, claimed that M9:5 abrogated 113 verses.[4] In fact, some Muslim scholars believe that M9:5 even abrogated many more verses, practically every verse that calls for peace and compassion.[5] Since the essence of the *naskh* doctrine is the abrogation of a verse (which is the conventional translation of *aayah*) or verses, then any abrogation must apply, at a minimum, to an entire verse. Therefore, Muslims who claimed or believed that M3:186 was abrogated must also accept the nullification of the entire verse, including the part of the verse that requests the believers to exercise patience and piety; otherwise, the abrogation applies only to part of the verse or a specific ruling within the verse. (Some Muslim clergy realized this problem and addressed it by introducing additional types of *naskh* that claim to abrogate part of the verse, such as a legal injunction within a verse, rather than the entire verse, thus contradicting the very verses that were used as the foundation of the concept as will be explained below.)

Another example of the application of *naskh* is instituting the punishment by the stoning of married adulterers in practically all Sunni and Shia jurisprudence schools. According to the Mushaf, *zina*, which is the publicly staged sexual intercourse between an unmarried man and a woman who are not married to each other, is punishable by one hundred lashes (or fifty in certain circumstances.)[6] However, according to widely accepted "Islamic" Sharia and the proponents of Hadith, if the *zina* offenders were married, then the punishment is death by stoning.

Notice that the Mushaf does not specify if the *zina* actors were married or not. It is highly improbable that this lack of specificity had been an oversight on the author of the Mushaf, especially since the punishment of stoning is the most severe, and what the Mushaf stipulates, namely lashes, does not compare in severity and implication.

The Mushaf did not restrict the punishment of lashes to non-married perpetrators of *zina*. The punishment of death, and specifically death-by-stoning, has roots in a few hadiths, but not in the Mushaf. The proponents of this punishment invoke *naskh,* along with narratives attributed to Umar ibn al-Khattaab, the second Righteous Caliph, where he was alleged to have said: "The following was revealed in the Qur'aan, 'And the *sheikh* and *sheikha*, if they commit *zina*, stone them affirmably.'"[7] The believers and interpreters of this alleged narration interpret *sheikh* and *sheikha* as a married male and a married female, respectively, despite the singular use of *sheikh* in the Mushaf to designate a male that had passed his prime years of strength. Nevertheless, the hadith attributed to ibn al-Khattaab implies, according to the stoning advocates, that the so-called stoning verse was part of the Mushaf and then it was removed, yet its applicability, or legal ruling, remained active; therefore, according to the stoning advocates, married adulterers should be stoned to death.

Another widely documented story is that Ayesha, the wife of the Prophet, was reported to have said that the stoning verse was transcribed on a piece of paper and during the preparation of the Prophet's body for burial, an animal entered Ayesha's room and ate the piece of paper.[8] The story attributed to Ayesha is used to provide another modality of how *naskh* took place. The biggest problem with the Ayesha story is the implication that *naskh* happened after the death of the Prophet. One also questions if the same verse in question was never written down on any other media or papers aside from the one that was eaten by the animal in Ayesha's bedroom. While these examples are provided here only to provide the reader with how *naskh* is claimed to have happened, it needs to be emphasized that one has to be cautious when giving such examples as there is no consensus amongst Muslim clergy (even within a single sect) on what had been abrogated in the first place.

Another example of *naskh* is to negate a Mushaf injunction that gives Muslims the choice between fasting and not fasting during the month of Ramadan, even if they have the ability to fast. M2:183 and

M2:184 specify that fasting was ordained on the followers of Muhammad. However, Allah also gives the choice to fast or not to those who are able to fast, while ending M2:184 with the definitive recommendation that fasting will bring more goodness. M2:185 addresses the followers of Muhammad who "witness the month" (Ramadan) to fast during its duration with allowance for the sick or travelers to postpone the fasting until later dates. Interestingly, M2:185 did not offer a choice of fasting for able people (neither sick nor travelling) as was the case in M2:184. Many earlier scholars considered the difference between the two verses as a clue that M2:185 abrogated M2:184 and thereby concluding that not fasting in Ramadan is not a choice that a healthy non-traveling Muslim has.[9]

The exegetes and traditional scholars of Islam have gone to extreme lengths to distance themselves from the possibilities spelled out by M2:184, namely the choice of fasting or not fasting for able-bodied Muslims who are neither sick nor on travel. Al-Jawziyya, a celebrated disciple of ibn Taymiyyah, claimed that fasting was ordained during the second Hijri year, and so the Prophet was given the choice of fasting or not for nine years until the complete abrogation of such permission was revealed in M2:185. Al-Jouziyya's claim implies that there was a nine-year gap in the revelation between M2:184 and M2:185. This means that the Mushaf was revealed in a fragmented fashion, that not even the entire content of one *surah* (chapter) was revealed in harmony or any contextual connection. If that were the case, the concept of a *surah* would be meaningless since the meaning of a verse cannot be understood independently of its preceding and possibly proceeding verses.

Nasikh is derived from the past tense, *nasakha*, which means "to transcribe". *Mansookh* is derived from the same root and it means "that which was transcribed". None of the two Arabic terms can be translated into any words that have a direct or indirect relationship to abrogation. The Arabic word for abrogation is *laghi*. This makes the concept of *naskh* especially problematic, not only because the correlation between the implication of *naskh* and the linguistic derivation is weak, if at all, but because it encroaches on the highest principles of Islam (including Sharia). This is the case because scholars within a specific Muslim sect did not have a consensus on the verses of the Mushaf that were abrogated and those that did the abrogation, if any. An illustrative example is the following list of scholars who commented or analyzed *naskh*, each mentioned here next to the number of verses he claimed to have been abrogated: Al-Zuhri (d. 123/742), 42; al-Nahhaas (d. 338/949) 138; ibn Salama (d. 167/783), 238; ibn al-Ata'iqi (d. 708/1308), 231; al-Suyutti (d. 911/1505), 20; Shah Wali Allah (d. 1176/1762) 5; while Abduh (d. 1323/1905) believed none were abrogated, and al-Khoei (d. 1413/1992) believes only one verse was abrogated.

This overwhelming data reinforces my claim that Muslims have no consensus on the applicability of the Mushaf. If two groups of Muslims believe in *naskh* and they differ on the verses that were abrogated, then these two groups, in practice, believe in two different Mushafs. Therefore, *naskh* is the most divisive concept, amongst Muslims, because it puts into dispute the very source of Islam. The confusion is compounded because, according to the framers of *naskh*, abrogation can take place without any textual reference in the Mushaf. The average Muslim is left to believe that the validity of *naskh* depends on the interpretative skills of theologians, skills that only they possess for reasons that only they know of.

On the assumption that the concept of *naskh* is valid, the lack of consensus in its application suggests that not all Muslims believe in the applicability or validity of the entire Mushaf. This is a stark conclusion that is directly and emphatically supported by the "science" of *naskh* itself. Absent of a clear Mushaf indication of one verse abrogating another, the *naskh* advocates imply contradiction or inconsistency between two verses or between a group of verses. This consequential belief is contradictory to the Mushaf that clearly states that it cannot have contradictions (see M4:82).

DOES *NASKH* MEAN ABROGATION?

The Mushaf contains four occurrences of the root and derivatives of *nasakha:* M2:106, 7:154, 22:52, and 45:29. These verses will be discussed below. Considering the context of all these verses, the linguistic and context-logical interpretation for *naskh* would be transcribing, reaffirming or documenting. Knowing that the Mushaf was revealed in and transformed into the form of the Arabic language in which the tribe of Quraish was well versed, it is highly unlikely that *naskh* was understood by Quraish as abrogation for the simple reason that there is no linguistic connection between *naskh* and abrogation. Consulting *Lisan al-Arab* (the most famous Arabic language dictionary compiled in 689/1290), however, does not provide any insight either since it provides a definition for *naskh* based on its interpretation by Muslim clergy as abrogation.[10] Clearly, several questions come to mind. If the companions of the Prophet realized that there are verses within the divine revelation that were nulled, they would have asked the Prophet then to clarify such potential confusion and not to leave the doors wide open for future generations (as recent as ours) to rule on the applicability or even the authenticity of the divine revelation.

Two factors could have contributed to the emergence of the *naskh*-as-abrogation theory. With the proliferation of the Hadith cottage industry in the first and second Islamic century (see Chapter 8), a body of knowledge was produced that turned out to be contradictory to certain Mushaf verses. The production of this knowledge was most likely guided by various economic, social, and political objectives. To align the Mushaf directives and rulings with the new knowledge, the Mushaf's language was reinterpreted, not through the language of Quraish, or by the Mushaf itself, but in light of the Hadith corpus, which contained significant and alarming contradictions to the Mushaf; it was as though a new language had to be devised to reconcile the new concepts in Hadith with the Mushaf.

It is difficult to ascertain whether the concept of *naskh* was the invention of non-Muslims who despised Islam, or of Muslim theologians or jurisprudents who were most likely struggling to reconcile a host of contradictions between the Mushaf and the Hadith corpus on the one hand, and contradictions between their interpretations of numerous verses of the Mushaf on the other.[11] Muslim scholars who objected to *naskh* attributed its origin to Jews or Christians who wanted to deviate the religion from its true source. These claims, while plausible, were intended to exonerate Muslims from anything wrong that have befallen them and to throw the blame on the typical "punching bags": the Jews and the Christians (a modus operandi that plagued Muslims of all ages). Nevertheless, the contradictions, which emerged in the multiple doctrines that became known collectively as Islam, had to be reconciled somehow. The only possible way to address these significant and stark contradictions was by either a complete denial or rejection of the Hadith doctrine altogether, or redefining the meanings of certain words in the Mushaf. Denial of the Hadith doctrine, however, would have created a major disruption and would have curtailed the privileges of the Umay-

Muslim's Greatest Challenge

yad and Abbasid empires (which patronized and facilitated the consolidation of the Hadith and the Sunnah doctrine) who derived their legitimacy from numerous hadiths and who used many hadiths as a population sedative. Therefore, a new language had to be invented that ascribed higher legislative authority to Hadith over the Mushaf. As a result, at the expense of preserving Hadith and its numerous contradictions, the divine revelation was put in doubt.

Despite claims by Muslim scholars that *naskh* can be traced to the Sunnah as did al-Shafi'i, or that the Prophet's companions devoted care to understanding *naskh*, its framers could not find any prophetic narratives that directly or indirectly alluded to the existence of *naskh*.[12] This is surprising, considering the powerful impact of *naskh* on Muslim jurisprudence, and its heightened importance to the degree that numerous Muslim scholars believe that disbelieving or rejecting *naskh* is a major sin amounting to *kufr*. Interestingly and surprisingly, the lack of any prophetic reference (authentic or weak) to *naskh* did not seem to warrant any consideration by its advocates.

The proponents of *naskh* based their concept on two verses. The first is M2:106

مَا نَنسَخْ مِنْ آيَةٍ أَوْ نُنسِهَا نَأْتِ بِخَيْرٍ مِّنْهَا أَوْ مِثْلِهَا ۗ أَلَمْ تَعْلَمْ أَنَّ اللَّهَ عَلَىٰ كُلِّ شَيْءٍ قَدِيرٌ

[What We *nansakh* of an *aayah* or make it forgotten, we bring one better than it or similar. Do not you know that Allah is capable of everything (or has hegemony over all things)]. The second is M16:101

وَإِذَا بَدَّلْنَا آيَةً مَّكَانَ آيَةٍ ۙ وَاللَّهُ أَعْلَمُ بِمَا يُنَزِّلُ قَالُوا إِنَّمَا أَنتَ مُفْتَرٍ ۚ بَلْ أَكْثَرُهُمْ لَا يَعْلَمُونَ

[And if We *baddalna* an *aayah* in place of another, and Allah understands what He reveals, they said you are a forger; indeed, the majority of them do not understand]. Without delving into the interpretation of the entire verse, we only focus on the underlined word *baddalna*, which had been interpreted by the framers of *naskh* to mean "We have abrogated". Derivatives of *baddala*, the root of *baddalna*, appear 44 times in the Mushaf. While Arabic words can have different meanings depending on their context, not a single context of the 44 occurrences comes close to hinting that *baddala* might imply abrogation or nullification.

The most logical and uncontroversial interpretation of *baddala* is "to exchange." But even if *baddala* implies abrogation, then M16:101 would not be meaningful.

Turning to M2:106, its most common interpretations have two major problems. The first problem is the interpretation or translation of the underlined word *nansakh* as "to abrogate". The second problem lies in translating *aayah* as a verse. As for the first problem, as explained earlier, there is no logical or linguistic connection between *naskh* and abrogation; therefore, to interpret *nansakh* as "to abrogate" defies the fundamental concept of language in the sense that a word designates a meaning (or multiple meanings, depending on the context) or a concept rather than anything one wishes.

To circumvent this challenge or irreconcilability between *nsakh* and abrogation, the framers of *naskh* created a second meaning framed within the Islamic Sharia's legal context (see Chapter 9). Since the Mushaf is neither a legal manuscript nor a manuscript of any specific field of study, its words cannot be understood as definitions of terms specialized to a particular field, including the field of law and jurisprudence. (For example, the word "resistance" in common English language implies the refusal to comply with something. However, in electrical engineering jargon, it implies a specific electrical property of objects.) The new language was somehow framed within an Islamic Jurisprudence or Islamic Sharia, and then imposed, projected or even forced on the entire religion of Islam. (An analogy would be to force the English speaking population in the entire world to use the word resistance as electrical engineers would use it in their practice.)

Under the framework of Sharia, when a Mushaf word is interpreted using the new language to serve a preconceived objective, its definition is typically preceded by the term *fi al-sharia,* which means that "in as far as Sharia is concerned", or "according to Sharia" the term in question has the stated definition. This new instrument of circumventing the original meaning of the Arabic word is in essence a fraud because of the fact that no explanation is given as to how the change of meanings of the words came about, or it could be the mechanism through which diversion in religion (*tahrif*) could be formalized or institutionalized. This circumvention of the true meaning of Arabic words has been used extensively by Muslim scholars without any jurisprudential oversight and by jurisprudents who projected their law discipline onto the Mushaf, as if the Mushaf was a legal text. The Mushaf, however, was not revealed as a legal text, nor was it revealed exclusively for theologians. Legal experts, Muslims or otherwise, can derive legislation based on the Mushaf principles, but the principles are not framed in any discipline-specific language. The Mushaf was revealed and transformed into an Arabic language form (a point that the Mushaf stressed emphatically).

The interpretation of *aayah*, to which we return shortly, is important to deconstructing the *naskh* myth. But first, let us consider a second verse that contains another derivative of *nasakha*, which is heavily used by the proponents of *naskh*, namely M45:29

$$\text{هَٰذَا كِتَابُنَا يَنطِقُ عَلَيْكُم بِالْحَقِّ ۚ إِنَّا كُنَّا نَسْتَنسِخُ مَا كُنتُمْ تَعْمَلُونَ}$$

[This is Our book speaks onto you in truth; we used to <u>nastansikh</u> what you have done]. Had the underlined *nastansikh* (a present form of the *nasakha*) been translated into abrogate, it would be meaningless for the Mushaf to imply "We used to nullify or abrogate what you used to do". However, the verse would be meaningful if *nastansikh* was translated as "to transcribe" or "to document" or "to record" or "to archive", especially considering that a book or record (*kitaabuna*) was mentioned in M45:29.

The third verse containing a derivative of *nasakha* is M7:154

$$\text{وَلَمَّا سَكَتَ عَن مُّوسَى الْغَضَبُ أَخَذَ الْأَلْوَاحَ ۖ وَفِي نُسْخَتِهَا هُدًى وَرَحْمَةٌ لِّلَّذِينَ هُمْ لِرَبِّهِمْ يَرْهَبُونَ}$$

[And when the anger subsided in Musa, he took the tablets and in their *nuskhatuha* was guidance and mercy for those who are fearful of their Lord]. Again, abrogation cannot have any relevance to the meaning or structure of the verse, but if *nuskhatuha* was translated as "its inscription", a meaningful sentence would emerge.

Now, let us look at the fourth and last verse containing a derivative of *nasakha*, M22:52

$$\text{وَمَا أَرْسَلْنَا مِن قَبْلِكَ مِن رَّسُولٍ وَلَا نَبِيٍّ إِلَّا إِذَا تَمَنَّىٰ أَلْقَى الشَّيْطَانُ فِي أُمْنِيَّتِهِ فَيَنسَخُ اللَّهُ مَا يُلْقِي الشَّيْطَانُ ثُمَّ يُحْكِمُ اللَّهُ آيَاتِهِ ۗ وَاللَّهُ عَلِيمٌ حَكِيمٌ}$$

[Never did We send a messenger or a prophet before you, but when he framed a desire, Satan threw (a thought) into his desire; then Allah *yansakhu* what Satan throws in, and Allah will then affirm His *aayaat*.] Most exegetes (if not all) translated *yansakhu* as "to abrogate", most likely guided by the overwhelming acceptance that *naskh* corresponds to abrogation according to the conventional interpretation of M2:106. However, the verse that immediately followed M22:52 reveals the unsuitability of such an interpretation. The conventional interpretation of M22:53 is likely one of the most controversial interpretations of any Mushaf verse. Here, the focus on this verse is purely on its relationship to the concept of *naskh*. Considering M22:53

لِيَجْعَلَ مَا يُلْقِي الشَّيْطَانُ فِتْنَةً لِلَّذِينَ فِي قُلُوبِهِم مَّرَضٌ وَالْقَاسِيَةِ قُلُوبُهُمْ ۗ وَإِنَّ الظَّالِمِينَ لَفِي شِقَاقٍ بَعِيدٍ

[So that he makes what Satan throws in a trial for those who have disease in their minds and for those who have hardened minds; and the oppressors will face a distant schism.] The unsuitability of translating *yansakhu* in M22:52 as "to abrogate" is evident since M22:52 reveals that Allah transformed what Satan threw in a trial for people with diseased minds. If what Satan threw in was abrogated, there would have not been any effect from Satan and thus there would not have been any trial.[13]

AAYAH VS. VERSE

A major problem in the *naskh* concept arises from interpreting *aayah* as verse, especially in M2:106. The Mushaf is composed of or divided into chapters. Each *surah* (chapter) is composed of verses. The beginning and end of a verse are designated by a symbol that typically takes the shape of a circle (referred to in Arabic as *najmah*).[14] The verse can be a complete sentence, part of a sentence, or even possibly more than one sentence. The singular and plural forms of the Arabic word *aayah* appear 382 times in the Mushaf, in 352 verses. In the vast majority of these verses, *aayah* or *aayaat* (plural of *aayah*) refers to a sign, an extraordinary or ordinary event, or a phenomenon, all used to support and validate the messages and messengers that Allah sent to humans. While *aayah* has a specific meaning (just like any other noun in Arabic that describes or is connected to a functionality), there could be different types of *aayaat*. There are *aayaat* that relate to cosmology, others to nature and still others to human behavior. According to the Mushaf, extraordinary events such as the feast-table that was sent to Jesus and his disciples and the splitting of the sea for Moses were *aayaat*. I will provide here only five examples out of hundreds given in the Mushaf. The first is M16:11

$$\text{يُنبِتُ لَكُم بِهِ الزَّرْعَ وَالزَّيْتُونَ وَالنَّخِيلَ وَالْأَعْنَابَ وَمِن كُلِّ الثَّمَرَاتِ إِنَّ فِي ذَٰلِكَ لَآيَةً لِّقَوْمٍ يَتَفَكَّرُونَ}$$

[He causes to grow for you plants and olives and palms and grapes and of all produce. Indeed in that there is an *aayah* for people who analyze.] Notice that this verse points to an *aayah* rather than the verse in itself being a sign, a phenomenon or a "miracle". The second example is M2:39

$$\text{وَالَّذِينَ كَفَرُوا وَكَذَّبُوا بِآيَاتِنَا أُولَٰئِكَ أَصْحَابُ النَّارِ هُمْ فِيهَا خَالِدُونَ}$$

[And those who made *kufr* and belie Our *aayaat*, those are the companions of the fire; they shall remain in it for eternity.] This verse warns those who made *kufr* and lied in Allah's *aayaat* of their hellfire destiny. Clearly, there is no sign in this verse and therefore, it cannot be an *aayah*. The third example is M41:53

$$\text{سَنُرِيهِمْ آيَاتِنَا فِي الْآفَاقِ وَفِي أَنفُسِهِمْ حَتَّىٰ يَتَبَيَّنَ لَهُمْ أَنَّهُ الْحَقُّ أَوَلَمْ يَكْفِ بِرَبِّكَ أَنَّهُ عَلَىٰ كُلِّ شَيْءٍ شَهِيدٌ}$$

[We will show them our *aayaat* in the horizons and in their own souls until it becomes apparent to them that it is the truth; is it not enough that your lord is a witness on all things.] The fourth example is M15:77

$$\text{إِنَّ فِي ذَٰلِكَ لَآيَةً لِّلْمُؤْمِنِينَ}$$

Naskh: Fraud in the Name of God

[Surely in that there is indeed a sign for the believer.] Each of these verses cannot be an *aayah*, but clearly, each is referring to one. The fifth example is M24:1

$$\text{سُورَةٌ أَنزَلْنَاهَا وَفَرَضْنَاهَا وَأَنزَلْنَا فِيهَا آيَاتٍ بَيِّنَاتٍ لَّعَلَّكُمْ تَذَكَّرُونَ}$$

[*Surah*, we have revealed it and ordained it and revealed within it apparent *aayaat* so you may be mindful.] Similarly, this verse, which serves as an introduction to M24, indicates that M24 contains within it apparent *aayaat*. The implication is that it also contains within it non-*aayaat*. Again, this verse itself cannot be an *aayah*.

Few verses refer to *aayaat* differently. These verses indicate that a specific set of *aayaat* are part of a *kitaab* as in M11:1

$$\text{الر كِتَابٌ أُحْكِمَتْ آيَاتُهُ ثُمَّ فُصِّلَتْ مِن لَّدُنْ حَكِيمٍ خَبِيرٍ}$$

[Alif Lam Raa, a *kitaab* whose *aayaat* have been fixed (or made clear) then they were explained in detail through a *hakim-khabir*.] This verse and few others with a similar structure, such as M10:1, 12:1, 13:1, 15:1, 28:2, and 31:2, indicate that *aayaat* are part (but not necessarily the entire content) of a *kitaab*. *Kitaab* does not uniformly designate either the Qur'aan or the Mushaf, but could be a parts of it. In fact, the Mushaf indicates that it has within it multiple *kutub* (plural of *kitaab*), as in M98:2, 3

$$\text{رَسُولٌ مِّنَ اللَّهِ يَتْلُو صُحُفًا مُّطَهَّرَةً}$$
$$\text{فِيهَا كُتُبٌ قَيِّمَةٌ}$$

[A messenger from Allah that recites scrolls purified. In it there are *kutub* that are dominating (or of high value).][15] Interestingly, the verse implies that there should be a differentiation between a *kitaab* and a *surah* (Mushaf chapter). These two verses indicate that the Mushaf contains multiple *kutub*. This would strongly suggest that the *kitaab* mentioned in M11:1 refers to certain verses in M11. Similarly, M10:1, 12:1, 13:1, 15:1, 28:2 and 31:2 suggest that each one of the respective Mushaf chapters contains a specific (and different) *kitaab*.

With the understanding that a verse and *aayah* are two different things, we revisit M2:106 to realize that this verse in itself is describing the *naskh* of an *aayah*. Since *aayah* refers to a sign, an event or a phenomenon, abrogating an *aayah* would be meaningless. Allah's only way of documenting (or archiving) his *aayaat* is only *naskh* in the revelations that He sent to humankind. In summary, M2:106 does not refer to verses but to the signs that Allah reveals and/or produces to indicate, to signal, to designate, or to focus attention on truths.[16] These *aayaat* were produced throughout the ages, at times accompanying prophets and messengers. Some of these *aayaat* have been transcribed in numerous divine revelations such as the Psalms of David, the Tablets of Moses, the Injil of Jesus and possibly others that have become forgotten and never transmitted from one generation to others. This is the most logical context of M2:106 whereby Allah affirms that He causes extraordinary events as they were documented in several revelations or, with time, have become forgotten, then he brings other *aayaat* similar to the earlier ones or better. To reinvent a new definition for *naskh* that contradicts the usage of the word *nasakha* and its derivatives as used in the Mushaf constitutes a "distortion of meaning" or diversion of the Massage; a diversion that the Mushaf refers to as *tahrif*.

Despite the obvious lack of connection between the word *naskh* and the concept of *naskh*, the assumption of its plausibility calls for few important questions. If *naskh* implied the nullification of certain Mushaf verses or parts of verses (legal, textual, or both, as had been theorized by numerous Muslim theologians and jurisprudents), then it would be expected that the Prophet, the very person who delivered the Message in the first place and who was sternly commanded to deliver what was revealed to him (see M5:67), must have indicated before he died if such nullification or abrogation took place. One would expect the Prophet to have mentioned *naskh* on at least one occasion that would have warranted inclusion in the Hadith corpus. The proponents of *naskh* appear to have overlooked this very crucial point despite the inclusion in the Hadith books of seemingly minor subjects such as details related to the private life of the Prophet, including his posture during urination.[17] It is highly abnormal that the complete absence of a concept as crucial as *naskh* in the entire Hadith corpus did not seem to warrant the concern of the *naskh* proponents. This is even more so considering that *naskh* was not mentioned even in weak (*thaeef*) hadiths.

SUNNAH ABROGATING THE MUSHAF

Based on available material from the Sunni and Shia sects, the concept of *naskh* never met any significant challenge, especially after the demise of the Mu'tazalites. By its wide acceptance, along with the canonization of Hadith as a doctrine that is equally significant to the Mushaf, it was conceivable that if the Mushaf and the Sunnah are both divine revelations, then one of them can abrogate the other. The Sunnah, however, was never considered as an independent revelation but had to be canonized through a process of filtration by the Muslim clergy who decided on what constitutes the Sunnah in the first place (through the processes of Hadith authentication). This unprecedented and unrestrained power of the clergy, a power that could not have been established without the support of the ruling elites, did what might have been conceived as the impossible during the life of the Prophet.

Deeply intoxicated with their power and privilege, prominent Muslim clergy of the second Muslim century claimed that certain Sunnah can abrogate certain Mushaf revelation. This claim translates to believing that a certain Prophetic narrative, i.e., a hadith, despite having a degree of authenticity stipulated by humans, can nullify the words of Allah. Thus the concept of *naskh* was extended to include abrogation of the Mushaf by Hadith. This type of abrogation, while not agreed upon by all Muslim sects, found support amongst the Hanafi and Maliki sects.[18] For instance, Anas ibn Malik (d. 93/712) and leading jurisprudents of the Hanafi and Shafi'i sects claimed that the Sunnah of the Prophet, if established by multiple chains (typically referred to in the annals of Hadith "science" as *mutawaatir*), then it can abrogate Mushaf verses. This incredible claim essentially establishes higher credence to narratives whose authenticity have been debated for centuries than the divine revelation.

While al-Shafi'i reaffirms his rejection of this type of *naskh*, in practice, he used it indirectly to establish the superiority of a certain hadiths over the Mushaf. An example is the well-known hadith amongst Sunni sects that stipulates that the receiver of Islam-mandated inheritance cannot be bequeathed. One version of this hadith appears in the al-Tirmidhi and abu Dawood collections as

$$\text{إِنَّ اللَّهَ قَدْ أَعْطَى كُلَّ ذِي حَقٍّ حَقَّهُ، فَلَا وَصِيَّةَ لِوَارِثٍ}$$

[It is affirmed that Allah has given every rightful owner his right, thus there is no will for an inheritor].[19] The problem with this so-called *wassiyya* hadith is that it is sharply contradicted by M2:180

$$\text{كُتِبَ عَلَيْكُمْ إِذَا حَضَرَ أَحَدَكُمُ الْمَوْتُ إِن تَرَكَ خَيْرًا الْوَصِيَّةُ لِلْوَالِدَيْنِ وَالْأَقْرَبِينَ بِالْمَعْرُوفِ حَقًّا عَلَى الْمُتَّقِينَ}$$

[and it was *kutiba* (made permissible or allowed) on you that if death is approaching one of you, it would be good for him/her that he leaves a will for the parents and closest of acquaintances a rightful duty for those who have piety.] This verse only establishes the allowance, permissibility, or recommendation to include biological parents and close acquaintances in the will. The verse, however, does not discuss the distribution of anything that is not willed or anything that is bequeathed in general. Distribution of inheritance, however, is left for other verses, such as M4:11,12. The proponents of the hadith above claimed that either the hadith or M4:11 or both abrogated M2:180. While some clergy, such as al-Shafi'i, disagreed with the claim that the Sunnah can abrogate the Mushaf, he and others still were in defense of the hadith despite its complete contradiction to the Mushaf. The defenders of the *wassiyya* hadith seem to have resorted to the *naskh* instrument despite the complementarity of M2:180 and M4:11.[20]

Naturally, an important question that comes to mind is how did the *naskh* proponents validate the claim that M2:180 abrogated M4:11? These scholars would cite a narrative claiming that ibn Abbas (d. 67/687) made the *naskh* claim, as reported in Sahih al-Bukhari:[21]

$$\text{عَنْ ابْنِ عَبَّاسٍ رَضِيَ اللَّهُ عَنْهُمَا قَالَ: كَانَ الْمَالُ لِلْوَلَدِ وَكَانَتِ الْوَصِيَّةُ لِلْوَالِدَيْنِ، فَنَسَخَ اللَّهُ مِنْ ذَلِكَ مَا أَحَبَّ، فَجَعَلَ لِلذَّكَرِ مِثْلَ حَظِّ الْأُنْثَيَيْنِ، وَجَعَلَ لِلْأَبَوَيْنِ لِكُلِّ وَاحِدٍ مِنْهُمَا السُّدُسَ، وَجَعَلَ لِلْمَرْأَةِ الثُّمُنَ وَالرُّبُعَ، وَلِلزَّوْجِ الشَّطْرَ وَالرُّبُعَ}$$

[Ibn Abbas said: The money used to belong to the offspring and the will used to be for the parents (*walidayn*), then Allah abrogated from that whatever he liked and then made the male inherit twice the portion of the female, and made for the parents (*abawyyn*) for each one the sixth, and made for the woman the eighth and quarter, and for the spouse a *shatr* and a quarter.] The contradictions and vagueness of this narrative are not of interest here, but what is noticeable is that this hadith does not mention or refer to M2:180 or M4:11, either explicitly or implicitly. So for the hadith to be used as a nullifier of Allah's revelation would give ibn Abbas, at the least, a divine status. Overall, there is no direct or indirect narrative attributed to the Prophet that would hint at any *naskh* between the above verses.

Absent of any significant challenge to *naskh*, its proponents laid the foundation for yet another concept: that of the "Godly wisdom" or "hidden philosophy" behind abrogation and how it was meant to make the religion easy for Muslims to gain more rewards and for non-Muslims who choose to convert to Islam.[22] A classical and widely used example of the supposed Godly wisdom behind *naskh* is the belief that the Islamic injunction against consuming intoxicating substances was revealed to sustainably transition the tribe of Quraish, who was used to excessive drinking, into giving up alcohol. Here, *naskh* is invoked to explain that M4:43 was first revealed to only prevent the new Muslims from praying while under the influence of alcohol, but later on, full prohibition was revealed in M5:90 when the community's alcohol drinking habit lessened. According to this logic, a person who converts to Islam at any time should follow the same "gradual" process of alcohol waning. But that is not practiced nor sanctioned by the very advocates of this alleged progressive/gradual style of Islam.

There are no historical records or hadiths available in the published literature, irrespective of whether they had strong or weak authentication, that give direct or indirect proof that some verses of the Mushaf have been abrogated by other verses that were revealed at later times. This fact explains why Muslim scholars never had consensus on which verses were abrogated and which did the abrogation. Deciding which verses were abrogated and which did the abrogation was left to the devices of an array of Muslim scholars and clergy and to their own interpretation of the Mushaf. No methodology was adopted even amongst the proponents of *naskh* in determining whether or not a certain verse was abrogated.

Even if one were to accept *naskh* as a principle derived from M2:106, its proponents never provided any sound reasoning of why certain verses abrogated others. By doing so, the *naskh* framers distorted the revelation. According to the Mushaf, this could potentially be a very grave sin, elevated to the level of haram since the act of attributing or ascribing something to Allah without scientific rationale is classified within the categories of haram stipulated by M7:33

$$\text{قُلْ إِنَّمَا حَرَّمَ رَبِّيَ الْفَوَاحِشَ مَا ظَهَرَ مِنْهَا وَمَا بَطَنَ وَالْإِثْمَ وَالْبَغْيَ بِغَيْرِ الْحَقِّ وَأَن تُشْرِكُوا بِاللَّهِ مَا لَمْ يُنَزِّلْ بِهِ سُلْطَانًا وَأَن تَقُولُوا عَلَى اللَّهِ مَا لَا تَعْلَمُونَ}$$

[State that my lord has only made haram the *fawahish*, those that are apparent and those that are hidden, and *ithm*, and *baghi* without (or not founded on) truth and to associate with Allah that for which He has not revealed any authority, and that you claim or attribute/ascribe to Allah things that you have no proof/rationale of.]

If *naskh* has no validation in the Sunnah and no validation in the Mushaf as discussed above, then it must have been expunged, extracted or theorized based on believing, or more descriptively reasoning, that what might appear to be a contradiction between two verses implies that one of the verses is no longer valid. This reasoning was based from its very beginning on the concept of contradictions and on logic, both of which are products of the mind. This means that the framers of *naskh*, of which Ahl al-Hadith (the group of Muslims that staunchly believe in Hadith/Sunnah as a major component of the religion) are a vast majority, believe in *akl* (mind/brain/reason) and not only *nakl* (transfer).

Concluding Thoughts

Naskh has no place in either reason or the Mushaf. It is a concept created to camouflage ignorance or provide an "Islamic" framework for subverting Allah's revelation, or possibly as a canonized instrument, along with Hadith, to justify economic, social or political objectives. Judging from numerous publications, the concept had been questioned by many scholars. Those who questioned it were severely attacked by many Muslim scholars as haters and enemies of Islam. Some *naskh* deniers were even elevated to the status of apostates. Ibn Hilal al-Nahwi said "Whoever says this thing (i.e., against abrogation) is not a believer, but rather a *kafir,* denying that with which Muhammad came. He must renounce his position or be killed".[23] Al-Nahhaas mentioned in his highly referenced book on *naskh* that several scholars prior to his time also did not believe in *naskh* entirely and that they were accused as being very close to *kufr*.[24] Abdulaziz ibn Baaz (d. 1420/1999), a former Grand Mufti of the Kingdom of Saudi Arabia, in response to an article that argued against the concept of abrogation stated: "That which he (the author) did is an act of clear disbelief, a repudiation of Islam, and denial of Allah the Glorious and His Prophet, on whom be peace, as any of the people of knowledge and faith who have read his article can perceive. It is obligatory upon the governing authority to have that man brought to the courts and ask that he retract his statements, and to rule upon him according to that which the pure Sharia summons".[25] Jafar al-Sadiq, one of the most respected Shia imams (the sixth) is alleged to have said "If a person does not know the *nasikh* and the *mansukh* and the *muhkam* and the *mutashabih*, they do not know the Qur'aan and they have no relation with the Qur'aan whatsoever." Considering the dramatic variation in interpreting and understanding *naskh* amongst Muslim scholars, according to al-Sadiq, most of them should be classified as ignorant of the Qur'aan. In a truly comical twist, Jews and Christians were brought into the fray to prove that *naskh* is valid by arguing that they were amongst the deniers of *naskh*.[26] This is so despite neither of these two groups believe in the Mushaf in the first place. Interestingly, the clergy of the Shia sect, all of whom are followers of Imam Sadiq, failed to have a consensus on what was abrogated and what was not.

Naskh is another controversial concept that was turned into "science", and that also served to distance Muslims from the Mushaf and to loosen their confidence in their ability to understand it or make attempts to interpret its verses without the tutelage of religious clergy and institutional hegemony. The concept of *naskh* is deeply entrenched in Muslim jurisprudence to the extent that key elements of al-Shafi's jurisprudence theory would come apart had it not been for *naskh* (al-Shafi'i's rulings on inheritance is a case in point). If the concept of *naskh* is abrogated, al-Shafi'i's *fiqh* rulings and those of many other Muslim scholars are in deep jeopardy. What is typically referred to as Islamic law and Islamic Sharia would also be in jeopardy. The stakes are so high for grand Muslim institutions to abrogate *naskh* altogether. When the advocates of *naskh* experience an indefensible challenge, they shy away from discussing specifics and in particular the implausibility of inconsistency between different verses of the Mushaf but insist on the validity of *naskh*, thus maintaining a consistent mercuriality through which many opinions can be accommodated.

Muslim's Greatest Challenge

Naskh has been used to justify extreme bloodshed and violence in the name of Islam. Whereas the Mushaf clearly states that guidance had come from Allah, so people have a free will according to M10:108 to accept the Lord's guidance or to reject it (see above). Many Muslim scholars followed the footsteps of al-Nahhaas (d. 338/949) who claimed that 113 verses are abrogated by M9:5, the so-called Sword verse, and 9 verses are abrogated by M9:29, the so-called Fighting verse.[27] The confusion is multiplied when Hadith is brought to support certain views. Here is an expert from the al-Jalalayn exegesis[28]

> Ibn Umar said that the Messenger of Allah said, "I have been commanded to fight the people until they testify that there is no deity worthy of worship except Allah and that Muhammad is the Messenger of Allah, establish the prayer and pay the *zakat*." This honorable *aayah* (9:5) was called the *aayah* of the Sword, about which al-Dahhak ibn Muzahim said, "It abrogated every agreement of peace between the Prophet and any idolater, every treaty, and every term." Al-Awfi said that ibn Abbas commented: "No idolater had any more treaty or promise of safety ever since *surah* Baqra'ah was revealed."

In their zeal to manufacture narratives to support the *naskh* concept, a thought that could have been overlooked by the framers of the above hadith is that the hadith claims that the Prophet did not honor the treaties that he held with non-Muslims. Nevertheless, the preponderance of historical narratives suggest that the *naskh* proponents were inclined into generalizing absolute violence, which could have served the objectives of states eager for expansion and wold have used every instrument in its disposal, most effective of which was religion. It is surprising that the *naskh* was not applied the other way around, namely to nullify the Sword and Fighting verses?

The zeal for *naskh* reached unusual extremes. To support the penalty of death by stoning for married adulterers, bizarre stories packaged as hadiths were sneaked into the Hadith corpus, thus giving them equal respect to prophetic narratives (irrespective of their authenticity). An example is a story by Amru ibn Maymoon. This story, which was included in Sahih al-Bukhari, is about a group of monkeys that stoned to death one of their members because it committed *zina*. Bizarre as it may sound, one can only speculate that it was included in Sahih al-Bukhari to give validation that stoning of married adulterers is so natural that even monkeys practice it.[29]

The *naskh* concept opened the door for a methodical canonized system practically justifying anything in the name of Islam despite Allah's insistence that the Mushaf is a fully-intact system of truths and instructions that cannot admit myths and illusions from either within it or from without (see M41:42). Over the ages, the *naskh* concept evolved to a labyrinth of information that became too complex for the "non-specialist" to comprehend. This maze of contradictory information, or the *naskh* corpus, had to be understood by the scholars of Islam since it was considered by numerous Muslim clergy as an important subject that would empower the clergy to understand and interpret the Mushaf. No matter how confusing or complex a body of knowledge is, it does not turn it into a science.

1 Brown, Jonathan. *Hadith*. Oneworld, 2009, p 271-273.
2 Fatoohi, Louay. *Abrogation in the Qur'an and Islamic Law*. Routledge, 2013.
3 Al-Zarqani, Muhammad Abdul-Adhim. *Manahil al-Irfan fi Uloom al-Qur'aan*. Dar al-Kitaab al-Arabi, 1995. Al-Baghdadi, Abi Mansour. *Al-Nasikh wa al-Mansookh*. Dar al-Adwa, [n.d.], pp. 13, 14. Abdo, Ehab Hasan. *Istihalat Wujood al-Naskh fi al-Qur'aan*. (Published online), 2004, pp. 251-260. This book contains the most exhaustive list of works that either supported or refuted *naskh*.
4 Fatoohi. *Abrogation*.
5 Fatoohi. *Abrogation*, p. 114.
6 Shahrour, Muhammad. *Nahwa Usool Jadeeda Lilfiqh al-Islami*. Dar al-Saqi, 2018, p. 294. Shahrour is arguably the first Muslim scholar to make this distinction.
7 Al-Zarqani. *Manahil*, p. 154.
8 Sunan ibn Majah Hadith collection, Kitaab al-Nikaah: "Ayesha said: 'The Verse of stoning and of breastfeeding an adult ten times was revealed, and the paper was with me under my pillow. When the Messenger of Allah died, we were preoccupied with his death, and a tame sheep came in and ate it.' "
9 According to M2:185, fasting is ordained on "who witnesses the month from within the group of believers." What "witnessing the month" means is an important and relevant question that was not considered by the proponents of *naskh*.
10 Ibn Manzur, Muhammad ibn Mukarram. *Lisan al-Arab*. 3rd ed., Dar Sader, 2000.
11 Some Muslim scholars attribute the first mention of *naskh* to Ali ibn abi Talib, the cousin of the Prophet, but the alleged narrative was never reported in the most prominent Hadith compendia. See al-Zarqani, *Manahil*, Vol. 2, p. 136.
12 Al-Shafi'i, Muhammad ibn Idris. *Al-Risala*. Dar al-Kutub al-Ilmiyyah, 1939, p. 222. Al-Hamadani, Mohammad ibn Musa (d. 548/1153), *al-Itibar fi al-Nasikh wa al-Mansookh min al-Akhbaar*. Da'erat al-Ma'arif al-Uthmanyya, 1940, p. 5.
13 M22:51 was interpreted by most prominent exegetes, such as ibn Kathir, al-Tabari and al-Baghawi, based on Hadith, to have been revealed when the Prophet had intermixed the revelation with verses inspired by Satan. Effectively, those exegetes and the relevant Hadith framers believed that the Prophet delivered satanic verses. Ironically, when Salman Rushdi suggested this in his book Satanic Verses, using

a mixture of fiction and non-fiction, the Muslim world erupted with fatwas calling for the death of Rushdi and numerous protests that spanned several continents, leading to many deaths. However, when a highly respected exegete such as ibn Kathir made the same suggestion that Rushdi did, no protests were registered. On the contrary, however, ibn Kathir continues to be elevated to a sainthood status.

14 *Najmah* also denotes a terrestrial star because they are separated from each other.

15 Shahrour, Muhammad. *Al-Kitaab wa al-Qur'aan: Ro'ya Jadeedah*. Dar al-Saqi, 2011, p. 54.

16 The realization that *aayah* is different from verse can have significant impact on interpreting the Mushaf in general. Particularly, it can shed light on understanding the difference between two important types of *aayaat*: the *muhkam* and the *mutashabih*. Under the conventional understanding that an *aayah* is a verse, the Mushaf had been divided into these two types. Muhammad Shahrour, in a more recent interpretation (see *Al-Kitaab wa al-Qur'aan*), realized that M3:7 strictly does not divide the Mushaf into two types of *aayaat* but three: the third type being neither muhkam nor mutashabih. However, if *aayah* does not mean verse, as claimed in this book, then a new interpretation of M3:7 would be needed.

17 See for instance the first group of hadiths in al-Tirmidhi's collection about the proper urination etiquette for Muslims.

18 Al-Baghdadi. *Al-Nasikh*, p. 47.

19 Abu Dawood, Kitaab Al-Wasayya, no. 2870. Surprisingly, this hadith, which has a significant economic and societal impact, is not included in either al-Bukhari or Muslim collections. Equally interesting is that the authenticity of this hadith continued to be debated until the 20th Century. Only recently was the hadith reclassified as *sahih* by al-Albani (d. 1420/1999), a prominent 20th century Salafi Muslim scholar of Hadith.

20 One cannot find any contradiction between M2:180 and M4:11. In fact, M4:11, the assumed abrogator of M2:180, emphasizes that the inheritance can be distributed only after the will is executed and after any loans (that the deceased did not pay in his lifetime) are paid. Also, notice that M2:180 focuses on the *waalidayyn*, which strictly refers to the biological parents. M4:11, on the other hand, mentions *abawayyhi*, which broadly denotes caregivers.

21 Sahih al-Bukhari, Kitaab al-Wasaya, no. 2747.

22 Al-Zarqani, *Manahil*, p. 153. According to al-Zarqani, the divine "wisdom" behind legal abrogation is to show the eloquence of the

Mushaf, and to provide the reciter of the Mushaf with the opportunity to gain additional rewards by increasing what the reciter can read. In the case of the absence of the stoning verse, which is an example of the textual abrogation, al-Zarqani argues that the divine "wisdom" behind removing the verse from the Mushaf is because of the abhorrence of the crime to the level that made it unfitting to be mentioned in the book of God.

23 Mustafa, Muhammad Salih Ali. *Al-Naskh fi al-Qur'aan al-Kareem*. Dar al-Qalam, 1988.
24 Al-Nahhaas, abu Ja'far. *Al-Nasikh wa al-Mansookh*. Al-Maktaba al-Aalamiyya, 1938, p. 4.
25 Ibn Baz, Abdul-Aziz ibn Abdu-Allah. "Clear Proof of the Disbelief of Whoever Claims it is Allowable for Anyone to Leave the Sharia of Muhammad." *Al-Dawa Magazine*, 1995.
26 Al-Zarqani. *Manahil*. Vol. 2, p. 147.
27 It is worth noting that the verses that related to violence were assigned specific names to give them presumably higher importance. However, we do not observe this practice applied to verses related to mercy or compassion.
28 Al-Mahalli, Jalal al-Deen and al-Toosi, Jalal al-Deen. *Tafsir al-Jalalayn*. Dar al-Hadith, [n.d.].
29 Sahih al-Bukhari, Kitaab Manaqib al-Ansaar, no. 3849. This story has caused so much debate amongst Muslims. The defenders of the story argue that ibn Maymoon was a highly credible and honest person. However, on the assumption that the credibility and honesty of ibn Maymoon is established, the inclusion of the story in a book that many Muslims consider to be the most important after the Mushaf is very suspicious. It is also impossible that the story of any credible person be suitable for inclusion in Sahih al-Bukhari, irrespective of whether or not he was a companion of the Prophet (incidentally, ibn Maymoon was not a companion)? The pressing question is what made the story of ibn Maymoon deserving of inclusion in Sahih al-Bukhari, or stated differently, why did the story of ibn Maymoon become part of the religion?

8

NEW DOCTRINES: SUNNAH AND HADITH

وَأَنزَلْنَا إِلَيْكَ الْكِتَابَ بِالْحَقِّ مُصَدِّقًا لِّمَا بَيْنَ يَدَيْهِ مِنَ الْكِتَابِ وَمُهَيْمِنًا عَلَيْهِ ۖ فَاحْكُم بَيْنَهُم بِمَا أَنزَلَ اللَّهُ ۖ وَلَا تَتَّبِعْ أَهْوَاءَهُمْ عَمَّا جَاءَكَ مِنَ الْحَقِّ ۚ لِكُلٍّ جَعَلْنَا مِنكُمْ شِرْعَةً وَمِنْهَاجًا ۚ وَلَوْ شَاءَ اللَّهُ لَجَعَلَكُمْ أُمَّةً وَاحِدَةً وَلَٰكِن لِّيَبْلُوَكُمْ فِي مَا آتَاكُمْ ۖ فَاسْتَبِقُوا الْخَيْرَاتِ ۚ إِلَى اللَّهِ مَرْجِعُكُمْ جَمِيعًا فَيُنَبِّئُكُم بِمَا كُنتُمْ فِيهِ تَخْتَلِفُونَ

And we have revealed to you the Book in truth, validating what is within it from the book and superseding/dominating it, so govern between them with what Allah has revealed to you and do not follow their desires that might conflict with what you have received in truth. To each of you, we have made a governance path and methodology, and if Allah had decided, He would have made you one nation, but so that He may subject you to a test in what He has provided to you, so rush to achieve goodness; to Allah is your return –all of you- so He may inform you of what you used to differ in.

M5:48

The Creation of New Doctrines

Never in the history of Muslims has a doctrine been more contentious and divisive than Hadith. The doctrine of Hadith divided the early Muslim communities with the same intensity it divided later ones. Hadith pitted one Muslim against his relatives, Arabs against non-Arabs, Ahl al-Sunnah wa al-Jama'ah against the Mu'tazalites and other sects, many powerful Muslim rulers against their subjects, and many Muslim subjects against their rulers. The Hadith doctrine initiated grand wars in the name of Allah and created numerous Muslim sects from extreme Shi'ism to extreme Sunnism and all other extremes in between. Hadith reduced women to cattle or "things" and created a culture among both women and men that perpetuated the belief that women were inherently inferior to men and can be equated to animals. Hadith instilled constant fear in Muslims; fear that deprived them of creativity and progress.

Never has there been a more effective barrier to understanding the Message of Islam than Hadith, which created a "religious" framework that altered Allah's revelation. Through sophistry and brilliant loopholes based on the same logic that the framers of Hadith despised, men authorized themselves to nullify Allah's words. The question arises as to how such an incredibly powerful doctrine was created; a doctrine that ended up being the de factor primary source for Muslims. This chapter is not about the authenticity of Hadith, about which many volumes of scholarly and non-scholarly works have been produced. Instead, this chapter is an attempt to shed light on how such a powerful doctrine was created, the message of which often contradicts the Message of Allah.

Hadith is an Arabic word that is derived from or related to the word *hadath* (an event that has already occurred), or possibly from the root *haddatha* (he narrated). Hadith refers to a written record about something the Prophet is believed to have said or did. (There are more elaborate definitions of Hadith; however, this definition is sufficiently inclusive without adding further confusing details.) Hadith is also broadly perceived as the tradition of the Prophet. What is believed by different Muslim sects to be the Prophet's tradition falls into two general categories based on the way the content of the information was transmitted. The first includes all direct transmissions starting with or containing the phrase "The Prophet said...". The second includes all indirect transmissions such as "The Prophet did...", or "Person X said the Prophet used to do...". A single Prophetic report, whether under the category of "said" or "did", henceforth will be referred to as a hadith, while the plural will be as hadiths.

The probability that a certain hadith is authentic, in that its content represents a factual report, varies. To determine the authenticity of Hadith, an elaborate system of classifications emerged, defining whether each hadith is: *sahih* (correct, authentic or true), which technically denotes a high probability of authenticity; *dhaeef* (weak), indicating a low probability of authenticity; and a variety of probabilistic degrees within these two extremes that led to additional classifications including *hasan* (good), *ghareeb* (strange), etc. These classifications can be varied and complex, using fluid criteria that are impossible to validate and rarely made explicit and clear. An example is a classification that depends on whether one or more people heard the Prophet directly and transmitted what they heard.

Overall, classification of Hadith became a labyrinth inaccurately and unjustifiably described as a science. In his treatise on the "sciences of Hadith," ibn al-Salah (d. 643/1245), a leading figure in Hadith studies and whose writings became part of Hadith curricula in major universities, classified Hadith into *sahih, hasan, thaeef, musnad, muttasil, marfoo, mawqoof, maqtoo, mursal, munqat'a, muthal* (which has several sub-categories), *mudallas, shath, munkar, mu'alal, muthtarib, mudarraj, mawthoo'a, maqloob, mashhoor, ghareeb, musalsal, nasikh, mansookh, mukhtalaf, muttafaq, muftaraq,* and *mo'talaf.*[1] (I have chosen not to translate these categories into English, as I may not capture their complexities and full meanings.) These classifications were created by scholars with varying objectives including extracting "Islamic" law or resolving particular legal or social problems of their times. Common to all types of classifications, however, is basing the criteria for authenticity on the modality of transmission (typically referred to in Arabic as *sanad*). To the best of my knowledge, no Hadith classification system has ever been devised that was based on the text of the Hadith itself (typically referred to in Arabic as *matn*) or on any non-*sanad* criteria such as compatibility with the Mushaf or consistency with historical or scientific records. Out of the tens of criteria extensively outlined and researched in his treatise on Hadith, ibn Salah did not include a single criterion related to the *matn*. In fact, the primary interest amongst the key framers of the Hadith science was the *sanad.* Even if two *sanad*-approved or *sanad*-verified hadiths were admittedly contradictory in meaning, according to the

Hadith scientists themselves, the two hadiths were considered authentic.[2]

The Sunnah describes the tradition of the Prophet. Hadith is essentially the documentation (oral or written) of the Sunnah. The Sunnah is derived from the Arabic term *sann'ah* (created as an example for others to emulate). For Muslims, the Sunnah, when not associated with a specific person, is understood to be a body of knowledge that describes the practices of the Prophet that should be emulated in the pursuit of the straight path. It is regarded as a "best practice" manual for good and pious Muslims. For instance, trimming the mustache, growing the beard, and whether or not a shoe can be put on while a person is standing are all believed to be included in the directives of the Sunnah (of course, with variance depending on each Muslim sect). However, some practices of the Prophet that were reported within the body of Hadith were never canonized as part of the Sunnah for no clear reason by Hadith scholars. The Sunnah also covers worship rituals. For example, additional prayers before and after the mid-day prayers are considered to be Sunnah in the sense that they are not obligatory. The common understanding that the Sunnah designates non-obligatory acts can be problematic since many "Islamic" rulings came into being through the Prophet's tradition such as, for example, the manner in which Muslims perform the daily prayers and many other matters related to inheritance and marriage. The execution of all these acts is also considered part of the Sunnah, yet they are obligatory.

Typically, the terms Sunnah and Hadith are used interchangeably. While common usage conflates the two, it must be emphasized that Muslims' perception of the two is different. The Sunnah does not imply an obligation on Muslims while Hadith is believed to contain obligations. The question of the authenticity of Hadith is critical to most Muslims; this is because Muslims believe that what the Prophet did or said is essential to leading a proper Islamic life. This includes the smallest details from the orientation and position of the body during urination, to matters of governance. In other words, Muslims believe that the Sunnah, i.e., the way the Prophet conducted his daily life fourteen centuries ago, including hygienic practices, methods of distributing uncultivated lands, procedures for conducting wars, promulgation of treaties and political governance, all constitute the model for best behavior not only for Muslims but for all of humanity. For many Muslims, following the Sunnah leads to a perfect life. Reality demonstrates that this belief is not only unhelpful in achieving a perfect or a good life but is often contradictory to the direct instructions of the Mushaf, and might even be detrimental to one's well-being. In fact, Hadith, most often, is contradictory to the guidance of Allah as manifested in the Mushaf.

For most Muslims, the Sunnah is considered highly important to the point that many believe that without the Sunnah, Islam would be incomplete and the Mushaf would be incomprehensible. How the Mushaf compares in significance to the Sunnah is a contentious subject that was the root cause of many divisions and even wars within Muslim communities. The body of the Sunnah, or Hadith, was most likely the singular reason behind the rise of a variety of Muslim sects. The creation of the Sunnah as a doctrine emerged in the first Islamic century and its canonization is mostly attributed to al-Shafi'i. The status given to the Sunnah in early Muslim history reached epic proportions, a status that continues to be upheld in contemporary times and championed by the Muslim sects who protected the institution of the Sunnah to extraordinary extremes.

The Hadith corpus and its extensive commentaries contain audacious statements by leading Sunnah proponents such as al-Darimi (d. 255/869), Yahya ibn abi Kathir (d. 129/747) and al-Shatibi (d. 790/1388).[3] Al-Darimi dedicated an introductory chapter in his *Sunan* with the title "*Al-Sunnah Qadiya ala kitaab Allah*" (the Sunnah has higher legal authority than the book of Allah). When one learns of the presence of such a chapter in such a respected book, one falls under the impression that the Prophet must have provided sufficient indications or narratives to warrant dedicating such a title in the first place. The chapter's title is borrowed from a statement attributed to Yahya abi Kathir. Interestingly, abi Kathir had a mixed review from Hadith authenticators to the point that some even considered him a Hadith fabricator. Despite this, however, the major Hadith books did not find a problem using his narratives. Chapter 49 of al-Darimi's *al-Sunnah Qadiya ala Kitaab Allah,* contains only five hadiths, with only one attributed to the Prophet. This lone hadith, however, does not even support al-Darimi's and abi Kathir's claims that the Sunnah rules over the Mushaf. Ayyub al-Sakhtiyani (d. 131/748) went even further to claim that "the Qur'aan needs the Sunnah more than the Sunnah needs the Qur'aan."[4] This audacious claim found enthusiastic support amongst a wide sector of Muslims, whom I call the Sunnah-first proponents, and particularly Muslim empires who realized the emergence of a grand crack through which a variety of practices can be made to look as if they were part of Islam or be made as "Islamic". The audacious explicit claims by al-Darimi, abi Kathir, al-Sakhtiyani, and others who were less explicit, such as al-Shafi'i, were generalized by Hadith scholars without academic scrutiny or challenge as the understanding of early Sunni Muslims.[5]

While most, if not all, Muslims would reject the idea that there is anything higher in authority than the Mushaf, few question, however, the sources that gave credence to such claims. In theory, the Mushaf is held as the ultimate source of religious authority. In practice, however, the Sunnah is regarded with greater significance. Many Muslims hold a middle ground, believing that the Sunnah complements the Mushaf and that without the Sunnah, it is impossible to understand the Mushaf. The opinions of abi Kathir and al-Darimi, al-Sakhtiyani and al-Barbahari, were later propagated widely and presented as norms and as representative of the Sunni faith.[6] Jonathan Brown, a contemporary Hadith scholar claims "the normative legacy of the Prophet is known as the Sunnah, and, although it stands second to the Qur'aan in terms of reverence, it is the lens through which the holy book is interpreted and understood."[7] Brown goes further to claim that "the Qur'aan was not the most powerful source for understanding the Islamic message...the Qur'aan and the Sunnah functioned in tandem. Like a locked door without a key, the Qur'aan could not be accessed without the Sunnah. The Qur'aan contained the totality of God's message, but the Sunnah explained, adjusted and added to it in order to convey God's complete guidance."[8]

All the way from ibn abi Kathir of the first Muslim century to staunch advocates of the institution of the Sunnah of the fourteenth Hijri century, and those in between, including al-Shafi'i, a strong advocacy and deep zeal emerged for the Sunnah to the point of considering belief in Hadith as a fundamental tenet of Islam. The Sunnah proponents have transformed the perception of Islam's core and grandeur from a Message of guidance to humanity and mind-blowing prophecies about nature and the universe into a manual on how to perform the daily prayers and whether women can pluck their eyebrows. Regarding the ritual prayers, the assumed narrative (and the most touted) by the Sunnah proponents is that since the Mushaf did not spell out such details, and the Sunnah did, its eminence became validated.

The predominant thinking of the Sunnah proponents suggested that the core of Islam rests on dos and do nots, referred to typically as *takleef* (obligation). To their surprise, however, the Sunnah never answered what they considered to be important matters. A paramount example is the obligatory daily prayer that is repeatedly used to validate their de-facto propositions that the Sunnah is of higher level than the Mushaf. The Sunnah books, such as those of Sahih al-Bukhari and others, much to the surprise of many Muslims, do not contain instructions on how to perform the daily prayers. In more than seventy hadiths classified under the Prayer Chapter in Sahih al-Bukhari, the compendium that commands the highest respect amongst the majority of Muslims, not a single hadith spells out the details of the prayers, either in form or pronouncements. In fact, no direct or indirect instructions are available in any of the other hundreds of hadiths within Sahih al-Bukhari that relate to prayers. Most of the hadiths in the Prayer Chapter are related to peripheral subjects such as places where the prayers can be performed or related requirements of hygiene. In his entire collection, al-Bukhari did not document a single direct hadith attributed to the Prophet and dedicated to the specific movements that constitute the prayers.

Sahih al-Bukhari is not the only Hadith compendium that had no mention of how the prayers should be performed. Out of 300 hadiths grouped under the Prayers Chapter in Sunan al-Tirmidhi, another prominent Hadith collection, not a single one sheds light on the precise physical performance of the daily prayers. The other respected compendia, such as Sahih Muslim, Sunan abu Dawood, Sunan al-Nisaa'i and others, do not provide any instructions either. In reality and in practice, Muslims who do and who do not have the highest regards for al-Bukhari perform their daily prayers the same way. Clearly, either group did not learn how to pray from the Sahih books or Hadith in general. This fact invalidates the corner stone argument on which the Sunnah proponents build their case.

While the obligation of prayers is clearly established in the Mushaf, the details are neither available in the Mushaf nor in the written traditions of the Prophet. These details have been transmitted from one generation to the next through imitation, emulation and observation. Since the Mushaf did not differentiate, in form, the prayers of the followers of Muhammad from that of earlier people, there is a likelihood that the contemporary form of the prayers did not change significantly; however, the substance and the words used within it did.[9] Notice that the Mushaf provides details of how to complete the ablution required for the ritual prayers (see M5:6); it could have spelled out the details of the ritual prayers, but it did not. If the form was more important than the substance, then the Mushaf would have given explicit details on how the prayers should be performed.[10] The stark fact is that it did not.

The framers of such arguments, including al-Shafi'i who argued this point in his *al-Risala* treatise, appear to have envisioned the religion as a collection of rituals that needed perfect execution. Interestingly, the Sunnah did not provide details of these rituals, and when it is alleged that it did, as in the case of the required charity and ritual prayers, contradictions abound.

In Chapter 5, I argued that the personification and objectification of Allah was a factor that prevented understanding Him. The consequences led to conceptions that are alien to the Mushaf and having significant impact in shaping the behavior of the Muslims, and especially the perception of the faith by non-Muslims. Similar to the manner in which sensual interpretations of the Mushaf were appealing and expedient, despite their incoherence and contradiction to other parts of the Mushaf, it was easier to embrace Hadith since it embodied some sort of a physical manifestation or a physical realization of certain behaviors. Most people have a tendency to accept facts or information that their senses communicate to them more easily than that communicated through reason and logic. Reasoning mandates using the mind, which history proves is least appealing to most people. This is not implying that most people are incapable of understanding complex concepts but only to emphasize that humans have a tendency to gravitate towards the sensual more than the abstract and the intellectual. For instance, the flatness of the earth was more accepted than its roundness since the human eye sees a flat land around it. This was the case until someone provided a proof based on rational mathematical and physics-based reasoning. The immediate and the physically manifested that can be touched, tasted, smelled, seen, or heard are much more acceptable for most people than what can be deduced, induced, analyzed, synthesized or reasoned out. Creating a model for the perfect life based on the physical attributes of the Prophet is much more tangible and clear (as documented through Hadith) than following the Mushaf's guidance that is time-invariant and requires significant and highly concerted participation in a wide range of human experiences such as governance, economy, entertainment, culture, society, arts, etc. Copying a great work of art is certainly much easier than creating one. However, even when copying works of art, the historical context is a valuable factor in determining the value and relevance of the copied work. The Mushaf repeatedly calls upon the reader to exercise her intellectual capabilities. The Mushaf does not call for either uniqueness or difference in how it is understood but rather it calls for originality. If the "perfect life" could be modeled, there would be infinite models based on the infinite complexity of the human circumstance and experience. The Prophet lived a narrow set of circumstances, in number and scope, that are infinitesimal in comparison to the collective human experience. The knowledge base, experience of humanity, and the entire spectrum of all aspects of life, at the time of the Prophet, were significantly narrower than today.

If leading a proper "Islamic" life requires adherence to the Sunnah, there are more than 30,000 hadiths with additional expansive volumes of commentaries that would take the average Arabic-speaking Muslim a lifetime to go through. Even if one were to be content with the two Sahihs (those of al-Bukhari and Muslim), one has to read tens of volumes of commentaries and exegeses to understand what is deeply buried within these hadiths.[11] Since many hadiths were transmitted through their perceived meaning rather than verbatim (as will be discussed below), it will take further effort to determine the original meaning of the words of Hadith. Such task seems formidable, if not impossible. Even more surprisingly, the practice of "addition" to the hadiths, i.e., adding words to certain hadiths to look as if they were part of the authentic Prophetic saying, were not even frowned upon as long as these additions were made by "trustworthy" individuals.[12] Even then, an important question (if not the quintessential question upon which the entire Hadith science hinges) that was never answered is who determines the trustworthiness of a certain hadith transmitter and what is the definition of trustworthiness.

Giving the words that Muhammad uttered the same standing and reverence as those of the Mushaf, as originally conceived and articulated by al-Shafi'i, opened the door to the emergence of multiple doctrines in Islam, instead of the Mushaf as the only one.[13] If the perfect life for Muslims requires the emulation of a snapshot of the life of the Prophet who lived in the seventh century in Arabia, a relatively underdeveloped and minimally sophisticated society, then Islam is void of its time-invariant and eternal character. This understanding rests on the assumption that the transmitted snapshots of the Prophet's actions and sayings are accurate and not distorted by the cultural and linguistic prism of a chain of transmitters and commentators who had natural human limitations. If the life of Muhammad in Medina was the perfect model for eternity, then of what value is the Mushaf to Muslims and humanity at large? The implication of human agency is then severely curtailed if not nullified.

There is no reason or any directive within the Mushaf to believe that emulating the Prophet in every aspect of his life brings the Muslim closer to piety or to Allah. Emulating the Prophet is a personal choice and, as I will argue in this chapter, has nothing to do with Islam and does not necessarily increase the piety of a believer. In fact, it is arguable that emulating the Prophet has created polarization and divisions within the Muslim communities throughout history and has created more harm than good, even when considering a seemingly benign (or trivial) Sunnah recommendation as growing a beard. To believe that such facial hairstyle for men is "Islamic" simply because it is alleged (in the form of a hadith) that the Prophet asked his followers to let their beards grow, leads to perceiving those without beards as less pious or religious, or less "Islamic".[14] Consequently, these "less pious" Muslims are considered as less qualified to comment on Islam, and, in general, such Muslims and their possible intellectual contribution become severely marginalized. On the other hand, "visibly pious" Muslims are rewarded with high respect within "Islamic" circles, even if they were intellectual, academic, or social failures. A more serious consequence, however, is that since the Hadith corpus is an amalgamation of contradictory narratives, accepting it as an Islamic doctrine was a significant catalyst in the emergence of different Muslim sects. Differences in essence should not be any cause for alarm, but many of these sects claimed the others are doomed to hellfire. The war-torn Muslim world is the direct outcome of Hadith.

WAS MUHAMMAD INFALLIBLE?

The belief by most Muslims that Muhammad's life was ideal severely limited their understanding of Islam as a petrified religion frozen in time and space. This confinement of the "ideal" life manifested itself in the Hadith and expansive commentaries on religion by Muslim scholars, and had the consequence of stifling Islam's global appeal as demonstrated by the geographical spread of Muslims around the world in contrast to Christianity, even if missionary activities were taken into account by both sides. A message frozen in time and space cannot have a strong appeal to a Muslim or a non-Muslim living in the twenty-first century, or even to a non-Muslim living during the first Muslim century in sub-Saharan Africa or in Europe. In contrast, the message of Christianity, which was validated locally (in time and space) by the miracles of Jesus, found appeal throughout the world as demonstrated by the spread of Christianity and its dominant presence in practically every continent and every corner of the world. Christian missionaries do not preach the sunnah of Jesus as far as how he attended to his bodily functions, or how he dressed, or whether or not he sported a beard. In fact, despite the numerous artistic depictions of Jesus having a beard and wearing a robe, such depictions hardly resonate with the average committed Christian.

The belief that the Prophet was perfect also led to believing in his infallibility. This belief, espoused by the majority of Muslims, sharply contradicts the Muhammad of the Mushaf, who is portrayed as a human who on occasions had erred in judgement or performed acts that were corrected by a divine revelation. The Mushaf emphasized that Muhammad did not possess any divine attributes at all. The Message, after all, was not Muhammad. The Message and its messenger were both infallible, not Muhammad the man, Muhammad the husband, Muhammad the father, Muhammad the governor, or Muhammad the Prophet. Muhammad the messenger is different from all the others. Irrespective of the status of the Sunnah in Islam, the Muhammad of the Mushaf is vastly different from Muhammad of Hadith. The Muhammad of Hadith does not complement the Mushaf's portrayal of Muhammad but sharply contradicts it. In fact, the Muhammad of Hadith represents a character that is contradictory to the Muhammad of the Mushaf. The Muhammad of the Mushaf cannot be the same Muhammad of the famed Prophet biographies that were written more than one hundred years after Muhammad died. The difference between the two Muhammads is so stark that it should prompt Muslims to think about who the real Muhammad was and whether there is any benefit from reconstructing an image of Muhammad outside the revelation, or an image that is not based on truth. Nevertheless, despite the difference between the two Muhammads, the Hadith itself never provides any indication to the infallibility of the Prophet.

Muslims elevated Muhammad to a status that was based neither on reality nor on Allah's revelation. The belief that Muhammad possessed divine characteristics significantly distances the Muslim from Islam rather than making him more pious because such an association, according to the Mushaf, amounts to *shirk* (the act of associating partners with Allah), which, according to the interpretation of practically all Muslims, is a great sin. Claiming that Muhammad had the capacity or was given the privilege of making eternal injunctions, including rulings on what is permissible or forbidden could also be considered technically as *shirk*, since it amounts to associating with Allah someone who has Allah's power and attributes. This is made explicit in the last phrase of M18:26

$$وَلَا يُشْرِكُ فِي حُكْمِهِ أَحَدًا$$

[and He does not share His rulings with anyone.]

Elevating Muhammad to a holy status could also suggest that Muslims were competing with the status or image of Jesus amongst most Christians. The underlying narrative of such competition is if Muhammad was proven to possess divine powers, he would have been superior to Jesus and therefore the superiority of Islam. Muslim culture is full of pseudo-hadiths (narratives with wide distribution that resonate within the Muslim culture as canonized hadiths, irrespective of their authenticity) that glorify the Prophet with divine attributes.

The concept of *ismah* (infallibility) has never been precisely defined. It is typically understood to mean "protection from errors and sins" in the sense that an infallible person does not commit errors or sins. The vast majority of Sunnis and practically all Shias believe that the Prophet possessed *ismah*, a privilege given to him by Allah. Shias go further and claim that all of their imams were granted *ismah*.[15] While Sunnis theoretically do not believe that anyone except the Prophet was granted such privilege, their practice, as guided by Hadith, suggests that not only the Prophet, but also the *sahaaba* (the companions of the Prophet) were deemed infallible. The rationale for the belief in the *ismah* of Prophet Muhammad, invoked by both Shias and Sunnis alike, cannot be found in the Mushaf. Here, I will focus only on the question of the infallibility of the Prophet rather than the imams and *sahaaba*.

New Doctrines: Sunnah and Hadith

Ismah is derived from *asamah,* an Arabic root word that means "to protect". M5:67 highlights the type of protection that the Messenger was granted in which Allah uses the present tense *ya'simakah*

$$\text{يَا أَيُّهَا الرَّسُولُ بَلِّغْ مَا أُنزِلَ إِلَيْكَ مِن رَّبِّكَ ۖ وَإِن لَّمْ تَفْعَلْ فَمَا بَلَّغْتَ رِسَالَتَهُ ۚ وَاللَّهُ يَعْصِمُكَ مِنَ النَّاسِ ۗ إِنَّ اللَّهَ لَا يَهْدِي الْقَوْمَ الْكَافِرِينَ}$$

[O you Messenger, convey what was revealed to you from your lord and if you did not then you would have not delivered His message and Allah *ya'simakah* from mankind; Allah does not guide the nation that conceals the truth.][16] *Ya'simakah* is used here in reference to mankind (*naas*). If one were to consider the context of the other twelve occurrences (in eleven verses) of the other derivatives of *asamah,* one finds them all related to the act of protection.[17] Surprisingly, the framers of the *ismah* concept never contested the interpretation of *ismah* as "protection" in those eleven verses. M5:67 commands the Messenger to convey the message and never be fearful as Allah promises to provide full protection from any harm that might come from people, specifically (as opposed to harm that might come from natural disasters). In light of the fact that no connection is established between infallibility and *ismah* in the entire Mushaf, the proponents of infallibility of the Prophet invoke the *fi al-sharia* definition, which bypasses the meaning of the Arabic words to fit a particular persuasion (see Chapter 9.)

A strong validation that Muhammad the prophet was not infallible can be found in several verses of the Mushaf. An important one is M33:1

$$\text{يَا أَيُّهَا النَّبِيُّ اتَّقِ اللَّهَ وَلَا تُطِعِ الْكَافِرِينَ وَالْمُنَافِقِينَ ۗ إِنَّ اللَّهَ كَانَ عَلِيمًا حَكِيمًا}$$

[O you Prophet, have awareness and cognisance of Allah and do not obey the truth-concealers (*kafireen*) and hypocrites; Allah was *aleem-hakim.*] If the Prophet were infallible, then there would be no need for Allah's warning and caution to the Prophet not to obey the truth-concealers. M33:1 implies that the Prophet either obeyed the truth-concealers and hypocrites or there was a possibility that he could have obeyed them. In either case, the Prophet would have committed an act contrary to Allah's dictates and direct command, which would have been an error or lapse in judgement on the part of the Prophet. This would invalidate the Prophet's infallibility if it meant full concordance with Allah's guidance, instructions and dictates. (It is important to note that M33:1 addressed the Prophet, not the Messenger; a point that we will return to later.)

Similarly, the 66ᵗʰ Chapter of the Mushaf (al-Tahreem) starts with another verse that admonishes the Prophet for making haram what had been made halal for him. M66:1 states

يَا أَيُّهَا النَّبِيُّ لِمَ تُحَرِّمُ مَا أَحَلَّ اللَّهُ لَكَ تَبْتَغِي مَرْضَاتَ أَزْوَاجِكَ وَاللَّهُ غَفُورٌ رَّحِيمٌ

[O Prophet, why do you eternally prohibit (make haram) what Allah has made eternally lawful for you, thereby seeking the satisfaction of your spouses, and Allah is forgiving-merciful.] If the Prophet were infallible, he would not have committed an error as serious as prohibiting a lawful act.[18]

While many Muslims overlook the implication of the above two verses for reasons that are not clear, Allah chose to archive specific prophetic experiences and put the above two verses at the helm of two important chapters in the Mushaf, effectively making an eternal archive of these Prophetic events. From the above and other verses, a clear image of the Prophet emerges, that of a man who made, or could have made mistakes, hence implying a fallible Prophet.

The human reality of Muhammad the Prophet did not accord well with those who elevated him to a super-human status. This elevation could have been the result of extreme love and admiration for the Prophet, or an aspiration for a high level of religious piety. Irrespective of all these motives, and without assuming a lurking nefarious conspiracy to destroy Islam, the outcome of the holy status attributed to the Prophet paved the way for the introduction of an entirely new doctrine, the Sunnah. This new doctrine was not discovered or created instantly but evolved over time and continues to evolve to this date. This ingenious concept has a built-in mechanism to tailor the religion as one wishes. Effectively, for Muslims, the Sunnah became Islam. The Mushaf was turned into an ornamentation to decorate with, to sing with, to achieve blessings from, to marginalize with, and to oppress with.

MUHAMMAD THE PROPHET VS. MUHAMMAD THE MESSENGER

Scholars of Islam are quick to point out that there is a distinct difference between a Prophet and a Messenger: a Messenger was requested and commissioned to deliver a precisely worded revelation containing a code of morality and ethics that was transformed into a document, whereas a prophet conveyed prophecies that contained either predictions of what would come in the future or descriptions of what had happened in the ancient past. Most likely, the prophecies were revealed to prophets and then were conveyed to communities orally. While many Muslim scholars recognized that a difference exists between a Messenger and a Prophet, though hardly reasonably articulated, most are quick to emphasize that a Messenger is necessarily a Prophet but a Prophet is not necessarily a Messenger. Interestingly, any recognized difference between the two stops there. This argument, which is not difficult to understand by the majority of Muslims, provides insufficient background to understand the functional relationship the Messenger or the Prophet would have had with his community and their subsequent religious implications and obligations.

Muslims have given very little attention to the particular usage of the roles of Prophet and Messenger in the Mushaf. Muhammad was a messenger and a Prophet. The fine distinction between the two capacities should evoke caution when considering the particular usage, in the Mushaf, of "Prophet" or "Messenger." To the best of my knowledge, Muhammad Shahrour was the first person ever to realize the contextual implications of each role as used in the Mushaf.[19] While a person might be called by a variety of descriptions, her name is different from adjectives or attributes that she might possess. While I might introduce a friend as a doctor, the usage here implies respect but is irrelevant unless I am introducing the doctor to professional colleagues within a medical context. If the Mushaf contains the words of the One who fashioned the precision of the DNA and sub-atomic particles and their physics, then one would expect that Allah had a precise purpose when He used the attribute "Prophet" instead of "Messenger" or vice versa. If Muslims consider the Mushaf as Allah's revelation, then they must believe it to be infinitely precise, or perfect. Despite consisting of words that the speakers of the Arabic language would find easier to understand than others, the producer of the Mushaf's words is not a man but the One who embodies all intelligence behind all things. Therefore, the Mushaf's words would require a completely different approach than if they were produced by a human. Muslims, thus, should start interpreting the Mushaf by considering Allah's words as very precise and that their choice is intended to convey a specific message that would otherwise be different had a different word been used. This methodology should replace the variety of inconsistent and variable Arabic grammar methodologies adopted and canonized by the Arabs throughout the ages.[20]

Within the context of the Mushaf, Prophet and Messenger are two words that cannot be interchangeable, as is the case with any other two words in the Mushaf. While people use synonyms interchangeably, the Mushaf is not a human production and Allah uses adjectives, attributes and names with precision that have significant purposes and implications.[21] Arabs might use some or many of the words of the Mushaf in their daily use of the Arabic language but cannot match the Mushaf's contextual and algorithmic precision. The assumption that any word appearing in a specific verse in the Mushaf can be interchanged with a different one is arbitrary and problematic, as it leads to diverging and conflicting interpretations of the Mushaf. If one believes that the Mushaf is a revelation from Allah, the Mushaf's linguistic structures and contexts are immune from contradictions and thus should be immune from interchangeability.

The distinction between the designations of Prophet and Messenger is fundamental to understanding the concept of the Sunnah and its validity. Muhammad was a Prophet and a Messenger. (The simultaneity is of little relevance here in the sense that a father can also be a carpenter.) Each of the two words describes a different attribute embodied within the same human being named Muhammad. The specific choice of either word would then strongly impact the interpretation of the Mushaf context. Most Muslims, and probably scholars and students of religion, agree that there is a distinction but they do not necessarily converge on a distinct meaning for both terms.[22]

To make understanding the difference possible, two examples are considered here. If a nurse was asked to follow the orders of a doctor, the implication is that the nurse would have to execute all orders dictated by the doctor related to, or in the context of, the defining relationship between her and the doctor and the capacity or profession of the doctor. The doctor can dictate to the nurse to take blood samples of a

New Doctrines: Sunnah and Hadith

certain patient, and the nurse has to comply with the request as mandated by her relationship with the doctor. However, the nurse is not at fault if she refuse an order to fill the gas tank of the doctor's car. Another example relates to the famous scientist Marie Curie. That was the name given to her by her ancestors and her parents. She was also a Professor at the University of Paris and a wife. A distinct attribute of Marie Curie confines the context to a specified relationship to others within the context. The invocation of Curie's professorship dictates a relationship to students or academic associates. Invocation of 'wife', however, dictates a relationship to a husband. It would have been improper and senseless to give an assignment to Curie's students instructing them to turn the assignment on a specific date to the wife. Her husband could have written a letter to his parents referring to matters related to their marital relationship. He could have used the word 'wife'. Had he chosen the word 'professor', he would have directed the recipient of his message to her professorial duties, which were disjointed from their marital relationship. Clearly, a wife can be a professor but not necessarily the converse; both professor and wife, when used in a sentence, specify the precise relevance to the context. As illustrated by these examples above, the precise usage of a profession or an attribute related to a professional capacity defines a specific relationship between the individuals mentioned or implied within the context given.

The interpretation of the Mushaf had been largely influenced by early Arab scholars whose language must have been strongly influenced by poetry, which was a dominant part of Arab culture, especially in the Arabian Peninsula.[23] Interchanging words that have close meanings or common designations had been, and continues to be, a mainstay of Arabic poetry. The outcome was sacrificing precision in lieu of seductive and soothing melodic poetry that served to entertain, mostly, than to convey a precise meaning. Because of the central role poetry played and particularly the strong oral tradition in the Arabian Peninsula, words used in poetry became a reference for their apparent meaning. For instance, many Arabs are eager to demonstrate that there are tens of names for the sword; however, all those words, except one, describe different attributes of the sword rather than provide an alternative name. Had the Mushaf been a book of Arabic poetry, imprecision might have been the norm. Allah anticipated (or predicted) humans' conflation of the Mushaf's style with that of poetry. This was explicitly stated in the Mushaf in response to or in anticipation of attempts by the Arabs to understand the text of the Mushaf in light of Arabic poetry (see M21:5, 36:69 and 69:41).

Establishing the importance of distinguishing between Prophet and Messenger within the Mushaf is a critical and major step towards understanding the proper context within which acts of obedience to Muhammad were established in the Mushaf. Most Muslim scholars and exegetes have based their arguments of obedience to Muhammad (the Prophet and Messenger) on several verses in the Mushaf or even on phrases within verses. The classical interpretation of these verses is problematic from different perspectives, including incorrect interpretations of the Arabic words and dismissing contextual relevance.

THE MESSENGER AS A GOOD EXAMPLE

M33:21 sets the tone for the importance of distinguishing the Prophet from the Messenger:

لَقَدْ كَانَ لَكُمْ فِي رَسُولِ اللَّهِ أُسْوَةٌ حَسَنَةٌ لِمَن كَانَ يَرْجُو اللَّهَ وَالْيَوْمَ الْآخِرَ وَذَكَرَ اللَّهَ كَثِيرًا

[There was for you (plural) in the Messenger of Allah an *uswah hasanah* (good example) for those who sought Allah and the Last Day and mentioned Allah plentifully]. Here, *uswah hasanah*, which is translated as 'good example', is commonly invoked as a holistic concept that encourages (or commands, as some scholars would argue) the Muslims to emulate the Messenger/Prophet. Allah could have produced different verses such as "there was for you in the Prophet an *uswah hasanah*..." or "there was for you in Muhammad an *uswah hasanah*..." The distinction can be better understood when a certain physics student is told, "You have in the Professor a good example" and let us assume the Professor in question is Einstein. Einstein's professorial attributes and physics knowledge and methodology are what the student needs to consider as the *uswah hasanah* here, not Einstein's personal behavior, which could have been unacceptable by some people, including his own students. First, the above verse does not mention any specific examples that Muslims need to emulate. Rather, an emphasis is made on a generic behavior that embodies the Message. Similar to the Professor example above, any behavior of Muhammad that is not based on or connected to the Message is excluded from the *uswah hasanah*. Second, the use of the past tense ("there was...") implies that the *uswah hasanah* in question applies to all believers in Muhammad and his Message. The use of the past tense in the Mushaf is not the same as its use in modern Arabic. If the past tense were to be understood as referring to something that is no longer taking place, the Messenger would have ceased to be an *uswah hasanah* while the revelation was taking place.

Since the emphasis in M33:21 is on the Messenger of Allah, the Mushaf makes it clear that Muhammad was not to be emulated in acts that were contrary to Allah's commands, so the *uswah hasanah* must relate to the behavior of Muhammad that is based solely on the Message. By going back to the beginning of M33, there exists the possibility that those addressed by M33:21 were contemporaries of the Prophet and were closely associated with him. This particular interpretation is plausible since it is based on the entire context of the verse.[24]

To support the contextual relevance of *uswah hasanah*, we look at the only two other occurrences of this phrase in the Mushaf. We find these in M60 where the *uswah hasanah* referred to that of Ibrahim and a group of people who were with him. The first of the two occurrences appear in M60:4

قَدْ كَانَتْ لَكُمْ أُسْوَةٌ حَسَنَةٌ فِي إِبْرَاهِيمَ وَالَّذِينَ مَعَهُ إِذْ قَالُوا لِقَوْمِهِمْ إِنَّا بُرَآءُ مِنكُمْ وَمِمَّا تَعْبُدُونَ مِن دُونِ اللَّهِ كَفَرْنَا بِكُمْ وَبَدَا بَيْنَنَا وَبَيْنَكُمُ الْعَدَاوَةُ وَالْبَغْضَاءُ أَبَدًا حَتَّى تُؤْمِنُوا بِاللَّهِ وَحْدَهُ إِلَّا قَوْلَ إِبْرَاهِيمَ لِأَبِيهِ لَأَسْتَغْفِرَنَّ لَكَ وَمَا أَمْلِكُ لَكَ مِنَ اللَّهِ مِن شَيْءٍ رَّبَّنَا عَلَيْكَ تَوَكَّلْنَا وَإِلَيْكَ أَنَبْنَا وَإِلَيْكَ الْمَصِيرُ

[There was for you an *uswah hasanah* in Ibrahim and those people who were with him, <u>in that they said to their nation we are disassociated from you and from what you worship that is beneath and reproach of Allah; we have rejected you and animosity and hatred has surfaced between us forever unless you believe in Allah alone,</u> except what Ibrahim expressed to his father that I will ask forgiveness for you...] The audience of this verse is the community of the faithful who believed in Muhammad as a messenger, as indicated by the first verse in M60, or people who lived during or after the revelation of the Mushaf. Since M60:4 was not revealed to the people of Ibrahim but to Muhammad's followers, clearly those followers were not contemporaries of Ibrahim. Therefore, following his (Ibrahim's) good example would have been meaningless unless the example was stated explicitly and reproduced in the Mushaf. Note how M60:4 explicitly detailed (underlined in the translation above) the *uswah hasanah* that is to be emulated from Ibrahim and his companions. Also, it is important to notice the exception from the *uswah hasanah* stated within the same verse.

The third occurrence of *uswah hasanah* appears in M60:6

لَقَدْ كَانَ لَكُمْ فِيهِمْ أُسْوَةٌ حَسَنَةٌ لِّمَن كَانَ يَرْجُو اللَّهَ وَالْيَوْمَ الْآخِرَ وَمَن يَتَوَلَّ فَإِنَّ اللَّهَ هُوَ الْغَنِيُّ الْحَمِيدُ

[There was for you (plural) in them an *uswah hasanah* (good example) for those who sought Allah and the Last Day, and who parts, then Allah free of need, the praiseworthy.] This verse is related to Ibrahim and was a reaffirmation of M60:4.

In summary, whenever *uswah hasanah* is mentioned in the Mushaf, it refers to a specific and well-defined behavior explicitly stated in the Mushaf, or a behavior associated with an attribute. The imperfection of Muhammad and Ibrahim as humans who lived in specific times and spaces exempted them from being absolute *uswah hasanah* for all humankind.

OBEDIENCE OF THE MESSENGER

The Mushaf contains 23 verses that demand obedience to the Messenger.[25] The Arabic word for obedience is *ta'ah*. In all of these verses, the imperative mood of obedience to the Messenger was associated in more than one way with Allah's obedience. The same imperative mood of *ta'ah* appeared in eight verses, all in M26, related not to Muhammad the Messenger but to the Messengers Noah, Hood, Salih, Loot and Shu'aib, with explicit reference to their messenger role.[26] In M33:66, *ta'ah* did not appear in the imperative mood but in the past tense; however, *ta'ah* remained associated with the Messenger.

Two important conclusions can be drawn from examination of all these verses. The first is that not one command of obedience was related to Muhammad the Prophet but rather to Muhammad the Messenger. The demands were either to "obey Allah and obey the Messenger" or to "obey Allah and the Messenger". This suggests that the Mushaf is indicating that there is a difference between the two types of obedience; one is demanded with a single use of the verb "obey", where Allah and the Messenger share the same verb, while the other is demanded with double use of the verb "obey: one for Allah and one for the Messenger.[27] (This distinction suggests that there are different types of obedience: one exclusive to Allah and the other shared by Allah and the Messenger. Further research is needed to address the difference between the two.) Based on all the verses that involved the word *ta'ah* and its derivatives, obedience was related to the Messenger. This strongly suggests and most likely affirms that obedience to Muhammad was exclusively related to his capacity as a messenger. Thus, Muhammad's obedience related to any matter that lies outside the body of the Message (i.e., the Mushaf) has to be excluded.

The obedience to the Messenger in all 23 verses in the Mushaf was a command to those who were associated with the Messenger during his life. In fact, the context of all 23 verses not only had relevance to the contemporaries of the Messenger but also had temporal context in the sense that obedience of the Messenger who died centuries ago is meaningless to someone living today. Another equally important consideration when studying the meaning and context of obedience is not to conflate it with following a person's way of life or following his tradition.

In two verses, M33:1 and M33:48, Muhammad the Prophet was warned not to obey the hypocrites. In M33:1, the reference to the Prophet was explicit, whereas in M33:48, it was implicit (as realized from the context and considering that M33:48 did not constitute a single sentence). This indicates that Muhammad either obeyed the hypocrites or could have obeyed the hypocrites. Had the Messenger been the subject instead of the Prophet, obedience of the Messenger becomes problematic, as it would entail obeying someone who could have made mistakes that include confusing the haram with the halal.

Not surprising that the Mushaf does not have any verse commanding the believers or Muslims to obey the Prophet. Any command within the Mushaf to obey the Messenger would then need to be understood in the context of Muhammad's capacity as a deliverer of a Message. Obeying the Messenger, as Allah commands in the Mushaf in different verses, strictly implies obeying the commands of Muhammad that are coincidental, emanating from, or relevant to the message embodied within the Mushaf. Just as the case of a nurse obeying a doctor is related to the medical profession and the "medical message", obeying the Messenger Muhammad cannot exceed the scope of his commands that are strictly related to the Message. Going beyond these confines should not be looked upon as disrespecting or marginalizing the Prophet. In fact, going beyond these limits constitute a direct violation of the Message that Muhammad conveyed in the first place.

The Mushaf precisely outlines the status of Muhammad in several verses. Giving Muhammad a status or designation that exceeds this status falls under the prohibition stated in M2:168-169

يَا أَيُّهَا النَّاسُ كُلُوا مِمَّا فِي الْأَرْضِ حَلَالًا طَيِّبًا وَلَا تَتَّبِعُوا خُطُوَاتِ الشَّيْطَانِ إِنَّهُ لَكُمْ عَدُوٌّ مُبِينٌ

إِنَّمَا يَأْمُرُكُم بِالسُّوءِ وَالْفَحْشَاءِ وَأَن تَقُولُوا عَلَى اللَّهِ مَا لَا تَعْلَمُونَ

[O you mankind, eat of whatever is in the earth lawful and good; and do not follow the steps of *al-shaytan*, he is an evident enemy to you. Surely he only commands you to odious (deeds) and *fawahish*, and to declare about Allah that which you have no understanding of.]

FOLLOWING THE FOOTSTEPS OF MUHAMMAD

Another term used in the Mushaf that is conflated with obedience is *ittiba* (to follow), which is derived from the past tense *ittaba'a*. While most Muslims believe that the Mushaf commands humanity, and the believers in particular, to follow the footsteps of Muhammad the Prophet, careful analysis of the Mushaf text does not provide substantiation for this commonly held belief. According to the Mushaf, *ittiba* can

New Doctrines: Sunnah and Hadith

indicate a reference to humans or intangibles, as in adhering to doctrines or concepts.

An example where *ittiba* appears in reference to humans is in M20:90

$$\text{وَلَقَدْ قَالَ لَهُمْ هَارُونُ مِن قَبْلُ يَا قَوْمِ إِنَّمَا فُتِنتُم بِهِ ۖ وَإِنَّ رَبَّكُمُ الرَّحْمَٰنُ فَاتَّبِعُونِي وَأَطِيعُوا أَمْرِي}$$

[And Harun had earlier said to them, O my people, surely you had been tempted by it and surely your Lord is al-Rahman, therefore *ittabyooni* (follow me) and *atee'oo* (obey) my command.] The plural imperative mode of *ittiba* is *ittabyooni*, the underlined word in the verse, which means "follow me". *Ittabyooni*, was followed by *atee'oo,* which is generally conflated with *ittiba*. Regardless of whether *atee'oo* means only "to follow" or something else, the verse makes a clear distinction between the act of following someone and that of obeying him or his commands.

Another illuminating verse is M18:66 where *ittiba* implies having a physical companionship or association. Sensitivity to this difference is critical to understanding key verses that associate obedience with the Messenger. The Mushaf does not contain any phrases commanding the believers of Muhammad to follow Allah, but rather, to obey Allah. The Prophet Muhammad requested the people with whom he was engaged to follow him if they loved Allah (see M3:31) but made it clear that he was following what Allah had revealed to him (see M6:50, 46:9, 10:15, 7:203). Therefore, the *ittiba* of a person, whether a Messenger, a Prophet, or a common man, implies that the human to be *ittiba*-ed must be a living being with a pulsing heart. *Ittiba* cannot apply to a dead person. Scrutiny of all Mushaf verses that include *ittaba'a* and its derivative strongly suggest that the *ittiba* of a human is not synonymous with obedience.[28]

A verse that is widely invoked to imply that Muslims are required to follow the tradition of the Prophet, including whatever he did and said is M4:65

$$\text{فَلَا وَرَبِّكَ لَا يُؤْمِنُونَ حَتَّىٰ يُحَكِّمُوكَ فِيمَا شَجَرَ بَيْنَهُمْ ثُمَّ لَا يَجِدُوا فِي أَنفُسِهِمْ حَرَجًا مِّمَّا قَضَيْتَ وَيُسَلِّمُوا تَسْلِيمًا}$$

[And indeed, by your Lord, they will never become *mu'minoon* (having *imaan*) until they ask you to become an arbitrator or a judge to resolve that which has emerged amongst them; then they will find in themselves no hardship (or difficulty) from believing in your judgement and they will accept in acceptance]. This verse can be applicable only to those who were contemporaries of the Messenger and does not apply to any two parties experiencing a conflict and who lived after the Prophet, since it is impossible to seek the judgment of a dead person. Assuming that this verse has universal applicability over time and space would require the Prophet to have made decisions that addressed all aspects of human life and that would have predicted all potential disputes that might occur until the Latter Day. This assumption is contradictory to the Mushaf, which emphatically states that the Prophet had no knowledge of the unseen and the future (see M72:26 and M27:65). The time-sensitive applicability of M4:65 may also be buttressed by M42:10

وَمَا اخْتَلَفْتُمْ فِيهِ مِن شَيْءٍ فَحُكْمُهُ إِلَى اللَّهِ ذَٰلِكُمُ اللَّهُ رَبِّي عَلَيْهِ تَوَكَّلْتُ وَإِلَيْهِ أُنِيبُ

[And in whatever things you differed about, then refer judgement on it to Allah. That is Allah my Lord, in Him I have put my trust and to him I return penitent.] While both M4:65 and M42:10 ask the followers of the Prophet to seek judgement from the Prophet and Allah, respectively, M4:65 is related to a conflict while M42:10 is related to having a difference.

The specificity of M4:65 to the Prophet's companions and community is supported by the fact that numerous Muslim clergy have issued millions of edicts on matters that were neither addressed in the Mushaf nor considered as part of the Hadith corpus. None have consulted the prophet on matters that had never arisen during his lifetime. In fact, the entire field of Usool al-Fiqh (see Chapter 9) was invented to answer emerging disputes, legal or otherwise, amongst Muslims. Extrapolating M4:56 to imply universal applicability is illogical and inconsistent with the context of the verse, which indicates temporal relevance to some of the companions of the Prophet whom Allah questioned regarding their sincerity in believing in the Messenger and in Allah. M4:65 was not the only a reference to the Prophet as an arbitrator; such status was also affirmed in M4:59

$$\text{يَا أَيُّهَا الَّذِينَ آمَنُوا أَطِيعُوا اللَّهَ وَأَطِيعُوا الرَّسُولَ وَأُولِي الْأَمْرِ مِنكُمْ ۖ فَإِن تَنَازَعْتُمْ فِي شَيْءٍ فَرُدُّوهُ إِلَى اللَّهِ وَالرَّسُولِ إِن كُنتُمْ تُؤْمِنُونَ بِاللَّهِ وَالْيَوْمِ الْآخِرِ ۚ ذَٰلِكَ خَيْرٌ وَأَحْسَنُ تَأْوِيلًا}$$

[O you who have become believers, obey Allah and obey the Messenger and those in command of your affairs from amongst you; and if you develop a dispute in a matter, refer it to Allah and the Messenger that is if you were believers in Allah and the Latter Day, that is of goodness and a better *ta'weela*.] Here again, the faithful are asked to willingly refer disputes to Muhammad in his capacity as a messenger, and to Allah, simultaneously. This verse most likely had a specific temporal context. However, if one were to generalize this verse to include all believers who lived after Muhammad passed away, then the resolution of any dispute has to be embodied within the Message.

M4:59 had been abused throughout history, having been used to quell democratic aspirations through demanding absolute obedience to the people in charge of political affairs. The request for obedience in M4:59 is directed at those in charge of the affairs and to the Messenger, simultaneously.[29]

"WHAT THE MESSENGER HAS GIVEN YOU"

A verse that often is invoked to demonstrate that whatever Muhammad said or did is to be emulated is M59:7

$$\text{مَّا أَفَاءَ اللَّهُ عَلَىٰ رَسُولِهِ مِنْ أَهْلِ الْقُرَىٰ فَلِلَّهِ وَلِلرَّسُولِ وَلِذِي الْقُرْبَىٰ وَالْيَتَامَىٰ وَالْمَسَاكِينِ وَابْنِ السَّبِيلِ كَيْ لَا يَكُونَ دُولَةً بَيْنَ الْأَغْنِيَاءِ مِنكُمْ ۚ وَمَا آتَاكُمُ الرَّسُولُ فَخُذُوهُ وَمَا نَهَاكُمْ عَنْهُ فَانتَهُوا ۚ وَاتَّقُوا اللَّهَ ۖ إِنَّ اللَّهَ شَدِيدُ الْعِقَابِ}$$

[And what Allah restored to His Messenger from the people of the towns - it is for Allah and for the Messenger and for *thi al-qurba* and orphans and *masakeen* and traveler so that it will not be a perpetual distribution amongst the rich from among you, and *ma aatakum* the Messenger, then take it; and what *ma nahaakum anhu* do not take it and be cognisant of Allah; indeed Allah is severe in penalty.] The misuse of this verse arises from interpreting *ma aatakum* as "that which the

Prophet has given or bequeathed to you in tradition and behavior" and interpreting *ma nahaakum* as "that which the Prophet has forbidden you from doing". The two roots of these two verbs, *aata* and *naha*, appear elsewhere in the Mushaf with meanings that can be understood from their respective contexts. Considering the entire verse and also the context informed by the two verses before and after it, the most likely correct meaning of *ma aatakum* is the Prophet's allocation of war bounty. Similarly, *ma nahaakum* would then be related to what the Prophet has asked the believers not to take from the war bounty.[30] In other verses of the Mushaf, *aata* is associated with *zakat* (obligatory charity). Similarly, for all other occurrences of the derivatives of *aata*, the meaning can be inferred directly from the context. In M2:38 the context is guidance, whereas in M2:271 the context refers to a tangible *sadaqat* (charity) and to whom it should be given. Interpreting the command of *ma aatakum* in M59:7 as a "tradition for you to emulate or follow" contradicts the context and therefore most likely is incorrect. Classical exegetes appear to have had sacrificed the contextual meaning of *aatakum* to support the grand notion of absolute obedience to the Prophet.

REVISITING THE SUNNAH

The Sunnah is a vaguely defined term, even amongst classical scholars of Islam. Generally, the Sunnah refers to words or actions that the Prophet is believed to have said or done. It also refers to other information transmitted about the Prophet directly or indirectly. Some even went to the extent of including the actions and sayings of the companions of the Prophet as the Sunnah. (There is no consensus among Muslim scholars on a definition for the Prophet's companions.[31]) Many scholars of Islam have divided the Sunnah into three different types: the *qawliyyah* Sunnah, words the Prophet uttered; the *amaliyyah* Sunnah, actions that the Prophet performed, and the *taqreeriyah* Sunnah, actions or words the Prophet witnessed or heard his companions doing or saying that he either affirmed or warned against.[32] A widely held understanding of the Sunnah is the collection of acts or behaviors that are worthy of divine reward if performed but do not lead to punishment in the hereafter if left unperformed. Many Muslims consider whatever Muhammad the Prophet and Muhammad the Messenger uttered to

New Doctrines: Sunnah and Hadith

have been a revelation, and consider his actions a result of Allah's inspiration and/or direct revelation. To a large extent, Muslims and Islam scholars use the Sunnah and Hadith interchangeably; however, Hadith is the text that documents the Sunnah.

Over time, the Sunnah became synonymous with almost everything involving the Prophet, from what he said to nearly everything he did. If the Prophet liked to eat squash or watermelon, then it became Sunnah to do so. If he ate with his hands, then eating with hands instead of forks, knives and spoons became a Sunnah. In fact, several books were written on Prophetic Medicine, which were a collection of hadiths with a wide range of degrees of authenticity that described cures for a host of ailments.[33] The evolution of the concept of the Sunnah turned Muhammad into a man of medicine. Take for instance *miswaak*, a teeth-cleaning twig made from the Salvadora Persica tree. Some hadiths report that the Prophet used *miswaak* for oral hygiene and therefore the use of *miswaak* became Sunnah. It is probable that the Prophet used *miswaak* for oral hygiene, and that *miswaak* was the most advanced oral hygiene technology in those days. As a leader and a father figure, the Prophet must have given advice to many people that he encountered and possibly recommended the use of *miswaak*. I would imagine that if the Prophet were to visit Muslims today and found people using the *miswaak*, he would be amused by such ancient and primitive dental hygiene methods. He would most likely recommend Oral B or more advanced oral hygiene tools. He would also be warning against the pervasive use of sugar in food products and might even suggest regular dental checkups.

While using *miswaak* is a matter of minimal significance, claiming that the *miswaak* is Sunnah and that its use in addition to other daily habits of the Prophet are superior to modern practices starkly contradicts the message of progress that the Mushaf advocates. In fact, the Mushaf emphatically warns against imitation of fathers, forefathers and previous generations. Adhering to reported habits and practices of the Prophet, even if true, that were entirely disconnected from the Message indeed sends the adherents fourteen centuries back and exemplifies a static religion disconnected from present reality.

Instead of framing whatever is reportedly attributed to the Prophet in historical and societal context, many Muslims seek validation of the Prophethood and, by extension, of Islam through researching the benefits of certain practices the Prophet is reported to have had, from using the *miswaak* to eating squash or black seeds. The subtext of these narratives suggests that Islam is a true religion if modern science can prove the remarkable effects of *miswaak* or black seeds on one's health.

There is no consensus on what the Sunnah is. In fact, confusion abounds amongst Muslims and their scholars on what deserves or qualifies to be part of the Sunnah. In essence, there is bewildering selectivity that mostly goes unnoticed and is not discussed in the Sunnah books. For example, since all hadiths are directly or indirectly related to the Prophet's life, it is perplexing that other information about a variety of aspects related to his daily life, such as his methods of transportation, were not included in the annals of the Sunnah. Why did specific practices such as using the *miswaak* become part of the Sunnah while waging war with the bow and arrow, which the Prophet is reportedly to have used during battles, did not? In fact, and most interestingly, despite the fact that the Prophet is reported to have explicitly instructed the Muslims to learn archery, this mode of warfare is not included within the Sunnah.

Based on multiple definitions used throughout history, the understanding of what the Sunnah entails continues to evolve with time. Irrespective of the label Sunnah or otherwise, many Muslims believe that the Prophet's actions were perfect and worth emulating. For the simplistic Muslims, the beard and the *miswaak* might represent behavioral models for higher piety, and consequently, rewards in the hereafter. For the sophisticated one, say a politician or a scholar, understanding how Muhammad forged treaties with his enemies is a sought after goal. The assumption by the sophisticated Muslim scholar is that forging treaties exactly as Muhammad did will bring the political practice in line with higher Islamic values and will make the treaty a perfect one; or, in the worst case scenario, if those goals are not achieved, it will bring the politician closer to Allah and all the subsequent rewards in the hereafter.

As described earlier, for many Muslim, the Sunnah of the Prophet implies doing something that invites a reward in the hereafter but refraining from it does not warrant punishment. In practice, however, things can be different. The Sunnah has become a source of legislation, binding on every Muslim, thus leading to a considerable confusion between acts that are commendable if performed and others that are obligatory (an example is the laws of inheritance). The books of Hadith contain many serious contradictions and violations of the Mushaf's injunctions.[34]

New Doctrines: Sunnah and Hadith

Numerous scholars of Islam claim that the Sunnah clarifies and provides an explanation for the Mushaf, but there is not one hadith that provides a clear unambiguous and uniform interpretation for any verse in the Mushaf. The claim that the Sunnah explains the Mushaf is typically demonstrated in a very strange, convoluted and patently ambiguous way that adds further confusion instead of explanation and clarification. This is typically demonstrated by citing a certain hadith as answering a specific question or addressing a particular situation or a problem, then the Mushaf is brought in to support the hadith, not the other way around. In other words, the starting point is the Hadith, not the Mushaf. For the case when a certain hadith presents an indisputable contradiction to the Mushaf, the instrument of abrogation is invoked, whereby the hadith is claimed to nullify or abrogate a Mushaf verse or part of it.[35] Numerous Muslim scholars elevated the status of the Sunnah to the point that some went as far as claiming that the religion of Islam is incomplete without the Sunnah and that the Sunnah can abrogate parts of the Mushaf.

The claim that the Sunnah helps or was intended to decipher (if needed) the Mushaf is typically based on M16:64

وَمَا أَنزَلْنَا عَلَيْكَ الْكِتَابَ إِلَّا لِتُبَيِّنَ لَهُمُ الَّذِي اخْتَلَفُوا فِيهِ وَهُدًى وَرَحْمَةً لِّقَوْمٍ يُؤْمِنُونَ

[And we have revealed the Book on (or upon) you only to *tobayyen* for them what they had differed on and a mercy to people who believe.] The underlined word *tobayyen* in this verse means 'to show' or 'to make apparent', not to explain or decipher; it is the opposite of to hide or to conceal. Therefore, the verse does not command the Prophet to explain or interpret the Book. Nevertheless, even if one assumed that *tobayyen* meant to explain, the explanation is strictly confined to a subject that is embedded within the Book, not outside of it, as the verse clearly indicates. Therefore, even under such an assumption, *tobayyen* would not be related to any new material, complementary, supplementary or contradictory to the Book.

Some Sunnah advocates claim that *tobayyen* implies interpretation of the Mushaf. However, the Mushaf refers to interpretation as *ta'weel*, while referring to the process of specifying or providing details or the process of classifications as *taf'seel*. It needs to be emphasized that irrespective of their meaning, Allah never asked the Prophet to make either *tafseel* or *ta'weel* of any Mushaf verse but only to make the verses apparent by informing the people around him of the contents of the verses. Simply, Muhammad had the revelation to present it to the people, not to keep it to himself. This testifies to the fact that Muhammad was a human with a free will. It was Muhammad's choice to follow the revelation and to reveal (*yobayyen*) it. These verses testify to the fact that the Prophet was not manipulated even by Allah.

There are two verses that sheds further light on the meaning of *tobayyen* and confirm the interpretation given above. The first is M2:159

$$\text{إِنَّ الَّذِينَ يَكْتُمُونَ مَا أَنزَلْنَا مِنَ الْبَيِّنَاتِ وَالْهُدَىٰ مِن بَعْدِ مَا بَيَّنَّاهُ لِلنَّاسِ فِي الْكِتَابِ أُولَٰئِكَ يَلْعَنُهُمُ اللَّهُ وَيَلْعَنُهُمُ اللَّاعِنُونَ}$$

[Those who *yaktumoon* (conceal) what We have revealed in clarifications and guidance after We *bayyannahu* (have made it apparent) to the people in the Book, those (people) will be excommunicated (from Allah's mercy) and they will be excommunicated by the excommunicators.] *Bayyannahu* is the past tense of *bayyanna,* from which *tobayyen* in M16:64 is derived. Here, Allah indicates that in addition to making the clarification, He provides the clarification within the Book; so the revelation by itself constitutes the clarification to which M2:159 and M16:64 refer.[36] Notice also the use of the verb *yaktumoon* (to conceal). The context implies that *tubayyen* is the antonym of *yaktum* (singular of *yaktumoon*). The second verse is M3:187

$$\text{وَإِذْ أَخَذَ اللَّهُ مِيثَاقَ الَّذِينَ أُوتُوا الْكِتَابَ لَتُبَيِّنُنَّهُ لِلنَّاسِ وَلَا تَكْتُمُونَهُ فَنَبَذُوهُ وَرَاءَ ظُهُورِهِمْ وَاشْتَرَوْا بِهِ ثَمَنًا قَلِيلًا ۖ فَبِئْسَ مَا يَشْتَرُونَ}$$

[And as Allah took the covenant of those who were given the book that you may *tubayynannahu* and do not *taktumoonahu* then they flung it beyond their backs then they traded it for little price.] The context indicates that *tubayynannahu* is the antonym of *taktumoonahu.*

Despite the meaning of the above verses and despite the fact that the body of Hadith does not include interpretation of the Mushaf, the vast majority of Muslims' scholarship has insisted that the Prophet explained and deciphered the Mushaf through the Sunnah, a claim that cannot be substantiated by reasoning, Hadith or any historical records.[37]

New Doctrines: Sunnah and Hadith

Despite the existence of numerous volumes of Mushaf exegeses, none is attributed to the Prophet, either directly or indirectly. This is an amazing and stark fact that continues to be dodged by many Muslim traditional and non-traditional scholars while others remain silent, undecided or possibly not interested in providing any explanation.

The claims that the Sunnah came to rule over the Mushaf started in the second Muslim century during times of empire expansion and consolidation of unprecedented wealth and power. The raison d'être of the empire was "Islamic" justifications. The fluidity and expansiveness of the Hadith was a key proponent of the "Islamic" empire and expectedly, its dominance had to be established by a host of courtiers. With time, and as explained earlier, the earlier unchallenged claims about Hadith gained credibility. One may argue that earlier works depended on archaic methodologies and lacked rigor and scrutiny. Modern scholarship, however, is assumed to be more advanced and should, at least from the academic/scholarly perspective, approach the Hadith scholarship outside the realm of emotionalism and "faith". From this perspective, the Hadith scholarship may be more fitting to possibly non-Muslim scholars (the "orientalists") than to Muslim scholars. An example is the work of Jonathan Brown who appears as a proponent of that claim that the Sunnah came to rule over the Qur'aan. Brown states without proof that "This was not an admission of any deficiency in the Qur'aan – rather it recognizes that the book required the Prophet's example and teachings in order to explain its verses and unlock its manifold meanings to an evolving community." He further claims, "Muslim schools of thought at various times have insisted, out of principle, that the words of a mere mortal, even Muhammad, could never conceivably carry more interpretive weight than the word of God. Yet they have all historically recognized that, whichever way one chooses to phrase it, the Prophet's legacy has profoundly informed and altered the way the Qur'aan's legal message has been understood."[38]

Brown's claim that the "Prophet's legacy" has profoundly altered the way the Qur'aan's message had been understood is reasonable if not accurate. It is highly likely that the alleged "Prophet's legacy" turned the practiced "Islam" into a static religion incapable of addressing the needs of an evolving humanity. The missing link here is that the Prophet's legacy was not only interpretive but was a behavioral model that is one of many sanctioned within the Mushaf (of course, on the assumption that what was transmitted to us in Hadith was true). Nevertheless, evidence points to other legacies rather than the Prophet's that truly altered the way the Mushaf's message had been understood. The preponderance of commentaries by prominent Muslim scholars, including some of those who reached near-godly status, that degraded the value of the Mushaf could have paved the way for such admission by Brown and others. The facts that the recorded "Prophet's example" as embodied in the Hadith corpus contradicted the verses of the Mushaf is a strong proof that it never unlocked its "manifold meanings" to any Muslim community, and above all created divisions and wars amongst Muslims themselves.

The massive amount of confusion within the Sunnah doctrine, which was firmly established on Hadith, led to the development of the so-called Hadith Sciences. These "sciences", as the case with the so-called Qur'anic Sciences, attempted to add a scientific veneer to a new doctrine that had no connection to science or its principles.

Hadith "Sciences"

Many Muslims of previous generations accepted the two Sahihs of al-Bukhari and Muslim as an authentic collection of Prophetic sayings, acts and norms. In their zeal to support the Hadith, many Muslim scholars and clergy consider these Sahihs as the most *sahih* (authentic or correct) books in existence immediately after the Mushaf. In their support of the Hadith, many Muslim scholars claim that the respect towards these two Sahihs (and some extend it to other Hadith collections) were largely based on the commentaries of major Muslim scholars, such as ibn al-Salah and al-Asqalani, who claimed "their books (i.e., the two Sahihs) are the most correct and authentic after the Book of Allah".[39] Al-Nawawi claimed that "the *umma* (the theoretical body of Muslims) is unanimous (i.e., made *ijma*) that these two books (i.e., the two Sahihs) are true and authentic.[40] Ibn Taymiyyah, who commands high respect amongst many Muslims, stated that "the community of scholars have agreed that there is no book more authentic after the Qur'aan than the books of al-Bukhari and Muslim".[41]

Amid an extraordinary enthusiasm of searching for clues on how the Prophet conducted his daily life, the technical definition for *sahih* was lost. Some Muslim scholars who succeeded al-Bukhari and who were aware of what he meant by *sahih* devised their own elaborate Hadith classification systems with several sub-categories of authenticity. With time, the entire classification system and all methodologies associated with Hadith became identified, by the framers of the Sunnah, as sciences. All these highly complex classifications and "sciences" discouraged many Muslims from questioning the authenticity of the Hadith corpus and its relevance to Islam. There could have been additional reasons for this discouragement including fearing that that any criticism of Hadith will be labeled as supporting the enemies of Islam. This backward extrapolation in time is fully justified by what has happened to 20th Century Muslim scholars who dared to provide a methodical and truly scientific critique of the entire Hadith "science". Expectedly, many others were deeply intimidated from delving into this "science" because of its intimidating complexity.

The entire system of collection and authentication of Hadith has to be recognized in its own right; simply as an elaborate system based on complex criteria that lacks consistency amongst Hadith transmitters. However, no matter how complex the entire Hadith authentication process is, it is not and has no resemblance to science.

The most elaborate efforts to document the Sunnah started in the second Muslim century by Umar ibn Abdulaziz (d. 101/720), the 8th Caliph of the Umayyad dynasty.[42] Given the absence of clear historical documents explaining his motives, and in light of his austere and pious personality unlike his Abbasid predecessors, ibn Abdulaziz could have been interested in stemming the tide of fabricated hadiths alleged to have reached over one million in number. Abdulaziz's efforts have been less methodical and can be categorized as an initiative from a political ruler. More sustained efforts to document the Hadith were led by al-Bukhari (d. 254/868), Muslim (d. 261/875), al-Tirmidhi (d. 279/892), abu Dawood (d. 275/888) and al-Nisa'i (d. 303/915). All of these Hadith collectors commenced their collection and authentication work in the third Hijri century. Parallel to this, the collectors individually developed their own methods to determine whether a certain hadith was authentic or not.

The advocates for the Sunnah as an Islamic doctrine from which legislation can be extracted were not necessarily from the same group that collected and attempted to authenticate hundreds of thousands of hadiths. Al-Shafi'i, for instance, one of the leading Muslim jurisprudents and a key proponent of the Sunnah as a parallel doctrine (see Chapter

9), preceded all major Hadith collectors and is not known as a Hadith collector or authenticator himself. The historical sequence suggests that al-Shafi'i's scholarship and innovations could have had a significant influence on Hadith collectors and possibly gave them the impetus for their efforts.

Such a broad categorization of the Sunnah and its perception as equal to the Mushaf was adopted by Sunni and Shia sects alike.[43] Realizing that it was impossible to determine with certainty the authenticity of Hadith, collectors and the scholars of Islam who preceded them introduced an elaborate system of classification that eventually led to the development of an authenticity spectrum: from the *dhaeef* (weak) hadith to *sahih* (correct) and a colorful range in between, such as *hasan* (good), *maudu* (forged), etc. It is important to note that there was no consistency in classification amongst all Hadith collectors. For instance, a *sahih* hadith for Muslim might not be a *sahih* one for al-Bukhari. In fact, not all Muslim hadiths are included in Sahih al-Bukhari and vice versa.[44] This is despite the fact that they were contemporaries and Muslim was a student of al-Bukhari. Based on the speculated authentication criteria that was surmised or speculated by later scholars (al-Bukhari never made explicit his criteria for his Hadith collection and classification), a *sahih* (authentic) hadith could have been classified by al-Bukhari as a *dhaeef* (weak).[45]

Methods for authentication of Hadith that were developed by Hadith collectors or by other scholars of Islam have evolved to become part of *Uloom al-Hadith* (Hadith Sciences). *Uloom* dealt with specific subjects related to Hadith, but were concerned with mostly the *isnaad* (the chain of transmitters) and, to a much lesser extent, the *matn* (the text of Hadith attributed to the Prophet).[46] From the Sunni side, the bulk of *Uloom al-Hadith* scholarship was concerned with those two subjects. The Shia sect, in theory, included compatibility of Hadith with the Mushaf.

Sanad involved verifying the sincerity of the transmitters and establishing their reputation as (mostly) men of honesty, integrity, excellent reputation and sound judgement. These criteria were the most important, if not all that mattered to decide, according to *Uloom al-Hadith,* whether a certain hadith was *sahih* (correct) or not. If the criterion of honesty was established for the entire chain of transmitters, say from al-Bukhari's time (third Hijri century) going back in time all the way to the Prophet (more than 200 years earlier), then al-Bukhari included a particular hadith in his compendium as authentic. (Of course, there are other requirements such as continuity in the chain of transmitters, etc.)

The criteria sufficient for al-Bukhari to label a certain hadith as *sahih* was different from that adopted by Muslim. (As stated above, al-Bukhari never documented his classification criteria, or if he did, none is available. In deciphering al-Bukhari's classification methodology, scholars of Hadith typically rely on either the writings of al-Bukhari's disciples or mere guesswork.) For example, al-Bukhari is claimed to have required a hadith to be *sahih* that two consecutive transmitters must have met with each other. However, Muslim relaxed this condition for his *sahih* criterion.[47]

The entire system of Hadith authentication hinged on determining with absolute certainty the sincerity of people who lived hundreds of years earlier. This is an incredible feat, if not impossible. From a scientific perspective, the probability of success in achieving such absolute certainty is extremely low, if not close to zero. To assume that al-Bukhari established beyond any doubt the sincerity of a chain of transmitters that spanned two hundred years implies that he had near-godly attributes that even Prophets did not possess. Indeed, this attribute had to be manufactured to add credibility, if not an aura of infallibility, to him and his work as many Muslims have come to believe. The "science" of hadith has become so complex and borders on the absurd when we realize that later Hadith classifiers considered two independent weak chains in the *sanad* (for example, the transmitters lacking trustworthiness or honesty) as sufficient to turn an independently classified hadith (using either of the two chains) into a *sahih* hadith.

The introduction of the English translation of Sahih Muslim by Muhammad Yahya indicates that Muslim divided the hadiths into three or four different categories.[48] The categories were based on Muslim's opinion of the transmitters, specifically on the attributes of the transmitters such as sincerity, truthfulness, precision in reporting, and others. A dispute (i.e., lack of Ijma) amongst the most prominent Hadith scholars is related to whether Muslim included all those categories in his Sahih collection. This dispute, however, has never been settled, while being dismissed by some scholars as of an "academic nature". But if all transmitters comprising a transmission chain were included in his Sahih, then it should be verifiable whether Muslim included the three categories of Hadith or only the first one. This is because all transmitters were supposed to be fully documented as far as their truthfulness and sincerity were concerned. On the assumption that Muslim died before completing his Sahih, it is highly unlikely that he died precisely on the day he completed the hadiths of the first category. Nevertheless, assuming that only the first category was included, in the introduction to his Sahih, Muslim stated:[49]

> Here we will introduce reports that are safer from fault than others, and purer, in that their narration of hadiths, reliable in what they reported, in whose narratives no severe differences are found in, nor erroneous confusion, as may be in the case with many *muhadithin* [reporters of Hadith] as is evident from the hadiths they narrated. So we will write down the reports of this type, and follow that with the reports in whose chains there are some people who are not known for their good memory and reliability, unlike those in the first category, on the basis that even though they are of a lower status than the first, they are still known to be truthful and knowledgeable.

Clearly, Muslim admitted that the first category includes reports of "safer fault" but not error free. Despite the divergence of opinion (i.e., lack of Ijma) by prominent scholars of Islam on the categories of hadiths and especially the competence of transmitters that were included in Sahih Muslim, there is a strong consensus amongst scholars of Hadith to accept Muslim's collection as authentic. Here is Muhammad Yahya again commenting in his introduction to the English translation:[50]

> The works of Imam Bukhari and Imam Muslim were not accepted just for their great technical skills. Rather, they were accepted because the rules and the methodologies they adopted were critically reviewed and then each Hadith they had listed was reviewed and probed critically and vigorously in the light of their own rules. And this critical work continued, unabated and with great vigour, for centuries.
>
> Among his critics were Imam Darqutni, Imam Hakim and several other scholars expert in the Science of Validation (al-Jarh wa al-Ta'dil). In the meanwhile, a vigorous criticism continued, supporting and opposing him. Even today, there is no bar on criticism of his works. As a result of this criticism and counter-criticism, all the Hadith scholars of the orthodox schools of Islamic jurisprudence are unanimous that the authentic collections of Bukhari and Muslim are

New Doctrines: Sunnah and Hadith

correct, next to the Qur'aan, and the ascription of the sayings and acts mentioned therein to the Messenger of Allah is right.

These amazing exaggerations by Yahya, possibly read by millions of Muslims, sound more like a reaffirmation of a belief rather than anything remotely connected to either scholarship or reality.[51]

The narrative of Muslim's introduction indicates that he was commissioned to compile his Sahih by someone. Muslim's modesty and conservative tones are evident from his introduction which contrasts sharply with the tone of leading Muslim imams and jurists including al-Juwayni (also known by the title Imam al-Haramain), a prominent Muslim jurist and Hadith scholar (d. 478/1085) who claimed that the Muslim *umma* had a consensus on the authenticity of the two Sahihs. Al-Juwayni, however, did not produce any proof of such broad claim. The height of the zeal towards the Sahihs is exemplified by a fatwa by Mohammad al-Nabulsi, a highly popular contemporary Muslim scholar who is deeply loved by many Muslims because of his *wasati* (middle-ground) approach and emphasis on the peaceful side of the religion (see Chapter 9 for a discussion on the *wasati* Islam.) Al-Nabulsi claimed that rejecting, or not accepting a Sahih hadith as an authentic narrative of the Prophet is sufficient to expel a Muslim from Islam, i.e., make him a *kafir*.[52]

All these amazing exaggerations and claims, such as "the *umma* is unanimous on the authenticity of Sahih Bukhari and Sahih Muslim", by a host of highly respected Muslim scholars and clergy that spanned hundreds of years are not only extreme but also blatantly false. All of this violent hyperbole by the champions of the Sunnah doctrine is despite Muslim implying with his very own words that the authenticity of the hadiths is a matter of probability.

Al-Bukhari essentially set the tone for all succeeding Hadith "Scientists" in that the authentication of Hadith became a matter of only verifying its *sanad*. Based on Hadith Science books, researching and establishing the compatibility of Hadith with the Mushaf was not considered a sufficiently worthy task to warrant its own authentication methodology. The most likely theoretical foundation for adopting such methodology, however, is the work of al-Shafi'i. By the time al-Bukhari embarked on his grand task of collecting hundreds of thousands of hadiths from all corners of the Muslim world, several early jurisprudents and scholars of Islam had already established that the Sunnah could override the

Mushaf. Thus, the question of the compatibility of Hadith with the Mushaf was no longer relevant, or the question of relevancy was degraded significantly.

THE SCIENCE OF THE IMPOSSIBLE (AKA ILM AL-RIJAAL)

To indulge in the titanic task of determining the sincerity, honesty and integrity of Hadith transmitters, another "science" had to be invented. Ilm al-Rijaal (the Science of Men) was intended as a methodology by which the sincerity, integrity and reputation of Hadith transmitters could be demonstrated. One of the most prominent scholars in this new "science" is al-Jarjani (d. 365/976) and al-Dimashki, (d. 774/1372).[53] The challenges brought by the methodology of al-Bukhari, namely the reliance on the sincerity and authenticity of the transmitters created the need for yet another "science", al-Jarh wa al-Ta'deel, which means to bring the character into disrepute and enhance the character. This additional "science" was intended to authenticate the characters of Hadith transmitters and determine whether they were trustworthy men. Some of the major books on al-Jarh wa al-Ta'deel were written more than hundreds of years after the death of al-Bukhari, which strongly indicates that many scholars of Hadith were not satisfied with al-Bukhari's own estimation of the reputation of the Hadith transmitters. This is attested by the fact that Muslim, a disciple of al-Bukhari, had different authentication criteria. In recent times, al-Albani, a highly respected Salafi scholar reclassified some of Sahih al-Bukhari hadiths from authentic to weak.[54] All this scholarship puts into question the very principles on which the validity of the Sahihs were established.

The methods used to decipher the honesty and credibility of transmitters of Hadith were subjective, often opaque and sometimes arbitrary. A transmitter deemed honest and trustworthy by one scholar was classified as untrustworthy by others.[55] In fact, looking carefully at one of these Ilm al-Rijaal books, one struggles to find any consistent methodology even within a single book, let alone a consistent acceptance (of someone as trustworthy) criteria. Therefore, it is difficult to find any justification for labeling the methods employed by authenticators of Hadith as scientific. As an example of the arbitrariness of these "sciences" is the case of Ismail ibn Ayyash. Abu Saleh al-Farra said about ibn Ayyash: "that man is not aware of what comes out of his head."

According to Hadith Sciences, both al-Farra and ibn Ayyash are part of the group of nobles who were considered trustworthy for transmitting Hadith and worthy enough to be included in al-Thahabi's (d. 748/1374) *Siyar a'Laam al-Nuba'la* 30-volume encyclopedia.[56] Despite this, al-Tirmidhi in his Jami has included a hadith (no. 2120) transmitted by ibn Ayyash while including testimonies from other Hadith transmitters who warned that no hadith should be accepted from ibn Ayyash and that he never transmitted from either people with or without credibility.

It is true that the definition of what constitutes sciences is a difficult subject. Some define science by the methods used to answer questions and observations.[57] Regardless of how science is defined and what constitutes the "scientific", consistency of definitions and compatibility with reality are paramount in any methods that are attributed to science. One could employ known scientific or scholarship methods to study Hadith. The outcome of these studies, however, does not result in something that might be referred to as Hadith Sciences. Studying the Hadith, irrespective of the methods used and irrespective of its authenticity or even the authenticity of the manuscripts that contained the numerous hadiths is different from framing the Hadith as a science. There is Hadith scholarship but not Hadith science.

A criterion that was used by the Hadith framers to test the trustworthiness of a certain hadith transmitter was what a select group of his contemporaries and others who were not his contemporaries thought of him.[58] This implied that members of this select group were not only sincere, honest, and trustworthy, but also were correct in their assessment of the personal characters of the entire chain of transmitters. In Hadith Sciences, a certain scholar's opinion became a widely accepted and respected method for evaluating the trustworthiness and scholarship of others. Essentially, opinions were packaged as methodologies and as science. A chain of authentication guesswork for assessing trustworthiness, all disguised as science, became part of Islam's "sciences", the "sacred knowledge", and the Muslim culture itself. Guesswork and opinions became a substitute for facts, the real ingredients of real science.

While there may be little indication to suggest that the intentions of Hadith collectors were anything but noble and sincere, the tasks they undertook in authenticating Hadith seem nearly impossible, if not dubious and absurd. We can always validate historical claims, or at least develop a sense of their authenticity by creating analogies to our times.

Take for example the task of determining whether someone who was an associate of Abraham Lincoln was a truthful man. Even today, with the substantial advancement of science, technology, data mining, real and artificial intelligence, record keeping, and the widespread availability of print media, it is difficult to determine with absolute certainty the sincerity, honesty and truthfulness of a contemporary, let alone someone who died a century ago. Even polygraph technology has severe limitations and is relevant to live subjects, not mummies. In fact, polygraph technology was designed to determine whether a live subject is lying or not, but not whether a live subject can determine if someone else, alive or dead, ever lied.

The emphasis on *sanad* and the entire knowledge corpus that evolved around it could have been a leading contributor to the pervasive cult culture that colored the vast majority of "Islamic scholarship". Such a culture could have made Muslims, their commoners and scholars alike, turn a blind eye towards serious claims that were referenced to strangers. These types of references are abundant in the works of major Muslim jurisprudents and exegetes and typically appear in phrases such as "some told us" and "some of the people of science/knowledge have told us".

In addition to the "trustworthiness" criteria that the Hadith scholars established, sectarian and political overtones played a major influence. For instance, the Sahihs of both al-Bukhari and Muslim rejected transmitters who were supporters of the Prophet's grandson Hussein. In fact, the sectarian influence on al-Bukhari's work can never be underestimated. The political leanings of the transmitter was a criterion used in the Hadith Sciences; a criterion that some transmitters did not even shy away from declaring. Ibn Sirin (d. 111/729), one of the Muslim scholars of the first century, is reported to have said: "They never asked about *sanad*, and when the great *fitna* (civil war) occurred, they said name for us your men, and then the Hadith of *ahl al-Sunnah* was accepted and the Hadith of *ahl al-bida* (innovators) were rejected." [59]

Despite all the apparent serious flaws of the two Sahihs and all other Hadith compendia, and more importantly, the attempts of their authors to achieve the impossible, some leading modern Hadith scholars bestowed upon these works and their authors lofty accolades that defy the human experience and border on the absurd. Here is Johnathan Brown in his introduction to *The Canonization of Al-Bukhari and Muslim*: "Finally, this book is not a criticism of al-Bukhari and Muslim or their

New Doctrines: Sunnah and Hadith

collections. The genius, rigor and dedication of those two scholars stand beyond my reach and abilities. To fully appreciate the *Sahihayn* within the context of the collection and criticism of hadiths is to move beyond a common first impression of the hadith tradition — that of an erratic and ultimately contrived game of religious telephone — to grasp the simple logic and eerie internal consistency of a widely scattered but uniformly dedicated community of scholars who, over the past 1,400 years, have repeatedly demonstrated that what we historians have deemed the limits of the possible for human memory and attention to detail simply need to be rethought."[60] Al-Bukhari and Muslim could have possessed genius and dedication, but their claimed scholarship, if it can be labeled as such, is deeply flawed and based on hypothetical premises and methodologies that are largely subjective and founded on the most fragile of human attributes: memory. (Of course, this is all under the assumption that what has reached us is the original works of al-Bukhari and Muslim.[61]) The inconsistency amongst Hadith scholars over the past 1400 years is too obvious to overlook. My own first impression of the Hadith tradition, to borrow the words of Brown, is indeed that of an erratic and "ultimately contrived game of religious telephone".

Non-Muslim western scholars have varying attitudes towards the Hadith corpus and all its "sciences". Some are intrigued at this body of knowledge but essentially feel impervious to criticizing it for fear of being attacked and humiliated for lacking all the canonized prerequisites, especially the "inner secrets" of the Arabic language. (Little did those non-Arabic speaking scholars realize that the Arabs themselves never had a consistent grammar and were struggling to make it consistent with the Mushaf's Arabic.) Others possibly were careful to criticize the "sciences" of Hadith for fear that they would be labeled as anti-Muslim or orientalists concealing hatred towards Islam and lurking silently to destroy it from within.

Examination of the Mushaf shows that the sincerity of the Prophet was not used as a condition for ascertaining the truth of his Message. After all, it is inconceivable that Muhammad was the only trustworthy man amongst the tribe of Quraish. Allah never invoked the character of Muhammad as a proof of the validity of the Message that he delivered but asked for acceptance of the revelation from all humans based on revealed signs (*aayaat*) that were included within the Mushaf (as an example, see M46:7). Despite his character, trust in Muhammad was never a cornerstone for validating the Message. Allah chose Muhammad to deliver the message most likely for specific reasons. However, these reasons were not expressed in the Mushaf.

The companions of the Prophet were surprisingly immune from the scrutiny of the "science" of al-Jarh wa al-Ta'deel. Their status precluded them from reproach and thus were deemed not to have made any errors, additions or deletions in documenting, reporting or transmitting the Hadith, a claim that can be refuted easily using the body of Hadith itself. Ayesha, one of the Prophet's wives, was reported in a certain Muslim Sahih hadith to have indicated that ibn Umar (who claimed in different hadiths that the Prophet said that the cries of the dead person inflict torture and pain on him) was not a liar but he could have made either a mistake or he could have forgotten what precisely the Prophet had said.[62] This admission by Muslim and al-Bukhari (and reaffirmed by al-Nawawi in his famous commentary on Sahih Muslim) brings to the forefront what most legal experts and psychologists know today, namely the fragility of the human memory. In fact, this hadith is important for different reasons. First, on the assumption that this hadith is true, the recollection of ibn Umar, a prominent and direct Hadith transmitter, had been put into question, and this was done by no other than the wife of the Prophet.[63] Second, this hadith, which is considered as *sahih* by Muslim, shows that Ayesha and some of the companions of the Prophet did not rule out the possibility that a Hadith transmitter could have been a liar. For the Ahl al-Sunnah wa al-Jama'ah who base their religion on *naql* (transmission, or Hadith) rather than *aql* (mind, intellect or rationality), their acceptance of this hadith as *sahih* should be sufficient to refute the theory that the companions of the Prophet were beyond reproach.

According to the doctrine of Hadith, the Muslim community in the early first Islamic century did not exclude the possibility that Hadith transmitters or even primary Hadith documenters were not trustworthy or even liars. Here is a hadith that sheds light on the credibility of abu Huraira, one of the most prominent Hadith narrators and one of the most referenced:

عَنْ أَبِي رَزِينٍ، قَالَ خَرَجَ إِلَيْنَا أَبُو هُرَيْرَةَ فَضَرَبَ بِيَدِهِ عَلَى جَبْهَتِهِ فَقَالَ أَلاَ إِنَّكُمْ تَحَدَّثُونَ أَنِّي أَكْذِبُ عَلَى رَسُولِ اللَّهِ صلى الله عليه وسلم لِتَهْتَدُوا وَأَضِلَّ أَلاَ وَإِنِّي أَشْهَدُ لَسَمِعْتُ رَسُولَ اللَّهِ صلى الله عليه وسلم يَقُولُ " إِذَا انْقَطَعَ شِسْعُ أَحَدِكُمْ فَلاَ يَمْشِ فِي الأُخْرَى حَتَّى يُصْلِحَهَا " .

[Abu Razeen narrated: "Abu Huraira came to us and he struck his forehead with his hand and said: 'Behold I you talk amongst yourself that I fabricate lies on the Messenger of Allah in order to guide you to the right path. In such a case, I would myself go astray. Listen. I bear testimony to the fact that I heard Allah's Messenger saying: When the thong of any one of you is broken, he should not walk in the second one until he has got it repaired.'"][64] According to Hadith Science, abu Razeen was a companion of the Prophet and that his trustworthiness was well established. If the early Muslim community, including the Prophet's companions who lived with and had direct access to abu Huraira, could not establish his credibility and trustworthiness, then it becomes doubtful if not impossible for someone who lived hundreds of years after to establish the trustworthiness of a chain of transmitters. The importance of this hadith cannot be diminished, especially when realizing that al-Bukhari included in his Sahih more than 440 abu Huraira hadiths.[65] (Another interesting aspect of this hadith is its placement within Sahih Muslim in the Chapter of Clothing and Ornamentation.)

While one cannot ascertain the correctness of this hadith, accepting it as authentic contradicts the system and methodologies dubbed as by Hadith Sciences and Sciences of Men. The possibility of making an error or forgetfulness in Hadith transmission is in full accord with the physiological and psychological human makeup and strongly contradicts the mythical superhuman image given to Hadith transmitters as people with incredible memory capacity to the point that the possibility of error or forgetfulness was null.[66] Any criticism of the superhuman character of these early scholars of Hadith is classically countered by producing arguments that cannot be either refuted or affirmed such as "this was Allah's way to protect the religion". To make all these exaggerations acceptable, elaborate legends were woven around the superhuman qualities of the likes of al-Bukhari and how he would travel thousands of miles only to determine, in subtle and clever ways, whether a particular Hadith transmitter was honest or not. These superhuman qualities are typically explained, without any proof, as a form of godly gifts (*karamaat*) that Allah bestows on his most sincere servants and most pious. Again, it is a claim that can be neither refuted nor proven. For those who disagreed with him during his lifetime, the Muslim narratives emphasize, were simply very envious of his intellectual prowess.

Perhaps in anticipation of such an outstanding exaggeration of the capabilities of al-Bukhari and others to verify the sincerity of men who lived over a span of hundreds of years, the Mushaf explicitly indicated that even the Prophet did not know which inhabitants of Medina were hypocrites and which were not. M9:10 states:

وَمِمَّنْ حَوْلَكُم مِّنَ الْأَعْرَابِ مُنَافِقُونَ وَمِنْ أَهْلِ الْمَدِينَةِ مَرَدُوا عَلَى النِّفَاقِ لَا تَعْلَمُهُمْ نَحْنُ نَعْلَمُهُمْ سَنُعَذِّبُهُم مَّرَّتَيْنِ ثُمَّ يُرَدُّونَ إِلَىٰ عَذَابٍ عَظِيمٍ

[And from those around you, from *al-a'raab,* there are hypocrites, and from the inhabitants of Madinah became ever-insurgent with hypocrisy you (singular) cannot tell who they are, we can determine who they are We will torment them twice then they will be returned to a great punishment.][67] The clarity of the verse leaves no doubt that the Prophet himself could not have determined the hypocrites from amongst his own companions. Those hypocrites, by definition, expressed sincerity and loyalty to Islam but concealed their real intentions.

SCIENCE OF VARIANCE

With time, questions arose as to the soundness of the Hadith authentication methods that were developed by earlier scholars of Hadith such as al-Tirmidhi, abu Dawood and even al-Bukhari. This prompted a revision of Hadith Sciences whereby transmission of Hadith by meaning rather than by precise wording (i.e., verbatim) became acceptable.[68] This major relaxation in Hadith transmission could have been politically motivated since the Hadith industry was strongly on the side of empires then. Nevertheless, the relaxation of the transmission criteria signaled a major devaluation of the credibility of Hadith. Consequently, many hadiths were transmitted by concept, expectedly as understood by the transmitter himself. To consolidate this new shift, the Hadith framers enacted complex criteria that must be found in the person who is qualified to transmit the Hadith by meaning.[69]

The transmission by meaning created more problems and added further mercuriality to the entire Hadith Science since the meaning of the Arabic words can differ amongst generations. It is impossible to give an example of how a specific hadith with specific words pronounced by the Prophet was transmitted while preserving the meaning. This is because had the original words of a specific hadith been known, it would have been presented using those words rather than different ones.

Transmitting Hadith by its meaning as understood by each person within the entire chain of transmitters is a serious flaw in the methodology of the Hadith Science. It assumes that the transmitter, in addition to having a reputation as a trustworthy individual, understood the precise meaning and context of the Prophetic sayings and that the Arabic words he used to document Hadith were immutable. The fact that numerous early scholars of Islam, including ibn Hanbal, al-Shafi'i, ibn Kathir and numerous others did not distinguish between words such as *nahi* (forbidding) and *tahrim* (forbidden by Allah), between *shahada* (witnessing) and *imaan* (belief), and between *imaan* and Islam, clearly indicate that Hadith transmitters, most likely, could have switched these words under the assumption that they were all synonymous.[70] An important example is confusing *nahi* with *tahrim*. Here are two hadiths in Sahih al-Bukhari related to whether or not it is permissible to eat the meat of domesticated donkeys:

نَهَى النَّبِيُّ صلى الله عليه وسلم عَنْ لُحُومِ الْحُمُرِ الْأَهْلِيَّةِ يَوْمَ خَيْبَرَ

[The Prophet asked to refrain from eating the meat of domesticated donkeys on the day of the battle of Khaibar.][71]

حَرَّمَ رَسُولُ اللَّهِ صلى الله عليه وسلم لُحُومَ الْحُمُرِ الْأَهْلِيَّةِ

[Allah's Messenger made haram the eating of the meat of domesticated donkeys.][72] Both of these hadiths were listed in Sahih al-Bukhari. Even the translation of these two hadiths into English confused the verb *naha* (refrained) with *man'a* (to forbade or to prevented).[73]

For English speakers who consult the USC-MSA translation of these two hadiths, the matter became even more confusing since *nahi* was translated as "made unlawful" and haram was translated as prohibited. Ibn Qudamah (d. 620/1223) commented that "the majority of the family of scholars take the stand that eating domesticated donkeys is haram." He also stated that "Ahmed said: 'Fifteen from the companions of the Prophet found it *makrooh* to eat it.' Ibn abd al-Bur said: 'There is no disagreement amongst the scholars of Islam today that it is haram.'"[74]

The two hadiths above, both part of the most respected Hadith book, must have been transmitted, at least one of them, by a meaning as understood it by one of its transmitters. This is because *tahrim* and *nahi* are two different words with severely different implications. Since the Prophet was elected by the people of Madinah as their governor, his duties and governance prerogatives must have included issuing proclamations and orders to his subjects related to all sorts of governance matters including regulating consumer goods. Al-Shafi'i, however, without providing any rationale, claimed that the Prophet's *nahi* implies *tahrim*.[75]

The disagreement amongst many Muslims regarding the permissibility of visiting graveyards could have also arisen because of ignoring the difference between *nahi* and *tahrim*. According to Sahih Muslim, the Prophet is reported to have said

نَهَيْتُكُمْ عَنْ زِيَارَةِ الْقُبُورِ فَزُورُوهَا

[I have *nahytukum* (discouraged you) from visiting the graveyards but now you can visit it.][76] If this hadith was transmitted by meaning, then one of the transmitters could have interchanged or confused *nahi* with *tahrim*, thus implying that the Prophet first made the visitation unlawful and then lawful. However, the Prophet, as a governor, could have discouraged his followers from visiting graveyards for several reasons and then later withdrew that discouragement, again, for all types of reasons that have to do with the social ethos of the Madinah society then.

A more profound example of possible transmission by meaning with more severe implications is represented by two important hadiths. The first is in Sahih Muslim:

أُمِرْتُ أَنْ أُقَاتِلَ النَّاسَ حَتَّى يَقُولُوا لاَ إِلَهَ إِلاَّ اللَّهُ فَمَنْ قَالَ لاَ إِلَهَ إِلاَّ اللَّهُ فَقَدْ عَصَمَ مِنِّي مَالَهُ وَنَفْسَهُ إِلاَّ بِحَقِّهِ وَحِسَابُهُ عَلَى اللَّهِ

[I have been ordered to fight people until they say/pronounce (*yaqoolo*) there is no god but Allah, and he who said no god but Allah then he secured from me protection of his money and life except for a right? His (other) affairs rest with Allah.][77] While the second is in Sahih al-Bukhari:

أُمِرْتُ أَنْ أُقَاتِلَ النَّاسَ حَتَّى يَشْهَدُوا أَنْ لاَ إِلَهَ إِلاَّ اللَّهُ وَأَنَّ مُحَمَّدًا رَسُولُ اللَّهِ، وَيُقِيمُوا الصَّلاَةَ، وَيُؤْتُوا الزَّكَاةَ، فَإِذَا فَعَلُوا ذَلِكَ عَصَمُوا مِنِّي دِمَاءَهُمْ وَأَمْوَالَهُمْ إِلاَّ بِحَقِّ الإِسْلاَمِ، وَحِسَابُهُمْ عَلَى اللَّهِ

[I have been ordered to fight people until they witness (*yash'hadoo*) that there is no god but Allah and that Muhammad is his Messenger, and to perform the ritual prayer and to dispense/give zakat. And if they have done all, then they secured from me protection of their blood and money except for a right? His (other) affairs rest with Allah.][78] Notice the similarity in the substance of the two hadiths, however, the framers of these two hadiths (their contradiction with the Mushaf has been discussed in Chapter 4) did not find it important to distinguish between two important verbs: *qala* and *shahida*. They failed to realize that even Allah did not ask either the followers of Muhammad or those of any other Prophet to witness that Allah is the only deity.

The transmission by meaning, or the conceptual transmission diminishes the value of not only the alleged authentic hadiths but also calls into question the highly detailed and respected Hadith exegeses such as those of al-Nawawi and al-Asqalani. These exegeses parse the grammatical meaning of the words of each hadith to discern its "true" meaning. Expectedly, if the words of a certain hadith differed, al-Nawawi's interpretation would differ as well. In fact, if Hadith transmission by meaning is acceptable, al-Nawawi's and al-Asqalani's works are irrelevant to those interested in Islam or in the Sunnah of the Prophet.

Any phrase or saying, whether originating from the Prophet or any other person, is relevant to its context. It is possible that for a specific true hadith, the first person in its chain of transmitters could have understood the hadith within its context but never reported the context. Other later transmitters could have transmitted the same hadith based on their interpretation of the earlier interpretation while lacking the context that was available to the former transmitters.

CANONIZATION OF CONTRADICTIONS

The sheer absurdity of the assumptions put forth by the proponents of the Hadith Sciences and on which the authenticity of the Hadith was established is glaring. Sahih al-Bukhari and other collections are full of contradictions. To reconcile these numerous contradictions, one more "science" was created. Uloom Mukhtalaf al-Hadith (the Sciences of Conflicting Hadith) and al-Mawdu'at (The Fabricated Ones) was invented to answer, most likely, what might be judged to be an outcry by many people (scholars and laymen alike) towards the contradictions between numerous hadiths and the Mushaf.[79]

There are two types of contradictions. The first type is contradictions within the body of Hadith and the second is contradictions between the Hadith and the Mushaf. There are numerous examples of the first category, with some having blatant contradictions and inconsistencies that are virtually impossible to reconcile. A prominent and illustrative example is reconciling numerous hadiths that relate to the Prophet's directives about documenting his words or actions. Some of these hadiths claim the Prophet strongly warned against documenting anything related to himself, while others claim that the Prophet permitted the practice.[80] Some of the proponents of documenting the Hadith argue that the prohibition on documenting the Prophet's words came on the seventh Hijri year. Particularly, in one hadith, abu Hurairah claimed that the Prophet prohibited writing Hadith and that he ordered the destruction of anything that was written about him.[81] In this hadith, abu Hurairah stated that he complied and destroyed all that he had written once he heard the Prophet's orders. Since abu Hurairah was reported to have accompanied the Prophet for approximately two years, if the practice of documenting the Hadith was allowed later on, a small number of hadiths should have reached us through abu Hurairah. This leads us to an important intentional or unintentional omission by the earliest of Hadith transmitters (who heard the Prophet directly): the missing time stamp. Including a time stamp (and a location stamp) should have never been a burden on the first Hadith transmitters considering that some of their hadiths contain elaborate details and names of people and places.

An example of the second type of hadiths that contradict the Mushaf are those that permit sexual intercourse between married couples during menstruation.[82] These hadiths are in stark contradiction to M2:222 explicitly asking men to distance themselves from their spouses during menstruation. In their attempts to reconcile this stark contradiction, Hadith scholars ended in bizarre arguments that many of the Hadith proponents have apparently decided to avoid altogether.[83] In fact, the hadiths permitting sexual intercourse during menstruation were even contradictory to other hadiths found in a single Hadith collection.

There are too many other examples to list here and are partially detailed below when comparing Muhammad of the Mushaf to Muhammad of the Hadith.

To help in reconciling some Mushaf-contradictory and Hadith-contradictory hadiths, the concept of *Naskh* (abrogation), which was applied generously to the Mushaf verses (see Chapter 7) was also applied to Hadith. The applicability of the *Naskh* concept to Hadith has two subcategories. The first is abrogation of Hadith by Hadith, and the second is abrogation of the Mushaf by Hadith. This ingenious loophole created an instrument by which any contradiction between any two hadiths can be resolved. Numerous Muslim scholars invoked this loophole repeatedly without providing any proof that a single hadith was abrogated aside from mere opinions that were not even referenced to any alleged Prophetic narrative or behavior.[84]

A prominent example is the will (bequeathing) hadiths in Sahih al-Bukhari and Jami al-Tirmidhi that contradict M2:180.[85] (These particular hadiths were discussed earlier in Chapter 7.) While many Muslim scholars frowned upon the extreme opinion that the Sunnah can abrogate the Mushaf, we find that the vast majority of Muslim scholars continued to champion the authenticity of such will hadiths.[86] This is despite their admission that there were different opinions on how M2:18 was abrogated. Even under the rubric of abrogation, leading Muslim scholars were not able to reach consensus to resolve a myriad of Hadith contradictions.[87] While one would expect that such controversial hadiths would be rejected altogether, they are being used today to support critical "Islamic" legislations and opinions, and continue to be part of the implementable Sharia, affecting millions of Muslims socially and economically.

There is yet a third category of hadiths that were, at face value, neither contradictory to other hadiths nor to the Mushaf. An example of this type is one in Sahih al-Bukhari that claims that women were created from a rib (presumably, the rib of Adam) and another that claims the sun goes to Allah's throne every day and seeks permission to prostrate.[88] To avoid explaining the bizarreness of such hadiths, some scholars interpreted them metaphorically. Those particular scholars did not provide any reason why the interpretations of such hadiths had to assume a metaphorical nature or, absent the context of these hadiths, when a metaphorical interpretation overrides the literal, apparent, or the true one.

Many Muslim jurisprudents and clergy established a host of instruments reaching unexpected extremes in linguistic sophistry and denial of reason to silence any criticism of the Hadith corpus even at the cost of reshaping the interpretation of the Mushaf in the shadow of Hadith. Excessive enthusiasm of certain scholars towards Hadith could have been encouraged by al-Shafi'i's ideas and theories, however, the body of knowledge that evolved in the process, including the so-called sciences of Hadith, created a dangerous if unintended new doctrine. The new thinking that emerged from Hadith "sciences" helped to shape a mercurial culture amongst Muslims that created an "Islamic" mechanism to justify nearly anything. The numerous contradictions in alleged Prophetic narratives and Hadith sciences helped to shape the mercurial Muslim who either manipulates the religion to justify whatever he or she feels is expedient, or remains close to Islam but in a superficial way. This emerging Muslim character is tormented as it sees contradictions that Allah's gift of human reasoning cannot reconcile. The only ties this character has to Islam is through threads of nostalgia and human relationships or sheer fear. At the end, Islam becomes more of a culture than a universal guiding philosophy.

SUNNAH AND HADITH: NEW DOCTRINES

The Sunnah and Hadith emerged as new doctrines competing with the Mushaf. Based on the writings of al-Shafi'i that have reached us, it is highly probable that he was the first to develop the theoretical foundations for the Sunnah as an Islamic doctrine that parallels the Mushaf in not only reverence amongst Muslims but as a primary and at times supreme source of legislation. Effectively, al-Shafi'i's *al-Risala* treatise opened the door to the "Islamization" of all aspects of life (see Chapter 9), and in the process created a major diversion of Muslims' and non-Muslims' energy from focusing on the Mushaf to obsession with purely legislative matters canonized as "Islamic."[89] Ahl al-Sunnah wa al-Jamma'ah specifically and the proponents of the Sunnah and Hadith in general claimed that the Sunna is a second *wahi* (divine revelation). It is difficult to ascertain the origin of this grand claim.[90] Most likely, it started rather implicitly by al-Shafi'i and then gained wider acceptance with time. Today, acceptance of the *wahyayyn* (two divine revelations) has become widely spread amongst diehard Hadith proponents and

New Doctrines: Sunnah and Hadith

particularly the Salafi sect.[91] These claims largely hinge on M53:3,4

$$\text{وَمَا يَنطِقُ عَنِ الْهَوَىٰ}$$
$$\text{إِنْ هُوَ إِلَّا وَحْيٌ يُوحَىٰ}$$

[And he does not utter or pronounces what is based on his inclination or what he desires. Affirmatively, it (هو) is/he but a revelation that is revealed]. Based on these two verses, the *wahyayyen* advocates claim that every word that Muhammad uttered was a divine revelation to be treated just like the Mushaf. They would justify the claim by interpreting the pronoun *huwa* (هو) as referring either to what Muhammad uttered or to Muhammad himself.[92] This would in turn imply that Muhammad, the man, was a revelation. The problem with this interpretation is the fact that Muhammad was a human who was born to a known mother and father, and who lived only once. It would have been impossible for Muhammad to have been revealed. Therefore, the pronoun *huwa* cannot refer to Muhammad the man, the Prophet or even the Messenger. Notice that the pronoun is exclusively (using the Arabic إلا) referring to what proceeded it, the *wahi*. Therefore, neither Muhammad nor the act of pronunciation are *wahi*. M36:69 further validates this interpretation:

$$\text{وَمَا عَلَّمْنَاهُ الشِّعْرَ وَمَا يَنبَغِي لَهُ ۚ إِنْ هُوَ إِلَّا ذِكْرٌ وَقُرْآنٌ مُبِينٌ}$$

[And We did not teach him poetry and it was not befitting/allowed for him; indeed it (هو) was nothing but *thikr* and clear/apparent Qur'aan.] This verse, which has a similar linguistic structure to M53:4, gives strong validation to the above interpretation since هو here cannot refer to either Muhammad or poetry but to *thikr* and Qur'aan, both of which proceeded هو. Notice that the pronoun هو can refer to non-tangibles such as guidance (M6:71), Allah's signs (M29:49), and truth (M8:32). Therefore, based purely on linguistic analysis, M53:3 and 53:4 do not provide any evidence that every word uttered by Muhammad was a revelation. In fact, there is no reason to assume that the revelation is utterance. Had that been the case, Muhammad would have been a god in the form of a human.

The claim that everything the Prophet said was a *wahi* is sharply contradicted by numerous verses where the Prophet was warned from carrying out acts that were contrary to Allah's teachings as explained earlier; most notably M66:1 (discussed earlier in this chapter), which indicates that the Prophet said things that were contrary to the revelation. Nevertheless, if the Sunnah as documented by Hadith is a second *wahi*, the proponents of the two *wahyayyn* should accept applying the classification of Hadith to this second wahi as well. This would then imply that the second *wahi* could be *sahih wahi* (authentic), *dhaeef wahi* (weak), *hasan wahi* (good), *ghareeb wahi* (strange), etc.

Based on general writings of al-Shafi'i, and particularly his *al-Risala* treatise, one can sense a raging debate in the early centuries of Islam between two camps. The first camp consisted of those who believed in the Mushaf as the only revelation and source of legislation. The second was the advocates of the Sunnah as supplementary, complementary and even at times supreme to the Mushaf. The proponents of the Sunnah doctrine typically argue that the Sunnah alone was able to give important details related to the daily ritual prayers, *hajj*, and how much of one's wealth to be given in *zakat*. Their narrative goes further to imply that Islam would be incomplete without the Sunnah. Some have even claimed that the Mushaf is in need of the Sunnah more than the Sunnah is in need of the Mushaf.[93]

It was discussed above that not one hadith in Sahih al-Bukhari attributed to the Prophet explained the number of times the Muslim has to prostrate during prayers or what should be said during the different acts of the prayer. One cannot find the Details of *hajj* in Sahih al-Bukhari either. All these claims suggest that the most important value Islam adds to one's life is the precise bodily movements in the daily ritual prayers and the specific details of the *hajj* rituals. Even the amount of *zakat* was not mentioned in the Mushaf, not to be left to Sunnah but to be left to human common sense and particularities.

When questioned about the absence in Sahih al-Bukhari of any details related to the ritual prayers, the proponents of the Hadith doctrine typically invoke a hadith where the Prophet instructed the believers to pray the way he prayed. Indeed, for Muslims, the Messenger's deeds are to be emulated by the Muslims but not the Prophet's deeds. These were the precise instructions of the Mushaf. In fact, Muslims have been praying without guidance from any of the six Hadith Compendia for centuries and never a significant dispute arose (as far as my knowledge is concerned) between them regarding the prayers. One wonders whether the Muslims who never had access to Sahih al-Bukhari, or who lived during the first two Islamic centuries performed the prayers correctly. Equally, interesting questions arise as to why Allah included in the Mushaf details of ablution while not giving details of the daily ritual prayers or the details of the *hajj*. If details, in general, were left to the domain of the Sunnah, why would stoning the married adulterer, a very grave type of punishment, be left to the Sunnah while the details of the ablution, which is clearly of much less significance, be left to the Mushaf? These important questions cannot be answered by guesswork or through the interpretation of God's mind (i.e., the philosophical underpinnings behind Allah's instructions).

The reliance on Hadith had the effect of distancing Muslims from the conceptual framework of Islam and moved them closer to a predominantly performance-based framework (possibly diminishing the conceptual implications of specific acts of worship). To the followers of Muhammed, the ritual prayers are important just like everything else in the Mushaf. However, perhaps the importance of the details of the ritual prayers pales in comparison to the spectrum of priorities in the life of Muslims in particular or the life of a human being in general. Perhaps Allah intended some latitude in these rituals that can accommodate human physical limitations and unexpected turns in one's health and agility.

One could only speculate as to why the precise mechanical movements of the ritual prayers were not detailed in the Mushaf. Perhaps those rituals are not part of the structure and ethos of any diverse or multi-denominational community such as the one the Prophet established in Madinah. Rituals are obligations towards Allah, not towards the community and thus can hardly define or characterise a community. This can be fully attested by the relationship between the ritual prayers and the functioning of the society in predominantly Muslim countries. From a theoretical perspective, whether a Muslim performs her prayers or not is irrelevant to the functioning of a community or to a social harmony between its members. Indeed, the prayer has the potential to increases one's piety and thus can lead to virtue and indirectly or partially to the well-being of the community. However, the performance and specific details of the prayers are not a guarantee for a healthy community.[94]

Despite the intricate classifications of Hadith, weak and dubious hadiths inundated the Mushaf exegeses. Grand exegetes such as ibn Kathir, al-Qurtubi and others used weak hadiths extensively in their exegeses despite knowing and even admitting that many of the hadiths they used were of dubious origin. Despite that many Muslim scholars, jurisprudents and clergy considered the use of weak hadiths not binding as far as "Islamic" legislation is concerned, weak hadiths were considered useful for Mushaf interpretation.[95] This modus operandi reflects either double standards towards Hadith in general or an attitude towards the Mushaf that it is not worthy of a precise and rational interpretation to the point of using myth, legends, and stories to aid in its understanding, or both. Relaxing the rules for Mushaf interpretation confirms the discussion presented earlier (Chapter 6) that understanding the Mushaf is secondary to the life of Muslims.

MUHAMMAD OF THE MUSHAF VS. MUHAMMAD OF HADITH

The Mushaf embodies Islam and all that needs to be known about Islam. For Muslims, it is expected that everything outside the Mushaf should be subjected to the principles and guidelines of the Mushaf. In other words, the Mushaf is the primary and complete source for the religion, not other material whose authenticity is constantly speculated and debated and yet to be fully validated. If Allah wanted the believers to be aware of specific practices, He would have spelled them out within the Mushaf. If Muslims needed to know anything about the man to whom Allah chose to be his last Messenger, they need look no further than the Mushaf.

The Sunnah and Hadith evolved with time to achieve a status that qualifies them to be parallel to the Mushaf. Effectively a parallel religion emerged that is characteristically and substantively different from the religion of Allah. The new religion, despite being different, cannot be justified as complementary to the Mushaf. This religion extensively expanded the scope of prohibitions (*tahrim*) and presented an image of Muhammad so radically different from the one presented by the divine revelation.

The Hadith portrayed Muhammad: as a pedophile;[96] as a sexual pervert who flirted with foreign women;[97] as a selfish person to the point of using religion to achieve his own salvation and satisfaction;[98] as vengeful and bloodthirsty;[99] as a temperamental leader who did not follow due process and who sought satisfaction from torture;[100] to have been irrational to the point of ordering executions without trial or even giving the accused an opportunity to defend himself;[101] to have allowed his men followers to fondle the breasts of foreign women;[102] as a highwayman;[103] as a leader who condoned deception;[104] as disobeying Allah's Mushaf commands;[105] as an untrustworthy leader who broke the covenants and treaties he established with neighboring tribes;[106] to have been a magician making water spring from (or between or through) his hands;[107] as a future teller.[108] If all these stories are true then the Muhammad of Hadith is not the Muhammad of the Mushaf but a dramatically different character, or the Muhammad of Hadith decided to go against the Mushaf. It is impossible to foresee a third alternative.

The Mushaf stressed that Muhammad was a human, a husband, a Prophet and a Messenger. Muhammad the human: could have been killed (M3:144); had made errors in judgement (M80:1); was misguided until he received guidance from Allah (M93:7); and never knew his ultimate fate (M46:9). The Mushaf gives no indication that Muhammad was a perfect human. Was Muhammad the "chosen" or the "selected" as many Muslims claim?[109] The Mushaf states that Adam, Noah, Ibrahim and the progeny of Imraan were chosen above all humanity (chosen is possibly the most accurate translation of *istafa* in M3:33), but Muhammad was not amongst this group. Was Muhammad better than all other Prophets and Messengers? The Mushaf does not engage in such favoritism discourse, perhaps because it is irrelevant. Was Muhammad born as a Messenger or did he evolve to a status that was eventually deserving of the Prophethood and deliverer of the final Message? The Mushaf might give indications that shed light on such a question, but, again, perhaps such a question has little relevance to the Message and to Islam.

Biographies of the Prophet, such as those compiled and written by ibn Ishaq (d. 159/770), ibn Hisham (d. 218/833), al-Waqidi (d. 207/823), and ibn Sayyid al-Naas (d. 734/1334), have been based on records of varying authenticity, historical fragments, imagination, exaggerations, myths, legends, and fabrications. For the majority of Muslims, the most trusted biography of the Prophet is that of ibn Hisham. Ibn Hisham, however, was not the originator of the biography that bears his name; he edited and abridged the original work of ibn Ishaq. Ibn Ishaq was born 75 years after the death of the Prophet, so when he embarked on his project of documenting the Prophet's life and history of early Islam, he was almost two generations apart from the era of his historical material.

If it were a monumental challenge to document and authenticate the Prophet's words and deeds (Hadith), to produce a Prophet biography, ibn Ishaq and ibn Hisham should have operated under similar and very stringent rules. This is the case if the biographies were intended for anything of religious value such as Islamic legislation or worship. However, this was not the case. None of their works were subjected to the scrutiny of the Hadith Sciences despite their serious and numerous flaws. Muslim scholars, however, had a chequered and mostly unfavorable opinion of ibn Ishaq. Malik, the de facto founder of the Maliki sect and the compiler of al-Muwatta, one of the early Hadith collections, and who was a Hadith scholar in his own right, was a contemporary of ibn Ishaq. Malik believed that ibn Ishaq was not trustworthy and that he transmitted heavily from recent converts to Islam.[110] According to Tahdheeb al-Tahdheeb, one of the major Hadith Science books, Ahmed ibn Hanbal, the founder of the Hanbali sect, did not believe that all solitary reports of ibn Ishaq were reliable. In fact, ibn Hanbal considered ibn Ishaq a Hadith fabricator.[111]

Ibn Ishaq's Prophet biography contains fairy-tales, legends, fabrications and possibly some truths. If historical narratives build upon a factual event to convey a non-truthful message, or vice-versa, it can be argued that the entire narrative is either deceptive, untruthful or fictional. Interestingly, the introduction to ibn Hisham's work stated that ibn Ishaq was commissioned by the Abbasid Caliph al-Mansour to write a history book for his son; a book that spans the period from the creation of Adam all the way to the Prophet's era. If true, this would suggest that ibn Ishaq was a courtier, a close associate or a patron of the Caliph. A grand commission as such could have entailed a heavy financial compensation. Ibn Ishaq most likely was eager to satisfy the contract with the Caliph by producing voluminous material that needed fecund imagination. In modern academic jargon, ibn Ishaq should have declared the source of his funding, otherwise the integrity of his work would be in doubt.

Ibn Sayyid al-Naas (d. 734/1334) based his biography of the Prophet, *Uyoon al-A'thaar*, largely on ibn Ishaq and al-Waqidi. Al-Naas's rich imagination and fabrication of elaborate stories about the Prophet, including intricate details about the Prophet's personal life, are highly suspect. This is especially the case since sources for his stories were missing. To spice up his biography, and possibly for promotional purposes, al-Naas inundated his stories with Prophetic miracles that even the most extreme of Hadith transmitters were cautious to include in their compendia. One might argue that al-Naas's scholarship was compatible with his time. Such a claim, however, is difficult to substantiate considering the scholarship demonstrated during much earlier periods in human history. (Similar arguments are commonly invoked in defense of the celebrated Muslim clergy. Al-Shafi'i and ibn Kathir, for example, narrated numerous hadiths and stories and attributed them to unknown people.[112])

Despite the scholarship methodologies of yesteryear, modern scholarship methods, which are the most advanced methods known to mankind, constitute the right prism that Muslims need to use to understand any works written about their religion or their Prophet. There is hardly any reason to give credence to al-Naas's work. Surprisingly, some prominent Muslim academics and scholars think otherwise, as exemplified by the introduction to a modern printing of *Uyoon al-A'thaar*. The introduction reveals the admiration bestowed upon al-Naas by modern academics describing his methodology:[113]

> He [al-Naas] simplified the works of two major luminaries of the Prophet's biography and history of the battles, namely ibn Ishaq and al-Waqidi, and made apologies for the attacks those two luminaries suffered by those who discredited their works which are considered the foundation for all that followed... and he [al-Naas] was cautious in authenticating the Prophet's biography based on the Qur'aan revelation and the Sunnah, and when he could not find authentication in these two sources, he resorted to the biography books that he himself heard or was authenticated by others, and some of these books have never reached us, thus *Uyoon al-Athar* came to fill the void.

The academics that bestow such unusual and vacuous accolades are a victim of a Muslim culture created by Hadith that inculcated into the innermost psyche of Muslims that humanity is in a perpetual decline. Therefore, no criticism of such "golden age" luminaries would be tolerated despite their fictional contributions that can never pass the academic standards of either today or yesteryear.

The harm of these biographies extend beyond their impact on Muslims. These mostly fictional biographies were an important substance for non-Muslims who wanted to understand Islam. From the perspective of an outsider, a way to understand a cult, nation, religious group or any collective is to understand its leader: how he conducted his life in general; how he dealt with society, his companions, his wives, his enemies, the poor, etc. The impression such a leader gives matters significantly in shaping one's view of a religion. This is especially the case with Islam and Muslims since Muslim scholars and clergy have created a buffer zone (i.e., the parallel doctrine of Sunnah) that made it next to impossible to present Islam to non-Muslims in a language they can understand and analyze, and by turning Islam into a deeply complex theological sophistry. Thus, naturally, the Prophet's biographies become the de facto introduction to Islam. If other than a Muslim had produced these mostly fictional and incredulous works, he would have been dubbed as an Orientalist (with its assumed deeply negative connotation) or a sworn enemy of Islam who wanted to chisel its foundation.

Some non-Muslim scholars provided biographies for the Prophet by mostly translating the works of ibn Ishaq and al-Waqidi. Most notable amongst these is William Muir (d. 1323/1905). Muir's extensive research of the history of the Prophet could have most likely formed his conclusions about Islam. In fact, it is likely that Muir and many who read the ibn Ishaq and ibn Hisham biographies could have formed a particular opinion of the Prophet that would have crushed any appetite for any further interest in Islam.[114] Muir's and other's (including Salman Rushdie) infatuation with the idea that the Prophet was possessed by demons originated from Muslims rather than from Christian evangelists, Christian colonizers or Jews. Despite Muir's Christian faith and evangelism, Muslims should scrutinize the work of Muir by using the same prism that scrutinizes the works of ibn Ishaq and other fictional Muslim writers. Uttering the *shahada* (the pronouncement that Allah is the only God and Muhammad is His Messenger) cannot be a guarantee for trustworthiness.

Allah archived in the Mushaf what He wanted humanity to know about Muhammad. The Muslim is not obliged to accept anything about Muhammad that falls outside the Mushaf. If a Muslim does not accept that Muhammad is the master of all humanity, then that Muslim has not violated his religion. However, if a Muslim elevates Muhammad, the Prophet and the Messenger, to a status that is contradictory to the Mushaf, or gives Muhammad an attribute exclusive to Allah, or associates a divine attribute to the Prophet, then that Muslim has introduced an addendum to Islam or even fabricated additional articles of faith. A Muslim who accepts that Muhammad shared with Allah the authority of *tahrim* (declaring acts as haram) and that Muhammad is capable of knowing the future, has most likely distanced himself from piety. In fact, these acts or beliefs constitute associating partners with God, which is the essence of *shirk*.

Concluding Thoughts

The Sunnah doctrine diverted Muslims from following Allah's pure message towards a labyrinth of contradictions. This diversion diminished the spirit of Islam and perpetuated myths rather than enforcing the truths that the Mushaf came to emphasize in the first place. This diversion diminished confidence in the religion by its own adherents. The Hadith "sciences" championed this attempt to connote a scientific veneer to a collection of mere opinions and guesswork.

If the present is any lesson for understanding the past, today we find that the Hadith doctrine has many benefactors who show unusual zeal to support it at the cost of Allah's divine words. For those benefactors, any criticism of certain hadiths is immediately equated with rejecting the path of the Prophet and his Sunnah. Even rejecting some hadiths that projects the Prophet as a pedophile and womanizer renders the Muslim, in the eyes of the Hadith proponents, as an enemy of the Sunnah and, by extension, of the Prophet and of Islam. It is difficult to suspect that these Hadith benefactors are benefiting from their admiration for the Prophet. The benefit, for many, stems from the privilege and power derived from fake hadiths sanctified by the elevation of Hadith to the status of the Mushaf, if not higher.

The Hadith benefactors were divided amongst clergy, academics and especially rulers and their courtiers (a good example is Muawiyah, the founder of the Umayyad dynasty, who was the primary benefactor from the Hadith cottage industry that proliferated during his reign.)[115] The first two provided the theoretical background for Hadith "sciences" while the rulers, mostly of Muslim majority countries, reaped the ultimate fruits for having a system through which the populations could be controlled and preoccupied with an overload of vacuous and never-ending rituals that hardly leave any quality time and energy for questioning the functioning and legitimacy of despots.

The Hadith corpus also helped governments to benefit immensely from agitating the masses to justify hostility and even war against other countries. The Hadith system is expandable as needed and can always be called upon to justify political interests such as making peace overtures or treaties with violators of the most basic of human rights (as was the case of animosity or rapprochement that some Muslim countries had with the State of Israel; all of which was sanctioned by the Hadith). The system is so confusing and complex that it shielded itself from criticism from non-Muslim scholars. Above all, the system is largely despot-friendly because of its built-in provisions that yield, totally, to the rulers, kings and despots for making the "righteous and guided" judgements that benefit the *umma*. At the same time, the system is a strong advocate of violence and war since it rewards whoever comes to power legally or illegally; the victor through violence is the *amir* who must be obeyed.

The perceived triumphalism of Ahl al-Hadith over the rationalists who were historically lumped together under the derogatory collective of the Mu'tazilites and/or Khawarij (umbrella designations that came to define the enemies of Ahl al-Hadith, Ahl al-Sunnah wa al-Jama'ah, the Umayyads and the Abbasids) was summarized in al-Shafi'i's repeatedly-touted argument that "without the Sunnah and Hadith, how could Muslims know the details of prayer or the Ramadan fast?" If al-Shafi'i and other luminaries of his time understood the religion as the proper execution of the ritual prayer, or an imposition of all types of restrictions on the fasting Muslim, or the proper "Islamic" behavior when urinating, then their age can hardly be classified as the Golden Age of Islam, but rather as the age of caging Islam.

This seemingly primitive and narrow understanding of what religion is all about has segregated the believers of the Message from the majority of humanity simply because this majority does not follow identical procedures in specific worship rituals. The Hadith devalued the concept of values that are the foundations for healthy societies. The quintessential factor for uniting the Muslims became a mere mechanical performance such as starting the Ramadan fast on the same date or lining up in one place for collective prayers. The true quintessential factor for uniting the Muslims ceased to be the ultimate truth and the quest for fairness and justice.

Hadith transform many Muslims into a cult. In this cult, justice and fairness ceased to be universal values. In this cult, the net worthiness of a Muslim became his practice of rituals rather than upholding the values of Islam. If a Jew or Christian committed war crimes, this cult reacted vehemently with outrage, but if a Muslim committed equally reprehensive war crimes, the cult turned a blind eye.

Since the Hadith implied that the human civilization is in decline, then there is not much hope in the future simply because the best of people and the best of times are all behind us, and the best of humanity's goodness and potential are not only capped but also ever shrinking. If the opposite, then the immutable principles of the Mushaf, presented with full details, are the key to guidance. The behavior of early Muslims cannot be turned into a religion. If al-Shafi'i and other Muslim scholars of his time were not able to understand or decipher some of the injunctions of the Mushaf, say the inheritance verses, then either the Mushaf was deficient or its correct interpretation has yet to be arrived at by future generations. This would not exclude the possibility that the Prophet himself was not equipped to understand even some of the *ahkam* (rulings) of the Mushaf. If he did, there would have never been such a wide range of disagreements even within not so many years from the time of his death. If the divine revelations were in harmony with humans' evolution and development, then it is not extreme to accept the possibility that some injunctions of the Mushaf needed people who are scientifically more apt to understand them than the early Muslim society.

Muhammad was a Messenger as M3:144 expresses. He was entrusted to deliver the Message and was warned to deliver it fully (see M5:67). Contrary to a popular belief amongst many Muslims, Muhammad did not know the future, past, or the unseen, except whatever was revealed within the Mushaf. Muhammad was not asked to explain or interpret the Mushaf. Some of the Mushaf does not need any interpretation as it is direct and self-explanatory, while the interpretation of other parts depends on the evolution of humans' scientific competency and knowledge.

Muhammad was not a model to be emulated by the billions of people who were to be born after his death. The Sunnah doctrine has deprived Muslims of their agency and the immense responsibility to adapt to the ever-changing world; it petrified their universe in contradiction to the principle of *tasbeeh* (continuous change and adaption) that governs every constituent of the universe.[116] The Sunnah and Hadith reduced Islam to imitating every act the Prophet is reportedly to have done and every act that the Prophet recommended or commanded his followers to do.

The Sunnah created a new Muslim. By following the Sunnah, this

Muslim becomes contented that he is doing the right thing. This Muslim is no longer in need to expend any intellectual effort to understand the universe and how to adjust his behavior to be in harmony with reality. The Sunnah and Hadith doctrines created a culture of imitation that, as Muhammad Shahrour brilliantly put it, a culture that is incapable of producing knowledge. The predominant Muslim culture looks backward for references, for role models and for inspiration. The Sunnah made this culture suspended between a mythical past and the pleasures of the hereafter, leaving the present to the "infidels". The infatuation with the past "color-blinded" the Muslims to view the first two Hijri centuries as the Golden Age of Islam; perhaps it was the golden age of those empires that used Islam to justify their expansion and conquest. Since nothing comes closer to gold in value, expectedly, it must be downhill thereafter.

Hadith created a new religion that aggressively competes with the Message of Islam. This new Hadith doctrine or parallel religion slowly evolved over hundreds of years and contributed in a large way to preventing the expansion of the Message of Islam from reaching humanity at large. Despite the claims of the fastest growing religion, Muslims constitute a mere fraction of the world's population. An increase in the number of the faithful has been due, mostly, to the forces of biological reproduction, nothing else.

During a recent encounter with a Muslim friend who was not comfortable with some of the ideas presented in this chapter, he exclaimed "but how will I perform...", and he went on to list a variety of daily functions, some of which were religious rituals and some were not. My friend's innocence is a product of the perception the Hadith has successfully inculcated in the minds of Muslims; that Islam came to control and regulate every aspect of life, and by implication, depriving the human being from any agency. The Hadith created a culture whereby the more one subjects one's life to the dictates of Hadith and by implication control over every aspect of life, the higher the piety and closeness to Allah. The alternative is human emancipation as the Mushaf intended it.

Islam will never reach universal appeal as long as Muslims consider Hadith or Sunnah to be one of its fundamental doctrines. A claim that is widely championed by Muslims is tolerance. The reality on the ground, however, tells of a different story, a story of severe intolerance. Killings of Muslims by Muslims has become commonplace. Severely

New Doctrines: Sunnah and Hadith

discrediting and attacking Muslims by Muslims is rampant and takes all forms from caustic and virulent personal attacks to murder. All this violence is carried out in the name of protecting Islam despite the belief by the alleged Islam and Sunnah protectors and the Hadith proponents that Allah has guaranteed to protect the religion. Perhaps the Hadith framers know deep down in their hearts, and correctly, that Allah did not guarantee the protection of the Hadith or Sunnah doctrines; hence the ever flinging sects claiming to be the defenders of the Sunnah and *ansar* al-Sunnah.

Anyone who champions the Mushaf as the primary source of Islam is labeled as *munkir al-Sunnah* (denier or rejecter of the Sunnah). The intolerance of those Muslims stems from no other source than the doctrine they champion the most, whereas those who advocate the Mushaf as the primary and the only source of Islam derive their concept of tolerance from the Mushaf itself. The first camp are quick to use most virulent labels at those who disagree with them, while the second camp come very close to the concept of tolerance as expressed in the Mushaf.[117] It is noticeable that the ferocity and intensity with which the Mushaf advocates have been attacked by Muslims pales in comparison to any attacks against "infidels" or those who support infidels in everything they do and is against Islam. The proponents of Hadith invoke M16:125 when arguing or engaging non-Muslims:

ادْعُ إِلَىٰ سَبِيلِ رَبِّكَ بِالْحِكْمَةِ وَالْمَوْعِظَةِ الْحَسَنَةِ وَجَادِلْهُم بِالَّتِي هِيَ أَحْسَنُ إِنَّ رَبَّكَ هُوَ أَعْلَمُ بِمَن ضَلَّ عَن سَبِيلِهِ وَهُوَ أَعْلَمُ بِالْمُهْتَدِينَ

[Call (this is addressed either to everyone or to the Prophet) to the way of your Lord with wisdom and good admonition, and carry out debates with them in the best way, Your Lord understands (more than anyone else) who have deviated away from His way, and He understands (more than anyone else) best who is right-guided.] One hopes that the staunch Sunnah supporters use the same Mushaf guidance to debate with those who champion the Mushaf above all.

The debate raging today in the Muslim world that questions all falsehoods being turned into religious doctrines also raged in the first two centuries as exemplified by the debates between al-Shafi'i and others.[118] The difference between then and now is that access to information has now become available to practically everyone. All Hadith compendia and the works of Malik, al-Shafi'i, ibn Hanbal, al-Nawawi, al-Asqalani, etc. are readily available within seconds for anyone with access to the Internet. All the scholarship of those scholars, clergy and jurisprudents is exposed for all to see and to judge for accuracy and authenticity. However, what is similar today to yesteryear is the power structure that the Hadith Sciences and Hadith and Sunnah doctrines helped produce. These "sciences" created powerful institutions that hypnotized Muslims to accept that the Hadith *ulama* (scholars) are the ones to seek answers for topics ranging from cosmology to gynecology.

When critique of Hadith Sciences started, all good manners that the *ulama* were expected to have and all the virtues of humility and wisdom the *ulama* are commanded to use in their debates, were all forsaken. The incredible mercuriality in the Hadith Sciences was perfectly tolerated by the *ulama* for so many centuries; a mercuriality that can turn the halal into haram and vice-versa as one wishes. However, doubting the authenticity of the two Sahihs was sufficient to toss the Muslim out of the *umma* body. This amazing violence of the *wasati ulama* is indeed rational — their thrones, not Islam, were under attack.

---

1. Ibn al-Salah, abu Amr. *Uloom al-Hadith.* Dar al-Fikr, 2002. This book is highly regarded in Hadith Sciences and is part of the curricula at several Muslim universities.
2. Fawzi, Ibrahim. *Tadween al-Sunnah.* Riad el-Rayyes Books, 1994, p. 29.
3. Al-Darimi, Abdullah. *Sunan al-Darimi.* Bab al-Sunnah Qadiya ala Kitaab Allah, no. 49, pp. 473-475. Al-Shatibi, abu Ishaq. *Al-Muwafiqat.* Vol. 4, Dar ibn Affan, 1997, pp. 309-313.
4. Brown, Jonathan. *Hadith.* Oneworld, 2009, p. 151. Al-Barbahari, abu Muhammad. *Sharh al-Sunnah.* Dar Makkah International, 2014, p. 71.
5. Brown, Jonathan. *Misquoting Muhammad.* Oneworld, 2014, p. 37. Brown. *Hadith*, p. 150.
6. Al-Barbahari. *Sharh.* p. 71.
7. Brown. *Hadith*, p. 3.
8. Brown. *Misquoting*, p. 37.
9. It is worth noting that Arab Christians use the Arabic word *salaat* for prayers unlike their co-religionists who do not speak Arabic.

New Doctrines: Sunnah and Hadith

10. The Mushaf stressed *khushoo* (complete concentration and submission) as an important element in performing *salaat* (see M23:2), but never was explicit on the form. *Khushoo*, however, could have broader meaning and could be unrelated to the daily ritual prayers.
11. Most notably, *al-Minhaj fi Sharhi Sahih Muslim* by al-Nawawi, and *fath al-Baree fi Sharh Sahih al-Bukhari*, by al-Asqalani.
12. Al-Kannouji, abi al-Tayyeb. *Al-Hittah fi Thikr al-Sihah al-Sittah*. Dar al-Jeel, [n.d.], pp. 232, 254.
13. Al-Shafi'i, Muhammad ibn Idris. *Al-Risala*. Dar al-Kutub al-Ilmiyyah, 1939. Aal-Shafi'i created a foundation for legislation that was later canonized as integral to Islam.
14. According to some Shia scholars, such as Ali al-Sistani (d. 1349/1930), shaving the beard is haram.
15. Shia imams are descendants of the Prophet.
16. In practically all English translations that I came across, *kafireen* in M5:67 was translated as disbelievers. Disbelievers is a synonym for infidels (see Fuller, Graham, *A World without Islam*, Little, Brown and Company, 2010). This translation legitimizes violence by extremist Muslims against non-Muslims and alienates Muslims from developing sufficient and serious interest in Islam.
17. See M3:101,103, 4:146,175, 10:27, 11:43, 12:32, 22:78, 33:17, and 40:33.
18. Even the Shias' interpretation of M66:1 does not deny the wrongdoing of the Prophet, yet the Shias not only attribute infallibility to the Prophet but also his imam descendants.
19. Shahrour, Muhammad. *Al-Sunnah al-Rasooliyya wa al-Sunnah al-Nabawiyya*. Dar al-Saqi, 2011, p.102.
20. Dhaif, Shawki. *Al-Madaris al-Nahawiyyah*. 7th ed., Dar al-Ma'arif, 1968.
21. Intermixing names, attributes and adjectives leads to confusing the names of Allah with his attributes.
22. Some even do not differentiate between the two at all as in Brown, Jonathan, *Hadith*, p. 9, where M8:1 was translated as "Obey God and His prophet".
23. Al-Shafi'i, for example, was a poet and is reported to have memorized thousands of poems.
24. Despite the introduction by al-Shafi'i of the concept of specificity vs. generality of the verses of the Mushaf, most, if not all works of exegeses ignore the context of the verses as if the verses of the Mushaf were randomly positioned and as if the title of Chapters and the specific placement of verses within a contextual structure is irrelevant to

its meaning.
25. See M 2:32, 3:132, 4:13, 4:59, 4:64, 4:69, 4:80, 5:92, 8:1, 8:20, 8:46, 9:71, 24:52, 25:54, 25:56, 33:33, 33:66, 33:71, 47:33, 48:17, 49:14, 58:13, 64:12, 81:21
26. See M26:108,110,126,131,144,150,163,179.
27. Shahrour. *Al-Sunnah,* p. 110.
28. Paying careful attention to the meaning of *ittiba,* particularly its applicability to either intangibles (such as concepts, principles, revelations) or to living beings, helps the interpretation of other verses that have been given broad context and applicability. Most notably M2:143, which is typically understood to imply that all Muslims have been made a middle nation so that they may be a witness to all mankind and that the Messenger was made a witness on all Muslims. The distinction between the two applications of *ittiba* indicate that the Muslims addressed in M2:143 were only those who were associates (living with) of the Prophet.
29. It is noteworthy to emphasize how the Mushaf have differentiated between the nature of the conflict in the three verses M42:10, 4:59 and 4:65. Three different Arabic words were used: اِخْتَلَفْتُمْ (differed), شَجَرَ (emerging conflict) and تَنَازَعْتُمْ (dispute).
30. See al-Tabari's *tafsir* where he makes a similar argument.
31. Al-Suyuti, Jalal al-Deen. *Tadween al-Raawee.* Vol. 1, 2nd ed., Maktaba al-Kawthar, 1994. Al-Zahrani, Mohammad. *Tadween al-Sunnah al-Nabawiyyah.* Dar al-Hijrah, 1996, p. 14. Ibn al-Salah. *Uloom,* p. 293.
32. Al-Zahrani. *Tadween,* p. 14. Abu Rayyah, Mahmoud. *Adhwa ala al-Sunnah al-Muhammadiyyah.* 6th ed., Dar al-Ma'aarif, 1957. Fawzi. *Tadween,* p. 29.
33. Al-Jewziyyah, ibn Qayyem. *The Medicine of the Prophet.* Islamic Text Society, 1998. Al-Suyuti, Jalal al-Deen. *The Medicine of the Prophet.* Ta-Ha, 2015.
34. There are numerous examples including the prayers and fasting of Muslim women during menstruation, sexual intercourse for women during menstruation, fasting in Ramadan, inheritance laws, Hajj rituals, deception in marriage and divorce rules.
35. Al-Nahhaas, abu Ja'far. *Al-Nasikh wa al-Mansookh.* Al-Maktaba al-Alamiyya, 1938, p. 7. Al-Shafi'i. *Al-Risala,* p. 140. While al-Shafi'i claims that the Sunnah cannot abrogate the Mushaf, he used specific hadiths to claim that some Mushaf verses abrogated others. This is not sufficient ground to assume that al-Shafi'i believed that the Sunnah can abrogate the Mushaf, yet his argument is an indirect way to

prove the same. Amongst Shias, al-Khoei (d. 1412/1992), a highly influential Twelver Shia Islamic scholar, claimed that consensus or uninterrupted hadiths can abrogate the Mushaf, see al-Khoei, abu al-Qasim. *Al-Bayan fi Tafsir al-Qur'aan.* Anwar al-Huda, 1981.

36. In M2:159 Allah uses the pronoun we. Customarily and traditionally, the use of we in the Mushaf is considered as the royal we or majestic plural. Several years ago, my daughter who was 20 at that time raised the question as to why Allah refers to Himself in some verses using the singular pronoun and in others using the plural one. Careful attention to M2:159 and M16:64 suggests that Allah's use of the majestic plural is not related to highness, greatness or any other exaggerated attribute but rather to a proper use of the pronoun. When Allah uses we, He is describing an action that was performed not only by Himself.

37. Al-Zarqani, Muhammad Abdul-Adhim. *Manahil al-Irfan fi Uloom al-Qur'aan.* Dar al-Kitaab al-Arabi, 1995, p. 29.

38. Brown, *Hadith,* pp. 150,151.

39. Al-Asqalani, Ahmed ibn Ali ibn Hajar. *Fath al-Baree fi Sharh Sahih al-Bukhari.* Vol. 1, Dar al-Ma'rifa, 2001, p. 74.

40. Al-Nawawi, abu Zakaria Yahya ibn Sharaf. *Tahtheeb al-Asma wa al-Lughaat.* Vol. 1, Dar al-Kutub al-Ilmiyyah, [n.d.], p. 74.

41. Ibn Taymiyyah, Taqi al-Deen Ahmad. *Majmoo al-Fataawi.* Vol. 20, King Fahd Complex for Printing the Noble Mushaf, [n.d.], p. 321.

42. Al-Mutairi, Hakim Ubaisan. *Tarikh Tadween al-Sunnah wa Shubhat al-Mustashriqeen.* Kuwait University, 2002.

43. Hashim Al-Husaini. *Al-Mawdw'aat fi al-Aa'thaar wa al-Akhbaar.* Dar al-Ta'aruf, 1987, p. 13.

44. Ibn al-Salah, abu Amr. *Uloom al-Hadith.* Sa'adah Press, 1908.

45. Brown, Jonathan. *The Canonization of al-Bukhari and Muslim: The formation and Function of the Sunni Hadith Canon.* Brill Publisher, 2007.

46. Ibn al-Salah. *Uloom.*

47. Brown. *The Canonization,* p. 71.

48. Ibn al-Hajjaj, abu al-Hussain Muslim. *Sahih Muslim.* Translated by Nasiruddin al-Khattaab, 4th ed., Darussalam, 2007.

49. Ibn al-Hajjaj. *Sahih.*

50. Ibn al-Hajjaj. *Sahih.*

51. Most works on Islam that are collectively grouped under Islamic heritage are disconnected from rigorous scholarship. Scholarship and academic integrity were absent in most of these works. Since these major works that constitute Islamic heritage were never

questioned or scrutinized for accuracy and references, it has given rise to a culture that looks upon serious scholarship and careful analysis as works of the enemies of Islam. It is indeed a travesty that the English translation of one of the most important works in Islamic heritage, that of Sahih Muslim, will have this introduction.

52. http://www.amazighworld.org/arabic/human_rights/index_show.php?id=6194. Accessed 27 February 2019.
53. Al-Jarjani, abi Ahmad. *Al-Kamil fi Dua'afa al-Rijal.* Vol. 1, Maktabat al-Rushd, [n.d.]. Al-Dimashki, abi al-Fida ibn Kathir. *Al-Takmeel fi al-Jarh wa al-Ta'deel wa Ma'rifat al-Thiqat wa al-Dua'fa wa al-Majaheel.* Vol. 1, Markaz al-Numan, 2011.
54. Abu Abdul-Rahman, Muqbil. *Al-Shafa'a.* 3rd ed., Dar al-Aa'thar, 1999, p. 264. Ilal, Rachid. *Sahih al-Bukhari: Nihayat Ustoora.* Dar al-Watan, 2017. Al-Albani, Muhammad Nasser. Dhaeef al-Jam'I al-Saghir wa Ziyadatahu. Al-Maktab al-Islami, 1988.
55. Al-Sharayri, Mansour Mahmoud Muhammad. "Hadith al-Wasiyya bil-Thaqalyen: Dirasa Hadithiyya." *Umm al-Qura Magazine for Sharia Sciences and Islamic Studies*, no. 51, 2011, pp. 77, 126.
56. Al-Thahabi, Shams al-Deen. *Siyar a'Laam al-Nubala.* 11th ed., Mu'assassat al-Risalah, 1996. https://www.islamweb.net/newlibrary/display_book.php?ID=1373&bk_no=60&flag=1. Accessed 1 March 2019.
57. Di Francia, G. Toraldo. *The Investigation of the Physical World.* Cambridge University Press, 1981.
58. Ibn al-Salah. *Uloom.*
59. Itr, Noor al-Deen. *Manhaj al-Naqd fi Uloom al-Hadith.* 2nd Ed., Dar al-Fikr, 1979, p. 55.
60. Brown. *The Canonization,* p. xxii.
61. Ilal. *Sahih.* This book is arguably the first to question the origin of Sahih al-Bukhari and to highlight the availability of different versions, none of which could be traced to al-Bukhari himself.
62. Sahih Muslim, Kitaab al-Jana'iz, nos. 928a, 927h, 929a.
63. See al-Nawawi's interpretation of Sahih Muslim. Available online: https://archive.org/details/shsm01. Accessed 1 March 2019.
64. Sahih Muslim, Kitaab al-Libs wa al-Zeena, no. 2098a. In the www.sunnah.com translation of this hadith, the phrase أَنِّي أُكْذِبُ عَلَى رَسُولِ اللَّهِ was translated as "I attribute wrongly to Allah's Messenger (certain things)." An accurate translation would be "I fabricate lies on the Messenger of Allah."
65. Hamza, Muhammad. *Al-Hadith al-Nabawi wa Makanatahoo fi al-*

66. *Fikr al-Islami.* Al-Markaz al-Thaqafi al-Arabi, 2015, p. 139.
67. Itr. *Manhaj,* p. 54.
68. The Arabic word *al-a'raab* was left untranslated as I am not confident of any translation to state here.
69. Ibn al-Salah. *Uloom,* pp. 45, 63.
70. Hamza, Muhammad. *Al-Hadith al-Nabawi wa Makanatahoo fi al-Fikr al-Islami.* Al-Markaz al-Thaqafi al-Arabi, 2015, p. 325.
71. See for instance the different classical exegeses of M3:18 where *imaan,* knowledge, witnessing, all were considered as synonyms.
72. Sahih al-Bukhari, Kitaab al-Thaba'ih wa al-Sayd, no. 5521.
73. Sahih al-Bukhari, Kitaab al-Thaba'ih wa al-Sayd, no. 5527.
74. The important difference between *nahi* and *man'a* provides an understanding of the following phrase in M29:45: إِنَّ الصَّلَاةَ تَنْهَى عَنِ الْفَحْشَاءِ وَالْمُنْكَرِ [Surely the prayer *tanha* on/of *fahisha* and *mun'kur*]. A sample of common Mushaf translations of *tanha* are: forbids, prevents, prohibits, restrains, and deter. Surprisingly, none came close to the meaning of *nahi,* which can best be translated as call to refrain. An excellent example was provided by Muhammad Shahrour where he explained that a physician makes *nahi* regarding smoking cigarettes but the government can make *man'a* (aptly translated as prohibition) of smoking in certain buildings or in public places.
74. Ibn Qudamah, Muwaffiq al-Deen. *Al-Maghni.* Dar Aalam al-Kutub, 3rd ed., 1997.
75. Al-Shafi'i. *Al-Risala,* p. 343.
76. Sahih Muslim, Kitaab al-Jana'iz, no. 977a. (Only part of the full hadith is stated.)
77. Sahih Muslim, Kitaab al-Imaan, no. 21a.
78. Sahih al-Bukhari, Kitaab al-Imaan, no. 25.
79. Ibn Qutaybah, Abdullah. *Ta'weel Mukhta'laf al-Hadith.* Al-Maktab al-Islami, 1999. Al-Hasany, Hashim Maroof. *Al-Mawdoa'at fi al-Aa'thar wa al-Aakhbar.* Dar al-Ta'aruf Lilmatboo'at, 1987, p. 13. Ibn Qutaybah (d. 276/889) was one of the earliest Muslim scholars to address the contradictions within Hadith.
80. Abu Raiyyah, Mahmoud, *Adhwa'a ala al-Sunnah al-Muhammadiyah,* 6th ed., Dar al-Ma'aarif, 1957, pp. 29-26.
81. Abu Raiyyah, Mahmoud. *Adhwa'a ala al-Sunnah al-Muhammadiyah.* 6th ed., Dar al-Ma'aarif, 1957, p. 19.
82. Sahih al-Bukhari, Kitaab al-Haidh, no. 303. Sunan abu Dawood, no. 267.
83. In www.sunnah.com, a website of Hadith proponents, *yubashirna*

was translated as embracing or fondling; however, *mubashara* in the Mushaf implies sexual intercourse (see M2:187). The Hadith reconcilers would consult a variety of sources to make the argument that *mubashara* can be of different types, but even if *mubashara* in Sunan abu Dawood and Sahih al-Bukhari hadiths meant embracing, which implies touching or having close proximity between the husband and his wife, this would contradict clear Mushaf instructions stating that during menstruation, men should leave women alone and not come close to them as clearly stated in M2:222.

84. Sahih al-Bukhari, Kitaab al-Nikaah, no. 5119. This is a highly controversial hadith where the Prophet was alleged to have allowed for a temporary relationship between a man and a woman outside contractual marriage.

85. Sahih al-Bukhari, Kitaab al-Wasaaya, no. 2747. Jami al-Tirmidhi, Kitaab alWasaaya ann Rasool Allah, no. 2120.

86. Al-Mahalli, Jalal al-Deen and al-Toosi, Jalal al-Deen. *Tafsir al-Jalalayn*. Dar al-Hadith, [n.d.], p. 34. Abrogation of the Mushaf by the Sunnah is typically considered an extreme opinion. However, this web site http://bayanelislam.net/, which is a depository of topics and answers by a group of leading contemporary Muslim scholars, shows otherwise. The list of scholars who provide answers on this site include: Muhammad abu al-Noor, former Minister of Awkaf, Egypt; Ahmed Hashim, former President of al-Azhar University; Abdullah al-Muslih, Muhammad Bashar, Vice President of the Arabic Language Mujamma; Muhammad Jawhary, former Dean of the Usool al-Deen College, al-Azhar University; Mahmoud Umarah, former Dean of Usool al-Deen College, al-Azhar University; Abdulhamid Madkoor, Professor of Islamic Philosophy, Sciences College, Cairo University; and Muhammad al-Julayned, Islamic Philosophy Professor, Sciences College, Cairo University. Therefore, it is inaccurate to dismiss the claim that the Sunnah can abrogate the Mushaf as an extraordinary and rare opinion.

87. Itr. *Manhaj*, pp. 39-46. Here we see how Muslim Scholars have gone to great lengths and used heavy sophistry in their attempts to reconcile contradictory hadiths. Despite that many hadiths paid attention to careful details, two important pieces of information were conspicuously absent from Hadith: place and time. Yet, despite the introduction of the concept of abrogation in Hadith, there was no consensus by leading Muslim scholars on how to reconcile the contradictions between a large number of hadiths and the Mushaf and contradictions within Hadith.

88. Sahih al-Bukhari, Kitaab al-Nikaah, no. 5186. Sahih al-Bukhari, Kitaab Bad'a al-Khalq, no. 3199.
89. Al-Shafi'i. *Al-Risala*.
90. Trabishi, George. *Min Islam al-Qur'aan ila Islam al-Hadith*, 3rd ed., Dar al-Saqi, 2015, p. 185.
91. https://www.youtube.com/watch?v=4i5lkqPhH5Y. Accessed March 2, 2019. Al-Uwaid, Abdulaziz. *Usool al-Fiqh ind al-Sahaaba*. 25th ed., al-Wai al-Islami, 2011, p. 37. Al-Jewziyyah, ibn Qayyem. *Kitaab al-Rooh*. Dar al-Turath, 2003, p. 93. Al-Jewziyya considered the Sunnah as *hikmah*
92. Al-Baghdadi, abu Bakr. *Al-Kifaayah fi Ilm al-Riwaayah*. Al-Maktaba al-Ilmiyyah, [n.d.], p. 8, 12. To the best of my knowledge, the only exegete who interprets M53:3 and M58:4 as a reaffirmation that the Sunnah is a *wahi* is al-Sa'di.
93. Itr. *Manhaj*, p. 22.
94. The Mushaf referred to the daily ritual prayer as *iqaamat al-salah*. Elsewhere in the Mushaf, *al-salah* appeared without *iqaamat*. Therefore, the phrase *iqaamat al-salah* is not synonymous with *al-salah*. Despite this, however, there is a strong connection between the two in the sense that both are means of connecting with Allah.
95. Al-Nawawi, abu Zakaria Yahya Ibn Sharaf. *Al-Athkar*. Dar al-Rayyan Lilturath, al-Dar al-Masriyyah al-Lubnaniah, 1988, p. 27.
96. Sahih Al-Bukhari, Kitaab al-Nikaah, no. 5133. Eghbariyya, Musa Mahmoud. *Al-Buloogh wa al-Rushd fi al-Sahria al-Islamiyya*. Dar al-Kutub al-Ilmiyyah, 2011, p. 139. Eghabriyya lists the opinions of some jurisprudents who believed that a man is allowed to have sexual intercourse with a woman (as a wife) as long as she reaches the age of nine, even if she has not reached puberty.
97. Sahih al-Bukhari, Kitaab al-Jihaad, no. 2788. The placement of this hadith in the Book of Fighting in the Cause of Allah is noteworthy.
98. Sahih Muslim, Kitaab al-Salah, no. 384. Sunan abi Dawood, Kitaab al-Salah, no. 523. Sunan ibn Majah, Kitaab al-A'than wa al-Sunnah feeha, no. 722.
99. Sunan abi Dawud, Kitaab al-Hudood, no. 4361.
100. Sunan abi Dawud, Kitaab al-Hudood, no. 4364.
101. Ibn Taymiyyah, Taqi al-Deen Ahmad. *Al-Sarim al-Maslool ala Shatim al-Rasool*. Vol. 2, al-Ramadi, 1997, p. 121.
102. Sahih Muslim Kitaab al-Ridha, no. 1453 b.
103. Sahih al-Bukhari, Kitaab al-Jihad, [no number].
104. Sahih al-Bukhari, Kitaab al-Hiyyal, nos. 6957, 6960,
105. Sahih al-Bukhari, Kitaab al-Haidh, no. 303. Sunan abu Dawood, no.

267.
106. See ibn Kathir's interpretation of M9:5 and the hadiths therein.
107. Sahih Al-Bukhari, Kitaab al-Wudu, no. 169.
108. Sahih al-Bukhari, Kitaab al-Istisqa, no. 1036.
109. Many Muslims attributed the name Mustafa (Chosen) to the Prophet.
110. Al-Naas, abi al-Fath ibn Muhammad ibn Sayyid. *Uyoon al-A'thaar fi Funoon al-Maghazi wa al-Shama'el wa al-Siyar.* Vol. 1, Dar ibn Kathir, 1977, p. 66. Al-Naas, however, claims that Malik and ibn Ishaq reconciled their differences.
111. Al-Asqalani, Ahmed ibn Ali ibn Hajar. *Tahdheeb al-Tahdheeb.* Vol. 9, Da'ira Ma'arif Nizamia, 1908, p.43.
112. Al-Shafi'i. *Al-Risala*, pp. 79, 93, 107, 113, 139, 140, 142, 150, 187, 189, 200, 292.
113. Al-Naas. *Uyoon.*
114. Muir, William. *The Life of Mahomet.* Vol. 4, Smith, Elder and Co, 1861, pp. 78, 79. The following is a passage from Muir's book: "As a counterpart to this incident, and showing the certainty of Paradise secured by the mere profession of Islam, I may transcribe the following tradition. Al-Aswad, the shepherd of one of the Jews of Kheibar, came over to Mahomet, and declared himself a believer. Abandoning his flock, the straightway joined the Moslem army and fought in its ranks. He was struck by a stone and killed, before he had yet as a Moslem offered up a single prayer. But he died fighting for the faith, and therefore had secured a Martyr's crown. Surrounded by a company of his followers, Mahomet visited the corpse, which had been laid out for him to pray over. When he drew close to the spot, he abruptly stopped and looked another way. "Why dost thou thus avert thy face!" asked those about him. "Because," said Mahomet, "two black-eyed houries of Paradise, his wives, are with the martyr now; they wipe the dust from off his face, and fondly solace him." Muir's following footnote to this passage is very telling: "Neither can I vouch for this story, but like the last, it illustrates the spirit of Islam, and the teaching of Mahmomet, under the influence of which such tales grew up."
115. Three hadiths exemplify how Hadith was used to justify despotism: (1) The Messenger of Allah said, "Whosoever obeys me, obeys Allah; and he who disobeys me, disobeys Allah; and whosoever obeys the Amir (leader), in fact, obeys me; and he who disobeys the Amir, in fact, disobeys me." (Sahih al-Bukhari, Kitaab al-Ahkam, no. 7137). (2) The Messenger of Allah said: "The best of your rulers are those whom you love and who love you, who invoke God's blessings

New Doctrines: Sunnah and Hadith

upon you and you invoke His blessings upon them. And the worst of your rulers are those whom you hate and who hate you and whom you curse and who curse you. It was asked (by those present): Shouldn't we overthrow them with the help of the sword? He said: No, as long as they establish prayer among you. If you then find anything detestable in them. You should hate their administration, but do not withdraw yourselves from their obedience. (Sahih Muslim, Kitaab al-Imarah, no. 1855a. (3) Hudhayfa ibn al-Yaman reported: I asked, "O Messenger of Allah, we were living in an evil time and Allah brought us good which we live in now. Will there be evil after this good?" The Messenger of Allah, peace and blessings be upon him, said, "Yes." I said, "And any good after this evil?" The Prophet said, "Yes." I said, "And any evil after this good?" The Prophet said, "Yes." I said, "How will it be?" The Prophet said, "Rulers after me will come who do not follow my guidance and my tradition. Some of their men will have the hearts of devils in a human body." I said, "O Messenger of Allah, what should I do if I live to see that time?" The Prophet said, "You should listen and obey them even if the ruler strikes your back and takes your wealth, even still listen and obey." (Sahih Muslim, Kitaab al-Imarah, no. 1847b). Interestingly, the last hadith is contradictory to the following one in Sahih al-Bukhari, Kitaab al-Jihaad wa al-Sayir, no. 2955: Narrated ibn Umar: The Prophet said, "It is obligatory for one to listen to and obey (the ruler's orders) unless these orders involve one disobedience (to Allah); but if an act of disobedience (to Allah) is imposed, he should not listen to or obey it."

116. http://shahrour.org/?topic=سؤال-عن-التسبيح. Accessed 17 March 2019.
117. In recent years, the al-Azhar University found its institution severely threatened by Islam Behairy, a young Egyptian scholar. Behairy requested that Sahih al-Bukhari be reconsidered for further authentication. In April of 2015, in an apparent collusion between the state and al-Azhar, which is the primary Muslim religious institution in Egypt, Behairy was thrown in jail for his curiosity and benign recommendations only to be released by a presidential pardon after spending a year in jail.
118. Al-Shafi'i never named anyone of the many people whom he debated in his al-*Risala* treatise.

9

LEGISLATION BEYOND THE REVELATION

قُلْ تَعَالَوْا أَتْلُ مَا حَرَّمَ رَبُّكُمْ عَلَيْكُمْ ۖ أَلَّا تُشْرِكُوا بِهِ شَيْئًا ۖ وَبِالْوَالِدَيْنِ إِحْسَانًا ۖ وَلَا تَقْتُلُوا أَوْلَادَكُم مِّنْ إِمْلَاقٍ ۖ نَّحْنُ نَرْزُقُكُمْ وَإِيَّاهُمْ ۖ وَلَا تَقْرَبُوا الْفَوَاحِشَ مَا ظَهَرَ مِنْهَا وَمَا بَطَنَ ۖ وَلَا تَقْتُلُوا النَّفْسَ الَّتِي حَرَّمَ اللَّهُ إِلَّا بِالْحَقِّ ۚ ذَٰلِكُمْ وَصَّاكُم بِهِ لَعَلَّكُمْ تَعْقِلُونَ

Declare/proclaim/promulgate: come I will recite what your Lord has prohibited on you, that you do not associate anything with Him, and to those who gave birth to you provide good treatment, and do not kill your children fearing poverty, We will provide for you and them, and do not approach *fawahish*, what is apparent of them and what is concealed, and do not kill the soul which Allah has forbidden except through right, this has He entrusted you with that you may understand through reason.

M6:151

THE EVOLUTION OF RELIGIOUS DOCTRINES

The religion of Islam as concluded by the Message of Muhammad and preceded by earlier Prophets and Messages was intended for all humans without any discrimination or favoritism. The story of the Message of Muhammad has strong similarities to the story of the Messages of Jesus

Legislation Beyond the Revelation

and Moses before him. All were intended for humanity and were to be the only divine revelation to provide guidance for all of humankind. With time, however, other material and doctrines were added to those messages. The added material was purely human-made, replete with contradictions and inconsistencies. The contradictions were then justified by yet another set of doctrines and religious instruments. This is because a doctrine based on a set of contradictions is flawed from its very core; it cannot be fixed. Such doctrine can only defend itself by further growth. This growth, however, can only be possible by adding further contradictions.

Eventually, the amalgamation of the divine revelation with a newly added huge package of "religious" material required experts to navigate through this incredible maze. These experts became scholars of religion. With the passage of time, the added material became religious doctrine and canon, and eventually became viewed as part of the divine revelations.

The new doctrine that was claimed to be part of Islam, namely the Hadith/Sunnah, extended the religious authority (i.e., the divine authority) to the Prophet. Still, however, the new domain was restricted and became narrower with the passage of time since numerous Muslim scholars started scrutinizing this new doctrine for "authenticity". To further expand the domain of religion, the legislative authority had to be extended beyond the Prophet. To this end, ingenious instruments were created that opened the door for humans to legislate in the name of Allah.

In extending the domain of legislation to humans, Muslims were no exception from the adherents of other religions. In this chapter, I will discuss the major doctrines that have become accepted by the majority of Muslims as part of Islam and largely never questioned. This chapter focuses on the purely human-made instruments that evolved to a level that gave Muslim jurisprudents the power to provide divine legislation. This ushered in the beginning of the Muslim clergy.

Muslims' Greatest Challenge
DEEN AND *ILM*

The *deen* is largely understood by Muslims as a synonym for Islam and as the English counterpart of the word "religion". According to the Mushaf, the finality of the *deen* was stated within M5:3

الْيَوْمَ أَكْمَلْتُ لَكُمْ دِينَكُمْ وَأَتْمَمْتُ عَلَيْكُمْ نِعْمَتِي وَرَضِيتُ لَكُمُ الْإِسْلَامَ دِينًا

[On this day, I have completed your religion for you and finalized my providence on you and contently approved Islam as your religion.] With the revelation of this verse, Allah categorically emphasized that *deen* was completed on "this very day," presumably the day on which the verse was revealed. The *deen* that Allah emphasized as only acceptable to Him or only considered by Him (see M3:19) is mentioned in the singular form throughout the Mushaf. From this important piece of information, coupled with the Mushaf's declaration that in Allah's consideration the only *deen* is Islam, we can safely conclude that there is no plurality of *deen* in Allah's consideration, and that there is only one *deen* that Allah accepts.[1]

The word *muslimoon* (Muslims) appears repeatedly in the Mushaf. There is no sufficient information from the Mushaf itself to conclude that *muslimoon* always implies those who adhere or follow the religion (*deen*) of Islam. All this suggests is that Muslims are not necessarily the only people following the *deen*. Additionally, careful attention must be paid to three Mushaf words: *milla*, *umma* and *Sharia*, all of which are commonly conflated with *deen*. In fact, M2:62 provides strong evidence that the category of Muslims is not parallel to those of Jews, Christians or other groups:

إِنَّ الَّذِينَ آمَنُوا وَالَّذِينَ هَادُوا وَالنَّصَارَىٰ وَالصَّابِئِينَ مَنْ آمَنَ بِاللَّهِ وَالْيَوْمِ الْآخِرِ وَعَمِلَ صَالِحًا فَلَهُمْ أَجْرُهُمْ عِندَ رَبِّهِمْ وَلَا خَوْفٌ عَلَيْهِمْ وَلَا هُمْ يَحْزَنُونَ

[Surely those who *aamanoo* (believed) and those who *hadoo* and the *Nasara* and the Saabi'een, whoever believed in Allah and the Latter Day and have done suitable (good-righteous) deeds, then they will have their reward provided by their Lord and there shall be no fear on them and they will not grieve.] Suffice it to notice that Muslims are not mentioned here, but those who believed. (Going further into this verse is beyond the scope of this book.)[2]

Consequently, all of the revelations to each of the Prophets were consistent with and complementary to each other, all forming the complete *deen*. If the revelations constituted a singular *deen*, then what is the reason for their spread over thousands of years? The Mushaf provides a succinct summary of numerous revelations and their dominant themes that strongly relate to the evolution of humanity. For example, the theme of Prophet Noah's message was worshipping Allah (see M7:59). As societies evolved, the introduction of fundamental concepts of justice such as fairness in trade became necessary as human's living modalities were transformed from fragmented family and tribal entities to more complex settlements and cities (see M7:85).[3]

Because the revelations were spread over thousands of years, the Mushaf indicates that humans had been constantly evolving since Adam (whether Adam designates a specific human being or a group of people will not be discussed in this book). For example, the most ancient of revelations mentioned in the Mushaf, which preceded Prophet Noah, involved Angels, as indicated by M23:24. This could have been an indication of a primitive behavior of the early humans that required a "super-being" to direct those "primitive" humans towards a specific concept, perhaps the oneness of God or something different. Later on, Moses and Jesus and the revelations that accompanied them were supported and validated by extraordinary physical events or "miracles", but not Angels. These miracles could have been needed then as humans were likely inclined towards the sensual rather than the abstract; perhaps an indication of less developed intellectual faculties. The final messenger, however, was not an Angel and did not produce any miracles. The authentication of the final message must have been provided within itself. Its validation and "proof of authenticity" must be information that can be processed by the more mature and evolved humans with abilities to abstract, analyze and synthesize.

Muhammad delivered an entire and complete *deen* but this *deen* was also fully consistent with, and a continuation of, the *deen* that previous prophets conveyed. This can be understood with a simple analogy to the field of physics. Physics is one; there cannot be two physics.[4] Our understanding of certain physical phenomena might be wrong, but this does not change the fact that there is only one physics underlying such phenomenon whether we understand it or not. There could be different physical or mathematical models to explain gravitational attraction between bodies; nevertheless, gravity is governed by one physics. Delivering the concepts of physics to a student is gradual and consistent with the student's intellectual ability and maturity in relevant subjects.

Islam's requirements for the followers of Muhammad to accept and believe the prophets that preceded Muhammad could not have been an act of appeasement or magnanimity towards Christians and Jews but rather an affirmation that the *deen* of Allah is one, and that it was delivered in parcels by prophets ending with Muhammad in compatibility with the evolving abilities of humans, particularly evolution in their intellectual capacity and functions. Muhammad's message embodied by the Mushaf served as a summary and conclusion for the *deen*. Muhammad was the last part of the chain of guidance that was promised by Allah to Adam in M2:38

قُلْنَا اهْبِطُوا مِنْهَا جَمِيعًا ۖ فَإِمَّا يَأْتِيَنَّكُم مِّنِّي هُدًى فَمَن تَبِعَ هُدَايَ فَلَا خَوْفٌ عَلَيْهِمْ وَلَا هُمْ يَحْزَنُونَ

[We declared/proclaimed/promulgated that you should descend/relocate from it all of you, and then if you receive from me guidance, then whomever follows or adheres to my guidance, there will not be no fear concerning them and they will not be in grieve]. The piecewise revelation of the *deen*, culminating with Muhammad's message, moreover suggests compatibility and consistency with humans' evolution in societal development in all its multi-faceted aspects and possibly evolution in intellectual capacity and functionality.

A natural question would arise as to what lent credibility to Muhammad the Messenger? What proof did Muhammad have that validated his prophecy and that could have come directly from Allah? After all, the prophecies of Jesus and Moses were supported and validated by extraordinary or uncommon phenomena such as the splitting of the sea (Moses) and curing the diseased and bringing life to the dead (Jesus). The connected and amalgamated narratives of the Prophets in the Mushaf indicate strong parallels in revelation modalities between all Prophets in the sense that a validation was needed for people to believe or accept the different messages. If Muhammad's message was final, its "validation" had to be embedded within the revelation itself and it had to be independent of time and space since it was intended for all people, not related to specific time or space.

If the validation of the Message is embedded within the Mushaf and presented in the form of a language, then it must be a type of validation that can only be understood through reasoning. The human brain could have evolved during the period between Adam and Muhammad to diminish reliance on the sensual.[5] The final message revealed to Muhammad had to be compatible with the evolution of humans, and if it were intended for all humans after Muhammad, then its validity had to be embedded within the Mushaf, and such validity needed human intellectual ability. Any other "messages" made by man, such as the doctrines of the Sunnah and Hadith, cannot validate Muhammad's prophecy and the Mushaf as divine revelation.

Understanding that the *deen* is complete has profound implications for Muslims' daily life. It is almost impossible to find a Muslim, a follower of Muhammad and a believer in the Mushaf who would disagree that the *deen* is complete. After all, M5:3 (see above) is too clear to dispute its contextual meaning even if the meaning of *deen* is not clear. In reality, however, Muslims' behavior and practice do not reflect their acceptance of the completeness of *deen*. The completion of *deen* implies that we cannot add to or subtract from it; nothing more is forthcoming that can be considered part of the *deen*. If the *deen* is part of the revelations to Muhammad, then the *deen* is embodied within the Mushaf. If the *deen* explains what haram is, then no one has the authority to label any act as haram beyond what had been precisely stated in the Mushaf.

If a certain science is complete, there can be no scientists in that field. Once a scientific discipline is complete, it moves to the industry or to professional practice. A practice can be refined, improved and even re-evaluated. A scientist is a producer of new knowledge; he is different from a practitioner who puts knowledge to practice. A holder of a Doctorate of Philosophy degree is not necessarily a scientist. However, a person who never attended college can be a scientist. Examples of practitioners are lawyers and medical doctors. A lawyer needs to understand the law before she practices it. A medical doctor can be sued in court if he does not follow established and approved medical practices and procedures. If the science of nuclear physics is complete then we can certainly learn this science but we cannot produce nuclear scientists anymore. Society can then produce more people knowledgeable in nuclear science but not scientists of nuclear science. Consequently, using the Arabic term *ilm* (loosely translated as science), there can be no *alim* (loosely translated as scientist) or *ulama* (plural of *alim*) in nuclear science anymore. It is possible to have people who are *a'rifeen* (knowledgeable) in nuclear science but not *ulama* in nuclear science.

Ma'rifa is the Arabic term for knowledge. *Ma'rifa* is not science. If the *deen* had been completed, then it is impossible to have *ulama* in *deen*. It is possible to have people who are knowledgeable in *deen*, such as those who know all that is designated in the Mushaf as haram, or those who have an understanding of the subject of inheritance as explained in the Mushaf. We can also have scholars in Islam. These people have studied and understood a wide range of topics related to Islam and became experts in it. The purpose of having experts in a certain practice is to convey and explain the subjects of the practice to those less capable or less fortunate to have the means or time to know and understand such subjects. The purpose of experts is also to add value to society through providing services and products. The existence of *ulama* in a certain subject implies the availability of people who can create knowledge in certain fields. Therefore, *ulama* in *deen* is an impossibility because there is nothing left in *deen* to be created or introduced.

The Mushaf verses that contain *ilm* and all related derivatives need to be understood in light of the important distinction between *ilm* and *ma'rifa*, all the way from the story of Adam to every word that is derived from the root *a'lima*. Most importantly, the concept of *ulama* in *deen*, as a means of adding new material to the religion, can be considered a form of *shirk*. This is because *shirk* is defined as attributing or associating Allah's abilities to humans. Using *ilm* and *ma'rifa* interchangeably is not only imprecise, but leads to significant misunderstandings. (This mix-up further cloaks a very important *Mushaf* objective that is essential to understand Allah Himself.) Understanding the difference between *ilm* and *ma'rifa* helps shed light on the question of whether Allah knows the future or not; a question that has baffled Muslim and non-Muslim philosophers for centuries and added significant confusion to the highly controversial subject of predestination (see Chapter 3).

Science and *ulama* cannot be relevant in any way to the amalgamation of contradictions dubbed as "Qur'anic Sciences". *Ilm* and *ulama* are two words that were associated historically with Muslim scholars or, specifically, scholars of Islamic jurisprudence and Mushaf exegesis. Realizing and understanding the distinction between *ilm* and *ma'rifa* leads

Legislation Beyond the Revelation

to an important conclusion: that there is no such thing as *uloom al-deen* (sciences of the *deen*). By the very definition of *ilm, uloom al-deen* connotes innovation in the *deen*. Whenever the Mushaf references *ulama* or "people of *Ilm*", the predominant understanding amongst Muslims is that there is a connection or reference to the scholars of jurisprudence or the scholars of other established fields related to the Mushaf, the Sunnah, and Hadith. To illustrate this misinterpretation, we consider M35:27-28

أَلَمْ تَرَ أَنَّ اللَّهَ أَنْزَلَ مِنَ السَّمَاءِ مَاءً فَأَخْرَجْنَا بِهِ ثَمَرَاتٍ مُخْتَلِفًا أَلْوَانُهَا وَمِنَ الْجِبَالِ جُدَدٌ بِيضٌ وَحُمْرٌ مُخْتَلِفٌ أَلْوَانُهَا وَغَرَابِيبُ سُودٌ

وَمِنَ النَّاسِ وَالدَّوَابِّ وَالْأَنْعَامِ مُخْتَلِفٌ أَلْوَانُهُ كَذَلِكَ إِنَّمَا يَخْشَى اللَّهَ مِنْ عِبَادِهِ الْعُلَمَاءُ إِنَّ اللَّهَ عَزِيزٌ غَفُورٌ

[Have you not seen/observed that Allah sends down from the heaven water which We used to bring out therewith produce with varying colors, and from the mountains are streaks white and red, of different colors, and black crags. And from humans and land-based animals (*dawaab*) and domesticated animals (*an'aam*) variety of colors; indeed those who are fearful and mindful of/towards Allah, from amongst His people (those who follow Allah and those who do not) are the *ulama*. Allah is indeed *Aziz*-forgiving.] As these two verses indicate, the *ulama* mentioned in M35:28 are those who are most mindful of Allah. However, since *ulama* designates a broad category of scientists, the context of M35:28 narrows the reference to the sciences of biology, zoology, geography, anthropology and possibly others. In fact, those *ulama* need not be followers of Muhammad, as the word *ebad* in M35:28 refers to humans that either obey or disobey Allah.[6] Therefore, the *ulama* in the above verse have no association with the man-made subject of Hadith Science discussed in earlier chapters. The context of M35:27-28 suggests that the *ulama* are those who are studying and contributing to understanding and advancing humans' knowledge of the material world. The *ulama* in these verses have nothing to do with "Qur'anic Sciences" either.

A nearly universal practice amongst Muslims is to use part of M35:28, namely, انما يخشى الله من عباده العلماء, [indeed those who are fearful and mindful of/towards Allah, from amongst His people (those who follow Allah and those who do not) are the *ulama*] to bestow a unique status on the framers of Hadith or even a certain young graduate of a religious school. This practice has contributed to stunting the intellectual and scientific growth and advancement in Muslims societies. This partial verse has been used for too long to elevate the status of students of Islam to unimaginable heights and reverence. A turbaned graduate of al-Azhar or Qum is immediately qualified to be amongst the deeply mindful of Allah, along with a wholly unjustified society-bestowed reverence.[7] In fact, a student who finishes a four-year university program in Islamic studies at one of the clergy-approved religious schools becomes an expert on subjects ranging from cosmology to gynecology.[8]

Science, which helps societies to advance and prosper, had been turned into the "sciences of religion". Muslim scholars frowned upon the sciences that were related to the laws of the material world. In fact, anything that had to do with the material world was perceived as least important or secondary to *uloom al-Deen*. The Mushaf, however, emphasized the opposite. The sciences of the material world, precisely, were emphasized as the means to decipher Allah's signs (*aayaat*) to achieve validation of the revelation. Reality, and the means to understand reality and progress, were all decimated at the altar of the "sciences of religion."

Confusing *ilm* with *ma'rifa* led to a catastrophic misunderstanding of important Mushaf verses that reveal the attributes of Allah. Specifically, the confusion led to ignoring the difference between the *ma'roof* and the *ma'loom*. *Ma'roof* refers to information that is already available. *Arifa* implies acquiring information that was already produced or known. *Ma'roof* also implies "recognition" as in the story of Yousuf when he recognized (*fa'arafahum*) his siblings (see M12:58).

Not recognizing the difference between *ilm* and *ma'rifa* has implications that go beyond correctly positioning the status of *ulama* within the Mushaf context. In fact, it can lead to a philosophical (or perhaps theological) confusion concerning whether Allah "knows" the future or not. For instance, in M8:23

وَلَوْ عَلِمَ اللَّهُ فِيهِمْ خَيْرًا لَأَسْمَعَهُمْ وَلَوْ أَسْمَعَهُمْ لَتَوَلَّوْا وَهُم مُّعْرِضُونَ

[And had Allah *alima* that they possessed goodness, He would have made them hear, and had He made them hear, they would have strayed away in objection and denial.] Almost all the circulated English translations of this verse translate *alima* as "have known", "have seen" or "have found". The problem with all these translations is that the Arabic equivalent of "had known" is *arifa*. *Alima* would indicate that Allah was able to correctly predict their future behavior and thus He arrived at the knowledge (*ma'rifa*) that they would have adopted a specific behavior. The word *ilm* and its derivatives appear more than 850 times in the Mushaf. A corresponding English word could be determined only after the precise analysis of how the word or its derivative had been used in the Mushaf context. The overriding theme implied by *ilm*, nevertheless, is most likely to be a general understanding, or understanding the cause behind an event, a phenomenon or a behavior. Understanding, in turn, leads to predicting an effect due to a cause.

Within certain reservations, one could translate *ilm* as science, but one has to be cautious not to stretch this translation too far. According to this carefully relaxed translation, a chemistry scientist (*aa'lim*), guided by a full understanding of the laws of nature, would be able to predict what would happen if oxygen is mixed with hydrogen under specific conditions, even if such an experiment had never taken place before. Predicting an effect based on a cause means knowing some or all the laws of physics, biology, etc., and more broadly, the laws of nature. Before the start of the experiment, the chemistry scientist can be described as having the *ilm* of the reaction. He would correctly predict the outcome by virtue of him knowing all factors that are part of and that influence the experiment.

When the Mushaf explains, referring to Allah, that within Him is the *ilm*, we cannot infer that within Him is the knowledge but rather Allah has full comprehension of all laws governing nature, i.e., the ultimate super intelligence of the universe. Twenty years ago, the weatherman had a very crude prediction of future weather and temperature. Today, the science of weather forecasting has advanced significantly that enables prediction of tomorrow's weather with a high degree of accuracy, but not certainty. The more advanced the science of weather forecasting, the higher the prediction accuracy (i.e., future knowledge). If humans possess absolute *ilm* and all prevailing conditions (the so-called "initial conditions" and "boundary conditions" in mathematical jargon), then their prediction would converge closer to future reality. Mathematical models are good predictors, but not absolute science.

Confusing *ilm* with *ma'rifa* leads to misunderstanding Mushaf verses that relate to acts of worship and obligations, not only to questions of seemingly philosophical relevance. One example is highlighted by considering the last phrase of M2:184

$$وَأَن تَصُومُوا خَيْرٌ لَّكُمْ إِن كُنتُمْ تَعْلَمُونَ$$

[And if you fast, it has goodness for you if only you *talamoon*.] Similar to M8:23, all available English translations interpret *talamoon* as "you knew". If this was the correct translation, then those who fast during Ramadan did not know before the revelation of this verse that fasting was good for them. But if that was the case, and if *talamoon* meant "you knew," there is redundancy and additional language in the verse that would not be needed. Allah could have revealed only وَأَن تَصُومُوا خَيْرٌ لَّكُمْ [And if you fast, it has goodness for you]. Once this is declared, the goodness of fasting becomes known as the phrase indicates. However since *talamoon* is derived from *ilm*, then the meaning in M2:184 implies an encouragement to understand and learn (the essential elements of science) how fasting can lead to goodness and betterment of the person.

The word *ulama* is different from the phrase *ulu al-ilm*. Based on the usage of *ulu* (those who are characterized as possessing a certain quality or a tangible object) in the Mushaf, *ulu*-something is a group of people who are not necessarily connected with each other in space and time. *Ulu al-ilm* implies a group of people that were provided with knowledge and its sources and tools (i.e., the understanding of where the knowledge came from). *Ulama* is a group of people who achieved the ability to infer or create knowledge. Einstein was a scientist of physics since he created new information that was never known before. Einstein was an *aalim* of physics. In addition to his *aalim* attribute, Einstein was a scholar of physics and a professor of physics.

Ulu al-ilm might or might not be *ulama*. To illustrate this further, take a person who was given the ingredients and procedure for making bread. All this information constitutes knowledge (*ma'arifa*). Once the person is informed as to why each ingredient is needed and why each stage in the baking process is needed, that person becomes one who has the *ilm* of bread making. Still the person is not an *aalim* in bread making. If and when this person generates new knowledge in bread making, he or she becomes an *aalim* of bread making.

This brings us to a very critical juncture. If the *deen* is complete, there can be no scientists in the *deen* as discussed above. This also implies that there can be no *ulama* (plural of *aalim*) in the *deen*. Thus, the *deen* can neither be extended nor be a domain for innovation. If the *deen* is the "science", so to speak, for what is haram, then there can be no further addition to what is haram, since the domain of *tahrim* (eternal prohibition) is tightly sealed, and forever. Anyone, irrespective of her or his scholarly erudition or piety, who stretches the domain of the *deen* or adds to it is strictly in violation of the Mushaf dictates. An analogy can also be made to a practicing lawyer, say in a country like the USA. This lawyer is a professional in the sense that she follows the dictates of the law. She uses the tools learned in law school to understand cases that might come her way. However, this lawyer cannot introduce legislation in her capacity as a practicing lawyer. In the USA, the legislator is the US Congress. Not even the judiciary branch of the government is empowered to introduce or create legislation. However, even the legislators cannot go beyond the bounds of the constitution. Therefore, all the classifications that were created by Muslim jurisprudents such as *mandoob* (recommended), *makrooh* (disliked), *mustahab* (good to do), *mubaah* (permissible), etc., have nothing to do with the *deen*. The Mushaf explicitly stated all that falls under the haram; everything else is permissible.

DEEN, SHARIA AND LEGISLATION

The product of Islamic legislation is Islamic law or Sharia. Since there is a wide disagreement amongst Muslims on the principles of Islamic legislation, one would expect that the outcome of this legislation will not be accepted uniformly either by Muslims. This is why the concept of Sharia is highly contentious and stands on thin ice.

Embodied within the Mushaf, Allah provided a constitution for governing humans' behavior; however, the process of legislation and the outcome and content of the legislation were left for the people. This is highly similar to the legislative system of the USA. In Islam, the *deen* is the constitution. The term Sharia, used widely amongst Muslims, is not the *deen*. If Sharia is used to imply legislation, then it is extremely important that it be differentiated from the *deen*. It is also important that Muslims define what they mean by Sharia and, more importantly, reference the definition to the Mushaf.

No matter how much knowledge one can achieve in the so-called "sciences" of religion, no one can acquire the authority to create or invent a new *deen*, add to it, or even "revitalize" or "renew" it. Many Muslims of the Salafi persuasion are, in theory, adamant in championing the sole authority of Allah as the only legislator, thereby implying that all legislative bodies in any country represent a transgression against Allah.[9] For example, in the Kingdom of Saudi Arabia, which patronizes the Hanbali sect, there are no legislative bodies and no written constitution since the Mushaf is considered as the sole legislative document and authority. A problem with the Hanbalis (and in general, the Salafis) is that their very own doctrine created the possibility for infinite legislative instruments through mere guesswork (using various innovative instruments such as Sunnah, Ijma, and Qiyaas), as we show below.

Hikmah is another important Mushaf term that had been conflated with wisdom. Amongst contemporary Arabs, *hikmah* is typically and commonly understood to mean wisdom. The Mushaf, however, associates *hikmah* with Allah's revelations. For instance, in M2:151

$$\text{كَمَا أَرْسَلْنَا فِيكُمْ رَسُولًا مِّنكُمْ يَتْلُو عَلَيْكُمْ آيَاتِنَا وَيُزَكِّيكُمْ وَيُعَلِّمُكُمُ الْكِتَابَ وَالْحِكْمَةَ وَيُعَلِّمُكُم مَّا لَمْ تَكُونُوا تَعْلَمُونَ}$$

[Just as We have sent amongst you a Messenger from yourselves (from amongst you), to deliver Our *aayat* (signs) to you, and to favor you and to teach you the Book and (the) *hikmah*, and to teach you that which you never understood before.] Also in M2:231

$$\text{وَإِذَا طَلَّقْتُمُ النِّسَاءَ فَبَلَغْنَ أَجَلَهُنَّ فَأَمْسِكُوهُنَّ بِمَعْرُوفٍ أَوْ سَرِّحُوهُنَّ بِمَعْرُوفٍ وَلَا تُمْسِكُوهُنَّ ضِرَارًا لِّتَعْتَدُوا وَمَن يَفْعَلْ ذَٰلِكَ فَقَدْ ظَلَمَ نَفْسَهُ وَلَا تَتَّخِذُوا آيَاتِ اللَّهِ هُزُوًا وَاذْكُرُوا نِعْمَتَ اللَّهِ عَلَيْكُمْ وَمَا أَنزَلَ عَلَيْكُم مِّنَ الْكِتَابِ وَالْحِكْمَةِ يَعِظُكُم بِهِ وَاتَّقُوا اللَّهَ وَاعْلَمُوا أَنَّ اللَّهَ بِكُلِّ شَيْءٍ عَلِيمٌ}$$

[And when you (plural) divorce women and they have reached their term, either retain them according to acceptable terms or release them according to acceptable terms, and do not keep them, intending harm, to transgress, and whoever does that has oppressed himself. And do not take the signs of Allah in mockery. And recognize Allah's bounty and what he has revealed to you of the Book and *hikmah* by which He admonishes you. And be cautious of Allah and understand that Allah, of all things, is *aleem*.] The verse explicitly states that *hikmah* is part of the revelation, and that it is used (in addition to the Book) as an instrument of admonition. If *hikmah* is part of the revelation, it cannot be wisdom. In fact, the context in the above verse strongly suggests that *himka* is related to governance. In fact, the root verb for *hikmah* is *hakama*, which means "to make a judgement". Wisdom, on the other hand, cannot be taught but can only be acquired. (See also M5:110 which specifies that *hikmah* was taught to Jesus.)

The *deen* commandments that relate to governance and community welfare can only be based on the revelation, not on post-Prophetic doctrines including the Sunnah, Ijma or Qiyaas, as we discuss in this chapter. Linguistically and contextually, M2:231 unequivocally indicates that Allah's revelation is related to governance. Therefore, the *deen* is a part of the revelation. Anything that was not revealed has nothing to do with the *deen*. Can it be that simple? If the answer is yes, then entire "*deens*", those parallel doctrines created by humans, will be rendered null and void with severe political and economic implications for their benefactors and, to a lesser extent, for their patrons.

IJTIHAD: THE INITIAL TRANSFER OF DIVINE AUTHORITY

Based on a few hadiths of questionable authenticity, Muslim scholars constructed religious concepts and doctrines that bestowed divine authority upon a class of human legislators. Acquiescence and indifference from the vast majority of Muslims helped buttress Ijtihad and other concepts as highly regarded *deen*-based institutions without any genuine challenge. Ijtihad is an Islamic legal term referring to independent reasoning or the thorough exertion of a jurist's mental faculty in finding a solution to a legal question.[10] The concept of Ijtihad was expunged from thin interpretations of a few hadiths and Mushaf verses by a few individuals, and then canonized as a principle of Islamic legislation.

The concept of Sharia originated from confusion surrounding the functions of jurists, jurisprudents and governors. Governors rule and are supposed to uphold and enforce the law. Jurisprudents or legislators develop or create the law, and Jurists execute the law. Jurists cannot exceed the rules or bounds that jurisprudents enact. Several transmitted hadiths indicate that the Prophet dispatched learned people to distant lands, such as Yemen, to teach recent converts to Islam their new religion.[11] The Prophet's emissaries were teachers of Islam, instructing the new Muslims how to perform certain religious rituals and most likely sharing what was revealed of the Mushaf up to that time (since the revelations continued until the end of the Prophet's life). The other emissaries were judges who helped arbitrate disputes and assist in governance based on the revelation and practices of the Prophet and the nascent governance system established in Madinah.

In those days, life was much less complex than today in terms of technology, transportation, economy, etc., and therefore the laws of governance were much fewer in comparison. It is likely that at the time of the early Muslim community in Madinah, the *ahkam* (injunctions) of the Mushaf presented a significant portion of the law to those relatively simple communities that embraced Islam. Several hadiths suggest that the judges whom the Prophet sent to distant lands were instructed to first use the Mushaf, then the practice of the Prophet (the Sunnah), and if the subject matter of dispute was not explicit in either, then they would use Ijtihad.

The earliest appearance of the word Ijtihad comes from several hadiths, two of which are particularly important because of their wide adoption. Whether these hadiths are true (*sahih*) or not is not of significance here, they are important only as far as the origin of the concept of Ijtihad is concerned. The first hadith is part of Sunan abu Dawood:[12]

أنَّ رَسُولَ اللَّهِ صلى الله عليه وسلم لَمَّا أرَادَ أنْ يَبْعَثَ مُعَاذًا إلى الْيَمَنِ قالَ " كَيْفَ تَقْضِي إذا عَرَضَ لَكَ قَضَاءٌ " . قالَ أقْضِي بِكِتَابِ اللَّهِ . قالَ " فإنْ لَمْ تَجِدْ فِي كِتَابِ اللَّهِ " . قالَ فَبِسُنَّةِ رَسُولِ اللَّهِ صلى الله عليه وسلم . قالَ " فإنْ لَمْ تَجِدْ فِي سُنَّةِ رَسُولِ اللَّهِ صلى الله عليه وسلم وَلاَ فِي كِتَابِ اللَّهِ " . قالَ أجْتَهِدُ رَأيِي وَلاَ آلُو . فَضَرَبَ رَسُولُ اللَّهِ صلى الله عليه وسلم صَدْرَهُ وَقالَ " الْحَمْدُ لِلَّهِ الَّذِي وَفَّقَ رَسُولَ رَسُولِ اللَّهِ لِمَا يُرْضِي رَسُولَ اللَّهِ"

Legislation Beyond the Revelation

[When the Messenger of Allah intended to send Mu'ath ibn Jabal to the Yemen, he (the Prophet) asked: How will you judge when the occasion of deciding a case/arbitration arises? He replied: I shall judge in accordance with Allah's Book. He asked: (What will you do) if you do not find any guidance in Allah's Book? He replied: (I shall act) in accordance with the Sunnah of the Messenger of Allah SAAWS. He asked: (What will you do) if you do not find any guidance in the Sunnah of the Messenger of Allah SAAWS and in Allah's Book? He replied: I shall do my best to form an opinion and I shall spare no effort. The Messenger of Allah SAAWS then patted him on the breast and said: Praise be to Allah Who has helped the messenger of the Messenger of Allah to find something which pleases the Messenger of Allah.][13] It seems likely that the context of this hadith was the Prophet interviewing candidates for the position of a judge for a certain region in Yemen. In such context, Mu'ath was essentially quizzed by the Prophet on his decision-making process. Mu'ath answered by invoking the word *ajtahid*, by which he meant that he would spare no effort and exert diligence in achieving a just judgement that, based on the wording of the hadith, will not be based on either the Mushaf or the Sunnah. This means that the outcome of Mu'ath's Ijtihad was not based on the *deen*.

The hadith's core theme is the responsibilities of the judge and the decision-making process he or she adopts to reach a just decision. There are indications, however, that this hadith is a forgery, particularly the reference to the Sunnah of the Messenger. The Sunnah became canonized many years after the death of the Prophet, so invoking it at a much earlier time, and by the Prophet himself, is suspicious (let alone the Prophet praising himself using the *salawaat*). Additionally, the Sunnah of the Messenger was a "work in progress" and could not have been completed as a system for jurisdiction by the time Mu'ath was dispatched to Yemen.

The second hadith is part of the Sahih al-Bukhari collection:

عَمْرِو بْنِ الْعَاصِ، أَنَّهُ سَمِعَ رَسُولَ اللَّهِ صلى الله عليه وسلم يَقُولُ " إِذَا حَكَمَ الْحَاكِمُ فَاجْتَهَدَ ثُمَّ أَصَابَ فَلَهُ أَجْرَانِ، وَإِذَا حَكَمَ فَاجْتَهَدَ ثُمَّ أَخْطَأَ فَلَهُ أَجْرٌ

[Amr ibn al-Aas heard the Prophet saying "If a governor makes a ruling, striving to apply his reasoning (Ijtihad) and he is correct, then he will have two rewards. If a judge makes a ruling, striving to apply his reasoning and he is mistaken, then he will have one reward."][14] Notice that in the first hadith, the Prophet was considering appointing a judge/arbiter to Yemen and most likely he was interviewing a few candidates. The arbiter is not a teacher but assumed (from the hadith) to possess knowledge of the *ahkam* from the Mushaf and the Sunnah. In the second hadith, the word *ha'kem* (ruler/governor) was used instead of *qadhi* (judge/arbiter).

The word *ha'kem* does not mean a judge or arbiter, but rather a ruler or governor. At their face values, the two hadiths address different subjects: the first is the qualification of a judge while the second is the rewards of the ruler/governor. The word *ajtahid* appeared in the first hadith while *ijtahada* appeared in the second. Both are derived from *juhd* (to exert an effort, which can be towards a noble or sinister goal). *Ajtahid* means "I will exert my utmost effort" while *ijtahada* means "he exerted his utmost effort". Ijtihad, as a major canonized legislative concept, was essentially extracted from these two hadiths.

Based on the common use of the above two hadiths, the distinction between jurisprudence, governorship and executing judgements had been confused.[15] (This confusion is compounded when recalling that the framers of Hadith allowed its transmission by meaning as discussed earlier in Chapter 8.) The common interpretations of the two hadiths confused "judge" with "governor" and vice versa. Aside from their distinctive meanings, neither the judge nor the governor is endowed with authority to create legislation.

It is likely that this example of imprecision amongst many Muslims was the origin of a misunderstanding that gave the class of jurisprudent vast powers that eventually endowed them with a divine status. Therefore, Ijtihad in practicing arbitration (or even issuing verdicts) evolved into legislation. Legislation in turn, as the years passed, was elevated to the status of religious legislation, which is strictly the domain of the *deen*. Such evolution in the mandate and power of judges was facilitated by the natural status the jurists had in the early day of Islam. They had to be the most learned in the new religion since they had to extract their judgments from the Mushaf along with other precedential cases interpreted or explained by the Prophet. Those highly respected jurists ranged from the likes of Malik, who lived in Madinah and was recognized as the founder of the Maliki sect, to al-Shafi'i, the de facto founder of the Shafi'i sect, who lived a hundred years later.

Legislation Beyond the Revelation

The class of jurists, naturally, had a close relationship to the power centers since it was (and largely remains) impossible for such a profession to be disconnected from governance. (Even today, the president/king/governor of many countries plays a key role in the appointment of judges to the highest court of the land. This is the case even in Western democracies such as the USA.) Since the jurists were the most learned in the new religion, they were treated, expectedly, with reverence and high respect. Supported by the concept of Ijtihad, the vast majority of Muslims looked towards this particular class of jurists who emerged during the first two Muslim centuries, as legislators. Muslims turned to the jurists in search of answers to issues and questions that neither the Mushaf nor the Messenger had discussed. All matters that the Prophet is alleged to have engaged with, verbally or physically, those jurists reconsidered and reframed within a religious broad legislative framework simply by virtue of associating the verbal or physical acts with the Prophet. This reframing led to the most severe damage to Muslim societies and initiated the petrification of the Muslim culture. Willingly or unwillingly, those jurists planted the seeds of regression that stunted the growth of Muslims for the past one thousand years.

Whenever a class of people emerges in any society, it has a tendency to preserve and enhance its privileges. The elevation of the class of jurists to a near-divine status, and by implication, authority, was partially a result of this class wishing to preserve the privileges acquired by virtue of their profession and high status in society. The tyranny, extreme authoritarianism and expansionism of the Umayyad and Abbasid rulers made it inconceivable that jurists remained an impartial body, drawing parallels to how the jurists and Islam's legislative bodies were and continue to be courted directly by rulers, at least amongst Sunni sects. Prominent modern day examples are the al-Azhar in Egypt, which, in modern times, have become a de facto ministry of the Egyptian government, and the Hanbali-Wahabi clergy in Saudi Arabia, who are directly appointed by the king. Over the years, and under the pressure of marginalization inflicted on Muslims by Muslim clergy (see Chapter 2), most Muslims have become accustomed to accepting a haram ruling from a certain "Islamic" figure despite the Mushaf's stark reprimand of the Prophet for assuming the authority of *tahrim* (see M66:1).

The Sunnah doctrine was discussed extensively in Chapter 8, however, this doctrine has had a severe impact on legislation and on what later became known as the body of Sharia. Here is an example to illustrate this impact. The two hadiths above are considered the backbone of the concept of Ijtihad; however, they address two different contexts (jurists vs. governors). If the two hadiths were transmitted by meaning, it is likely that at least one individual within the chain of transmitters that spanned some 200 years misunderstood or disregarded the difference between judging and governing.[16] Perhaps the difference was not important to some. Even today, many Muslims do not realize the significance of the difference between the two terms. Nevertheless, even if one assumes that the two hadiths were authentic and were transmitted verbatim, one cannot find within them elements worthy of canonizing Ijtihad as a unique religious concept worthy of importance.

Some scholars of Islam refer to some Mushaf verses as an additional proof of the validity of Ijtihad. Two verses are typically used to justify Ijtihad. The first one is M9:122

وَمَا كَانَ الْمُؤْمِنُونَ لِيَنفِرُوا كَافَّةً فَلَوْلَا نَفَرَ مِن كُلِّ فِرْقَةٍ مِّنْهُمْ طَائِفَةٌ لِّيَتَفَقَّهُوا فِي الدِّينِ وَلِيُنذِرُوا قَوْمَهُمْ إِذَا رَجَعُوا إِلَيْهِمْ لَعَلَّهُمْ يَحْذَرُونَ

[And it was not for the believers to go forth all at once; for there should separate from every division of them a group to obtain understanding in the *deen* and warn their people when they return to them that they might be cautious.] While the burden of proof lies on those who invoke this verse to validate the concept of Ijtihad, nevertheless, based on this verse, one might argue that it is a remarkable stretch to make any connection between *deen* and Ijtihad. Another verse used often to create validity for Ijtihad is M29:69

الَّذِينَ جَاهَدُوا فِينَا لَنَهْدِيَنَّهُمْ سُبُلَنَا وَإِنَّ اللَّهَ لَمَعَ الْمُحْسِنِينَ

[And those who strive for Us (*jahadoo*), We will surely guide them to Our ways. And indeed, Allah is with those who do good deeds.] Based on this verse, making a connection between "striving for" and the canonized concept of Ijtihad is like trying to fit a square peg into a round hole. Nevertheless, despite the fragility of the above arguments as a validation for Ijtihad, Muslim clergy and scholars provide a preponderance of material disguised as evidence. Despite the irrelevance of this additional material, it typically has an overwhelming effect on most Muslims.[17]

Most, if not all traditional Muslim jurists and scholars bestowed upon Ijtihad a prominent place in the body of Islamic law despite the lack of any substantive connection between Ijtihad and *deen*. Since the concept of Ijtihad gave Muslim clergy extraordinary powers, it was not surprising that it was stretched and elevated to a high status, even to the extent of recognizing its essence as the devotion to the study of religion in general.[18] Of course, all this extraordinary elevation happened surreptitiously without providing any rationale whither from the Mushaf or Hadith.

Despite the frail connection between Hadith and the Mushaf, on the one hand, and Ijtihad on the other, as a canonized concept, the very authenticity of the bedrock of Ijtihad (i.e., the two hadiths) had been questioned and in fact degraded centuries after their induction into the Hadith corpus. Upon re-visiting the authenticity of these two hadiths, al-Albani, a prominent 20th Century Salafi scholar, devalued the authenticity of abu Dawood's hadith to *tha'if* (weak) from its earlier classification as *sahih* (authentic). Al-Albani's devaluation of the hadith was accepted by many scholars indicating, not only the fluidity of the Hadith classification methodologies, but also the weakness of the concept of Ijtihad in the first place.

The elevation of Ijtihad to a prominence exclusive only to the Mushaf and the Sunnah is expressed in secondary books on Usool al-Fiqh.[19] Amin Islahi went as far as claiming that Ijtihad is a fundamental source of Islamic Law, third only to the Qur'aan and the Sunnah.[20] Kamali goes even further by stating that Ijtihad is the "most important source of Islamic law next to the Qur'aan and the Sunnah."[21] Such emphatic support for Ijtihad and making it as important as the Mushaf and the Sunnah, in as far as expunging legislation is concerned, is made despite the claim by Kamali that "The presence of an element of speculation in *ijtihad* implies that the result arrived at is probably correct, while the possibility of it being erroneous is not excluded."[22] Here is a stark admission that, if the instrument of Ijtihad is accepted, then religious legislation can be flawed, or essentially leading to unjust rulings and laws. It is perplexing how far the proponents of the Ijtihad are willing to go, even at the expense of compromising their own religion.

The over-enthusiasm of the proponents of Ijtihad to frame it within a religious context and to give it religious legitimacy could have been motivated by their discomfort with the severely limiting classical alternative, which is the exclusion of any unprecedented opinions or legislations. This alternative is conventionally presented using classical phrases such as "closing the doors of Ijtihad" or "closure of the gates of Ijtihad." Since the connection between Ijtihad and the Mushaf or the Sunnah is frail, the Ijtihad proponents must have had different motives to champion the concept. A likely motive could have been creating an opening through which the Sharia can be interpreted to be "compatible" with the times or to be flexible or to be "less harsh".

When one realizes how feeble the concept of Ijtihad is, one finds the question of the opening or closing of the doors of Ijtihad to be simply irrelevant to Islam. The advocates and champions of Ijtihad were gasping for any "religious" link, no matter how weak, in order to escape from the cloaks of age-old authority-sanctioned legislation canonized as "Islamic". The liberal camp, on the one hand, wanted to "open the doors of Ijtihad" in order to relax what is perceived as severe, radical or literal interpretations of Sharia. The conservative camp, on the other hand, while adamant on keeping the doors of Ijtihad tightly shut, were in contradiction with their own fundamental religious dictates, namely Hadith, which is nothing but open-ended Ijtihad.

Ijtihad took a life of its own, like a snowball increasing in size and momentum. Ijtihad started from a convoluted interpretation of an alleged Prophetic narrative and then framed as a canonized and sanctified doctrine. In the typical modus operandi of classical Muslim jurists, once a concept is canonized, then its *hukm* (religious ruling), *shuroot* (conditions), *man'huj* (methodology), who can become a *mujtahid* (the one who makes Ijtihad), *shuroot al-mujtahid* (qualifications of the one who is sanctioned to perform Ijtihad), etc., become extensive topics of yet one more layer of "sciences". Take for example the concept of the *hujjah* (religious authority). Here again is Kamali: "The *mujtahid* is thus the authority (*hujjah*) for himself. His is the duty to provide guidance to those who do not know, but he himself must remain in close contact with the sources."[23] In complete disregard for context and language, Kamali cites M16:43 to validate his extraordinary and unjustified claim. He further claims that "This is also the purport of another Qur'anic *aayah* which enjoins those who do not possess knowledge: Then ask those who have knowledge (*ahl al-dhikr*) if you yourselves do not know (al-Nahl 16:43). Thus only those who do not know may seek guidance from others, not those who have the ability and knowledge to deduce the correct answer themselves. The *ahl al-dhikr* in this *aayah* refers to the *ulama*, regardless as to whether they actually know the correct ruling of an issue or not, provided they have the capacity to investigate and find out."[24] Kamali provides no rationale to explain how *ahl al-dhikr* refers to *ulama* or justifies any connection between the two.

Outside of any deep sentimental and emotional attachment to religious scholars and clergy, one finds Kamali's conclusions very problematic at many levels. Kamali's deductions and consequent conclusions were based on flawed interpretations of the Mushaf, and on using confusing and unauthentic Hadith that was transmitted with disregard for words and their precise meanings. Kamali's scholarship is a reflection of how the "Islamic sciences" worked hand-in-hand with the "sciences" of marginalization (see Chapter 2) to discourage or even frighten all but the most liberated minds from questioning such invalidated and highly irrelevant conclusions.

The theory of Ijtihad also proposed or imposed requirements for who is capable, or authorized to perform Ijtihad. In general, these requirements are imprecise and vary between and within Muslim sects.[25] These requirements are problematic in the sense that they are open-ended and not easily verifiable since they rely upon knowledge of Arabic, especially its grammar (with all of its inconsistencies and exceptions). This last requirement is often invoked if all else fails to disqualify a new *mujtahid* who comes from outside the class of *mujtahids* sanctioned by the canonized religious institutions. What is typically referred to as Arabic grammar, furthermore, is not self-consistent and differs from the Mushaf grammar (some of the most common *tafaasir* demonstrate numerous disagreements on linguistic interpretations of various verses including, particularly, the grammatical structure of verses). In light of the abundance of Arabic grammar schools, one wonders which grammar the *mujtahid* should command.[26]

Another requirement for the *mujtahid* is knowledge of Hadith. However, confusion abounds as to which hadiths are true and which are not, which are to be interpreted as commands for action and which simply reflect the practice of the Prophet during a particular time.

A third requirement for the *mujtahid* is to understand the *nasikh* and the *mansookh* in the Mushaf (see Chapter 7). Even if one assumed that the theory of Naskh (abrogation) is sound, the most erudite in the so-called sciences of the Qur'aan have never reached a consensus on which verses were abrogated and which were not (the number of verses believed to be abrogated ranged from one to hundreds; see Chapter 7).

Another requirement for the *mujtahid* is knowledge of *Asbab al-Nuzool* (reasons behind the revelation). This is yet another very problematic requirement. Muslim scholars differed widely on the alleged *asbab* leading to confusing and contradictory interpretations of the Mushaf (see Chapter 6 for more on *Asbab al-Nuzool*).

In summary, the *mujtahid* is required to be aware of a collection of contradictory body of information. Expectedly, the probability of the *mujtahid* arriving at a flawed religious law or a religious ruling becomes high.

Ijtihad (and Ifta, as we show later) can be conceived as a continuing and methodical effort by empires desperate to maintain legitimacy through Islam. Jurists are not likely to be fully independent of the governance and political system of which they are part. The connection between the Umayyad and Abbasid Caliphs and Muslim jurists and Hadith collectors could shed further light on this subject. Since both persecution and appeasement of prominent Muslim jurists is evident from historical records, it is conceivable that the Umayyad and Abbasid empires courted jurists, jurisprudents, Hadith collectors and religious figures who would establish legitimacy for the empire and its rulers' claim to governance. Today's religious landscape is a strong indication of what could have happened in the past.

External influence by a variety of benefactors has never been scrutinized to a degree commensurate with the role that Hadith plays in Muslim societies. What is happening today can help us understand what happened in the past. The reality of the present shows that the governments that drive their legitimacy from Islam are keen on having religious bodies that interpret the religion for political ends. Confluence of rulers and courtiers of the "religious" variety has never been unique to Muslims.[27] Other powerful players in commerce and society could have motives in using Hadith to further their own interests. For example, in the introduction to his Sahih, Muslim ibn al-Hajjaj repeatedly cited a person who apparently commissioned his Hadith project. The mystery shrouding this potential benefactor suggests that he could have subsidized Muslim's work financially.[28] Another example is the potential influence of al-Mansour on what has become widely accepted as the biography of the Prophet. According to ibn Hisham, the author of the famed biography of the Prophet, ibn Ishaq, whose biography of the Prophet was the basis on which ibn Hisham based his work, was commissioned by the Abbasid Caliph al-Mansour to write a history book for his son. This commission likely entailed a hefty compensation commensurate with a Caliph who ruled over wide swaths of nations and tribes.

Subduing the subjects of empires often benefitted religious and scholarly elites who were convenient tools that made the masses conform to the dictates of the rulers in the name of religion. Irrespective of the context and the interpretation of Karl Marx's opinion about religions, ample evidence throughout history confirms the manipulation of religions to tranquilize the masses. This is strongly evident in the history of Muslims.

USOOL AL-FIQH

The ill-conceived concept of Ijtihad could have paved the way for the emergence of Usool al-Fiqh. The literal translation of Usool al-Fiqh is the foundations of *fiqh*. *Fiqh* is a religiously canonized term that originates from the past tense *faqiha*, which means "to be fully educated or having strong competency in a specific subject". A broad definition of Usool al-Fiqh is the methods by which the rules of Sharia are derived. While Fiqh in itself is an invented concept, Usool al-Fiqh, as a science or pseudo-science, established the foundation for the emergence of multiple doctrines and helped to solidify these doctrines within the canons of Islam.

Basing their reasoning on the concept of Ijtihad, the framers of Usool al-Fiqh built into their doctrine a self-exoneration clause to absolve the *mujtahid* of any consequence of his Ijtihad, and consequently, of any accountability. In fact, the problem with two hadiths discussed above is not confined to confusing the duty of the governor with that of the jurists, but the creation of many problems that helped provide foundations for myriads of loopholes. According to Usool al-Fiqh, the *mujtahid* will receive a divine reward even if he made a blunder in his Ijtihad.[29] By admitting the possibility of error as a result of Ijtihad, the framers of Usool al-Fiqh, once more, inserted into religion the possibility and even acceptability of flawed legislative ruling. This means that their Sharia, which they claim to be purely Allah's legislation, allows for flaws. To put it in more candid terms, a religious ruling canonized under *al-hukm al-shar'i* (the ruling of Sharia) can admittedly be flawed or outright wrong. This Sharia-by-extension, or essentially the "Islamization" of legislation, provided the mechanism, in theory and in practice, for flawed legislation. This flawed legislation is aptly characterized as "Islamic".

The possibility of committing errors in religious legislation, as admitted by the framers of Usool al-Fiqh, can have significant implications, especially when considering what is perceived largely as an Islamic penal code. In this domain, there cannot be room for errors as the consequences can be extremely severe not only for individuals subjected to the penal code that is extracted by the Muslim scholars, but also for the entire society.

To see how the fuzziness of Usool al-Fiqh muddied the legislation landscape, we focus on how Islam places universal limits on any man-made penal code while not giving any specificity to punishments. However, upper limits on punishment in Islam are largely, if not universally, confused with punishment itself.[30] *Hudood* is an Arabic term that means limits, however, in *Fiqh*, it denotes punishments. (The Mushaf uses the word *qasas* for punishment, which comes from the root *qassa*, meaning "to extract from".) The Mushaf is explicit in its severe warning to those who exceed the *hudood* that Allah specified in the Mushaf.[31] However, Allah never threatens people with severe punishment if they do not exceed the *hudood*.[32]

The jurists who created canons of religious legislation out of thin air were the same who imposed punishments of chopping hands and feet for the *hirabah* offense. (*Hirabah*, typically translated as war against Allah and His Messenger, had been used expansively and frequently by Muslim rulers to justify political persecution in the name of Islam and under the guise of Islamic prosecution.) In fact, the class of jurists, intoxicated by their newly assumed religious authority and empowered by the subservience and religious naivety of many Muslims, created the environment for the likes of prominent Muslim jurisprudents to extract bizarre legislation effectively legalizing incest.[33] Using legislative doctrines based on alleged Prophetic directives and narratives and spun from amusing extrapolations of out-of-context Mushaf verses, famed Muslim jurisprudents legalized marrying one's daughter if she was a product of *zina* (adultery). Despite the absurdity of such legal opinions and their violation of the most basic of human values and norms, the

Legislation Beyond the Revelation

Muslim clergy behind these edicts, Muslims were made to believe, would still net a reward in the hereafter since these religious edicts were made under the rubric of Ijtihad.

Another consequence of the canonization of Ijtihad was the concept of *takleef* (to create obligation). *Mukallaf* is aptly translated as the one who is obliged or required to do certain things. Strictly speaking, *takleef* pertains only to *fardh,* which is the obligation a Muslim has towards Allah. *Takleef* towards Allah is something that the Muslim needs to do purely for Allah, thus it is outside the sphere of either interference or accountability from any human, group or government. However, in Usool al-Fiqh, the concept of *takleef* was expanded enormously, incapacitating the Muslim with obligations.[34] The Mushaf uses the term *fardh* to refer to a short enumerated list of obligations stated explicitly in the Mushaf. When the Muslim clergy extended the concept of *takleef* beyond the Mushaf, they essentially canonized a new form of slavery in the name of Islam.

Despite their omnipresence in Muslims' religious lexicon, *takleef* and *fardh* were imprecise constructs that created specific categories of muddied religious obligations with no parallels in the Mushaf. In Usool al-Fiqh, *fardh* includes prayers and fasting amongst other practices or rituals. However, the Mushaf uses *kutiba* rather than *furidha* in as far as fasting is concerned. In the case of the daily ritual prayers, *kitaab* is used in addition to a direct command. Therefore, the daily ritual prayers do not fall under the same category of fasting. The framers of Usool al-Fiqh did not focus on the precise distinction between the Mushaf terms and their implications, thus forging new categories that added multiple layers of complexity — and certainly a lot of confusion — to a religion that was intended for all humans, their erudite and their illiterates.

While Ijtihad is considered as a precursor to Usool al-Fiqh, newly constructed sources of religious legislation such as Ijma (consensus) and Qiyaas (analogy) were used to buttress its validity. In the words of Kamali, "The *ulema* of *Usool* are in agreement that the *mujtahid* is bound by the result of his own Ijtihad".[35] Such unsubstantiated statements dot the landscape of the Ijtihad discourse. The rules of Ijtihad are alarmingly convoluted to the point that it is impossible to point out the origin of the myriads of concepts that were derived from it.

Muslims' Greatest Challenge
IFTA

Ifta is the act of issuing a religious ruling, opinion or edict by a Muslim religious authority who could be either an individual with scholarly attributes, an independent religious group, or a governmental religious organization. This concept was created to strengthen the authority of the legislative branch with yet another "religious" instrument. Despite clear instructions in the Mushaf that rendering a religious ruling is Allah's prerogative alone (see M4:127,176), the Muslim clergy were defiant and went to the extent of creating an Ifta institution that subjected practically everything in existence into a haram-halal ruling.[36]

Many Muslims believe that nearly any new invention, whether tangible or conceptual, had to be ruled upon to determine whether it is halal (permissible) or haram (eternally prohibited).[37] The outcome of Ifta is a fatwa, which is generally considered (with considerable vagueness in its definition) as a religiously mandated ruling, or conventionally glorified using an "Islamic" lexicon as *al-hukm al-shar'i* (the Sharia ruling).[38] The person, typically a Muslim clergy, who issues a fatwa is called a *mufti*. While the Mushaf spelled out the few and exclusive list of all things that are eternally forbidden, the Ifta institutions subjected the halal to their oppressive and overbearing dictates and musings. These rulings encompassed practically everything that one can think of, from wearing a cap to playing chess or cards, all required a fatwa as to whether these acts were halal or not.[39] (Muhammad Rashid Rida, a prominent 20th Century reformer, issued more than 1,060 fatwas.[40] Several other prominent Muslim scholars and clergy of the 20th Century issued thousands of fatwas.[41]) The Ifta became a profitable enterprise since the majority of Muslims truly believed that they can lead a better life by knowing the *al-hukm al-shari'*. Perhaps many Muslims were focused on rewards rather than doing what is suitable for their time and place, a call that had been repeated numerous times in the Mushaf.

By creating the assumption that everything in existence needs to be tagged as either halal or haram, the Muslim clergy robbed Muslims of their liberty and freedom and imprisoned them into a suffocating fatwa jail. Whereas the Mushaf explicitly and severely restricted the haram domain, the Muslim clergy severely restricted the halal domain. Take for example Yusuf al-Qaradawi, a contemporary and a highly prominent Muslim clergy, who dedicated an expansive book entitled *The Lawful and the Prohibited in Islam (al-Halal wal Haram fil Islam)*.[42] Al-

Legislation Beyond the Revelation

Qaradawi is explaining to his subjects the domain of the halal, seemingly trying to pick up what Allah left uncompleted. Al-Qaradawi invades practically everything that the Muslim faces in life, commenting on playing chess to "Relaxing the Mind". Here is an expert from al-Qaradawi's fatwa on what he considers as prohibited crops:[43]

> It is haram to cultivate a plant, such as hashish and the like, which is haram for eating or which has no other known use except what is harmful. The case of tobacco is of this nature; whatever the classification of smoking, whether haram or *makruh*, the growing of tobacco is similarly classified. We ourselves prefer to classify smoking as haram.
> It is not a valid excuse for the Muslim to say that he is growing the haram crop in order to sell it to non-Muslims, for the Muslim is never permitted to be a party to the propagation of what is haram. This is similar to a Muslim's raising pigs in order to sell them to Christians, which is clearly unlawful. As we have seen, even a halal item such as grapes cannot be sold to others if it is known that they will use them to make wine.

The rationale for al-Qaradawi's fatwas are presumably the instruments of Usool al-Fiqh that I will discuss below. What is relevant here, however, is the laxity through which a haram fatwa can be issued. Notice the phrase "We ourselves prefer to classify smoking as haram." So according to al-Qaradawi, an eternal prohibition became a matter of preference. Such an extraordinary presumption of authority goes largely unnoticed if not fueling further admiration for al-Qaradawi and other *muftis*, who are regarded as an asset to Muslims as they navigate the halal-haram landscape.

Al-Qaradawi goes even further to claim that raising pigs to sell to Christians is "clearly unlawful". This is an extraordinary extrapolation from the Mushaf, which specifically prohibited eating the meat of pigs. Is eating or using anything else a haram? The Mushaf specifically prohibited the meat of pigs. According to the Mushaf, meat is different from skin and bones and fat. Nevertheless, al-Qaradawi did not validate his extrapolation. The presumption that he is from *ahl al-thikr*, perhaps, is sufficient to fend off any criticism of his fatwas. A certain Muslim might not tolerate anything else coming from the pig, but that is his prerogative and preference, both of which have nothing to do with religion.

By virtue of the Ifta institution, the Islamic concept of *uboodiyyat* (freedom towards Allah) was turned into bondage to the ruling elites who kept the Muslim masses constantly off-balance by using fear.[44] One can watch numerous TV programs across the Muslim world where callers seek the fatwas of Muslim clergy on matters ranging from the permissibility of wearing a type of jeans and the legal length of men's beards all the way to the legality of residing in the "non-Muslim" West. The Muslim clergy hypnotized the marginalized Muslim masses to make them believe that the road to paradise had to go through the *muftis*. This trivialized the religion by reducing it to dos and don'ts and gutted it from its sole.

Muftis endowed themselves with extraordinary powers. Here is al-Qaradawi's understanding of the status of the Mufti:[45]

> Imam al-Shatibi said: "The Mufti has a standing within the *umma* similar to that of the Prophet (SAAW) in as far as the Sharia *ahkam* are concerned. He says to them: 'this is halal and this is haram'." And ibn Qayyem [al-Jewziyyah] considered the Mufti as the signatory for Allah *jalla jallaluhu* similar to the vice-regents that the caliphs and kings appoint to sign on their behalf. And they are [Muftis] the ones that he [al-Jewziyyah] authored for them his book: *A'laam al-Muwaq'een ann Rab al-Aa'lameen*, so which status is more worthy of this status?

Effectively, the Mufti became a god. The halals and harams became playing fields of past and contemporary Muslim clergy. The halal and haram became variables subject to change if the Mufti see the need.[46] Since the Muftis are traditionally appointed by the rulers, the needs have become decisively that of the ruler.

A case in point is the recent government directive to allow women to drive cars in the Kingdom of Saudi Arabia. This is a stark illustration of how the religious institutions, represented by their grand Muftis, can be coaxed to lavish legitimacy on government policies when desired. The Council of Senior Scholars in the Kingdom, a government body appointed directly by the king, issued a statement supporting the new decree allowing women to drive by stating that "the Kingdom of Saudi Arabia was established on the Book and the Sunnah, and we are in agreement with our rulers in everything that they deem as beneficial for the country and the people, and this is what is essentially implied by the Sharia based allegiance".⁴⁷ The statement by the Council is extraordinary in the sense that it has practically assigned Allah's powers to the ruler. This Council is the same one that believed that it was against Sharia for women to drive cars only hours before the King issued his directive.

ALLAH'S LEGISLATION VERSUS HUMANS' LEGISLATION

Irrespective of being the outcome of a conspiracy, docility, machinations, or subservience, the religious system that evolved pacified and petrified the Muslim mind. The objective of a good Muslim was confined to finding the ruling on every act in order to either avoid hellfire or to be rewarded in the hereafter. Pious Muslim women became terrified to expose a strand of their hair. Such pacifism, selfishness (in search of rewards) and constant paranoia and fear helped shape the Muslim psyche. The psyche became either fearful, or content and careless, attributes that are the ingredients for docility and retrogress. The binary Muslim became disinterested in issues of justice, governance, poverty, pollution, politics, innovation, etc. The world became a side-note. The most important existential questions in the re-engineered Muslim mind have become confined within the halal-haram binary. Everything else became a waste of time, a mere low worldly affair (dubbed typically as *al-hayyat al-dunya*, the lower world) not worthy of attention and in fact, viewed with scorn.⁴⁸

Because of the canonization of Usool al-Fiqh, to render a judgement (by a judge) in a court of law or legal arbitration was extended to legislation. Jurists were confused with jurisprudents. Legislation was muddied with arbitration. The Mushaf made it explicit that Allah's legislation is made available within the Mushaf. Anything outside the Mushaf will therefore be humans' legislation. In three different very important verses, Allah stresses that only His revelation is to be used for enacting *ahkam*, i.e., legislation. Here are the last phrases of M5:44,45,47, respectively:

ومَن لَّمْ يَحْكُم بِمَا أَنزَلَ اللَّهُ فَأُولَٰئِكَ هُمُ الْكَافِرُونَ

[and who does not judge by what Allah has revealed are those who are truth deniers (*kafiroon*)]

وَمَن لَّمْ يَحْكُم بِمَا أَنزَلَ اللَّهُ فَأُولَٰئِكَ هُمُ الظَّالِمُونَ

[and who does not judge by what Allah has revealed are those who are the oppressors (*thalimoon*)].

وَمَن لَّمْ يَحْكُم بِمَا أَنزَلَ اللَّهُ فَأُولَٰئِكَ هُمُ الْفَاسِقُونَ

[and who does not judge by what Allah has revealed are those who are the rebellious (*fasiqoon*)].

In numerous discussions with Muslims, I faced questions such as is it halal or haram for men to shake hands with women. The answer is that it has nothing to do with the religion. If some cultures, not only Muslim cultures, feel it is inappropriate for different reasons, then for men not to shake hands with women is part of that culture. There might be positive or negative aspects to such a cultural norm, but, irrespectively, it has nothing to do with religion. The halal-haram tag is different from realizing which practice is suitable (*salih*) for society and which is not. The incredibly important concept of doing what is suitable for the society has been sacrificed, along with the society itself, for no other reason but accumulating rewards.

Here, the question arises as whether humans in general and Muslims in particular need legislation beyond the Mushaf? Based on the human experience over many centuries and based on the evolution of new technologies and services, the answer is an emphatic affirmative. New legislation will always be needed as long as humans exist, and as long as their societies continue to evolve in complexity and sophistication. This new legislation, however, cannot be a divine legislation, and thus cannot be subjected to the halal-haram binarity. Recognizing that humans can legislate is not a transgression against the *deen* as long as human's legislation is concerned with anything outside the sphere of Allah's legislation.[49]

If one chooses to interpret legislation as Sharia, then there are two types of Sharia: Allah's Sharia and human's Sharia; both share the same

Legislation Beyond the Revelation

name but have separate domains. Allah's legislation has an exceptionally narrow scope since it deals with the makeup of the human being (regulating the primordial instincts/behavior such as aggression related to theft, violence or murder, and mating). One can divide Allah's legislation into two parts. The first part is a private matter between Allah and humans. Since Allah created (in the sense that was discussed earlier) humans, he has a special relationship with them individually. In this part, any commandments or instructions that Allah directs to humans is outside the sphere of other humans' intervention. The second part is related to the relationship between Allah and human societies. This part is enforceable within the concept of *hudood* (limits). The *hudood* provide the upper limit to punishments that are related to specific offenses.

When the class of jurisprudents become endowed with legislative powers that were given to them by themselves and by the religious elite and patrons of the religious elite (benefactors of the political and ruling establishment), then religion becomes distant from it source. All of a sudden the Mushaf's concept of *shirk* (association) becomes real and current, and no longer a theoretical construct. The Mufti became the modern mini-god.

Completely untamed while heavily regulated by the governing elite, the fatwa industry became wide-spread penetrating all aspects of life from the bedroom and the bathroom to politics. The use of fatwas became a direct political instrument. On January 6, 2016, the Minister for Religious Affairs (*awqaf*) of Egypt, Muhammad Juma, issued a fatwa stating that demonstrating against the Egyptian ruling authority is "a complete crime, haram from the Sharia point of view, and contradictory to the path of the *deen*".[50] This is a classic example where the new demigods (cloaked by the canons of Ijtihad, Ifta, *mujtahid*, *mufti*, etc.) work hand-in-glove with the ruling elites to sanctify the oppression and transgression of ruthless dictators and despots, in the name of the *deen*.

Interestingly, prominent Muslim scholars would issue fatwas that are completely contradictory. An example is a fatwa by al-Qaradawi declaring visiting al-Aqsa Masjid in Jerusalem a haram as long as it is under Israeli occupation.[51] Remarkably, al-Qaradawi's fatwa is contradicted by yet another fatwa by Ali Goma, the former Grand Mufti of Egypt.[52] The same *mufti* contradicted the rulings of the four major Sunni sects in approving the handshaking between a man and a foreign woman (not *muhram*), claiming that the handshaking is permissible as long as the intention of the man is benevolent and for the purpose of reconciliation.[53]

Muslims may point to the Catholic Church for its authoritarianism but they overlook that each of their own sects have many Popes with authority exceeding that of the Catholic Church. In the Catholic Church, the process of issuing edicts might be highly authoritarian, but it appears to remain centralized. Amongst Sunni sects, the process is expansive and at times out of control. The concept of the fatwa essentially codified the *deen*.

It is difficult to determine when the position of the *mufti* or Grand Mufti was established. Nowadays, this institution is adopted in many Muslim and non-Muslim countries and regions. In countries with a Sunni Muslim majority, the appointment of the Grand Mufti is primarily influenced by the political establishment. For instance, in Turkey and Saudi Arabia, the president or the King appoints the Grand Mufti.[54] In Egypt, the Grand Mufti is appointed by the President.[55] In some Shia sects, the equivalent of a Grand Mufti is assumed by the position of the Grand Ayatollah. This position remained outside of the political establishment until the consolidation of the Wilayat al-Faqih (Rule of the Jurisprudent) by Khomeini, which led to the amalgamation of the position with the political system in the Islamic Republic of Iran.[56]

In both the Sunni and Shia sects, the Grand Mufti or the Grand Ayatollah are either appointed by the political ruler or elected by an assembly of people with specific qualifications and who hold religious persuasions and ideologies favorable to the political establishment. This means that the highest authority of interpreting the law and the dispensing of "religious" legislation is sanctioned by the political establishment, or by people connected to or appointed by the religiopolitical establishment. Notice the similarity to the Catholic Church where a new Pope is elected by Cardinals who were themselves appointed by a previous Pope. A similar process is used to elect the head of the Coptic Church in Egypt. Clearly, there are strong parallels between the Sunnis, the Shias, the Catholics and the Copts — and possibly other religious sects — in the way they create religious legislative authority.

Legislation Beyond the Revelation
THE CANONS OF USOOL AL-FIQH

While human-made legislation is distinct from a divine one, it can be inspired by it or connected to it in spirit. However, irrespective of how the human legislation is arrived at, it remains strictly a human legislation outside the boundary of *deen,* and, specifically, outside the Mushaf.

Human-made legislation deals with the regulation of society, ensuring there is justice and protection for members of a social group or nation. Usool al-Fiqh extended legislation in the name of Allah, thereby Islamizing (i.e., making something part of Islam) what is exclusively human-made legislation. Generally, the four canons of Usool al-Fiqh are the Mushaf, the Sunnah, Ijma and Qiyaas. (Other sects, such as the Malikis, use the opinion of the People of Madinah as a secondary source after the Sunnah.[57]) The first of these four canons embodies Allah's laws, while the remaining three fall into the sphere of human-made laws and regulations, or human Sharia. Even if the Sunnah introduced legislation beyond the Mushaf, this would fall outside any legal regime imposed by Allah (see Chapter 8).

Ijma is the second most fundamental concept on which legislation is based. This concept is deeply shrouded in sophistry and confusion. Ijma is derived from the Arabic word *ajma'a*, which implies either "to determine", "to agree upon by a group of people" or to "achieve consensus". Ijma is conventionally (and loosely) defined as the consensus of the community of jurisprudents.[58] It is recognized as an instrument by which "Islamic" legislation can be established regarding a specific subject that the Mushaf or the Sunnah did not address. No one can define with certainty when precisely Ijma emerged as a canon of Usool al-Fiqh. Al-Shafi'i's *al-Risala* treatise indicates that Ijma was an instrument that al-Shafi'i and possibly his contemporaries or precedents used for religious legislation.

Al-Shafi'i's support of Ijma rested upon feeble arguments. He argued that according to a few hadiths, the Prophet asked his followers to adhere to *luzoom jama'at al-Muslemeen*.[59] The phrase can be translated as "to be associated with the Muslims", or "to be close to the Muslims", or "to be part of the group of Muslims." Al-Shafi'i argued that the Prophetic phrase does not imply physical association since it is impossible to ask someone to be associated with people who are dispersed over different regions. Therefore, al-Shafi'i's inferred that *luzoom* implies "to follow or to be associated with the group of Muslims in what they make halal and what they make haram, and obedience in both."⁶⁰ He further claimed, "Whoever said what the Muslim congregation believes or says, then he has fulfilled the requirement of *luzoom* in the Prophetic command. And whoever rejects what the Muslim congregation believes or says, then he has strayed away, contradicted, or differed from the congregation of which [the Prophet] commanded to be a part."⁶¹

Association or being part of a group indeed can imply either physical proximity or proximity in faith, aspiration, feelings, or any other aspect that is not tangible. In either interpretation, and on the assumption that the phrase, which is part of a hadith in this case, is authentic, the difference between a Prophetic command and an encouragement could have been lost during the transmission of the hadith. (If the Sunnah is a revelation as much as the Mushaf is, as was discussed in Chapter 8, and the Mushaf revelation has extra-Mushafic context, one would expect that the Sunnah revelation to have a context too that parallels the Mushaf's *Asbab al-Nuzool*).

Al-Shafi'i's reasoning that concludes that Ijma as an instrument of legislation followed from the "*luzoom jama'at al-Muslemeen*" hadith is flawed. Nevertheless, al-Shafi'i reiterates his conviction that "This kind of [legal] knowledge is an example of what I have already discussed [namely], that no one at all should [give an opinion] on a specific matter by merely saying: It is permitted or prohibited, unless he is certain of [legal] knowledge, and this knowledge must be based on the Qur'aan and the Sunnah, or [derived] from Ijma and Qiyaas".⁶² These words represent al-Shafi'i's own understanding of the rationale behind the validity of Ijma. Other Muslim scholars, however, attributed al-Shafi'i's and other jurisprudents' acceptance of Ijma to the Mushaf. In his treatise on Ijma, Yaqoob al-Bahusein, a 20th Century Muslim scholar, stated that al-Shafi'i and other jurisprudents attributed the validity of Ijma to M4:115.⁶³ The fact that this verse has nothing to do with legislation explains the difficulty one senses that al-Shafi'i experienced in justifying his Ijma concept according to al-Bahusein's own narrative. Interestingly, al-Bahusein does not use al-Shafi'i's own logic to justify Ijma.

The followers of al-Shafi'i had even harder times validating Ijma to the point that they narrated stories with doubtful authenticity. Al-Subki (d. 771/1370), a leading Shafi'i scholar of the 14th Century, narrates a story about how al-Shafi'i proved the validity of Ijma. Despite the supernatural aspects of the story that also includes the presence of al-Khadr, a figure that many Muslims believed to have accompanied the Prophet Musa, al-Shafi'i ends up attributing the validity of Ijma to M4:115. Interestingly, M4:115 was never part of his proof of Ijma in either *al-Risala* or al-Umm, his two treatises where he outlined his philosophy of Usool al-Deen.[64] (There is no value in discussing M4:115 here as it has no relevance to Ijma.)

The origin of Ijma has never been clear. Maalik ibn Anas was reported to have used Ijma before al-Shafi'i, which suggests that al-Shafi'i was a proponent of Ijma rather than its creator.[65] The word Ijma could have also originated or derived from *jama'ah* (a group). One hadith that is widely cited to stress the importance of being part of the group is that of Muawiyah, the founder of the Umayyad dynasty:[66]

عَنْ مُعَاوِيَةَ بْنِ أَبِي سُفْيَانَ، أَنَّهُ قَامَ فِينَا فَقَالَ أَلاَ إِنَّ رَسُولَ اللَّهِ صلى الله عليه وسلم قَامَ فِينَا فَقَالَ " أَلاَ إِنَّ مَنْ قَبْلَكُمْ مِنْ أَهْلِ الْكِتَابِ افْتَرَقُوا عَلَى ثِنْتَيْنِ وَسَبْعِينَ مِلَّةً وَإِنَّ هَذِهِ الْمِلَّةَ سَتَفْتَرِقُ عَلَى ثَلاَثٍ وَسَبْعِينَ ثِنْتَانِ وَسَبْعُونَ فِي النَّارِ وَوَاحِدَةٌ فِي الْجَنَّةِ وَهِيَ الْجَمَاعَةُ"

[Muawiyah ibn abi Sufiyan stood among us and said: Beware! The Apostle of Allah stood among us and said: Beware! The people of the Book before were split up into seventy-two sects, and this community will be split into seventy three: seventy two of them will go to Hell and one of them will go to Paradise, and it is the majority group.][67] The Umayyads were keen on using Islam to justify political ends and to establish legitimacy for their empire and its expansion. This hadith and many others of the same genre have the hallmarks of politically motivated fabrications to serve the political ends of the Umayyad dynasty.[68] Specifically, this hadith and others were used to justify that those who follow the Umayyads are the only "saved" group. Consequently, another dire implication of Muawiyah's hadith was the death of political pluralism in Muslim-dominated societies.

Not all Muslims throughout history believed in Ijma. The al-Shu'arah, historically referred to by their opponents and later by most Muslims as al-Khawarij (typically denoting the group that split from Ali ibn abi Talib, the fourth Righteous Caliphs, during the battle of Saffin), and the Abadhis are two Muslim sects who date their origin to the first Muslim century. Both groups never recognized Ijma and Qiyaas as sources of legislation.

The concept of Ijma is muddied by contradictions and inconsistencies. For instance, what had been agreed upon by a certain generation, scholars of Islam, jurisprudents or any group, might not be agreed upon by a different generation. This implies an inconsistency of the religion that uses Ijma is one of its legislative doctrines (whether Islam, Christianity, Judaism or other creeds). This built-in feature of Ijma renders Sharia as a variable. In fact, the definitions of Ijma are numerous and there is no agreement between Muslim sects or even Muslims within a single sect on a consistent definition of Ijma itself. Abu al-Husayn al-Basri (d. 436/1045) defined it as "Agreement of a group on a certain matter by action or abandonment".[69] Al-Juwayni considered Ijma as "the agreement of the *umma*, or the agreement of its *ulama* on a ruling from Sharia".[70] Al-Ghazali (d. 504/1111) defines Ijma as "Agreement of the community of Muhammad, specifically, on a religious question or matter", while al-Amidi (d. 630/1233) defines it as the "Agreement of all the people of binding and loosing who belong to the community of Muhammad, in a certain period of time, on a rule about a certain incidence".[71]

After al-Shafi'i, most, if not all Sunni Muslim scholars accepted Ijma as a canonized religious instrument, as if it were an article of faith. According to ibn al-Mundhir (d. 319/931), Ijma was applied to 765 different and wide ranging subjects from the type of punishment for those who steal intoxicants to the proper method to divide a single pearl between a group of people.[72] One interesting and noticeable subject that al-Mundhir lists is *zina* (adultery) and the state of becoming intoxicated from alcohol. He concludes that because of Ijma, *zina* and becoming intoxicated were both haram. However, one can easily conclude that both are haram from the Mushaf itself rather than any other Usool al-Fiqh instrument.

Thus, even if Ijma was an instrument of expunging legislation, its relevance to matters that were addressed in the Mushaf is questionable. Overriding the Mushaf in legislation appears as if the Mushaf is not considered a legislative authority unless the Muslim clergy reach a consensus. Nevertheless, ibn al-Mundhir's Ijma treatise is missing important information such as which group of jurisprudents or scholars made Ijma and what were their qualifications. In fact, it is not clear when ibn al-Mundhir lived, whether there was an Ijma database and whether it was shared and authenticated by the people who made the Ijma. Ibn al-Mundhir's Ijma treatise suggests that Ijma evolved as an overbearing and intrusive instrument of control and intimidation, all in the name of Islam.

Legislation Beyond the Revelation

Scholars differed widely on who can make Ijma. Malik confined Ijma to the people of Madinah and no one else.[73] According to ibn al-Salah, Ijma is founded on his claim that the *umma* in its entirety is infallible and cannot make a mistake.[74] But ibn al-Salah never clarified which group of people are qualified to make Ijma. On the one hand, ibn al-Salah claimed that the entire *umma* is empowered to make Ijma, and on the other, he claimed that Ijma can be made only by those "worthy" of making Ijma from the *umma*. Al-Affani, a 20th Century scholar of Islam, confines Ijma to *ahl al-ilm* (people of knowledge/science).[75] This equivocation on who is empowered to make Ijma strongly suggests major confusion surrounding the concept. It seems that with time, the frailty of Ijma as a religious doctrine has become more apparent, driving its proponents and framers to continuously recalibrate earlier definitions and provide additional "validation."

From the point of view of the Mushaf, Ijma constitutes a major transgression against Islam. To clarify this, we turn to M7:33

قُلْ إِنَّمَا حَرَّمَ رَبِّيَ الْفَوَاحِشَ مَا ظَهَرَ مِنْهَا وَمَا بَطَنَ وَالْإِثْمَ وَالْبَغْيَ بِغَيْرِ الْحَقِّ وَأَن تُشْرِكُوا بِاللَّهِ مَا لَمْ يُنَزِّلْ بِهِ سُلْطَانًا وَأَن تَقُولُوا عَلَى اللَّهِ مَا لَا تَعْلَمُونَ

[Say/pronounce that my Lord has only made haram the fawahish, what is apparent of them and what is concealed, and *ethm*, and to seek things and gains without right, and that you associate with Allah that which He has not revealed an authority, and that you say/pronounce/promulgate/decree about Allah that which you have no understanding of or science of.][76] The first part of the verse is accepted and implemented by practically all Muslim scholars without much debate. The last two phrases (underlined) represent a stark warning to attributing anything to Allah that is not based on either revelation or genuine understanding. This covers a wide range of behaviors and actions from knowingly concocting fake science to issuing religious edicts under any guise, including Ijma.

Despite the feebleness of the Ijma doctrine, the enthusiasm for it has been overwhelming amongst the majority of both Shia and Sunni Muslim clergy. Examples of this enthusiasm are expressed by al-Baydawi (d. 482/1089), a Hanafi scholar who claimed that "One who rejects the doctrine of Ijma rejects the religion at large. This is because the orbit of all the fundamentals of religion and their returning point is the Ijma of Muslims." Al-Sarakhsi (d. 490/1097), another Hanafi scholar, goes to the extent of claiming that "One who denies the validity of Ijma seeks to indirectly demolish religion per se." Al-Juwayni, a Shafi'i scholar, claimed that "Ijma is the strap and support of the Sharia and to it the Sharia owes its authenticity."[77]

Despite unsubstantiated contradictory and dubious claims of its validity by a host of Muslim scholars of previous centuries, contemporaries such as Ahmad Hassan claimed "It must be noted ... that unlike the Qur'aan and the Sunnah, Ijma does not directly partake of divine revelation. As a doctrine and proof of Sharia, Ijma is basically a rational proof. The theory of Ijma is also clear on the point that it is a binding proof."[78] Hassan, despite his belief that Ijma is a theory, still insists that it is a "binding proof".

This enthusiasm for Ijma is neither universal nor consistent throughout history. Ibn Taymiyyah, the godfather of Salafism, was not an adherent of the concept since he could not find it to have a logical connection to either the Mushaf or the Sunnah. Mahmoud Shaltut, the former Grand Imam of al-Azhar, said of Ijma "and I barely know anything that has become common between people as one of the foundation of Usool al-Sharia in Islam and had been discussed widely and contested by different schools of thought as had been argued and experienced."[79]

Despite wide disagreements (i.e., absence of Ijma) by Muslim scholars on most, if not all, aspects of Ijma, it continues to be a canonized constituent of Usool al-Fiqh amongst the majority of Shias and Sunnis. It is a poorly justified loophole to allow humans to be associates (*shareek*) of Allah in legislation. It also serves political objectives when used very often as an instrument of subjugation and control. In fact, the way the concept is typically invoked brings to the forefront questions of ethics, sincerity and honesty about some of its proponents. Take for example al-Nawawi's commentary on certain hadiths in Sahih Muslim related to the extraordinarily bizarre subject of suckling of the elder. Al-Nawawi claimed "these hadiths are unanimous in those who suckled (from one woman) are not allowed (haram) to marry the woman they suckled from, and that the *umma* has made Ijma on this."[80] Al-Nawawi does not provide any support for his claim that the *umma* had unanimously agreed on such opinion or ruling, let alone failing to explain to his audience and his followers what he meant by *umma*. (Even when

Legislation Beyond the Revelation

invoked in the Mushaf, comprehending the word *umma* requires understanding its context.)

Other invocations of Ijma include phrases such as "All Muslim jurisprudents are unanimous (made Ijma) on such and such." Interestingly, the framers and proponents of Ijma invoke the *umma* too often as the body that is qualified to make Ijma, yet these proponents do not give a clear definition of the *umma*. The Mushaf characterizes a group with a common behavior as *umma*. Thus, Ijma can lead to the making of an *umma*, not the other way around. Nevertheless, who is qualified to make Ijma is a highly contentious issue that is equally fluid in practically every aspect of Ijma. According to Kamali: "In regard to the rules of *fiqh*, it is the Ijma of the *fuqaha* alone which is taken into account."[81] The question naturally arises as to whether the *fuqaha* that belong to certain factions, such as the Khawarij, the Shias, or those who might have been charged with heresy and *bid'ah* (innovation in religion), would be qualified to participate in Ijma. Going further, one needs to know who is authorized to level the charge of heresy. Is it the ruler? Any ruler? An oppressive ruler? Who are those people of *bid'ah*? It needs to be kept in mind that the definition of who is a *faqih* differs between Muslim sects.

QIYAAS AND ISTIHSAAN AND THE NEW FOUNDATIONS

Qiyaas and Istihsaan are the fourth and fifth pillars of Usool al-Fiqh. Qiyaas describes the process of reasoning by analogy or deductive analogy, while Istihsaan is the process of making the best choice based on certain criteria. Irrespective of its origin in Muslim history, the instrument of Qiyaas became a fully canonized doctrine of Sunnism. Specifically, when the Mushaf, the Sunnah and Ijma does not provide a ruling on a certain matter that might arise, the *hukm al-shar'i* (the ruling of Islamic Sharia) can then be extracted or deduced. The Qiyaas instrument, despite being firmly based on logic and reasoning, was fully embraced by Ahl al-Sunnah wa al-Jamma'ah. This is surprising since this Muslim sect fiercely rejected *akl* (mind) and reasoning when navigating the religion landscape.

Istihsaan, the fifth cannon of Usool al-Fiqh, emerged as a legalistic principle whereby jurists select a ruling based on balancing its impact on society in comparison to all other possible rulings. Most likely Istihsaan, perhaps under a different designation, was a purely legal principle exercised by jurists before Islam, and for the purpose of extracting the best ruling in terms of fairness while considering its impact on society. However, many prominent Muslim jurists seem to have canonized Istihsaan as an Islamic principle and evolved it to denote choosing between legal rulings produced by different scholars.[82]

Istihsaan has effectively been extended to imply that the *faqih* may choose what he is most comfortable with amongst different religious rulings while presenting the ruling as "Islamic" or within an Islamic framework. Istihsaan had gone beyond its strict legalistic scope to encompass practically everything under the *deen* that is subjected to Ijtihad. Al-Shafi'i and most Muslim clergy did not make a clear distinction between Ijtihad and Istihsaan. In fact, numerous rulings by al-Shafi'i and many other Muslim clergy never provided the origin or the particular Usool al-Fiqh instrument on which their fatwas were based. This was the case especially when the fatwas carried profound implications as in the case of *jizya*, the poll tax on non-Muslims.[83]

Through its transformation into a full-blown religious doctrine, Istihsaan became the modus operandi for the type of Muslim scholars who claim to be a *wasati* (i.e., following the "middle ground"). The *wasati* methodology essentially gave rise to the concept of multiple Islams. If there is a middle-ground Islam (i.e., *wasati*), then there must be a radical Islam, a conservative Islam, a liberal Islam, a feminist Islam, etc. Istihsaan added additional mercuriality to an already fluid and contradictory set of doctrines.

The doctrines of Ijma, Qiyaas, and Istihsaan have no foundation in either the Mushaf or the Sunnah. All are based on convoluted interpretations of certain verses of the Mushaf and alleged hadiths. These instruments are severely detrimental to Muslims as they completed the transformation of jurisprudents into minor gods and partners with Allah in as far as having the authority to legislate and make the haram declaration. Consequently, these new doctrines facilitated a grand hegemony of jurists and jurisprudents over the Muslim masses.

The absence of any challenge to the theory of Ijtihad opened a Pandora's Box replete with all types of religious foundations leading to the possibility of infinite "Islamic" legislation. Ijtihad, which encouraged Muslim jurists to develop the doctrines of Ijma, Qiyaas, and Istihsaan,

Legislation Beyond the Revelation

produced yet additional instruments of legislation, that of *qawa'id* (foundations) or *usool* (legal maxims). *Qawa'id* (commonly used to denote *usool* too) refers to the rules or principles that Muslim scholars constructed to facilitate religious rulings and edicts related to a variety of acts that appear to have a common theme.

The origin of the *qawa'id* is not certain; however, they most likely evolved slowly with the evolution of Islamic jurisprudence in general. There are some hints that suggest that they were canonized hundreds of years after the death of the framers of Usool al-Fiqh. One particular *qa'ida* (singular of *qawa'id*) with far reaching impact is one that states that there can be no Ijtihad if a clear text (*nuss*) is available. This is typically understood by most Muslims to mean that if there is a clear ruling that stems from either the Mushaf or Hadith, then Ijtihad becomes irrelevant. The problem with this *qa'ida* is that the Hadith can be either authentic or not. Furthermore, the framers of this *qa'ida* included Ijma as the third component of the "text", the first two being the Mushaf and Hadith. The inclusion, however, is attributed to al-Jewziyyah, a 14th Century Salafi disciple of ibn Taymiyyah.[84] This *qa'ida* with its far reaching impact is essentially founded on the flawed concept of Ijma.

These *qawa'id* ranged in number from a few to almost one hundred. Examples include *Sadd al-Tharai'ih* (prevention of excuses), *al-Daroorat Tubeeh al-Mahdoorat* (necessities permit the forbidden) and others that were generated circuitously from peculiar interpretations of either a few Mushaf verses or from certain hadiths. Few Muslims (scholars or commoners) cared to investigate the validity of such *qawa'id*. For instance, *al-Daroorat Tubeeh al-Mahdoorat* was derived from the last sentence of M5:3

حُرِّمَتْ عَلَيْكُمُ الْمَيْتَةُ وَالدَّمُ وَلَحْمُ الْخِنْزِيرِ وَمَا أُهِلَّ لِغَيْرِ اللَّهِ بِهِ وَالْمُنْخَنِقَةُ وَالْمَوْقُوذَةُ وَالْمُتَرَدِّيَةُ وَالنَّطِيحَةُ وَمَا أَكَلَ السَّبُعُ إِلَّا مَا ذَكَّيْتُمْ وَمَا ذُبِحَ عَلَى النُّصُبِ وَأَنْ تَسْتَقْسِمُوا بِالْأَزْلَامِ ذَٰلِكُمْ فِسْقٌ الْيَوْمَ يَئِسَ الَّذِينَ كَفَرُوا مِنْ دِينِكُمْ فَلَا تَخْشَوْهُمْ وَاخْشَوْنِ الْيَوْمَ أَكْمَلْتُ لَكُمْ دِينَكُمْ وَأَتْمَمْتُ عَلَيْكُمْ نِعْمَتِي وَرَضِيتُ لَكُمُ الْإِسْلَامَ دِينًا <u>فَمَنِ اضْطُرَّ فِي مَخْمَصَةٍ غَيْرَ مُتَجَانِفٍ لِإِثْمٍ فَإِنَّ اللَّهَ غَفُورٌ رَحِيمٌ</u>

[It was made haram for you the dead animals, blood, the flesh of swine, and that which has been dedicated to other than Allah, and that was killed by strangling or by a violent blow or by a head-long fall or by the goring of horns, and those from which a wild animal has eaten, except what you slaughtered before death, and those which are sacrificed on stone altars, and that you seek decision through divining arrows; that is grave disobedience. This day those who disbelieve have despaired of defeating your religion; so fear them not, but fear Me. This day I have completed for you your religion and completed My favor upon you and have approved for you Islam as religion. But whoever is forced by severe hunger with no inclination to sin - then indeed, Allah is Forgiving and Merciful.] Clearly, the entire verse is related to forbidden foods where Allah gives permission for the hungry and those having no alternatives to eating forbidden foods such as pig's meat. The permission is strictly related to eating forbidden foods at time of need. For the purpose of further buttressing the *qa'ida*, specific sentences were extracted from two other verses, namely M5:3 and M6:119. In his comprehensive and detailed PhD thesis, Kamil claims that the source of this *qa'ida* is the underlined sentence in M5:3 (see above) in addition to the following two sentences from M2:173 and M6:119[85]

فَمَنِ اضْطُرَّ غَيْرَ بَاغٍ وَلَا عَادٍ فَلَا إِثْمَ عَلَيْهِ

وَقَدْ فَصَّلَ لَكُم مَّا حَرَّمَ عَلَيْكُمْ إِلَّا مَا اضْطُرِرْتُمْ إِلَيْهِ

These two sentences, however, are incomplete. When the entire verses are considered, a different conclusion emerges. First, M2:173

إِنَّمَا حَرَّمَ عَلَيْكُمُ الْمَيْتَةَ وَالدَّمَ وَلَحْمَ الْخِنزِيرِ وَمَا أُهِلَّ بِهِ لِغَيْرِ اللَّهِ فَمَنِ اضْطُرَّ غَيْرَ بَاغٍ وَلَا عَادٍ فَلَا إِثْمَ عَلَيْهِ إِنَّ اللَّهَ غَفُورٌ رَحِيمٌ

[Emphatically, it was made haram on you dead animals, blood, the flesh of swine, and that which has been dedicated to other than Allah, and if whoever has no alternative, neither seeking this situation nor transgressing, there is no sin upon him. Indeed, Allah is Forgiving Merciful.] The second, M6:119

وَمَا لَكُمْ أَلَّا تَأْكُلُوا مِمَّا ذُكِرَ اسْمُ اللَّهِ عَلَيْهِ وَقَدْ فَصَّلَ لَكُم مَّا حَرَّمَ عَلَيْكُمْ إِلَّا مَا

Legislation Beyond the Revelation

$$\text{اضْطُرِرْتُمْ إِلَيْهِ وَإِنَّ كَثِيرًا لَيُضِلُّونَ بِأَهْوَائِهِم بِغَيْرِ عِلْمٍ إِنَّ رَبَّكَ هُوَ أَعْلَمُ بِالْمُعْتَدِينَ}$$

[And why should you not eat of from that upon which the name of Allah has been mentioned and He has explained in detail to you what He has made haram on you, excepting that to which you are compelled and indeed many lead others astray through their own inclinations without understanding, indeed your Lord is most understanding of the transgressors.]

Clearly the context of above two verses relates to food. To give even more support to the *qa'ida*, Kamil uses only the underlined part of yet another verse: M16:16

$$\text{مَن كَفَرَ بِاللَّهِ مِن بَعْدِ إِيمَانِهِ إِلَّا مَنْ أُكْرِهَ وَقَلْبُهُ مُطْمَئِنٌّ بِالْإِيمَانِ وَلَٰكِن مَّن شَرَحَ بِالْكُفْرِ صَدْرًا فَعَلَيْهِمْ غَضَبٌ مِّنَ اللَّهِ وَلَهُمْ عَذَابٌ عَظِيمٌ}$$

[Whoever makes *kufr* in Allah after his *imaan*, except for one who was forced while his mind is secure in *imaan*, but those who lead someone to accept *kufr*, upon them is wrath from Allah, and for them is a great punishment.] Here, the context is not food but rather forcible conversion from *imaan* to *kufr*; a very specific context with no grounds for extracting any maxim or any *qa'ida*, let alone *al-Daroorat Tubeeh al-Mahdoorat*.

Using the underlined part of M16:16 to validate the *qa'ida* constitutes a lack of academic rigor and poor scholarship that were ignored or overlooked by the supervisors of Kamil's thesis.[86] Perhaps the institution that supported the thesis did not expect any challenge to this (or all other *qawa'id*) because of the assumption that it was already validated, and, therefore, questioning its validity would be perceived as a transgression against Islam. Kamil's thesis and the vast majority of others granted by Muslim religious institutions suggest that the only academic activities or scholarship that they sanction would be to provide a new summary, tabulation, classification, or repackaging of what had already been accepted as part of Islam.

Kamil's distortion of the messages carried in the above verses is typical of the modus operandi of the vast majority of the scholars of Islam. Going to any means to justify pre-conceived notions is summarized by

377

a poignant declaration by abi al-Hasan al-Karkhi (d. 240/854), who was the most prominent figure amongst the jurisprudents of the Hanafi sect of his time and believed to be the first to write specifically on Islamic legal maxims. According to al-Karkhi,

كل آية تخالف قول أصحابنا فإنها تحمل على النسخ أو على الترجيح والأولى أن تحمل "على التأويل من جهة التوفيق"

"Any verse that contradicts what our companions have said, that verse should be considered as either abrogated, or weighed, but it is preferred that it is interpreted in a way that supports our assertions."[87]

Another widely used *qa'ida* is *Sadd al-Tharai'ih* (prevention of excuses). This is typically invoked to label certain acts as haram because they are believed or assumed to lead to another act that is already recognized as haram. One can see from the outset that this is an expansive rule indeed. An example of its application includes preventing women from driving in the Kingdom of Saudi Arabia (prior to 2018). Scholars, mostly of the Hanbali sect, have argued that for women to drive is haram since it can facilitate women meeting and flirting with men outside of marriage, which in turn can lead to *zina*. Since the concept of the *qawa'id* is flawed in the first place, it is expected that the application of this particular *qa'ida* would lead to inconsistencies and contradictions. For instance, according to this *qa'ida*, one would expect that men too should be prevented from driving since they would also be likely to use driving to meet and flirt with women. The same reasoning should ban the use of personal computers since they can be used to watch pornography, along with cars since they can be turned into killing machines.

One might argue that the framers of these *qawa'id* or Islamic maxims did not intend them to be absolute. For instance, the framers argue that the *al-Daroorat Tubeeh al-Mahdoorat* does not sanction committing adultery if one does not have the means to be married. A large number of exceptions are in fact available in Usool al-Fiqh books.[88] The exceptions, however, represent open-ended interpretations and opinions that add a myriad of confusion. If one were to consider the exceptions associated with a single maxim, one is better off considering the verse itself from which the maxim was extracted. In fact, the entire verse, as discussed above, clearly confines the exception as implied by the context. Some of the *qa'waid* were essentially a rewording of a sentence

Legislation Beyond the Revelation

within a Mushaf verse. For Muslims, however, the Mushaf is the quintessential Usool al-Fiqh. Why not keep it as such and refer to it for its verses containing the maxims that all Muslims should adhere to. The *qu'waid* created yet another shield between the Muslims and the divine revelation.

Usool al-Fiqh evolved with the rise of Muslim Empires. These empires were created in the name of religion and thus, their sustainability, continuity and expansion, all had to come from the religion. Usool al-Fiqh provided a mechanism through which all kinds of "Islamic" legislation can be churned to justify anything the rulers wanted. Usool al-Fiqh paved the way for bizarre dissection of the world into *dar al-harb* (the land of war) and *dar al-silm* (the land of peace) and a system of discrimination and oppression against all individuals who did not believe in the Prophecy and Message of Muhammad.[89]

Starting with the Umayyad and Abbasid dynasties, during which Usool al-Fiqh were firmly established, up until the Ottoman Empire which gave great importance to the office of the Mufti to consolidate religious authority and make it an instrument of the state, Usool al-Fiqh evolved to work as a coercive measure on the one hand and providing legitimacy for empires on the other. A prominent example is the laws of inheritance. To support the Abbasid claim to power, the empire's religious clergy turned governance into a bequeathable property. Debate raged between supporters of Sunnis and Shias on whether uncles have precedent in inheritance over daughters of the deceased. Here, Usool al-Fiqh was used to serve purely political objectives.

Another example is whether a Muslim can bequeath a portion of his money or property to his relatives, spouse, or anyone from the pool of heirs sanctioned in the Mushaf. Here, we find leading jurists and founders of Muslim jurisprudence schools, such as al-Shafi'i and ibn Hanbal, denying such permissibility by resting their argument on the following hadith:[90]

إِنَّ اللَّهَ قَدْ أَعْطَى كُلَّ ذِي حَقٍّ حَقَّهُ فَلاَ وَصِيَّةَ لِوَارِثٍ

[Affirmably, Allah has given every rightful owner his right, so there is no will for an heir] despite being contradictory to M2:180

Muslims' Greatest Challenge

$$\text{كُتِبَ عَلَيْكُمْ إِذَا حَضَرَ أَحَدَكُمُ الْمَوْتُ إِن تَرَكَ خَيْرًا الْوَصِيَّةُ لِلْوَالِدَيْنِ وَالْأَقْرَبِينَ بِالْمَعْرُوفِ حَقًّا عَلَى الْمُتَّقِينَ}$$

[*kutiba* on you (plural) when death approaches one of you if he leaves wealth a bequest for the parents and near relatives according to what is acceptable; a duty upon the righteous.] The vast majority of Muslim scholars have championed the above will hadith fiercely, and are not shy to admit that the hadith and verse are in contradiction. To favor the hadith, they invoke the abrogation doctrine, specifically that the inheritance verses at the beginning of M4 have abrogated M2:180.[91] But even on the assumption that the instrument of abrogation is valid (see Chapter 7), Muslim clergy are in disagreement as to accurately determining the verses that were abrogated, and whether the abrogation was through a different verse, a hadith or both. In fact, even for those who advocated that the verse in question was abrogated, in a classic modus operandi of Muslim clergy, no proof of this specific abrogation was provided. Al-Karkhi's maxim truly encapsulated the means by which jurisprudents went to extremes to justify the objectives that benefited the ruling dynasties. Al-Karkhi's edacious maxim suggests that he lived at a time where the Mushaf, the only legislative canon in Islam, was viewed with the least importance. Today, the vast majority of Muslim clergy seem to have adopted al-Karkhi's maxim to the fullest.

Usool al-Fiqh was one of several factors that created an oppressive dominance of the clergy over every aspect of life. Another two important factors were the interpretation of two Mushaf words: *ibtila* and *ibada*.

Ibtila appears in M67:2

$$\text{الَّذِي خَلَقَ الْمَوْتَ وَالْحَيَاةَ لِيَبْلُوَكُمْ أَيُّكُمْ أَحْسَنُ عَمَلًا وَهُوَ الْعَزِيزُ الْغَفُورُ}$$

[He who created death and life in order to *yablu'wakum* who amongst you will have the best of deeds and He is the Aziz and more merciful.] *Yablu'wakum* is derived from *ibtila*, which is conventionally translated to imply severe test or hardship. If that was the case, then, according to this verse, life indeed should be nothing but hardship. This misunderstanding paved the way for accepting hardship as a true validation of Allah's revelation. In fact, with this understanding, the religion itself was perceived as hardship. The problem here is that those who interpreted *ibtila* as hardship overlooked that *ibtila* can be a very good thing indeed as in M21:35

$$كُلُّ نَفْسٍ ذَائِقَةُ الْمَوْتِ ۗ وَنَبْلُوكُم بِالشَّرِّ وَالْخَيْرِ فِتْنَةً ۖ وَإِلَيْنَا تُرْجَعُونَ$$

[Every soul will taste death and We will *nablwakum* you with evil and with good as trial; and to Us you will be returned.]

The second factor is the interpretation of *ibada*. Muhammad Shahrour convincingly demonstrated that *ibada* implies one of two opposite acts: willful obedience or willful disobedience.[92] This is not to say that the two opposite meanings are present in every occurrence of the term or its derivatives, but rather the correct meaning depends on the context.

The evidence for the two possible and opposite meanings of *ibada* is available within the Mushaf. Particularly, the verse used to support the interpretation of *ibada* as obedience only is M51:56

$$وَمَا خَلَقْتُ الْجِنَّ وَالْإِنسَ إِلَّا لِيَعْبُدُونِ$$

[And I did not create jinn and humans but only to *yabu'doon*.] All available English translations interpret *yabu'doon* as "to worship me" or "to serve me". However, the reality contradicts this interpretation in the sense that not all people worship or serve Allah (also as evidenced from the Mushaf). Thus if the conventional understanding is correct, according to this verse, Allah has failed to come true on his promise and that Allah's will was never fulfilled. If *ibada* in M51:56 means only obedience, then the entire religion, and by extension all aspects of life, are turned into obedience. Naturally, this would then entail that there must be many rules to adhere to in order to cover every single act the human makes. Expectedly, the more obedience, the more one is fulfilling Allah's promise, and the more obedience, the more validation of the Mushaf. As seen from numerous hadiths, obedience to the ruling elites also becomes more palatable and perhaps even a religious prerogative.

Concluding Thoughts

Usool al-Fiqh evolved as a highly intrusive set of instruments canonized as Islamic. Irrespective of the objectives that the Usool al-Fiqh framers had in mind, these new doctrines operated to regulate the Muslims' life from the time he wakes up to the time he sleeps – and even then, how he sleeps. Every single movement of the Muslim and every single act was subjected to the invasiveness of the Muslim clergy. The framers of Usool al-Fiqh embedded within their doctrines rules that provided for unlimited expansion. Kamali, a champion of Usool al-Fiqh, affectionately summarizes how intrusive Usool al-Fiqh became:

> [U]nlike its Western counterpart, Islamic jurisprudence is not confined to commands and prohibitions, and far less to commands which originate in a court of law. Its scope is much wider, as it is concerned not only with what a man must do or must not do, but also with what he ought to do or ought not to do, and the much larger area where his decision to do or to avoid doing something is his own prerogative. Usool al-fiqh provides guidance in all these areas, most of which remain outside the scope of Western jurisprudence.[93]

Human's legislation can fall under one or more of three categories. It can be derived from or inspired by the Mushaf, which is implicitly in accordance with the Allah's dictates; it can be derived from non-Mushaf sources while simultaneously not being contradictory to the Mushaf or not exceeding the upper limits (*hudood*) imposed by the Mushaf; or it can be derived from sources other than the Mushaf while being contradictory to the Mushaf. The first two categories can be perceived as Islamically-inspired legislation but not Islamic legislation.

The clergy have hypnotized the Muslim *umma* into believing that the clergy are indispensable. Most Muslims believe that there are numerous questions that have not been addressed directly and explicitly in the Mushaf such as polygamy. Should there be or not be polygamy. M4:3 addresses the case of orphans, but not a generic or specific directive about polygamy. Therefore, what does the Mushaf say about polygamy. The answer is that the Mushaf does not say anything. Does this mean the Muslim man can marry as many women as he wishes? The answer is that it is up to him and up to the laws of the land where he lives. In addition, marriage requires mutual consent. Islam has nothing to do with how many women a Muslim man can marry. Governments around the world regulate the halal and the haram but they never enforce the haram. For something to be halal does not mean that it is good or bad, for either the individual or society; it simply belongs to a class of behaviors that need to be evaluated by the relevant actors and its suitability to society and the individual. This bring up the issue of agency and freedom. Eating halal beef and French fries is certainly halal, as there is not one Muslim who would contest this claim. However, eating beef and fries everyday for several months can lead to a heart disease, arteries blockage and early death. The individual Muslim needs to make these choices independently of the intrusiveness of the Muslim clergy.

Usool al-Fiqh created a foundation, no matter how feeble, for the emergence of doctrines that parallel the Mushaf and that carry similar or higher weight in comparison to the divine revelation. The instigators of these new doctrines were likely the Umayyad and Abbasid rulers, who scavenged the Muslim landscape for scholars willing to bestow legitimacy on their brutal campaigns of conquest and subjugation of Muslim and non-Muslims. Usool al-Fiqh became a rich and regenerative religious medium that helped establish whatever the rulers wished for, such as dividing the world into *Dar al-Harb* (land of war) and *Dar al-Islam* (land of Islam), a division that is based on the concept of superiority, expansionism and the presumption of eternal hostility between Muslims and non-Muslims. Usool al-Fiqh opened the door wide to reframing the religion in a way to preoccupy the Muslim masses with trivial matters that are advocated as gates to salvation. Usool al-Fiqh and their Muslim clergy became a strong foundation for protecting despotism.

Usool al-Fiqh confused the division between Allah's legislation and that of humankind. Allah's legislation is fully described in the Mushaf. The Mushaf is an immutable constitution for humanity; only a few specifics apply to the followers of Muhammad. Part of Allah's legislation is non-enforceable, while other parts are. Humans, on the other hand, are entitled to legislate depending on the complexity and advancement of their societies. Most importantly, however, human legislation is outside the realm of the *deen*; it is not subjected to the halal-haram binary. For emphasis, nothing outside the Mushaf can be designated as haram. The central problem that Muslims have continued to reel from is the transformation of human-made legislation into religious legislation.

In the midst of this sea of confusion and contradictions that were facilitated by the doctrines of Usool al-Fiqh, a wide spectrum of rulings emerged. These rulings were based on mere opinions and not Allah's legislation. What could have started as a fully legitimate jurisprudential scholarship became widely accepted, by Muslims, as a canonized Islamic legislation (with the assumption that it is either divine or related to the divine). The concept of *takleef* and *hukm al-shar'i* invaded the legislative landscape with minimal resistance. The early framers of Usool al-Fiqh, backed by their benefactors, used a proven primordial tactic that deprived people of their rational ability — fear. Islam was refashioned from a religion based on guidance and freedom into a religion based on fear and control. Hellfire was made awaiting to engulf women who dared expose a few strands of their hair in front of men, wicked Angels waited to hang sinful women from their breasts, single-horned beasts waited to smash the head of a deceased person if he or she failed to correctly answer a question. A four-year university program in Usool al-Fiqh turned a graduate into a universal scholar with expertise ranging from gynecology to cosmology.

Towards the end of the 19th Century, many Muslim scholars believed that the wide-scale misfortunes of Muslims might be resolved if only Muslims would return to the spirit of Islam. Some notable and influential scholars of the late 19th Century, such as Ismail Farooqi and Taha Jaber al-Alwani, further argued that to solve the problems of humanity at large, all things needed to be Islamized. This led to a frenzy to Islamize everything, Islamization of art, sociology, economics, knowledge, etc. The thinking of the champions of Islamization was that Muslims ruled all over the globe and enjoyed their golden age when all things were "Islamic". This Islamization drive was essentially an extension of the Islamization of legislation. While the process of Islamization did not go as far as making certain knowledge haram and other halal, it was moving with that spirit.

The quintessential Islamization that was overlooked was the Islamization of Usool al-Fiqh. It can be argued that the solution to the Muslims' abyss could very much be the de-Islamization of all that the framers of Usool al-Fiqh turned into Islamic. De-Islamization of legislation is what is needed. This would be the very first step for Muslims to achieve their true religious freedom and their freedom of thought that can culminate in their freedom from the hegemony of the state and its religious courtiers. This would be the very step for Muslims to achieve their long-awaited renaissance.

1. Abu Rayyah, Mahmoud. *Deen Allah Wahid ala Alsinat al-Rusul.* Dar al-Karnak, [n.d.]. In recent years, several scholars have stressed the oneness of the religion. Abu Rayya seems to be the earliest person, at least of 20th Century Muslim scholars who devoted an entire book to this concept.
2. This particular verse is deeply profound in its impact on how Muslims view other people. This verse lists four categories of people, but does not refer to them uniformly. One can refer to a group or a sect by its name, say as in *Nasara* (most likely the followers of Jesus), or by an attribute such as "those who did so and so". This fine categorization is apparent in this verse. The first two groups are those who believed and those who *hadoo*. These characterizations are interesting and important. If those who believed referred to Muslims, why did Allah not list the Muslims instead? Similarly, if those who *hadoo* were the Jews, why did Allah not list the Jews instead? Nevertheless, the rewards are given not to members of the four groups but to members from within those groups who fulfill three conditions: belief in Allah, belief in the Latter Day and doing good deeds.
3. Shahrour, Muhammad. *Al-Qasas al-Qur'aani: Qiraa'ah Mu'aasira.* Dar al-Saqi, 2010, p. 77.
4. This analogy was inspired by a discussion with one of my graduate students who shall remain anonymous.
5. Reference to mathematics could help illustrate this point. If Isaac Newton's Principia Mathematica was revealed in its entirety in the 10th Century BC, it would be inconceivable that it would have had any effect then since a host of mathematical preliminaries were not established at that time.
6. Shahrour, Muhammad. *Al-Kitaab wa al-Qur'aan: Ro'ya Jadeedah.* Dar al-Saqi, 2011. Shahrour is perhaps the first person on record to expose the meaning of the word *ebad.* Shahrour showed that the Arabic word *ebad* could have two possible and opposite meanings: to obey or to disobey. Just like other Arabic words that imply two opposite meanings, the correct meaning is discerned from its context.
7. Al-Azhar University and Qum Seminaries are considered the highest seats of religious learning for the Sunni and Shia sects, respectively.
8. I attended a Muslim conference in the 1980s that included a prominent Muslim scholar who gained fame due to his political activities and writings. The conference organized a closed women-only session with this activist where Muslim women would be free to ask him about matters related to women's reproductive health and organs. This was despite the fact that this Muslim scholar/activist did not

have any formal training in Islam or even Sharia.
9. These philosophies mushroomed to full-blown expressions of rejecting anything that does not fit the "traditional" form of "Islamic" government. The concept of the "Islamic" government is either a theoretical construct or a model based on fragmented historical records that mixed truths with myths. See Qutb, Sayyid. *Ma'aalim fi al-Tariq*. Arab Center for Studies and Research, 2012.
10. Rabb, Intisar. "*Ijtihad*" *The Oxford Encyclopedia of the Islamic World*, edited by John L. Esposito, Oxford University Press, 2009.
11. Al-Owaid, Abdul-Aziz ibn Muhammad. *Usool al-Fiqh ind al-Sahaaba*. Kuwait Ministry of Waqf and Islamic Affairs, 2011.
12. Sunan abu Dawood, Kitaab al-Aqdhiya, no. 3592.
13. Notice that the Messenger praised himself by invoking the *salawaat* in this hadith. The salawaat is abbreviated as SAAWS (*sallah Allah alaihi wa sallam*).
14. Sahih al-Bukhari, Kitaab al-E'tisaam bi al-Kitaab wa al-Sunnah, no. 7352. Sunan abu Dawood, Kitaab al-Aqdhiya, no. 3574.
15. Kamali, Mohammad Hashim. *Principles of Islamic Jurisprudence*. 3rd ed., Islamic Texts Society, 1991, p. 372, 373. Al-Owaid. *Usool*, pp. 38-40.
16. Ibn al-Salah, abu Amr. *Uloom al-Hadith*. Sa'adah Press, 1908. Abu Rayyah, Mahmoud. *Adwa ala al-Sunnah al-Muhammadiyyah*. 6th ed., Dar al-Ma'aarif, 1957, pp. 45, 63.
17. One can sense a style in numerous books on Sharia and Fiqh where the advocated validity of a specific matter (*hukm*, etc.) is provided from Hadith, Sunnah, and surprisingly, when it is convenient, reason and logic are also used despite severe contempt for both amongst the Hadith and Sunnah framers in general.
18. Kamali. *Principles*, p. 373.
19. I define secondary books as those that compile the opinions of prominent Muslim scholars and clergy of Islam rather than give the original sources for their opinions.
20. Islahi, Amin Ahsan. *Islamic Law, Concept and Codification*. Islamic Publications, 1979, p. 109.
21. Kamali. *Principles*, p. 366.
22. Kamali. *Principles*, p. 367.
23. Kamali. *Principles*, p. 370.
24. Kamali. *Principles*, p. 371.
25. Kamali. *Principles*, p. 366.
26. Dhaif, Shawki. *Al-Madaris al-Nahawiyyah*. 7th ed., Dar al-Ma'arif, 1968. Dhaif discusses the emergence of different schools of Arabic

grammar in the second Muslim century and beyond.
27. The histories of Christians, Jews, Hindus and even Buddhists suggest many parallels.
28. Ibn al-Hajjaj, abul Hussain Muslim. *Sahih Muslim*. Translated by Nasiruddin al-Khattaab, Darussalam, 2007.
29. Sahih al-Bukhari, Kitaab al-E'tisaam bi al-Kitaab wa al-Sunnah, no. 7352.
30. Shahrur, Muhammad. *The Qur'an, Morality and Critical Reason: The Essential Muhammad Shahrur*. Translated by Andreas Christmann, Brill, 2009, p. 178.
31. See for example M2:229, 4:14, and 65:1.
32. Islam concurs with earlier revelations such as Judaism and Christianity (and most likely others) on unacceptable conducts. However, Islam came to put upper limits on punishments of transgressions with virtually no lower limits. For example, the wrongness of adultery and murder are immutable; however, the punishment of such wrongs or offenses could have possibly changed and finally been constrained by an upper limit as stated in the Mushaf.
33. Ibn Uthaymeen, Muhammad ibn Saleh. *Al-Sharh al-Mum'the ala Zad al-Mustaqni*. Vol. 7, Dar ibn al-Jewzy, 2003, pp. 39, 40. Ibn Uthaymeen provides a legal ruling legalizing marriage to a daughter that is a product of adultery. Ibn Uthaymeen reaffirms rulings widely attributed to Malik and al-Shafi'i, who argued that the daughter in such case is not a legal daughter since the biological parents were not married according to Islam.
34. Kamali. *Principles*, p. 321.
35. Kamali. *Principles*, p. 370.
36. Omar Awwass in his PhD dissertation entitled *Fatwa: the Evolution of an Islamic Legal Practice and its Influence on Muslim Society* (UMI Dissertation Publishing, UMI Number: 3623102) canonized the concept of Ifta using the following argument: "As the authoritative text for Muslims, the Qur'aan's responsive engagement of people's inquiries and concerns provided the epistemological legitimation for the validation of this practice in Muslim life. In other words, fatwa gained its acceptability as a valid form of legal practice and law production because it was something that was enunciated and practiced by the authoritative discourse of Islam (i.e. the Qur'aan)". The problem with Awass's reasoning and conclusion is that all inquiries documented in the Mushaf were answered by Allah, not even the Prophet.
37. Ibn Taymiyyah. *Fatawa al-Nisa*. Translated by Sayed Gad, [n.d.]

38. For some religiopolitical Muslim sects, such as Hizb al-Tahrir, demanding *al-hukm al-shar'i* became a highly intimidating tactic in their legal and social discourse.
39. Ibn Taymiyyah, Ahmed. *Majmoo'a al-Fatawa*. Saudi Ministry of Islamic Affairs, Dawa and Guidance, 2004. This is a 37-volume compendium of edicts issued by ibn Taymiyyah on a wide range of human behaviors. Ibn al-Mundhir. *Al-Ijma*. 2nd ed., Maktabat al-Furqan, 1999. Ibn al-Mundhir lists 765 religious questions on which he claimed the Muslim clergy made consensus. There must be many other questions on which consensus was not achieved.
40. Rida, Muhammad Rashid. *Fatawa al-Imam Muhammad Rashid Rida*. Dar al-Kitaab al-Jadeed, 2005. This 6-volume compendium contains more than 1060 fatwas in 2,774 pages.
41. Al-Qaradawi, Yusuf. *Moojibat Tagh'eer al-Fatwa fi Asrina*. Al-Ittihad al-Aalami li Ulama al-Muslimeen [n.d.], pp. 9, 10.
42. Al-Qaradawi, Yusuf. *The Lawful and the Prohibited in Islam*. American Trust Publications, [n.d.].
43. Al-Qaradawi. *The Lawful,* p. 130.
44. Notice that the Mushaf stresses *uboodiyat*, but the root of this term comes from *abada*. The brilliant exposition by Muhammad Shahrour, possibly the first ever of its kind, strongly indicates that *abada* has two possibilities, all in one: to obey willingly or to disobey willingly (see http://shahrour.org/?page_id=12. Accessed on 17 March 2019). This suggests that the concept of freedom is conceptualized in the Mushaf as *uboodiyat*.
45. Al-Qaradawi. *Moojibat,* p. 11. Al-Qaradawi attributes al-Shatibi's statement to vol. 4, p. 244 of al-Shatibi's *al-Muwafiqat*. However, no such statement was found in *al-Muwafiqat*.
46 Al-Qaradawi. *Moojibat,* p. 244.
47. http://www.alquds.co.uk/?p=797800. Accessed 17 March 2019.
48. Al-Tabari, abi Ja'far. *Ikhtilaaf al-Fuqa'ha*. Dar al-Kutub al-Aa'lamiyya, 1999. While the main objective of this book is to list more than 70 cases or questions that the Muslim clergy have differed on, it demonstrates that those clergy believed that almost everything in society needed their certification regarding its permissibility. The job of the Muslim clergy became tagging everything as either halal or haram.
49. Muslims must still make sure that their understanding of the Mushaf is correct. A case in point is the subject of inheritance (*earth*) and will (*wassyyah*), which have never been resolved in a way that does not contradict the Mushaf, but rather have been understood in light of

the practices of earlier Muslims irrespective of the correctness of such practices.

50. http://www.alquds.co.uk/?p=462445. Accessed 10 March 2019.
51. http://islam.ru/en/content/news/visit-occupied-jerusalem-haram-qaradawi]. Accessed 10 March 2019.
52. Ibid.
53. http://www.alquds.co.uk/?p=723812. Accessed 10 March 2019.
54. Hatina, Meir (ed.). *Guardians of Faith in Modern Times: 'Ulama' in the Middle East (Social, Economic and Political Studies of the Middle East and Asia)*, Brill, 2008, pp. 232. In the Kingdom of Saudi Arabia, the office of the Mufti was created in 1953 by King Abdul Aziz, the founder of the Kingdom. In 1969, King Faisal abolished the office and replaced it with The Ministry of Justice. In 1993, the Mufti position was restored.
55. In 2013, one year after the Egyptian revolution that toppled Husni Mubarak, al-Azhar elected the Grand Mufti through votes by senior scholars, but the appointment needed ratification by the sitting president of the county. The resemblance to the Catholic Church is stark. A stark difference between the two, however, is the political independence of the Catholic Church.
56. The Supreme Leader in post-revolution Iran assumes the position of the highest political and spiritual authority. Two-thirds majority of the 88-member Assembly of Experts elects the Supreme Leader.
57. The Malikis do not specify a particular period in which the Madinah people lived.
58. Fawzi, Ibrahim. *Tadween al-Sunnah*. Riad el-Rayyes Books, 1994, p. 116. Ibn Anas (aka Mailk), al-Shafi'i and al-Ghazali all had different definitions for Ijma.
59. Al-Shafi'i, Muhammad ibn Idris. *Al-Umm*. Daar al-Wafa, 2001, p. 220.
60. Al-Shafi'i. *Al-Umm*, pp. 220-223.
61. Al-Shafi'i. *Al-Umm*, pp. 220-223.
62. *Al-Shafi'i. Al-Risala*. Translated by Majid Khadduri, 2nd ed., the Islamic Texts Society, 1987, p. 78.
63. Al-Bahusein, Yaqoob. *Al-Ijma*. Maktabat al-Rushd, 2008, p. 219.
64. Al-Subki, Taj al-Deen. *Tabaqat al-Shafiyya al-Kubra*. Vol. 2, Dar Ihya al-Kutub al-Arabiyya, 1964, p. 245.
65. Fawzi. *Tadween*, p. 116.
66. Sunan abu Dawood, Kitaab al-Sunnah, no. 4597.
67. Rustum, Sad. *Al-Fi'ruq wa al-Matha'hib al-Islamiyya munth al-Bidayah*. Al-Awa'el, 2004, p. 388.

68. Fawzi. *Tadween,* pp. 77-97.
69. Al-Bahusein, Yaqoob. *Al-Ijma.* Maktabat al-Rushd, 2008, p. 21.
70. Al-Bahusein. *Al-Ijma,* pp. 20-26.
71. Al-Bahusein. *Al-Ijma,* p. 26. Al-Bahusein claims that there were tens of definitions of Ijma. Farooq, Mohammad Omar. *Towards our Reformation from Legalism to Value-Oriented Islamic Law and Jurisprudence.* The International Institute of Islamic Thought, 2011.
72. Ibn al-Mundhir. *Al-Ijma.* 2nd ed., Maktabat al-Furqan, 1999.
73. Fawzi. *Tadween,* p. 116. It is not clear whether Malik ibn Anas implied the people of Madinah who were living at his time or in any other period in history.
74. Ibn al-Salah. *Uloom,* p. 28.
75. Al-Affani, Syed Hussein. *Riyadh al-Jannah fi al-Rudd ala al-Madrasa al-Akliyya wa Munkiri al-Sunnah.* Dar al-Affani, 2005, p. 12.
76. *Ethm* is a specific Mushafic word that gives the general connotation of retardation or regress. See http://shahrour.org/?page_id=12. Accessed March 17 2019.
77. Hasan, Ahmad. *The Doctrine of Ijma: A Study of the Juridical Principle of Consensus.* [n.d.].
78. Hasan. *The Doctrine.*
79. Fawzi. *Tadween,* p. 117.
80. http://library.islamweb.net/newlibrary/display_book.php?idfrom=4306&idto=4397&bk_no=53&ID=638. Accessed 10 March 2019.
81. Kamali. *Principles,* p. 174. Al-Shawkani, Muhammad. *Irshad al-Fuhool ila Tahqiq al-Haqq min Ilm al-Usool.* Dar ibn al-Jewzy, [n.d.], p.71.
82. It is difficult, if not impossible, to know how certain practices evolved to be part of Islam's legislative canons. In fact, there are numerous practices that once given an Arabic designation or name, they become considered by mostly non-Arabs as connected somehow to Islam. For example, many Muslims consider the *rihla,* which literally means a trip or a journey, as an Islamic concept whereby a group of dedicated Muslims embark on a journey to seek divine knowledge. Examples abound in what is referred to as Islamic economics such as *mudarabah, iktinaz, mukhabarah,* etc.
83. Al-Shafi'i, Muhammad ibn Idris. *Al-Risala.* Dar al-Kutub al-Ilmiyyah, 1939, p. 503. Al-Shafi'i. *Al-Umm,* p. 479.
84. Al-Zarqa, Ahmed. *Sharh al-Qawa'id al-Fiqhiyya.* 2nd ed., Dar al-Qalam, 1989, p. 147. http://majles.alukah.net/t59330/. Accessed 17 March 2019.

85. Kamil, Umar Abdullah. *Al-Qawa'id al-Fiqhiyya al-Kubra wa Atharuha fi al-Mu'aamalaat al-Maliyyah.* [n.d.]. Al-Azhar University, PhD dissertation, p. 125. http://iefpedia.com/arab/wp-content/uploads/2009/08/-القواعد-الفقهية-الكبرى-واثرها-في-المعاملات-المالية .
86. One of the supervisors of the thesis was Ali Goma, the former grand Mufti of Egypt.
87. Shabbar, Saeed. *Al-Ijtihad wa al-Tajdeed fi al-Fikr al-Islami al-Mua'sir.* The International Institute of Islamic Thought, 2016, p. 19.
88. Al-Zarqa. *Sharh,* p. 185.
89. The *jizya* is an excellent example (see Chapter 4).
90. Jami al-Tirmidhi, Kitaab al-Wasaaya, no. 2120.
91. It is noteworthy that al-Tirmidhi assigned to this hadith a grade of *hasan* rather than *sahih*. Al-Albani, a 20th Century Muslim scholar of Hadith elevated the grade of the hadith to *sahih*. See Chapter 7 for more discussion on inheritance.
92. http://shahrour.org/?page_id=12. Accessed on 17 March 2019.
93. Kamali. *Principles*, p. 7.

10

TOWARDS A MUSLIM RENAISSANCE

تِلْكَ الدَّارُ الْآخِرَةُ نَجْعَلُهَا لِلَّذِينَ لَا يُرِيدُونَ عُلُوًّا فِي الْأَرْضِ وَلَا فَسَادًا وَالْعَاقِبَةُ لِلْمُتَّقِينَ

That last abode we will transform it for those who do not seek neither superiority on Earth nor corruption/rottenness (on Earth), and the eventual outcome is for the *mutaqeen*.

M28:83

In 1993, in the Haram of Madinah, the second most important site for Muslims after Mecca, and where the tomb of the Prophet is located, a morning worshipper by the name of Ali Mukhtar Abdul-Aaal was performing his pre-dawn prayers when he saw the entourage of an important visitor. This important visitor turned out to be the deposed president of Egypt, Hosni Mubarak, who was paying a visit to the tomb of the Prophet. Ali managed to get close to Mubarak and shouted at him, Mr. President, "Have cognizance and fear of Allah and rule with what Allah has revealed." In a matter of hours, Ali was detained by the Saudi police and within few days, he was shipped to Egypt to be severely tortured and jailed for 15 years. Abdul-Aaal was never charged with any crime.[1] His ordeal started in one of Muslims' holiest places (*haram*) where a Muslim should feel safe and secure more than any other place on earth.

Muslims' Greatest Challenge

By any standards, historical or contemporary, this story is chilling. More chilling still is the fact that no "Islamic" organization came to Abdul-Aaal's support. No Muslim group championed Ali's case or highlighted the brutality he suffered, the loss of 15 years of his life, for separating him from his loved ones and from his freedom, all for uttering few words in a Muslim holy sanctuary. It is even harder to imagine, in the 21st Century that such injustice could happen anywhere outside the Muslim world. The big question is why such injustice happens amidst people who claim to be the followers of a Prophet who was sent as a mercy to humankind. The answer must be related to Muslims' worldview, which was not shaped by the Mushaf. This worldview was instead shaped by the parallel doctrines that have come to be recognized as "Muslim tradition".

The Muslim tradition left Muslims in limbo. Muslims distanced themselves from the Mushaf using the pretext that only the *ulama* are capable of understanding a book that was sent as a guidance for all humanity including, a brilliant physicist and my grandmother who never attended school. But this pretext turned out to be hollow: the *ulama*, after all, turned out to be simply repeaters of what was said and done hundreds of years earlier. At distant times, when writing material was scarce, someone who memorized some of the Hadith and some verses of the Mushaf was very valuable to his or her Muslim community. In fact, that person was given the title *hafidh* (memorizer). Today, online search engines have replaced the Muslim clergy.

With the advent of the internet, the monopoly on knowledge has disappeared, possibly forever. The entire Mushaf, popular Mushaf *tafaasir*, practically the entire canonized Hadith corpus, and commentaries on Hadith, are now all available at the fingertips of any smartphone user. Since there is no compulsion in religion, one can leave the Mushaf at will and adopt whatever philosophy or doctrines one wishes. But the Muslims who effectively abandoned the Mushaf while retaining their Muslim identity have left it for vacuous "Islamic" doctrines full of contradictions. These Muslims do not find the injustice of depriving a man of 15 years of his life as a concern worth making noise about. After all, which chapter in Sahih al-Bukhari is dedicated to justice, freedom and human rights? These new Muslims divorced themselves from agency, placing the *hukm al-shari* above the principles of justice. These Muslims divorced themselves from their humanity, the very essence of their being as the Mushaf stresses.

Hardly any Muslim organization is interested or dedicated solely to protecting human rights for the likely reason that Muslim's tradition or canonized doctrines deprived Muslims from reality and pushed them to the practice of accumulation of rewards. Muslims became self-centered, despising this world (i.e., reality) and focusing only on the hereafter. The doctrines that overshadowed Islam created a me-first culture. The new doctrines would exalt the believers to do good deeds, not for the sake of goodness but for the sake of accumulating reward points (i.e., *ajr*). The clergy would exalt the believer to visit the sick, not primarily because the sick need consolation and support, but because there are rewards for performing such a visit. Muslims became deprived of the spirit of the religion and life, focusing only on the physical form. The Muslims view the world in a binary lens: *kufr* vs. Islam, halal vs. haram, and *ajr* worthy vs. non-*ajr* worthy. This view turned out to be the most harmful to Muslim societies, resulting in relegating them to irrelevance and to living on the margins of civilizations.

Human rights became a side note in the consideration of the average Muslim, since according to the parallel doctrines that many Muslims had adopted, this world ceases to be important. The average Muslim would values spending time in a Masjid to accumulate rewards (*ajr*) than spending time working with an organization that defends human rights. Any hesitation in choosing between the masjid and the human rights organization disappears if Christians, Jews or non-Muslims run these organizations.

The parallel doctrines violently isolated the Muslims from the Mushaf. Human rights and freedom were absent from the "Muslim tradition" since they were never principles or doctrines that the Umayyad or Abbasid dynasties championed. (The Hadith and Sunnah doctrines were brought to full fruition during the reign of these two dynasties). The doctrines of "tradition" helped creating different cultures. At the individual level, these doctrines created a culture of selfishness (the *ajr*-based culture). At the collective level, two types of Muslim groups emerged: The pacifists, such as the Sufi-like sects who emphasized spirituality and isolation from participatory living, and the *khilaafa* advocates, whose highest goals was ascending to (or usurping) power.

Searching for the halal and haram in everything deprived Muslims of the quintessential methods of progress, including searching for what is beneficial and what is not. The other type of binarization, that of labeling people as Muslim or not, also stifled effective and genuine engagement with humanity at large.

Years of mental slavery have created the binary Muslim. This binary Muslims insists on viewing everything as halal or haram. The binary Muslim is conditioned to view whatever is abhorrent or repugnant as haram. From shaking hands between males and females to slavery, the Muslim mind seeks a ruling or a fatwa for its halalness or haramness. The reason behind Adam's creation has been forgotten, never understood, or used merely as a filler for "Islamic" children's stories. Take for example slavery. While slavery in its historical and classic form is not a burning issue for Muslims to be concerned with at this time, the idea that slavery is not haram as dictated by the Mushaf puts the binary Muslim in a quandary: the assumed sub-narrative would make Islam look like a barbaric or unjust religion. The binary Muslim wants a quick religious ruling on slavery.

The insatiable urge for seeking the ruling on slavery and thousands of other matters, actions, technologies, inventions, behaviors and even using the modern toilet, has led to two dangerous consequences. First, it created a demand for more clergy while enlarging their authority and perceived importance to the Muslim community. Second, it deprived the Muslims of active social engagement and meaningful debate to carefully and continuously assess the trade-off between the benefits and drawbacks of all things in life. The fact that slavery is not haram is not an encouragement to institutionalize it. In the same vein, not all things that are halal are good for humans. Some are in fact extremely harmful.

The infatuation with the past and the insistent marginalization of Muslims made them look to the past for salvation and improvement in all facets of life. Muslims' feeling that the best is behind them and that the best of people lived long ago diminished their self-realization of the potential to advance and contribute to civilizations, and to have sufficient power to ensure their security and independence. The concept of tradition was conflated with the past. Tradition became the epitome of idealism that deprived Muslims from using the past to refine and improve their present. Emulating the "learned scholars" of the past became the aspirations of modern *ulama*. These *ulama* dig deep into the past for whatever ibn Taymiyyah, al-Ghazali, al-Shafi'i, al-Nawawi, al-Jewziyyah, ibn Kathir, or other historic figures commented on in search of rulings to please fatwa-hungry Muslims.

Looking into the past became a downward spiral. The Muslims rejected the two essential elements of progress, evolution and feedback. Emulating the past became desirous, with nostalgia for the past and for the days "the nations bowed at the Muslims' feet" becoming Muslims' dream.

The Muslim clergy, with acquiescence from the marginalized Muslim masses, turned history into a religion. The behaviors and actions of the companions of the prophet, the generation that succeeded the companions, the next generation and so on, all became canonized religion. What the Righteous Caliphs did became unquestionable religion, even if they believed that the Mushaf that we have today is incomplete. No longer would Muslims seek an answer from the Mushaf but from history, irrespective of its authenticity. Muslims became encapsulated within the past. Whenever "reformers" try to free Muslims from this bondage, the overbearing pressure of the Muslim tradition quashes them.

For the preconditioned Muslim mind, the future is static, all was fixed when Allah created the universe millions of years ago. Since all future events including one's earnings, health, and time of death are all fixed, there is little genuine incentive to do any serious planning of one's own. The overwhelming weight of the Hadith and Sunnah doctrines and their penetration into the psyche of Muslims frightens many Muslims from challenging the doctrine of predestination. If a Muslim experiences abuse, torture or imprisonment, it is all swallowed as Allah's will, predestined to happen. Therefore, the pious, God-fearing Muslim should accept all these miseries with patience and open arms.

For example, the Mushaf elevated patience, as a virtue or a practice, to a level equal to that of *salat*. However, this extremely important practice has become a justification for subservience and servitude. Lost on the Muslim mind that patience is not an end in itself but rather a means to achieve ends. The new parallel doctrines deprived the Muslim of any incentive to do anything or to have hope for the future, only to wait for the end and to accept one's "fate" with grace, patience and as a form of *ibadat* (worship). In this manner, the past became a source of Muslims' retardation and the future left beyond their control and irrelevant to their will. The human will has been obliterated despite its prominence in Allah's revelation. At the end, the Muslims became frozen in time, living on the margins of civilizations.

Muslims' Greatest Challenge

Whereas the Mushaf encouraged Muslims to participate in life and stressed the importance of governance, the Muslim clergy, armed with their parallel doctrines, discouraged participation in governance and projected it as participation in politics. The clergy encouraged seclusion and isolation; they also encouraged static and ceremonial participation, such as in congregational prayers and similar activities. In such condoned collective activities, the monologue of the ruling elites and their sanctioned clergy is dominant. The concept of participation becomes vacuous. Participation in form was emphasized but not in substance. Congregational prayers were encouraged only because of the additional rewards it brings to Muslims rather than its political and societal implications. Masajid (mosques) are open for the "business" of *ajr* accumulation, not for any other purpose. Outside the *ajr* activities, the masajid are locked.

While the Mushaf stressed the substance and never mentioned the forms, Muslims' participation in life and in worship contradicted the Mushaf by heavily focusing on the form rather than the substance. Muslim clergy became obsessed with details, whereas the Mushaf never mentioned details. Allegedly, the raison d'être of the Hadith corpus was providing the details that the Mushaf intentionally did not incorporate. Since Islam was completed with the conclusion of the revelation, the details that were added later on could not have been part of Islam. Allah did not send prophets and Angels to instruct humans how to cleanse themselves. After all, cats know how to cleanse themselves without any revelation. Humans do not need a prophet to remind them to defend themselves and their land if attacked. Allah commanded Muslims to give charity, but never specified how much. Allah encouraged Muslims to perform Hajj and Umra, but never gave details. Allah encouraged Muslims to fast because, according to the revelation, it is good for humans to fast. The clergy, however, made fasting an act of worship and created an entire code of conduct during fasting and even an entire fiqh of fasting. Under the guise of *tibyaan* (clarification), a new religion was created as an addendum, or replacing to the revelation.

Muslim clergy became a professional class concerned with preserving the "guild" in the same way artisans, carpenters, lawyers, medical doctors, teachers, welders and other professionals put considerable effort to ensure the survival of their profession. Their biggest selling point was that without the clergy, Islam would disappear. However, this selling point is only to preserve their guild. Allah promised that He would preserve the religion, no one else. The Muslim clergy have inserted themselves between the Muslims and Allah. These clergy are the key impediment to Muslim emancipation. If Muslims are satisfied with Allah's revelation, then they should live under the shadow of their creator, no one else.

The people of religions evolve in similar, and, perhaps, natural ways. Christians evolved throughout the past two thousand years to where they are now. The evolution of Christianity starkly parallels the evolution of Muslims. Christians turned Jesus into a God. Muslims claimed that Muhammad was empowered with Godly attributes, thus effectively making him a partner with God. Christians institutionalized religion by creating the concept of the Church that regulates and controls how religion is dispensed to the masses. Muslims created the concept of Rijaal al-Deen (the men of religion) which culminated in religious institutions, such as al-Azhar, that monopolized religion and dispensed its consumables to the masses. Muslims created religious institutions that were given the authority to issue fatwas and religious ruling for what is haram and what is halal. Christians considered the Godly revelation not only the words of Jesus but also those of other disciples and saints.[2] Muslims also added the Hadith and the Sunnah as an integral part of Islam and as a divine revelation. Christians created the concept of the Papal infallibility and religious authority. Muslims made the Prophet infallible and elevated the status of his companions to virtual infallibility. Christians considered Jesus the Spirit of God. Shia Muslims named some Imams the Spirit of God. Christians at some point in their history restricted reading the Bible and persecuted anyone who attempted to translate it from Latin into English.[3] While Muslim clergy did not preach against translation of the Mushaf into other languages or explicitly restricted its distribution, they, however, claimed that the Mushaf cannot be understood without the clergy. The Christians for years kept the Bible in Latin. Muslim clergy used Arabic grammar to shield the Muslims from the Mushaf.

The Christians revolted against the dominance of the Church, against the petrification of religion and against the Church clergy who acted as gatekeepers to Paradise. The revolt came through a period of inquiry and learning that could have been influenced by the interaction between Christians and Muslims through Spain and Sicily. Ironically, that exchange between the two peoples was symmetrical whereby Muslims inherited Europe's medieval ethos. Nevertheless, all these factors led to Christians achieving their Renaissance and emancipation from the Church.

Are Muslims heading towards their long-awaited renaissance and emancipation from all dead and living Muslim clergy and all parallel doctrines that came to replace Islam?

---

1. http://mubasher.aljazeera.net/news/-وفاة-الرجل-الذي-قال-لمبارك-اتق-الله-فاعتقله-15-عاما
2. Michale D. Googan, editor. *The Illustrated Guide to World Religions*. Oxford University Press, 2003.
3. https://www.huffingtonpost.com/bernard-starr/why-christians-were-denied-access-to-their-bible-for-1000-years_b_3303545.html.
HTTP://WWW.ALOHA.NET/~MIKESCH/BANNED.HTM

Bibliography

Abdo, Ehab Hasan. *Istihalat Wujood al-Naskh fi al-Qur'aan.* (Published online), 2004.

Abu Abdul-Rahman, Muqbil. *Al-Shafa'a.* 3rd ed., Dar al-Aa'thar, 1999.

Abu Rayyah, Mahmoud. *Adwa'a ala al-Sunnah al-Muhammadiyyah.* 6th ed., Dar al-Ma'aarif, 1957.

Abu Rayyah, Mahmoud. *Deen Allah Wahid ala Alsinat al-Rusul.* Dar al-Karnak, [n.d.].

Ahmad, Aziz. *History of Islamic Sicily.* Columbia University Press, 2000.

Al'aika, Sultan and al-Ssahib, Muhammad. *Asbab Tafawuk al-Sahaaba fi Thabt al-Hadith.* Dar ibn Aljaoozi, 2010.

Al-Affani, Sayed ibn Hussein. *Riyadh al-Jannah fi al-Rudd ala al-Madrasa al-Akliyya wa Munkiri al-Sunnah.* Dar al-Aaffani, 2006.

Al-Ahmadi, Abdullah ibn Salman. *Al-Masa'el wa al-Rasa'el.* Vol. 2, Dar Taybeh, 1991.

Al-Akl, Nasir ibn Abdul Karim. *Al-Itijahat al-Aklanyya al-Haditha.* Dar al-Fadhylah, 2001.

Al-Albani, Muhammad Nasser. Dhaeef al-Jam'I al-Saghir wa Ziyadatahu. Al-Maktab al-Islami, 1988.

Al-Asqalani, Ahmed ibn Ali ibn Hajar. *Fath al-Baree fi Sharh Sahih al-Bukhari.* Vol. 1, Dar al-Ma'rifa, 2001

Al-Asqalani, Ahmed ibn Ali ibn Hajar. *Tahdheeb al-Tahdheeb.* Vol. 9, Da'ira Ma'arif Nizamia, 1908.

Al-Athari, abu al-Zahra'a. *Ia'that al-Nathar fi Tahqiq Qawl al-Bukhari Fihi Nathar,* [.n.d.].

Al-Baghdadi, Abi Mansour. *Al-Nasikh wa al-Mansookh.* Dar al-Adwa, [n.d.].

Al-Baghdadi, abu Bakr. *Al-Kifaayah fi Ilm al-Riwaayah.* Al-Maktaba al-Ilmiyyah, [n.d.].

Al-Bahusein, Yaqoob. *Al-Ijma.* Maktabat al-Rushd, 2008.

Al-Barbahari, abu Muhammad. *Sharh al-Sunnah.* Dar Makkah International, 2014.

Al-Darmi, AbdAllah ibn Abd al-Rahman. *Sunan al-Darmi* (*aka Musnad al-Darmi*). Dar al-Mughni, 2000.

Al-Dimashki, abi al-Fida ibn Kathir. *Al-Takmeel fi al-Jarh wa al-Ta'deel wa Ma'rifat al-Thiqat wa al-Dua'fa wa al-Majaheel.* Vol. 1, Markaz Al-Numan, 2011.

Al-Fahid, Nasir ibn Hamad. *Haqiqat al-Hadharah al-Islamiyya.* Manbar al-Tawheed wa al-Jihad, [n.d.].

Al-Hamadani, Mohammad ibn Musa. *Al-Itibar fi al-Nasikh wa al-Mansookh min al-Akhbaar. Da'erat al-Ma'arif al-Uthmanyya,* 1940.

Al-Hasany, Hashim Maroof. *Al-Mawdoa'at fi al-Aa'thar wa al-Aakhbar*. Dar al-Ta'aruf Lilmatboo'at, 1987.

Al-Jarjani, abi Ahmad. *Al-Kamil fi Dua'afa al-Rijal*. Vol. 1, Maktabat al-Rushd, [n.d.].

Al-Jewziyya, ibn Qaiyyem. *Shifa al-Aleel fi al-Qada wa al-Qadar*. Almaktaba Altawfeeqyyah, [n.d.].

Al-Jewziyyah, ibn Qayyem. *Kitaab al-Rooh*. Dar al-Turath, 2003.

Al-Jewziyyah, ibn Qayyem. *The Medicine of the Prophet*. Islamic Text Society, 1998.

Al-Kannouji, abi al-Tayyeb. *Al-Hittah fi Thikr al-Sihah al-Sittah*. Dar al-Jeel, [n.d.].

Al-Khamis, Mohammad ibn Abdulrahman. *Etikaad al-A'imma al-Arba'ah: abi Hanifa wa Malik wa al-Shafi'i wa Ahmed*. Dar al-Ismah, 1992.

Al-Khoei, abu al-Qasim. *Al-Bayan fi Tafsir al-Qur'aan*. Anwar al-Huda, 1981.

Al-Mahalli, Jalal al-Deen and al-Toosi, Jalal al-Deen. *Tafsir al-Jalalayn*. Dar al-Hadith, [n.d.].

Al-Mutairi, Hakim Ubaisan. *Tarikh Tadween al-Sunnah wa Shubhat al-Mustashriqeen*. Kuwait University, 2002.

Al-Naas, abi al-Fath ibn Muhammad ibn Sayyid. *Uyoon al-A'thaar fi Funoon al-Maghazi wa al-Shama'el wa al-Siyar*. Vol. 1, Dar ibn Kathir, 1977.

Al-Nahhaas, abu Ja'far. *Al-Nasikh wa al-Mansookh*. Al-Maktaba al-Alamiyya, 1938.

Al-Nawawi, abu Zakaria Yahya ibn Sharaf. *Al-Athkaar*. Dar al-Rayyan Lilturath, al-Dar al-Masriyyah al-Lubnaniah, 1988.

Al-Nawawi, abu Zakaria Yahya ibn Sharaf. *Al-Minhaj fi Sharhi Sahih Muslim*. Al-Mutba'ah al-Masriyyah, 1929.

Al-Nawawi, abu Zakaria Yahya ibn Sharaf. *Tahtheeb al-Asma wa al-Lughaat*. Vol. 1, Dar al-Kutub al-Ilmiyyah, [n.d.].

Al-Owaid, Abdul-Aziz ibn Muhammad. *Usool al-Fiqh ind al-Sahaaba*. Kuwait Ministry of Waqf and Islamic Affairs, 2011.

Al-Qaradawi, Yousuf. *Moojibat Tagh'eer al-Fatwa fi Asrina*. Al-Ittihad al-Aalami li Ulama al-Muslimeen [n.d.].

Al-Qaradawi, Yusuf. *The Lawful and the Prohibited in Islam*. American Trust Publications, [n.d.].

Al-Razi, abu Jafar. *Al-Kafi*. 3rd ed., vol. 1, Dar al-Hadith, 1972.

Al-Sa'di, Abdur-Rahman ibn Nasir. *Tayseer al-Kareem al-Rahman fi Tafsir Kalam al-Mannan (Tafsir al-Sa'di)*. 2nd ed., Dar al-Salam, 2002.

Al-Sadr, Baqar. *Iqtisaduna*. Al-Alami, 2010.

Al-Sadr, Baqar. *Falsafatuna*. Dar al-Ta'aaruf, 1980.

Al-Shafi'i, al-Imam Muhammad ibn Idris. *Al-Risala fi Usul al-Fiqh*. Translated by Majid Khadduri. 2nd ed., Islamic Text Society, 1961.

Al-Shafi'i, Muhammad ibn Idris. *Al-Risala*. Dar al-Kutub al-Ilmiyyah, 1939.

Al-Shafi'i, Muhammad ibn Idris. *Kitaab al-Umm*. Dar al-Wafa, 2001.

Al-Sharayri, Mansour Mahmoud Muhammad. "Hadith al-Wasiyya bil-Thaqalyen: Dirasa Hadithiyya." *Umm al-Qura Magazine for Sharia Sciences and Islamic Studies*, no. 51, 2011.

Al-Shatibi, abu Ishaq. *Al-Muwafiqat*. Vol. 4, Dar ibn Affan, 1997.

Al-Shawkani, Muhammad. *Irshad al-Fuhool ila Tahqiq al-Haqq min Ilm al-Usool*. Dar ibn al-Jewzy, [n.d.].

Al-Subki, Taj al-Deen. *Tabaqat al-Shafiyya al-Kubra*. Vol. 2, Dar Ihya al-Kutub al-Arabiyya, 1964.

Al-Suyuti, Jalal al-Deen. *Tadween al-Raawee*. Vol. 1, 2nd ed., Maktaba al-Kawthar, 1994.

Al-Suyuti, Jalal al-Deen. *The Medicine of the Prophet*. Ta-Ha, 2015.

Al-Suyuti, Jalal al-Deen. *Al-Itqaan fi Uloom al-Qur'aan*. King Fahd Complex for Printing the Noble Mushaf, 2005.

Al-Tabari, abi Ja'far. *Ikhtilaaf al-Fuqa'ha*. Dar al-Kutub al-Aa'lamiyya, 1999.

Al-Tabari, Muhammad ibn Jarir. *Jami al-Bayaan ann Taweel al-Qur'aan (Tafsir al-Tabari)*. Dar al-Kutub al-Ilmiyyah, 2009.

Al-Thahabi, Shams al-Deen. *Siyar a'Laam al-Nubala*. 11th ed., Mu'assassat al-Risalah, 1996.

Al-Tusi, abu Ja'far Muhammad ibn Hasan. *Tahdhib al-Ahkaam*. Vol. 10, Dar al-Ta'aaruf, [n.d.].

Al-Uwaid, Abdulaziz. *Usool al-Fiqh ind al-Sahaaba*. 25th ed., al-Wai al-Islami, 2011.

Al-Wahidi, Ali ibn Ahmad. *Asbaab al-Nuzool*. Royal A'al al-Bayt Institute for Islamic Thought, 2008.

Al-Zahrani, Mohammad. *Tadween al-Sunnah al-Nabawiyyah*. Dar al-Hijrah, 1996.

Al-Zarqa, Ahmed. *Sharh al-Qawa'id al-Fiqhiyya*. 2nd ed., Dar al-Qalam, 1989.

Al-Zarqani, Muhammad Abdul-Adhim. *Manahil al-Irfan fi Uloom al-Qur'aan*. Dar al-Kitaab al-Arabi, 1995.

Awwass, Omar. *Fatwa: the Evolution of an Islamic Legal Practice and its Influence on Muslim Society* (UMI Dissertation Publishing, UMI Number: 3623102).

Bosworth, Clifford Edmund. *The Islamic Dynasties*. Columbia University Press, 1996.

Brown, Jonathan. *Hadith*. Oneworld, 2009.

Brown, Jonathan. *Misquoting Muhammad.* Oneworld, 2014.
Brown, Jonathan. *The Canonization of al-Bukhari and Muslim: The formation and Function of the Sunni Hadith Canon.* Brill Publisher, 2007.
Cahen, Cl., Inalcik, Halil and Hardy, P. "Djizya". *Encyclopaedia of Islam,* edited by P. Bearman, Th. Bianquis, C.E. Bosworth, E. van Donzel, and W.P. Heinrichs. 2nd ed., Accessed 29 August 2016.
Chomsky, Noam. *On Power and Ideology.* South End Press, 1990.
Chossudovsky, Michel. *America's War on Terrorism.* 2nd ed., Center for Research on Globalization, 2005.
Coulson, Noel. *A History of Islamic Law.* Edinburgh University Press, 1984.
Czerepinski, Kareema. *Tajweed Rules of the Qur'aan.* Sarawar, Part 1, 2003.
Dhaif, Shawki. *Al-Madaris al-Nahawiyyah.* 7th ed., Dar al-Ma'arif, 1968.
Di Francia, G. Toraldo. *The Investigation of the Physical World.* Cambridge University Press, 1981.
Eghbariyya, Musa Mahmoud. *Al-Buloogh wa al-Rushd fi al-Sahria al-Islamiyya.* Dar al-Kutub al-Ilmiyyah, 2011.
Farooq, Mohammad Omar. *Towards our Reformation from Legalism to Value-Oriented Islamic Law and Jurisprudence.* The International Institute of Islamic Thought, 2011.
Fatoohi, Louay. *Abrogation in the Qur'an and Islamic Law.* Routledge, 2013.
Fawzi, Ibrahim. *Tadween al-Sunnah.* Riad el-Rayyes Books, 1994.
Hamza, Muhammad. *Al-Hadith al-Nabawi wa Makanatahoo fi al-Fikr al-Islami.* Al-Markaz al-Thaqafi al-Arabi, 2015.
Hasan, Ahmad. *The Doctrine of Ijma: A Study of the Juridical Principle of Consensus.* [n.d.].
Hashim al-Husaini. *Al-Mawdw'aat fi al-Aa'thaar wa al-Akhbaar.* Dar al-Ta'aruf, 1987.
Hatina, Meir (ed.). *Guardians of Faith in Modern Times: 'Ulama' in the Middle East (Social, Economic and Political Studies of the Middle East and Asia),* Brill, 2008.
Ibn al-Hajjaj, abu al-Hussain Muslim. *Sahih Muslim.* Translated by Nasiruddin al-Khattaab, 4th ed., Darussalam, 2007.
Ibn al-Munther. *Al-Ijma.* 2nd ed., Maktabat al-Furqan, 1999.
Ibn al-Salah, abu Amr. *Uloom al-Hadith.* Dar al-Fikr, 2002.
Ibn al-Salah, abu Amr. *Uloom al-Hadith.* Sa'adah Press, 1908.
Ibn Anas, Malik. *Al-Muwatta,* 3rd ed., Diwan Press, 2014.
Ibn Baz, Abdul-Aziz ibn Abdu-Allah. "Clear Proof of the Disbelief of Whoever Claims it is Allowable for Anyone to Leave the Sharia of

Muhammad." *Al-Dawa Magazine*, 1995.

Ibn Hanbal, Ahmed. *Al-Rudd ala al-Jahamiyyah wa al-Zanadiqah*. Dar al-Thabaat, 2003.

Ibn Hanbal, Ahmed. *Kitaab al-Sunnah*. Al-Matb'ah al-Salafiyyah, 1930.

Ibn Hanbal, Ahmed. *Usool Ahl al-Sunna*.

Ibn Hisham, abi Abdulmalik. *Al-Seerah al-Nabawiyya*. Dar al-Fikr, 1965.

Ibn Ishaq, Muhammad. *Al-seerah al-Nabawiyya (Seerat ibn Ishaq)*. Dar al-Kutub al-Ilmiyyah, 2004.

Ibn Kathir, abu al-Fida Imaduddin Ismail. *Book of Evidences: The Miracles of the Prophet*. Translated by Ali Mwinyi Mziwa and ibn R. Ramadhan, Dar al-Ghad, 2001.

Ibn Kathir, abu al-Fida Imaduddin Ismail. *Stories of the Prophet*, Darussalam, 2003.

Ibn Kathir, abu al-Fida Imaduddin Ismail. *Stories of the Prophets*. Darus-Salam Publications, 2016.

Ibn Kathir, abu al-Fida Imaduddin Ismail. *Tafseer al-Qur'aan al-Azeem (Tafsir ibn Kathir)*. Dar al-Salaam, 2012.

Ibn Khaldun. *Al-Muqaddimah*. Vol. 1, Dar al-Awdah, 1981.

Ibn Khaldun. *Al-Muqaddimah: An Introduction to History* Abridged Edition. Translated by Franz Rosenthal. Abridged and edited by N. J. Dawood. Princeton University Press, 2015.

Ibn Manzur, Muhammad ibn Mukarram. *Lisan al-Arab*. 3rd ed., Dar Sader, 2000.

Ibn Qudamah, Muwaffiq al-Deen. *Al-Maghni*. Dar Aalam al-Kutub, 3rd ed., 1997.

Ibn Qutaybah, Abdullah. *Ta'weel Mukhta'laf al-Hadith*. Al-Maktab al-Islami, 1999.

Ibn Taymiyyah, Taqi al-Deen Ahmad. *Al-Sarim al-Maslool ala Shatim al-Rasool*. Al-Ramadi, 1997.

Ibn Taymiyyah, Taqi al-Deen Ahmad. *Al-Sarim al-Maslool ala Shatim al-Rasool*. Vol. 2, 2nd ed., Dar al-Tawsweeq al-Duwliyya, 2007.

Ibn Taymiyyah, Taqi al-Deen Ahmad. *Majmoo al-Fataawi*. Vol. 20, King Fahd Complex for Printing the Noble Mushaf, [n.d.].

Ibn Taymiyyah, Taqi al-Deen Ahmed. *Majmoo'a al-Fatawa*. Saudi Ministry of Islamic Affairs, Dawa and Guidance, 2004.

Ibn Taymiyyah. *Fatawa al-Nisa*. Translated by Sayed Gad, [n.d.]

Ibn Uthaymeen, Muhammad ibn Saleh. *Al-Sharh al-Mum'the ala Zad al-Mustaqni*. Vol. 7, Dar ibn al-Jewzy, 2003.

Ilal, Rachid. *Sahih al-Bukhari: Nihayat Ustoora*. Dar al-Watan, 2017.

Islahi, Amin Ahsan. *Islamic Law, Concept and Codification*. Islamic Publications, 1979.

Itr, Noor al-Deen. *Manhaj al-Naqd fi Uloom al-Hadith*. 2nd Ed., Dar al-

Fikr, 1979.

Jami al-Tirmidhi. www.sunnah.com.

Kamali, Mohammad Hashim. *Principles of Islamic Jurisprudence*. 3rd ed., Islamic Texts Society, 1991.

Kamil, Umar Abdullah. *Al-Qawa'id al-Fiqhiyya al-Kubra wa Atharuha fi al-Mu'aamalaat al-Maliyyah*. [n.d.]. Al-Azhar University, PhD dissertation.

Keller, Nuh Ha Mim. *The Concept of Bid'ah in the Islamic Shari'a*. The Muslim Academic Trust, 1999.

Khomeini, Roohallah. *Islam and Revolution: Writings and Declarations of Imam Khomeini*. Translated and annotated by Hamid Algar, Mizan Press, 1981.

Kurzman, Charles and Ernst, Carl. "Islamic Studies in U.S. Universities". *Review of Middle East Studies*, vol. 46, Middle East Studies Association of North America (MESA), 2012.

Lacey, Robert. *The Kingdom: Arabia and the House of Saud*. Harcourt Brace Jovanovich, 1981.

Luntz, Frank. *The Israel Project's 2009 Global Language Dictionary*. available at: https://www.transcend.org/tms/wp-content/uploads/2014/07/sf-israel-projects-2009-global-language-dictionary.pdf. Accessed 6 February 2019.

Michot, Yahya. "Ibn Taymiyyah's 'New Mardin Fatwa'. Is genetically modified Islam (GMI) carcinogenic? *The Muslim World*, Hartford Seminary, Blackwell Publishing Ltd., 2011.

Muir, William. *The Life of Mahomet*. Vol. 4, Smith, Elder and Co, 1861.

Murtadha, Muhammad Mahmoud. *Falsafat al-Ismah ind al-Shia*. Dar al-Wila'a, 2015.

Musnad Fatimah al-Zahra. Dar al-Safwah, [n.d.].

Mustafa, Muhammad Salih Ali. *Al-Naskh fi al-Qur'aan al-Kareem*. Dar al-Qalam, 1988.

Mutahari, Murtadha. *Al-Nabi al-Ummi*. MSA of US & Canada (PSG), [n.d.].

Ouzon, Zakareya. *Jinayat Seebaaway*. Riyad al-Rayyes Books, 2002.

Qutb, Sayyid. *Fi Thilal al-Qur'aan*. Dar al-Shurooq, 2008.

Qutb, Sayyid. *Ma'aalim fi al-Tariq*. Arab Center for Studies and Research, 2012.

Rabb, Intisar. "*Ijtihad*" *The Oxford Encyclopedia of the Islamic World*, edited by John L. Esposito, Oxford University Press, 2009.

Rida, Muhammad Rashid. *Fatawa al-Imam Muhammad Rashid Rida*. Dar al-Kitaab al-Jadeed, 2005.

Riyadh al-Saliheen, www.sunnah.com.

Rustum, Sad. *Al-Fi'ruq wa al-Matha'hib al-Islamiyya munth al-Bidayah*, al-

Awa'el, 2004.
Sabiq, Sayyid. *Fiqh al-Sunnah*. Vol. 2, Dar al-Kitaab al-Arabi, 1973.
Sahih al-Bukhari. www.sunnah.com.
Sahih Muslim. www.sunnah.com.
Said, Edward. *Orientalism*. Vintage, 1979.
Shabbar, Saeed. *Al-Ijtihad wa al-Tajdeed fi al-Fikr al-Islami al-Mua'sir*. The International Institute of Islamic Thought, 2016.
Shah, Muhammad Sultan. *Evolution and Creation*. Society for Interaction of Religion-Science and Technology, 2010.
Shaheen, Jack. "Arab and Muslim Stereotyping in American Popular Culture". *Occasional Papers Series*, Center for Muslim-Christian Understanding, Georgetown University, 1997.
Shaheen, Jack. *Guilty: Hollywood's Verdict on Arabs After 9/11*. Olive Branch Press, 2007.
Shahrour, Muhammad. *Al-Kitaab wa al-Qur'aan: Ro'ya Jadeedah*. Dar al-Saqi, 2011.
Shahrour, Muhammad. *Al-Qasas al-Qur'aani: Qiraa'ah Mu'aasira*. Vol. 1, Dar al-Saqi, 2010.
Shahrour, Muhammad. *Al-Sunnah al-Rasooliyya wa al-Sunnah al-Nabawiyya*. Dar al-Saqi, 2011.
Shahrour, Muhammad. *Nahwa Usool Jadeeda Lilfiqh al-Islami*. Dar al-Saqi, 2018.
Shahrur, Muhammad. *The Qur'an, Morality and Critical Reason: The Essential Muhammad Shahrur*. Translated by Andreas Christmann, Brill, 2009.
Sunan abi Dawood. www.sunnah.com.
Sunan ibn Majah. www.sunnah.com.
Tabatabaa'i, Muhammad Husayn. *Al-Mizan*. Al-Aa'la, 1997.
Trabishi, George. *Min Islam al-Qur'aan ila Islam al-Hadith*, 3rd ed., Dar al-Saqi, 2015.
Translations of the Mushaf. www.quran.com
Ullmann, Manfred. *Islamic Medicine*. Edinburgh University Press, 1740.
Watt, William Montgomery. *Islamic Political Thought*. Edinburgh University Press, 1987.
Williamson, Jeffrey G. and Clingingsmith, David. *India's Deindustrialization in the 18th and 19th Centuries* (PDF). Harvard University, 2005.

INDEX

A

a'immah, 206, 207
a'lam, 198
aa'lim, 344
aalim, 345, 346
aamanoo, 337
aata, 286
aatakum, 285
aayaat, 72, 95, 97, 162, 168, 188, 247, 248, 249, 250, 259, 302, 343
aayah, 239, 244, 245, 246, 247, 248, 249, 250, 256, 259, 356
Abadhi, 22
Abbasid, 5, 12, 13, 19, 51, 65, 101, 116, 130, 243, 293, 316, 352, 357, 358, 380, 384, 396
abd, 98, 306
Abdo, Ehab Hasan, 258, 402
Abdo, Muhammad, 182
Abi Kathir, 265
Abi Sufiyan, 370
abrogation, 124, 141, 214, 238, 239, 241, 242, 243, 244, 245, 246, 247, 250, 251, 253, 254, 259, 289, 309, 331, 357, 381
abrogator, 188, 236, 259
Abu Abdul-Rahman, Muqbil, 328, 402
Abu Dawood, 152, 162, 251, 267, 293, 304, 330, 332, 349, 354, 388, 391
Abu Hanifa, 74, 105, 117, 132, 133, 134, 156, 167, 183, 403
Abu Rayyah, Mahmoud, 327, 387, 388, 402
Adam, 77, 80, 170, 174, 178, 309, 315, 316, 338, 339, 340, 341, 397
adhriboohun, 66, 67
Afghanistan, 4, 110, 111, 116
Ahkam, 333
Ahl al-Adl, 17
Ahl al-Bait, 124, 207
ahl al-bida, 300
ahl al-dhikr, 356
Ahl al-Hull wa al-Aqd, 226
ahl al-ilm, 372
Ahl al-Sunnah wa al-Jama'ah, 172, 178, 230, 262, 302, 320

Ahmad, Aziz, 402
Ahruf, 219, 220, 221
ajr, 45, 160, 180, 203, 216, 217, 396, 399
ajtahid, 350, 351
akl, 59, 254, 375
aklani, 59
Aklanis, 60, 102
aklanism, 59
aklanyyoon, 59
Al'aika, Sultan, 52, 402
Al-Affani, Sayed ibn Hussein, 102, 402
Al-Ahmadi, Abdullah ibn Salman, 158, 402
Al-Akl, Nasir ibn Abdul Karim, 102, 402
al-albab, 58
Al-Alwani, Taha Jaber, 385
Al-Athari, abu al-Zahra'a, 52, 402
al-awaam, 34
Al-Azhar, 18, 37, 52, 208, 220, 232, 331, 334, 343, 352, 373, 391, 400
Al-Baghdadi, Abi Mansour, 258, 402
Al-Baghdadi, abu Bakr, 331, 402
Al-Bahusein, Yaqoob, 391, 392, 402
Al-Albani, 48, 155, 259, 298, 328, 354, 393, 402
Al-Baqara, Surah of, 188
Al-Barbahari, abu Muhammad, 325, 402
Al-Baydawi, 373
Al-Bukhari. *See* Sahih al-Bukhari
al-Buraaq, 177
Al-Darmi, AbdAllah ibn Abd al-Rahman, 106, 402
al-Daroorat Tubeeh al-Mahdoorat, 376, 378, 380
Al-Dimashki, abi al-Fida ibn Kathir, 328, 402
Al-Fahid, Nasir ibn Hamad, 17, 402
Al-Farabi, 171, 178
Al-Ghazali, 371
Al-Hamadani, 258, 402
Alhasan, 207
Al-Hasany, Hashim Maroof, 330, 403
Alhussein, 207
alim, 18, 179, 341
alima, 344
Al-Jahiz, 171
al-Jarh wa al-Ta'dil, 296
Al-Jarjani, 298, 328, 403

Al-Jewziyya, 52, 182, 183, 327, 331, 403
Al-Juwayni, 297, 371, 373
Al-Kafi., 52, 157, 403
Al-Kannouji, 51, 325, 403
Al-Karkhi, abi al-Hasan, 379
Al-Khamis, 105, 156, 183, 403
al-khawaas, 34
Al-Khawarizmi, 178
Al-Khazini, 171
Al-Khoei, 242, 327, 403
Al-Mahalli, 186, 260, 330, 403
Al-Manar, 66, 186, 195
al-Mas'udi, 171
almaytah, 204
Al-Mizan, tafsir, 206
Al-Mutairi, 328, 403
al-Muwatta, 234, 316, 405
Al-Naas, 317, 332, 403
Al-Nahhaas, 239, 254, 260, 327, 403
Al-Nawawi, 25, 292, 327, 331, 374, 403
Al-Owaid, 388, 403
al-Qaida, 111, 112
Al-Qaradawi, 362, 363, 390, 403
al-Qurtubi, 66, 161, 186, 193, 195, 202, 314
Al-Razi, 52, 157, 186, 195, 220, 403
Al-Ridha, Imam, 143
Al-Risala, 116, 212, 219, 231, 268, 310, 312, 334, 369, 370
Al-Sa'di, 186, 205, 215, 331, 232, 403
Al-Sadiq, Jafar, 186, 255
Al-Sadr, 403
Al-Sakhtiyani, 265, 266
Al-Sha'raawi, 108
Al-Shafi'i, 39, 40, 42, 105, 116, 117, 119, 132, 133, 154, 155, 156, 167, 183, 212, 219, 231, 233, 234, 244, 251, 252, 255, 258, 265, 266, 268, 269, 293, 294, 297, 305, 306, 310, 312, 317, 320, 321, 324, 325, 326, 327, 330, 331, 332, 334, 352, 369, 370, 371, 375, 381, 389, 391, 392, 397, 403, 404
Al-Sharayri, 328, 404
Al-Shatibi, 325, 404
Al-Shawkani, 392, 404
Al-Subki, 370, 391, 404
Al-Suyuti, 186, 327, 404
Al-Tabarani, 224, 234
Al-Tabari, 106, 390, 404
Al-Thahabi, 328, 403

Al-Tirmidhi, 120, 152, 155, 224, 251, 259, 267, 293, 299, 304, 393
Al-Tusi, 157, 404
Al-Uwaid, 331, 404
Al-Wahidi, 233, 404
Al-Zahrani, 231, 327, 404
Al-Zarqa, 392, 393, 404
Al-Zarqani, 37, 52, 53, 103, 104, 208, 220, 221, 232, 233, 234, 258, 259, 260, 327, 404
Al-Zuhri, 242
amaliyyah
  Sunnah, 286
amputation, 146, 147, 148
ansar al-Sunnah, 323
apostasy, 9, 10, 11, 15, 142, 143, 144, 157, 167
aql, 58, 60, 302
aqta, 146
Arabian Peninsula, 59, 112, 113, 114, 277
Arabness, 37, 70
Arabs, 37, 42, 44, 59, 63, 64, 65, 68, 71, 104, 107, 128, 154, 209, 218, 223, 225, 227, 229, 232, 233, 262, 276, 277, 301, 347, 392, 408
arifa, 343
asbab. *See* Asbab al-Nuzool
Asbab al-Nuzool, 185, 208, 210, 212, 213, 214, 215, 217, 227, 228, 233, 357, 369
Ash'aris, 59, 60, 102
Al-Asqalani, 31, 46, 220, 292, 307, 324, 325, 327, 332, 401
atee'oo, 283
awqaf, 366
Awwass, Omar, 404
ayadihum, 174

B

ba'th, 78
baddala, 244
baddalna, 244
Badr, 36, 125, 126
Bahrain, 113
baraka, 218
bashar, 28, 96, 170, 182
batil, 21, 94, 95, 98, 165, 179, 186
Bayyannahu, 290
Bible, 32, 400
bid'ah, 62, 71, 374

biology, 2, 169, 188, 342, 344
Bosworth, Clifford Edmund, 404
British Empire, 5, 113
Brown, Jonathan, 231, 258, 325, 326, 328, 404, 405
Buddhism, 3, 16, 143, 237
Byzantine, 23

C

Cahen, Cl., 156, 405
Cambridge, 9, 51, 329, 405
causality, 14, 55, 70, 71, 72
Chechen wars, 111
chemistry, 2, 162, 166, 210, 344
Chicago, University of, 31
Chomsky, Noam, 17, 405
Chossudovsky, Michel, 154, 405
Christendom, 49, 128
Christianity, 11, 16, 25, 95, 143, 186, 237, 271, 371, 389, 400
Christians, 14, 17, 27, 28, 36, 108, 127, 136, 154, 165, 168, 172, 175, 194, 231, 243, 255, 272, 325, 337, 339, 362, 363, 389, 396, 400
Church, 10, 11, 14, 32, 170, 367, 368, 391, 400
Clingingsmith, David, 17, 408
Coulson, Noel, 405
Curie, Marie, 277
Czerepinski, Kareema, 234, 405

D

dar al-harb, 380
dar al-silm, 380
Darwin, Charles, 9
Dawkins, Richard, 177
Day of Accountability, 56, 57, 78, 79, 91, 127, 145, 160, 174, 175, 178
day of judgement, 68
Day of Resurrection, 67, 83
Der'eya, 112
Dhaif, Shawki, 326, 388, 405
dharaba, 66, 67
Di Francia, G. Toraldo, 51, 329, 405
Dr. Suess, 81
duaa, 98, 166, 167

E

Eghbariyya, Musa Mahmoud, 332, 405
Egypt, 48, 112, 207, 330, 334, 352, 366, 367, 368, 393, 394
Einstein, Albert, 10, 185, 278, 345
El-Ssahib, Muhammad, 52, 402
enlightenment, 14
Ernst, Carl, 17, 407
Europe, 10, 14, 271, 400
European
    Colonialism, 12
    Renaissance, 174

F

fahisha, 138, 329
Faisal, King
    of the Kingdom of Saudi Arabia, 391
faqaha, 58
Faraday, Michael, 20
Farooq, Mohammad Omar, 392, 405
Farooqi, Ismail, 385
fasiqoon, 365
fatalism, 13
Fatiha, 163, 164
Fatimah
    daughter of the Prophet, 108, 109, 216, 233, 407
Fatoohi, Louay, 157, 258, 405
fatwa, 134, 158, 297, 361, 362, 366, 367, 389, 397
fawahish, 201, 236, 254, 282, 335, 372
Fawzi, Ibrahim, 325, 391, 405
fi al-istilah, 69, 70, 104
fiqh, 255, 358, 374, 383, 399
fitna, 11, 118, 120, 121, 154, 300
France, 5, 17
Friday, sermon of, 34, 36, 43, 45, 49, 52, 98, 225
furidha, 360
Furqan, 189, 219, 390, 392, 405

G

Galileo, 11
Ghali, 87, 105, 161
ghareeb, 106, 157, 263, 312
grand Mufti, 364

H

ha'kem, 351
hadath, 262
haddatha, 262
hadoo, 307, 337, 387
hajj, 109, 216, 312, 313
Hamza, Muhammad, 329, 405
Hanbali, 22, 154, 316, 347, 352, 379
haqq, 21, 94, 100, 164, 165, 169, 179
haram, 32, 111, 115, 135, 201, 204, 215, 236, 253, 254, 274, 281, 305, 319, 324, 325, 340, 341, 346, 353, 361, 362, 363, 364, 365, 366, 367, 369, 371, 372, 374, 376, 377, 378, 379, 384, 385, 386, 390, 391, 394, 396, 397, 400
Hardy, 156, 405
Harvard, 17, 19, 408
hasan, 263, 294
  wahi, 312
Hasan, Ahmad, 392, 405
Hashim Al-Husaini, 328, 405
Hatina, Meir, 391, 405
hidayah, 191
hikmah, 189, 197, 331
Hinduism, 3, 16
Hirabah, 150
hisaab, 78
Hood, Prophet, 280
Horn of Africa, 112
hudood, 135, 139, 359, 366, 383
huffadh, 41
hujjat, 18

I

ibada, 381, 382, 383
Iblis, 178
ibn Abbas, 121, 133, 142, 195, 199, 200, 202, 203, 252, 253, 256
Ibn Abbas, 194, 199, 252
ibn Abdulaziz, Umar, 293
ibn Abdulwahhab, 17, 112, 113, 154
Ibn al-Ata'iqi, 242
Ibn al-Hajjaj, abu al-Hussain Muslim, 328, 405
ibn al-Mundhir, 371, 372
Ibn al-Mundhir, 372, 390, 392
ibn al-Salah, 263, 292, 372
Ibn al-Salah, abu Amr, 51, 234, 325, 328, 388, 405
Ibn Anas, Malik, 234, 405
Ibn Arabi, 15
ibn Bajah, 171
Ibn Baz, Abdul-Aziz ibn Abdu-Allah, 260, 405
Ibn Hanbal, 40, 52, 103, 105, 116, 130, 155, 174, 182, 231, 406
Ibn Hanbal, Ahmed, 52, 103, 105, 155, 182, 231, 406
Ibn Hayyan, 15
Ibn Hisham, 214, 234, 315, 316, 318, 358
Ibn Hizam, 219
Ibn Ishaaq, 214
Ibn Ishaq, 315, 316, 317, 318, 332, 358, 406
Ibn Jabal, Mu'ath, 350
Ibn Jubair, Said, 193
Ibn Kathir, 11, 17, 39, 60, 66, 80, 86, 87, 105, 106, 120, 154, 161, 167, 168, 172, 173, 174, 176, 182, 186, 194, 195, 202, 203, 204, 205, 211, 215, 230, 231, 232, 258, 305, 314, 317, 332, 397, 403, 406
Ibn Khaldun, 52, 171, 182, 406
Ibn Mahdi, Abdulrahman, 129
Ibn Manzur, Muhammad ibn Mukarram, 104, 233, 258, 406
Ibn Mas'ud, Abdullah, 78
Ibn Maymoon, Amru, 141, 256, 260
Ibn Miskawaih, 171
Ibn Naf'i, Uqba, 23
Ibn Qudamah, 305, 330, 406
Ibn Qudamah, Muwaffiq al-Deen, 330, 406
Ibn Qutaybah, Abdullah, 330, 406
Ibn Rushd, 171, 178
Ibn Salah, 25, 263
Ibn Salama, 242
Ibn Sina, 15, 171
Ibn Taymiyyah, 17, 26, 27, 31, 48, 51, 116, 130, 131, 133, 134, 135, 154, 155, 156, 158, 167, 168, 171, 172, 176, 205, 211, 233, 241, 292, 327, 332, 373, 376, 389, 390, 397, 406, 407
Ibn Uthaymeen, 389, 406
Ibrahim, Prophet, 95, 101, 279, 280, 315
ibtila, 381, 382
Ifta, 357, 361, 363, 367, 389
ihsaan, 45, 88, 89
ijaza, 18
ijma. *See* Ijma

Ijma, 25, 51, 295, 296, 347, 348, 361, 368, 369, 370, 371, 372, 373, 374, 375, 376, 390, 391, 392, 402, 405
ijtahada, 351
Ijtihad, 13, 26, 198, 202, 232, 348, 349, 350, 351, 352, 353, 354, 355, 356, 357, 358, 359, 360, 361, 367, 375, 376, 388, 393, 407, 408
Ikhwan, 113
Ikrama, hadith of, 142, 143
Ilal, Rachid, 157, 328, 406
ilm, 195, 204, 207, 341, 342, 343, 344, 345, 346
Ilm, 341
   peopole of, 342
Ilm al-Rijaal, 298
Ilm Mukhtalaf al-Hadith, 80
imaan, 88, 89, 107, 122, 128, 134, 145, 166, 211, 284, 305, 329, 378
imamat, 151, 206
Imamat, 151
Imami
   sect, 22
immolating, 215
Imraan
   progeny of, 315
Inalcik, Halil, 156, 405
incantation, 161, 163
infallibility, 27, 49, 51, 69, 124, 133, 177, 201, 202, 203, 207, 271, 272, 273, 274, 295, 326, 400
infidels, 12, 117, 128, 166, 322, 323, 325
insaan, 170, 182
Internet, 6, 324
iqra, 44
Iran, 2, 4, 5, 6, 146, 150, 367, 391
Iranian
   revolution, 3, 4, 6, 7
Iraq, 4, 110, 111, 157
Isfahani, Raghib, 171
Ishaq
   Prophet, 214, 215
ISIS, 111, 112
Islahi, Amin Ahsan, 388, 406
Islamic World, 15, 388, 407
ismah, 69, 104, 272, 273
Ismail, Prophet, 182, 214, 215, 298, 385
ismat, 27, 124
isnaad, 294
Isra, 97, 108, 177, 183
Israel, 3, 107, 111, 154, 230, 320, 407
istafa, 315

Istihsaan, 374, 375, 376
ittaba'a, 282, 283
ittabyooni, 283
Ittabyooni, 283
ittiba, 282, 283, 326

J

Ja'fari
   sect, 22, 117
jahadoo, 354
Jahamiyya, 60
Jamal, battle of, 35, 154
Jami al-Tirmidhi, 155, 234, 309, 330, 393, 407
jannah, 174
jawwad, 44, 223
Jesus, 25, 27, 95, 97, 108, 125, 248, 250, 271, 272, 335, 338, 339, 348, 387, 400
Jews, 29, 36, 107, 108, 120, 127, 128, 136, 139, 140, 142, 151, 154, 173, 175, 194, 231, 243, 255, 318, 332, 337, 339, 387, 389, 396
Jibril
   Angel, 88, 89
   hadith of, 87, 89, 90
jihad, 112, 115, 127, 155
jizyah, 126, 136, 137, 138

K

kafir, 12, 125, 128, 129, 132, 143, 168, 254, 297
kafireen, 273, 325
kafiroon, 73, 365
Kamali, Mohammad Hashim, 388, 407
Kamil, Umar Abdullah, 393, 407
karama, 226
karamaat, 40, 42, 303
kataba, 76, 82, 83, 85, 106
kataba la'kum, 82
Keller, Nuh Ha Mim, 102, 407
Khadijah
   wife of the Prophet, 93
khalaf, 36, F41
khalaqa, 74, 169
khalq, 72, 74, 168, 169, 170, 180
Khan, Muhsin
   Mushaf translation, 87, 161
khateeb, 45
Khawarij, 320, 371, 374

khilafa, 77
Khomeini, 51, 154, 367, 407
Khomeini, Roohallah, 407
khutba, 49
Kingdom of Saudi Arabia, 112, 146, 150, 157, 195, 255, 347, 364, 379, 391
kitaab, 76, 83, 86, 90, 213, 249, 265, 360
kufr, 9, 10, 11, 12, 15, 51, 62, 71, 111, 128, 129, 132, 145, 182, 201, 244, 248, 255, 378, 396
kuloob, 54, 61
kun fayakoon, 72, 73, 165, 170, 172, 177, 178
Kurzman, Charles, 17, 407
kutiba, 82, 84, 85, 252, 360, 381
kutub, 249

L

Lacey, Robert, 17, 154, 407
laghi, 241
Latter Day, 56, 88, 284, 285, 337, 387
Lebanon, 6
Libya, 4
Lisan al-Arab, 69, 104, 209, 233, 242, 258, 406
Loot, Prophet. *See* Lut
Luntz, Frank, 154, 407
luzoom, 369

M

ma'loom, 343
ma'rifa, 91, 195, 207, 341, 342, 343, 344, 345
Madani, 214
Madinah, 115, 117, 213, 304, 306, 313, 349, 352, 368, 372, 391, 392, 394
Mahdi, Hasan, 183
makrooh, 306
man'huj, 355
mandoob, 346
mansookh, 188, 208, 227, 236, 237, 263, 357
Mantiqees, 60, 102
Mardin Fatwa, 134, 156, 407
Marx, Karl, 8, 358
mashi'ah, 81, 178
Mathematics, 190
matn, 263, 294
Meccai, 214

Medicine
  Prophetic, 218
  Prophetics, 287
Medina, 18, 35, 64, 117, 135, 139, 140, 270, 304
menstruation, 152, 158, 308, 327, 330
Michot, Yahya, 156, 407
Middle East, 2, 3, 4, 5, 6, 17, 112, 114, 391, 405, 407
miracles, 71, 94, 95, 97, 98, 99, 108, 162, 165, 271, 317, 338
Miraj, 97, 108, 177, 183
miswaak, 287, 288
mo'jiza, 95
Mongols, 174
Moses, 95, 129, 140, 148, 180, 207, 228, 248, 250, 336, 338, 339
mu'minoon, 134, 284
Mu'tazalites, 4, 17, 59, 60, 102, 195, 230, 233, 251, 262, 320
mubaah, 346
Mubarak, Hosni, 391, 394
mufti, 18, 31, 52, 130, 361, 367
muhadithin, 296
muhram, 367
Muir, William, 318, 332, 333, 407
mujtahid, 355, 356, 357, 359, 361, 367
Mukallaf, 360
Murtadha, Muhammad Mahmoud, 104, 407
mushrikeen, 123, 124, 125, 126, 197, 238
Muslims Brotherhood, Society of, 48
Musnad Fatimah al-Zahra, 109, 233, 407
Mustafa, Muhammad Salih Ali, 260, 407
Mutahari, Murtadha, 107, 407
mutaqeen, 188, 226, 230, 394
mutawaatir, 251

N

nablwakum, 382
naha, 286, 305
nahaakum, 285
nahi, 305, 306, 329
Nahj al-Balagha, 207, 232
nahytukum, 306
Najaf, 18
najmah, 247
nak'ala, 147
nakallan, 146
nakl, 254
nansakh, 244, 245

Nasara, 337, 387
nasikh, 188, 208, 227, 236, 237, 255, 263, 357
nastansikh, 246
Newtonian
   mechanics, 8, 100
nika'lan, 147, 149
Noah, 125, 280, 315, 338
North Africa, 3
nushooz, 66, 67
nuskhatuha, 246
nuss, 376

O

olu al-ilm, 195
olu al-Ilm, 195
Ottoman Empire, 380
Ottoman, domain, 4
ou'too, 137
Ouzon, Zakareya, 231, 407

P

Pakistan, 4, 116
Palestinian
   territories, 111
Palestinians, 111
paradise, 5, 75, 128, 186, 223, 363
Paris, University of, 277
people of knowledge, 195, 255, 372
People of the Book, 125, 126
Persians, 107, 117, 218
physics, 2, 20, 30, 43, 55, 56, 100, 102, 188, 209, 268, 275, 278, 338, 340, 344, 345
Pickthall
   Mushaf translation, 87, 105, 161
predestination, 13, 74, 75, 76, 78, 82, 83, 87, 88, 90, 91, 106, 107, 210, 341, 398
Prophethood, 22, 23, 93, 96, 135, 142, 193, 287, 315

Q

qa'ida, 376, 377, 378, 379
qaala, 21
Qadaris, 86, 106
qadha, 72, 74, 76, 90, 107
qadhi, 351
qadr, 90

Qairawan, 23
qalb, 60, 61, 82, 102
qara'ah, 224
qata'ah, 146, 148
qatta'ah, 146, 148, 158
qawa'id, 376, 379, 380
qawl, 72
qawliyyah
   Sunnah, 286
qawwamoon, 66
qira'aat, 219, 220, 221
Qiyaas, 347, 348, 361, 368, 369, 371, 374, 375, 376
Qudsi, hadith, 74, 75, 105
Qum, 18, 343, 387
Quraish, 36, 37, 94, 96, 193, 219, 221, 231, 234, 242, 243, 253, 301
Qutb, Sayyid, 48, 52, 86, 106, 186, 187, 388, 407

R

Rabb, Intisar, 388, 407
rajm, 138, 139, 140, 141
Ramadan, 40, 88, 89, 133, 216, 240, 320, 321, 327, 345
renaissance, 14, 386, 401
Rida, Muhammad Rashid, 390, 407
Riddah Wars, 117, 142
Ridha, Rashid, 186
Rijaal al-Deen, 400
Rijal, 66, 328, 403
Riyadh al-Saliheen, 234, 407
Rumi, Jalal al-Deen, 171
ruqiyah, 163

S

Saabi'een, 337
Sababiyyah, 70
Sabiq, Sayyid, 51, 408
sadaqat, 137, 286
Sadd al-Tharai'ih, 376, 379
Saffin, battle of, 35, 371
sahaaba, 24, 25, 35, 36, 38, 90, 117, 205, 226, 272
sahaabi, 25, 37
Sahih al-Bukhari, 25, 31, 34, 38, 39, 46, 48, 51, 52, 79, 83, 89, 105, 106, 108, 122, 127, 135, 139, 141, 142, 143, 152, 154, 155, 156, 157, 158, 162,

163, 173, 182, 183, 224, 230, 232, 234, 252, 256, 259, 260, 267, 294, 298, 305, 307, 308, 309, 312, 325, 327, 328, 329, 330, 331, 332, 333, 334, 351, 388, 389, 395, 402, 406, 408
Sahih International, 66, 87, 103, 106, 161
Sahih Muslim, 78, 80, 87, 88, 89, 105, 106, 107, 152, 155, 232, 267, 295, 296, 297, 302, 303, 306, 325, 328, 329, 330, 332, 333, 374, 389, 403, 405, 408
Sahihayn, 301
Said, Edward, 17, 408
salaat, 161, 199, 325
Salaf, 117, 119, 124, 131
Salafi, 15, 22, 31, 38, 48, 67, 103, 112, 115, 116, 130, 131, 172, 211, 259, 298, 311, 347, 354, 376
Salafis, 20, 48, 51, 59, 63, 70, 116, 117, 131, 174, 178, 203, 347
Salafism, 112, 115, 116, 373
Salah, Raed, 107
salawaat, 160, 161, 350, 388
saleh, 179
Salvadora Persica, 287
samma'ma, 184
sana'a, 74
sanad, 263, 295, 297, 300
sann'ah, 264
Satan, 54, 247, 258
Satanic, verses, 11, 258
Shabbar, Saeed, 393, 408
Shah Wali Allah, 242
Shah, Muhammad Sultan, 182, 408
shahada, 186, 194, 195, 305, 318
Shaheen, Jack, 154, 408
shahid, 194, 195
Shahrour, Muhammad, 102, 105, 106, 138, 157, 182, 183, 213, 229, 230, 231, 233, 235, 258, 259, 275, 322, 326, 329, 382, 387, 390, 408
Shahrour, Muhammad. *See* Shahrour, Muhammad, *See* Shahrour, Muhammad
Sham, 111, 120
shareek, 373
Sharia, 30, 31, 69, 111, 133, 149, 157, 239, 241, 245, 255, 260, 309, 328, 337, 346, 347, 349, 353, 355, 358, 359, 361, 363, 364, 366, 368, 371, 373, 375, 388, 404, 405
sheikh, 18, 27, 240

sheikha, 240
Shia
   sect, 4, 6, 25, 29, 53, 104, 117, 124, 142, 143, 157, 186, 187, 206, 207, 239, 251, 255, 294, 325, 327, 367, 373, 387, 400, 407
shirk, 124, 125, 128, 272, 319, 341, 366
Shu'aib, Prophet, 280
shuroot, 355
Sicily, 51, 400, 402
Somalia, 4
Spain, 400
sudoor, 54, 61, 184
Sufi, 6, 217, 396
Sunan, 80, 106, 108, 154, 162, 258, 265, 267, 325, 330, 332, 349, 388, 391, 402, 408
Sunan abi Dawood, 332, 408
Sunan al-Nisaa'i, 267
Sunan ibn Majah, 154, 258, 332, 408
Sword, hadith, 122, 123, 124, 127
Sword, verse of, 124, 256
Sykes-Picot, treaty of, 17
Syria, 4

T

ta'ah, 280, 281
Ta'beean, 226
Tabatabaa'i, 29, 52, 86, 187, 206, 207, 408
Tabatabaa'i, Muhammad Husayn, 52, 408
taf'seel, 289
tafaasir, 186, 187, 193, 195, 200, 201, 204, 205, 208, 213, 356, 395
tafsir, 106, 186, 187, 189, 194, 195, 198, 200, 203, 204, 205, 206, 213, 227, 228, 229, 326
Tafsir al-Jalalayn, 186, 187, 260, 330, 403
tahrif, 245, 250
tajweed, 40, 44, 45, 208, 220, 223, 224, 225
takleef, 267, 360, 385
taktumoonahu, 290
talaa, 21, 224
talamoon, 345
taqreeriyah
   Sunnah, 286
taqwa, 35, 39, 41, 125, 126, 230
taraaduf, 209, 232
tarteel, 224, 229

thaeef, 48, 106, 250, 263
thalimoon, 365
thikr, 29, 30, 31, 68, 99, 103, 213, 225, 227, 311, 363
tobayyen, 289, 290
Torah, 29, 139, 140, 157, 174, 187
Trabishi, George, 331, 408
Trinity, 129
tubayyen, 290
Tunisia, 23

U

u'qatta'anna, 148
uboodiyyat, 363
ulama, 19, 208, 324, 341, 342, 343, 345, 346, 356, 371, 395, 397
Ullmann, Manfred, 408
uloom al-deen, 342
Uloom al-Hadith, 51, 52, 234, 294, 325, 328, 329, 388, 405, 406
uloom al-Qur'aan, 208
Ulu al-ilm, 345, 346
Umar
    Abdullah ibn, 133
    ibn, 122, 139, 200, 256, 302
    ibn al-Khattab, 211, 219, 240
    Righteous Caliph, 121, 133, 141, 149
Umayyad
    dynasty, 5, 12, 13, 19, 51, 101, 116, 120, 130, 144, 243, 293, 320, 352, 357, 370, 380, 384, 396
umma, 17, 25, 50, 206, 292, 297, 320, 324, 337, 363, 371, 372, 374, 384
ummy, 92, 93
ummyyoon, 93
Umra, 216, 399
USA, 114, 346, 347, 352

uswah hasanah, 278, 279, 280
Uyoon al-A'thaar, 317, 332, 403

W

Wahhabism, 7, 17, 112, 113, 114, 115, 116, 154
Wars of Rebellion. *See* Ridda Wars
wasati, 6, 297, 324, 375
wassiyya, 252
Williamson, Jeffrey G, 17, 408
WWI, 4, 5

Y

yaktum, 290
yaktumoon, 290
yansakhu, 247
Yemen, 4, 146, 349, 350, 351
yobayyen, 290
you'too, 126, 136, 137
Yousuf, Prophet, 35, 148, 207, 343, 390, 403

Z

zaany, 138
Zaidi
    sect, 22
zakat, 84, 88, 89, 123, 124, 127, 133, 136, 137, 152, 238, 256, 286, 307, 312
Zamakshari, 195
zandaqa, 11, 15, 22, 51, 71, 201
zina, 138, 139, 140, 141, 142, 239, 240, 256, 360, 371, 379
Zoroastrians, 127, 136

www.ingramcontent.com/pod-product-compliance
Lightning Source LLC
Chambersburg PA
CBHW060348080526
44583CB00012B/220